TABLE OF CONTENTS

A COLD WIND BLOWS...

Although the battle for Outland still rages, both the Alliance and the Horde have been forced to move their focus back to Azeroth and to look northward to the cold, forbidding continent of Northrend, where new threats are emerging. From deep within Icecrown Citadel the Lich King exerts his icy grip on his minions, readying his forces for an all-out assault.

Unable to put aside their longstanding conflict even in the face of this new threat, both the Alliance and Horde are drawing separate battle lines and making preparations to stop the Lich King's forces. No strangers to the ways of the Scourge, both sides understand that to fail here is to lose far more than Northrend.

World of Warcraft is a living, breathing, ever-changing world, and the newly rediscovered continent of Northrend is no exception. Its challenges and experiences are like nothing you have faced so far: they will put your abilities to the test. Intrepid explorers need every advantage they can get. With this guide we've given you a powerful tool to get you started in this harsh but beautiful land.

Within These Pages

A New Continent

Wrath of the Lich King brings with it the entire new continent of Northrend to explore, with new allies, new foes, new dungeons and raids, and much more. With the release of the expansion your level 70 characters can now start earning experience again. With new quests, new factions, and new PvP areas there is no shortage of things to do!

In addition to the new content there are many changes and additions to gameplay. This chapter gives you everything you need to understand these changes so you can get started experiencing the new content right away.

Interface and Statistics Changes

Player Window

If you've run more than a few dungeons or raids you are familiar with this scenario: Your guild works really hard and spends a good chunk of time to take down a boss. Everyone is excited—until the loot drops. You've seen this particular piece of cloth Plus Healing gear before. It is a really good piece, but since it is cloth healing gear it is only really good for priests and both of the priests in your raid already have it. With the change to Spell Power, that same cloth piece is now potentially useful to any cloth wearer in your raid. So, what was a good drop for two or three of your raiders, may now be useful for a lot more.

While DPS casters may not notice much difference in the actual numbers listed on their Character Window, Healers may see a decrease. Don't worry! This doesn't indicate a loss of healing power. All healing spells have been modified to benefit from Spell Power so that the amount you heal for is roughly the same as it was before.

Miss vs. Resist

You can now more concretely see how your Hit Rating stacks up when casting spells. Your combat log now differentiates between a spell that misses the target and one which is resisted. Both events were formerly recorded as a Resist, so it could be difficult to see how Hit Rating influenced your performance.

Spell Power is not the only stat that has been consolidated. You no longer have separate Hit Rating, Critical Strike Rating, and Haste Rating for melee and spells. These stats now modify both. This is especially useful for classes that fill multiple roles. A Shaman or a Druid may need to switch out fewer pieces of gear when moving from DPS to Healing for example. The less gear you need to carry with you, the better.

Spell Pushback

In the past, casters could be continually interrupted by melee attacks while attempting to cast and had to rely on instant cast spells, or luck, in close combat. Now, the first two hits you take add 0.5 seconds each to the casting time of a spell, while during a channeled spell each of those two hits decreases the spell's duration by 25%. After the first two hits there is no further effect (other than the damage you take of course) to your casting. Go ahead and wind up that Frostbolt or Fireball!

Stat Changes

As you look over your character screen and items, you most likely notice a few changes. One of the most significant is the introduction of Spell Power. Before, you had separate Plus Damage and Plus Healing amounts listed on gear and items. Now, those have been consolidated under one stat—Spell Power. This is an important change because it greatly affects what gear can be used by what class. For example, in the past gear usually had either a Plus Damage or a Plus healing component, making it clear whether or not it was intended for a healing or DPS class. That same item now would just have Spell Power, making it equally valuable to healers and damage dealing casters.

While this does mean there is a bit more competition for gear, it also means that that same piece of gear is more useful to more people, which is a very good thing.

Pets and Mounts

No matter how big your bags are or how many bank spaces you purchase, it seems you can always use more room. A new Pets tab has been added to your Character Info window to help free up some space in your bags. This tab holds both your vanity pets, under Companions, and your Mounts. To switch between the two use the tabs at the top of the window. To place a pet or mount in your Pets tab, right click on it in your inventory, much like you would use an item. Once the pet or mount is added to your Pets tab, it disappears from your inventory, freeing up some space. Each page holds up to twelve pets or mounts, and as you fill them up, new pages are added, so you will never run out of room. Now you no longer have to choose which pets to carry around in your bag; your whole menagerie can come with you!

Interface

Northrend

Racial Abilities

Barber Shop

PVE

Phasing

To bring out a pet or a mount, just open up your Pets tab and click on the Summon button for Companions, or the Mount button for Mounts. You can dismiss your pets by again clicking on this same button. To quickly access your most used pets and mounts you can drag their icon from your Pets tab onto one of your Action Bars where you can summon and mount the same way you always have. The Pets window is convenient for everyone, but is a very useful addition for those players who like to collect various pets or who like to use different mounts. Now you can bring your companions along on your adventurers, and still have room for more loot!

Glyph spaces open up with Minor spaces unlocking at levels fifty, and seventy. As their name suggests, Major Glyphs tend to have a more significant impact on your abilities, often increasing damage, reducing cooldowns, or adding additional effects to a spell or ability. Minor Glyphs function in much the same way, but their changes are generally less significant, but still very useful.

Much like Gems or Enchantments, Glyphs basically augment your abilities the same way the former two items augment your equipment and can be changed in much the same way. To inscribe a Glyph right click on it in your inventory then click on the appropriate space in your Glyphs tab. Again, like Gems and Enchantments, Glyphs can be removed or overwritten, but doing so destroys them. You can remove a Glyph at anytime by shift-right clicking it or by placing another Glyph in its spot. Once inscribed, a Glyph becomes part of your abilities and you don't have to do anything extra to get the benefits from it. For more information on Inscription, including Glyph recipes, see the Crafting chapter of this guide.

CURRENCY

Gold may be the bedrock of Azeroth economy but it is not the only currency you deal in. Keeping track of all the various means of tender used to entail looking through your inventory, PvP window, and bank to see how many of the various points, badges, etc., that you had. The new Currency tab in your character Info window lets you see all of that at a glance. Here you can see your Arena Points, Honor Points, Badges, Emblems, Marks of Honor, and even other means of currency like the new Venture Coins or Stone Keeper's Shards, even when they are stored in your bank.

The Currency tab organizes the various items and points into categories such as PvP or Miscellaneous. By clicking on a particular currency you can open up the Currency Options. Here you can choose to move a particular currency to an Unused category. You can still view currency marked as Unused, but it is under its own category, and not mixed in with your other forms of currency. Under Currency Options you can also choose to show that currency when you open your backpack, right underneath your money. With these options, the Currency tab makes it easier overall for you to track your assets.

KEEPING TRACK OF TIME

Time flies when you are having fun, but there are a couple of new ways to keep track of it by using the Clock and Event Calendar functions on your mini-map.

CLOCK

At the bottom of your mini-map is the Clock. Mouse over it to see the Realm Time and Local Time. To open up your Clock Settings, click it. Here you can choose to display your local time on the clock instead of the realm time. Being able to see both lets you keep track of time in your world and in Azeroth so you are always on time for raids and other events.

From here you can also access the Stopwatch. Click on the Stopwatch icon in the upper right corner of the Clock Settings to bring up the Stopwatch and press play to start it running. You can pause it using the same button or reset it using the button on the right. The Stopwatch can be used to time anything you want. Use it to see how long it takes you to wipe the floor with your dueling partner or time yourself while fighting a tough mob just to see how quickly you can do it.

The clock also includes an Alarm function. This is very useful if you know you only have so much time to play, or want to remind yourself of a real world or in-game obligation. Use the drop down menus to select the appropriate hour and minutes, in five minute increments. Make sure if you have Use Local Time checked that you set it with that in mind. You can then type in a short message to yourself to go along with the alarm. At the appointed time, a bell rings and your message pops up in your chat window and in the center of your screen. Your clock also pulses until you click it to turn off the alarm. You can make sure you are never late for that guild meeting, dungeon run, or even work, ever again.

GLYPHS

Glyphs are an exciting new way to customize your character's skills and talents. Each character now has a Glyph tab in their Spellbook & Abilities Window. In it you see six circles, three large and three small. These are spaces in which you can inscribe different class specific Glyphs. Much like Jewelcrafting produces gems for other characters' socketed items, Scribes (those who have the Inscription profession) produce Glyphs for you to inscribe in these spaces in your spellbook.

There are two types of Glyphs: Major, which can be inscribed onto the larger circles, and Minor, which fill the smaller ones. Not all six circles are open to you at first, but as you level they become available to you. At level 15 you gain access to your first Major and Minor glyph spaces. At levels thirty, and eighty your other two Major

CALENDAR

As the event creator, or as an invitee, you can see who else has been invited, as well as if they have accepted or declined the invitation. If only real life events were this easy to manage! The tabs running along the right side of the event information indicate how many of each class have accepted the invitation.

For times when you aren't in game, you can still monitor your events from The Armory webpage <www.armory.com>. Though you can't create events from here, after logging in you can see the calendars for each of your characters and respond, just as you would in game!

There is a lot going on in World of Warcraft and the Event Calendar is designed to help you keep track of it all! Located on the top right hand corner of your mini-map, the Calendar displays today's date. Click on it to bring up the full Calendar.

The Calendar displays one month at a time and you can move back and forth between the months by using the arrows on each side of the name of the month. At its most basic, the Calendar displays the World Events taking place each month. By using the Filters drop down menu in the upper right corner you can also see other events such as Battleground Holidays, The Darkmoon Faire, Active Raid Lockouts and Resets, and Weekly Holidays such as the Stranglethorn Fishing Extravaganza. To get more information on an event, just click on it to get a short description. By using the Calendar you can make sure always know what's going on so you can plan accordingly.

CUSTOMIZING YOUR EXPERIENCE

Since the launch of the Burning Crusade, there have been a lot of changes to the Interface Options. Whereas you used to have only a few, albeit useful, options, you now have much more detailed control over how you view and interact with the game. The interface options are divided into easy to navigate categories. Just select the category on the left and you can view all of its options to the right. This makes it much easier to find what you need quickly and allows you to customize your interface to a great degree.

Tracking events is great, but the calendar also offers you the opportunity to set up your own events. To create an event, right click on the day for which you wish to hold your event. This brings up the event creation menu.

The first thing you need to do is to type in a name for your event. You can use approximately thirty characters, so be descriptive, but not too descriptive. Next, select what type of event you are hosting from the dropdown menu: Raid, Dungeon, PvP, Meeting, or Other. If you select Raid or Dungeon, this brings up another menu listing all of the raid or dungeon locations, separated into Classic, The Burning Crusade, or Wrath of the Lich King. Choose the location for your event and you are ready to set the time. Next you can add a description of your event in the box provided. The last thing you need to do is decide who to invite. Enter each player's name in the space provided at the bottom of the window and click Invite.

AGGRO WARNING

There are several useful new options, among them is the Aggro Warning. This allows you to see how close you are to pulling aggro on your target. As you get closer and closer to passing whoever has aggro, your portrait goes from yellow to red. You can also see your percentage of the aggro by mousing over the target and viewing it in the tooltip which pops up. Once you reach 100%, that monster is coming for you! You can find this option under the Display category.

While your Macros and Key Bindings menus have not changed, they are now saved server side instead of on your local machine. This means that if you want to log on to the game using a different computer, your macros and key bindings are right there waiting for you. You no longer have to spend time setting everything up again each time you switch computers!

Once invited, each player's Calendar pulses a glowing question mark to indicate they have a pending invite. When you receive an invite, click on your calendar and you see this same question mark on the day of the event. To respond, click on the event, look over the details, and either decline or accept the invitation. Once you accept, the event is marked on your calendar and can be viewed at any time.

It's a Changing World

Besides being able to access the new continent of Northrend, there are a few changes to the old world as well. For starters, you can now visit the Ruins of the Scarlet Enclave on the eastern edge of the Eastern Plaguelands. Acherus: The Ebon Hold, home to the Death Knights can be seen floating overhead.

While the Ebon Hold is an addition to the old world, there have been a couple of subtractions as well. The city of Dalaran, which once stood on the shore of Lordamere Lake, has been moved to Northrend by the Kirin Tor, leaving a smoking crater behind. The floating necropolis, Naxxramas, has left the skies above the Eastern Plaguelands and moved to Northrend as well.

Traveling to Northrend

Getting to Northrend is easy for travelers. There are new Zeppelin towers near both the Undercity and Orgrimmar for the Horde. The Undercity Zeppelin offers transport to Vengeance Landing in Howling Fjord, located on the southwestern tip of Northrend. From Orgrimmar you can take the zeppelin to Warsong Hold, in the Borean Tundra on southeastern Northrend. Alliance ships now sail to Northrend from Menethil Harbor to Valgarde in Howling Fjord and from the newly opened Stormwind Harbor to Valiance Keep in the Borean Tundra.

Much like Shattrath in Outland, the Kirin Tor's city, Dalaran, hosts portals to all of the major cities of each faction, including Shattrath, in both Sunreaver's Sanctuary for the Horde, and The Silver Enclave for the Alliance. As a floating city, Dalaran is unreachable from the ground until you have completed a quest. If you wish to visit the city before then, the best thing to do is to find a friendly mage or warlock to portal or summon you there. Remember though that you are asking
for their time and reagents and if you are lucky enough to find a kind soul to do this for you, make sure you are very appreciative. Once you reach Dalaran you can pick up the flight path and use the Crystal in the building across from Krasus' Landing to teleport to the Violet Stand in the Crystalsong Forest below. Once you do this you can then use the crystal there to reach Dalaran from that location as well.

Cold Weather Flying

You may be thinking to yourself, "Flight Paths? Who needs Flight Paths? I've got a flying mount!" However, your land mounts are about to see more use than they have in awhile. Flying in Northrend takes a special skill called Cold Weather Flying. This can be learned from a Cold Weather Flying Trainer at level 77 and lets you use your flying mounts on the continent. Prior to that you need to make your way across the land the old fashioned way, dodging hostile mobs and clearing the way to where you need to go. If you play on a PvP server, you may want to find a group of friends to quest with to discourage higher level characters from swooping down on their flying mounts looking for a quick kill.

Racial Abilities

Many of the racial traits have been revamped and rebalanced for the expansion; some have been removed, while others have been added. Below is a list of all the racial abilities currently in the game.

Blood Elf

Arcane Affinity

This passive ability increases your Enchanting Skill, giving you a small head start on that profession. While this is not a new skill, it still gives you an advantage in the expansion as you can access recipes sooner than other Enchanters as you level up your profession.

Arcane Torrent

Silences all nearby enemies for a few seconds and restores some of your base Energy, Mana, or Runic Power, depending on your class. This skill has been drastically changed. Now, the former Mana Tap component has been removed so you don't have to build up charges in order to use Arcane Torrent, which also frees up a spot on your Action Bar. Having an extra silence ability is great during tough PvE battles but really shines when used in PvP. Often that extra Mana, Energy, or Runic Power can mean the difference between victory and defeat.

Magic Resistance

This passive skill reduces the chance you will be hit by spells. This is a very useful skill. Some of the other races get resistances to certain schools of magic, but this skill gives you some resistance to all of them, making it a superior skill. It is so superior that Blood Elves only get three racial abilities, while other races get at least four.

Draenei

Gemcutting

This passive ability increases your Jewelcrafting skill, giving you an advantage over other races in that profession. The added points let you skill up on lower level materials for a bit longer, which can save you a pocket full of gold at higher skill levels.

Gift of the Naaru

This ability heals the target of damage over time. The amount healed is based on the caster's Spell Power or Attack Power, whichever is higher. Unlike other spells, the casting time on this ability does not increase when you take damage and it is not effected by the Global Cooldown.

Heroic Presence

Formerly, Draenei had either Inspiring Presence, or Heroic Presence, depending on their class. The two have now been combined under Heroic Presence. This passive ability increases the chance to hit with all spells and attacks for you and all nearby party members. It is a nice addition when soloing, and is really great at increasing your group's damage output since it effects everyone.

Shadow Resistance

This passive ability reduces your chance of being hit by Shadow spells.

CHANGES

Interface

Northrend

Racial Abilities

Barber Shop

PvE

Phasing

DWARF

Find Treasure

Allows you to sense nearby treasure, making it appear on the minimap. This functions like a form of tracking and you can select it from the list on your mini-map.

Frost Resistance

This passive ability reduces the chance you will be hit by Frost spells.

Gun Specialization

This passive ability increases your chance to critically hit with Guns.

Mace Specialization

This passive ability increases your expertise with Maces and Two-Handed Maces.

Stoneform

While active, this ability grants immunity to Bleed, Poison, and Disease effects, and also increases Armor. Stoneform has always been a very useful racial, especially in PvP, and will continue to be so with the expansion. The addition of Death Knights means that one more class is going to come at you with Diseases, and Stoneform definitely gives you an advantage when facing Death Knights on the battlefield. Cleansing their diseases can cripple their damage output, giving you the upper hand, not to mention how useful Stoneform is against the deadlier poisons and Bleed effects new talents have given to other classes.

GNOME

Arcane Resistance

This passive ability reduces the chance you will be hit by Arcane Spells.

Engineering Specialization

This passive ability increases your Engineering skill, giving you an advantage when starting this profession. You can access schematics before other races, giving you more chances to skill up on them while they are orange. This increases your chances of skilling up, and having more options allows you to use cheaper, easier to get materials in many cases.

Escape Artist

This ability allows you to escape the effects of any immobilization or movement speed reduction effect and can no longer be resisted.

Expansive Mind

This passive ability increases your Intellect, always useful for casters.

HUMAN

Diplomacy

This passive ability increase your reputation gains. This makes it easier for humans to raise their reputation with various factions. With the addition of the new factions in Northrend, this can be very useful.

Every Man for Himself

This ability removes all movement impairing effects and all effects which cause loss of control of your character and shares a cooldown with similar abilities. Highly useful in both PvE and PvP situations, it has a fairly short cooldown, so it can be used several times during an Arena match or other encounters.

Mace Specialization

This passive ability increases your expertise with Maces and Two-Handed Maces.

Perception

This passive ability increase your Stealth detection which can be an advantage in PvP situations. This ability has been changed to a passive ability and lets humans detect stealthed characters as if they were one level lower than they are.

Sword Specialization

This passive ability increases your expertise with Swords and Two-Handed Swords.

The Human Spirit

This passive ability increases your Spirit. The amount of increase has been decreased so it doesn't create a balance issue.

NIGHT ELF

Nature Resistance

This passive ability reduces the chance you will be hit by Nature spells.

Quickness

This passive ability reduces the chance that melee and ranged attackers will hit you.

Shadowmeld

Activate this ability to slip into the shadows, reducing the chance for enemies to detect your presences. Shadowmeld lasts until you cancel it or until you move. Any threat is restored versus enemies still in combat upon cancellation of this effect. The changes to Shadowmeld have made this ability much more useful. In effect, it functions much like a Rogue's Vanish, in that it can get you out of a dangerous situation. Though you can't move while using it, getting creatures to ignore you, and PvP foes to detarget you, is very, very useful.

Wisp Spirit

This passive ability transforms you into a wisp upon death, increasing your speed.

ORC

Axe Specialization

This passive ability increases your expertise with Axes and Two-Handed Axes.

Blood Fury

When used, Blood Fury increases your melee attack power and your spell damage. This ability no longer causes you to receive 50% less healing from all sources, making it even more useful!

Command

This passive ability increases the damage done by your Death Knight, Hunter, and Warlock pets.

Hardiness

The duration of Stun effects on you is reduced by this passive ability.

TAUREN

Cultivation

This passive skill increases your Herbalism skill, making it easier to get those higher level herbs as you level your skill.

Endurance

This ability has changed from augmenting your total health to your base Health. This means that it is not affected by health increases like scrolls, elixirs, or potions.

Nature Resistance

This passive ability reduces the chance you will be hit by Nature spells.

War Stomp

War Stomp stuns up to five nearby enemies.

PRIEST RACIAL SPELLS

Priests no longer have a distinct spell for each race, so you don't have to choose a particular race to get what you want from the class. Some of these spells have become trainable at Priest Trainers while others are now part of the Priest's talent tree.

TROLL

Beast Slaying

This passive ability increases the damage you to versus Beasts.

Berserking

Berserking increases your casting and attack speed. The increase scales up the more seriously you are injured and no longer has an activation cost.

Bow Specialization

This passive ability increases your chance to critically hit with Bows.

Da Voodoo Shuffle

The duration of all movement impairing effects is reduced by this passive ability. This new ability is a boon to all trolls, especially in PvP.

Regeneration

This passive ability increases the rate of Health regeneration and a percentage of total Health regeneration may continue during combat.

Throwing Specialization

Your chance to critically hit with Throwing Weapons is increased by this passive ability.

UNDEAD

Cannibalize

When activated, regenerates a percentage of health over time. Only works on Humanoid or Undead corpse. Any movement, action, or damage take while Cannibalizing cancels the effect.

Shadow Resistance

This passive ability reduces your chance of being hit by Shadow spells, but does not give as much protection as other classes' Resistance racials.

Underwater Breathing

Your breath lasts longer underwater because of this passive ability. After all, you are Undead, how much air can you possible need? This ability has been changed so that you can breath underwater for almost ten minutes, much longer than you could before.

Will of the Forsaken

This instant ability removes any Charm, Fear, or Sleep effects from you but no longer gives you a lasting immunity from such effects. This change means that you can no longer "pop" this ability ahead of time if you think you are in danger, but must instead wait until you have been effected.

CHANGES

Interface

Northrend

Racial Abilities

Barber Shop

PVE

Phasing

Shave and a Haircut

Not all of the new features found in this expansion are just about exploring new regions or improving your character, some, like the Barbershop, are just plain fun! If you are in need of a new 'do, head to one of the Barbershops located in all of the major cities. Once there, have a seat in the chair and you are greeted with three options: Hair Style, Hair Color, and Features.

Click through the options to try out different combinations. You can even check out hairstyles that originally belonged to other races, though you are still limited to those belonging to your same gender. Once you have the look you want, click OK to leave the barber chair with your new look!

A new haircut may not increase your DPS, get you better equipment, or make you a more effective healer, but it can be epic, nonetheless.

The Price of Change

Beauty doesn't come cheap and the price of a new look varies depending on your standing with the city where the Barbershop is located, so visiting one where your reputation is the highest saves you a bit of cash.

Grand Master Crafting

Crafters who had previously reached the maximum amount of skill in their chosen profession can now speak to a Grand Master Trainer to become Grand Masters themselves. This new tier of crafting lets you skill up to 450 and adds many new recipes to the game, giving crafters many new useful items with which to raise their skill.

Each profession has been granted unique recipes, many of which are comparable with dropped gear, raising the demand for player-crafted items. Crafters are also much more interdependent than they once were. For example, Scribes can produce Vellum which Enchanters can then use to store enchantments. This allows them to be traded or even sold in the Auction House, which is a significant change to how Enchanters conduct their trade. Blacksmiths can now add sockets to some items, creating a greater demand for quality gems produced by Jewelcrafters. Overall, these changes are a great benefit to crafters and other players alike!

Though all crafters can learn the skills taught by their trainers, they also gain recipes from drops, from purchasing them once they have enough reputation with certain factions, and in some cases, through research. For example, with Inscription, the only way to learn how to make Minor Glyphs is through Minor Inscription Research. Once a day a Scribe can use this ability to produce a random amount of scrolls which they already know and they have a chance of learning a new Minor Glyph recipe. Alchemists have something similar in Northrend Alchemy Research. Once a week an Alchemist can take a group of Northrend herbs and attempt to discover a new Alchemy recipe. All of this insures that not all crafters have the exact same catalog as other members of their profession.

Many of the professions also offer boons that affect much more than just their crafted items. Abilities like the Herbalist's Lifeblood, or the Skinner's Master of Anatomy provide benefits that cross over onto the battlefield. For more information on the various professions and a list of recipes for each, check out the Crafting section of this guide.

New PvE Rewards

Wrath of the Lich King offers several new dungeon and raid challenges, and includes a new reward system for running these new Raids and Heroic Dungeons in Northrend.

Emblem of Heroism

Can be looted off of bosses in ten-man raids and in Heroic five-man dungeons.

Name	ExtendedCost	Stats
Frozen Orb	10 Emblem of Heroism	Tradeskill Item.
Libram of Renewal	15 Emblem of Heroism	Libram: Reduces the mana cost of Holy Light.
Libram of Reciprocation	15 Emblem of Heroism	Libram: Your Judgement of Command spell has a chance to grant haste.
Libram of Obstruction	15 Emblem of Heroism	Libram: Your Judgement ability also increases your shield block value.
Totem of the Elemental Plane	15 Emblem of Heroism	Totem: Your Lightning Bolt spell has a chance to grant haste.
Totem of Forest Growth	15 Emblem of Heroism	Totem: Reduces the base mana cost of Chain Heal.
Totem of Splintering	15 Emblem of Heroism	Totem: Increases the attack power bonus on Windfury Weapon attacks.
Idol of Lush Moss	15 Emblem of Heroism	Idol: Increases the spell power on the periodic portion of your Lifebloom.
Idol of Steadfast Renewal	15 Emblem of Heroism	Idol: Increases the damage dealt by Wrath by 70.
Idol of the Ravenous Beast	15 Emblem of Heroism	Idol: Increases the damage dealt by Shred by 203.
Sigil of Haunted Dreams	15 Emblem of Heroism	Sigil: Your Blood Strike and Heart Strikes have a chance to grant haste.
Lillehoff's Winged Blades	15 Emblem of Heroism	Thrown: Physical 186-279, 1.8, 129.2 +19 Agility, +27 Stamina, Equip: Improves critical strike rating by 27., Increases attack power.
Pendant of the Outcast Hero	25 Emblem of Heroism	+45 Agility, +51 Stamina, Equip: Improves critical strike rating by 38., Increases attack power.
Chained Military Gorget	25 Emblem of Heroism	+41 Strength, +75 Stamina, Equip: Increases defense rating by 33., Equip: Increases your dodge rating by 32., Equip: Improves hit rating by 21.

Name	ExtendedCost	Stats
Encircling Burnished Gold Chains	25 Emblem of Heroism	+49 Stamina, +38 Intellect, +34 Spirit, Equip: Improves hit rating by 25., Increases spell power.
Lattice Choker of Light	25 Emblem of Heroism	+37 Stamina, +38 Intellect, Equip: Improves critical strike rating by 34., Increases spell power., Restores some mana per 5 sec.
Ward of the Violet Citadel	25 Emblem of Heroism	+49 Stamina, +34 Intellect, Equip: Improves hit rating by 38., Equip: Improves critical strike rating by 25., Increases spell power.
Handbook of Obscure Remedies	25 Emblem of Heroism	+43 Stamina, +36 Intellect, +38 Spirit, Equip: Improves haste rating by 25., Increases spell power.
Sundial of the Exiled	40 Emblem of Heroism	Equip: Improves critical strike rating by 84., Your harmful spells have a chance to increase your spell power by 590 for 10 secs.
Valor Medal of the First War	40 Emblem of Heroism	Equip: Increases your dodge rating by 84., Increases dodge rating.
Mirror of Truth	40 Emblem of Heroism	Equip: Improves critical strike rating by 84., Chance on critical hit to increase your attack power by 1000 for 10 secs.
The Egg of Mortal Essence	40 Emblem of Heroism	Equip: Increases spell power by 98., Your direct healing and heal over time spells have a chance to increase your haste rating by 505 for 10 secs.
Verdungo's Barbarian Cord	40 Emblem of Heroism	Plate: 1261, Socket Bonus: +4 Strength, Socket: Yellow, +58 Strength, +99 Stamina, Equip: Improves critical strike rating by 48., Equip: Improves haste rating by 30.
Waistguard of Living Iron	40 Emblem of Heroism	Plate: 1261 Socket Bonus: +6 Stamina, Socket: Yellow, +57 Strength, +88 Stamina, Equip: Increases defense rating by 44., Equip: Increases your dodge rating by 25., Equip: Increases your parry rating by 32.
Magroth's Meditative Cincture	40 Emblem of Heroism	Plate: 1261, Socket Bonus: +5 Spell Power, Socket: Yellow, +49 Stamina, +51 Intellect, Equip: Improves critical strike rating by 38., Equip: Improves haste rating by 40., Increases spell power.
Vereesa's Silver Chain Belt	40 Emblem of Heroism	Mail: 705, Socket Bonus: +8 Attack Power, Socket: Blue, +57 Agility, +69 Stamina, +34 Intellect, Equip: Improves hit rating by 28., Increases attack power., Increases armor penetration rating.
Beadwork Belt of Shamanic Vision	40 Emblem of Heroism	Mail: 705, Socket Bonus: +4 Haste Rating, Socket: Yellow, +49 Stamina, +50 Intellect, Equip: Improves haste rating by 44., Increases spell power., Restores some mana per 5 sec.
Jorach's Crocolisk Skin Belt	40 Emblem of Heroism	Leather: 317, Socket Bonus: +4 Agility, Socket: Blue, +40 Agility, +61 Stamina, Equip: Improves critical strike rating by 46., Equip: Increases your expertise rating by 38., Increases attack power.
Vine Belt of the Woodland Dryad	40 Emblem of Heroism	Leather: 317, Socket Bonus: +4 Spirit, Socket: Yellow, +49 Stamina, +51 Intellect, +38 Spirit, Equip: Improves critical strike rating by 40., Increases spell power.
Plush Sash of Guzbah	40 Emblem of Heroism	Cloth: 169, Socket Bonus: +4 Hit Rating, Socket: Yellow, +49 Stamina, +52 Intellect, Equip: Improves haste rating by 42., Equip: Improves hit rating by 33., Increases spell power.

Name	ExtendedCost	Stats
Elegant Temple Gardens' Girdle	40 Emblem of Heroism	Cloth: 169, Socket Bonus: +4 Spirit, Socket: Yellow, +57 Stamina, +48 Intellect, +43 Spirit, Increases spell power., Restores some mana per 5 sec.
Balanced Heartseeker	40 Emblem of Heroism	Dagger: Heirloom
Venerable Dal'Rend's Sacred Charge	40 Emblem of Heroism	One-handed Sword: Heirloom
Polished Spaulders of Valor	40 Emblem of Heroism	Plate: Heirloom, Experience gained from killing monsters increased.
Champion Herod's Shoulder	40 Emblem of Heroism	Mail: Heirloom, Experience gained from killing monsters increased.
Mystical Pauldrons of Elements	40 Emblem of Heroism	Mail: Heirloom, Experience gained from killing monsters increased.
Stained Shadowcraft Spaulders	40 Emblem of Heroism	Leather: Heirloom, Experience gained from killing monsters increased.
Preened Ironfeather Shoulders	40 Emblem of Heroism	Leather: Heirloom, Experience gained from killing monsters increased.
Tattered Dreadmist Mantle	40 Emblem of Heroism	Cloth: Heirloom, Experience gained from killing monsters increased.
Rolfsen's Ripper	50 Emblem of Heroism	Dagger: Physical 170-317, 1.7, 143.2 +39 Stamina, Equip: Improves haste rating by 50., Increases attack power.
Grasscutter	50 Emblem of Heroism	Sword: Physical 160-299, 1.6, 143.4 +25 Agility, +39 Stamina, Equip: Improves critical strike rating by 38., Increases attack power.
Pride	50 Emblem of Heroism	Fist Weapon: Physical 251-467, 2.5, 143.6 +39 Stamina, Equip: Improves hit rating by 50., Increases attack power.
Devout Aurastone Hammer	50 Emblem of Heroism	One-handed Mace: Heirloom
Swift Hand of Justice	50 Emblem of Heroism	Trinket: Heirloom. Increases haste, heals you for a percentage of your maximum health whenever you kill a target that yields experience or honor.
Discerning Eye of the Beast	50 Emblem of Heroism	Trinket: Heirloom. Increases Spell Power, heals you for a percentage of your maximum health whenever you kill a target that yields experience or honor.
Gloves of the Lost Conqueror	60 Emblem of Heroism	Armor Token: These tokens can be turned in to a specific vendor to purchase parts of an armor set unique to your class.
Gloves of the Lost Protector	60 Emblem of Heroism	Armor Token: These tokens can be turned in to a specific vendor to purchase parts of an armor set unique to your class.
Gloves of the Lost Vanquisher	60 Emblem of Heroism	Armor Token: These tokens can be turned in to a specific vendor to purchase parts of an armor set unique to your class.
Bloodied Arcanite Reaper	65 Emblem of Heroism	Two-Handed Axe: Heirloom
Charmed Ancient Bone Bow	65 Emblem of Heroism	Bow: Heirloom
Dignified Headmaster's Charge	65 Emblem of Heroism	Staff: Heirloom
Chestguard of the Lost Conqueror	80 Emblem of Heroism	Armor Token: These tokens can be turned in to a specific vendor to purchase parts of an armor set unique to your class.
Chestguard of the Lost Protector	80 Emblem of Heroism	Armor Token: These tokens can be turned in to a specific vendor to purchase parts of an armor set unique to your class.
Chestguard of the Lost Vanquisher	80 Emblem of Heroism	Armor Token: These tokens can be turned in to a specific vendor to purchase parts of an armor set unique to your class.
Reins of the Wooly Mammoth	200 Emblem of Heroism	Mount: Summons and dismisses a rideable Wooly Mammoth. This is a very fast mount.

Interface

Northrend

Racial Abilities

Barber Shop

PVE

Phasing

Emblem of Valor

Can be looted off of bosses in twenty-five man raids.

Name	ExtendedCost	Stats
Ring of Invincibility	25 Emblem of Valor	+28 Agility, +55 Stamina, Equip: Improves critical strike rating by 43., Equip: Improves haste rating by 38., Increases attack power.
Signet of the Impregnable Fortress	25 Emblem of Valor	+38 Strength, +84 Stamina, Equip: Increases defense rating by 56., Equip: Improves hit rating by 27., Equip: Increases your expertise rating by 21.
Band of Channeled Magic	25 Emblem of Valor	+42 Stamina, +41 Intellect, +32 Spirit, Equip: Improves haste rating by 43., Increases spell power.
Renewal of Life	25 Emblem of Valor	+48 Stamina, +41 Intellect, Equip: Improves critical strike rating by 28., Increases spell power., Restores 17 mana per 5 sec.
Hammerhead Sharkskin Cloak	25 Emblem of Valor	Cloth: 154, +28 Agility, +61 Stamina, Equip: Improves haste rating by 32., Equip: Improves critical strike rating by 43., Increases attack power.
Platinum Mesh Cloak	25 Emblem of Valor	Cloth: 154, +41 Strength, +84 Stamina, Equip: Increases defense rating by 38., Equip: Increases your dodge rating by 37., Equip: Improves hit rating by 32.
Disguise of the Kumiho	25 Emblem of Valor	Cloth: 154, +48 Stamina, +38 Intellect, +37 Spirit, Equip: Improves haste rating by 41., Increases spell power.
Cloak of Kea Feathers	25 Emblem of Valor	Cloth: 154, +42 Stamina, +43 Intellect, Equip: Improves haste rating by 28., Increases spell power., Restores 17 mana per 5 sec.
Bladed Steelboots	40 Emblem of Valor	Plate: 1580, +75 Strength, +112 Stamina, Equip: Improves critical strike rating by 53., Equip: Improves hit rating by 43.
Kyzoc's Ground Stompers	40 Emblem of Valor	Plate: 1580, +75 Strength, +111 Stamina, Equip: Increases defense rating by 50., Equip: Increases your dodge rating by 33., Equip: Increases your parry rating by 34.
Sabatons of Rapid Recovery	40 Emblem of Valor	Plate: 1580, +73 Stamina, +50 Intellect, Equip: Improves haste rating by 49., Increases spell power., Restores some mana per 5 sec.
Pack-Ice Striders	40 Emblem of Valor	Mail: 884, +49 Agility, +75 Stamina, +40 Intellect, Equip: Improves hit rating by 39., Increases attack power., Increases armor penetration rating.
Treads of Coastal Wandering	40 Emblem of Valor	Mail: 884, +64 Stamina, +53 Intellect, Equip: Improves critical strike rating by 50., Increases spell power., Restores some mana per 5 sec.
Boots of Captain Ellis	40 Emblem of Valor	Leather: 398, +37 Agility, +85 Stamina, Equip: Improves critical strike rating by 43., Equip: Improves haste rating by 55., Increases attack power.
Rainey's Chewed Boots	40 Emblem of Valor	Leather: 398, +64 Stamina, +57 Intellect, +55 Spirit, Increases spell power., Restores some mana per 5 sec.
Xintor's Expeditionary Boots	40 Emblem of Valor	Cloth: 212, +55 Stamina, +57 Intellect, +55 Spirit, Equip: Improves hit rating by 43., Increases spell power.
Slippers of the Holy Light	40 Emblem of Valor	Cloth: 212, +64 Stamina, +55 Intellect, +57 Spirit, Equip: Improves haste rating by 37., Increases spell power.

Name	ExtendedCost	Stats
Mantle of the Lost Conqueror	60 Emblem of Valor	Armor Token: These tokens can be turned in to a specific vendor to purchase parts of an armor set unique to your class.
Mantle of the Lost Protector	60 Emblem of Valor	Armor Token: These tokens can be turned in to a specific vendor to purchase parts of an armor set unique to your class.
Mantle of the Lost Vanquisher	60 Emblem of Valor	Armor Token: These tokens can be turned in to a specific vendor to purchase parts of an armor set unique to your class.
Wristbands of the Sentinel Huntress	60 Emblem of Valor	Plate: 1005, +56 Strength, +61 Stamina, Equip: Increases your expertise rating by 32., Equip: Improves critical strike rating by 56.
Bracers of Dalaran's Parapets	60 Emblem of Valor	Plate: 1005, +43 Strength, +84 Stamina, Equip: Increases defense rating by 37., Equip: Increases your parry rating by 38., Equip: Improves hit rating by 28.
Zartson's Jungle Vambraces	60 Emblem of Valor	Plate: 1005, +55 Stamina, +38 Intellect, Equip: Improves haste rating by 41., Increases spell power., Restores some mana per 5 sec.
Armguard of the Tower Archer	60 Emblem of Valor	Mail: 563, +38 Agility, +55 Stamina, +31 Intellect, Equip: Improves hit rating by 28., Equip: Improves haste rating by 30., Increases attack power.
Pigmented Clan Bindings	60 Emblem of Valor	Mail: 563, +55 Stamina, +38 Intellect, Equip: Improves haste rating by 28., Increases spell power., Restores 17 mana per 5 sec.
Wristwraps of the Cutthroat	60 Emblem of Valor	Leather: 253, +38 Agility, +55 Stamina, Equip: Improves haste rating by 41., Increases attack power., Increases armor penetration rating.
Bands of the Great Tree	60 Emblem of Valor	Leather: 253, +48 Stamina, +41 Intellect, +28 Spirit, Increases spell power., Restores 17 mana per 5 sec.
Wraps of the Astral Traveler	60 Emblem of Valor	Cloth: 135, +48 Stamina, +41 Intellect, +43 Spirit, Equip: Improves hit rating by 28., Increases spell power.
Cuffs of the Shadow Ascendant	60 Emblem of Valor	Cloth: 135, +42 Stamina, +43 Intellect, Equip: Improves haste rating by 38., Increases spell power., Restores some mana per 5 sec.
Legplates of the Lost Conqueror	75 Emblem of Valor	Armor Token: These tokens can be turned in to a specific vendor to purchase parts of an armor set unique to your class.
Legplates of the Lost Protector	75 Emblem of Valor	Armor Token: These tokens can be turned in to a specific vendor to purchase parts of an armor set unique to your class.
Legplates of the Lost Vanquisher	75 Emblem of Valor	Armor Token: These tokens can be turned in to a specific vendor to purchase parts of an armor set unique to your class.

Like the Badges of Justice found in Burning Crusade dungeons, these can be spent at certain merchants to purchase some really stunning pieces of Binds on Pickup (BoP) equipment. These require level 80 and are far superior to the equipment you have come across before.

In addition to the BoP pieces, you can also choose to spend your Emblems on pieces of Binds to Account (BtA) Heirloom items. Heirloom items can be mailed to any character on your account. The statistics on these items change depending on the level of the character who owns it. This gives any character a superior blue quality item to use for that slot starting at level 1 and going all the way to level 80. In effect, instead of spending your gold to purchase equipment for your other characters, you can now spend your Emblems to do the same thing. This not only helps you equip other characters, it also insures that you always have a use for the Emblems once you've purchased anything the character earning them needs. This is a great benefit all around. For example, maybe your guild or group of friends really needs you to bring your healer to help them out with a run, but another of your characters really needs the gear upgrades. You can help out your friends with whatever character is most needed, but still earn gear for that other character.

There is an Emblem of Heroism Quartermaster and an Emblem of Valor Quartermaster in both the Sunreaver's Sanctuary, for Horde, and The Silver Enclave, for Alliance, in Dalaran. There are a few other merchants, such as the Jewelry Vendor in Dalaran, who take Emblems in trade as well.

NEW DUNGEONS (5 MAN CONTENT)

	DUNGEON NAME	LEVEL RANGE	LOCATION
	Ahn'kahet: The Old Kingdom	73-75	Dragonblight
	Azjol-Nerub	72-74	Dragonblight
	Caverns of Time: The Culling of Stratholme	78-80	Tanaris
	Drak'Tharon Keep	74-76	Grizzly Hills
	Gundrak	76-78	Zul'Drak
	The Nexus	71-73	Borean Tundra
	The Oculus	80	Borean Tundra
	Ulduar: Halls of Lightning	78-80	Storm Peaks
	Ulduar: Halls of Stone	78-80	Storm Peaks
	Utgarde Keep	70-72	Howling Fjord
	Utgarde Pinnacle	80	Howling Fjord
	Violet Hold	75-77	Dalaran

Sharing Quests

You can now share quests with group members no matter where they are, and you can also share quests by linking them in the Chat Window. Daily Quests can be shared now as well, as long as you picked them up on the same day you are trying to share them. Make sure everyone has the relevant quests to save time when preparing for a dungeon run.

NEW RAIDS (10 AND 25 MAN CONTENT)

	DUNGEON NAME	LEVEL RANGE	LOCATION
	Naxxramas	80+	Dragonblight
	The Nexus: The Eye of Eternity	80+	Borean Tundra
	The Obsidian Sanctum	80+	Dragonblight
	The Vault of Archavon	80+	Wintergrasp

All four raids offer challenging ten-man content and Heroic level 25-man content if you are feeling adventurous!

PHASING

Northrend is a dynamic place and one of the ways the game handles this is through Phasing. With Phasing, a single location can have different appearances and NPC's depending on the experience of the player. For example, Dun Niffelem, home to the Sons of Hodir, is not always a friendly place. If you visit it when you first enter the Storm Peaks, you find the frost giants to be quite hostile. However, after doing a certain quest line you become friendly with them and their city transforms into a friendly quest hub complete with vendors for you. You haven't entered an instance, but rather a different phase of the same city. For instance, if you have a group member who has not done the correct quests yet, they see a much different Dun Niffelem than you do, even though you are technically in the same physical location. You and everyone else who is friendly or above with the Sons of Hodir are in the same phase of Dun Niffelem. Your group member, who is not with you, is in an earlier phase.

This allows the world you experience to reflect your actions in it. Phasing is used in several quests to reflect the changes you are making in the world, making for a much more immersive experience. Phasing can present a problem when grouping. In many cases characters that are not on the same steps of a quest are in different phases, making it difficult, and sometimes impossible to aid each other. When this happens, the best thing to do is to take the time to catch up your group mate to where you are in the quest line, or to form a group of people on the same phase as you. Though this sometimes can take a bit more effort, it is well worth the time. Phasing makes for a much more dynamic world and seeing it change with your actions can be a more satisfying completion to a quest than the reward itself.

FOCUS TARGETS

You can now easily set focus targets. Select the target you want to set as your focus, right click on it and select Set Focus. You can set a Focus Cast Key in the Combat panel of your Interface Options. This way, when casting a spell or ability and holding down that key, it targets your focus target rather than your main target. You can clear your focus target by again right clicking on the focus frame and selecting Clear Focus. This is especially useful for crowd control and cleansing spells.

PLAYER VS. PLAYER

Whether you just like the occasional duel or arena match, or prefer to pit your skills against other players in a large scale conflict, this expansion has something for everyone interested in PvP. The seedy Underbelly of Dalaran offers an open area for

dueling, compete with spectators. You can experience two new arenas, one in the Underbelly and the other in the heart of Orgrimmar. You can battle over a powerful Titan Artifact in Strand of the Ancients, a unique new Battleground off the coast of Dragonblight. In Wintergrasp, you can participate in zone-wide PvP unlike anything you've experienced before. We've provided detailed information on these new PvP offerings in the PvP section of this guide.

CHANGES

Interface

Northrend

Racial Abilities

Barber Shop

PVE

Phasing

DEATH KNIGHT

Death Knights are the first hero class ever available in World of Warcraft, and as such, are pretty special. These elite warriors wear plate, making them pretty tough on the battlefield. They can wield either two-handed weapons or can dual wield one-handed weapons to great effect. This class is great for soloing and more than capable of filling either a tank or DPS slot in almost any group or raid. In addition to their martial prowess, Death Knights wield the power of runes to utilize class specific melee abilities and spells, making them unlike any of the previously existing classes.

Jirak

These runes create a unique resource management system very different from energy, rage, or mana, but with a little practice it is easy to use. Every Death Knight has two Blood Runes, Frost Runes, and Unholy Runes. Each ability you use requires certain runes, just like a spell may cost other classes a certain amount of mana. As you use your abilities, the runes are used, but they refresh fairly quickly throughout the fight. This means that you can't really "spam" a single ability, but instead must utilize diverse abilities that require different runes during a battle. Familiarizing yourself with your abilities and knowing which abilities require which runes becomes important, especially in longer battles. As Death Knights use their abilities, they also build up Runic Power which they can unleash in devastating attacks by using certain abilities. Much like Rage, Runic Power decays once you are out of battle, so use it or lose it!

SCARLET ENCLAVE

Scarlet Enclave Legend

1 Death's Breach	8 Havenshire Farms	15 Chapel of the Crimson Flame
2 Havenshire Mine	9 Crypt of Remembrance	16 Scarlet Overlook
3 Havenshire Stables	10 New Avalon Inn	17 King's Harbor
4 Havenshire Lumber Mill	11 New Avalon Forge	18 The Noxious Glade
5 Mailbox	12 New Avalon Town Hall	19 Browman Mill
6 Light's Point Tower	13 Scarlet Hold	20 Light's Hope Chapel
7 Light's Point	14 Scarlet Tavern	

Creating a Death Knight

To create a Death Knight you must already have a character of level 55 or greater on your account. One of your existing characters does not become a Death Knight; it is a completely new and separate character. Once you have a level 55 character you can make a Death Knight on any realm where you have a level 55 character or above. The usual rules apply: You must have an open character slot to create a Death Knight and you can't create a Death Knight of an opposing faction on a PvP server. For instance, you can't create a Horde Death Knight on a PvP server where you already have Alliance characters.

Once you have created your character you are ready to get started in Acherus: The Ebon Hold!

Quests

The Death Knight quest chain detailed below takes your from your starting level of 55 through at least level 58 and prepares you for playing your Death Knight in the wider world. You spend these first few levels playing through a story arc that gives you the opportunity to learn about your character and get practical experience using the Death Knight's unique abilities in a variety of situations. These quests cannot be skipped, and you wouldn't really want to anyway, so enjoy your time here before rejoining your friends and guild mates.

The information below gives you everything you need to complete every quest in this chain, including hints and tips on using your abilities and dealing with the challenges each quest provides. The majority of quests here are linear, meaning you complete one, then get the next step, and so on. When more than one quest is available at once, we have noted it so you can be sure to take care of them without having to retrace your steps. Each quest you complete teaches you something about your character and has an impact on the world around you. Take your time and enjoy this unique starting area.

IN SERVICE OF THE LICH KING

Quest Giver:	The Lich King
Goal:	Speak to Instructor Razuvious
Prerequisite:	N/A
Rewards:	N/A
Bonus Talents Earned:	N/A

Anger, cruelty, vengeance—The Lich King has gifted you all of these things as one of his chosen. Seek out Instructor Razuvious within Acherus: The Ebon Hold to begin your journey.

THE EMBLAZONED RUNEBLADE

Quest Giver:	Instructor Razuvious
Goal:	Locate a battle-worn sword. Use the Runeforge to create the blade.
Prerequisite:	In Service Of The Lich King
Rewards:	Runed Soulblade, Learn: Runeforging
Bonus Talents Earned:	N/A

Search the nearby weapon racks for an old, worn sword. Take it to the nearby Runeforge to transform it into a Runed Soulblade. Once you have done this, return to Instructor Razuvious to receive your new weapon.

RUNEFORGING: PREPARATION FOR BATTLE

Quest Giver:	Instructor Razuvious
Goal:	Use your Runeforging ability to engrave a rune upon your Runed Soulblade.
Prerequisite:	The Emblazoned Runeblade
Rewards:	N/A
Bonus Talents Earned:	N/A

Runeforging is a skill unique to Death Knights. You start with only two choices: Rune of Cinderglacier or Rune of Razorice, but gain more as you progress in levels. Runeforging is a valuable way to add attributes to your weapons, and should not be overlooked. To complete this quest, approach one of the Runeforges and open up your Runeforging crafting window. Select which Rune you which to engrave and apply it to your weapon. You must be near a Runeforge in the Ebon Hold to use Runeforging. Once you are done, return to Instructor Razuvious.

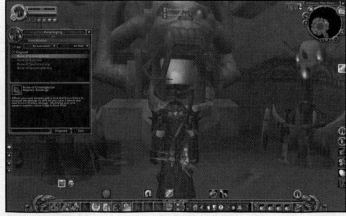

Runeforging

Runeforging is a class ability exclusive to the Death Knight. With it, you can emblazon your weapon with specific runes to suit your individual play style or the situation. These runes function much like enchantments. You can have only one on your weapon at a time, and you can also only have either a rune or an enchantment, not both, on one weapon.

Runeforging functions much like a profession. Once you learn the skill after completing the **Runeforging: Preparation for Battle** quest, you can use the Runeforging icon to bring up a list of available runes. Head to a Runeforge, available in the Ebon Hold, and select which rune you want to try and place it on your weapon. Most Runeforging recipes can be used on any weapon, but some can only be used on 1H or 2H specifically. While you can only use your Runeforging skill near a Runeforge, you can change your runes as often as you wish, at no cost, so experiment with them all to see what works best for you. While you only start with a few Runes, you gain more as you level.

	Rune of Cinderglacier	Has a chance to increase the damage of your next two attacks that deal Frost or Shadow damage.
	Rune of Lichbane	Adds extra weapon damage as Fire damage or a higher percentage of damage versus Undead targets.
	Rune of Razorice	Causes extra weapon damage as Frost damage and has a chance to increase Frost vulnerability.
	Rune of Spellbreaking	Deflects a percentage of all spell damage and reduces the duration of Silence effects. Requires 1H Rune Weapon.
	Rune of Spellshattering	Deflects a percentage of all spell damage and reduces the duration of Silence effects. Requires 2H Rune Weapon.
	Rune of Swordbreaking	Increases Parry chance and reduces the duration of Disarm effects. Requires 1H Rune Weapon.
	Rune of Sword-shattering	Increases Parry chance and reduces the duration of Disarm effects. Requires 2H Rune Weapon.
	Rune of the Fallen Crusader	Has a chance to heal you and increase your total Strength for a short time.

THE ENDLESS HUNGER

Quest Giver:	Instructor Razuvious
Goal:	Use the key to free an unworthy initiate and face them in battle.
Prerequisite:	Runeforging: Preparation For Battle
Rewards:	N/A
Bonus Talents Earned:	N/A

In the center of this floor are several Initiates that have proven themselves unworthy of becoming Death Knights. Use the key that Razuvious gives you to unlock one from his or her chains. They don their armor and equipment and face you in battle for the chance to earn their freedom. This is your first taste of battle as a Death Knight. Though you only have a few abilities at this point, they are more than enough to take down one of these cretins. As you use your abilities, notice how your runes are used up and then refreshed. This becomes very important in later battles, so you want to get used to keeping an eye on them. Once you have emerged victorious, return to Instructor Razuvious.

HOME SWEET HOME

Acherus: The Ebon Hold is home to the Lich King's legion of Death Knights, and later, to the Knights of the Ebon Blade. Here you find merchants, trainers, and the all important Runeforge. There is even a training dummy set up in the center for your use, after you have completed this quest line. Though you can eventually visit all the cities of Azeroth, Acherus is the closest thing a Death Knight has to a home.

THE EYE OF ACHERUS

Quest Giver:	Instructor Razuvious
Goal:	Report To The Lich King
Prerequisite:	The Endless Hunger
Rewards:	N/A
Bonus Talents Earned:	N/A

Now that Instructor Razuvious has seen to it that you are equipped with a weapon and know how to use it, **The Lich King** has a task for you.

DEATH COMES FROM ON HIGH

Quest Giver:	The Lich King
Goal:	Use the Eye of Acherus to Analyze structures in New Avalon
Prerequisite:	The Eye Of Acherus
Rewards:	N/A
Bonus Talents Earned:	N/A

Use the Eye of Acherus Control Mechanism to either side of the Lich King to gain control of an Eye of Acherus. With it you can analyze important structures in New Avalon like the Scarlet Hold, the Forge, the Town Hall, and the Chapel of the Crimson Flame. Once you have used the Control Mechanism, you can control the direction of the Eye as you would your normal movement. Head toward the large red arrows which point out your major targets. When you are near each one, use the Siphon of Acherus to target the structure and gather technical information about it. The Scarlet Crusade doesn't take kindly to your spying, and attack if they see you. Use Shroud to move about the town unseen. If you collect information or enter combat, the Shroud is broken, and nearby Crusade members begin attacking the Eye. If this happens you can move out of their range but sometimes the best defense is a good offense. If the soldiers notice your spying attempts, use the Summon Ghouls on Scarlet Crusade ability. This ability calls forth your Scourge allies to rise out of the ground and attack the Scarlet Crusade, giving you time to move the rather fragile Eye to safety. Once you have gathered all the information you need, use the icon on the taskbar to return to your body. If the eye is destroyed, you can use the Control Mechanism to gain another.

THE MIGHT OF THE SCOURGE

Quest Giver:	The Lich King
Goal:	Report to Highlord Darion Mograine
Prerequisite:	Death Comes From On High
Rewards:	Dominion Over Acherus, Bladed Ebon Amulet
Bonus Talents Earned:	N/A

Take the red teleporter at the base of the steps to reach the Hall of Command to speak with Highlord Darion Mograine. The Dominion Over Acherus buff allows you to move more quickly while in the Ebon Hold. From now on you gain this buff every time you enter Acherus.

REPORT TO SCOURGE COMMANDER THALANOR

Quest Giver:	Highlord Darion Mograine
Goal:	Report to Scourge Commander Thalanor
Prerequisite:	The Might Of The Scourge
Rewards:	N/A
Bonus Talents Earned:	N/A

Go up the stairs, past the teleporter to reach Scourge Commander Thalanor. Speak with him to requisition a Gryphon to take to you to Death's Breach, the camp below the Ebon Hold.

THE SCARLET HARVEST

Quest Giver:	Scourge Commander Thalanor
Goal:	Report to Prince Valanar
Prerequisite:	Report To Scourge Commander Thalanor
Rewards:	N/A
Bonus Talents Earned:	N/A

Ride the Gryphon provided by Commander Thalanor to reach Death's Breach, below the Ebon Hold. Speak to Prince Valanar upon your arrival.

IF CHAOS DRIVES, LET SUFFERING HOLD THE REINS

Quest Giver:	Prince Valanar
Goal:	Slay 10 Scarlet Crusaders or Scarlet Peasants and 10 Citizens of Havenshire
Prerequisite:	The Scarlet Harvest
Rewards:	Valanar's Signet Ring
Bonus Talents Earned:	1

Head west, down the hill into Havenshire. You can find paths leading down from Death's Breach at either end of the camp. Once there, slay ten Scarlet Crusaders or Scarlet Peasants and ten Citizens of Havenshire. The Peasants are easily slain; they don't really fight back at all. The Crusaders put up more of a fight! Be careful that you don't get overwhelmed by the Crusaders, many of whom patrol somewhat close together. The Citizens can be found further in Havenshire, trying to run to the safety of New Avalon. Before setting out to complete this quest be sure to pick up **Grand Theft Palomino** and **Tonight We Dine in Havenshire** as they can easily be done at the same time.

They're Getting Away!

The Citizens of Havenshire are trying their best to run to the perceived safety of New Avalon. Use your Death Grip ability to whisk them back to you where you can finish them off.

BONUS TALENT POINTS

Beginning with **If Chaos Drives, Let Suffering Hold the Reins**, Many quests award you Bonus Talent Points upon completion. By the time you have finished all of the Death Knight chain of quests you have the correct number of talent points for your level.

GRAND THEFT PALOMINO

Quest Giver:	Salanar the Horseman
Goal:	Steal a horse from the Havenshire Stables
Prerequisite:	Accepting If Chaos Drives, Let Suffering Hold The Reins
Rewards:	N/A
Bonus Talents Earned:	1

Salanar is in need of horses to shape into proper Deathchargers! Head down into Havenshire and make your way to the Stables. Once there, select a horse and ride it back to Salanar. While most of the Scarlet Crusade guarding this area are no match for you, be on the look out for Kitrik, the stable master. He has no patience for horse thieves and if he catches you on one of his he reposes it immediately, and you must try again. He is an elite foe and much too tough for any single Death Knight. Like any good thief, your best bet is to avoid his notice altogether.

TONIGHT WE DINE IN HAVENSHIRE

Quest Giver:	Orithos the Sky Darkener
Goal:	Retrieve 15 Saronite Arrows
Prerequisite:	Accepting If Chaos Drives, Let Suffering Hold The Reins
Rewards:	Sky Darkener's Shroud of Blood, Sky Darkener's Shroud of the Unholy, Shroud of the North Wind
Bonus Talents Earned:	1

The Saronite arrows used by Orithos' archers give them spectacular range and damage, allowing them to stop the fleeing Citizens of Havenshire dead in their tracks. Unfortunately, Saronite is rare here so Orithos asks you to retrieve the spent arrows. The arrows are scattered throughout Havenshire. Complete this quest while working on **If Chaos Drives, Let Suffering Hold the Reins**.

DEATH'S CHALLENGE

Quest Giver:	Olrun the Battlecaller
Goal:	Win duels against 5 Death Knights
Prerequisite:	Accepting If Chaos Drives, Let Suffering Hold The Reins
Rewards:	Insignia of the Scourge
Bonus Talents Earned:	1

Death's Challenge is a rite of passage for all Death Knights. You must challenge five Death Knights, either other players or the Death Knight Initiates found in Death's Breach. You only receive credit for winning, so use your abilities to the fullest in each battle. Remember to use your diseases effectively for maximum damage output—your challenger surely will. Once you have been victorious five times, return to Olrun.

RELICS

The Sigil of the Dark Rider is the first Relic you receive as a Death Knight. These can be powerful pieces of equipment so always be on the lookout for upgrades to your relic.

INTO THE REALM OF SHADOWS

Quest Giver:	Salanar the Horseman
Goal:	Slay a Dark Rider of Acherus
Prerequisite:	Grand Theft Palomino
Rewards:	Summon Deathcharger, Sigil Of The Dark Rider
Bonus Talents Earned:	2

Once you accept this quest you are transported to the Shadow Realm. Make your way down into Havenshire and look for the Dark Rider. You don't have to worry about running into any Scarlet Crusade here; they don't patrol the Shadow Realm. The Rider can be a tough foe, but one you can solo with little difficulty as long as you make use of your abilities. Once he has fallen, climb atop his mount and lead it back to Death's Breach. Once you are there use the Horseman's Call to summon Salanar and exit the Shadow Realm. If when doing this quest something should happen and you should leave the Shadow Realm prematurely, speak to Salanar and he helps you return. Completing this quest earns you the right to summon your own Deathcharger! This very fast mount serves you well throughout your travels.

GOTHIK THE HARVESTER

Quest Giver:	Prince Valanar
Goal:	Seek out Gothik the Harvester
Prerequisite:	Into The Realm Of Shadows
Rewards:	N/A
Bonus Talents Earned:	N/A

The Lich King's Grand Necromancer, Gothik the Harvester, has arrived in Death's Breach. Seek him out and offer your aid.

THE GIFT THAT KEEPS ON GIVING

Quest Giver:	Gothik the Harvester
Goal:	Use the Gift of the Harvester on Scarlet Miners to transform them.
Prerequisite:	Gothik The Harvester
Rewards:	Soul Harvester's Charm
Bonus Talents Earned:	1

Place the Gift of the Harvester on your hotbar for easy access and head down into Havenshire and enter the mine. Use the Gift of the Harvester on each Scarlet Miner you come across. It either turns them into a Ghoul, and they become your pet, or they turn into a Scarlet Ghost. The Ghosts are aggressive, so when one appears send it to its final resting place and move on to use the Gift on another Miner. Once you have gathered up five ghouls you are ready to return to Gothik. Your small army of ghouls is useful should you face members of the Scarlet Crusade on your way out of the mine.

AN ATTACK OF OPPORTUNITY

Quest Giver:	Gothik the Harvester
Goal:	Speak with Prince Valanar.
Prerequisite:	The Gift That Keeps On Giving
Rewards:	N/A
Bonus Talents Earned:	N/A

Prince Valanar is ready to finish off the Scarlet Fleet once and for all! Speak with him in Death's Breach to lend your sword to the cause.

MASSACRE AT LIGHT'S POINT

Quest Giver:	Prince Valanar
Goal:	Make your way behind enemy lines. Use a ship's cannon to destroy 100 Scarlet Defenders.
Prerequisite:	An Attack Of Opportunity
Rewards:	Plated Saronite Bracers
Bonus Talents Earned:	1

Prince Valanar has concocted a plan to deal a devastating blow to the Scarlet Crusade fools. Return to Havenshire Mine and locate a mine car outside, near the outhouse. Climb inside the mine car and an unsuspecting Scarlet Miner pulls you behind enemy lines onto one of the Scarlet ships. Once there, use their own cannons against all of the Scarlet Defenders on the beach.

Each cannon comes equipped with the ability to fire at range, as well as with an Electro-magnetic Pulse. Use the cannon to fire on the troops below you on the beach. You can easily aim it by using your movement keys and can control its arc by using the two arrows on the left hand side of the interface. Once they realize what is happening, the Defenders turn their own cannon fire on you. Use the cannon to destroy theirs! They also send troops up to the ship to try to stop you. When this happens, use the Electro-magnetic Pulse to destroy nearby enemies. Once you have destroyed 100 of the Defenders, call down the Scourge Gryphon to make your escape.

VICTORY AT DEATH'S BREACH!

Quest Giver:	Prince Valanar
Goal:	Deliver Prince Valanar's Report to Highlord Darion Mograine.
Prerequisite:	Massacre At Light's Point
Rewards:	Ornate Saronite Legplates
Bonus Talents Earned:	3

Deliver news of the victory over Scarlet forces! You can find Highlord Darion Mograine within Acherus.

THE WILL OF THE LICH KING

Quest Giver:	Highlord Darion Mograine
Goal:	Report to Prince Valanar.
Prerequisite:	Victory At Death's Breach
Rewards:	N/A
Bonus Talents Earned:	N/A

After delivering your report you find Death's Breach changed. Having taken Havenshire, the Scourge forces now move onward to New Avalon! Return to Death's Breach and report to Prince Valanar to aid in wiping out the Scarlet Crusade!

THE CRYPT OF REMEMBRANCE

Quest Giver:	Prince Valanar
Goal:	Report to Prince Keleseth.
Prerequisite:	The Will Of The Lich King
Rewards:	N/A
Bonus Talents Earned:	N/A

Now that Havenshire has fallen, Prince Valanar sends you forward to the Crypt of Remembrance which lies to the south. Once there speak to his brother, Prince Keleseth, to do your part in the coming battle. On your way to the Crypt, stop in the field to speak with Noth the Plaguebringer.

THE PLAGUEBRINGER'S REQUEST

Quest Giver:	Noth the Plaguebringer
Goal:	Bring Noth an Empty Cauldron, an Iron Chain, and 10 Crusader Skulls.
Prerequisite:	The Will Of The Lich King
Rewards:	The Plaguebringer's Girdle
Bonus Talents Earned:	2

On your way to the Crypt of Remembrance, you see Noth the Plaguebringer in the center of the pumpkin patch. He is trying to construct a Plague Cauldron but needs certain items to complete his work. To find the Empty Cauldron make your way to the basement of New Avalon's Inn. The Chain can be found in New Avalon's Forge. The Skulls can be found on any Crusader—you just need to take them! Once you have collected all of these items, return to Noth. Before embarking on this quest, be sure to visit the Crypt of Remembrance to pick up **Nowhere To Run And Nowhere To Hide** as well as **Lambs To The Slaughter**.

NOTH'S SPECIAL BREW

Quest Giver:	Noth the Plaguebringer
Goal:	Place 20 Skulls inside the Cauldron
Prerequisite:	The Plaguebringer's Request
Rewards:	Noth's Special Brew x5
Bonus Talents Earned:	N/A

This repeatable quest gives you something to do with all those leftover skulls you've collected while killing all of those Scarlet Crusaders in New Avalon. Place twenty of them in Noth's Cauldron to receive 5 bottles of Noth's Special Brew. This brew restores a portion of your health and runic power, so it comes in very handy during a tough fight. Stock up to be well prepared for any future challenges.

NOWHERE TO RUN AND NOWHERE TO HIDE

Quest Giver:	Prince Keleseth
Goal:	Assassinate the Mayor of New Avalon and find the New Avalon Registry.
Prerequisite:	The Will Of The Lich King
Rewards:	N/A
Bonus Talents Earned:	2

Keleseth wishes to strike fear into the heart of New Avalon in a way that a mere assault on its gates will not. Head into the town and make your way past the defenders and citizens to the Town Hall. Once inside, assassinate Mayor Quimby. He presents no challenge but be ready for a Councilman or two to try to stop you on your way in. Once the Mayor is dead, pick up the Registry at the back of the room and return to Keleseth. Before embarking on this quest, be sure to speak with Baron Rivendare in the Crypt of Remembrance to pick up the quest, **Lambs To The Slaughter**.

LAMBS TO THE SLAUGHTER

Quest Giver:	Baron Rivendare
Goal:	Slay 10 Scarlet Crusade Soldiers and 15 Citizens of New Avalon
Prerequisite:	The Will Of The Lich King
Rewards:	Greaves of the Slaughter
Bonus Talents Earned:	2

Head into New Avalon and slay the Scarlet Crusade and the Citizens. Any of them count towards this quest, so you can kill whomever you come across. You can get a good start on completing this quest while heading toward the Town Hall for **Nowhere To Run And Nowhere To Hide**. Once you are finished, return to Baron Rivendare.

LIKE YOU NEEDED ANOTHER REASON TO KILL THE SCARLET CRUSADE...

Fighting the Scarlet Crusade gives you a great opportunity to use your Raise Dead ability. This spell summons a Ghoul to fight alongside of you. You need a humanoid corpse or a handful of Corpse Dust to raise your smelly little friend, but with New Avalon just full of potential dead humanoids, why waste perfectly good Corpse Dust?

HOW TO WIN FRIENDS AND INFLUENCE ENEMIES

Quest Giver:	Prince Keleseth
Goal:	Persuade the Scarlet Crusade into talking about the Crimson Dawn.
Prerequisite:	Nowhere To Run And Nowhere To Hide
Rewards:	Keleseth's Signet Ring
Bonus Talents Earned:	2

Prince Keleseth has learned much in his travels—including how to get information out of almost anyone! Equip the "Persuaders" he gives you as your weapons and do battle with members of the Scarlet Crusade in New Avalon. Make sure you equip both of them! The persuaders have a chance or working on any of the Crusade, so it doesn't matter which ones you battle. Some of the Crusade hold onto their convictions very tightly and die before revealing any information. Keep trying though and eventually one of them cracks under your torture. By using these Persuaders you soon learn the truth about the Crimson Dawn!

THE PATH OF THE RIGHTEOUS CRUSADER

Quest Giver:	Orbaz Bloodbane
Goal:	Steal the New Avalon Patrol Schedule
Prerequisite:	Behind Scarlet Lines
Rewards:	Bloodbane's Gauntlets Of Command
Bonus Talents Earned:	2

Orbaz has found out that the Scarlet Crusade keeps a schedule of all their patrols in the Scarlet Hold and he has tasked you with stealing it. Before embarking on this quest, pick up **Brothers In Death** from Thassarian which becomes available upon accepting this quest. Head northeast of the tavern to find the hold. It is the largest building in New Avalon and is easy to spot. You need to fight your way past several members of the Crusade to reach the Hold. Once inside, be prepared for a few more fights and head up the steps in the center to reach the large room at the top of the keep. The New Avalon Patrol Schedule is sitting in plain sight on the table in the back, but it is guarded by Scarlet Commander Rodrick! The Commander is a bit more challenging than the rank and file Crusaders, but he is still soloable as long as you pay attention to the battle and make full use of your abilities. Take him out and grab the Patrol Schedule from the table and return to Orbaz.

BEHIND SCARLET LINES

Quest Giver:	Prince Keleseth
Goal:	Report to Orbaz Bloodbane
Prerequisite:	How To Win Friends And Influence Enemies
Rewards:	N/A
Bonus Talents Earned:	N/A

Prince Keleseth has sent some of his most trusted agents behind enemy lines and he now sends you to offer them your sword. They have set up base in the Scarlet Tavern, near the southern end of New Avalon, behind a pair of orchards near the Chapel of the Crimson Flame. Make your way to the tavern, taking out any Scarlet Crusade who try to stop you.

BROTHERS IN DEATH

Quest Giver:	Thassarian
Goal:	Find Koltira Deathweaver.
Prerequisite:	Accepting The Path Of The Righteous Crusader
Rewards:	N/A
Bonus Talents Earned:	1

Breaking through the Scarlet lines was costly, but Thassarian is concerned about one Death Knight in particular, Koltira Deathweaver. He was last seen being dragged into the Scarlet Hold. Make your way inside the hold and down the stairs near the center. The staircase to the cellar lies directly underneath the stairs leading up and can be easy to miss. Speak with Koltira once you reach the cellar. You can complete this quest at the same time as **The Path Of The Righteous Crusader**, since both lead you into the Scarlet Hold.

BLOODY BREAKOUT

Quest Giver:	Koltira Deathweaver
Goal:	Slay High Inquisitor Valroth and take his head to Thassarian.
Prerequisite:	Brothers In Death
Rewards:	Saronite War Plate
Bonus Talents Earned:	2

You free Koltira from the rack, but he is badly hurt and needs your help to get his revenge on these Scarlet dogs! Once you accept this quest, waves of Scarlet Crusade members begin coming down the stairs. Koltira Deathweaver is too weak to fight with you but he does provide an Anti-Magic Shell throughout the battle. Try to remain within it at all times. Use your Death Grip to pull the casters toward you. They don't do a lot of damage, but by using Koltira's Shell you can avoid much of what they do.

Once you have dealt with several of these small waves, High Inquisitor Valroth arrives. He is much more dangerous than the underlings you have been dealing with. Make sure you stay within Koltira's Shell as much as possible. Valroth has a knockback ability that knocks you out of the protective shield. When this hits you, scramble back into the Anti-Magic Shell as quickly as possible. If you don't, the High Inquisitor's Smite eats you alive. As long as you stay under Koltira's Shell you can deal with High Inquisitor Valroth with little danger. Once he falls to the ground, take his head back to Thassarian at the Scarlet Tavern.

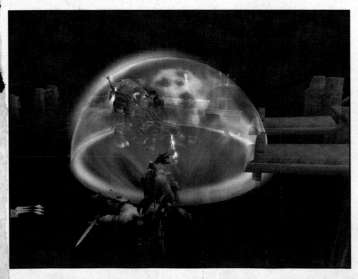

A CRY FOR VENGEANCE!

Quest Giver:	Thassarian
Goal:	Report to Knight Commander Plaguefist.
Prerequisite:	Bloody Breakout
Rewards:	N/A
Bonus Talents Earned:	N/A

Thanks to your rescue of Koltira, Thassarian is now aware that the Crusade is executing captured Death Knights in the Chapel of the Crimson Flame! Head due west of the inn to reach the Chapel. Once there, report to Knight Commander Plaguefist.

A SPECIAL SURPRISE

Quest Giver:	Knight Commander Plaguefist
Goal:	Execute an Argent Dawn Prisoner.
Prerequisite:	A Cry For Vengeance!
Rewards:	N/A
Bonus Talents Earned:	1

Commander Plaguefist has arranged a special treat for you! Enter the long building behind the Chapel. Here you find several Argent Dawn prisoners, one of each race. Approach the one of your own race and listen to their story. When they have finished their sentimental babbling, do your duty and execute the prisoner. If another Death Knight is already speaking with your prisoner, you need to wait until they are finished and have slain the prisoner before you can begin. Return to Knight Commander Plaguefist when you are finished.

A SORT OF HOMECOMING

Quest Giver:	Knight Commander Plaguefist
Goal:	Return to Thassarian.
Prerequisite:	A Special Surprise
Rewards:	Signet of the Dark Brotherhood
Bonus Talents Earned:	2

Return to the Scarlet Tavern and let Thassarian know that the Chapel of the Crimson Flame will soon be reduced to ash.

A MEETING WITH FATE

Quest Giver:	Orbaz Bloodbane
Goal:	Reach High General Abbendis at King's Harbor.
Prerequisite:	Ambush At The Overlook
Rewards:	N/A
Bonus Talents Earned:	2

Put on the Scarlet Courier's clothes and in this disguise, make your way to King's Harbor, southeast of the Scarlet Overlook. Don't engage anyone in combat on the way so that you don't ruin your disguise. Speak with High General Abbendis once you arrive.

AMBUSH AT THE OVERLOOK

Quest Giver:	Orbaz Bloodbane
Goal:	Strike down the Scarlet Courier.
Prerequisite:	A Sort Of Homecoming
Rewards:	N/A
Bonus Talents Earned:	1

Head out of the tavern and across the orchard towards New Avalon to reach the Scarlet Overlook. Once there, use the Makeshift Cover given to you by Orbaz Bloodbane. Once your cover is in place, the Scarlet Courier appears! He fights valiantly for his life but you should have no problem finishing him off. Take him down and rob him of his clothes. Orbaz has more work for you once you have finished.

THE SCARLET ONSLAUGHT EMERGES

Quest Giver:	High General Abbendis
Goal:	Deliver The Path of Redemption to Orbaz Bloodbane.
Prerequisite:	A Meeting With Fate
Rewards:	N/A
Bonus Talents Earned:	1

High General Abbendis is fooled by your disguise. Thinking you are the Scarlet Courier, she gives you a message for one of her comrades. Instead, deliver The Path of Redemption to Orbaz Bloodbane. It tells him all he needs to know about the Scarlet Onslaught. Be sure to read this before turning it over to him. It tells the story of how the Scarlet Crusade becomes the Scarlet Onslaught in Northrend.

SCARLET ARMIES APPROACH...

Quest Giver:	Orbaz Bloodbane
Goal:	Deliver The Path of Redemption to Highlord Darion Mograine.
Prerequisite:	The Scarlet Onslaught Emerges
Rewards:	Blood-soaked Saronite Plated Spaulders
Bonus Talents Earned:	3

Take the portal that Orbaz Bloodbane opens for you to Acherus and deliver the news of the approaching Scarlet armies to Highlord Darion Mograine.

THE SCARLET APOCALYPSE

Quest Giver:	Highlord Darion Mograine
Goal:	Seek out the Lich King.
Prerequisite:	Scarlet Armies Approach
Rewards:	N/A
Bonus Talents Earned:	N/A

The Scarlet Crusade has mustered their forces for one final, doomed stand. Seek out the Lich King in Death's Breach. He has work for you.

AN END TO ALL THINGS...

Quest Giver:	The Lich King
Goal:	Use a Frostbrood Vanquisher to destroy 150 Scarlet Soldiers and 10 Ballistas.
Prerequisite:	The Scarlet Apocalypse
Rewards:	Greathelm of the Scourge Champion
Bonus Talents Earned:	6

When you return to Death's Breach, you find the landscape much changed once again. The Scourge has pushed the assault into New Avalon and the Lich King orders you to help finish off the desperate Scarlet forces. Use the Horn of the Frostbrood he gives you to call forth a Frostbrood Vanquisher and ride it towards New Avalon. You can easily control the mount with your normal movement keys. The Vanquisher has two abilities, Frozen Deathbolt and Devour Humanoid. The Frozen Deathbolt is used to deal massive amounts of damage to both the Scarlet Crusade and their ballistae. Devour Humanoid lets you grab a quick snack to replenish the Vanquisher as you fight.

Once you reach New Avalon, target the ballistae on the ground. Unlike the ones on the walls, these massive weapons are surrounded by Scarlet Crusade forces, so you kill two Scarlet birds with one Deathbolt! Aim for the ballista and you take out the Scarlet Crusade as collateral damage. If you still need more ballistae afterwards, go for the ones on the walls. These fools are making their last stand and they know it and they throw everything they've got at you. Their arrows damage the Vanquisher, but the main danger is from the large bolts fired by the ballistae. When you see one fire, move

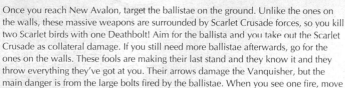

quickly out of the way to avoid taking a heavy hit of damage. If your ride begins taking too many hits, back off out of danger and scoop up a few Scarlet Crusade from the edges to regenerate. Once you are ready, return to terrorizing them! If you should lose your Vanquisher, use the Horn of the Frostbrood to summon another. Once you have completed your task, return to the Lich King at Death's Breach.

THE LICH KING'S COMMAND

Quest Giver:	The Lich King
Goal:	Report to Scourge Commander Thalanor at Browman Mill.
Prerequisite:	An End To All Things…
Rewards:	N/A
Bonus Talents Earned:	N/A

With the destruction of the Scarlet Crusade forces, there is only one thing standing in the path of the Lich King—Light's Hope Chapel. Go northwest out of Death's Breach, through the cave and into the Noxious Glade. Take the path leading out of the glade to reach Browman Mill where Scourge Commander Thalanor awaits.

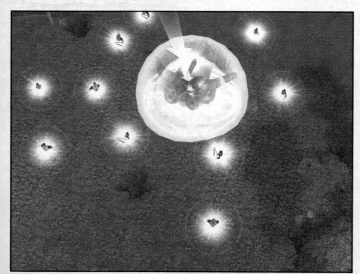

THE LIGHT OF DAWN

Quest Giver:	Scourge Commander Thalanor
Goal:	Defeat the forces of the Argent Dawn and uncover the Light of Dawn.
Prerequisite:	The Lich King's Command
Rewards:	Learn: Deathgate and Greataxe of the Ebon Blade or Greatsword of the Ebon Blade
Bonus Talents Earned:	6

Once the armies have assembled, follow Highlord Darion Mograine into battle. Be sure to stay with the Scourge forces. If you engage the forces of the light without them you are killed rather quickly. Join your fellow Death Knights in battling the defenders. Stick close to the other Scourge fighters and wear down your opponents. This is a massive battle and though your numbers are far greater, your foes stand upon holy ground and won't give way easily.

The forces of the Scourge are gathering at Browman Mill for an all out assault against Light's Hope Chapel. Once you arrive, notice the timer in the upper right portion of your screen. This lets you know if the event has already started. If it hasn't, speak to Highlord Darion Mograine to begin the event. He calls upon the Scourge armies to rise up and prepare for battle!

Once many of the defenders of the light have been defeated, Highlord Tirion Fordring arrives, putting a stop to the battle. Once this happens, you need to only wait and watch events unfold. When it is all over, you are able to complete your quest. Fordring speaks with Highlord Darion Mograine, revealing much about his past, but the Lich King soon arrives to take matters into his own hands.

The Lich King launches an attack against Fordring, and only aid from an unexpected source stops him from killing Fordring and turns the tide of battle. With Ashbringer in hand, Highlord Tirion Fordring stands against the Lich King, forcing him into a retreat.

Though you will never again be what you once were in life, having thrown off the yoke of your master, you and your fellow Death Knights now have a new purpose—the eradication of the Scourge and the destruction of the Lich King!

TAKING BACK ACHERUS

Quest Giver:	Highlord Darion Mograine
Goal:	Return to Acherus: The Ebon Hold.
Prerequisite:	The Light of Dawn
Rewards:	N/A
Bonus Talents Earned:	N/A

Now that you have broken the chains that bound you to the Lich King, it is time to take back Acherus! Use the Death Gate spell to return to The Ebon Hold. Once there report to Highlord Darion Mograine.

DEATH GATE

Your Death Gate spell allows you to return to the Ebon Hold whenever you wish. You need to use it when you want to visit your trainer or use your Runeforging skill. Death Gate makes it very convenient for you to pop back to Acherus whenever you need. When adventuring in Outland or Northrend just set your hearth to a convenient location, such as Shattrath, and use your Death Gate spell to visit the Ebon Hold, take care of your business, then hearth back to your home point.

THE BATTLE FOR THE EBON HOLD

Quest Giver:	Highlord Darion Mograine
Goal:	Slay 10 Scourge and Help Kill Patchwerk.
Prerequisite:	Taking Back Acherus
Rewards:	N/A
Bonus Talents Earned:	N/A

The Lich King may have retreated to Icecrown, but The Ebon Hold still houses some of his servants in the form of Abominations, Val'kyr Battle-maidens, and Scourge Necromancers. Use the teleporter to reach the second floor. Once there engage and defeat at least ten Scourge. In the center is Patchwerk, a colossal abomination. He is too tough for you take on by yourself. Seek out the aid of your brothers and sisters of the Ebon Blade to take him down. You don't need to bring your own group, just help other Death Knights take him out. The battle continues, even after you have completed your quest so once you have done your part to clean up Acherus, use the teleporter to return to Highlord Darion Mograine. Which quest you receive next depends on whether your character was a member of the Alliance or the Horde before becoming a Death Knight.

WARCHIEF'S BLESSING

Faction:	Horde
Quest Giver:	Highlord Darion Mograine
Goal:	Deliver the letter to Thrall.
Prerequisite:	The Battle For The Ebon Hold
Rewards:	N/A
Bonus Talents Earned:	N/A

Highlord Darion Mograine knows that for the Knights of the Ebon Blade to survive, they must make allies. Deliver the letter, given to Mograine on your behalf by Lord Tirion Fordring, to Thrall in Orgrimmar. There is a convenient portal on the balcony behind Highlord Darion Mograine.

The citizens of Orgrimmar are not happy to see a monster like you walking their streets, but their loathing is a small price to pay for the crimes you have committed while in service to the Lich King. Until you speak with Thrall you are unable to utilize any of the town's services such as the bank or merchants. Make your way into the Valley of Wisdom to reach Grommash Hold, where you can find the Warchief.

WHERE KINGS WALK

Faction:	Alliance
Quest Giver:	Highlord Darion Mograine
Goal:	Deliver the letter to King Varian Wrynn.
Prerequisite:	The Battle For The Ebon Hold
Rewards:	N/A
Bonus Talents Earned:	N/A

Highlord Darion Mograine knows that for the Knights of the Ebon Blade to survive, they must make allies. Deliver the letter, given to Mograine on your behalf by Lord Tirion Fordring, to King Varian Wrynn in Stormwind. There is a convenient portal on the balcony behind Highlord Darion Mograine.

Stormwind's citizens have suffered during battles with the Scourge and they do not forgive easily. You are unable to interact with any of the merchants or other city services until you speak with King Wrynn. Deliver the letter and he agrees to form an alliance with the Knights of the Ebon Blade against the Scourge! You are now welcome among the cities of the Alliance.

Upon completing the Death Knight chain of quests you should be at least level 58 and ready to take on the world. This is the perfect level to start questing in Outland. Because you were formerly a hero of your faction, you know all of the Flight Paths in Azeroth and don't have to spend time and effort revisiting all of them. This makes it very convenient for you to get around. You also start with a Bandaging Skill of 275, so you are ready to learn Heavy Runecloth Bandaging before jumping into battle. Visit the appropriate First Aid Trainer, found in Theramore for the Alliance and Hammerfall for the Horde, to pick up this skill and you are ready to start questing in Outland!

Abilities

Death Knights have some very unique abilities. Though they are very definitely a melee class, their manipulation of runes grants them devastating strikes, virulent diseases, and a host of other abilities designed to make them formidable opponents. There are three distinct groups of abilities, each tied to the runes used to cast them (though some of the more powerful abilities take more than one rune type to use): Blood, Frost, and Unholy. No matter how you choose to allocate your talent points, all of these abilities are at your disposal.

BLOOD

Blood Boil

Causes any of the Death Knight's diseases on the target, and all enemies nearby the target, to painfully erupt, dealing Shadow damage.

While this does consume your diseases, it is a great way to deal a burst of damage to the enemies surrounding you. It works especially well after Pestilence when the diseases have been spread around to nearby targets. If your foe is still standing after using Blood Boil, begin applying your diseases again, share them with Pestilence, and hit the Blood Boil again!

Blood Presence

This ability strengthens the Death Knight with the presence of blood, increasing damage and healing the Death Knight by a percentage of the damage dealt. Only damage dealt to targets that grant experience or honor can trigger this heal. Only one Presence may be active at a time.

Blood Presence is one of the three different presences you can use. Much like a warrior's stances, you are always in a presence. You just need to select the right one for the circumstances. Blood Presence is great for soloing most things since its healing component cuts down on the time you need to recuperate between battles, and added damage is always good.

Blood Strike

Instantly strike the enemy, causing a percentage of weapon damage plus some extra damage. It also deals with additional damage per disease.

Blood Strike is best used when you have already placed all of your diseases on the target. Since each disease causes extra damage, load the target up and then Blood Strike for maximum effect.

Blood Tap

Immediately activates a Blood Rune and temporarily converts it into a Death Rune. This rune counts as a Blood, Unholy, or Frost Rune.

Blood Tap is a highly useful ability and the more you familiarize yourself with your various abilities and their rune costs, the more often you use it. For example, you may wish to use a few moves in a row that require Frost runes to activate, but you aren't using your Blood runes at the moment. Use Blood Tap to convert an unneeded Blood Rune into a Death Rune and you've got the runes required to execute your plan. This gives you a bit more flexibility when deciding which abilities to use in a fight. With its fairly short cooldown, Blood Tap can come into play usually at least once per battle.

Dark Command

Commands the target to attack you, but has no effect if the target is already attacking you.

Dark Command functions much like a warrior's Taunt ability. It is great for peeling mobs off of healers and overzealous DPS classes and forcing the enemy to pay attention to you. It is extremely useful for a tanking Death Knight and shouldn't be relegated to the back page of your action bars, even if you never tank. This ability is great for saving those more squishy members of your party who find themselves with too much unwanted attention from mobs. Keep it handy and your group will thank you.

Death Pact

The Death Knight sacrifices an undead minion, healing you for a percentage of his or her maximum health.

Death Pact makes your Ghoul even more useful by trading your Ghoul's life for some of yours. While this does consume your Ghoul, you can always raise another. After all, you raised him from the dead—he kind of owes you.

Forceful Deflection

This passive ability increases your Parry Rating by a percentage of your total Strength.

This is one of the reasons why Strength is so important to a Death Knight, the other being for additional Attack Power. Parry helps with tanking quite a bit as any damage you can avoid is damage that doesn't have to be healed.

Pestilence

Causes Shadow damage to the target and all nearby targets and spreads any diseases on the target to the additional targets.

This ability is great at spreading around the pain. Pestilence is very useful when tanking multiple mobs, or to add that little bit extra of DPS. Pile up diseases on your main target, then use Pestilence to infect any other nearby targets. Once they have ticked a bit, finish them off with Blood Boil for explosive damage.

Strangulate

Strangulates an enemy, silencing them for a short time and deals Shadow damage at the end of the Silence.

Casters are the bane of any melee class but Strangulate gives you a way to fight back against their constant magical muttering. Use Strangulate to interrupt their spells, giving you a few precious seconds to act. When the Silence wears off, your target is hit with that blast of Shadow damage, adding injury to the insult.

FROST

Chains of Ice

The heavy chains shackle the target, reducing their movement to zero. The target regains a percentage of their movement each second.

Chains of Ice is a great method of crowd control. While it doesn't lock your target down like a mage's frost nova or a hunter's trap, it works well, especially against other melee classes. Sure, they are still going to come at you, but by the time they get within reach you have had enough time to load them up with diseases before they can even so much as scratch your armor with their weapon, giving you the upper hand.

Empower Rune Weapon

Empower your rune weapon, immediately activating all your runes and generating a decent amount of Runic Power.

This is great for tough battles when you need all the extra power you can get. While the cooldown keeps you from using it in every battle, it is short enough that you can use it almost every time you find yourself in trouble—or when you just want to deliver a particularly devastating beat down.

Frost Fever

Frost Fever deals Frost Damage over time and reduces the target's melee and ranged attack speed.

This passive effect is caused by using Icy Touch and other Frost spells. Your Attack Power gives you a bonus to the damage caused. As you use your Frost abilities, you have the chance to apply this disease to the target. Once applied it behaves like any other disease and can be effected by abilities like Pestilence and Blood Boil.

Frost Presence

The Death Knight takes on the presence of frost, increasing your total health and armor contribution from items, while reducing spell damage taken. It also increases the threat you generate. Only one Presence may be active at a time.

Frost Presence is mostly used for tanking and keeping yourself alive during tough battles. It is great at increasing your survivability and with the addition of added threat it most often the best presence for tanking.

Horn of Winter

The Death Knight blows the Horn of Winter, increasing the total Strength and Agility of all party or raid members nearby.

This buff only lasts a short time, but it gives a significant bonus to these stats. While it does require Runic Power, the cost is not that great and can easily be absorbed during a battle to improve your fellow party members.

Icebound Fortitude

The Death Knight freezes his blood to become immune to Stun effects and reduce all damage taken by a great percentage for a short time. This does not remove existing Stun effects.

This is great when fighting mobs that stun, or just for tanking, to give your healers some help. The relatively low cooldown time makes it highly useful. Any ability that mitigates the damage you take is a good thing. Though it does cost Runic Power, don't let that discourage you from using it often. The cost is not very great and though you may have to wait a moment before accumulating more Runic Power, the damage mitigation is more than worth the small trade off in damage dealing.

Icy Touch

Chills the target for Frost damage and infects them with Frost Fever, a disease that reduces melee and ranged attack speed.

Icy Touch is one of the mainstays of your arsenal, great because it causes damage and a disease. Make it one of the first spells you cast on any incoming foe.

Mind Freeze

Smash the target's mind with cold, interrupting spellcasting and preventing any spell in that school from being cast for a short time.

Unlike Strangulate, this silencing ability costs Runic Power but is highly useful when fighting casters. Hit them with Strangulate, then as it wears off and you have built up Runic Power use Mind Freeze. The more you can stop a caster from casting, the less harmful she is. Use Mind Freeze to interrupt that annoying heal or big damage spell.

Obliterate

A brutal instant attack that deals weapon damage plus some extra damage. It also deals additional damage per disease, but consumes the diseases.

Stack up all of your diseases on the target then Obliterate them! If that doesn't knock your opponent of their feet, start applying the diseases again and try it once more!

Path of Frost

The Death Knight's freezing aura creates ice beneath his feet, allowing him and his party or raid to walk on water for a time. This also works while mounted, but any damage cancels the effect.

It sure is a lot easier than trying to swim in full plate!

Rune Strike

Instantly strike the target for a percentage of weapon damage plus additional damage. Rune Strike is only useable after an attack is dodged or parried. Rune Strike cannot be dodged, blocked, or parried..

Keep Rune Strike on an easily visible portion of your action bar so you can see when it becomes active. It is a pretty powerful strike, so be sure to use it every time it comes up.

Runic Focus

Unlike most casters, a Death Knight's spells cause double damage on critical hits. Critical hits from casters normally do not approach double damage without talents. Death Knightsneed no such talents.

UNHOLY

Anti-Magic Shell

This spell surrounds the Death Knight in an Anti-Magic Shell, absorbing a high percentage of the damage dealt by harmful spells and preventing the application of harmful magical effects. Damage absorbed by Anti-Magic Shell energizes the Death Knight with additional Runic Power.

While the Anti-Magic shell only lasts for a few seconds, it is very useful. Pop it up in a fight to not only eliminate a great deal of the damage you would otherwise take but to grab that extra Runic Power. This ability makes it cost practically nothing to use.

Army of the Dead

Summons an entire legion of Ghouls to fight for the Death Knight. The Ghouls swarm the area, taunting and fighting anything they can. While channeling Army of the Dead, you take less damage equal to your Dodge and Parry chance.

Army of the Dead is a great way to deal with a group of foes. Though they don't last very long, the army is great at getting the attention of enemies and occupying them for a few precious seconds, allowing you to get a handle on the battle. This ability has a moderately long cooldown, so you want to use it when it counts. Also, like any other mindless pet your Ghoul army can be a bit overzealous. Make sure you are in an area conducive to such a large ghoulish group before summoning them so you don't end up with extra mobs you weren't counting on.

Blood Plague

A passive ability that creates a disease dealing Shadow damage over time. It also has a chance to remove one heal over time effect whenever it does damage. It is caused by Plague Strike and other abilities.

An extra disease is always a good thing, and the extra damage is always welcome but Blood Plague's ability to remove Heal Over Time effects is its greatest asset. This way, instead of your diseases competing with a HoT, you eliminate it and do the damage you came to do.

Death and Decay

Corrupts the ground targeted by the Death Knight, causing Shadow damage every second that the target remains in the area for a short time. This ability produces a high amount of threat.

Death and Decay is great for tanking multiple mobs. Place it on the ground and gather up the threat from the nearby foes. It is also very useful anytime your target, such as a mob that doesn't run or a zealous PvP player, is reluctant to leave your vicinity. As long as they are close to you they keep soaking up the damage, and the extra threat, for the duration of this spell.

Death Coil

Fires a blast of unholy energy, causing Shadow damage to an enemy target or healing damage from a friendly Undead target.

Death Coil is an awesome use of Runic Power, allowing you to dump quite a bit of it into this powerful blast. It is also great for healing your Ghoul pet. While this may not always be a smart use of Runic Power on your short lived Ghouls, by spending talents in the Unholy tree you get the ability to have a longer lived Ghoul, making Death Coil a valuable heal.

Death Gate

It opens a gate which the Death Knight can use to return to the Ebon Hold.

This spell is invaluable for every Death Knight. Not only can you easily visit your trainer to train or respec, you can also quickly access a Runeforge. Set your hearth in a convenient place and use Death Gate to travel back to Acherus to attend to your Death Knight needs and hearth back to wherever you are currently adventuring.

Death Grip

Harnessing the unholy energy that surrounds and binds all matter, Death Grip draws the target toward the Death Knight and forces the enemy to attack the Death Knight for a few seconds.

Death Knights don't use ranged weapons so Death Grip is most obviously useful for pulling mobs, but is also beneficial in other ways. For instance, whether you are the tank or not, Death Grip lets you pull mobs off of healers and casters, or anyone who just can't handle the aggro at the moment. At the very least it gives that person time to get a heal off or maybe dump their threat. This can make all the difference in a close fight. When you are the tank this just gives you one more way to keep all the enemies focused on you. Death Grip is also perfect for mobs, or players in PvP, that think they are going to run away. Unlike abilities that root them in place, Death Grip not only stops their flight, but jerks them right back to you, in range to use any and all of your abilities. Its cooldown time means you won't be able to use it more than once or twice a fight, but it is one of the most powerful tools in your arsenal, so learn to use it well.

Death Strike

A deadly weapon attack that deals a percentage of weapon damage plus extra damage then heals you for a percentage of the damage done for each of the diseases on the target.

Death Strike is massively useful at making up for the damage you take during battle. Lay down your diseases on a target then Death Strike for maximum return on your rune expenditure. You get to deal damage and heal yourself—always a good combination.

Plague Strike

A vicious strike that deals a percentage of weapon damage plus additional damage. It also infects the target with Blood Plague, a disease dealing Shadow damage over time. Plague Strike removes one heal over time effect from the target.

Damage is good to have, but the real strength of this strike lies in its ability to inflict Blood Plague. This strong damage over time ability not only deals out additional pain, but has a good chance to remove heal over time effects each time it does damage. By not competing with a heal, your diseases are just that much more devastating.

Raise Dead

It does what it says: raises a Ghoul to fight by your side. If no humanoid corpse that yields experience or honor is available, you must supply Corpse Dust to complete the spell. If the corpses of friendly players are raised, they have control over the Ghoul. You can only have one Ghoul at a time with this ability.

Your Ghoul is your staunchest ally. Though his brain is a bit rotten, he attacks anything you command him to, adding a substantial amount of damage to your own output. To summon a Ghoul all you need is a humanoid corpse or Corpse Dust. Corpse Dust is available from reagent vendors throughout Azeroth, so you should always be able to summon your Ghoul if need be. In areas where humanoid corpses are plentiful, keep him out to give you the advantage. Corpse Dust isn't cheap, but you should always keep a stack on you for emergencies. You can also cast this on fellow players, once they are deceased that is. Sure, they won't obey your commands like your usual Ghoul, but it is fun to raise your friends from the dead!

Unholy Presence

The ability infuses the Death Knight with unholy fury, increasing your attack speed and movement speed and reducing the global cooldown of all abilities. Only one presence may be active at one time.

Unholy Presence is great for providing DPS, particularly in groups. With it you are more vulnerable than in Frost or Blood Presence, but you gain an increase to your damage output that more than makes up for it.

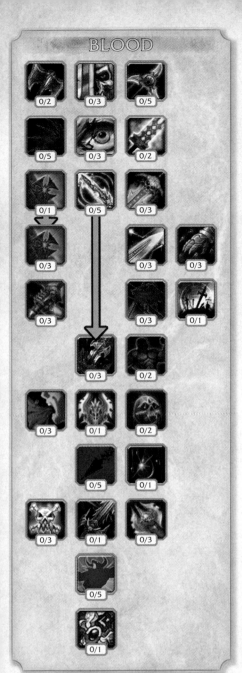

TALENTS

As with your abilities, the Death Knight's Talents are divided up between three trees: Blood, Frost, and Unholy. Each offers unique talents which strengthen your character in different ways. While there is no right way or wrong way to spec, each tree has its own strengths. Which path you choose should depend on what skills you wish to augment the most, which talents are most useful to your style of play, and most importantly, what is the most fun for you. Take time to play with various builds to see what you like the best. Remember, no talent spec is ever set in stone and a quick trip to your trainer in the Ebon Hold and a bit of your hard earned cash lets you rebuild your talents whenever you want.

BLOOD

The Blood talent tree revolves mostly around dealing physical damage and keeping yourself healed. It is great for soloing or questing. It also works really well with other DPS classes, getting the most benefit from other classes' debuffs that decrease armor for example. Good for generating Runic Power and reducing threat, it is not often used for tanking, but works really well as a DPS spec, giving you the extra power you need to take enemies down quickly.

Butchery

Whenever you kill an enemy that grants experience or honor, you generate Runic Power. In addition you generate a smaller amount of Runic Power every few seconds while in combat.

Subversion

Increases the critical strike chance of Blood Strike, Heart Strike, and Obliterate, and reduces threat generated while in Blood or Unholy Presence.

Blade Barrier

Whenever you have no Blood Runes active, your Parry chance is increased for the next few seconds.

35

Bladed Armor

Your Attack Power is increased depending on your armor value.

Scent of Blood

You have a chance after being struck by a ranged or melee hit to gain the Scent of Blood effect, causing your next melee hit to generate Runic Power.

Two-Handed Weapon Specialization

Increases the damage you deal with two-handed melee weapons.

Rune Tap

Converts 1 Blood Rune into a percentage of your maximum health.

Dark Conviction

Increases your chance to critically hit with weapons, spells and abilities.

Death Rune Mastery

Whenever you hit with Death Strike or Obliterate there is a chance that the Frost and Unholy Runes become Death Runes when they activate.

Improved Rune Tap

Increases the health provided by Rune Tap and lowers the cool down on it as well.

Spell Deflection

You have a chance equal to your Parry chance of taking less damage from a direct damage spell.

Vendetta

Heals you for a percentage of your maximum health whenever you kill a target that yields experience or honor.

Bloody Strikes

Increases the damage and the bonus damage from diseases of your Blood Strike and Heart Strike.

Veteran of the Third War

Increases your total Strength, Stamina, and Expertise.

Mark of Blood

Place a Mark of Blood on an enemy. Whenever the marked enemy deals damage to a target, that target is healed for a percentage of its maximum health.

Bloody Vengeance

Gives you a bonus to the Physical damage you deal for a short time after dealing a critical strike from a weapon swing, spell, or ability. This effect stacks up to three times.

Abomination's Might

Your Blood Strikes and Heart Strikes have a chance and your Obliterates have a greater chance to increase the attack power of raid members nearby for a short period of time. This also increases your total Strength.

Bloodworms

Your weapon hits have a chance to cause the target to spawn Bloodworms. Bloodworms attack your enemies, healing you as they do damage for a short time or until they are killed.

Hysteria

Induces a friendly unit into a killing frenzy for a short time. The target is Enraged, which increases their physical damage but causes them to suffer damage equal to a percentage of their maximum health every second.

Blood Aura

All party or raid members near the Death Knight are healed by a percentage of the damage they deal. Only damage dealt to targets that grant experience or honor can trigger this heal.

Sudden Doom

Your Blood Strikes and Heart Strikes have a chance to make your next Death Coil consume no Runic Power and critically hit if cast within a short amount of time.

Vampiric Blood

Increases the amount of health generated through spells and effects for a time.

Will of the Necropolis

Reduces the cooldown of your Anti-Magic Shell. In addition, when you are low on health, your total armor increases.

Heart Strike

Instantly strikes the enemy, causing a percentage of weapon damage, additional damage, and bonus damage per disease. Also prevents the target from using Haste effects for a short time.

Might of Mograine

Increases the critical strike damage bonus of your Blood Boil, Blood Strike, Death Strike, Heart Strike, and Obliterate abilities.

 ## Blood Gorged

When you are close to full health, you deal more damage. Also increases your expertise.

 ## Dancing Rune Weapon

Unleashes all available Runic Power to summon a second rune weapon that fights on its own for a short time, doing the same attacks as the Death Knight.

FROST

The Frost line has many talents that deal with damage mitigation, making it popular with tanking Death Knights. This doesn't mean that you don't deal decent damage with Frost, you certainly can, but how you deal the damage is much different than with other specs. Many of talents in the Frost line revolve around infecting your target with Frost Fever and then hitting them hard and fast. Like the Blood spec you have some very useful group abilities as well.

 ## Improved Icy Touch

Your Icy Touch does additional damage and your Frost Fever reduces melee and ranged attack speed by an additional amount.

 ## Glacier Rot

Diseased enemies take more damage from your Icy Touch, Howling Blast and Frost Strike.

 ## Toughness

Increases your armor value from items and reduces the duration of all movement slowing effects.

 ## Icy Reach

Increases the range of your Icy Touch, Chains of Ice and Howling Blast.

 ## Black Ice

Increases your Frost damage.

 ## Nerves of Cold Steel

Increases your chance to hit with one-handed melee weapons and increases the damage done by your offhand weapon.

 ## Icy Talons

You leech heat from victims of your Frost Fever, so that when their melee attack speed is reduced, yours increases for a short time.

 ## Lichborne

Draw upon unholy energy to become undead for a short time. While undead, you are immune to Charm, Fear, and Sleep effects and your horrifying visage causes melee attacks to have an additional chance to miss you.

 ## Annihilation

Increases the critical strike chance of your melee special abilities. In addition there is a chance that your Obliterate does its damage without consuming diseases.

 ## Runic Power Mastery

Increases your maximum Runic Power.

 ## Killing Machine

After landing a critical strike from an auto attack, there is a chance your next Icy Touch, Howling Blast or Frost Strike will be a critical strike.

 ## Frigid Dreadplate

Reduces the chance melee attacks will hit you.

 ## Chill of the Grave

Your Chains of Ice, Howling Blast, Icy Touch and Obliterate generate additional Runic Power.

 ## Deathchill

When activated, makes your next Icy Touch, Howling Blast, Frost Strike or Obliterate a critical hit.

 ## Improved Icy Talons

Your Icy Talons effect increases the melee attack speed of your entire group or raid for a short time. In addition, it increases your melee attack speed at all times.

 ## Merciless Combat

Your Icy Touch, Howling Blast, Obliterate and Frost Strike do additional damage when striking targets with low health.

 ## Rime

Increases the critical strike chance of your Icy Touch and Obliterate and casting Icy Touch has a chance to cause your next Howling Blast to consume no runes.

Endless Winter

Your Chains of Ice has a chance to cause Frost Fever and the Runic Power cost of your Mind Freeze is reduced.

Howling Blast

Blasts the target with frigid wind dealing Frost damage to all nearby enemies. Deals double damage to targets infected with Frost Fever.

Frost Aura

All party or raid members near the Death Knight gain spell resistance.

Chilblains

Victims of your Frost Fever disease are Chilled, reducing movement speed for a short time.

Blood of the North

Increases Blood Strike damage. In addition, whenever you hit with Blood Strike or Pestilence there is a chance that the Blood Rune becomes a Death Rune when it activates.

Unbreakable Armor

Increases your armor, your total Strength, and your Parry for a short time.

Acclimation

When you are hit by a spell, you have a chance to boost your resistance to that type of magic for a short time.

Frost Strike

Instantly strikes the enemy, causing weapon damage plus Frost damage

Guile of Gorefiend

Increases the critical strike damage bonus of your Blood Strike, Obliterate, Howling Blast, and Frost Strike abilities and increases the duration of your Icebound Fortitude.

Tundra Stalker

Your spells and abilities deal more damage to targets infected with Frost Fever and increases your expertise. Increases the damage done by Icy Touch and increases your expertise.

Hungering Cold

Purges the earth around the Death Knight of all heat. Enemies close by are trapped in ice, preventing them from performing any action for a short period of time and infecting them with Frost Fever. Enemies are considered Frozen, but any damage other than diseases breaks the ice.

UNHOLY

While diseases are important in all Death Knight builds, the Unholy talent line specializes in talents that increase the damage and duration of your diseases, making them your primary source of damage. Though your pet is not the focus of this talent tree, putting points into it does get you several talents that work with your pet specifically to increase its usefulness.

Vicious Strikes

Increases the critical strike chance and critical damage bonus of your Plague Strike, Death Strike, and Scourge Strike.

Morbidity

Increases the damage and healing of Death Coil and reduces the cooldown on Death and Decay.

Anticpation

Increases your Dodge chance.

Epidemic

Increases the duration of Blood Plague and Frost Fever.

Virulence

Increases your chance to hit with your spells and reduces the chance that your spells and diseases can be cured.

Unholy Command

Reduces the cooldown of your Death Grip ability.

Ravenous Dead

Increases your total Strength and the contribution your Ghouls get from your Strength and Stamina.

Outbreak

Increases the damage of Plague Strike, Pestilence and Blood Boil.

Necrosis

Your auto attacks deal an additional amount of Shadow damage.

Corpse Explosion

Causes a corpse to explode dealing Shadow damage to all nearby enemies. Uses a nearby corpse if the target is not a corpse. Does not affect mechanical or elemental corpses.

On a Pale Horse

You become as hard to stop as death itself. The duration of all Stun and Fear effects used against you is reduced and your mounted speed is increased. This does not stack with other movement speed increasing effects.

Blood-Caked Blade

Your auto attacks have a chance to cause a Blood-Caked Strike, which hits for a percentage of weapon damage plus a percentage for each of your diseases on the target.

Shadow of Death

Increases your total Strength and Stamina. In addition, whenever you die, you return to keep fighting as a Ghoul for a short time.

Summon Gargoyle

A Gargoyle flies into the area and bombards the target with Nature damage modified by your attack power.

Impurity

Your spells receive an additional benefit from your attack power.

Dirge

Your Death Strike, Obliterate, Plague Strike and Scourge Strike generate additional Runic Power.

Magic Suppression

You take less damage from all magic. In addition, your Anti-Magic Shell absorbs additional spell damage.

Reaping

Whenever you hit with Blood Strike or Blood Boil there is a chance that the Blood Rune becomes a Death Rune when it activates.

Master of Ghouls

The Ghoul summoned by your Raise Dead spell is considered a pet and is under your control. Unlike normal Death Knight Ghouls, your pet does not have a limited duration.

Desecration

Your Plague Strikes have a chance to cause the Desecrated Ground effect. Targets in the area are slowed by the grasping arms of the dead while you cause additional damage while standing on the unholy ground.

Anti-Magic Zone

Places a large, stationary Anti-Magic Zone that reduces spell damage done to party or raid members inside it. The Anti-Magic Zone lasts for a period of time or until it has absorbed its maximum amount of damage.

Unholy Aura

All party or raid members near the Death Knight move faster. This effect does not stack with other movement improving effects.

Night of the Dead

Your next ten Plague Strikes and Scourge Strikes lower the cooldown of Raise Dead and Army of Dead with each strike.

Crypt Fever

Your diseases also cause Crypt Fever, which increases the damage of other diseases on the target.

Bone Shield

The Death Knight is surrounded by whirling bones. While at least one bone remains, he takes less damage from all sources and deals more damage with all attacks, spells, and abilities. Each damaging attack that lands consumes one bone.

Wandering Plague

When your diseases damage an enemy, there is a chance equal to your melee critical strike chance that they cause additional damage to the target and all enemies very close by. Ignores any target under the effect of a spell that is cancelled by taking damage.

Ebon Plaguebringer

Your Crypt Fever morphs into Ebon Plague, which increases vulnerability to magic, in addition to increasing the damage done by diseases. Improves your critical strike chance with weapons and spells at all times.

Scourge Strike

An unholy strike that deals weapon damage as Shadow damage plus additional damage, and bonus damage per each disease.

Rage of Rivendare

Your spells and abilities deal more damage to targets infected with Blood Plague. Also increases your expertise.

Unholy Blight

A vile swarm of unholy insects surround the Death Knight for a small radius. Enemies caught in the area take Shadow damage per second and are considered diseased.

CLASSES

TEN MORE LEVELS!

The opening up of Northrend has increased the level cap ten more levels—all the way to 80! The new continent is full of challenges to help you reach this goal. These extra ten levels give you the chance to increase your skill with many of your current abilities, as well as to learn many new ones.

Every class has seen some changes, some more than others of course. To keep things balanced many old familiar abilities have been tweaked slightly, or in some cases extensively, to make them fit the world as a whole. Before you start worrying that your character has been bruised by the nerfbat, keep in mind that every class has become more powerful, and by extension, more useful in a wider variety of situations.

As is the case with Outland, you will find no class trainers in Northrend. The one exception to this being that the Kirin Tor provides mage trainers in Dalaran. To visit your trainer and get your hands on your new abilities, you must return to one of the major cities of your faction. For your first few levels in Northrend you can leave your Hearthstone set in Shattrath or one of the capital cities in Kalimdor or the Eastern Kingdoms to make traveling back to your trainer a bit easier. Of course you have to make the trip back the old fashioned way then. Once you reach Dalaran, set your Hearthstone there. Much like Shattrath did for Outland, Dalaran functions as a central travel hub for Northrend. From Dalaran you can take one of the portals found in the Sunreaver's Sanctuary for Horde, or The Silver Enclave for Alliance, straight back to your trainer at the capital city of your choice.

NEW AND REVISED TALENTS

As if the new abilities weren't enough to get you excited, your characters are also going to earn ten more Talent Points to play with. Each talent tree has gained two more tiers, making the deepest talent in each one cost 51 Talent Points. Every class has been given some truly awesome new Talents on which to spend those points, but those extra points give you more than just access to these new abilities, they also give you choice.

With ten more Talent Points to play with you have more room to experiment. Spend them all in one tree to specialize or spread them around to pick up different Talents. With so many options, there isn't really a right way or a wrong way to spec. What's important is learning how your Talents affect how you play. Try different things, even if they are wildly different from the builds you've used before. Switching specs isn't always cheap, but you earn enough money in Northrend to cover the cost of experimenting. The time you spend is well worth it when it comes to really knowing your character and that is a much better advantage than any particular Talent or Ability will ever be.

NEW CLASS ABILITIES AND TALENTS

With so many changes to the abilities and talents, we've given you all the information you need to see the possibilities for your character. This chapter discusses the abilities and talents for each class so you can plan for your drive to level 80!

With so many changes to the abilities and talents we felt it was important to give you a full look at what you have available to your class. You will find many new names on these lists, and even more changes to familiar abilities. These additions have also effected how classes augment each other, so take a look at not only your class, but the others as well.

Classes

Druid

Hunter

Mage

Paladin

Priest

Rogue

Shaman

Warlock

Warrior

Druid Abilities

Druids are getting some pretty extensive additions and revisions to their abilities and talents. Some of the shapeshift forms have received changes which make them more viable in different circumstances. Many spells and talents now can be used by the Druid in various forms. This will greatly affect how you play. You may find yourself having to switch back to caster form less frequently, or even using your shapeshift forms more often in battle because of this.

Underused, or niche, abilities have been given an overhaul to make them more widely useable. For example, you can now cast Entangling Roots indoors! You may find yourself no longer relying on the same few familiar spells, but instead dusting off those rarely used abilities and giving them a larger role in your everyday play.

In addition to the new abilities that come with working your way towards level 80, you now have access to a whole host of new Talents. There are significant changes to all three Druid Talent trees.

BALANCE

 ### BARKSKIN

The druid's skin becomes as tough as bark. All damage taken is reduced. While protected, damaging attacks will not cause spellcasting delays. This spell is usable while stunned, frozen, incapacitated, feared or asleep. Usable in all forms.

Now that this is useable in all forms, Barkskin is going to see a lot more use. Use it to protect yourself while you get off a heal, or other spell, or to mitigate the damage you take while you are incapacitated on some way.

 ### CYCLONE

Tosses the enemy target into the air, preventing all action but making them invulnerable for a few seconds. Only one target can be affected by your Cyclone at a time.

 ### ENTANGLING ROOTS

Roots the target in place and causes Nature damage over time. Damage caused may interrupt the effect.

Answering the prayer of many Druids, Entangling Roots is now useable indoors. This is a significant change! Now you have an effective method of crowd control that works anywhere, and on a variety of targets.

 ### FAERIE FIRE

Decreases the armor of the target. While affected, the target cannot stealth or turn invisible.

Faerie Fire is also effective against the improved Night Elf ability, Shadowmeld.

 ### HIBERNATE

Forces the enemy target to Sleep. Any damage will awaken the target. Only one target can be forced to hibernate at a time. Only works on Beasts and Dragonkin.

 ### HURRICANE

Creates a violent storm in the target area causing Nature damage to enemies and greatly increasing the time between melee, ranged attacks and spells. Druids must channel to maintain the spell.

This ability no longer has a cooldown which means you can unleash it as much as you want, or at least as much as you can bear the high mana cost. If you have Omen of Clarity, Hurricane is the perfect spell to use when it procs—lots of AoE damage at no cost. Hurricane can also now produce critical damage. As a Balance spell this makes it very useful in Moonkin form, which also mitigates the mana cost when it critically hits.

 ### INNERVATE

Greatly increases the target's Spirit based mana regeneration and allows full mana regeneration while casting.

 ### MOONFIRE

Burns the enemy for Arcane damage and then additional Arcane damage over time.

Moonfire comes with a moderate to hefty mana cost. This doesn't mean you shouldn't use it, it can be a very, very useful offensive spell. However, it is most mana efficient with its DoT portion is able to tick for its entire duration.

 ### NATURE'S GRASP

While active, any time an enemy strikes the caster they are afflicted by Entangling Roots.

As with some other abilities, Nature's Grasp has moved form your Talent tree to being a trainable ability. It can also now be used indoors, and while shapeshifted, making it a very effective buff to keep on as much as possible, especially considering it has no mana cost.

 ### SOOTHE ANIMAL

Soothes the target beast, reducing the range at which it will attack you. Only affects Beasts and Dragonkin targets.

Now that this is instant cast, it is even more useful for getting you past tricky areas where beasts are just waiting to eat you.

 ### STARFIRE

Causes Arcane damage to the target.

 ### TELEPORT: MOONGLADE

Teleports the caster to the Moonglade.

 ### THORNS

Thorns sprout from the friendly target causing Nature damage to attackers when hit.

 ### WRATH

Causes Nature damage to the target.

FERAL COMBAT

AQUATIC FORM

Shapeshift into aquatic form, increasing swim speed and allowing the druid to breathe underwater. Also protects the caster from Polymorph effects. The act of shapeshifting also frees the caster of Polymorph and Movement Impairing effects.

BASH

Stuns the target and interrupts spellcasting for a short time.

BEAR FORM

Shapeshift into Bear form, increasing attack power, Armor contribution from items, and Stamina. The act of shapeshifting also frees the caster of Polymorph and Movement Impairing effects. You can also use various bear abilities.

CAT FORM

Shapeshift into cat form, increasing melee attack power plus Agility. Also protects the caster from Polymorph effects and allows the use of various cat abilities. The act of shapeshifting frees the caster of Polymorph and Movement Impairing effects.

CHALLENGING ROAR

Forces all nearby enemies to focus attacks on you.

Use it when your Growl is on cooldown to give yourself some extra time to build up threat or when Growl is on cooldown to make sure you've got the enemy's attention. Its cooldown has been greatly reduced, so get used to working it into your normal rotations.

CLAW

Claw the enemy, causing additional damage. Awards one combo point.

COWER

You Cower, causing no damage but lowering your threat a large amount, making the enemy less likely to attack you.

DASH

Increases movement speed by a large amount while in Cat Form for a short time. Does not break prowling.

DEMORALIZING ROAR

The druid roars, decreasing nearby enemies' melee attack power.

DIRE BEAR FORM

Shapeshift into dire bear form, increasing melee attack power, armor contribution from items, and Stamina. Also protects the caster from Polymorph effects and allows the use of various bear abilities. The act of shapeshifting frees the caster of Polymorph and Movement Impairing effects.

ENRAGE

Generates rage over time, but reduces base armor in Bear Form and in Dire Bear Form.

FAERIE FIRE(FERAL)

Decreases the armor of the target. While affected, the target cannot stealth or turn invisible. Deals damage and additional threat when used in Bear Form or Dire Bear Form.

This is an example of a talent that has been made into a trainable ability, so all druids can access it.

FELINE GRACE

Reduces damage from falling.

FEROCIOUS BITE

Finishing move that causes damage per combo point and converts each extra point of energy into additional damage. Damage is increased by your attack power.

FLIGHT FORM

Shapeshift into Flight Form, increasing movement speed and enabling you to fly. Cannot be used in combat and can only be used in Outland or Northrend. The act of shapeshifting frees the caster of Polymorph and Movement Impairing effects.

FRENZIED REGENERATION

Converts rage per second into health for a short time. Each point of rage is converted into a small percentage of max health.

GROWL

Taunts the target to attack you, but has no effect if the target is already attacking you.

The cooldown on this ability has been slightly reduced, making it easier to keep the mob's attention on you. You may also notice that the range is larger. This gives you much more control over a battlefield.

LACERATE

Lacerates the enemy target, dealing bleed damage and making them bleed over time and causing a high amount of threat. Damage is increased by attack power. This effect stacks up to five times on the same target.

MAIM

Finishing move that causes damage and incapacitates the target. Additional damage caused may interrupt the effect. The victim's spellcasting is also interrupted. Causes more damage and lasts longer per combo point.

MAUL

A strong attack that increases damage and causes a high amount of threat. Effects which increase Bleed damage also increase Maul damage.

POUNCE

You Pounce, stunning the target and causing damage over time. Must be prowling. Awards 1 combo point.

PROWL

Allows the Druid to prowl around, but reduces your movement speed by a moderate amount. Lasts until cancelled.

RAKE

Rake the target for bleed damage and additional amount of damage over time. Awards 1 combo point.

RAVAGE

Ravage the target, causing a great deal of damage. Must be prowling and behind the target. Awards 1 combo point.

RIP

Finishing move that causes damage over time. Damage increases per combo point and by your attack power.

SAVAGE ROAR

Finishing move that increases attack power by a moderate amount. Lasts longer per combo point.

SHRED

Shred the target, causing a good deal of damage. Must be behind the target. Awards 1 combo point. Effects which increase Bleed damage also increase Shred damage.

SWIFT FLIGHT FORM

Shapeshift into swift flight form, increasing movement speed by a great deal and allowing you to fly. Cannot use in combat. Can only use this form in Outland or Northrend. The act of shapeshifting frees the caster of Polymorph and Movement Impairing effects.

SWIPE

Swipe nearby enemies, inflicting damage. Damage increased by attack power.

This ability is great for holding aggro on multiple mobs. Use it anytime you have to tank more than one foe, or just use it when soloing to take out enemies quclly.

TIGER'S FURY

Increases damage done for a short time.

With it having no Energy cost, Tiger's Fury can be cast every time its cooldown is up to give you a damage boost.

TRACK HUMANOIDS

Shows the location of all nearby humanoids on the mini-map. Only one type of thing can be tracked at a time.

TRAVEL FORM

Shapeshift into travel form, increasing movement speed. Also protects the caster from Polymorph effects. Only useable outdoors. The act of shapeshifting frees the caster of Polymorph and Movement Impairing effects.

RESTORATION

ABOLISH POISON

Attempts to cure one poison effect on the target, and one more poison effects every tick for a short time.

CURE POISON

Cures one poison effect on the target.

GIFT OF THE WILD

Gives the Gift of the Wild to all party and raid members, increasing armor, attributes and all resistances.

HEALING TOUCH

Heals a friendly target for a moderate amount.

LIFEBLOOM

Heals the target over a few seconds. When Lifebloom completes its duration or is dispelled, the target instantly heals themselves. This effect can stack.

You may notice that Lifebloom doesn't heal for quite as much as it used to. While still a useful spell, it is now on par with other healing abilities.

MARK OF THE WILD

Increases the friendly target's armor, attributes and all resistances.

NOURISH

Heals a friendly target. Heals for an additional amount if you have a Rejuvenation, Regrowth, or Lifebloom effect active on the target.

REBIRTH

Returns the spirit to the body, restoring a dead target to life.

Druid

Hunter

Mage

Paladin

Priest

Rogue

Shaman

Warlock

Warrior

REGROWTH

Heals a friendly target and heals for an additional amount over time.

REJUVENATION

Heals the target over time.

REMOVE CURSE

Dispels one Curse from a friendly target.

This can now be used in your Tree of Life form as well.

REVIVE

Returns the spirit to the body, restoring a dead target to life. Cannot be cast when in combat.

TRANQUILITY

Heals all nearby group members. Druid must channel to maintain the spell.

DRUID TALENTS

BALANCE

STARLIGHT WRATH

=Reduces the cast time of your Wrath and Starfire spells.

GENESIS

-Increases the damage and healing done by your periodic damage and healing effects.

MOONGLOW

Reduces the Mana cost of your Moonfire, Starfire, Starfall, Wrath, Healing Touch, Regrowth and Rejuvenation spells.

NATURE'S MAJESTY

Increases the critical strike chance of your Wrath, Starfire, Starfall, Nourish and Healing Touch spells.

IMPROVED MOONFIRE

Increases the damage and critical strike chance of your Moonfire spell.

BRAMBLES

Damage from your Thorns and Entangling Roots is increased and damage done by your Treants is increased. In addition, damage from your Treants and attacks done to you while you have Barkskin active have a chance to Daze the target.

The new boost to your Treant damage makes this an even more useful talent. In addition, the chance to Daze your opponent gives you just that much more time to get in another attack of cast a quick heal.

NATURE'S GRACE

All spell criticals have a chance to grace you with a blessing of nature, reducing the casting time of your next spell.

NATURE'S SPLENDOR

Increases the duration of your Moonfire and Rejuvenation spells, your Regrowth spell and your Insect Swarm and Lifebloom spells.

NATURE'S REACH

Increases the range of your Balance spells and Faerie Fire(Feral) ability and reduces the threat generated by your Balance spells.

This new threat reduction really makes a difference when a fight requires you to cast a great deal.

VENGEANCE

Increases the critical strike damage bonus of your Starfire, Starfall, Moonfire, and Wrath spells.

CELESTIAL FOCUS

Gives your Starfire and Starfall spells a chance to stun the target and increases your spell haste.

Celestial Focus no longer gives you the pushback protection when casting wrath, but the critical strike bonus more than make up for it.

LUNAR GUIDANCE

Increases your spell power by a percentage of your total Intellect.

INSECT SWARM

The enemy target is swarmed by insects, decreasing their chance to hit and causing damage over time.

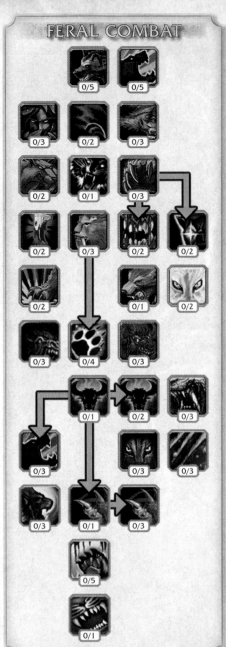

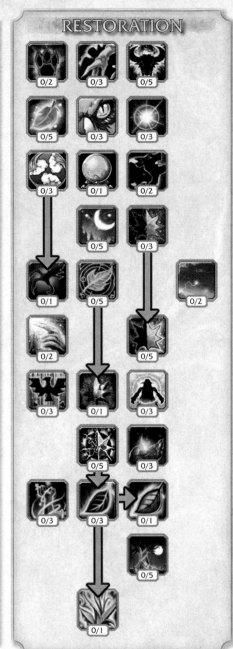

CLASSES

Druid

Hunter

Mage

Paladin

Priest

Rogue

Shaman

Warlock

Warrior

BALANCE

FERAL COMBAT

RESTORATION

IMPROVED INSECT SWARM

Increases your damage done by your Wrath spell to targets afflicted by your Insect Swarm and increases the critical strike chance of your Starfire spell on targets afflicted by your Moonfire spell.

DREAMSTATE

Regenerate mana equal to a percentage of your Intellect every few seconds, even while casting.

MOONFURY

Increases the damage done by your Starfire, Moonfire and Wrath spells.

This talent now has less ranks but gives the same effect, leaving you more free points to spend elsewhere.

BALANCE OF POWER

Increases your chance to hit with all spells and reduces the chance you'll be hit by spells.

MOONKIN FORM

Shapeshift into Moonkin Form. While in this form the armor contribution from items is greatly increased and all nearby party and raid members have their spell critical strike chance increased. Spell critical strikes in this form have a chance to instantly regenerate a percentage of your total mana. The Moonkin can only cast Balance and Remove Curse spells while shapeshifted. The act of shapeshifting frees the caster of Polymorph and Movement Impairing effects.

IMPROVED MOONKIN FORM

Your Moonkin Aura also causes affected targets to gain haste and you gain a percentage of your spirit as additional spell damage.

IMPROVED FAERIE FIRE

Your Faerie Fire spell also increases the chance the target will be hit by spell attacks, and increases the critical strike chance of your damage spells on targets affected by Faerie Fire.

OWLKIN FRENZY

Attacks done to you while in Moonkin form have a chance to cause you to go into a Frenzy, increasing your damage and causing you to be immune to push-back while casting Balance spells.

WRATH OF CENARIUS

Your Starfire spell and your Wrath spell gain an additional percentage of your bonus damage effects.

ECLIPSE

When you critically hit with Starfire, you have a chance of increasing damage done by Wrath. When you critically hit with Wrath, you have a chance of increasing your critical strike chance with Starfire.

Notice that the bonus has been increased but the cooldown has been increased. Even with the longer cooldown, the bonus damage makes this ability very powerful.

TYPHOON

You summon a violent Typhoon that does Nature damage when in contact with hostile targets, knocking them back.

This gives you an effective way to interrupt spellcasters from range. The knockback effect doesn't fling the target very far, but it is more than enough to interrupt their casting.

FORCE OF NATURE

Summons three treants to attack enemy targets for a short time.

GALE WINDS

Increases damage done by your Hurricane and Typhoon spells and increases the range of your Cyclone spell.

EARTH AND MOON

Your Wrath and Starfire spells apply the Earth and Moon effect, which increases spell damage taken. Also increases your spell damage.

Earth and Moon now has less ranks, but gives the overall same benefits. This gives you more points to spend somewhere else!

STARFALL

You summon a flurry of stars from the sky on all targets near the caster, each dealing Arcane damage. Also causes Arcane damage to all other enemies next to an enemy target.

FERAL COMBAT

FEROCITY

Reduces the cost of your Maul, Swipe, Claw, Rake and Mangle abilities.

FERAL AGGRESSION

Increases the attack power reduction of your Demoralizing Roar and the damage caused by your Ferocious Bite.

FERAL INSTINCT

Increases the damage done by your Swipe(Bear) ability and reduces the chance enemies have to detect you while prowling.

This ability no longer increases your threat while in Bear Form, but the extra damage works toward the same end.

SAVAGE FURY

Increases the damage caused by your Claw, Rake, Mangle(Cat), Mangle(Bear), and Maul abilities.

THICK HIDE

Increases your Armor contribution from items.

FERAL SWIFTNESS

Increases your movement speed in Cat Form and increases your chance to dodge while in Cat Form, Bear Form and Dire Bear Form.

This ability can now be used indoors!

SURVIVAL INSTINCTS

When activated, this ability temporarily grants you a percentage of your maximum health for while in Bear Form, Cat Form, or Dire Bear Form. After the effect expires, the health is lost.

This ability does not affect the Global Cooldown.

SHARPENED CLAWS

Increases your critical strike chance while in Bear, Dire Bear or Cat Form.

SHREDDING ATTACKS

Reduces the Energy cost of your Shred ability and the Rage cost of your Lacerate ability.

PREDATORY STRIKES

Increases your melee attack power in Cat, Bear, Dire Bear and Moonkin Forms by a percentage of your level and a percentage of any attack power on your equipped weapon.

PRIMAL FURY

Give you a chance to gain an additional amount of Rage anytime you get a critical strike while in Bear and Dire Bear Form and your critical strikes from Cat Form abilities that add combo points have a chance to add an additional combo point.

PRIMAL PRECISION

Increases your expertise, and you are refunded a percentage of the energy cost of a finishing move if it fails to land.

BRUTAL IMPACT

Increases the stun duration of your Bash and Pounce abilities and decreases the cooldown of Bash.

FERAL CHARGE

Teaches Feral Charge(Bear) and Feral Charge(Cat).

Feral Charge(Bear) causes you to charge an enemy, immobilizing and interrupting any spell being cast. This ability can be used in Bear Form and Dire Bear Form.

Feral Charge(Cat) causes you to leap behind an enemy, dazing them.

NURTURING INSTINCT

Increases your healing spells by a percentage of your Agility, and increases healing done to you while in Cat Form.

NATURAL REACTION

Increases your dodge while in Bear Form or Dire Bear Form, and you regenerate Rage every time you dodge while in Bear Form or Dire Bear Form.

HEART OF THE WILD

Increases your Intellect. In addition, while in Bear or Dire Bear Form your Stamina is increased and while in Cat Form your attack power is increased.

SURVIVAL OF THE FITTEST

Increases all attributes and reduces the chance you'll be critically hit by melee attacks.

LEADER OF THE PACK

While in Cat, Bear or Dire Bear Form, the Leader of the Pack increases ranged and melee critical chance of all nearby party members.

IMPROVED LEADER OF THE PACK

Your Leader of the Pack ability also causes affected targets to heal themselves for a percentage of their total health when they critically hit with a melee or ranged attack. The healing effect cannot occur more than once every few seconds. In addition, you gain a percentage of your maximum mana when you benefit from this heal.

CLASSES

Druid

Hunter

Mage

Paladin

Priest

Rogue

Shaman

Warlock

Warrior

Primal Tenacity

Reduces the duration of Fear effects, and reduces all damage taken while stunned.

Protector of the Pack

Increases your attack power in Bear Form and Dire Bear Form, and for each friendly player in your party when you enter Bear Form or Dire Bear Form, damage you take is reduced while in Bear Form and Dire Bear Form.

Predatory Instincts

While in Cat Form, increases your damage from melee critical strikes and reduces the damage taken from area effect attacks.

Infected Wounds

Your Shred, Maul, and Mangle attacks cause an Infected Wound in the target. The Infected Wound reduces the movement speed of the target and the attack speed. Stacks up to two times.

King of the Jungle

While using your Enrage ability in Bear Form or Dire Bear Form, your damage is increased, and your Tiger's Fury ability also instantly restores energy.

Mangle

Mangle the target, inflicting damage and causing the target to take additional damage from bleed effects. This ability can be used in Cat Form or Dire Bear Form.

Improved Mangle

Reduces the cooldown of your Mangle(Bear) ability, and reduces the energy cost of your Mangle(Cat) ability.

Rend and Tear

Increases damage done by your Maul and Shred attacks on bleeding targets and increases the critical strike chance of your Ferocious Bite ability on bleeding targets.

Berserk

When activated, this ability causes your Mangle(Bear) ability to hit up to three targets and have no cooldown, and reduces the energy cost of all your Cat Form abilities. You cannot use Tiger's Fury while Berserk is active. Clears the effect of Fear and makes you immune to Fear for the duration.

Using Berserk also clears the cooldown on Mangle (Bear), letting you use it again right away.

RESTORATION

Improved Mark of the Wild

Increases the effects of your Mark of the Wild and Gift of the Wild spells.

Its number of ranks has been decreased, but not its effectiveness. This gives you more points to put into other Talents!

Nature's Focus

Reduces the pushback suffered from damaging attacks while casting Healing Touch, Wrath, Entangling Roots, Cyclone, Nourish, Regrowth and Tranquility.

Furor

Gives you a percentage chance to gain Rage when you shapeshift into Bear or Dire Bear Form, and you keep some of your Energy when you shapeshift into Cat Form, and increases your total Intellect while in Moonkin form.

Naturalist

Reduces the cast time of your Healing Touch spell and increases the damage you deal with physical attacks in all forms.

Subtlety

Reduces the threat generated by your restoration spells and reduces the chance your spells will be dispelled.

Natural Shapeshifter

Reduces the mana cost of all shapeshifting.

INTENSITY

Allows a percentage of your mana regeneration to continue while casting and causes your Enrage ability to instantly generate some Rage.

OMEN OF CLARITY

Each of the Druid's damage, healing spells and auto attacks has a chance of causing the caster to enter a Clearcasting state. The Clearcasting state reduces the Mana, Rage or Energy cost of your next damage, healing spell or offensive ability, making it cost no mana.

MASTER SHAPESHIFTER

Grants an effect which lasts while the Druid is within the respective shapeshift form.

Bear Form – Increases physical damage.

Cat Form – Increases critical strike chance.

Moonkin Form – Increases spell damage.

Tree of Life Form – Increases healing.

TRANQUIL SPIRIT

Reduces the mana cost of your Healing Touch, Nourish and Tranquility spells.

IMPROVED REJUVENATION

Increases the effect of your Rejuvenation spell.

NATURE'S SWIFTNESS

When activated, your next Nature spell with a short casting time becomes an instant cast spell.

GIFT OF NATURE

Increases the effect of all healing spells.

IMPROVED TRANQUILITY

Reduces threat caused by Tranquility and reduces its cooldown.

EMPOWERED TOUCH

Your Healing Touch spell gains an additional percentage of your bonus healing effects.

IMPROVED REGROWTH

Increases the critical effect chance of your Regrowth spell.

LIVING SPIRIT

Increases your total Spirit.

SWIFTMEND

Consumes a Rejuvenation or Regrowth effect on a friendly target to instantly heal them an amount equal to several ticks of Rejuvenation or several ticks of Regrowth.

NATURAL PERFECTION

Your critical strike chance with all spells is increased and critical strikes against you give you the Natural Perfection effect reducing all damage taken.

EMPOWERED REJUVENATION

The bonus healing effects of your healing over time spells is increased.

LIVING SEED

When you critically heal your target with Swiftmend, Regrowth, Nourish or Healing Touch spell you have a chance to plant a Living Seed on the target. The Living Seed will bloom when the target is next attacked.

REPLENISH

Your Rejuvenation spell has a chance to restore Energy, Rage, Mana or Runic power per tick.

TREE OF LIFE

Shapeshift into the Tree of Life. While in this form you increase healing received for all nearby party and raid members, and you can only cast Restoration, Innervate and Barkskin spells, but the mana cost of your healing over time spells is reduced by a moderate amount. The act of shapeshifting frees the caster of Polymorph and Movement Impairing effects.

IMPROVED TREE OF LIFE

Increases your armor contribution from items while in Tree of Life Form and increases your healing spell power by a percentage of your spirit while in Tree of Life Form.

GIFT OF THE EARTHMOTHER

Reduces the base global cooldown of your Rejuvenation, Lifebloom and Wild Growth spells.

WILD GROWTH

Heals up to five close by friendly party or raid members over time. The amount healed is applied quickly at first, and slows down as the Wild Growth reaches its full duration.

Druid

Hunter

Mage

Paladin

Priest

Rogue

Shaman

Warlock

Warrior

Hunter Abilities

Hunters have received quite a few changes with the expansion. Many of their abilities have been beefed up and changed to make them easier to use in a variety of situations. For example, all Aspects now have a reduced global cooldown, and even better, cost no mana. This makes it much easier to switch aspects as needed, even in the heat of battle. Hunters are also getting some much needed pet love. For starters, if speced deeply enough into the right line, you can now tame exotic pets. This means that creatures that before were off limits to Hunters are now fair game. If you've always wanted an adorable little Devilsaur for your very own, now's your chance!

The most significant change though, is not to Hunters themselves, but to their pets. The way you train and use your pets has drastically changed, starting with what you choose to tame. Before, Hunter's often shied away from taming lower level pets, even if they liked their look, because of the time it took to level them up. Now, any pet that is more than five levels below you is automatically leveled to be five levels below you when you tame it. All pet families also have one ability unique to their family. Stable-masters now have room for two additional pets, at a cost of course, so try taming something new or different from what you've usually used.

Loyalty, Training Points, and your Beast Training ability are all gone. You no longer have to learn skills by training various pets only to throw them by the wayside to teach the skill to your main pet or pets. Pets now learn all skills at their level, getting new ranks automatically as they gain levels. For customization, pets now have their own Talent tree. Every pet falls into one of three categories: Cunning, Ferocious, or Tenacious. You don't get to choose which tree to spec your pet into. For instance, bears are Tenacious and therefore have the Tenacity Talent tree, while cats use the Ferocity tree. You do get to choose how you spend points in that tree though. Beginning at level 20 pets earn their first Talent point and they get another point every four levels. The three Talent trees do share many useful talents but are very different as well. As for abilities, every pet can learn Growl, Cower, and either Bite or Claw (but not both). As mentioned above, every pet also has an ability unique to its family. Beyond that, the Talents you pick up determine a pet's other abilities. Things like Avoidance and Cobra Reflexes are Talents instead of skills now. Overall this new system gives you much more control over your pet, allowing you to customize it to fit your needs and play style.

BEAST MASTERY

 ### Aspect of the Beast

The hunter takes on the aspects of a beast, becoming untrackable and increasing the melee attack power of the hunter and the hunter's pet. Only one Aspect can be active at a time.

 ### Aspect of the Cheetah

The hunter takes on the aspects of a cheetah, increasing movement speed. If the hunter is struck they will be Dazed. Only one Aspect can be active at a time.

 ### Aspect of the Dragonhawk

The hunter takes on the aspects of a dragonhawk, increasing ranged attack power and chance to dodge. Only one Aspect can be active at a time.

 ### Aspect of the Hawk

The hunter takes on the aspects of a hawk, increasing ranged attack power. Only one Aspect can be active at a time.

 ### Aspect of the Monkey

The hunter takes on the aspects of a monkey, increasing chance to dodge. Only one Aspect can be active at a time.

 ### Aspect of the Pack

The hunter and group members within range take on the aspects of a pack of cheetahs, increasing movement speed. If you are struck under the effect of this aspect, you will be dazed. Only one Aspect can be active at a time.

 ### Aspect of the Viper

The hunter takes on the aspect of the viper, causing ranged attacks to regenerate mana but reducing your total damage done. Mana gained is based on the speed of your ranged weapon. Only one Aspect can be active at a time.

 ### Aspect of the Wild

The hunter and group members within range take on the aspect of the wild, increasing Nature resistance. Only one Aspect can be active at a time.

This aspect now gives much greater Nature Resistance, making it a must for some fights!

 ### Beast Lore

Gathers information about the target beast. The tooltip will display damage, health, armor, any special resistances, and diet. In addition, Beast Lore will reveal whether or not the creature is tameable and what abilities the tamed creature has.

 ### Call Pet

Summons your pet to you.

 ### Dismiss Pet

Dismiss your pet. Dismissing your pet will reduce its happiness.

 ### Eagle Eye

Zooms in the Hunter's vision. Only usable outdoors.

 ### Eyes of the Beast

Take direct control of your pet and see through its eyes.

 ### Feed Pet

Feed your pet the selected item. Feeding your pet increases happiness. Using food close to the pet's level will have a better result.

KILL COMMAND

Give the command to kill, increasing your pet's damage done from special attacks. Each special attack done by the pet reduces the damage bonus.

MASTER'S CALL

Your pet attempts to remove all root and movement impairing effects on the target, and cause them to be immune to all such effects for a few seconds.

MEND PET

Heals your pet over time.

REVIVE PET

Revive your pet, returning it to life with low health.

SCARE BEAST

Scares a beast, causing it to run in fear. Damage caused may interrupt the effect. Only one beast can be feared at a time.

TAME BEAST

Begins taming a beast to be your companion. Your armor is reduced while you focus on taming the beast. If you lose the beast's attention for any reason, the taming process will fail. Once tamed, the beast will be very unhappy and disloyal. Try feeding the pet immediately to make it happy.

MARKSMANSHIP

ARCANE SHOT

An instant shot that causes Arcane damage.

This shot no longer dispels magic effects.

AUTO SHOT

Automatically shoots the target until cancelled.

CONCUSSIVE SHOT

Dazes the target, slowing movement speed for a few seconds.

DISTRACTING SHOT

Distracts the target to attack you, but has no effect if the target is already attacking you.

FLARE

Exposes all hidden and invisible enemies within the targeted area.

HUNTER'S MARK

Places the Hunter's Mark on the target, increasing the ranged attack power of all attackers against your target. In addition, the target of this ability can always be seen by the hunter even if it stealths or turns invisible. The target also appears on the mini-map.

KILL SHOT

You attempt to finish the wounded target off, firing a long range attack dealing bonus weapon damage plus an additional amount. Kill Shot can only be used on enemies that have low health.

The damage on this ability has been decreased slightly, but it is still a powerful tool.

MULTI-SHOT

Fires several missiles, hitting multiple targets for an additional amount of damage.

RAPID FIRE

Increases ranged attack speed for a brief time.

SCORPID STING

Stings the target, reducing chance to hit with melee and ranged attacks for a short time. Only one Sting per Hunter can be active on any one target.

SERPENT STING

Stings the target, causing Nature damage over a short time. Only one Sting per Hunter can be active on any one target.

STEADY SHOT

A steady shot that causes unmodified weapon damage, plus an additional amount. Causes extra damage against Dazed targets.

Steady shot's bonus damage has been reduced slightly. This is due to the fact that it now takes ammo. You can increase your damage based on the ammo you use.

Classes

Druid

Hunter

Mage

Paladin

Priest

Rogue

Shaman

Warlock

Warrior

TRANQUILIZING SHOT

Attempts to remove an Enrage and Magic effect from an enemy target.

The cooldown on this has been reduced, making it even more effective during long battles.

VIPER STING

Stings the target, draining mana over a short time. Only one Sting per Hunter can be active on any one target.

VOLLEY

Continuously fires a volley of ammo at the target area, causing Arcane damage to enemy targets every second for a few seconds.

SURVIVAL

DETERRENCE

When activated, increases the chance to dodge and parry all melee and ranged attacks for a short time.

With a shorter cooldown, you will find yourself using this much more often.

DISENGAGE

You attempt to disengage from the target, leaping backwards. Must be facing the target.

EXPLOSIVE TRAP

Place a fire trap that explodes when an enemy approaches, causing Fire damage and burning all enemies for additional Fire damage over time to all within range. Only one trap can be active at a time.

FEIGN DEATH

Feign death which may trick enemies into ignoring you.

FREEZING ARROW

Fire a freezing arrow that places a Freezing Trap at the target location, freezing the first enemy that approaches, preventing all action for a short time. Any damage caused will break the ice. Only one trap can be active at a time.

FREEZING TRAP

Place a frost trap that freezes the first enemy that approaches, preventing all action for a short time. Any damage caused will break the ice. Only one trap can be active at a time.

FROST TRAP

Place a frost trap that creates an ice slick around itself for some time when the first enemy approaches it. All enemies within range will be slowed while in the area of effect. Only one trap can be active at a time.

IMMOLATION TRAP

Place a fire trap that will burn the first enemy to approach it over a short time. Only one trap can be active at a time.

MISDIRECTION

Threat caused by your next few attacks is redirected to the target party or raid member. Caster and target can only be affected by one Misdirection spell at a time.

MONGOOSE BITE

Attack the enemy for a moderate amount of damage.

You can now use this at anytime, not just after a Dodge!

RAPTOR STRIKE

A strong attack that increases melee damage.

SNAKE TRAP

Place a trap that will release several venomous snakes to attack the first enemy to approach. The snakes will die after a short time. Only one trap can be active at a time.

TRACK BEASTS

Shows the location of all nearby beasts on the mini-map. Only one form of tracking can be active at a time.

TRACK DEMONS

Shows the location of all nearby demons on the mini-map. Only one form of tracking can be active at time.

TRACK DRAGONKIN

Shows the location of all nearby dragonkin on the mini-map. Only one form of tracking ca be active at a time.

TRACK ELEMENTALS

Shows the location of all nearby elementals on the mini-map. Only one form of tracking can be active at a time.

TRACK GIANTS

Shows the location of all nearby giants on the mini-map. Only one form of tracking can be active at a time.

TRACK HIDDEN

Greatly increases stealth detection and shows hidden units within detection range on the mini-map. Only one form of tracking can be active at a time.

TRACK HUMANOIDS

Shows the location of all nearby humanoids on the mini-map. Only one form of tracking can be active at a time.

TRACK UNDEAD

Shows the location of all nearby undead on the mini-map. Only one form of tracking can be active at a time.

WING CLIP

Maims the enemy, reducing the target's movement speed for a brief time.

This ability no longer does damage, but because its main use has always been to slow down the target, its functionality hasn't really changed.

Classes

Druid

Hunter

Mage

Paladin

Priest

Rogue

Shaman

Warlock

Warrior

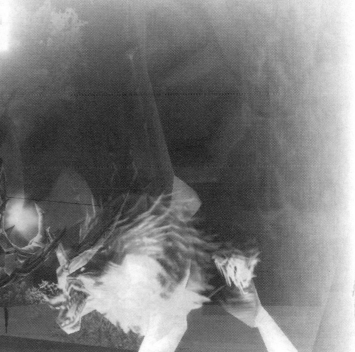

HUNTER TALENTS

BEAST MASTERY

IMPROVED ASPECT OF THE HAWK

While Aspect of the Hawk or Dragonhawk is active, all normal ranged attacks have a chance of increasing ranged attack speed for a brief time.

ENDURANCE TRAINING

Increases the Health of your pet and your total health.

FOCUSED FIRE

All damage caused by you is increased while your pet is active and the critical strike chance of your pet's special abilities is increased while Kill Command is active.

IMPROVED ASPECT OF THE MONKEY

Increases the Dodge bonus of your Aspect of the Monkey or Dragonhawk.

THICK HIDE

Increases the armor rating of your pets and your armor contribution from items.

IMPROVED REVIVE PET

Revive Pet's casting time is reduced, mana cost is reduced, and it increases the health your pet returns with.

PATHFINDING

Increases the speed bonus of your Aspect of the Cheetah and Aspect of the Pact, and also increases your speed while mounted. The mounted movement speed increase does not stack with other effects.

 ASPECT MASTERY

This new Talent improves your various aspects:

Aspect of the Viper – Reduces the damage penalty.
Aspect of the Monkey – Reduces the damage done to you while active.
Aspect of the Hawk – Increases the attack power bonus.
Aspect of the Dragonhawk – Combines the bonuses from Aspect of the Monkey and Hawk.

 UNLEASHED FURY

Increases the damage done by your pets.

 IMPROVED MEND PET

Reduces the mana cost of your Mend Pet spell and gives the Mend Pet spell a chance to cleanse a Curse, Disease, Magic or Poison effect from the pet each tick.

 FEROCITY

Increases the critical strike chance of your pet.

 SPIRIT BOND

While your pet is active, you and your pet will regenerate a slight amount of total health over time and this ability increases healing done to you and your pet.

 INTIMIDATION

Command your pet to intimidate the target on the next successful melee attack, causing a high amount of threat and stunning the target for a few seconds.

 BESTIAL DISCIPLINE

Increases the Focus regeneration of your pets.

 ANIMAL HANDLER

Increases your pet's chance to hit and reduces the cooldown of your Master's Call ability.

Animal Handler no longer increase your mounted speed, but gains usefulness with the Master's Call component.

 FRENZY

Gives your pet a chance to gain an attack speed increase for a short time after dealing a critical strike.

 FEROCIOUS INSPIRATION

When your pet scores a critical hit, all party members have all damage increased for a short time.

 BESTIAL WRATH

Send your pet into a rage causing additional damage for a short time. While enraged, the beast does not feel pity or remorse or fear and it cannot be stopped unless killed.

 CATLIKE REFLEXES

Increases your chance to dodge and your pet's chance to dodge.

 INVIGORATION

When your pet scores a critical hit with a special ability, you have a chance to instantly regenerate mana.

 SERPENT'S SWIFTNESS

Increases ranged combat attack speed and your pet's melee attack speed.

 LONGEVITY

Reduces the cooldown of your Bestial Wrath, Intimidation and Pet Special Abilities.

BEAST MASTERY

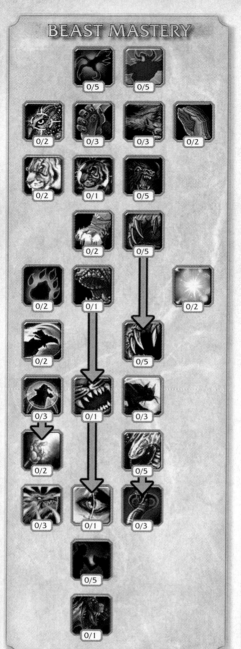

MARKMANSHIP

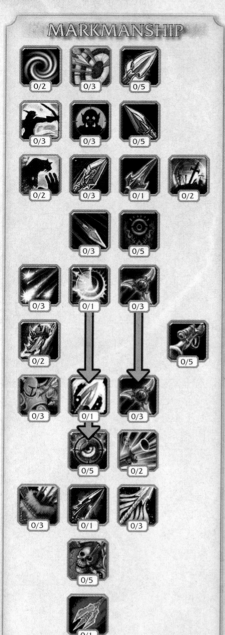

SURVIVAL

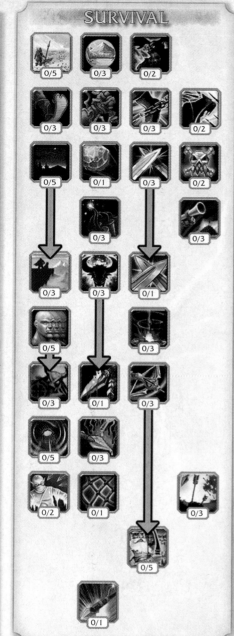

Druid

Hunter

Mage

Paladin

Priest

Rogue

Shaman

Warlock

Warrior

THE BEAST WITHIN

When your pet is under the effects of Bestial Wrath, you also go into a rage causing additional damage and reducing the mana costs of all your spells for a short time. While enraged, you do not feel pity or remorse or fear and you cannot be stopped unless killed.

KINDRED SPIRITS

Increases your pet's damage and you and your pet's movement speed while your pet is active. This does not stack with other movement speed increasing effects.

COBRA STRIKES

You have a chance when you critically hit with Arcane Shot, Steady Shot or Kill Shot to cause your pet's next few attacks to critically hit.

BEAST MASTERY

You master the art of Beast Training, teaching you the ability to tame Exotic pets and increasing your total amount of Pet Skill Points.

CAREFUL AIM

Increases your ranged attack power by an amount equal to a percentage of your Intellect.

IMPROVED HUNTER'S MARK

Increases the bonus attack power granted by your Hunter's Mark ability and reduces the mana cost of your Hunter's Mark ability.

MORTAL SHOTS

Increases the critical strike damage bonus of your ranged abilities.

GO FOR THE THROAT

Your ranged critical hits cause your pet to generate extra focus.

IMPROVED ARCANE SHOT

Increases the damage done by your Arcane Shot.

AIMED SHOT

An aimed shot that increases the ranged damage and reduces the healing done to that target.

Though it now has a slightly longer cooldown, Aimed Shot now takes less mana and is instant cast, making it much more useable.

RAPID KILLING

Reduces the cooldown of your Rapid Fire ability. In addition, after killing an opponent that yields experience or honor, your next Aimed Shot, Arcane Shot, or Chimera Shot causes additional damage.

IMPROVED STINGS

Increases the damage done by your Serpent Sting and Wyvern Sting and the mana drained by your Viper Sting. In addition, reduces the chance your Stings will be dispelled.

MARKSMANSHIP

IMPROVED CONCUSSIVE SHOT

Increases the duration of your Concussive Shot's daze effect.

FOCUSED AIM

Reduces the pushback suffered from damaging attacks while casting Steady Shot, and increases your chance to hit.

LETHAL SHOTS

Increases the critical strike chance with ranged weapons.

Efficiency

Reduces the Mana cost of your Shots and Stings.

 ## Concussive Barrage

Your successful Auto Shot, Multi-Shot and Volley attacks have a chance to Daze the target for a brief time.

 ## Readiness

When activated, this ability immediately finishes the cooldown on your other Hunter abilities.

 ## Barrage

Increase the damage done by your Multi-Shot, Aimed Shot, and Volley spells.

 ## Combat Experience

Increases your total Agility and Intellect.

 ## Ranged Weapon Specialization

Increases the damage you deal with ranged weapons.

 ## Piercing Shots

Your Steady Shot and Aimed Shot abilities ignore some of your target's armor.

 ## Trueshot Aura

Increases the attack power of party and raid members within range.

This ability has been improved by working for a whole raid!

 ## Improved Barrage

Increases the critical strike chance of your Multi-Shot and Aimed Shot abilities and reduces the pushback suffered from damaging attacks while channeling Volley.

 ## Master Marksman

Increase your critical strike chance and reduces the Mana cost of your Steady Shot.

 ## Rapid Recuperation

Reduces the mana and focus of all shots and abilities by you and your pet while under the effect of Rapid Fire, and you gain a slight amount of mana back every few seconds for a brief time when you gain Rapid Killing.

 ## Wild Quiver

You have a chance to shoot an additional shot when doing damage with your Auto Shot, dealing additional Nature damage. Wild Quiver consumes no ammo.

 ## Silencing Shot

A shot that deals some weapon damage and Silences the target for a few seconds.

 ## Improved Steady Shot

Your Steady Shot hits have a chance to increase the damage done by your next Aimed Shot, Arcane Shot or Chimera Shot and reduce the mana cost of your next Aimed Shot, Arcane Shot or Chimera Shot.

 ## Marked for Death

Increases the damage done by your shots and the damage done by your pet's special abilities on marked targets, and increases the critical strike damage bonus of your Aimed Shot, Steady Shot, Kill Shot or Chimera Shot.

 ## Chimera Shot

You deal bonus weapon damage, refreshing the current Sting on your target and triggering an effect:

Serpent Sting – Instantly deals some of the damage done by your Serpent Sting.

Viper Sting – Instantly restores mana to you equal to some of the total amount drained by your Viper Sting.

Scorpid Sting – Attempts to Disarm the target for a short time.

Druid

Hunter

Mage

Paladin

Priest

Rogue

Shaman

Warlock

Warrior

SURVIVAL

 IMPROVED TRACKING

Increases all non-periodic damage done to targets that are being tracked.

This new ability incorporates the old Talents, Monster Slaying and Humanoid Slaying.

 HAWK EYE

Increases the range of your ranged weapons.

 SAVAGE STRIKES

Increases the critical strike chance of Raptor Strike, Mongoose Bite and Counterattack.

 SUREFOOTED

Reduces the duration of movement impairing effects.

This Talent has been moved up in the tree to make it easier for you to grab.

 ENTRAPMENT

Gives your Immolation Trap, Frost Trap, Explosive Trap, and Snake Trap a chance to entrap the target, preventing them from moving for a brief time.

 IMPROVED WING CLIP

Gives your Wing Clip ability a chance to immobilize the target for a brief time.

 SURVIVAL INSTINCTS

Reduces all damage taken and increases the critical strike chance of your Arcane Shot, Steady Shot, and Explosive Shot.

Survival Instincts used to be pretty deep into the tree, but now it has been moved up, making it easier for all Hunters to have it if they want.

 SURVIVALIST

Increases your Stamina.

 SCATTER SHOT

A short-range shot that deals some weapon damage and disorients the target for a few seconds. Any damage caused removes the effect. Turns off your attack when used.

 DEFLECTION

Increases your chance to parry and reduces the duration of all Disarm effects used against you. This does not stack with other Disarm duration reducing effects.

 SURVIVAL TACTICS

Reduces the chance your Feign Death ability and all trap spells will be resisted, and reduces the cooldown of your Disengage ability.

 T.N.T

Your Immolation Trap, Explosive Trap and Explosive Shot have a chance to stun targets for a few seconds when they land, and increases the chance your Explosive Shot will critically hit.

 LOCK AND LOAD

You have a chance when you trap a target and a chance when you deal periodic damage with your Serpent Sting to cause your next few Arcane Shot or Explosive Shot spells to trigger no cooldown, cost no mana and consume no ammo.

 HUNTER VS. WILD

Increases your and your pet's attack power and ranged attack power equal to a percentage of your total Stamina.

 KILLER INSTINCT

Increases your critical strike chance with all attacks.

 COUNTERATTACK

A strike that becomes active after parrying an opponent's attack. This attack deals damage and immobilizes the target for a brief time. Counterattack cannot be blocked dodged or parried.

The damage on this has been increased by a significant amount and it scales based on your Ranged Attack Power, making it a devastating attack.

 THRILL OF THE HUNT

Gives you a chance to regain some of the mana cost of any shot when it critically hits.

 MASTER TACTICIAN

Your successful ranged attacks have a chance to increase your critical strike chance with all attacks for a brief time.

 NOXIOUS STINGS

If Wyvern Sting is dispelled, the dispeller is also afflicted by Wyvern Sting lasting a percentage of the duration remaining, and increases all damage done by you on targets afflicted by your Serpent Sting.

 POINT OF NO ESCAPE

Increases the critical strike chance of all attacks on targets affected by your Frost Trap, Freezing Trap and Freezing Arrow.

This Talent has been reduced in ranks, but you get the same effect.

 TRAP MASTERY

Frost Trap and Freezing Trap – Increases the duration.

Immolation Trap and Explosive Trap – Increases the damage done.

Snake Trap – Increases the number of snakes summoned.

 SNIPER TRAINING

Increases the damage done by your Steady Shot, Aimed Shot and Explosive Shots if you are at long range from your target, and increases the critical strike chance of our Kill Shot ability.

 HUNTING PARTY

Your Arcane Shot, Explosive Shot and Steady Shot critical strikes have a chance to grant party or raid members mana regeneration equal to a percentage of the maximum mana per second.

 EXPLOSIVE SHOT

You fire an explosive charge into the enemy target, dealing Fire damage. The charge will blast the target every second for a few seconds. Each charge also deals Fire damage to all nearby enemies within range of the target.

 LIGHTNING REFLEXES

Increases your Agility.

 RESOURCEFULNESS

Reduces the mana cost of all traps and melee abilities and reduces the cooldown of all traps.

 EXPOSE WEAKNESS

Your ranged criticals have a chance to grant you Expose Weakness, increasing your attack power by a percentage of your Agility for a short time.

 WYVERN STING

A stinging shot that puts the target to sleep for a short time. Any damage cancels the effect. When the target wakes up, the Sting causes Nature damage over a brief time. Only one Sting per Hunter can be active on the target at a time.

CLASSES

Druid

Hunter

Mage

Paladin

Priest

Rogue

Shaman

Warlock

Warrior

Hunter Pet Talents

CUNNING

FEROCITY

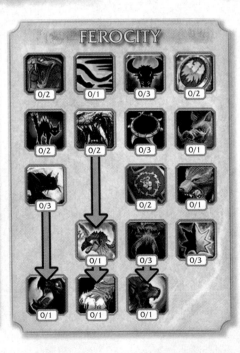

TENACITY

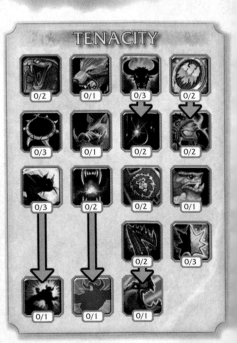

CUNNING

COBRA REFLEXES

Increases your pet's attack speed. Your pet hits faster but each hit does less damage.

DIVE

Increases your pet's movement speed for a time.

GREAT STAMINA

Increases your pet's total Stamina.

NATURAL ARMOR

Increases your pet's armor.

BOAR'S SPEED

Increases your pet's movement speed.

MOBILITY

Reduces the cooldown on your pet's Dive ability.

OWL'S FOCUS

Your pet has a chance after using an ability that the next ability will cost no focus if used within a few seconds.

SPIKED COLLAR

Your pet does additional damage with all attacks.

AVOIDANCE

Reduces the damage your pet takes from area of effect attacks by a significant amount.

LIONHEARTED

Reduces the duration of all Stun and Fear effects used against your pet by a moderate amount.

CARRION FEEDER

Your pet can generate health and happiness by eating a corpse. Will not work on the remains of elemental or mechanical creatures.

GREAT RESISTANCE

Your pet takes less damage from Arcane, Fire, Frost, Nature, and Shadow magic.

CORNERED

When at low health, your pet does moderately more damage and is less likely to be critically hit.

FEEDING FRENZY

Your pet does additional damage to targets that are low health.

WOLVERINE BITE

A fierce attack causing damage modified by pet level, that you pet can use after its target dodges. Cannot be dodged, blocked, or parried.

ROAR OF RECOVERY

Your pet's inspiring roar restores a significant amount of your mana over a short time.

BULLHEADED

Removes all movement impairing effects and all effects which cause loss of control of your pet.

CLASSES

Druid

Hunter

Mage

Paladin

Priest

Rogue

Shaman

Warlock

Warrior

FEROCITY

 ## COBRA REFLEXES

Increases your pet's attack speed. Your pet hits faster but each hit does less damage.

 ## DASH

Increases your pet's movement speed for a time.

 ## GREAT STAMINA

Increases your pet's total Stamina.

 ## NATURAL ARMOR

Increases your pet's armor.

 ## IMPROVED COWER

Your pet's cower also decreases damage taken for a short time.

 ## BLOODTHIRSTY

Your pet's attacks have a chance to increase its happiness by a small amount and heal a small percentage of its total health.

 ## SPIKED COLLAR

Your pet does additional damage with all attacks.

 ## BOAR'S SPEED

Increases your pet's movement speed.

 ## AVOIDANCE

Reduces the damage your pet takes from area of effect attacks by a significant amount.

 ## LIONHEARTED

Reduces the duration of all Stun and Fear effects used against your pet by a moderate amount.

 ## CHARGE

Your pet charges the enemy, immobilizing the target for a short time and increasing the pet's melee attack power for its next attack.

 ## HEART OF THE PHOENIX

When your pet dies, it miraculously returns to life with full health.

 ## SPIDER'S BITE

Increases the critical strike chance of your pet.

 ## GREAT RESISTANCE

Your pet takes less damage from Arcane, Fire, Frost, Nature, and Shadow magic.

 ## RABID

Your pet goes into a killing frenzy, increasing attack power. Successful attacks have a significant chance to increase attack power by an additional amount. This effect can stack up to five times.

LICK YOUR WOUNDS

Your pet heals itself over a few seconds while channeling.

 ### CALL OF THE WILD

Your pet roars, increasing the melee and ranged attack power of all nearby party members.

TENACITY

 ### COBRA REFLEXES

Increases your pet's attack speed. Your pet hits faster but each hit does less damage.

 ### CHARGE

Your pet charges an enemy, briefly immobilizing the target and increasing the pet's melee attack power for its next attack.

 ### GREAT STAMINA

Increases your pet's total Stamina.

 ### NATURAL ARMOR

Increases your pet's armor.

 ### SPIKED COLLAR

Your pet does additional damage with all attacks.

 ### BOAR'S SPEED

Increases your pet's movement speed.

 ### BLOOD OF THE RHINO

Increases your pet's total Stamina and increases all healing effects on your pet by a moderate amount.

 ### PET BARDING

Increases your pet's armor and chance to Dodge.

 ### AVOIDANCE

Reduces the damage your pet takes from area of effect attacks by a significant amount.

 ### GUARD DOG

Your pet's Growl generates additional threat and happiness.

 ### LIONHEARTED

Reduces the duration of all Stun and Fear effects used against your pet by a moderate amount.

 ### INTERVENE

Your pet runs at high speed towards a group member, intercepting the next melee or ranged attack made against them.

 ### GRACE OF THE MANTIS

Reduces the chance your pet is critically hit by melee attacks.

 ### GREAT RESISTANCE

Your pet takes less damage from Arcane, Fire, Frost, Nature, and Shadow magic.

 ### LAST STAND

Your pet temporarily gains a significant amount of its maximum health for a short time. After the effect expires, the health is lost.

 ### TAUNT

Your pet taunts the target to attack it for a few seconds.

 ### ROAR OF SACRIFICE

Your pet absorbs damage from a party or raid member, transferring a significant amount of damage take to the pet.

CLASSES

Druid

Hunter

Mage

Paladin

Priest

Rogue

Shaman

Warlock

Warrior

Mage Abilities

Mages have gained quite a few new abilities, but have seen the biggest change in the revision of their Talent trees. Many Talents have been revised and moved around, and quite a few have even had the number of ranks changed. All of these changes serve to make the most of the available abilities and Talents, no matter how the mage is speced. You will notice that many of the new Talents affect spells of all schools. This is great for when a certain boss or situation requires you to cast outside your comfort zone. These changes insure that many times you get the benefit from your Talents, even when you are casting in another line.

There is no perfect spec for a Mage. The importance lies in learning how to best use your abilities. Fire may still be the king of straight out DPS, but Arcane has the advantage when it comes to Mana and mobility. Frost lags a bit behind the other two schools when it comes to damage—they have to make up somehow for the awesome freezes and snares that they have, but they still produce devastating DPS.

The new spells and extra Talent points means that there are a lot of new combinations you haven't tried yet. Familiarize yourself with the changes and additions and try taking a look at your character with fresh eyes. There may not be a one size fits all way to play a Mage, but with so many options, there is certainly one that fits you.

ARCANE

 ### AMPLIFY MAGIC

Amplifies magic used against the targeted party member, increasing damage taken from spells and healing spells.

 ### ARCANE BLAST

Blasts the target with energy, dealing Arcane damage. Each time you cast Arcane Blast, the damage increases and mana cost increases.

Though the duration of Arcane Blast has been reduced, the change to increasing the damage instead of reducing the casting time gives this spell as much needed boost.

 ### ARCANE BRILLIANCE

Infuses all party and raid members with brilliance, increasing their Intellect.

 ### ARCANE EXPLOSION

Causes an explosion of arcane magic around the caster, causing Arcane damage to all nearby targets.

 ### ARCANE INTELLECT

Increases the target's Intellect.

 ### ARCANE MISSILES

Launches Arcane Missiles at the enemy, causing Arcane damage.

 ### BLINK

Teleports the caster forward, unless something is in the way. Also frees the caster from stuns and bonds.

 ### CONJURE FOOD

Conjures food, providing the mage and their allies with something to eat, regenerating health. Conjured items disappear if logged out for more than 15 minutes.

 ### CONJURE MANA GEM

Conjures a mana gem that can be used to instantly restore mana.

 ### CONJURE REFRESHMENT

Conjures refreshments, providing the mage and their allies with something to eat, regenerating health and mana. Conjured items disappear if logged out for more than 15 minutes.

 ### CONJURE WATER

Conjures water, providing the mage and their allies with something to drink, regenerating mana. Conjured items disappear if logged out for more than 15 minutes.

 ### COUNTERSPELL

Counters the enemy's spellcast, preventing any spell from that school of magic from being cast for a short time. Generates a high amount of threat.

 ### DAMPEN MAGIC

Dampens magic used against the targeted party member, decreasing damage taken from spells and healing from spells.

 ### EVOCATION

While channeling this spell, you gain a percentage of your total mana over a short time.

The cooldown on Evocation has been greatly reduced, which may change the way you manage your mana. Evocation was already a powerful tool, especially in prolonged battles. With its shorter cooldown it is now going to come into play in many more encounters.

INVISIBILITY

Fades the caster to invisibility over a few seconds, reducing threat each second. The effect is cancelled if you perform or receive any actions. While invisible, you can only see other invisible targets and those who can see invisible.

The time it takes for you to fade into invisibility has been reduced, making this much more viable as a means of escape rather than just an aggro reducing move.

MAGE ARMOR

Increases your resistance to all magic and allows a percentage of your mana regeneration to continue while casting. Only one type of Armor spell can be active on the Mage at any time.

MANA SHIELD

Absorbs damage, draining mana instead.

MIRROR IMAGE

Creates three copies of the caster nearby, which cast spells and attack the mage's enemies.

This spell is a powerful addition to your arsenal. When you cast it, three exact copies of you—right down to the buffs you have, appear and begin attacking your target. You bounce between them, and cannot move too far away. If you try, the images pull you back to them. Their damage output does not equal yours, but together they make an impressive addition to your damage output. Mirror Image is on a fairly short cooldown, so doesn't have to be saved for special occasions. Pull it out often to get used using this devastating, and fun, new spell.

POLYMORPH

Transforms the enemy into a sheep, forcing it to wander around. While wandering, the sheep cannot attack or cast spells but regains health at a fast rate.

REMOVE CURSE

Removes one Curse from a friendly target.

RITUAL OF REFRESHMENT

Begins a ritual that creates a refreshment table. Raid members can click the table to acquire Conjured Mana Biscuits. Requires the caster and two additional party members to complete the ritual. In order to participate, all players must right-click the refreshment portal and not move until the ritual is complete.

SLOW FALL

Slows falling speed. Requires a Light Feather each time it is used.

SPELLSTEAL

Steals a beneficial magic effect from the target.

FIRE

FIRE BLAST

Blasts the enemy for Fire Damage.

FIRE WARD

Absorbs Fire damage.

FIREBALL

Hurls a fiery ball that causes Fire damage and additional Fire damage over time.

FLAMESTRIKE

Calls down a pillar of fire, burning all enemies within the area for Fire damage and additional Fire damage over time.

FROSTFIRE BOLT

Launches a bolt of Frostfire at the enemy, causing Frostfire damage, slowing movement speed and causing additional Frostfire damage over time. If the target is more vulnerable to Frost damage, this spell causes Frost instead of Fire damage.

MOLTEN ARMOR

Causes Fire damage when hit, increases your chance to critically hit with spells and reduces the chance you are critically hit. Only one type of Armor spell can be active on the Mage at any time.

SCORCH

Scorch the enemy for Fire damage.

Classes

Druid

Hunter

Mage

Paladin

Priest

Rogue

Shaman

Warlock

Warrior

FROST

BLIZZARD

Ice shards pelt the target area doing Frost damage over time.

CONE OF COLD

Targets in a cone in front of the caster take Frost damage and are slowed.

FROST ARMOR

Increases Armor. If an enemy strikes the caster, they may have their movement slowed and the time between their attacks increased for a short time. Only one type of Armor spell can be active on the Mage at any time.

Frost Armor, along with your Ice Armor, Mage Armor, and Molten Armor no longer count as magical effects and therefore cannot be dispelled!

FROST NOVA

Blasts enemies near the caster for Frost damage and freezes them in place. Damage caused may interrupt the effect.

FROST WARD

Absorbs Frost damage.

FROSTBOLT

Launches a bolt of frost at the enemy causing Frost damage and slowing movement speed for a short time.

ICE ARMOR

Increases Armor and Frost resistance. If an enemy strikes the caster, they may have their movement slowed and the time between attacks increased. Only one type of Armor spell can be active on the Mage at any time.

ICE BLOCK

You become encased in a block of ice, protecting you from all physical attacks and spells for a short time, but during that time you cannot attack, move or cast spells. Also causes Hypothermia, preventing you from recasting Ice Block for a time.

ICE LANCE

Deals Frost damage to an enemy target. Causes triple damage against Frozen targets.

Mage Talents

ARCANE

0/2	0/3	0/5
0/3	0/2	0/5
0/2	0/3	0/3	0/1
0/2	0/2	0/3	0/3
0/2	0/1		0/5
0/3	0/3	0/2
0/3	0/1	0/3
	0/2	0/5
0/1	0/5	
0/3	0/2	
0/1		

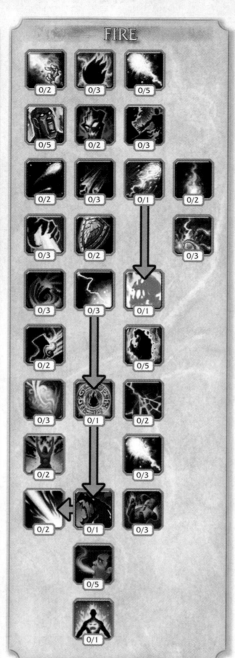

FIRE

0/2	0/3	0/5
0/5	0/2	0/3
0/2	0/3	0/1	0/2
0/3	0/2		0/3
0/3	0/3	0/1
0/2		0/5
0/3	0/1	0/2
0/2		0/3
0/2	0/1	0/3
	0/5	
	0/1	

FROST

0/3	0/5	0/3
0/3	0/2	0/3	0/3
0/3	0/1	0/3
0/2	0/3	0/3
	0/1	0/3	0/3
0/2	0/1	0/5
	0/2	0/2
0/3	0/1	0/3
	0/5	
	0/1	

Druid

Hunter

Mage

Paladin

Priest

Rogue

Shaman

Warlock

Warrior

ARCANE

ARCANE SUBTLETY

Reduces the chance your spells will be dispelled and reduces the threat caused by your Arcane spells.

ARCANE FOCUS

Increases your chance to hit and reduces the mana cost of your Arcane spells.

This Talent now only has three ranks instead of five, which clears up some points to spend elsewhere.

ARCANE STABILITY

Reduces the pushback suffered from damaging attacks while casting Arcane Missiles and Arcane Blast.

ARCANE FORTITUDE

Increases your armor by an amount equal to a percentage of your Intellect.

MAGIC ABSORPTION

Increases all resistances and causes all spells you fully resist to restore a percentage of your total mana.

ARCANE CONCENTRATION

Gives you a chance of entering a Clearcasting state after any damage spell hits a target. The Clearcasting state reduces the mana cost of your next damage spell by 100%.

MAGIC ATTUNEMENT

Increases the range of your Arcane spells and the effect of your Amplify Magic and Dampen Magic spells.

SPELL IMPACT

Increases the damage of your Arcane Explosion, Arcane Blast, Blast Wave, Fire Blast, Scorch, Fireball, Ice Lance and Cone of Cold spells.

STUDENT OF THE MIND

Increases your total Spirit.

FOCUS MAGIC

Increases the target's chance to critically hit with all spells. When the target critically hits the caster's chance to critically hit with spells is increased for a short time.

This ability is especially great when casters are grouped together. Just by casting this on each other they can seriously up the frequency of their critical hits, making them a force to be reckoned with on any field of battle.

ARCANE SHIELDING

Decreases the mana lost per point of damage taken when Mana Shield is active and increases the resistances granted by Mage Armor.

IMPROVED COUNTERSPELL

Your Counterspell also Silences the target for a few seconds.

ARCANE MEDITATION

Allows your mana regeneration to continue while casting.

TORMENT OF THE WEAK

Your Frostbolt, Fireball, Frostfire Bolt, Arcane Missiles, and Arcane Barrage abilities deal more damage to Snared Targets.

IMPROVED BLINK

Reduces the mana cost of Blink and after casting Blink your chance to be hit by all attacks and spells is reduced for a short time.

Well used by almost every Mage, this new and improved version of this Talent makes it even more useful, especially in a PvP or other fast paced setting.

PRESENCE OF MIND

When activated, your next Mage spell with a casting time of less than 10 seconds becomes an instant cast spell.

ARCANE MIND

Increases your total Intellect.

 INCANTER'S ABSORPTION

When you absorb damage your spell damage is increased by a percentage of the amount absorbed.

 ARCANE FLOWS

Reduces the cooldown of your Presence of Mind, Arcane Power and Invisibility spells.

 MIND MASTERY

Increases spell power by a percentage of your total Intellect.

 SLOW

Reduces target's movement speed by a good amount, increases the time between ranged attacks and increases casting time. Slow can only affect one target at a time.

 MISSILE BARRAGE

Gives your Arcane Blast, Arcane Barrage, Fireball, Frostbolt and Frostfire Bolt spells a chance to reduce the channeled duration of the next Arcane Missiles spell.

 NETHERWIND PRESENCE

Increases your spell haste.

 SPELL POWER

Increases critical strike damage bonus of all spells.

 ARCANE BARRAGE

Launches several missiles at the enemy target causing Arcane damage.

 PRISMATIC CLOAK

Reduces all damage taken and reduces the fade time of your Invisibility spell.

 ARCANE INSTABILITY

Increases your spell damage and critical strike chance.

ARCANE POTENCY

Increases the critical strike chance of your next damaging spell after gaining Clearcasting or Presence of Mind.

This change makes Arcane Potency a more valuable talent as its chance to go off has increased with the addition of Presence of Mind to its prerequisites.

 ARCANE EMPOWERMENT

Increases the damage of your Arcane Missiles spell by an amount equal to a percentage of your spell power and the damage of your Arcane Blast by a percentage of your spell power.

 ARCANE POWER

When activated, your spells deal more damage while costing more mana to cast.

Druid

Hunter

Mage

Paladin

Priest

Rogue

Shaman

Warlock

Warrior

BURNING DETERMINATION

When Interrupted or Silenced you have a chance to become immune to both mechanics.

WORLD IN FLAMES

Increases the critical strike chance of your Flamestrike, Pyroblast, Blast Wave, Dragon's Breath, Living Bomb, Blizzard and Arcane Explosion spells.

FLAME THROWING

Increases the range of your Fire spells.

IMPACT

Gives any of your damaging spells a chance to stun the target.

PYROBLAST

Hurls an immense fiery boulder that causes Fire damage.

The casting time on this has been reduced, though it is still longer than your other spells. The damage it deals more than makes up for the patience it requires to cast though.

BURNING SOUL

Reduces the pushback suffered from damaging attacks while casting Fire spells and reduces the threat caused by your Fire spells.

IMPROVED SCORCH

Your damaging Scorch spells have a chance to cause your target to become vulnerable to spell damage, increasing spell critical strike chance against that target. Stacks up to five times.

MOLTEN SHIELDS

Causes your Fire Ward and Frost Ward spells to have a chance to reflect the warded spell while active. In addition, your Molten Armor has a chance to affect ranged and spell attacks.

FIRE

IMPROVED FIRE BLAST

Reduces the cooldown of your Fire Blast spell.

INCINERATION

Increases the critical strike chance of your Fire Blast, Scorch, Arcane Blast and Cone of Cold spells.

IMPROVED FIREBALL

Reduces the casting time of your Fireball spell.

IGNITE

Your critical strikes from Fire damage spells cause the target to burn for a percentage of your spell's damage over a few seconds.

MASTER OF ELEMENTS

Your spell criticals will refund a percentage of their base Mana cost.

PLAYING WITH FIRE

Increases all spell damage caused and all spell damage taken.

CRITICAL MASS

Increases the critical strike chance of your Fire spells.

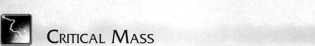

BLAST WAVE

A wave of flame radiates outward from the caster, damaging all enemies caught within the blast for Fire damage, knocking them back and dazing them.

This new knockback component really comes in handy when you are about to be overwhelmed. Hit Blast Wave, knock your enemies back, and use the precious few seconds to make your escape or wind up a devastating attack.

BLAZING SPEED

Gives you a chance when hit by a melee or ranged attack to increase your movement speed and dispel all movement impairing effects.

FIRE POWER

Increases the damage done by your Fire spells.

PYROMANIAC

Increases chance to critically hit and reduces the mana cost of all Fire spells.

COMBUSTION

When activated, this spell causes each of your Fire damage spell hits to increase your critical strike chance with Fire damage spells by 10%. This effect lasts until you have caused three critical strikes with Fire spells.

MOLTEN FURY

Increases damage of all spells against targets with low health.

FIERY PAYBACK

When low health all damage taken is reduced and your Pyroblast spell's cast time is reduced while the cooldown is increased.

EMPOWERED FIRE

Increases the damage of your Fireball and Frostfire Bolt spells by an amount equal to a percentage of your spell power.

The addition of Frostfire to this Talent just makes it that much more valuable to have. This insures that you are getting an advantage from it even in those situations where you can't depend on Fire to get the job done.

FIRESTARTER

Your damaging Blast Wave and Dragon's Breath spells have a chance to make your next Flamestrike spell instant cast.

DRAGON'S BREATH

Targets in a cone in front of the caster take Fire damage and are Disoriented for a few seconds. Any direct damaging attack will revive targets. Turns off your attack when used.

HOT STREAK

Any time you score 2 spell criticals in a row using Fireball, Fire Blast, Scorch, or Frostfire Bolt, you have a chance that the next Pyroblast spell cast within 10 sec will be instant cast.

BURNOUT

Increases your spell critical damage bonus with all Fire spells but your spell criticals cost an additional percentage of the spell's cost.

LIVING BOMB

The target becomes a Living Bomb, taking Fire damage over time. After the allotted time or when the spell is dispelled, the target explodes dealing Fire damage to all nearby enemies. This spell can only affect one target at a time.

Druid

Hunter

Mage

Paladin

Priest

Rogue

Shaman

Warlock

Warrior

FROST

 FROSTBITE

Gives your Chill effects a chance to freeze the target for a few seconds.

 IMPROVED FROSTBOLT

Reduces the casting time of your Frostbolt spell.

 ICE FLOES

Reduces the cooldown of your Frost Nova, Cone of Cold, Ice Block and Icy Veins spells.

 ICE SHARDS

Increases the critical strike damage bonus of your Frost spells.

 FROST WARDING

Increases the armor and resistances given by your Frost Armor and Ice Armor spells. In addition, gives your Frost Ward and Fire Ward a chance to negate the warded damage spell and restore mana equal to the damage caused.

 ELEMENTAL PRECISION

Reduces the mana cost and increases your chance to hit with Frost and Fire spells.

 PERMAFROST

Increases the duration of your Chill effects and reduces the target's speed.

PIERCING ICE

Increases the damage done by your Frost spells.

 ICY VEINS

Hastens your spellcasting, increasing spell casting speed and reduces the push-back suffered from damaging attacks while casting by 100%.

 IMPROVED BLIZZARD

Adds a chill effect to your Blizzard spell. This effect lowers the target's movement speed.

 ARCTIC REACH

Increases the range of your Frostbolt, Ice Lance, Deep Freeze and Blizzard spells and the radius or your Frost Nova and Cone of Cold spells.

This ability has been changed to include the new 51 point Talent, Deep Freeze.

 FROST CHANNELING

Reduces the mana cost of all spells and reduces the threat caused by your Frost spells.

 SHATTER

Increases the critical strike chance of all your spells against frozen targets.

 COLD SNAP

When activated, this spell finishes the cooldown on all Frost spells you recently cast.

 IMPROVED CONE OF COLD

Increases the damage dealt by your Cone of Cold spell.

 FROZEN CORE

Reduces the damage taken from all spells.

COLD AS ICE

Reduces the cooldown of your Cold Snap, Ice Barrier, Deep Freeze and Summon Water Elemental.

 ## WINTER'S CHILL

Gives your Frost damage spells a chance to apply the Winter's Chill effect, which increases the chance spells will critically hit the target. Stacks up to 5 times.

 ## SHATTERED BARRIER

Gives your Ice Barrier spell a chance to freeze all nearby enemies for a few seconds when it is destroyed.

 ## ICE BARRIER

Instantly shields you, absorbing damage. While the shield holds, spells will not be interrupted.

 ## ARCTIC WINDS

Increases all Frost damage you cause and reduces the chance melee and ranged attacks will hit you.

 ## EMPOWERED FROSTBOLT

Increases the damage of your Frostbolt spell by an amount equal to a percentage of your spell power and increases critical strike chance.

 ## FINGERS OF FROST

Gives your Chill effects a chance to grant you the Fingers of Frost effect, which treats your next two spells cast as if the target were Frozen.

 ## BRAIN FREEZE

Your Frost damage spells have a chance to cause your next Fireball spell to be instant cast and cost no mana.

 ## SUMMON WATER ELEMENTAL

Summon a Water Elemental to fight for the caster.

Your Water Elemental now has a longer range on its Waterbolt and Freeze. This means your pet no longer has to get such a close look at a monster to do damage. The Mana cost has been reduced on the Waterbolt while the Freeze now take a bit more mana. This balances out in a good way as most elementals spend a good deal of their time using Waterbolt.

 ## IMPROVED WATER ELEMENTAL

Increases the duration of your Summon Water Elemental spell and your Water Elemental restores mana to all party or raid members within a large radius.

 ## CHILLED TO THE BONE

Increases the damage caused by your Frostbolt, Frostfire Bolt and Ice Lance spells and reduces the movement speed of all chilled targets.

 ## DEEP FREEZE

Stuns the target. Only usable on Frozen targets.

Druid

Hunter

Mage

Paladin

Priest

Rogue

Shaman

Warlock

Warrior

Paladin Abilities

Paladins have seen quite a few changes to their Talents and abilities with the expansion. Many abilities have been tweaked to balance out with the Paladin's awesome arsenal. Talents have been moved around and in many cases had their ranks reduced to free up more points for you to spend on other useful Talents. These changes, as well as the additional Talent points you gain as you move toward level 80 allow you to pick up more Talents than ever. Everything that has been done focuses on making more of the Paladin's abilities useful in more situations.

All Auras now affect all party and raid members within range, making it easier for Paladins to buff their groups or raids. You will notice other changes as well. For instance, some abilities and Talents have been removed like Blessing of Light. Its effects remain however, folded into the abilities it effected. Judgment has been replaced by three separate, more specific, Judgment spells, all with their own effects. All of your Seals have also been reduced to just one rank, and all cost the same percentage of base Mana. Their overall duration has been increased and more importantly, they are no longer consumed with you use one of your Judgment spells. Instead, the effect can trigger by any of your weapon based special abilities. This makes a huge difference in how you manage your Seals and Judgments and may take a bit of practice to get used to. Paladins are not doubt happy to see that summoning their mount no longer costs mana, nor does it affect your global cooldown. These are just a few of the recent changes that are working to make the class even stronger than before.

Like other classes that can potentially fill multiple roles, Paladins often find themselves having to be prepared for any situation. Now that stats like Haste, chance to Hit and Crit are no longer exclusive to either spells or melee abilities, it makes it a bit easier to keep track of what you need. This consolidation also means that some pieces of gear can be good for a tanking, healing, or DPS role and you won't always have to carry around different sets, or at least not as much.

HOLY

BLESSING OF WISDOM

Places a Blessing on the friendly target, restoring mana every few seconds. Players may only have one Blessing on them per Paladin at any one time.

CLEANSE

Cleanses a friendly target, removing a poison effect, disease effect, and magic effect.

CONCENTRATION AURA

All party or raid members within range lose less casting or channeling time when damaged. Players may only have one Aura on them per Paladin at any one time.

CONSECRATION

Consecrates the land beneath the Paladin, doing Holy damage over a short time to enemies who enter the area.

Consecration now scales with attack power and spell power, giving this ability quite a punch.

DIVINE PLEA

You gain a percentage of your total mana over time, but the amount healed by your spells is reduced.

EXORCISM

Causes Holy damage to an Undead or Demon target.

The mana cost of this ability has been reduced and it also now scales with your attack power and spell power.

FLASH OF LIGHT

Heals a friendly target.

GREATER BLESSING OF WISDOM

Gives all members of the raid or group that share the same class with the target Greater Blessing of Wisdom, restoring mana every few seconds. Players may only have one Blessing on them per Paladin at any one time.

HOLY LIGHT

Heals a friendly target.

HOLY WRATH

Sends bolts of holy power in all directions, causing Holy damage and stunning all Undead and Demon targets within range for a few seconds.

While the radius of this spell has been reduced, so has its cooldown and it has become instant cast. There are plenty of places to make use of this spell in Northrend.

LAY ON HANDS

Heals a friendly target for an amount equal to the Paladin's maximum health and restores some of their mana.

This ability no longer drains all of your mana and its cooldown has been reduced, both of which make this a much more easily used ability.

PURIFY

Purifies the friendly target, removing a disease effect and a poison effect.

REDEMPTION

Brings a dead player back to life. Cannot be cast when in combat.

SACRED SHIELD

Each time the target takes damage they gain a Sacred Shield, absorbing damage and increasing the Paladin's chance to critically hit with Flash of Light for a short time. They cannot gain this effect more than once every few seconds.

SEAL OF LIGHT

Fills the Paladin with divine light, giving each melee attack a chance to heal the Paladin. Only one Seal can be active on the Paladin at any one time. Unleashing this Seal's energy will deal Holy damage to an enemy.

SEAL OF RIGHTEOUSNESS

Fills the Paladin with holy spirit, granting each melee attack additional Holy damage. Only one Seal can be active on the Paladin at any one time. Unleashing this Seal's energy will cause Holy damage to an enemy.

SEAL OF WISDOM

Fills the Paladin with divine wisdom, giving each melee attack a chance to restore a percentage of the Paladin's maximum mana. Only one Seal can be active on the Paladin at any one time. Unleashing this Seal's energy will deal Holy damage to an enemy.

SENSE UNDEAD

Shows the location of all nearby undead on the mini-map until cancelled. Only one form of tracking can be active at a time.

TURN EVIL

The targeted undead or demon enemy is compelled to flee for a short time. Damage caused may interrupt the effect. Only one target can be turned at a time.

Turn Undead was removed to make way for this new and improved version.

Classes

Druid

Hunter

Mage

Paladin

Priest

Rogue

Shaman

Warlock

Warrior

PROTECTION

DEVOTION AURA

Gives additional armor to party members within range. Players may only have one Aura on them per Paladin at any one time.

DIVINE INTERVENTION

The Paladin sacrifices himself to remove the targeted party member from harm's way. Enemies will stop attacking the protected party member, who will be immune to all harmful attacks but will not be able to take any action for some time.

The cooldown on this ability has been reduced.

DIVINE PROTECTION

Reduces all damage taken for a short time, but increases the time between your attacks. Once protected, the target cannot be protected by Divine Shield, Divine Protection or Hand of Protection for a time.

DIVINE SHIELD

Protects the Paladin from all damage and spells for a short time, but increases the time between attacks. Once protected, the target cannot be protected by Divine Shield, Divine Protection or Hand of Protection again for a time.

FIRE RESISTANCE AURA

Gives additional Fire resistance to all party members within range. Players may only have one Aura on them per Paladin at any one time.

FROST RESISTANCE AURA

Gives additional Frost resistance to all party members within range. Players may only have one Aura on them per Paladin at any one time.

HAMMER OF JUSTICE

Stuns the target for a brief time and interrupts spellcasting for a few seconds.

HAND OF FREEDOM

Places a Hand of Freedom on the friendly target, granting immunity to movement impairing effects for a short time. Players may only have one Hand on them per Paladin at any one time.

HAND OF PROTECTION

A targeted party member is protected from all physical attacks for a short time, but during that time they cannot attack or use physical abilities. Players may only have one Hand on them per Paladin at any one time. Once protected, the target cannot be protected by Divine Shield, Divine Protection or Hand of Protection again for a time.

HAND OF SACRIFICE

Places a Hand on the party member, transferring some damage taken to the caster. Players may only have one Hand on them per Paladin at any one time.

The duration has been decreased slightly while the cooldown has been increased to help balance this powerful ability.

HAND OF SALVATION

Places a Hand on the party or raid member, reducing their total threat every second for a short time. Players may only have one Hand on them per Paladin at any one time.

RIGHTEOUS DEFENSE

Come to the defense of a friendly target, commanding multiple enemies attacking the target to attack the Paladin instead.

This ability no longer costs mana and the global cooldown has been removed. In addition, its cooldown has been reduced. These changes make this ability much easier to work into your tanking rotation.

RIGHTEOUS FURY

Increases the threat generated by your Holy spells.

SEAL OF JUSTICE

Fills the Paladin with the spirit of justice for a few minutes, giving each melee attack a chance to stun for a few seconds. Only one Seal can be active on the Paladin at any one time. Unleashing this Seal's energy will deal Holy damage to an enemy.

SHADOW RESISTANCE AURA

Gives additional Shadow resistance to all party members within range. Players may only have one Aura on them per Paladin at any one time.

SHIELD OF RIGHTEOUSNESS

Slams the target with your shield, causing Holy damage equal to your block value plus an additional amount. This spell causes a high amount of threat.

SPIRITUAL ATTUNEMENT

A passive ability that gives the Paladin mana when healed by other friendly targets' spells. The amount of mana gained is equal to a percentage of the amount healed.

RETRIBUTION

AVENGING WRATH

Increases all damage and healing caused for a short time.

BLESSING OF MIGHT

Places a Blessing on the friendly target, increasing attack power. Players may only have one Blessing on them per Paladin at any one time.

CRUSADER AURA

Increases the mounted speed for all party members within range. Players may only have one Aura on them per Paladin at any one time. This does not stack with other movement speed increasing effects.

GREATER BLESSING OF MIGHT

Gives all members of the raid or group that share the same class with the target the Greater Blessing of Might, increasing attack power. Players may only have on Blessing on them per Paladin at any one time.

HAMMER OF WRATH

Hurls a hammer that strikes an enemy for Holy damage. Only usable on enemies that have low health.

This spell moved from the Holy line and brought with it a reduced mana cost and became instant cast, making it even more useful.

JUDGMENT OF JUSTICE

Unleashes the energy of a Seal spell to judge an enemy for a short time, preventing them from fleeing and limiting their movement speed. Refer to individual Seals for additional Judgment effect. Only one Judgment per Paladin can be active at any one time.

JUDGMENT OF LIGHT

Unleashes the energy of a Seal spell to judge an enemy for a short time, granting melee attacks made against the judged enemy a chance of healing the attacker. Refer to individual Seals for additional Judgment effect. Only one Judgment per Paladin can be active at any one time.

JUDGMENT OF WISDOM

Unleashes the energy of a Seal spell to judge an enemy, giving each attack a chance to restore some of the attacker's mana. Refer to individual Seals for additional Judgment effect. Only one Judgment per Paladin can be active at any one time.

RETRIBUTION AURA

Causes Holy damage to any enemy that strikes a party or raid member within range. Players may only have one Aura on them per Paladin at any one time.

SEAL OF BLOOD

All melee attacks deal additional Holy damage, but the Paladin loses health equal to a percentage of the total damage inflicted. Unleashing this Seal's energy will judge an enemy instantly causing Holy damage at the cost of health equal to a percentage of the damage caused.

SEAL OF CORRUPTION

Fills the Paladin with holy power, causing attacks to apply Blood Corruption, which deals additional Holy damage over time. Blood Corruption can stack multiple times. Only one Seal can be active on the Paladin at any one time. Unleashing this Seal's energy will deal Holy damage to an enemy, increased by a percentage of each application of Blood Corruption on the target.

Paladin Talents

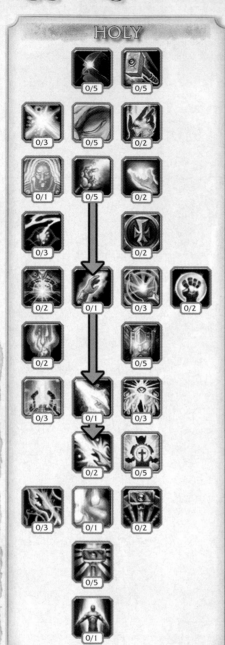

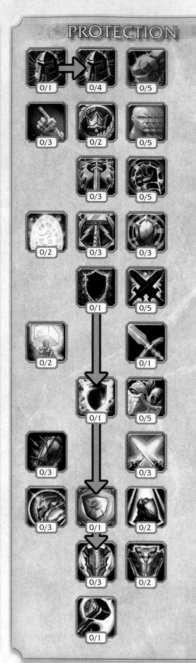

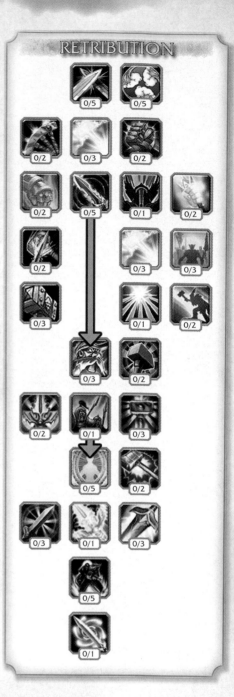

HOLY

SPIRITUAL FOCUS

Reduces the pushback suffered from damaging attacks while casting Flash of Light and Holy Light.

This Talent has been moved up to tier one of the tree. This makes this very useful talent more readily available to Paladins who are speced into other lines.

SEALS OF THE PURE

Increases the damage done by your Seal of Righteousness, Seal of Vengeance and Seal of Corruption and their Judgment effects.

This Talent takes the place of Improved Seal of Righteousness. It has been moved up to the top of the Talent tree making it easier to grab.

HEALING LIGHT

Increases the amount healed by your Holy Light, Flash of Light and the effectiveness of Holy Shock spells.

DIVINE INTELLECT

Increases your total Intellect.

UNYIELDING FAITH

Reduces the duration of all Fear and Disorient effects.

AURA MASTERY

Increases the radius of your Auras.

ILLUMINATION

After getting a critical effect from your Flash of Light, Holy Light, or Holy Shock heal spell you have a chance to gain mana equal to a percentage of the base cost of the spell.

IMPROVED LAY ON HANDS

Gives the target of your Lay on Hands spell a bonus to their armor value from items for a short time. In addition, the cooldown for your Lay on Hands spell is reduced.

IMPROVED CONCENTRATION AURA

Increases the effect of your Concentration Aura by an additional percentage and reduces the duration of any Silence or Interrupt effect used against an affected group member. The duration reduction does not stack with any other effects.

This ability has been moved over from Protection to the Holy tree.

IMPROVED BLESSING OF WISDOM

Increases the effect of your Blessing of Wisdom spell.

PURE OF HEART

Reduces the duration of Curse and Disease effects.

DIVINE FAVOR

When activated, gives your next Flash of Light, Holy Light, or Holy Shock spell a critical effect chance.

SANCTIFIED LIGHT

Increases the critical effect chance of your Holy Light and Holy Shock spells.

BLESSED HANDS

Reduces the mana cost and increases the resistance to Dispel effects of all Hand spells.

PURIFYING POWER

Reduces the mana cost of your Cleanse, Purify and Consecration spells and increases the critical strike chance of your Exorcism and Holy Wrath spells.

HOLY POWER

Increases the critical effect chance of your Holy spells.

LIGHT'S GRACE

Gives your Holy Light spell a chance to reduce the cast time of your next Holy Light spell.

HOLY SHOCK

Blasts the target with Holy energy, causing Holy damage to an enemy, or healing to an ally.

You can hit an ally with this spell at a much greater range than you can an enemy. Its cooldown has also been reduced, making it a much more viable spell.

BLESSED LIFE

All attacks against you have a chance to cause half damage.

INFUSION OF LIGHT

Your Holy Shock critical hits reduce the cast time of your next Flash of Light or Holy Light.

This Talent now gives a greater reduction to cast time than previously.

HOLY GUIDANCE

Increases your spell power by a percentage of your total Intellect.

SACRED CLEANSING

Your Cleanse spell has a chance to increase the target's resistance to Disease, Magic and Poison for a short time.

DIVINE ILLUMINATION

Reduces the mana cost of all spells for a short time.

Druid

Hunter

Mage

Paladin

Priest

Rogue

Shaman

Warlock

Warrior

Enlightened Judgments

Increases the range of your Judgment spells and increases your chance to hit.

Anticipation

Increases your chance to dodge.

This has been moved up the tree, making it easier for any Paladin to grab, no matter how they are speced.

Judgments of the Pure

Your Judgment spells increase your casting and melee haste.

This ability now has a longer duration.

Improved Righteous Fury

While Righteous Fury is active, all damage taken is reduced.

This Talent used to give an increase to the threat generated by Righteous Fury but that component has now been folded into the base spell.

Beacon of Light

The target becomes a Beacon of Light to all targets within range. Any heals you cast on those targets will also heal the Beacon. Only one target can be the Beacon of Light at a time.

Toughness

Increases your armor value from items and reduces the duration of all movement slowing effects.

PROTECTION

Blessing of Kings

Places a Blessing on the friendly target, increasing total stats. Players may only have one Blessing on them per Paladin at any one time.

Divine Guardian

While Divine Shield is active a percentage of all damage taken by party or raid members within range is redirected to the Paladin.

Improved Blessing of Kings

Increases the effectiveness of Blessing of Kings.

Improved Hammer of Justice

Decreases the cooldown of our Hammer of Justice spell.

Divine Strength

Increases your total Strength.

This talent has been moved to the top of the Talent tree, making it easier for any Paladin to use, even if they are speced deep into another line.

Improved Devotion Aura

Increases the armor bonus of your Devotion Aura and increases the amount healed on any target affected by your Devotion Aura.

Stoicism

Reduces the duration of all Stun effects and reduces the chance your spells will be dispelled.

Blessing of Sanctuary

Places a Blessing on the friendly target, reducing damage taken from all sources. In addition, when the target blocks, parries, or dodges a melee attack the target will gain rage, runic power, or some mana. Players may only have one Blessing on them per Paladin at any one time.

Guardian's Favor

Reduces the cooldown of your Hand of Protection and increases the duration of your Hand of Freedom.

Reckoning

Gives you a chance after being hit by any damaging attack that the next few weapon swings within a short time will generate an additional attack.

 REDOUBT

Increases your block value and damaging melee and ranged attacks against you have a chance to increase your chance to block.

The old ability of Shield Specialization has had its effects rolled into Redoubt.

 COMBAT EXPERTISE

Increases your Expertise, total Stamina and chance to critically hit.

 TOUCHED BY THE LIGHT

Increases your spell power by an amount equal to a percentage of your Stamina and increases the amount healed by your critical heals.

 AVENGER'S SHIELD

Hurls a holy shield at the enemy, dealing Holy damage, Dazing them and then jumping to additional nearby enemies.

The cast time has been greatly reduced and the duration has been increased.

 SACRED DUTY

Increases your total Stamina and reduces the cooldown of your Divine Shield and Divine Protection spells while reducing the attack speed penalty.

 GUARDED BY THE LIGHT

Reduces spell damage taken and reduces the mana cost of your Holy Shield, Avenger's Shield and Shield of Righteousness spells.

 ONE-HANDED WEAPON SPECIALIZATION

Increases all damage you deal when a One-Handed weapon is equipped.

 SHIELD OF THE TEMPLAR

Reduces all damage taken and increases the damage of your Holy Shield, Avenger's Shield and Shield of Righteousness spells.

 HOLY SHIELD

Increases chance to block for a short time and deals Holy damage for each attack blocked while active. Each block expends a charge.

The cooldown on this ability has been reduced, and its charges have been increased to blast your attackers with more Holy damage.

 JUDGMENTS OF THE JUST

Your Judgment spells also reduce the melee attack speed of the target.

 ARDENT DEFENDER

When you have low health, all damage taken is reduced.

 HAMMER OF THE RIGHTEOUS

Hammer the current target and up to two nearby additional targets, causing a huge boost to your main hand weapon damage per second as Holy damage.

Druid

Hunter

Mage

Paladin

Priest

Rogue

Shaman

Warlock

Warrior

RETRIBUTION

DEFLECTION

Increases your Parry chance.

BENEDICTION

Reduces the mana cost of all instant cast spells.

IMPROVED JUDGMENTS

Decreases the cooldown of your Judgment spells.

HEART OF THE CRUSADER

In addition to the normal effect, your Judgment spells will also increase the critical strike chance of all attacks made against that target.

IMPROVED BLESSING OF MIGHT

Increases the attack power bonus of your Blessing of Might.

VINDICATION

Gives the Paladin's damaging attacks a chance to reduce the target's attributes for a short time.

CONVICTION

Increases your chance to get a critical strike with all spells and attacks.

SEAL OF COMMAND

Gives the Paladin a chance to deal additional Holy damage. Only one Seal can be active on the Paladin at any one time. Unleashing this Seal's energy will Judge an enemy, instantly causing Holy damage. This attack will always be a critical strike if the target is stunned or incapacitated.

PURSUIT OF JUSTICE

Reduces the duration of all Disarm effects and increases movement and mounted movement speed. This does not stack with other movement speed increasing effects.

EYE FOR AN EYE

All criticals against you cause a percentage of the damage taken to the attacker as well. The damage caused by Eye for an Eye will not exceed half of the Paladin's total health.

SANCTIFIED SEALS

Increases your chance to critically hit with all spells and attacks and reduces the chance your Seals will be dispelled.

CRUSADE

Increases all damage caused and all damage caused against Humanoids, Demons, Undead and Elementals by an additional amount.

TWO-HANDED WEAPON SPECIALIZATION

Increases the damage you deal with Two-Handed melee weapons.

SANCTIFIED RETRIBUTION

Damage caused by targets affected by Retribution Aura is increased.

DIVINE PURPOSE

Reduces your chance to be hit by spells and ranged attacks and gives your Hand of Freedom spell a chance to remove Stun effects on the target.

VENGEANCE

Gives you a bonus to Physical and Holy damage you deal after dealing a critical strike from a weapon swing, spell, or ability. This effect stacks multiple times.

IMPROVED RETRIBUTION AURA

Increases the damage done by your Retribution Aura.

 ## SWIFT RETRIBUTION

Your Retribution Aura also increases casting, ranged and melee attack speeds.

 ## THE ART OF WAR

Increases the critical strike damage of your Judgment, Crusader Strike and Divine Storm abilities and when these abilities critically hit the cast time of your next Flash of Light is reduced.

 ## CRUSADER STRIKE

An instant strike that causes bonus weapon damage.

 ## REPENTANCE

Puts the enemy target in a state of meditation, incapacitating them for a while. Any damage caused will awaken the target. Usable against Demons, Dragonkin, Giants, Humanoids and Undead.

Remember that this ability still has a much shorter duration in PvP.

 ## SHEATH OF LIGHT

Increases your spell power by an amount equal to a percentage of your attack power and your critical healing spells heal the target for a percentage of the healed amount over a short time.

 ## JUDGMENTS OF THE WISE

Your Judgment spells have a chance to grant the Replenishment effect to party or raid members mana regeneration equal to a percentage of their maximum mana per second, and to immediately grant you a percentage of your base mana.

 ## RIGHTEOUS VENGEANCE

Increases critical damage bonus of your Judgment and Divine Storm spells.

 ## FANATICISM

Increases the critical strike chance of all Judgments capable of a critical hit and reduces the threat caused by all actions except when under the effects of Righteous Fury.

 ## DIVINE STORM

An instant weapon attack that causes Physical damage on multiple enemies within range. The Divine Storm heals several party or raid members totaling a percentage of the damage caused.

 ## SANCTIFIED WRATH

Increases the critical strike chance of Hammer of Wrath, reduces the cooldown of Avenging Wrath and while affected by Avenging Wrath a percentage of all damage caused bypasses damage reduction effects.

Classes

Druid

Hunter

Mage

Paladin

Priest

Rogue

Shaman

Warlock

Warrior

PRIEST ABILITIES

Most of the changes to come at the Priests have been in the form of tweaks to their already existing abilities, though they have received a few new Talents and gotten rid of or consolidated a few of the less used ones—Wand Specialization, for example. In most cases, your Talents have become more powerful and, perhaps more importantly, more flexible, giving you benefits no matter which line you put your Talent point into.

Like other healers, Priests have been greatly affected by the consolidation of plus healing and damage to Spell Power. Now, instead of balancing all of their Talents and gear to give mostly healing or damage—rarely both, they can concentrate instead on increasing their Spell Power to benefit their output overall, in healing and damage. While this doesn't mean that a Priest that is healing speced can suddenly put out the damage of a Shadow Priest, it does mean that when they do use their damage spells they are much more effective, and the reverse is true as well.

DISCIPLINE

 ### DISPEL MAGIC

Dispels magic on the target, removing two harmful spells from a friend or two beneficial spells from an enemy.

 ### FEAR WARD

Wards the friendly target against Fear. The next Fear effect used against the target will fail, using up the ward.

 ### INNER FIRE

A burst of Holy energy fills the caster, increasing armor. Each melee or ranged damage hit against the Priest will remove one charge.

 ### LEVITATE

Allows the caster to levitate, floating a few feet above the ground. While levitating, you will fall at a reduced speed and travel over water. Any damage will cancel the effect.

 ### MANA BURN

Destroy Mana from a target. For each Mana destroyed in this way the target takes some Shadow damage.

 ### MASS DISPEL

Dispels magic in a targeted radius, removing a harmful spell from each friendly target and a beneficial spell from each enemy target. This dispel is potent enough to remove Magic effects that are normally undispellable.

 ## POWER WORD: FORTITUDE

Power infuses the target increasing their Stamina.

 ## POWER WORD: SHIELD

Draws on the soul of the party member to shield them, absorbing damage. While the shield holds, spellcasting will not be interrupted by damage. Once shielded, the target cannot be shielded again for a short time.

 ## PRAYER OF FORTITUDE

Power infuses all party and raid members, increasing their Stamina.

 ## SHACKLE UNDEAD

Shackles the target undead enemy. The shackled unit is unable to move, attack or cast spells. Any damage caused releases the target. Only one target can be shackled at a time.

HOLY

 ### ABOLISH DISEASE

Attempts to cure a disease effect on the target, and another disease effect every few seconds for a short while.

 ### BINDING HEAL

Heals a friendly target and the caster. Causes a low amount of threat.

CURE DISEASE

Removes a disease from the friendly target.

DIVINE HYMN

You recite a Hymn, causing the closest enemies within range to become incapacitated for a short time, and heals the closest friendly targets within ranged over a short time. Incapacitated enemies take less damage while incapacitated and for a few seconds after the incapacitation ends. Damage caused may interrupt the effect on all incapacitated targets.

FLASH HEAL

Quickly heals a friendly target.

GREATER HEAL

A slow casting spell that heals a single target for a significant amount.

HEAL

Heals your target for a moderate amount.

HOLY FIRE

Consumes the enemy in Holy Flames that cause Holy damage and an additional amount of Holy damage over time.

Holy Fire has received a significant damage boost as well as a reduced casting time, but its duration has been slightly reduced.

HOLY NOVA

Causes an explosion of holy light around the caster, causing Holy damage to all enemy targets within range and healing all party members within range. These effects cause no threat.

This powerful spell has received a reduction on its mana cost, making it an even more powerful tool.

HYMN OF HOPE

You recite a Holy Hymn of Hope, restoring Mana every few seconds to all party members within range. The Priest must channel to keep the Hymn active.

LESSER HEAL

Heals your target for a moderate amount.

PRAYER OF HEALING

A powerful prayer that heals party members within range.

PRAYER OF MENDING

Places a spell on the target that heals the next time they take damage. When the heal occurs, Prayer of Mending jumps to a raid member within range. Jumps up to several times and lasts half a minute after each jump. This spell can only be placed on one target at a time.

This already powerful spell can now critically hit, giving your targets a much greater infusion of health.

RENEW

Heals the target over time.

RESURRECTION

Brings a dead player back to life. Cannot be cast when in combat.

SMITE

Smite an enemy for Holy damage.

SHADOW

DEVOURING PLAGUE

Afflicts the target with a disease that causes Shadow damage over time. A percentage of the damage caused by Devouring Plague heals the caster.

FADE

Fade out, temporarily reducing all your threat.

Druid

Hunter

Mage

Paladin

Priest

Rogue

Shaman

Warlock

Warrior

MIND SOOTHE

Soothes the target, reducing the range at which it will attack you. Only affects Humanoid targets.

This ability no longer has a max target level so you can try it on pesky higher level mobs when you need to sneak by and are feeling lucky.

MIND VISION

Allows the caster to see through the target's eyes. Will not work if the target is in another instance or on another continent.

PRAYER OF SHADOW PROTECTION

Power infuses the target's party, increasing their Shadow resistance.

PSYCHIC SCREAM

The caster lets out a psychic scream, causing multiple enemies within range to flee for a short time. Damage caused may interrupt the effect.

SHADOW PROTECTION

Increases the target's resistance to Shadow spells.

SHADOW WORD: DEATH

A word of dark binding that inflicts Shadow damage to the target. If the target is not killed by Shadow Word: Death, the caster takes damage equal to the damage inflicted upon the target.

SHADOW WORD: PAIN

A word of darkness that causes Shadow damage over time.

SHADOWFIEND

Creates a shadowy fiend to attack the target. Caster receives Mana when the Shadowfiend deals damage.

MIND BLAST

Blasts the target for Shadow damage.

MIND CONTROL

Controls a humanoid mind, but increases the time between its attacks.

MIND SEAR

Causes an explosion of shadow magic around the enemy target, causing Shadow damage every second for a several seconds to all enemies within range around the target.

Priest Talents

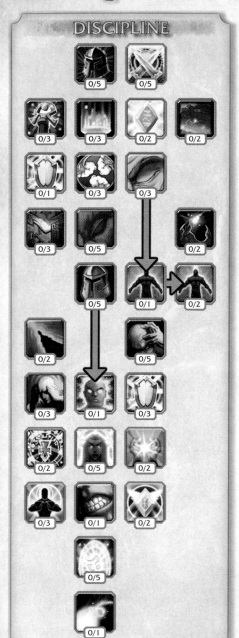

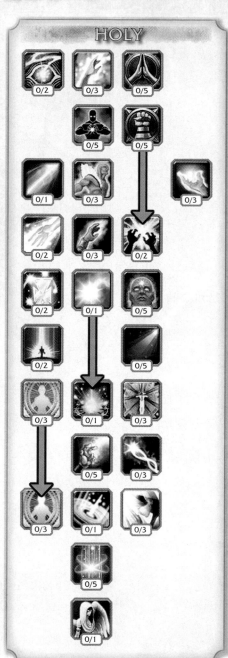

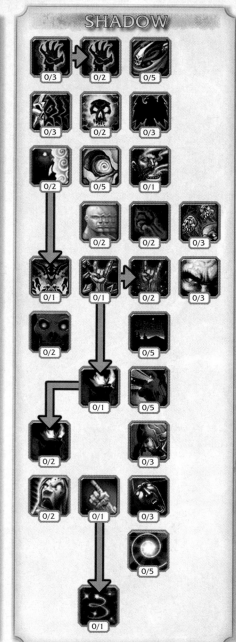

DISCIPLINE

UNBREAKABLE WILL

Reduces the duration of Stun, Fear, and Silence effects done to you.

TWIN DISCIPLINES

Increases the damage and healing done by your instant spells.

This new Talent acknowledges that most Priests aren't always all healing or all damage and helps them out in both roles.

SILENT RESOLVE

Reduces the threat generated by your Holy and Discipline spells and reduces the chance your spells will be dispelled.

IMPROVED INNER FIRE

Increases the effect of your Inner Fire spell and increases the total number of charges.

This no longer just gives you just plus healing, but with the Spell Power changes, increases your damage as well. In addition, it has been moved up in the tree making it more accessible to priests of all specs.

Classes

Druid

Hunter

Mage

Paladin

Priest

Rogue

Shaman

Warlock

Warrior

87

IMPROVED POWER WORD: FORTITUDE

Increases the effect of your Power Word: Fortitude and Prayer of Fortitude spells.

This talent has been moved up the tree one tier, letting Priests grab it a few levels earlier.

MARTYRDOM

Gives you a chance to gain the Focused Casting effect that lasts a short time after being the victim of a melee or ranged critical strike. The Focused Casting effect reduces the pushback suffered from damaging attacks while casting Priest Spells and decreases the duration of Interrupt effects.

IMPROVED POWER WORD: SHIELD

Increases the damage absorbed by your Power Word: Shield.

INNER FOCUS

When activated, reduces the Mana cost of your next spell and increases its critical effect chance if it is capable of a critical effect.

MEDITATION

Allows a percentage of your Mana regeneration to continue while casting.

ABSOLUTION

Reduces the Mana cost of your Dispel Magic, Cure Disease, Abolish Disease and Mass Dispel spells.

MENTAL AGILITY

Reduces the Mana cost of your instant cast spells.

IMPROVED MANA BURN

Reduces the casting time of your Mana Burn spell.

MENTAL STRENGTH

Increases your total Intellect.

DIVINE SPIRIT

Holy power infuses the target, increasing their Spirit.

IMPROVED DIVINE SPIRIT

Your Divine Spirit and Prayer of Spirit spells also increase the target's spell power by an amount equal to a percentage of the Spirit granted.

FOCUSED POWER

Increases damage and healing done by your spells. In addition, your Mass Dispel cast time is reduced.

Formerly this had a component that increased your chance to hit with Mind Blast and Mass Dispel but this component has been removed in favor of the increased damage and healing.

ENLIGHTENMENT

Increases your total Stamina and Spirit and increases your spell Haste.

FOCUSED WILL

After taking a critical hit you gain the Focused Will effect, reducing all damage taken and increasing healing effects on you. Stacks multiple times.

The increased healing component has been decreased a bit but is still significant.

POWER INFUSION

Infuses the target with power, increasing spell casting speed and reducing the Mana cost of all spells.

The cooldown on this ability has been reduced, letting you use it more often.

REFLECTIVE SHIELD

Causes a percentage of the damage absorbed by your Power Word: Shield to reflect back at the attacker. This damage causes no threat.

RENEWED HOPE

Increases the critical effect chance of your Flash Heal, Greater Heal and Penance spells on targets afflicted by the Weakened Soul effect.

 ## PAIN SUPPRESSION

Instantly reduces a friendly target's threat, reduces all damage taken and increases resistance to Dispel mechanics for a short time.

This powerful ability has had its cooldown increased to make up for its strength.

 ## RAPTURE

Causes you to gain up to a slight amount of your maximum Mana each time you heal with Greater Heal, Flash Heal or Penance, or damage is absorbed by your Power Word: Shield or Divine Aegis. Increasing the amount healed or absorbed increases the Mana gained.

 ## GRACE

Your Flash Heal, Greater Heal, and Penance spells have a chance to bless the target with Grace, reducing damage done to the target and increases all healing received from the Priest. This effect stacks multiple times.

 ## ASPIRATION

Reduces the cooldown of your Inner Focus, Power Infusion, Pain Suppression and Penance spells.

 ## BORROWED TIME

Grants spell haste for your next spell after casting Power Word: Shield, and increases the amount absorbed by your Power Word: Shield equal to a percentage of your spell power.

 ## DIVINE AEGIS

Critical heals create a protective shield on the target, absorbing a percentage of the amount healed.

 ## PENANCE

Launches a volley of holy light at the target, causing Holy damage to an enemy or healing to an ally over time.

Druid

Hunter

Mage

Paladin

Priest

Rogue

Shaman

Warlock

Warrior

HOLY

HEALING FOCUS

Reduces the pushback suffered from damaging attacks while casting any healing spell.

IMPROVED RENEW

Increases the amount healed by your Renew spell.

HOLY SPECIALIZATION

Increases the critical effect chance of your Holy spells.

SPELL WARDING

Reduces all spell damage taken.

DIVINE FURY

Reduces the casting time of your Smite, Holy Fire, Heal and Greater Heal spells.

DESPERATE PRAYER

Instantly heals the caster.

BLESSED RECOVERY

After being struck by a melee or ranged critical hit, heal for a percentage of the damage taken over a short time. Additional critical hits taken during the effect increase the healing received.

INSPIRATION

Increases your target's armor for a short time after getting a critical effect from your Flash Heal, Heal, Greater Heal, Binding Heal, Penance, Prayer of Healing or Circle of Healing spell.

HOLY REACH

Increases the range of your Smite and Holy Fire spells and the radius of your Prayer of Healing, Holy Nova, Divine Hymn and Circle of Healing spells.

IMPROVED HEALING

Reduces the Mana cost of your Lesser Heal, Heal, Greater Heal, Divine Hymn and Penance spells.

SEARING LIGHT

Increases the damage of your Smite, Holy Fire, Holy Nova and Penance spells.

HEALING PRAYERS

Reduces the Mana cost of your Prayer of Healing and Prayer of Mending spell.

SPIRIT OF REDEMPTION

Increases total Spirit and upon death, the Priest becomes the Spirit of Redemption for a short time. The Spirit of Redemption cannot move, attack, be attacked or targeted by any spells or effects. While in this form the Priest can cast any healing spell free of cost. When the effect ends, the Priest dies.

SPIRITUAL GUIDANCE

Increases spell power by a percentage of your total Spirit.

SURGE OF LIGHT

Your spell criticals have a chance to cause your next Smite or Flash Heal spell to be instant cast, cost no Mana, but be incapable of a critical hit.

SPIRITUAL HEALING

Increases the amount healed by your healing spells.

HOLY CONCENTRATION

Gives you a chance to enter a Clearcasting state after casting any critical Flash Heal, Binding Heal, or Greater Heal spell. The Clearcasting state reduces the Mana cost of your next Flash Heal, Binding Heal, or Greater Heal.

LIGHTWELL

Creates a Holy Lightwell. Members of your raid or party can click the Lightwell to restore health over a short time. Attacks done to you equal to a percentage of your total health cancel the effect.

The casting time has been reduced significantly, the number of charges doubled, and the cooldown has been reduced. All of these factors make this a much more viable spell.

BLESSED RESILIENCE

Critical hits made against you have a chance to prevent you from being critically hit again for a short time.

EMPOWERED HEALING

Your Greater Heal spell gains an additional percentage and your Flash Heal and Binding Heal gain an additional percentage of your bonus healing effects.

SERENDIPITY

If your Greater Heal or Flash Heal spells heal your target over maximum health, you are instantly refunded a percentage of the spell's Mana cost.

IMPROVED HOLY CONCENTRATION

Increases the chance you'll enter Holy Concentration and also increases your spell Haste for the next couple Greater Heal, Flash Heal or Binding Heal spells after you gain Holy Concentration.

CIRCLE OF HEALING

Heals several friendly party or raid members within range of the target.

This now heals the targets with the lowest health first as long as they are in range, which makes this a much more useable ability.

TEST OF FAITH

Increases healing and spell critical effect chance on friendly targets at or below half health.

DIVINE PROVIDENCE

Increases the amount healed by Circle of Healing, Binding Heal, Holy Nova, Prayer of Healing, Divine Hymn and Prayer of Mending, and reduces the cooldown of your Prayer of Mending.

GUARDIAN SPIRIT

Calls upon a guardian spirit to watch over the friendly target. The spirit increases the healing received by the target and also prevents the target from dying by sacrificing itself. This sacrifice terminates the effect but heals the target half their maximum health.

Classes

Druid

Hunter

Mage

Paladin

Priest

Rogue

Shaman

Warlock

Warrior

SHADOW

 ## SPIRIT TAP

Gives you a chance to gain a bonus to your Spirit after killing a target that yields experience or honor. For the duration, your Mana regenerates at an increased rate while casting.

 ## IMPROVED SPIRIT TAP

Your Mind Blast and Shadow Word: Death critical strikes increase your total Spirit. For the duration, your Mana regenerates at an increased rate while casting.

This new Talent can really help with Mana regeneration, especially to Shadow Priests or others who DPS frequently.

 ## BLACKOUT

Gives your Shadow damage spells a chance to stun the target for a brief time.

 ## SHADOW AFFINITY

Reduces the threat generated by your Shadow spells.

 ## IMPROVED SHADOW WORD: PAIN

Increases the damage done by your Shadow Word: Pain.

This Talent no longer has the component that increases the duration of this ability, but the additional damage more than makes up for it.

 ## SHADOW FOCUS

Increases your chance to hit with your Shadow spells and reduces the Mana cost of your Shadow spells.

The reduction in Mana cost is a new and very helpful component.

 ## IMPROVED PSYCHIC SCREAM

Reduces the cooldown of your Psychic Scream spell.

 ## IMPROVED MIND BLAST

Reduces the cooldown of your Mind Blast spell.

 ## MIND FLAY

Assault the target's mind with Shadow energy, causing Shadow damage and slowing their movement speed.

This ability now has the chance to critically hit, making it a devastating attack.

 ## VEILED SHADOWS

Decreases the cooldown of your Fade ability and reduces the cooldown of your Shadowfiend ability.

 ## SHADOW REACH

Increases the range of your offensive Shadow spells.

 ## SHADOW WEAVING

Your Shadow damage spells have a chance to increase the Shadow damage you deal for a short time.

 ## SILENCE

Silences the target, preventing them from casting spells.

The global cooldown has been removed from this ability.

 ## VAMPIRIC EMBRACE

Afflicts your target with Shadow energy that causes you to be healed, and other party members to be healed, for a percentage of any Shadow spell damage you deal.

 ## IMPROVED VAMPIRIC EMBRACE

Increases the healing received from Vampiric Embrace.

 ## FOCUSED MIND

Reduces the Mana cost of your Mind Blast, Mind Control, Mind Flay and Mind Sear spells.

MIND MELT

Increases the critical strike chance of your Mind Blast, Mind Flay and Mind Sear spells.

DARKNESS

Increases your Shadow spell damage.

SHADOWFORM

Assume a Shadowform, increasing your Shadow damage, reducing Physical damage done to you and threat generated. However, you may not cast Holy spells while in this form. Your Shadow Word: Pain, Devouring Plague, and Vampiric Touch abilities deal increased percentage damage equal to your spell critical strike chance.

Shadowform now also shows up in the UI over your left action bar like other shapeshifting abilities, making it more convenient for you to switch forms at need.

SHADOW POWER

Increases the critical strike damage bonus of your Mind Blast, Mind Flay, and Shadow Word: Death spells.

IMPROVED SHADOWFORM

Your Fade ability now has a chance to remove all movement impairing effects when used while in Shadowform, and reduces the casting or channeling time lost when damaged when casting any Shadow spell while in Shadowform.

MISERY

Your Shadow Word: Pain, Mind Flay and Vampiric Touch spells also increase the chance for harmful spells to hit for a short time and increases the damage of your Mind Blast, Mind Flay and Mind Sear spells by an amount equal to a percentage of your spell power.

PSYCHIC HORROR

Causes your Psychic Scream ability to inflict Psychic Horror on the target when the Fear effect ends. Psychic Horror reduces all damage done by the target for a brief time.

VAMPIRIC TOUCH

Causes Shadow damage over time to your target and causes party or raid members to gain a slight amount of their maximum Mana per second when you deal damage from Mind Blast.

PAIN AND SUFFERING

Your Mind Flay has a chance to refresh the duration of your Shadow Word: Pain on the target, and reduces the damage you take from your own Shadow Word: Death.

TWISTED FAITH

Increases your spell power by a percentage of your total Spirit, and your damage done by your Shadow Word: Pain and Mind Blast is increased if your target is afflicted by your Shadow Word: Pain.

DISPERSION

You disperse into pure Shadow energy, reducing all damage taken. You are unable to attack or cast spells, but you regenerate a percentage of your Mana every second for a short time. Dispersion can be cast while stunned, feared or silenced.

Classes

Druid

Hunter

Mage

Paladin

Priest

Rogue

Shaman

Warlock

Warrior

Rogue Abilities

The changes to Rogues have increased their bag of tricks and made them more powerful and versatile. Some Talents have been reduced in rank, freeing up points for other Talents. Others have been combined, like Fist Weapon Specialization and Dagger Specialization, or expanded to balance this class with the changes everyone is seeing. Your Energy regeneration should be smoother now, and therefore more predictable, making it easier to manage your abilities.

Perhaps the most significant change is the removal of the Poison skill. Don't worry, Rogues are still masters of the noxious art, but they no longer have to make their own poisons! All finished poisons can be bought from a convenient vendor, just like other reagents. Most of the poisons are familiar to you but a few have changed. For instance, Anesthetic Poison now also dispels one Enrage effect, and Crippling Poison has a greater movement reduction. More important than individual Poison changes however is the fact that they all now scale with your attack power. This makes an already powerful aspect of your class even more useful since attack power is so important to Rogues.

Less significant than the items above are a few minor, but helpful, changes as well. Vanish, one of a Rogue's most stunning abilities, no longer requires Flash Powder, making one less thing you need to cart around. Also, you no longer need a set of Thieves Tools to use Pick Lock and Disarm Trap. Now you've got even more bag space for poisons or loot!

ASSASSINATION

AMBUSH

Ambush the target, causing bonus weapon damage plus an additional amount to the target. Must be stealthed and behind the target. Requires a dagger in the main hand. Awards a combo point.

CHEAP SHOT

Stuns the target for a few seconds. Must be stealthed. Awards two combo points.

DEADLY THROW

Finishing move that reduces the movement of the target for a few seconds and causes increased thrown weapon damage.

DISMANTLE

Disarm the enemy, removing all weapons, shield or other equipment carried for a short time.

ENVENOM

Finishing move that consumes your Deadly Poison doses on the target and deals instant Poison damage. Following the Envenom attack you have an additional chance to apply Instant and Deadly Poison to targets for a second, plus and additional second per combo point. One dose consumed for each combo point.

The added chance to apply poisons is a powerful addition to this ability and should not be overlooked.

EVISCERATE

Finishing move that causes damage per combo point.

EXPOSE ARMOR

Finishing move that exposes the target, reducing armor per combo point.

GARROTE

Garrote the enemy, silencing them for a few seconds causing damage over time, increased by attack power. Must be stealthed and behind the target. Awards a combo point.

KIDNEY SHOT

Finishing move that stuns the target. Lasts longer per combo point.

RUPTURE

Finishing move that causes damage over time, increased by your attack power. Lasts longer per combo point.

SLICE AND DICE

Finishing move that increases melee attack speed. Lasts longer per combo point.

COMBAT

BACKSTAB

Backstab the target, causing bonus weapon damage plus an additional amount to the target. Must be behind the target. Requires a dagger in the main hand. Awards a combo point.

EVASION

Increases the Rogue's Dodge chance and reduces the chance ranged attacks hit the Rogue.

The cooldown on this has been significantly reduced.

FAN OF KNIVES

Instantly throw both weapons at all targets within range, causing full weapon damage.

FEINT

Performs a feint, causing no damage but lowering your threat by a large amount, making the enemy less likely to attack you.

GOUGE

Causes some damage, incapacitating the opponent for a few seconds, and turns off your attack. Target must be facing you. Any damage caused will revive the target. Awards a combo point.

The damage of this powerful attack is now based on your attack power.

KICK

A quick kick that interrupts spellcasting and prevents any spell in that school from being cast for a brief time.

This ability no longer has a damage component, but this shouldn't affect how you use it since its main purpose has always been to interrupt spell casting.

SHIV

Performs an instant Off-Hand weapon attack that automatically applies the poison from your Off-Hand weapon to the target. Slower weapons require more Energy. Awards a combo point.

SINISTER STRIKE

An instant strike that causes bonus damage in addition to your normal weapon damage. Awards a combo point.

SPRINT

Increases the Rogue's movement speed for a short time. Does not break stealth.

The cooldown on your Sprint ability has been significantly reduced, which is a great help especially in PvP.

SUBTLETY

BLIND

Blinds the target, causing it to wander disoriented for a brief time. Any damage caused removes the effect.

CLOAK OF SHADOWS

Instantly remove all existing harmful spell effects and increases your chance to resist all spells for a brief time. Does not remove effects that prevent you from using Cloak of Shadows.

The cooldown on this ability has been increased slightly to make up for its power.

DETECT TRAPS

Greatly increased chance to detect traps.

DISARM TRAP

Disarm a hostile trap.

This ability now requires you to be in Stealth but has had its rang increased and its cast time reduced. In addition, you no longer to carry around Thieves Tools for this, freeing up a bag space.

DISTRACT

Throws a distraction, attracting the attention of all nearby hostiles for a short time. Does not break stealth.

PICK POCKET

Pick the target's pocket.

SAFE FALL

Reduces damage from falling.

SAP

Incapacitates the target. Must be stealthed. Only works on Humanoids, Beasts, Demons, and Dragonkin that are not in combat. Any damage caused revives the target. Only one target may be sapped at a time.

STEALTH

Allows the Rogue to sneak around, but reduces your speed.

TRICKS OF THE TRADE

A current party or raid member becomes the target of your Tricks of the Trade. The threat caused by your next attack and all actions taken for several seconds afterwards are transferred to the target. In addition, all damage caused by the target is increased during this time.

VANISH

Allows the Rogue to Vanish from sight, entering an improved stealth mode for a short time. Also breaks movement impairing effects.

The cooldown on this has been significantly reduced, making it easier to use this more often, instead of only in dire situation. It also no longer requires the use of Flash Powder. No more hitting your Vanish button to remove yourself from a sticky situation only to find you've run out!

Classes

Druid

Hunter

Mage

Paladin

Priest

Rogue

Shaman

Warlock

Warrior

ROGUE TALENTS

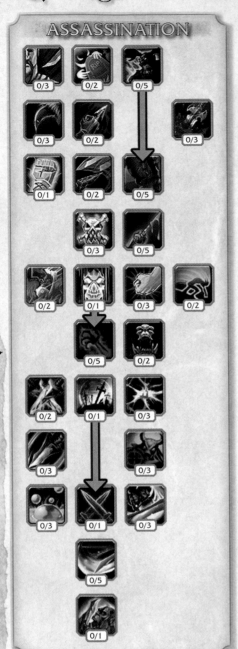

ASSASSINATION

COMBAT MASTERY

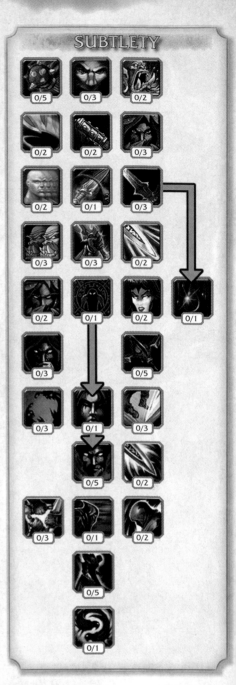

SUBTLETY

ASSASSINATION

IMPROVED EVISCERATE

Increases the damage done by your Eviscerate ability.

REMORSELESS ATTACKS

After killing an opponent that yields experience or honor, gives you an increased critical strike chance on your next Sinister Strike, Hemorrhage, Backstab, Mutilate, Ambush or Ghostly Strike.

MALICE

Increases your critical strike chance.

RUTHLESSNESS

Gives your melee finishing moves a chance to add a combo point to your target.

BLOOD SPATTER

Increases the damage caused by your Garrote and Rupture abilities.

Classes

Druid

Hunter

Mage

Paladin

Priest

Rogue

Shaman

Warlock

Warrior

 PUNCTURING WOUNDS

Increases the critical strike chance of your Backstab ability and the critical strike chance of your Mutilate ability.

 VIGOR

Increases your maximum Energy.

 IMPROVED EXPOSE ARMOR

Reduces the Energy cost of your Expose Armor ability.

This Talent used to increase the duration of Expose Armor, but with the lessened Energy cost you can make up for it by pummeling your target with more attacks during its new duration.

 LETHALITY

Increases the critical strike damage bonus of all combo moves.

 VILE POISONS

Increases the damage dealt by your poisons and Envenom ability and gives your poisons an additional percentage chance to resist dispel effects.

 IMPROVED POISONS

Increases the chance to apply Instant and Deadly Poison to your target.

 FLEET FOOTED

Reduces the duration of all movement impairing effects and increases your movement speed. This does not stack with other movement speed increasing effects.

Instead of raising your chance to resist movement impairing effects, this now decreases the duration. You may find that you are afflicted a bit more by movement impairing effects, but with the duration decreases and your own movement speed increased, they won't be as much of a danger.

 COLD BLOOD

When activated, increases the critical strike chance of your next offensive ability.

 IMPROVED KIDNEY SHOT

While affected by your Kidney Shot ability, the target receives additional damage from all sources.

 QUICK RECOVERY

All healing effects on you are increased. In addition, your finishing moves cost less Energy when they fail to hit.

 SEAL FATE

Your critical strikes from abilities that add combo points have a chance to add an additional combo point.

 MURDER

Increases all damage caused against Humanoid, Giant, Beast and Dragonkin targets.

 DEADLY BREW

When you apply Instant, Wound or Mind-Numbing poison to a target, you have a chance to apply Crippling Poison.

 OVERKILL

Abilities used while stealthed, and for a brief time after breaking stealth, cost less Energy.

 DEADENED NERVES

Reduces all damage taken.

This Talent has been reduced to three ranks, but you still get about the same effect.

 FOCUSED ATTACKS

Your melee critical strikes have a chance to give you some Energy.

 FIND WEAKNESS

Offensive ability damage increased.

This is now a passive Talent, letting you get all the effect without any effort.

 MASTER POISONER

Increases the critical hit chance of all attacks made against any target you have poisoned and reduces the duration of all Poison effects applied to you.

 MUTILATE

Instantly attack with both weapons for an additional amount of damage with each weapon. Damage is increased against Poisoned targets. Awards two combo points.

This ability no longer requires you to be behind the target, meaning it can get much more use.

 TURN THE TABLES

Whenever anyone in your party or raid blocks, dodges, or parries an attack your chance to critically hit with all combo moves is increased for a short time.

CUT TO THE CHASE

Your Eviscerate and Envenom abilities have a chance to refresh your Slice and Dice duration to its maximum.

HUNGER FOR BLOOD

Enrages you, increasing all damage caused. If used while a Bleed effect is afflicting you, it will attempt to remove it and refund Energy. This effect can be stacked multiple times.

COMBAT

IMPROVED GOUGE

Increases the effect duration of your Gouge ability.

IMPROVED SINISTER STRIKE

Reduces the Energy cost of your Sinister Strike ability.

DUAL WIELD SPECIALIZATION

Increases the damage done by your Off-Hand weapon.

This very useful Talent has been moved up to the top of the Talent tree, giving easy access to any Rogue who wants to grab it.

IMPROVED SLICE AND DICE

Increases the duration of your Slice and Dice ability.

DEFLECTION

Increases your Parry chance.

This Talent has been reduced to three ranks, freeing up points to spend elsewhere.

PRECISION

Increases your chance to hit with weapon and poison attacks.

The added chance to hit with poison is a nice addition to this already useful ability.

ENDURANCE

Reduces the cooldown of your Sprint and Evasion abilities and increases your total Stamina.

RIPOSTE

A strike that becomes active after parrying an opponent's attack. This attack deals bonus weapon damage and slows their melee attack speed. Awards a combo point.

While it no longer disarms a target, slowing your opponent's attack is a great benefit.

CLOSE QUARTERS COMBAT

Increases your chance to get a critical strike with Daggers and Fist Weapons.

This takes the place of the Dagger Specialization and also affects Fist Weapons, helping to make it worth a Rogue's time to use Fist Weapons.

IMPROVED KICK

Gives your Kick ability a chance to Silence the target for a few seconds.

IMPROVED SPRINT

Gives a chance to remove all Movement Impairing effects when you activate your Sprint ability.

LIGHTNING REFLEXES

Increases your Dodge chance.

AGGRESSION

Increases the damage of your Sinister Strike, Backstab, and Eviscerate abilities.

This Talent has been moved up to the top of the tree to make it easier for Rogues of all specs to use.

MACE SPECIALIZATION

Your attacks with maces ignore up to a percentage of your opponent's armor.

This ability no longer stuns enemies, but the increase in damage you can do with it more than makes up for the change.

BLADE FLURRY

Increases your attack speed. In addition, attacks strike an additional nearby opponent.

SWORD SPECIALIZATION

Gives you a chance to get an extra attack on the same target after hitting your target with your sword.

WEAPON EXPERTISE

Increases your Expertise.

BLADE TWISTING

Increases the damage dealt by Sinister Strike and Backstab, and your damaging melee attacks have chance to Daze the target for a brief time.

The movement speed reduction on this Daze is significant, letting you get in even more hits on your target.

VITALITY

Increases your Energy regeneration rate.

ADRENALINE RUSH

Increases your Energy Regeneration rate considerably for a short time.

NERVES OF STEEL

Reduces damage taken while affected by Stun and Fear effects.

THROWING SPECIALIZATION

Increases the range of Throw and Deadly Throw and gives your Deadly Throw and Fan of Knives abilities a chance to interrupt the target for a few seconds.

COMBAT POTENCY

Gives your successful Off-Hand melee attacks a chance to generate Energy.

UNFAIR ADVANTAGE

Whenever you dodge an attack you gain an Unfair Advantage, striking back for a percentage of your Main Hand weapons' damage. This cannot occur more than once per second.

SAVAGE COMBAT

Increases your total attack power and all physical damage caused to enemies you have poisoned is increased.

PREY ON THE WEAK

Your critical strike damage is increased when the target has less health than you (as a percentage of total health).

KILLING SPREE

Step through the shadows from enemy to enemy within range, attacking an enemy with both weapons until multiple assaults are made. Can hit the same target multiple times. Cannot hit invisible or stealthed targets.

NERVES OF STEEL

Reduces damage taken while affected by Stun and Fear effects.

THROWING SPECIALIZATION

Increases the range of Throw and Deadly Throw and gives your Deadly Throw and Fan of Knives abilities a chance to interrupt the target for a few seconds.

COMBAT POTENCY

Gives your successful Off-Hand melee attacks a chance to generate Energy.

UNFAIR ADVANTAGE

Whenever you dodge an attack you gain an Unfair Advantage, striking back for a percentage of your Main Hand weapons' damage. This cannot occur more than once per second.

SURPRISE ATTACKS

Your finishing moves can no longer be dodged, and the damage dealt by your Sinister Strike, Backstab, Shiv, Hemorrhage and Gouge abilities is increased.

Classes

Druid

Hunter

Mage

Paladin

Priest

Rogue

Shaman

Warlock

Warrior

DIRTY TRICKS

Increases the range of your Blind and Sap abilities and reduces the Energy cost of your Blind and Sap abilities.

CAMOUFLAGE

Increases the speed while stealthed and reduces the cooldown of your Stealth ability.

ELUSIVENESS

Reduces the cooldown of your Vanish and Blind abilities and your Cloak of Shadows ability.

GHOSTLY STRIKE

A strike that deals bonus weapon damage and increases your chance to dodge for a brief time. Awards a combo point.

SERRATED BLADES

Causes your attacks to ignore some of your target's Armor and increases the damage dealt by your Rupture ability. The amount reduced increases with your level.

SETUP

Gives you a chance to add a combo point to your target after dodging their attack or fully resisting one of their spells. This cannot happen more than once per second.

The chance to gain a combo point has been significantly increased.

INITIATIVE

Gives you a chance to add an additional combo point to your target when using your Ambush, Garrote, or Cheap Shot ability.

The chance for this Talent to activate has been increased.

IMPROVED AMBUSH

Increases the critical strike chance of your Ambush ability.

SUBTLETY

RELENTLESS STRIKES

Your finishing moves have a chance per combo point to restore Energy.

MASTER OF DECEPTION

Reduces the chance enemies have to detect you while in Stealth mode.

OPPORTUNITY

Increases the damage dealt with your Backstab, Mutilate, Garrote and Ambush abilities.

SLEIGHT OF HAND

Reduces the chance you are critically hit by melee and ranged attacks and increases the threat reduction of your Feint ability.

HEIGHTENED SENSES

Increases your Stealth detection and reduces the chance you are hit by spells and ranged attacks.

CHEAT DEATH

You have a chance that an attack which would otherwise kill you will instead reduce you to a percentage of your maximum health. In addition, all damage taken is reduced for a few seconds (modified by Resilience). This effect cannot occur more than once per minute.

Druid

PREPARATION

When activated, this ability immediately finishes the cooldown on your Evasion, Sprint, Vanish, Cold Blood and Shadowstep abilities.

SINISTER CALLING

Increases your total Agility and increases the percentage damage bonus of Backstab and Hemorrhage.

Hunter

Mage

DIRTY DEEDS

Reduces the Energy cost of your Cheap Shot and Garrote abilities. Additionally, your special abilities cause more damage against targets at low health.

WAYLAY

Your Ambush critical hits have a chance to reduce the target's melee and ranged attack speed and movement speed for a short time.

Paladin

Priest

HEMORRHAGE

An instant strike that deals bonus weapon damage and causes the target to Hemorrhage, increasing any Physical damage dealt to the target. Awards a combo point.

HONOR AMONG THIEVES

When anyone in your group critically hits with a damage or healing spell or ability, you have a chance to gain a combo point on your current target. This effect cannot occur more than once every second.

Rogue

Shaman

MASTER OF SUBTLETY

Attacks made while stealthed, and for a brief time after breaking stealth, cause additional damage.

SHADOWSTEP

Attempts to step through the shadows and reappear behind your enemy and increases movement speed for a few seconds. The damage of your next ability is increased and the threat caused is reduced.

This ability can no longer be used while you are rooted, so you may have to depend on Vanish to get you out of roots.

Warlock

Warrior

DEADLINESS

Increases your attack power.

FILTHY TRICKS

Reduces the cooldown of your Tricks of the Trade and Distract abilities and also your Preparation ability.

ENVELOPING SHADOWS

Reduces the damage taken by area of effect attacks.

SLAUGHTER FROM THE SHADOWS

Reduces the Energy cost of your Backstab and Ambush abilities and the Energy cost of your Hemorrhage.

PREMEDITATION

When used, adds two combo points to your target. You must add to or use those combo points within the time limit or the combo points are lost.

The duration of Premeditation has been increased and its cooldown decreased letting you use this powerful ability more often.

SHADOW DANCE

Enter the Shadow Dance, allowing the use of Sap, Garrote, Ambush, Cheap Shot, Premeditation, Pickpocket and Disarm Trap regardless of being stealthed.

Shaman Abilities

As with other classes, Shamans are receiving some much needed additions and changes to give them more versatility. Some Talents have been removed while others have received pretty extensive revisions to give Shamans the aforementioned versatility as well as things like extra DPS and more healing power. Along with these changes comes a basic change for all totems. They now deal Physical, not Magical damage, which can make quite a difference when it comes to resistances.

The recent change to Spell Power has also made things a bit easier for the Shaman. Before you had to balance your gear very carefully, or carry around multiple sets, to effectively move between damage and healing. Now that Spell Power effects both you may find that you don't need to haul around that extra gear, or at least not all of it.

Some of the changes made don't affect just the Shaman but have to do with how you function in a group. For example, the Tranquil Air totem has been removed completely. It was a very effective way to help manage threat in a group but with the modifications to base threat and changes to tanking abilities, it just wasn't needed anymore. Instead, you are now free to let the tank handle the threat and lay down one of your other very useful totems instead.

ELEMENTAL COMBAT

 ### CHAIN LIGHTNING

Hurls a lightning bolt at the enemy, dealing Nature damage and jumping to additional nearby enemies. Each jump reduces the damage. Affects three total targets.

 ### EARTH SHOCK

Instantly shocks the target with concussive force, causing Nature damage. It also interrupts spellcasting and prevents any spell in that school from being cast for a few seconds.

 ### EARTHBIND TOTEM

Summons an Earthbind Totem at the feet of the caster for that slows the movement speed of nearby enemies.

 ### FIRE NOVA TOTEM

Summons a short lived Fire Nova Totem. Unless it is destroyed before it reaches the end of its duration, the totem inflicts Fire damage to nearby enemies.

 ### FLAME SHOCK

Instantly sears the target with fire, causing Fire damage immediately and Fire damage over time.

 ### FROST SHOCK

Instantly shocks the target with frost, causing Frost damage and slowing movement speed by a great deal. Causes a high amount of threat.

 ### HEX

Transforms the enemy into a frog. While Hexed, the target cannot attack or cast spells. Damage caused may interrupt the effect. Only one target can be Hexed at a time. Only works on Humanoids and Beasts.

 ### LAVA BURST

You hurl molten lava at the target, dealing Fire damage. If your Flame Shock is on the target, Lava Burst will consume the Flame Shock, causing Lava Burst to critically hit.

 ### LIGHTNING BOLT

Casts a bolt of lightning at the target causing Nature damage.

 ### MAGMA TOTEM

Summons a Magma Totem at the feet of the caster that causes Fire damage to nearby creatures every few seconds.

 ### PURGE

Purges the enemy target, removing two beneficial magic effects.

 ### SEARING TOTEM

Summons a Searing Totem at your feet that repeatedly attacks an enemy for Fire damage.

STONECLAW TOTEM

Summons a Stoneclaw Totem at the feet of the caster that taunts nearby creatures to attack it. Enemies attacking the Stoneclaw Totem have a chance to be stunned. Stoneclaw Totem also protects your other totems, causing them to absorb damage.

The health of your Stoneclaw Totem is based on your total health, so the hardier you are, the longer it holds its own.

WIND SHOCK

Instantly blasts the target with a gust of wind, causing no damage but lowering your threat, making the enemy less likely to attack you, and interrupts spellcasting and prevents any spell in that school from being cast for a few seconds.

ENHANCEMENT

ASTRAL RECALL

Yanks the caster through the twisting nether back to your bind location. Speak to an Innkeeper to change your home location.

BLOODLUST

Increases melee, ranged, and spell casting speed by a moderate amount for all party and raid members. After the completion of this effect, those affected will become Sated and unable to benefit from Bloodlust again for a few minutes.

EARTH ELEMENTAL TOTEM

Summons an elemental totem that calls forth a greater earth elemental to protect the caster and allies.

FAR SIGHT

Changes the caster's viewpoint to the targeted location. Only useable outdoors.

FIRE RESISTANCE TOTEM

Summons a Fire Resistance Totem at the feet of the caster that increases the Fire resistance of nearby party members.

FLAMETONGUE TOTEM

Summons a Flametongue Totem at the feet of the caster. Nearby party members have their spell damage and healing increased.

FLAMETONGUE WEAPON

Imbue the Shaman's weapon with fire, increasing total spell damage. Each hit causes additional Fire damage, based on the speed of the weapon. Slower weapons cause more Fire damage per swing.

Classes

Druid

Hunter

Mage

Paladin

Priest

Rogue

Shaman

Warlock

Warrior

FROST RESISTANCE TOTEM

Summons a Frost Resistance Totem at the feet of the caster. The totem increases nearby party members' Frost resistance.

FROSTBRAND WEAPON

Imbue the Shaman's weapon with Frost. Each hit has a chance of causing additional Frost damage and slowing the target's movement speed.

The movement speed reduction has been greatly increased, making this great against fleeing foes.

GHOST WOLF

Turns the Shaman into a Ghost Wolf, increasing speed by a good amount. Only useable outdoors.

GROUNDING TOTEM

Summons a Grounding Totem at the feet of the caster that will redirect one harmful spell cast on a nearby party member to itself, destroying the totem. Will not redirect area of effect spells.

LIGHTNING SHIELD

The caster is surrounded by three balls of lightning. When a spell, melee or ranged attack hits the caster, the attacker will be struck for Nature damage. This expends one lightning ball. Only one ball will fire every few seconds. Only one Elemental Shield can be active on the Shaman at any one time.

NATURE RESISTANCE TOTEM

Summons a Nature Resistance Totem at the feet of the caster that increases the Nature resistance of nearby party members.

ROCKBITER WEAPON

Imbue the Shaman's weapon, increasing its damage per second.

The higher level ranks of Rockbiter have been removed. Your Windfury Weapon works as a replacement after level 30.

SENTRY TOTEM

Summons an immobile Sentry Totem at your feet that allows you to see the area near the totem and warns of enemies that attack it. Right click on the buff to switch back and forth between totem sight and Shaman sight.

STONESKIN TOTEM

Summons a Stoneskin Totem at the feet of the caster. The totem protects nearby party members, increasing their armor.

Though it no longer reduces physical damage, the increase in armor more than makes up for it.

STRENGTH OF EARTH TOTEM

Summons a Strength of Earth Totem at the feet of the caster. The totem increases the strength and agility of all nearby party members.

This now covers the increased agility for which you formerly needed the Grace of Air totem.

WATER BREATHING

Allows the target to breathe underwater for ten minutes.

WATER WALKING

Allows the friendly target to walk across water. Any damage cancels the effect.

Shapeshifting no longer cancels this effect, so feel free to bring your Ghost Wolf out to play!

WINDFURY TOTEM

Summons a Windfury Totem at the feet of the caster. The totem provides melee and ranged haste to all nearby party members.

WINDFURY WEAPON

Imbues the Shaman's weapon with wind. Each hit has a chance of dealing additional damage equal to two extra attacks with extra attack power.

WRATH OF AIR TOTEM

Summons a Wrath of Air Totem at the feet of the caster. The totem provides spell Haste to all nearby party members.

RESTORATION

ANCESTRAL SPIRIT

Returns the spirit to the body, restoring a dead target to life. Cannot be cast in combat.

CHAIN HEAL

Heals the friendly target then jumps to heal additional nearby targets. If cast on a party member the heal will only jump to other party members. Each jump reduces the effectiveness of the heal. Heals three total targets.

CURE DISEASE

Cures one disease on the target.

CURE POISON

Cures one poison on the target.

DISEASE CLEANSING TOTEM

Summons a Disease Cleansing Totem at the feet of the caster that attempts to remove one disease effect from nearby party members every few seconds.

EARTHLIVING WEAPON

Imbues the Shaman's weapon with earthen life. Increases healing done and each heal has a chance to proc Earthliving on the target, healing an additional amount over time.

This new spell is great and providing extra healing during tough fights.

HEALING STREAM TOTEM

Summons a Healing Stream Totem at the feet of the caster that heals nearby group members.

HEALING WAVE

Heals a friendly target.

LESSER HEALING WAVE

Heals a friendly target.

MANA SPRING TOTEM

Summons a Mana Spring Totem at the feet of the caster that restores Mana to nearby group members.

POISON CLEANSING TOTEM

Summons a Poison Cleansing Totem at the feet of the caster that attempts to remove one poison effect from nearby party members every few seconds.

REINCARNATION

Allows you to resurrect yourself upon death with a percentage of your health and mana.

TOTEMIC CALL

Returns your totems to earth, giving you a percentage of the Mana required to cast each totem destroyed by Totemic Call.

TREMOR TOTEM

Summons a Tremor Totem at the feet of the caster that shakes the ground around it, removing Fear, Charm and Sleep effects from party members within 30 yards. Lasts 2 min.

WATER SHIELD

The caster is surrounded by three globes of water, granting Mana per five seconds. When a spell, melee or ranged attack hits the caster, some mana is restored to the caster. This expends one water globe. Only one globe will activate every few seconds. Only one Elemental Shield can be active on the Shaman at any one time.

Druid

Hunter

Mage

Paladin

Priest

Rogue

Shaman

Warlock

Warrior

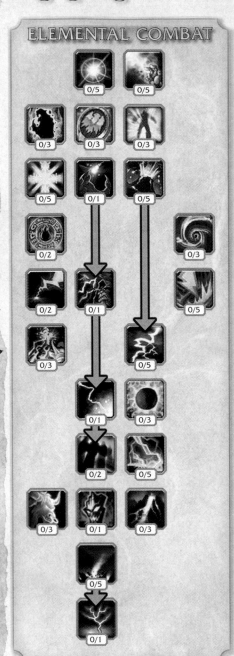

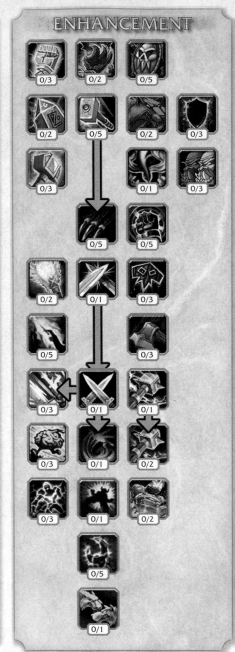

ELEMENTAL COMBAT

0/5	0/5	
0/3	0/3	0/3
0/5	0/1	0/5
0/2		0/3
0/2	0/1	0/5
0/3		0/5
0/1	0/3	
0/2	0/5	
0/3	0/1	0/3
0/5		
0/1		

ENHANCEMENT

0/3	0/2	0/5
0/2	0/5	0/2	0/3
0/3		0/1	0/3
0/5	0/5	
0/2	0/1	0/3
0/5		0/3
0/3	0/1	0/1
0/3	0/1	0/2
0/3	0/1	0/2
0/5		
0/1		

RESTORATION

0/5	0/5	
0/2	0/5	0/5
0/3	0/5	0/1	0/3
0/5	0/5	
0/3	0/1	0/3
0/5		
0/5	0/1	0/1
0/2	0/2	0/3
0/3	0/1	0/2
0/5		
0/1		

ELEMENTAL

CONVECTION

Reduces the mana cost of your Shock, Lightning Bolt, Chain Lightning and Lava Burst spells.

CONCUSSION

Increases the damage done by your Lightning Bolt, Chain Lightning, Thunderstorm, Lava Burst and Shock spells.

CALL OF FLAME

Increases the damage done by your Fire Totems and damage done by your Lava Burst spell.

ELEMENTAL WARDING

Reduces damage taken from Fire, Frost and Nature effects.

ELEMENTAL DEVASTATION

Your offensive spell crits increase your chance to get a critical strike with melee attacks for a short time.

UNRELENTING STORM

Regenerate mana equal to a percentage of your Intellect every few seconds, even while casting.

REVERBERATION

Reduces the cooldown of your Shock spells.

ELEMENTAL PRECISION

Increases your chance to hit with Fire, Frost and Nature spells and reduces the threat caused by Fire, Frost and Nature spells.

Though the bonus to your chance to hit has been reduced, the threat reduction has been greatly increased.

ELEMENTAL FOCUS

After landing a critical strike with a Fire, Frost, or Nature damage spell, you enter into a Clearcasting state. The Clearcasting state reduces the mana cost of your next two damage or healing spells by a significant amount.

This now has a chance to proc off of Lesser Healing Wave and Healing Wave and can effect all healing spells, making it much more useful.

LIGHTNING MASTERY

Reduces the cast time of your Lightning Bolt, Chain Lightning, and Lava Burst spells.

ELEMENTAL FURY

Increases the critical strike damage bonus of your Searing, Magma, and Fire Nova Totems and your Fire, Frost, and Nature spells.

This talent now requires you to have Elemental Focus.

ELEMENTAL MASTERY

When activated, this spell gives your next Fire, Frost, or Nature damage spell a 100% critical strike chance and reduces the mana cost by 100%.

IMPROVED FIRE NOVA TOTEM

Increases the damage done by your Fire Nova Totem and your Fire Nova Totem has a chance to reduce the movement speed of all targets damaged by it.

ELEMENTAL SHIELDS

Reduces all damage taken and increases the damage done by your Lightning Orbs, the mana gained from your Mana Shield Orbs, and the healing done by your Earth Shield Orbs.

EYE OF THE STORM

Reduces the pushback suffered from damaging attacks while casting Lightning Bolt, Chain Lightning, Lava Burst and Hex spells.

ELEMENTAL OATH

Your spell critical strikes grant your party or raid members within a large radius Elemental Oath, increasing spell critical strike chance.

ELEMENTAL REACH

Increases the range of your Lightning Bolt, Chain Lightning and Lava Burst spells, and increases the radius of your Thunderstorm spell.

LIGHTNING OVERLOAD

Gives your Lightning Bolt and Chain Lightning spells a chance to cast a second, similar spell on the same target at no additional cost that causes half damage and no threat.

CALL OF THUNDER

Increases the critical strike chance of your Lightning Bolt, Chain Lightning and Thunderstorm spells.

ASTRAL SHIFT

When stunned, feared or silenced you shift into the Astral Plane reducing all damage taken for the duration of the stun, fear or silence effect.

Druid

Hunter

Mage

Paladin

Priest

Rogue

Shaman

Warlock

Warrior

TOTEM OF WRATH

Summons a Totem of Wrath at the feet of the caster. The totem increases spell power for all party and raid members, and increases the critical strike chance of all attacks against all nearby enemies.

LAVA FLOWS

Increases the range of your Flame Shock, and increases the critical strike damage bonus of your Lava Burst spell.

STORM, EARTH AND FIRE

Reduces the cooldown of your Chain Lightning spell, your Earth Shock's range is increased and the periodic damage done by your Flame shock is increased.

THUNDERSTORM

You call down a bolt of lightning, energizing you and damaging nearby enemies. Restores mana to you and deals Nature damage to all nearby enemies, knocking them back.

ENHANCEMENT

ENHANCING TOTEMS

Increases the effect of your Strength of Earth and Flametongue Totems.

EARTH'S GRASP

Increases the health of your Stoneclaw Totem and the radius of your Earthbind Totem.

This Talent has been moved up to the top of the tree, making it easier to grab, even if you spec deeply into one of the other two lines.

ANCESTRAL KNOWLEDGE

Increases your Intellect.

GUARDIAN TOTEMS

Increases the amount of armor increased by your Stoneskin Totem and reduces the cooldown of your Grounding Totem.

THUNDERING STRIKES

Improves your chance to get a critical strike with all spells and attacks.

IMPROVED GHOST WOLF

Reduces the cast time of your Ghost Wolf spell.

IMPROVED SHIELDS

Increases the damage done by your Lightning Shield Orbs, increases the amount of mana gained from your Water Shield Orbs and increases the amount of healing done by your Earth Shield Orbs.

ELEMENTAL WEAPONS

Increases the damage caused by your Windfury Weapon effect, increases the spell damage on your Flametongue Weapon and increases the bonus healing on your Earthliving Weapon.

SHAMANISTIC FOCUS

Reduces the mana cost of your shock spells.

ANTICIPATION

Increases your chance to dodge, and reduces the duration of all Disarm effects used against you. This does not stack with other Disarm duration reducing effects.

FLURRY

Increases your attack speed for your next few swings after dealing a critical strike.

TOUGHNESS

Increases your armor value from items and reduces the duration of movement slowing effects.

IMPROVED WINDFURY TOTEM

Increases the melee haste granted by your Windfury totem.

 ## SPIRIT WEAPONS

Gives a chance to parry enemy melee attacks and reduces the threat generated by your melee attacks.

 ## MENTAL DEXTERITY

Increases your Attack Power by a percentage of your Intellect.

This means that Intellect is not part of an either or equation when choosing gear, giving you more effective options, no matter your spec.

 ## UNLEASHED RAGE

Causes your critical hits with melee attacks to increase all party and raid members' attack power if they are fairly near you. Lasts 10 sec.

 ## WEAPON MASTERY

Increases the damage you deal with all weapons.

 ## DUAL WIELD SPECIALIZATION

Increases your chance to hit while dual wielding.

 ## DUAL WIELD

Allows One-Hand and Off-Hand weapons to be equipped in the Off-Hand.

 ## STORMSTRIKE

Instantly attack with both weapons. In addition, the next two sources of Nature damage dealt to the target from the Shaman are increased.

 ## MENTAL QUICKNESS

Reduces the mana cost of your instant cast Shaman spells and increases your spell power by an amount equal to a percentage of your attack power.

 ## LAVA LASH

You charge your Off-Hand weapon with lava, instantly dealing 100% off-hand Weapon damage. Damage is increased if your Off-Hand weapon is enchanted with Flametongue.

 ## IMPROVED STORMSTRIKE

Increases the amount of Stormstrike charges and reduces the cooldown.

 ## STATIC SHOCK

You have a chance to hit your target with a Lightning Shield Orb charge when you deal melee attacks and abilities, and increases the number of charges of your Lightning Shield.

 ## SHAMANISTIC RAGE

Reduces all damage taken and gives your successful melee attacks a chance to regenerate mana equal to a percentage of your attack power.

 ## EARTHEN POWER

Your Earthbind Totem has a chance to also remove all snare effects from you and nearby friendly targets when it pulses.

 ## MAELSTROM WEAPON

When you deal damage with a melee weapon you have a chance to reduce the cast time of your next Lightning Bolt, Chain Lightning, Lesser Healing Wave, Chain Heal or Healing Wave spell.

The chance to proc has been reduced slightly for this ability, but it also affects your Chain Heal.

 ## FERAL SPIRIT

Summons two Spirit Wolves under the command of the Shaman.

CLASSES

Druid

Hunter

Mage

Paladin

Priest

Rogue

Shaman

Warlock

Warrior

Ancestral Healing

Increases your target's armor value for a short time after getting a critical effect from one of your healing spells.

Tidal Focus

Reduces the mana cost of your healing spells.

Improved Water Shield

When you gain a critical effect from your Healing Wave, Lesser Healing Wave or Riptide spells, you have a chance to instantly consume a Water Shield Orb.

Healing Focus

Reduces the pushback suffered from damaging attacks while casting any Shaman healing spell.

Tidal Force

Increases the critical effect chance of your Healing Wave, Lesser Healing Wave and Chain Heal by a significant amount. Each critical heal reduces the chance by a small amount.

This new Talent replaces Totemic Mastery.

Healing Grace

Reduces the threat generated by your healing spells and reduces the chance your spells will be dispelled.

RESTORATION

Improved Healing Wave

Reduces the casting time of your Healing Wave spell.

Restorative Totems

Increases the effect of your Mana Spring and Healing Stream Totem.

Totemic Focus

Reduces the mana cost of your totems.

Tidal Mastery

Increases the critical effect chance of your healing and lightning spells.

Improved Reincarnation

Reduces the cooldown of your Reincarnation spell and increases the amount of health and mana you reincarnate with.

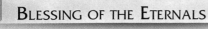

BLESSING OF THE ETERNALS

Increases the critical effect chance of your spells and increases the chance to apply the Earthliving heal over time effect on the target when they are at or under 35% total health.

IMPROVED CHAIN HEAL

Increases the amount healed by your Chain Heal spell.

Druid

Hunter

Mage

Paladin

Priest

Rogue

Shaman

Warlock

Warrior

HEALING WAY

Your Healing Wave spells have a chance to increase the effect of subsequent Healing Wave spells on that target. This effect will stack up to three times.

NATURE'S BLESSING

Increases your healing by an amount equal to a percentage of your Intellect.

Nature's Blessing no longer increases your spell damage and its effect on your healing has been reduced. This was necessary because of the changes to Spell Power and should not effect the overall efficacy of this talent.

NATURE'S SWIFTNESS

When activated, your next Nature spell with a casting time less than ten seconds becomes an instant cast spell.

ANCESTRAL AWAKENING

When you critically heal with your Healing Wave, Lesser Healing Wave or Riptide you summon an Ancestral spirit to aid you, instantly healing the nearby member of your raid or party with the lowest percentage of their health.

FOCUSED MIND

Reduces the duration of any Silence or Interrupt effects used against the Shaman. This effect does not stack with other similar effects.

EARTH SHIELD

Protects the target with an earthen shield, reducing casting or channeling time lost when damaged by a moderate amount and causing attacks to heal the shielded target. This effect can only occur once every few seconds. Earth Shield can only be placed on one target at a time and only one Elemental Shield can be active on a target at a time.

PURIFICATION

Increases the effectiveness of your healing spells.

IMPROVED EARTH SHIELD

Increases the amount of charges for your Earth Shield and increases the healing done by your Earth Shield.

NATURE'S GUARDIAN

Whenever a damaging attack is taken that reduces you to low health, you have a chance to heal a percentage of your total health and reduce your threat level on that target.

TIDAL WAVES

You have a chance after you cast Chain Heal or Riptide to lower the cast time of your next Lesser Healing Wave or Healing Wave spell. In addition, your Healing Wave gains an additional percentage of your bonus healing effects as does your Lesser Healing Wave.

MANA TIDE TOTEM

Summons a Mana Tide Totem at the feet of the caster that restores a percentage of total mana every few seconds to nearby group members.

RIPTIDE

Heals a friendly target and continues healing for several seconds. Your next Chain Heal cast on that primary target within that time consumes the healing over time effect and increase the amount of the Chain Heal.

Riptide is now affected by Ancestral Awakening and Improved Water Shield as well, increasing your chance to get back some mana or increase healing.

CLEANSE SPIRIT

Cleanse the spirit of a friendly target, removing one poison effect, one disease effect, and one curse effect.

You no longer have to try to get rid of these debuffs separately. This new spell does it all!

Warlock Abilities

Warlocks deal impressive damage through the careful combination of damage spells, Dots, and pets, and their new Talents and abilities reflect this role. In many cases abilities have had their damage increased or their mana cost reduced, making them more efficient for the Warlock to use. Talents have been consolidated and moved in the tree to give you access to some important Talents earlier on. In addition, summoning your Dreadsteed or Felsteed no longer costs any mana and does not affect your global cooldown so that your mounts work just like everyone else's.

The most significant change to the Warlock is the way your pets are now handled. All of the Demon Master Trainers have vanished! Instead, all demon abilities and spells are automatically learned as pets gain levels. Gone are the days where you have to spend coin to not only train yourself but your pesky demonic friends as well.

There have been some changes to the demon abilities. For example, they automatically learn Avoidance at level 10. Blood Pact now works for the entire raid, making it unnecessary to stick a Warlock in a particular group. Consume Shadows now also greatly increases nearby allies' Stealth detection. Some abilities have been removed completely and new ones put in their place, like Fel Intelligence and Shadow Bite have replaced Paranoia and Tainted Blood on your Felhunter. Overall, your pets have received the same love given to the other classes in the game, making them better, stronger, and more fearsome.

AFFLICTION

 ### CORRUPTION

Corrupts the target, causing Shadow damage over time.

 ### CURSE OF AGONY

Curses the target with agony, causing Shadow damage over time. This damage is dealt slowly at first, and builds up as the Curse reaches its full duration. Only one Curse per Warlock can be active on any one target.

 ### CURSE OF DOOM

Curse the target with impending Doom, causing Shadow damage after a minute. If the target yields experience or honor when it dies from this damage, a Doomguard is summoned. Cannot be cast on players.

The Doomguard now has increased Health and Mana.

 ### CURSE OF RECKLESSNESS

Curses the target with Recklessness, increasing melee attack power but reducing armor. Cursed enemies do not flee. Only one Curse per Warlock can be active on any one target.

 ### CURSE OF ELEMENTS

Curses the target, reducing Arcane, Fire, Frost, Nature and Shadow resistances and increasing magic damage taken. Only one Curse per Warlock can be active on any one target.

 ### CURSE OF TONGUES

Forces the target to speak in Demonic, increasing the casting time of al spells. Only one Curse per Warlock can be active on any one target.

 ### CURSE OF WEAKNESS

Target's melee attack power is reduced. Only one Curse per Warlock can be active on any one target.

 ### DEATH COIL

Causes the enemy target to run in horror for a few seconds and causes Shadow damage. The caster gains all the damage caused in Health.

 ### DRAIN LIFE

Transfers Health from the target to the caster.

 ### DRAIN MANA

Transfers Mana from the target to the caster.

 ### DRAIN SOUL

Drains the soul of the target, causing Shadow damage over time. If the target is at low Health, Drain Soul causes many times more damage. If the target dies while being drained, and yields experience or honor, the caster gains a Soul Shard. Soul Shards are required for other spells.

 ### FEAR

Strikes fear in the enemy, causing it to run in fear. Damage caused may interrupt the effect. Only one target can be feared at a time.

 ### HOWL OF TERROR

Howl, causing multiple enemies within range to flee in terror for a short time. Damage caused may interrupt the effect.

 ### LIFE TAP

Converts Health into Mana. Spirit increases quantity of Health recovered.

 ### SEED OF CORRUPTION

Imbeds a demon seed in the enemy target, causing Shadow damage over time. When the target takes damage or dies, the seed inflicts Shadow damage to all other enemies within range of the target. Only one Corruption spell per Warlock can be active on any one target.

DEMONOLOGY

 ## BANISH

Banishes the enemy target, preventing all action but making it invulnerable for a time. Only one target can be banished at a time. Only works on Demons and Elementals.

 ## CREATE FIRESTONE

While applied to target weapon it increases damage dealt by direct spells and spell critical strike.

 ## CREATE HEALTHSTONE

Creates a Healthstone that can be used instantly restore Health. Conjured items disappear if logged out for more than 15 minutes.

 ## CREATE SOULSTONE

Creates a Soulstone. The Soulstone can be used to store one target's soul. If the target dies while his soul is stored he is able to resurrect with a percentage of his health and mana.

 ## DEMON ARMOR

Protects the caster, increasing armor and increasing the amount of Health generated trough spells and effects by a moderate amount. Only one type of Armor spell can be active on the Warlock at any time.

 ## DEMONIC CIRCLE: SUMMON

You summon a Demonic Circle at your feet. You can only have one Demonic Circle active at a time.

 ## DEMONIC CIRCLE: TELEPORT

You teleport to your Demonic Circle.

 ## DETECT INVISIBILITY

Allows the friendly target to detect lesser invisibility.

 ## ENSLAVE DEMON

Enslaves the target demon, up to level 84, forcing it to do your bidding. While enslaved, the time between the demon's attacks is increased and its casting speed is slowed. If you repeatedly enslave the same demon, it becomes more difficult with each attempt.

 ## EYE OF KILROGG

Summons an Eye of Kilrogg and binds your vision to it. The eye moves quickly but is very fragile.

 ## FEL ARMOR

Surrounds the caster with fel energy, increasing spell power plus additional spell power equal to a percentage of your Spirit. In addition, you regain a percentage of your maximum Health every few seconds. Only one type of Armor spell can be active on the Warlock at any time.

This can no longer be dispelled.

 ## HEALTH FUNNEL

Gives Health to the caster's pet every second for a short time as long as the caster channels.

 ## INFERNO

Summons a meteor from the Twisting Nether, causing Fire damage and stunning all enemy targets in the area for a few seconds. An Infernal rises form the crater, under the command of the caster for a minute.

Your Infernal has significantly increased Health, Damage, and Armor and has had its cooldown reduced by a large amount. However, its duration has been reduced significantly as well.

 ## RITUAL OF DOOM

Begins a ritual that sacrifices a random participant's Health to summon a Doom-guard. The Doomguard must be immediately enslaved or it attacks the ritual participants. Requires the caster and four party members to complete the ritual. In order to participate, all players must right-click the portal and not move until the ritual is complete.

 ## RITUAL OF SOULS

Begins a ritual that creates a Soulwell. Raid members can click the Soulwell to acquire a Fel Healthstone. The Soulwell lasts for a few minutes or until all charges are taken. Requires the caster and two party members to complete the ritual. In order to participate, all players must right-click the soul portal and not move until the ritual is complete.

The charges on this ability have been greatly increased to make it easier for large raids to grab a Healthstone.

 ## RITUAL OF SUMMONING

Begins a ritual that summons the targeted group member. Requires the caster and two party members to complete the ritual. In order to participate, all players must be out of combat and right-click the portal and not move until the ritual is complete.

 ## SENSE DEMONS

Shows the location of all nearby demons on the mini-map until cancelled. Only one form of tracking can be active at a time.

 ## SHADOW WARD

Absorbs shadow damage.

 ## SOULSHATTER

Reduces the threat for all enemies within range.

Classes

Druid

Hunter

Mage

Paladin

Priest

Rogue

Shaman

Warlock

Warrior

Summon Felhunter

Summons a Felhunter under the command of the Warlock.

Summon Voidwalker

Summons a Voidwalker under the command of the Warlock.

Your Voidwalker has had its Health, Damage and attack power increased.

Summon Imp

Summons an Imp under the command of the Warlock.

Unending Breath

Allows the target to breathe underwater for a long period of time.

Summon Succubus

Summons a Succubus under the command of the Warlock.

Your Succubus has had her Health and armor increased, increasing her overall survivability.

DESTRUCTION

Hellfire

Ignites the area surrounding the caster, causing Fire damage to the caster and Fire damage to all nearby enemies every second.

Searing Pain

Inflict searing pain on the enemy target, causing Fire damage. Causes a high amount of threat.

Immolate

Burns the enemy for Fire damage and then an additional amount of Fire damage over time.

Shadow Bolt

Sends a shadowy bolt at the enemy, causing Shadow damage.

Incinerate

Deals Fire damage to your target and an additional amount of Fire damage if the target is affected by an Immolate spell.

Shadowflame

Targets in a cone in front of the caster take Shadow damage and an additional amount of Fire damage over time.

Rain of Fire

Calls down a fiery rain to burn enemies in the area of effect for Fire damage over time.

Soul Fire

Burn the enemy's soul, causing Fire damage.

Talents

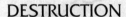

AFFLICTION

Improved Curse of Agony

Increases the damage done by your Curse of Agony.

Improved Corruption

Increases the damage done by your Corruption and increases the critical strike chance of your Seed of Corruption.

Suppression

Increases your chance to hit with Affliction spells, and reduces the Mana cost of your Affliction spells.

Frailty

Increases the amount of attack power reduced by your Curse of Weakness and reduces the amount of attack power granted by your Curse of Recklessness.

This Talent takes the place of Improved Curse of Weakness.

AFFLICTION

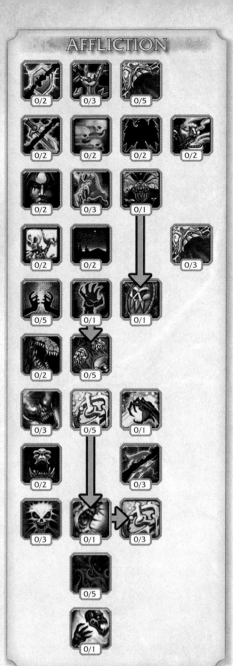

DEMONOLOGY

DESTRUCTION

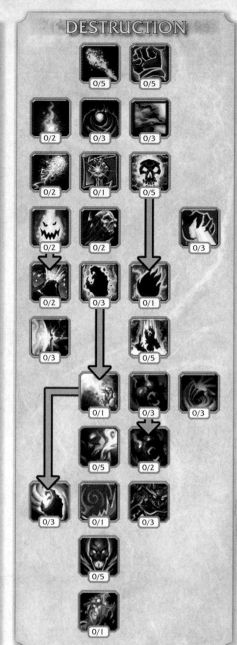

Druid

Hunter

Mage

Paladin

Priest

Rogue

Shaman

Warlock

Warrior

 ## IMPROVED DRAIN SOUL

Returns a percentage of your maximum Mana if the target is killed by you while you drain its soul. In addition, your Affliction spells generate less threat.

 ## IMPROVED LIFE TAP

Increases the amount of Mana awarded by your Life Tap spell.

 ## SOUL SIPHON

Increases the amount drained by your Drain Life and Drain Soul spells by an additional amount for each Affliction effect on the target.

 ## IMPROVED FEAR

Causes your Fear spell to inflict a Nightmare on the target when the fear effect ends. The Nightmare effect reduces the target's movement speed for a brief time.

 ## FEL CONCENTRATION

Reduces the pushback suffered from damaging attacks while casting Drain Life, Drain Mana, Drain Soul, Unstable Affliction, and Haunt.

 ## AMPLIFY CURSE

Reduces the global cooldown of your Curses.

GRIM REACH

Increases the range of your Affliction spells.

NIGHTFALL

Gives your Corruption and Drain Life spells a chance to cause you to enter a Shadow Trance state after damaging the opponent. The Shadow Trance state reduces the casting time of your next Shadow Bolt spell.

EMPOWERED CORRUPTION

Increases the damage of your Corruption spell by an amount equal to a percentage of your spell power.

SHADOW EMBRACE

Your Shadow Bolt and Haunt spells apply the Shadow Embrace effect, increasing all periodic damage dealt to the target by you and reduces all periodic healing done to the target. Stacks two times.

SIPHON LIFE

Transfers Health from the target to the caster every few seconds.

CURSE OF EXHAUSTION

Reduces the target's movement speed for a short time. Only one Curse per Warlock can be active on any one target.

IMPROVED FELHUNTER

Your Felhunter regains some of its maximum Mana each time it hits with its Shadow Bite ability, and increases the effect of your Felhunter's Fel Intelligence.

This new Talent makes this already formidable pet, even more daunting.

SHADOW MASTERY

Increases the damage dealt or life drained by your Shadow spells.

ERADICATION

Your Corruption ticks have a chance to increase your spell casting speed for a short time. This effect cannot occur more than once every half minute.

This new Talent serves to increase your overall DPS.

CONTAGION

Increases the damage of Curse of Agony, Corruption and Seed of Corruption and reduces the chance your Affliction spells will be dispelled.

DARK PACT

Drains some of your summoned demon's Mana, returning all of it to you.

The amount of mana you get has been significantly increased.

IMPROVED HOWL OF TERROR

Reduces the casting time of your Howl of Terror spell.

MALEDICTION

Increases the damage bonus effect of your Curse of the Elements spell and increases your spell damage.

DEATH'S EMBRACE

Increases the amount drained by your Drain Life while your Health is low and increases the damage done by your Shadow spells when your target is low Health.

UNSTABLE AFFLICTION

Shadow energy slowly destroys the target, causing Shadow damage over time. In addition, if the Unstable Affliction is dispelled it will cause damage to the dispeller and Silence them for a brief time.

The Silence effect has been reduced.

PANDEMIC

Each time you deal damage with Corruption or Unstable Affliction you have a chance equal to your spell critical strike chance to deal additional damage.

EVERLASTING AFFLICTION

Your Corruption, Siphon Life and Unstable Affliction spells gain an additional percentage of your bonus spell damage, and your Drain Life and Haunt spells have a chance to reset the duration of your Corruption spell on the target.

HAUNT

You send a ghostly soul into the target, dealing Shadow damage and increasing all damage done by your damage over time effects of the target for a short time. When the Haunt spell ends or is dispelled, the soul returns to you, healing you for all the damage it did to the target.

DEMONOLOGY

IMPROVED HEALTHSTONE

Increase the amount of Health restored by your Healthstone.

IMPROVED IMP

Increases the effect of your Imp's Firebolt, Fire Shield, and Blood Pact spells.

DEMONIC EMBRACE

Increases your total Stamina.

IMPROVED HEALTH FUNNEL

Increases the amount of Health transferred by your Health Funnel spell and reduces the initial Health cost. In addition, your summoned Demon takes less damage while under the effect of your Health Funnel.

DEMONIC BRUTALITY

Increases the effectiveness of your Voidwalker's Torment, Consume Shadows, Sacrifice and Suffering spells and increases the attack power bonus of your Felguard's Demonic Frenzy effect.

FEL VITALITY

Increases the Stamina and Intellect of your Imp, Voidwalker, Succubus, Felhunter and Felguard and increases your maximum Health and Mana.

This Talent takes the place of both Fel Stamina and Fel Intellect.

IMPROVED SUCCUBUS

Reduces the cast time of your Succubus' Seduction and increases the duration of your Succubus' Seduction and Lesser Invisibility spells.

SOUL LINK

When active, a percentage of all damage taken by the caster is taken by your Imp, Voidwalker, Succubus, Felhunter, Felguard, or enslaved demon instead. That damage cannot be prevented. Lasts as long as the demon is active and controlled.

FEL DOMINATION

Your next Imp, Voidwalker, Succubus, Felhunter and Felguard Summon spell has its casting time reduced and its Mana cost reduced.

DEMONIC AEGIS

Increases the effectiveness of your Demon Armor and Fel Armor spells.

UNHOLY POWER

Increases the damage done by your Voidwalker, Succubus, Felhunter and Felguard's melee attacks and your Imp's Firebolt.

MASTER SUMMONER

Reduces the casting time of your Imp, Voidwalker, Succubus, Felhunter and Felguard Summoning spells by a few seconds and reduce the Mana cost.

DEMONIC SACRIFICE

When activated, sacrifices your summoned demon to grant you an effect. The effect is canceled if any Demon is summoned.

Imp – Increases your Fire damage.

Voidwalker – Restores a percentage of your total Health every few seconds.

Succubus – Increases your Shadow damage.

Felhunter – Restores a percentage of your total Mana every few seconds.

Felguard – Increases your Shadow and Fire damage and restores a percentage of your total Mana every few seconds.

MASTER CONJURER

Increases the effects granted by your conjured Firestone and Spellstone.

MANA FEED

When you gain Mana from Drain Mana or Life Tap spells, your summoned demon gains a percentage of the Mana you gain.

MASTER DEMONOLOGIST

Grants both the Warlock and the summoned demon an effect as long as that demon is active.

Imp – Increases your Fire damage and increases the critical effect chance of your Fire spells.

Voidwalker – Reduces Physical damage taken.

Succubus – Increases your Shadow damage and increases the critical effect chance of your Shadow spells.

Felhunter – Reduces all spell damage taken.

Felguard – Increases all damage done and reduces all damage taken.

IMPROVED ENSLAVE DEMON

Reduces the Attack Speed and Casting Speed penalty of your Enslave Demon spell and reduces the resist chance.

DEMONIC RESILIENCE

Reduces the chance you'll be critically hit by melee and spells and reduces all damage your summoned demon takes.

Druid

Hunter

Mage

Paladin

Priest

Rogue

Shaman

Warlock

Warrior

DEMONIC EMPOWERMENT

Grants the Warlock's summoned demon Empowerment:

Succubus – Instantly vanishes, causing the Succubus to go into an improved Invisibility state. The vanish effect removes all stuns, snares and movement impairing effects from the Succubus.

Voidwalker – Increases the Voidwalker's Health and its threat generated from spells and attacks for a short time.

Imp – Increases the Imp's spell critical strike chance for a short time.

Felhunter – Dispels all magical effects from the Felhunter.

Felguard – Increases the Felguard's attack speed and breaks all stun, snare and movement impairing effects and makes your Felguard immune to them.

DEMONIC KNOWLEDGE

Increases your spell damage by an amount equal to a percentage of the total active demon's Stamina plus Intellect.

DEMONIC TACTICS

Increases melee and spell critical strike chance for you and your summoned demon.

FEL SYNERGY

Your Summoned Demons share an additional percentage of your Armor, Intellect and Stamina and you have a chance to heal your pet for a percentage of the amount of damage done by you.

IMPROVED DEMONIC TACTICS

Increases your summoned demons critical strike chance equal to a percentage of your critical strike chance.

SUMMON FELGUARD

Summons a Felguard under the command of the Warlock.

Your Felguard's health has been moderately increased.

DEMONIC EMPATHY

When you or your pet critically hits with a spell or ability, the other's damage done by their next few spells or abilities is increased.

DEMONIC PACT

Your pet's criticals apply the Demonic Pact effect to your party or raid members. Demonic Pact increases spell power by a percentage of your Spell damage for a short time. Does not work on Enslaved demons.

METAMORPHOSIS

You transform into a Demon for a short time. This form increases your armor by a large amount, damage done and reduces the chance you'll be critically hit by melee attacks and reduces the duration of stun and snare effects by half. You gain some unique demon abilities in addition to your normal abilities.

DESTRUCTION

IMPROVED SHADOW BOLT

Your Shadow Bolt critical strikes increase Shadow damage dealt until some non-periodic damage sources are applied.

The critical strike chance has been slightly decreased, but is still quite significant.

BANE

Reduces the casting time of your Shadow Bolt, Chaos Bolt and Immolate spells and your Soul Fire spell.

AFTERMATH

Gives your Destruction spells a chance to daze the target for a brief time.

This has been reduced from five ranks to two, but gives you a comparable effect.

MOLTEN CORE

Your Shadow spells and damage over time effects have a chance to increase the damage of your Fire spells for a short time.

CATACLYSM

Reduces the Mana cost of your Destruction spells and increases the chance to hit with your Destruction spells.

DEMONIC POWER

Reduces the cooldown of your Succubus' Lash of Pain spell and reduces the casting time of your Imp's Firebolt spell.

SHADOWBURN

Instantly blasts the target for Shadow damage. If the target dies within several seconds of Shadowburn, and yields experience or honor, the caster gains a Soul Shard

RUIN

Increases the critical strike damage bonus of your Destruction spells.

INTENSITY

Reduces the pushback suffered from damaging attacks while casting or channeling any Destruction spells.

DESTRUCTIVE REACH

Increases the range of your Destruction spells and reduces the threat caused by your Destruction spells.

IMPROVED SEARING PAIN

Increases the critical strike chance of your Searing Pain spell.

PYROCLASM

Gives your Rain of Fire, Hellfire, Conflagrate and Soul Fire spells a chance to stun the target for a few seconds.

IMPROVED IMMOLATE

Increases the initial damage of your Immolate spell.

DEVASTATION

Increases the critical strike chance of your Destruction spells.

NETHER PROTECTION

After being hit with a spell, you have a chance to gain Nether Protection, reducing all damage by that spell school for a brief time.

EMBERSTORM

Increases the damage done by your Fire spells and reduces the cast time of your Incinerate spell.

CONFLAGRATE

Ignites a target that is already afflicted by your Immolation or Shadowflame, dealing Fire damage and consuming Shadowflame spell.

SOUL LEECH

Gives your Shadow Bolt, Shadowburn, Chaos Bolt, Soul Fire, Incinerate, Searing Pain and Conflagrate spells a chance to return Health equal to a percentage of the damage caused.

BACKLASH

Increases your critical strike chance with spells and gives you a chance when hit by a physical attack to reduce the cast time of your next Shadow Bolt or Incinerate spell. This effect lasts a short time and will not occur more than once every several seconds.

SHADOW AND FLAME

Your Shadow Bolt, Chaos Bolt and Incinerate spells gain an additional percentage of your bonus spell damage effects.

IMPROVED SOUL LEECH

Your Soul Leech effect also restores Mana to you and your summoned demon equal to a percentage of your maximum Mana.

BACKDRAFT

When you cast Conflagrate, the cast time of your next three Destruction spells is reduced.

SHADOWFURY

Shadowfury is unleashed, causing Shadow damage and stunning all enemies within range for a few seconds.

This spell can now be cast while moving and the duration of its Stun component has been increased.

EMPOWERED IMP

Increases the damage done by your Imp and all critical hits done by your Imp have a chance to increase your spell critical hit chance for your next spell.

FIRE AND BRIMSTONE

Increases the damage of your Immolate spell by an amount equal to a percentage of your spell power, and the critical strike chance of your Conflagrate spell is increased if the Immolate on the target has only a few seconds remaining.

CHAOS BOLT

Sends a bolt of chaotic fire at the enemy, dealing Fire damage. Chaos Bolt cannot be resisted, and pierces through all absorption effects.

The change to Fire damage affects how this can be resisted.

Druid

Hunter

Mage

Paladin

Priest

Rogue

Shaman

Warlock

Warrior

Warrior Abilities

Warriors have received a great deal of attention. Many of their talents and abilities have been retooled so that they function well in more than one role the Warrior finds herself in. Strength now not only increases attack power, but also increases block value, potentially making the same piece of gear function well for both a DPS Warrior or a Tank.

Several Talents have seen their ranks reduced or, like Improved Taunt for example, been removed altogether to free up points for many of the new Talents that increase DPS or help with Rage generation and spending. All warriors have seen their DPS increase which is not only good for taking out the enemy but is also a key component of threat generation.

Threat generation has been greatly increased. This is a very good thing especially considering the devastating DPS and awesome healing power many of the other classes can provide. With changes to Defensive Stance and other abilities like Thunder Clap and Shockwave, Warriors are much more effective at tanking multiple mobs than they once were. Additions like Titan's Grip give DPS Warriors new options for dishing out the pain as well. Overall the changes have made Warriors much more effective and versatile.

ARMS

 ### Battle Stance

A balanced combat stance.

 ### Charge

Requires Battle Stance. Charge an enemy, generate Rage and stun it. Cannot be used in combat.

 ### Hamstring

Requires Battle Stance or Berserker Stance. Maims the enemy, reducing movement speed.

This move no longer causes damage, but this doesn't affect its usefulness as the point is to slow your enemy down so you can deal out the damage with your other attacks.

 ### Heroic Strike

A strong attack that increase melee damage and causes a high amount of threat. Causes additional damage against Dazed targets.

 ### Heroic Throw

Throws your weapon at the enemy causing damage based on attack power. This ability causes a high amount of threat.

This new ability works very well for pulling since it generates so much threat, giving you a head start on building it up against the target. It is also fun and useful against fleeing targets in PvP.

 ### Mocking Blow

Requires Battle Stance or Defensive Stance. A mocking attack that causes weapon damage, a moderate amount of threat and forces the target to focus attacks on you for a short time.

Now that this can be used in Defensive Stance, Mocking Blow is going to see much more use. It is yet another tool you can use to keep your foe focused on you.

 ### Overpower

Requires Battle Stance. Instantly overpower the enemy, causing weapon damage. Only useable after the target dodges. The Overpower cannot be blocked, dodged or parried.

Though this ability lost its bonus damage, its low Rage cost makes it still one of your most valuable attacks.

 ### Rend

Requires Battle Stance, Defensive Stance. Wounds the target causing them to bleed.

 ### Retaliation

Requires Battle Stance. Instantly counterattack any enemy that strikes you in melee. Melee attacks made from behind cannot be counterattacked. A maximum of 20 attacks will cause Retaliation.

 ### Thunder Clap

Requires Battle Stance or Defensive Stance. Blasts nearby enemies increasing the time between their attacks and doing damage to them. Damage is increased by attack power. This ability causes additional threat.

The cooldown has also been decreased and Thunder Clap now affects all target within range. This makes it an even more effective tool for keeping up threat on multiple mobs.

FURY

 ### Battle Shout

The Warrior shouts, increasing the attack power of all nearby raid and party members.

 ### Berserker Rage

Requires Berserker Stance. The Warrior enters a berserker rage, becoming immune to Fear, Sap, and Incapacitate effects and generating extra rage when taking damage.

This ability is now useable in all stances, making it much more useful. It has always been great for use in PvP, but now gives you another tool for use when tanking as well.

120

CHALLENGING SHOUT

Forces all nearby enemies to focus attacks on your for a short time.

The cooldown on this ability has been reduced, meaning it can become a bigger part of your threat management, especially when tanking multiple mobs. While you can't rely on it alone of course, it is a very useful addition to your toolbox.

CLEAVE

A sweeping attack that does your weapon damage plus bonus damage to the target and its nearest ally.

COMMANDING SHOUT

Increases the maximum health of all nearby party and raid members.

DEMORALIZING SHOUT

Reduces the melee attack power of all nearby enemies.

ENRAGED REGENERATION

You regenerate a percentage of your total health over a short time. This ability requires an Enrage effect, consumes all Enrage effects and prevents any from affecting you for the full duration.

EXECUTE

Requires Battle Stance or Berserker Stance. Attempt to finish off a wounded foe, causing damage and converting each extra point of Rage into additional damage. Only usable on enemies that have less than 20% health.

INTERCEPT

Requires Berserker Stance. Charge an enemy, causing damage based on attack power and stunning it.

INTIMIDATING SHOUT

The Warrior shouts, causing enemies close by to cower in fear. Up to five total nearby enemies will flee in fear.

PUMMEL

Requires Berserker Stance. Pummel the target, interrupting spellcasting and preventing any spell in that school from being cast for a few seconds.

Pummel has lost its damage component, but this change won't have too much of an effect on its use as its main purpose has always been to interrupt spellcasting anyway.

Druid

Hunter

Mage

Paladin

Priest

Rogue

Shaman

Warlock

Warrior

RECKLESSNESS

Requires Berserker Stance. Your next few special ability attacks have an additional 100% chance to critically hit but all damage taken is increased.

The cooldown on this ability has been reduced, allowing you to be reckless more often which can really increase your damage output. In situations where taking the extra damage as well isn't an issue, Recklessness is a powerful tool.

 ## SLAM

Slams the opponent, causing weapon damage plus bonus damage.

 ## VICTORY RUSH

Requires Battle Stance, Berserker Stance. Instantly attack the target. Can only be used after you kill an enemy that yields experience or honor. Damage is based on your attack power.

 ## WHIRLWIND

Requires Berserker Stance. In a whirlwind of steel you attack nearby enemies, causing weapon damage to each enemy.

PROTECTION

 ## BLOODRAGE

Generates Rage at the cost of health, and then generates additional rage over time.

 ## DEFENSIVE STANCE

A defensive combat stance. Decreases damage taken and damage caused by a small amount. Increases threat generated by a substantial amount.

The increase in threat generated helps you keep the mob's attention when faced with group members who are doing increased damage due to their new abilities and Talents.

 ## DEVASTATE

Requires One-Handed Melee Weapon. Sunder the target's armor causing the Sunder Armor effect. In addition causes a percentage of weapon damage plus bonus damage per each application of Sunder Armor on the target. The Sunder Armor effect can stack up to five times.

 ## DISARM

Requires Defensive Stance. Disarm the enemy's weapon for a short time.

The Rage cost of this ability has been reduced, making it a better choice on which to spend your Rage than it often was in the past.

 ## INTERVENE

Requires Defensive Stance. Run at high speed towards a party member, intercepting the next melee or ranged attack made against them as well as reducing their total threat.

 ## REVENGE

Requires Defensive Stance. Instantly counterattack an enemy. Revenge is only usable after the Warrior blocks, dodges, or parries an attack.

 ## SHIELD BASH

Requires Battle Stance or Defensive Stance. Bash the target with your shield, interrupting spell casting and preventing any spell in that school from being cast for a few seconds.

 ## SHIELD BLOCK

Requires Defensive Stance. Increases your chance to block and your block value.

 ## SHIELD SLAM

Slam the target with your shield, causing damage modified by your shield block value. Dispels one magic effect on the target and also causes a high amount of threat.

 ## SHIELD WALL

Requires Defensive Stance. Reduces all damage taken for a period of time.

 ## SPELL REFLECTION

Requires Battle Stance, Defensive Stance. Raise your shield, reflecting the next spell cast on you.

 ## STANCE MASTERY

Passive Ability. You retain some of your Rage points when you change stances.

SUNDER ARMOR

Sunders the target's armor, reducing it for each Sunder Armor and causes a high amount of Threat. The amount of Threat is increased by attack power. Sunder Armor can be applied up to five times and lasts until it is cancelled.

TAUNT

Taunts the target to attack you, but has no effect if the target is already attacking you.

Though Improved Taunt has been removed from your Talent tree, this ability has been changed so that the cooldown equals what that Talent used to give you, freeing up a few points to spend somewhere else. This is great news for any warrior!

Classes

Druid

Hunter

Mage

Paladin

Priest

Rogue

Shaman

Warlock

Warrior

WARRIOR TALENTS

ARMS

IMPROVED HEROIC STRIKE

Reduces the rage cost of your Heroic Strike ability.

DEFLECTION

Increases your Parry chance.

IMPROVED REND

Increases the bleed damage done by your Rend ability.

IMPROVED CHARGE

Increases the amount of Rage generated by your Charge ability.

IRON WILL

Reduces the duration of all Stun and Charm effects used against you.

TACTICAL MASTERY

You retain additional rage when you change stances. Also greatly increases the threat generated by your Bloodthirst and Mortal Strike abilities when you are in Defensive Stance.

ARMS

FURY

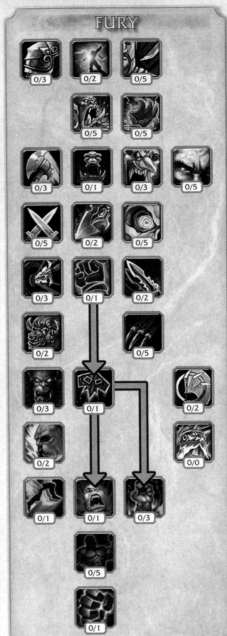

PROTECTION

IMPROVED OVERPOWER

Increases the critical strike chance of your Overpower ability.

ANGER MANAGEMENT

Generates Rage over time.

IMPALE

Increases the critical strike damage bonus of your abilities.

DEEP WOUNDS

Your critical strikes cause the opponent to bleed, dealing a percentage of your melee weapon's average damage over a few seconds.

TWO-HANDED WEAPON SPECIALIZATION

Increases the damage you deal with Two-Handed melee weapons.

TASTE FOR BLOOD

Whenever your Rend ability causes damage, you have a chance of allowing the use of your Overpower ability for a few seconds.

Druid

Hunter

Mage

Paladin

Priest

Rogue

Shaman

Warlock

Warrior

 ## POLEAXE SPECIALIZATION

Increases your chance to get a critical strike and the critical damage caused with Axes and Polearms.

 ## MORTAL STRIKE

A vicious strike that deals weapon damage plus bonus damage and wounds the target, reducing the effectiveness of healing a great deal for a short time.

 ## SWEEPING STRIKES

Requires Battle Stance or Berserker Stance. Your next five melee attacks strike an additional nearby opponent.

 ## STRENGTH OF ARMS

Increases your total Strength, Stamina and your Expertise.

 ## MACE SPECIALIZATION

Your attacks with maces ignore a percentage of your opponent's armor

 ## IMPROVED SLAM

Decreases the swing time of your Slam ability.

 ## SWORD SPECIALIZATION

Gives you a chance to get an extra attack on the same target after hitting your target with your Sword. This effect cannot occur more than once every few seconds.

 ## IMPROVED MORTAL STRIKE

Increases the damage caused by your Mortal Strike ability and reduces the cooldown.

 ## IMPROVED INTERCEPT

Reduces the Cooldown of your Intercept ability.

 ## UNRELENTING ASSAULT

Reduces the cooldown of your Overpower and Revenge abilities.

 ## IMPROVED HAMSTRING

Gives your Hamstring ability a chance to immobilize the target.

 ## SUDDEN DEATH

Your melee critical hits have a chance of allowing the use of Execute regardless of the target's health. In addition you keep a small amount of rage after using Execute.

 ## TRAUMA

Your melee critical strikes increase the effectiveness of Bleed effects on the target for a time.

 ## ENDLESS RAGE

You generate more Rage from damage dealt.

 ## SECOND WIND

Whenever you are struck by a Stun or Immobilize effect you generate Rage and Health over time.

 ## BLOOD FRENZY

Increases your attack speed. In addition, your Rend and Deep Wounds abilities also increase all physical damage caused to that target.

WRECKING CREW

Your melee critical hits Enrage you, increasing all damage caused.

BLADESTORM

Instantly Whirlwind all nearby targets and for a short while you perform a whirlwind attack every second. While under the effect of Bladestorm, you can move but cannot perform any other abilities but you do not feel pity, remorse, or fear and you cannot be stopped unless killed.

FURY

ARMORED TO THE TEETH

Increases your attack power depending on your armor value.

BOOMING VOICE

Increases the area of effect and duration of your Battle Shout, Demoralizing Shout and Commanding Shout.

CRUELTY

Increases your chance to get a critical strike with melee weapons.

IMPROVED DEMORALIZING SHOUT

Increases the melee attack power reduction of your Demoralizing Shout.

UNBRIDLED WRATH

Gives you a chance to generate additional Rage when you deal melee damage with a weapon.

IMPROVED CLEAVE

Increases the bonus damage done by your Cleave ability.

PIERCING HOWL

Causes all nearby enemies to be Dazed, reducing movement speed for a short time.

BLOOD CRAZE

Regenerates a percentage of your total Health over a few seconds after being the victim of a critical strike.

COMMANDING PRESENCE

Increases the melee attack power bonus of your Battle Shout and the health bonus of your Commanding Shout.

DUEL WIELD SPECIALIZATION

Increases the damage done by your Off-Hand weapon.

IMPROVED EXECUTE

Reduces the Rage cost of your Execute ability.

ENRAGE

Gives you a chance to receive a damage bonus after being the victim of a damaging attack.

PRECISION

Increases your chance to hit with melee weapons.

DEATH WISH

When activated you become enraged, increasing your physical damage but increasing all damage taken.

Death Wish no longer makes you immune to Fear effect so you need to adjust your tactics accordingly.

WEAPON MASTERY

Reduces the chance for your attacks to be dodged and reduces the duration of all Disarm effects used against you. This does not stack with other Disarm duration reducing effects.

 ## RAMPAGE

Your melee critical hits cause you to go on a rampage, increasing the ranged and melee critical hit chance of all party and raid members for a short time.

 ## IMPROVED BERSERKER RAGE

The Berserker Rage ability generates more Rage when used.

 ## BLOODSURGE

Your Bloodthirst critical hits have a chance of making your next Slam instant for a few seconds.

 ## FLURRY

Increases your attack speed for your next few swings after dealing a melee critical strike.

 ## UNENDING FURY

Increases the damage done by your Slam, Whirlwind and Bloodthirst abilities.

 ## INTENSIFY RAGE

Reduces the cooldown of your Bloodrage, Berserker Rage, Recklessness and Death Wish abilities.

 ## TITAN'S GRIP

Allows you to equip Two-Handed Axes, Maces and Swords in one hand. Also reduces your chance to hit with damage-dealing abilities that require a weapon.

The reduction in damage is to balance the fact that you are wielding a Two-Handed weapon. This gives you a much wider pool of possible weaponry to pull from and Two-Handed weapons usually give you higher stats. Plus, its just fun. If you are concerned with the chance to hit reduction you can gear for plus to hit to make up for it.

 ## BLOODTHIRST

Instantly attack the target causing damage. In addition, the next few successful melee attacks restore a small percentage of your maximum health. Damage is based on your attack power.

PROTECTION

 ## IMPROVED BLOODRAGE

Increases the Rage generated by your Bloodrage ability.

 ## IMPROVED WHIRLWIND

Increases the damage of your Whirlwind ability.

 ## FURIOUS ATTACKS

Your normal melee attacks have a chance to reduce all healing done to the target. This ability can stack up to two times.

 ## IMPROVED BERSERKER STANCE

Increases attack power and reduces threat while in Berserker Stance.

 ## SHIELD SPECIALIZATION

Increases your chance to block attacks with a shield and has a chance to generate Rage when a block occurs.

 ## HEROIC FURY

Removes any Immobilization effects and refreshes the cooldown of your Intercept ability.

IMPROVED THUNDER CLAP

Reduces the cost of your Thunder Clap ability and increases the damage and the slowing effect.

Druid

Hunter

Mage

Paladin

Priest

Rogue

Shaman

Warlock

Warrior

INCITE

Increases the critical strike chance of your Heroic Strike, Thunder Clap and Cleave abilities.

SHIELD MASTERY

Increases your block value and reduces the cooldown of your Shield Block ability.

ANTICIPATION

Increases your Dodge chance.

TOUGHNESS

Increases your armor value from items and reduces the duration of all movement slowing effects.

LAST STAND

When activated, this ability temporarily grants you a percentage of your maximum health for a time. After the effect expires, the health is lost.

The cooldown on this ability has been reduced, letting you use it much more often. Pop it whenever you know your healer needs an extra few seconds to get caught up on healing you.

IMPROVED SPELL REFLECTION

Reduces the chance you'll be hit by spells and when the ability is used it reflects the first spell cast against the two closest party members.

IMPROVED REVENGE

Increases the damage of your Revenge ability and gives you a chance to stun the target.

IMPROVED DISARM

Reduces the cooldown of your Disarm ability and causes the target to take additional damage while disarmed.

PUNCTURE

Reduces the Rage cost of your Sunder Armor and Devastate abilities.

IMPROVED DISCIPLINES

Reduces the cooldown of your Shield Wall, Retaliation and Recklessness abilities.

CONCUSSION BLOW

Stuns the opponent for a few seconds and deals damage based on attack power.

GAG ORDER

Gives your Shield Bash and Heroic Throw abilities a chance to Silence the target and increases the damage of your Shield Slam ability.

ONE-HANDED WEAPON SPECIALIZATION

Increases physical damage you deal when a One-Handed melee weapon is equipped.

IMPROVED DEFENSIVE STANCE

While in Defensive Stance all spell damage is reduced and when you Block, Parry or Dodge an attack you have a chance to become Enraged, increasing melee damage caused.

VIGILANCE

Focuses your protective gaze on a group or raid target, reducing their damage taken and transfers a percentage of the threat they cause to you. In addition, each time they are hit by an attack your Taunt cooldown is refreshed. This effect can only be on one target at a time.

FOCUSED RAGE

Reduces the Rage cost of your offensive abilities.

VITALITY

Increases your total Strength and Stamina and your Expertise.

SAFEGUARD

Reduces damage taken by the target of your Intervene ability.

WARBRINGER

Your Charge ability is now usable while in combat and in any stance. In addition, your Charge, Intercept and Intervene abilities will remove all movement impairing effects.

Along with Intercept and Intervene, this makes your Charge ability even more useful, giving you one more way to get to a party member when they gain unwanted aggro.

DEVASTATE

Sunder the target's armor causing the Sunder Armor effect. In addition, causes a percentage of weapon damage plus bonus damage for each application of Sunder Armor on the target.

CRITICAL BLOCK

Your successful blocks have a chance to block double the normal amount and increases your chance to critically hit with your Shield Slam ability.

SWORD AND BOARD

Increases the critical strike chance of your Devastate ability and when your Devastate or Revenge ability deals damage it has a chance of refreshing the cooldown of your Shield Slam ability and reducing its cost for a few seconds.

DAMAGE SHIELD

Whenever you take damage from or block a melee attack you cause damage equal to a percentage of your block value.

SHOCKWAVE

Sends a wave of force in front of the Warrior, causing damage based on attack power and stunning all enemy targets in a frontal cone.

Druid

Hunter

Mage

Paladin

Priest

Rogue

Shaman

Warlock

Warrior

NEW ZONES

Each of the following zone maps and legends includes helpful information such as the quest hubs, trainers, and specialty merchants found in each region. Alliance NPC's are marked in **blue**, the Horde are in **red**, and those neutral NPC's who deal with both factions are in **yellow**. Each letter in the legend corresponds to a location on the map so that you can easily find what you need. We've also included a resource legend for each zone. Here you can find information on the Ore, Herbs, and Factions found in the area. Look over the maps and legends to get an idea of what each zone offers and where you need to go to make sure you grab all of the important quests.

BOR'GOROK
OUTPOST

FIZZCRAN
AIRSTRIP

The
NEXUS

AMBER LEDGE

COLDARRA

GARROSH'S
LANDING

WARSONG HOLD

RIPLASH STRAND

RIPLASH RUINS

BOREAN TUNDRA

A WARSONG HOLD

B VALIANCE KEEP

C RIPLASH RUINS

SHOLAZAR BASIN

THE GEYSER FIELDS

TEMPLE CITY OF EN'KILAH

TAUNKA'LE VILLAGE

DEATH'S STAND

KASKALA

KEEP

NEW ZONES

Borean Tundra

Crystalsong Forest

Dalaran

Dragonblight

Grizzly Hills

Howling Fjord

Icecrown

Sholazar Basin

The Storm Peaks

Zul'Drak

K GARROSH'S LANDING

J COLDARRA

I WINTERFIN RETREAT

H AMBER LEDGE

G FIZZCRANK AIRSTRIP

D RIPLASH STRAND

E KASKALA

F TEMPLE CITY OF EN'KILAH

BOREAN TUNDRA

Located on the southwestern edge of the continent, Borean Tundra was chosen as one of the landing sites for both the Alliance and the Horde's journey to Northrend, and both have set up command posts in this harsh land. Foes like the Kvaldir and Skadir trouble the shores while Scourge forces lay claim to parts of the area and other dangerous creatures make this their home.

Though the territory is hostile, there are allies to be had here as well. In Kaskala, the Tuskarr battle to drive the Kvaldir from their shores and welcome any help they can get. The mages of the Kirin Tor are here in force, at Amber Ledge and the Transitus Shield inside of Coldarra. They care not if you are Alliance or Horde but welcome any who would aid them in their cause. D.E.H.T.A. (Druids for the Ethical and Humane Treatment of Animals), a radical portion of the Cenarion Expedition, ask for help from any who would aid them in their quest to thwart Hemet Nessingwary and those who follow the infamous butcher. The Winterfin Murlocs can also use your help in their home far to the north. The Taunka, stoic ancestral cousins of the Tauren, have an outpost here as well. They have allied themselves with the Horde and can use the help of their newfound allies.

Along with Howling Fjord, Borean Tundra is one of the starting zones of Northrend, with quests for players level 68-72. The towns of both the Horde and Alliance offer many quests and the peoples of this land can use your help as well. Be sure to visit the D.E.H.T.A. Encampment, in central Borean Tundra, Winterfin Retreat along the northwestern shore and Kaskala on the western coast to pick up more quests.

Legend

Herbs

Goldclover
Tiger Lily
Firethorn
Deadnettle
Frost Lotus

Minerals

Cobalt
Rich Cobalt

Reputation Information

Valiance Expedition (Alliance)
The Kalu'ak (Both)
Kirin Tor (Both)
The Hand of Vengeance (Horde)
The Taunka (Horde)
Warsong Offensive (Horde)
Cenarion Expedition (Both)

1 Valiance Keep

Old Man Colburn (Quest Giver)
Counselor Talbot (Quest Giver)
Medic Hawthorn (Quest Giver)
General Arlos (Quest Giver)
Private Brau (Quest Giver)
Sergeant Hammerhill (Quest Giver)
Airman Skyhopper (Quest Giver)
Harbinger Vurenn (Quest Giver)
Recruitment Officer Blythe (Quest Giver)
James Deacon (Quest Giver)
Leryssa (Quest Giver)
Midge (Quest Giver)
Admiral Cantlebree (Quest Giver)
Vindicator Yaala (Quest Giver)
Hilda Stoneforge (Quest Giver)
Mark Hanes (Quest Giver)
Magister Dath'omere (Quest Giver)
Fendrig Redbeard <Grand Master Mining Trainer>
Argo Strongstout <Grand Master Blacksmithing Trainer>
Brynna Wilson <Grand Master First Aid Trainer>
Rollick MacKreel <Grand Master Cooking Trainer>
Old Man Robert <Grand Master Fishing Trainer>
Kirea Moondancer <Grand Master Herbalism Trainer>
Falorn Nightwhisper <Grand Master Alchemy Trainer>
Sock Brightbolt <Grand Master Engineering Trainer>
Darin Goodstitch <Grand Master Tailoring Trainer>
Alestos <Grand Master Jewelcrafting Trainer>
Rosemary Bovard <Grand Master Leatherworking Trainer>
Trapper Jack <Grand Master Skinning Trainer>
Tink Brightbolt <Grand Master Inscription Trainer>
Alexis Marlowe <Grand Master Enchanting Trainer>
Logistics Officer Silverstone <Alliance Vanguard Quartermaster>

2 Farshire

Gerald Green (Quest Giver)
Jeremiah Hawning (Quest Giver)
Wendy Darren (Quest Giver)

3 Farshire Mine

Plagued Grain (Quest Giver)
William Allerton (Quest Giver)

4 Scalding Pools

Iggy "Tailspin" Cogtoggle (Quest Giver)

5 Fizzcrank Airstrip

Abner Fizzletorque (Quest Giver)
Mordle Cogspinner (Quest Giver)
Crafty Wobblesprocket (Quest Giver)
Fizzcrank Fullthrottle (Quest Giver)
Jinky Wingnut (Quest Giver)

6 Magmoth

Bonker Togglevolt (Quest Giver)

7 Death's Stand

Corporal Venn (Quest Giver)

8 Thassarian (Quest Giver)

9 Bixie Wrenchshanker (Quest Giver)

10 Talramas

Tinky Wickwhistle (Quest Giver)

1 Riplash Strand

Karuk (Quest Giver)

2 Shrine of Scales

Veehja (Quest Giver)

3 D.E.H.T.A. Encampment

Arch Druid Lathorius (Quest Giver)
Killinger the Den Watcher (Quest Giver)
Hierophant Cenius (Quest Giver)
Zaza (Quest Giver)

4 Coldrock Quarry

Etaruk (Quest Giver)
Elder Atkanok (Quest Giver)

5 Amber Ledge

Librarian Donathan (Quest Giver)
Librarian Garren (Quest Giver)
Librarian Normantis (Quest Giver)
Surristrasz (Quest Giver)
Warmage Anzim (Quest Giver)
Archmage Evanor (Quest Giver)
Librarian Ingram <Inscription Supplies>

6 Transitus Shield

Archmage Berinard (Quest Giver)
Raelorasz (Quest Giver)
Librarian Serrah (Quest Giver)
Kerlstrasza (Quest Giver)

7 Winterfin Retreat

King Mrgl-Mrgl (Quest Giver)
Brglmurgl (Quest Giver)
Mrmrglmr (Quest Giver)
Cleaver Bmurglbrm (Quest Giver)
Ahlurglgr <Clam Vendor>

8 Winterfin Caverns

Lurgglbr (Quest Giver)

9 Khu'nok the Behemoth (Quest Giver)

10 Kaskala

Utaik (Quest Giver)
Ataika (Quest Giver)

1 Warsong Hold

Warsong Recruitment Officer (Quest Giver)
High Overlord Saurfang (Quest Giver)
Sauranok the Mystic (Quest Giver)
Ambassador Talonga (Quest Giver)
Endorah (Quest Giver)
Garrosh Hellscream (Quest Giver)
Wind Master To'bor (Quest Giver)
Magistrix Kaelana (Quest Giver)
Orn Tenderhoof <Grand Master Cooking Trainer>
Fishy Ser'ji <Grand Master Fishing Trainer>
Crog Steelspine <Grand Master Blacksmithing Trainer>
Brunna Ironaxe <Grand Master Mining Trainer>
Chief Engineer Leveny <Grand Master Engineer>
Eorain Dawnstrike <Grand Master Enchanting Trainer>
Adelene Sunlance <Grand Master Inscription Trainer>
Geba'li <Grand Master Jewelcrafting Trainer>
Raenah <Grand Master Tailoring Trainer>
Tansy Wildmane <Grand Master Herbalism Trainer>
Arthur Henslowe <Grand Master Alchemy Trainer>
Nurse Applewood <Grand Master First Aid Trainer>
Gara Skullcrush <Horde Expedition Quartermaster>

Zend'li Venomtusk <Poison Supplies>

2 Mightstone Quarry

Overlord Razgor (Quest Giver)
Quartermaster Holgoth (Quest Giver)
Foreman Mortuus (Quest Giver)
Shadowstalker Barthus (Quest Giver)
Shadowstalker Luther (Quest Giver)
Warden Nork Bloodfrenzy (Quest Giver)
Ith'rix's Hardened Carapace (Quest Giver)

3 Warsong Farms Outpost

Shadowstalker Ickoris (Quest Giver)
Shadowstalker Canarius (Quest Giver)
Farmer Torp (Quest Giver)

4 Shadowstalker Getry (Quest Giver)

5 Coast of Echoes

Gorge the Corpsegrinder (Quest Giver)
Mobu (Quest Giver)
Walter of Pal'ea (Quest Giver)
Mootoo the Younger (Quest Giver)

6 Bloodspore Plains

Scout Tungok (Quest Giver)
Bloodmage Laurith (Quest Giver)
Primal Mighthorn (Quest Giver)

7 Gammoth

Massivo Glowing Egg (On top of Gammoth) (Quest Giver)

8 Steeljaw's Caravan

Grunt Ragefist (Quest Giver)
Longrunner Proudhoof (Quest Giver)

9 Bor'gorok Outpost

Spirit Talker Snarlfang (Quest Giver)
Overlord Bor'gorok (Quest Giver)
Ortrosh (Quest Giver)
Supply Master Taz'ishi (Quest Giver)

10 Ruins of Eldra'nath

Imperean (Quest Giver)

11 Magmoth

Farseer Grimwalker's Spirit (Inside Cave at bottom) (Quest Giver)

12 Scalding Pools

Crashed Recon Pilot (Quest Giver)

13 Talramas

Longrunner Bristlehorn (Quest Giver)

14 Sage Highmesa (Quest Giver)

15 Taunka'le Village

Sage Earth and Sky (Quest Giver)
Greatfather Mahan (Quest Giver)
Fezzix Geartwist (Quest Giver)
Greatmother Taiga (Quest Giver)
Dorain Frosthoof (Quest Giver)
Iron Eyes (Quest Giver)
Chieftain Wintergale (Quest Giver)
Durm Icehide (Quest Giver)
Sage Aeire (Quest Giver)
Mother Tauranook (Quest Giver)
Wind Turner Buruh (Quest Giver)
Tiponi Stormwhisper <Grand Master Skinning Trainer>
Awan Iceborn <Grand Master Leatherworker>

New Zones

Borean Tundra

Crystalsong Forest

Dalaran

Dragonblight

Grizzly Hills

Howling Fjord

Icecrown

Sholazar Basin

The Storm Peaks

Zul'Drak

THE
DECREPIT FLOW

VIOLET STAND

FORLORN WOODS

CRYSTALSONG FOREST
DRAGONBLIGHT

Ⓐ WINDRUNNER'S OVERLOOK

Ⓑ SUNREAVER'S COMMAND

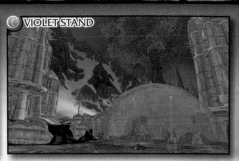

Ⓒ VIOLET STAND

THE STORM PEAKS

SUNREAVER'S
COMMAND

THE
NBOUND THICKET

WINDRUNNER'S
OVERLOOK

K THE DECREPIT FLOW

J DALARAN

I THE RUINS OF SHANALAR

H THE RUINS OF SHANALAR

G THE UNBOUND THICKET

D TO ICE CROWN

E THE AZURE FRONT

F THE GREAT TREE

137

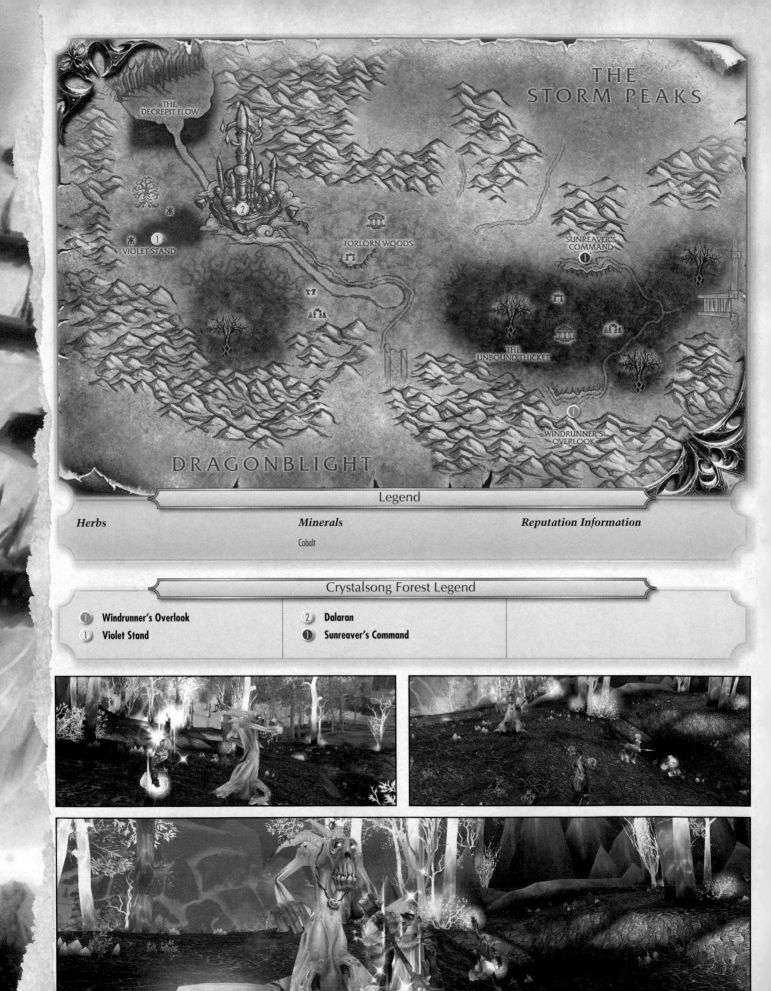

THE STORM PEAKS

THE DECREPIT FLOW

VIOLET STAND ①

② (Dalaran)

FORLORN WOODS

SUNREAVER'S COMMAND ①

THE UNBOUND THICKET

WINDRUNNER'S OVERLOOK ①

DRAGONBLIGHT

Legend

Herbs	Minerals	Reputation Information
	Cobalt	

Crystalsong Forest Legend

① Windrunner's Overlook	② Dalaran
① Violet Stand	① Sunreaver's Command

CRYSTALSONG FOREST

Crystalsong Forest lies at the center of Northrend, making it a waypoint for those traversing the continent. The hauntingly beautiful crystalline landscape is home to several types of creatures, some of which are hostile to all travelers. Both the Horde and the Alliance have set up small outposts in the east where travelers can purchase supplies or speak to a flight master.

Far to the northwest is the Great Tree. It alone is untouched by the crystal which gives this area its name. Running through the center of the forest is the Twilight Rivulet, a serene spot for fishing. In the west lies the Violet Stand, outpost of the Kirin Tor. Here you can find transport to the mage city of Dalaran which floats far above the forest.

139

DALARAN

- ANTONIDAS MEMORIAL
- SUNRI SANC
- MAGUS COMMERCE EXCHANGE
- THE VIOLET CITADEL
- RUNEWEAVER SQUARE
- THE SILVER ENCLAVE
- THE EVENTIDE

DALARAN

Ⓐ RUNEWEAVER SQUARE

Ⓑ KRASUS' LANDING

Ⓒ THE VIOLET HOLD

Borean
Tundra

Crystalsong
Forest

Dalaran

Dragonblight

Grizzly Hills

Howling Fjord

Icecrown

Sholazar Basin

The Storm
Peaks

Zul'Drak

K THE UNDERBELLY ENTRANCE

J ANTONIDAS MEMORIAL

I THE BANK OF DALARAN

H EXOTIC PETS

G SUNREAVER'S SANCTUARY

KRASUS'
LANDING

THE
VIOLET HOLD

D THE VIOLET CITADEL

E BARBERSHOP

F THE SILVER ENCLAVE

DALARAN

The mage city of Dalaran once stood on the shores of Lordamere Lake in the Eastern Kingdoms. Now, facing the threat of Malygos and the Blue Dragonflight, the mages of the Kirin Tor have transported the city in its entirety to float above the Crystalsong Forest in the heart of Northrend.

The city is an oasis of civilization on this continent of conflict. Here you can find trainers for all professions, merchants selling everything from the mundane to the exotic, and even a barbershop should you need to update your look. The Kirin Tor rule the city from the Violet Citadel at the western side of the city while the Violet Hold, their prison, lies in the east.

Though the Kirin Tor allies itself neither with the Horde nor the Alliance it has allowed each a section of the city open only to their members. The Silver Enclave is a haven for members of the Alliance and Sunreaver's Sanctuary provides the same service for the Horde. Within these areas you can find portals to all the major cities of the old world as well as to Shattrath. You can also join various battlegrounds here or take it easy in the tavern.

Every city, no matter how well run has a seedier side. Beneath the clean, well lit city streets lies the Underbelly. Here you find a few merchants which don't quite fit into the Magus Commerce Exchange as well as a less formal tavern, Cantrips and Crows. The Underbelly also boasts the Circle of Wills. Here adventurers can satisfy their honor with the duels not allowed above. This area is also home to goblins involved with the arena circuit and is the best place to come if you are spoiling for a fight.

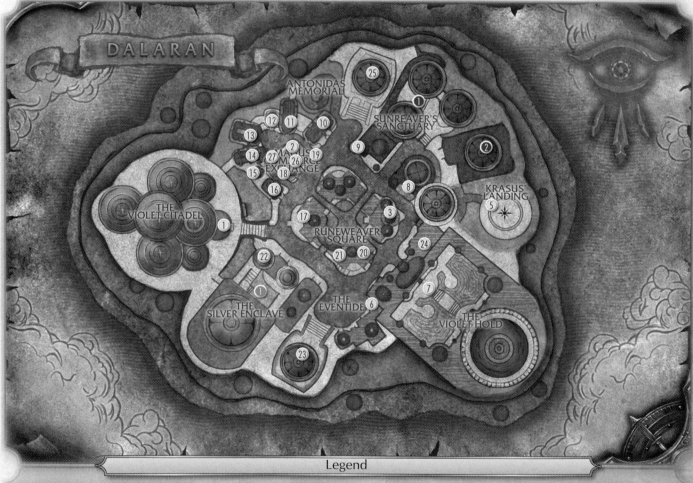

Legend

Herbs

Minerals

Reputation Information

Kirin Tor
The Silver Covenant
The Sunreavers

Borean Tundra

Crystalsong Forest

Dalaran

Dragonblight

Grizzly Hills

Howling Fjord

Icecrown

Sholazar Basin

The Storm Peaks

Zul'Drak

Dalaran Legend

① **The Silver Enclave**

Alliance Brigadier General (Quest Giver)
Arcanist Ivrenne <Emblem of Heroism Quartermaster>
Arcanist Adurin <Emblem of Valor Quartermaster>
Katherine Lee <Grand Master Cooking Trainer>
Zidormi <Keepers of Time>

① **The Violet Citadel**

Rhonin (Quest Giver)
Archmage Alvareaux <Kirin Tor Quartermaster>

② **Rin Duoctane (Quest Giver)**

③ **Archmage Celindra (Quest Giver)**

④ **Shifty Vickers (Quest Giver)**

⑤ **Krasus Landing**

Archmage Pentarus (Quest Giver)
Sky-Reaver Klum (Quest Giver)
Officer Van Rossem (Quest Giver)
Hira Snowdawn <Cold Weather Flying Trainer>

⑥ **Marcia Chase <Grand Master Fishing Trainer>**

⑦ **The Violet Hold**

Archmage Timear (Quest Giver)
Archmage Lan'dalock (Quest Giver)
Warden Alturas (Quest Giver)

⑧ **Mei Francis <Exotic Mounts>**

Breanni <Pet Supplies>

⑨ **Barbershop**

Kizi Copperclip <Barber>

⑩ **Tanks for Everything**

Alard Schmied <Grand Master Blacksmithing Trainer>
Imindril Spearsong <Weaponsmithing Trainer>
Orland Schaeffer <Armorsmithing Trainer>

⑪ **All That Glitters Prospecting Co.**

Jedidiah Handers <Grand Master Mining Trainer>

⑫ **Like Clockwork**

Findle Whistlesteam <Gnome Engineering Trainer>
Didi the Wrench <Goblin Engineering Trainer>
Justin Oshenko <Grand Master Engineering Trainer>

⑬ **Legendary Leathers**

Diane Cannings <Grand Master Leatherworking Trainer>
Derik Marks <Grand Master Skinning Trainer>
Manfred Staller <Elemental Leatherworking Trainer>
Andellion <Dragonscale Leatherworking Trainer>
Namha Moonwater <Tribal Leatherworking Trainer>

⑭ **Talismanic Textiles**

Lalla Brightweave <Spellfire Tailoring Specialist>
Charles Worth <Grand Master Tailoring Trainer>
Ainderu Summerleaf <Mooncloth Tailoring>
Linna Bruder Shadoweave <Shadoweave Tailoring Specialist>

⑮ **First to Your Aid**

Olisarra the Kind <Grand Master First Aid Trainer>

⑯ **Simply Enchanting**

Enchanter Nalthanis <Grand Master Enchanting Trainer>
Vanessa Seller <Shard Trader>

⑰ **The Wonderworks**

Jepetto Joybuzz <Toymaker>
Clockwork Assistant <Jepetto's Companion>

⑱ **The Scribes' Sacellum**

Professor Pallin <Grand Master Inscription Trainer>

⑲ **Dorothy Egan <Grand Master Herbalism Trainer>**

⑳ **Dalaran Visitor Center**

Elizabeth Ross <Tabard Vendor>
Andrew Matthews <Guild Master>

㉑ **Curiosities and More**

Debbie Moore <Trinkets & Charms>

㉒ **Sisters Sorcerous**

Endora Moorehead <Magical Goods>

㉓ **Dalaran Merchants' Bank**

㉔ **The Hunter's Reach**

Jarold Puller <Specialty Ammunition>

㉕ **The Bank of Dalaran**

㉖ **The Agronomical Apothecary**

Linzy Blackbolt <Grand Master Alchemy Trainer>

㉗ **Cartier and Co. Fine Jewelry**

Timothy Jones <Grand Master Jewelcrafting Trainer> (Quest Giver)
Harold Winston <Jewelry Vendor>

㉘ **Circle of Wills**

Zom Bocom <Apprentice Arena Vendor>
Xazi Smolderpipe <Arena Vendor>
Nargle Lashcord <Veteran Arena Vendor>
Kanika Goldwell <Arena Organizer>
Schembari "Uncle Sal" Shearbolt <Arena Battlemaster>
"Baroness" Llana <Arena Organizer>

① **Sunreaver's Sanctuary**

Horde Warbringer (Quest Giver)
Magister Brasael <Emblem of Valor Quartermaster>
Magistrix Lambriesse <Emblem of Herosim Quartermaster>

② **The Filthy Animal**

Awilo Lon'gomba <Grand Master Cooking Trainer>

ICECROWN

WINTERGRASP

ICEMIST VILLAGE

AZJOL NERUB

AGMAR'S HAMMER

STARS' REST

GALAKROND REST

MOA'KI HARBOR

DRAGONBLIGHT

Ⓐ WYRMREST TEMPLE

Ⓑ THE RUBY DRAGONSHRINE

Ⓒ ICEMIST VILLAGE

K ANGRATH'AR

J VENOMSPITE

I AZJOL NERUB

H WINTERGARDE KEEP

G STARS' REST

VICE

LIGHT'S TRUST

Naxxramas

WINTERGARDE KEEP

A

EST
E

VENOMSPITE

B

THE
FORGOTTEN SHORE

NEW
HEARTHGLEN

Borean
Tundra

Crystalsong
Forest

Dalaran

**Dragon-
blight**

Grizzly Hills

Howling Fjord

Icecrown

Sholazar Basin

The Storm
Peaks

Zul'Drak

D THE EMERALD DRAGON SHRINE

E LAKE INDU'LE

F NEW HEARTHGLEN

DRAGONBLIGHT

Located in the south of Northrend, the large area known as Dragonblight contains vast expanses of frozen tundra populated by dangerous indigenous creatures as well as by the incursion of Scourge. Dragons of all flights make this their final resting place and the hard frozen ground is punctuated with the gleaming bones of these majestic creatures rising up through the ice and snow. Its eastern and western borders are marked by Scourge strongholds, Azjol-Nerub and Naxxaramas respectively. In the north, Angrathar, the Wrath Gate, looms, blocking the entrance to the stronghold of Arthas himself, Icecrown Citadel.

At the heart of this land lies Wyrmrest Temple. Here the remaining Dragonflights have formed an accord and, under the leadership of Alexstrasza the Life-Binder, seek to stop the Blue Dragonflight. Dragonblight is also home to several Dragonshrines, final resting places for powerful dragons. These have recently come under attack from the Scourge who seek to use these remains to their own ends and the Wyrmrest Accord needs aid to help drive out this menace.

In western Dragonblight lies the entrance to the ancient kingdom of the Nerubians, Azjol-Nerub. Their underground cities once held great knowledge and treasure, and were a shining testament to their civilization. Now, Azjol-Nerub lies in ruins, populated by those Nerubians who have given their allegiance to the Lich King and have become members of the Scourge! In the east, the imposing necropolis Naxxramas floats above the landscape, casting a shadow over the land. The Scourge are not the only foes to be found in this harsh land. Most notably, the Scarlet Onslaught has moved into the area in force, with troops at Scarlet Point and in greater numbers at New Hearthglen.

The Alliance and Horde forces have set up outposts here in this bleak land and can use your help in their efforts. In addition, the Argent Crusade seeks the aid of any who would align themselves with their cause and the Kalu'ak of Mo'aki Harbor in the south reward those that would help them as well.

Legend

Herbs

Goldclover
Talandra's Rose
Tiger Lily

Minerals

Cobalt
Rich Cobalt

Reputation Information

Valiance Expedition (Alliance)
The Kalu'ak (Both)
Kirin Tor (Both)
The Hand of Vengeance (Horde)
The Taunka (Horde)
Warsong Offensive (Horde)
Argent Crusade (Both)
The Wyrmrest Accord (Both)

Dragonblight Legend

① **Wintergarde Keep**
Vas the Unstable (Quest Giver)
Inquisitor Hallard (Quest Giver)
High Commander Halford Wyrmbane (Quest Giver)
Gryphon Commander Urik (Quest Giver)
Zelig the Visionary (Quest Giver)
Commander Eligor Dawnbringer (Quest Giver)
Highlord Leoric Von Zeldig (Quest Giver)
Siege Engineer Quarterflash (Quest Giver)
Commander Lynore Windstryke (Quest Giver)
Rodney Wells (Quest Giver)

② **Cavalier Durkon (Quest Giver)**

③ **The Carrion Fields**
Legion Commander Yorik (Underground) (Quest Giver)

④ **Wintergarde Mausoleum**
Yord "Calamity" Icebeard (Underground) (Quest Giver)
Ambo Cash (Underground) (Quest Giver)

⑤ **Dawn's Reach**
Orik Trueheart (Quest Giver)

⑥ **Plunderbeard (Underground-from Wintergarde Mausoleum entrance) (Quest Giver)**

⑦ **Thorson's Post**
Duke August Foehammer (Quest Giver)

⑧ **Wintergarde Mine**
Slinkin the Demo-gnome (Quest Giver)

⑨ **7th Legion Front**
Legion Commander Tyralion (Quest Giver)

⑩ **Stars' Rest**
Warden Jodi Moonsong (Quest Giver)
Courier Lanson (Quest Giver)

⑪ **Fordragon Hold**
Highlord Bolvar Fordragon (Quest Giver)

⑫ **The Dragon Wastes**
Ceristrasz (Quest Giver)

⑬ **Moa'ki Harbor**
Emissary Skyhaven (Quest Giver)

❶ **Emerald Dragonshrine**
Nishera the Garden Keeper (Quest Giver)

❷ **Moa'ki Harbor**

Elder Ko'nani (Quest Giver)
Trapper Mau'l (Quest Giver)
Tua'kea (Quest Giver)
Toalu'u the Mystic (Quest Giver)
Sairuk <Kalu'ak Quartermaster>

❸ **The Pit of Narjun**
Killix the Unraveler (Quest Giver)

❹ **Moonrest Gardens**
Ethenial Moonshadow (Quest Giver)

❺ **Indu'le Village**
Elder Mana'loa (Quest Giver)

❻ **Ruby Dragonshrine**
Ruby Brooch (Drops off Dahlia Suntouch inside tree) (Quest Giver)

❼ **Wyrmrest Temple**
Aurastrasza (Quest Giver)
Chromie (Quest Giver)
Nalice (Quest Giver)
Lord Itharius (Quest Giver)
Alexstrasza the Life-Binder (Quest Giver)
Tariolstrasz (Quest Giver)
Lord Afrasastrasz (Quest Giver)
Cielstrasza <Wyrmrest Accord Quartermaster>

❽ **Maw of Neltharion**
Serinar (Quest Giver)

❾ **The Dragon Wastes**
Nozzlerust Supply Runner (Quest Giver)

❿ **Nozzlerust Post**
Narf (Quest Giver)
Zivlix (Quest Giver)
Xink (Quest Giver)

⑪ **The Crystal Vice**
Zort (Quest Giver)
Ko'char the Unbreakable (Quest Giver)

⑫ **Light's Trust**
Crusader Valus (Quest Giver)

⑬ **Dawn's Reach**
Tilda Darathan (Quest Giver)

⑭ **Wrecked Crab Trap (Bottom of sea floor) (Quest Giver)**

❶ **Venomspite**
Chief Plaguebringer Middleton (Quest Giver)
High Executor Wroth (Quest Giver)
Apothecary Vicky Levine (Quest Giver)
Quartermaster Bartlett (Quest Giver)
Spy Mistress Repine (Quest Giver)
Deathguard Molder (Quest Giver)
Hansel Bauer (Quest Giver)
Josric Fame <Grand Master Blacksmithing Trainer>
Apothecary Wormwick <Master Alchemy Trainer>

❷ **New Hearthglen**
Agent Skully (Quest Giver)

❸ **Agmar's Hammer**
Image of Archmage Aethas Sunreaver (Quest Giver)
Senior Sergeant Juktok (Quest Giver)
Overlord Agmar (Quest Giver)
Soar Hawkfury (Quest Giver)
Captain Gort (Quest Giver)
Doctor Sintar Malefious (Quest Giver)
Greatmother Icemist (Quest Giver)
Koltira Deathweaver (Quest Giver)
Valnok Windrager (Quest Giver)
Earthwarden Grife (Quest Giver)
Messenger Torvus (Quest Giver)
Apothecary Bressa <Master Alchemy Trainer>
Borus Ironbender <Grand Master Blacksmithing Trainer> (Quest Giver)

❹ **Westwind Refugee Camp**
Blood Guard Roh'kill (Quest Giver)
Emissary Brighthoof (Quest Giver)

❺ **Icemist Village**
Banthok Icemist (Quest Giver)

❻ **Vargastrasz (Quest Giver)**

❼ **Lake Indu'le**
Mage-Commander Evenstar (Quest Giver)

❽ **Dragon's Fall**
Rokhan (Quest Giver)
Kontokanis (Quest Giver)

❾ **Kor'kron Vanguard**
Saurfang the Younger (Quest Giver)

❿ **Moa'ki Harbor (Quest Giver)**
Envoy Ripfang (Quest Giver)

Borean Tundra

Crystalsong Forest

Dalaran

Dragon-blight

Grizzly Hills

Howling Fjord

Icecrown

Sholazar Basin

The Storm Peaks

Zul'Drak

ZUL'DRAK

DRAK'THARON KEEP

URSOC'S DEN

SILVERBROOK

WESTFALL ENCAMP

BLUE SKY LOGGING GROUNDS

ZEB'HALAK

GRIZZLEMAW

GRANITE SPRINGS

AMBERPINE LODGE

CONQUEST HOLD

VOLDRUNE

VENTURE BAY

GRIZZLY HILLS

HO

Ⓐ VOLDRUNE

Ⓑ CONQUEST HOLD

Ⓒ VENTURE BAY

K SILVERBROOK

J WESTFALL BRIGADE ENCAMPMENT

I THOR MODAN

H DRAKIL'JIN RUINS

G BLOODMOON ISLE

THOR
MODAN

BLOODMOON
ISLE

DRAKIL'JIN
RUINS

CAMP
ONEQWAH

DUN ARGOL

LING FJORD

F GRIZZLEMAW

E DUN ARGOL

F BLACK RIVER LOGGING CAMP

GRIZZLY HILLS

The lush green forests of Grizzly Hills may look peaceful upon first glance, but just as the landscape gives shelter to the herds of wild horses and other creatures who make their home here, it also hides those with more insidious motives.

Both the Alliance and Horde have set up camps in Grizzly Hills, each eager to control the resources in this lumber-rich area. Nowhere is this more evident than at the Blue Sky Logging Grounds in the north. Here, both factions battle over the area, seeking the lumber for their own uses. In the south, Venture Bay is ostensibly run by the Venture Co. but the Alliance and Horde battle it out for control of the harbor.

Though the tensions between the Alliance and the Horde are fierce as always, theirs is not the only struggle taking place here. At the center of Grizzly Hills lies Grizzlemaw where the Frostpaw Furbolgs do battle with the Redfangs over control of their sacred areas. The Iron Rune Dwarves are stripping the land, and the Taunka of Camp Oneqwah seek to stop them. The Grizzly Hill Giants also do their part to stop the Iron Rune Dwarves at Thor Modan. Just off the eastern shore lies Bloodmoon Isle, home to Shadowfang Tower and the mysterious Bloodmoon Worgen, and in the northwest lies the former troll stronghold of Drak'Tharon Keep. Only the stoutest adventurers now brave its Scourge-infested halls.

The conflicts in Grizzly Hills provide plenty of paying work for an adventurer, level 73-75, of either the Horde or Alliance. Be sure to visit your faction's camps to get started and do your part in the battle for Grizzly Hills!

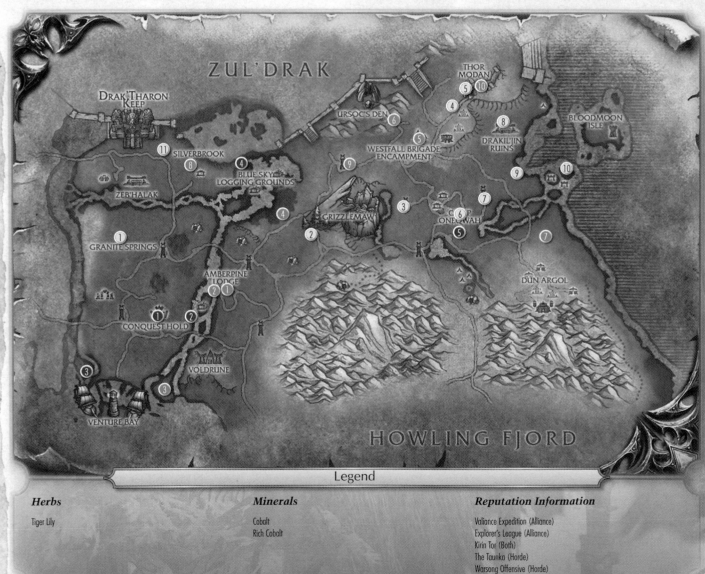

Legend

Herbs

Tiger Lily

Minerals

Cobalt
Rich Cobalt

Reputation Information

Valiance Expedition (Alliance)
Explorer's League (Alliance)
Kirin Tor (Both)
The Taunka (Horde)
Warsong Offensive (Horde)

Grizzly Hills Legend

① Amberpine Lodge
Hierophant Thayreen (Quest Giver)
Lieutenant Dumont (Quest Giver)
Master Woodsman Anderhol (Quest Giver)
Amberseed (Quest Giver)
Woodsman Drake (Quest Giver)

Aspen Grove Post
Ivan (Quest Giver)

② Blackriver Logging Camp
Scout Captain Carter (Quest Giver)

③ Venture Bay
Baron Freeman (Quest Giver)
Lieutenant Stuart (Quest Giver)
Sergeant Downey (Quest Giver)

④ Blue Sky Logging Grounds
Sergeant Hartsman (Quest Giver)
Rheanna (Quest Giver)
Pipthwack (Quest Giver)
Synipus (Quest Giver)

⑤ Westfall Brigade Encampment
Captain Gryan Stoutmantle (Quest Giver)
Brugar Stoneshear (Quest Giver)
Squire Percy (Quest Giver)
Torthen Deepdig (Quest Giver)

⑥ Hollowstone Mine
Petrov (Quest Giver)

⑦ Prospector's Point
Raegar Breakbrow (Quest Giver)
Mountaineer Kilian (Quest Giver)

⑧ Silverbrook
Caged Prisoner (Quest Giver)

Sergei (Quest Giver)
Katja (Quest Giver)

⑨ Heartwood Trading Post
Emily (Quest Giver)

⑩ Thor Modan
Surveyor Orlond (Quest Giver)

① Granite Springs
Drakuru (Quest Giver)
Prigmon (Quest Giver)
Mack Fearsen (Quest Giver)
Samir (Quest Giver)

② Ruuna's Camp
Ruuna the Blind (Quest Giver)

③ White Pine Trading Post
Sasha (Quest Giver)

④ Thor Modan
Fallen Earthen Warrior (Quest Giver)
Battered Journal (Quest Giver)

⑤ Boulder Hills
Kurun (Quest Giver)

⑥ Duskhowl Den
Sasha (Quest Giver)

⑦ Redwood Trading Post
Hugh Glass (Quest Giver)

⑧ Drakil'jin Ruins
Harrison Jones (Quest Giver)

⑨ Squatter's Camp
Harkor (Quest Giver)
Kraz (Quest Giver)

⑩ Ruins of Tethys

Gavrock (Quest Giver)

⑪ Bonesnap's Camp
Captured Trapper (Quest Giver)

① Conquest Hold
Conqueror Krenna (Quest Giver)
Sergeant Nazgrim (Quest Giver)
Hidetracker Jun'ik (Quest Giver)
Provisioner Lorkran (Quest Giver)
Magistrix Phaelista (Quest Giver)
Gorgonna (Quest Giver)
Windseer Grayhorn (Quest Giver)
Grennix Shivwiggle (Quest Giver)
Sergeant Thurkin (Quest Giver)

② Blackriver Logging Camp
Raider Captain Kronn (Quest Giver)

③ Venture Bay
Stone Guard Ragetotem (Quest Giver)
Gurtor (Quest Giver)
General Khazgar (Quest Giver)
Centurion Kaggrum (Quest Giver)

④ Blue Sky Logging Grounds
Aumana (Quest Giver)
Commander Bargok (Quest Giver)
Lurz (Quest Giver)
Grekk (Quest Giver)

⑤ Camp Oneqwah
Soulok Stormfury (Quest Giver)
Scout Vor'takh (Quest Giver)
Tormak the Scarred (Quest Giver)
Sage Paluna (Quest Giver)
Prospector Rokar (Quest Giver)

Borean
Tundra

Crystalsong
Forest

Dalaran

Dragonblight

**Grizzly
Hills**

Howling Fjord

Icecrown

Sholazar Basin

The Storm
Peaks

Zul'Drak

GJALERBRON

CAMP WINTERHOOF

APOTHECARY CAMP

SKÖRN

WESTGUARD KEEP

UTGA

EMBER CLUTCH

KAMAGUA

VALGARD

THE ANCIENT LIFT

NEW AGAMAND

SCALAWAG POINT

HOWLING FJORD

A KAMAGUA

B SCALAWAG POINT

C THE ANCIENT LIFT

Borean
Tundra

Crystalsong
Forest

Dalaran

Dragonblight

Grizzly Hills

**Howling
Fjord**

Icecrown

Sholazar Basin

The Storm
Peaks

Zul'Drak

K CAMP WINTERHOOF

J VENGEANCE LANDING

I EMBER CLUTCH

H GJALERBRON

G GIANTS' RUN

D UTGARDE KEEP

E NEW AGAMAND

F VALGARDE

GIANTS' RUN

VENGEANCE
LANDING

NIFFLEVAR

EXPLORERS' LEAGUE
OUTPOST

153

HOWLING FJORD

The breathtaking cliffs and green forests of Howling Fjord belie the dangers of the area. Both the Alliance and Horde have sent expeditions here to create a foothold on the continent of Northrend and as always tensions are rife between the two factions. However, these long standing hostilities are but a small part of the challenges adventurers face. New enemies, such as the Vrykul, have given their allegiance to the Lich King and make their home here as they prepare their forces for battle. Their stronghold, Utgarde Keep, lies at the center of Howling Fjord and their forces hold pockets of land throughout the area.

While there are a host of new foes here, there are also new allies to be made. The Kalu'ak make their home in the village of Kamagua on the Isle of Spears, off the western coast of Howling Fjord. These staunch Tuskarr earn their living primarily by fishing and whaling and welcome the aid of both Alliance and Horde members in defending their land from the recent attacks. Howling Fjord is also home to the Taunka. Like their ancestral relations the Tauren, the Taunka are a hardy people who have given their allegiance to the Horde in the ongoing struggle against the forces of the Lich King.

This zone contains a multitude of quests for both Horde and Alliance and along with Borean Tundra, is one of the beginning zones you visit when coming to Northrend. There are several quest hubs for adventurers level 68-72 at both the Alliance and Horde towns and outposts, and some of the denizens of Howling Fjord need your help as well. No matter your faction, visit the Frozen Glade in the northern part of the zone, Scalawag Point, off the southwestern coast, and the village of Kamagua, on the Isle of Spears, to offer your services and pick up some decent gold and equipment along the way!

Legend

Herbs

Goldclover
Tiger Lily

Minerals

Cobalt Node
Rich Cobalt

Reputation Information

The Hand of Vengeance (Horde)
The Taunka (Horde)
Horde Expedition (Horde)
Argent Crusade (Alliance)
Explorers' League (Alliance)
Valiance Expedition (Alliance)
The Kalu'ak (Both)

Howling Fjord Legend

1 Valgarde

Macalroy (Quest Giver)
Vice Admiral Keller (Quest Giver)
Beltrand McSorf (Quest Giver)
Thoralius the Wise (Quest Giver)
Guard Captain Zorek (Quest Giver)
Baron Ulrik von Stromhearth (Quest Giver)
Anchorite Yazmina <Grand Master First Aid Trainer>
Bernadette Dexter <Grand Master Leatherworking Trainer>
Frederic Burrhus <Grand Master Skinning Trainer>
Ounhulo <Grand Master Jewelcrafting Trainer>
Grumbol Stoutpick <Grand Master Mining Trainer>
Tisha Longbridge <Grand Master Engineering Trainer>
Rosina Rivet <Grand Master Blacksmithing Trainer>
Fayin Whisperleaf <Grand Master Herbalism Trainer>
Lanolis Dewdrop <Grand Master Alchemy Trainer>
Bram Brewbaster <Master Cooking Trainer>
Benjamin Clegg <Grand Master Tailoring Trainer>
Elizabeth Jackson <Grand Master Enchanting Trainer>
Byron Welwick <Grand Master Fishing Trainer>
Sorely Twitchblade <Poison Supplier>
Logistics Officer Brighton <Alliance Vanguard Quartermaster>

2 Daggercap Bay

Harold Lagras (Underwater) (Quest Giver)

3 Wyrmskull Village

Pulroy the Archaeologist (Quest Giver)
Scout Valory (Quest Giver)
Zedd (Quest Giver)
Defender Mordun (Quest Giver)

4 Utgarde Catacombs

Glorenfeld (Quest Giver)
Ares the Oathbound (Quest Giver)
Daegarn (Quest Giver)

5 Lieutenant Icehammer (Quest Giver)

6 Ivald's Ruin

Donny (Quest Giver)

7 Explorers' League Outpost

Stanwad (Quest Giver)
Walt (Quest Giver)
Hidalgo the Master Falconer (Quest Giver)

8 Ember Spear Tower

Scout Knowles (Quest Giver)

9 Westguard Keep

Captain Adams (Quest Giver)
Bombardier Petrov (Quest Giver)
Chef Kettleblack (Quest Giver)
Cannoneer Ely (Quest Giver)
Sapper Steelring (Quest Giver)
Explorer Abigail (Quest Giver)
Old Man Stonemantle (Quest Giver)

Peppy Wrongnozzle (Quest Giver)
Quartermaster Brevin (Quest Giver)
Father Levariol (Quest Giver)
Mage-Lieutenant Malister (Quest Giver)

10 Fort Wildervar

Foreman Colbey (Quest Giver)
Lieutenant Maeve (Quest Giver)
Gil Grisert (Quest Giver)
Prospector Belvar (Quest Giver)
Christopher Sloan (Quest Giver)
Researcher Aderan (Quest Giver)
Trapper Jethan (Quest Giver)

11 Steel Gate

Overseer Irena Stonemantle (Quest Giver)
Engineer Feknut (Quest Giver)
Watcher Moonleaf (Quest Giver)
Steel Gate Chief Archaeologist (Quest Giver)

12 Skorn

Westguard Sergeant (Quest Giver) (Summoned)

13 Chillmere Coast

Explorer Jaren (Quest Giver)

14 Lunk-Tusk (Quest Giver)

1 The Ancient Lift

Orfus of Kamagua (Quest Giver)

2 Kamagua

Elder Atuik (Quest Giver)
Grezzix Spindlesnap (Quest Giver)
Anuniaq (Quest Giver)
Tanaika <Kalu'ak Quartermaster>

3 Scalawag Point

"Silvermoon" Harry (Quest Giver)
Handsome Terry (Quest Giver)
Scuttle Frostprow (Quest Giver)
Taruk (Quest Giver)
Zeh'gehn (Quest Giver)
Annie Bonn (Quest Giver)

4 Ember Clutch

Ember Clutch Ancient (Quest Giver)

5 The Frozen Glade

Lurielle (Quest Giver)

6 Ulfang (Quest Giver)

7 Chillmere Coast

Old Icefin (Quest Giver)

8 Captain Ellis (Quest Giver)

1 Vengeance Landing

High Executor Anselm (Quest Giver)
Pontius (Quest Giver)
Apothecary Lysander (Quest Giver)
Roberta Jacks <Grand Master Skinning Trainer>
Gunter Hansen <Grand Master Leatherworking Trainer>
Marjory Kains <Grand Master Herbalism Trainer>

Emil Autumn <Grand Master Enchanting Trainer>
Wilhelmina Renel <Grand Master Alchemy Trainer>
Thomas Kolichio <Cooking Trainer>
Carter Tiffens <Grand Master Jewelcrafting Trainer>
Kristen Smythe <Grand Master Blacksmithing Trainer>
Jonathan Lewis <Grand Master Mining Trainer>
Sally Tompkins <Grand Master First Aid Trainer>
Booker Kells <Grand Master Inscription Trainer>
Jamesina Watterly <Grand Master Engineering Trainer>
Alexandra McQueen <Grand Master Tailoring Trainer>
Angelina Soren <Grand Master Fishing Trainer>

2 Bleeding Vale

Dark Ranger Lyana (Quest Giver)

3 Derelict Strand

Apothecary Hanes (Quest Giver)

4 Dragonskin Map (Quest Giver)

5 Captain Harker (Quest Giver)

6 Vengeance Lift

Sergeant Gorth (Quest Giver)
Longrunner Nnnik (Quest Giver)

7 Lydell's Ambush

Lydell (Quest Giver)

8 Ghostblade Post

Ranger Captain Areiel (Quest Giver)
Scribe Seguine (Quest Giver)

9 New Agamand

Chief Plaguebringer Harris (Quest Giver)
Plaguebringer Tillinghast (Quest Giver)
"Hacksaw" Jenny (Quest Giver)
Cormath the Courier (Quest Giver)
Tobias Sarkhoff (Quest Giver)
David Marks <Poison Vendor>

10 Apothecary Camp

Apothecary Malthus
Apothecary Grick
Apothecary Anastasia

11 Steel Gate

Sage Mistwalker
Longrunner Skycloud

12 Skorn

Winterhoof Brave (Quest Giver) (Summoned)

13 Camp Winterhoof

Celea Frozenmane (Quest Giver)
Ahota Whitefrost (Quest Giver)
Wind Tamer Kagan (Quest Giver)
Nokoma Snowseer (Quest Giver)
Sage Edan (Quest Giver)
Junat the Wanderer (Quest Giver)
Longrunner Pembe (Quest Giver)
Chieftain Ashtotem (Quest Giver)
Greatmother Ankha (Quest Giver)

Borean Tundra

Crystalsong Forest

Dalaran

Dragonblight

Grizzly Hills

Howling Fjord

Icecrown

Sholazar Basin

The Storm Peaks

Zul'Drak

ICECROWN

SHOLAZAR BASIN

ONSLAUGHT HARBOR

THE SHADOW VAULT

ALDUR'THAR

JOTUNHEIM

YMIRHEIM

THE FLESHWERKS

CORP'RETHAR

ICECROWN CITADEL

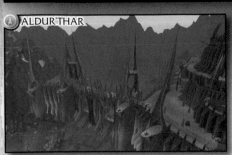

A ALDUR'THAR

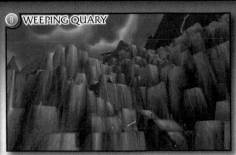

B WEEPING QUARY

C SCOURGEHOLME

K ICECROWN CITADEL

J THE FLESHWERKS

I MORD'RETHAR

H CORP'RETHAR

G BALARGARDE FORTRESS

SINDRAGOSA'S
FALL

MORD'RETHAR

ARGENT
VANGUARD

D ORDRIM'S HAMMER

E THE SKYBREAKER

F THE SHADOW VAULT

157

Icecrown

The frozen region known as Icecrown is composed mainly of the Icecrown Glacier which has slammed into the continent of Northrend. Unlike the snowy tundra of the Dragonblight or the windswept mountains of the Storm Peaks, Icecrown is not merely cold. The ground is not frozen nor covered by snow—it is solid ice. Nothing grows here. Nothing lives.

At the southern end of the zone lies Icecrown Citadel, stronghold of the Lich King. The citadel surrounds the Frozen Throne from which Arthas commands his legions of undead. Though you have no doubt dealt with the Scourge in your travels through Northrend, you have never seen them in such numbers as exist in Icecrown. They are legion, spreading across the ice, doing the bidding of their monarch without question, without doubt, without rest.

The number of the Scourge are so great that the Alliance and Horde forces in the area are headquartered on great flying battleships lest they be overrun by sheer numbers. Both the Skybreaker, for the Alliance, and Orgrim's Hammer, for the Horde, provide relatively safe bases from which to launch their reconnaissance missions into Icecrown. Both sides have allied with the Knights of the Ebon Blade in an attempt to thwart the Lich King's plans. Though his minions far outnumber the opposing forces, there are those who are not content with servitude to the Lich King and can be turned into allies as well.

Adventurers, level 77-80, who dare these icy wastes find that their skills are much needed by their faction, as well as by members of the Argent Crusade and others. Make use of what allies you find, no matter where you find them.

Legend

Herbs	Minerals	Reputation Information
Icethorn	Saronite	Knights of the Ebon Blade
Lichbloom	Rich Saronite	Argent Crusade
	Titanium	Warsong Offensive
		Valiance Expedition

Icecrown Legend

① The Skybreaker
High Captain Justin Bartlett (Quest Giver)
Thassarian (Quest Giver)
Knight-Captain Drosche (Quest Giver)
Absalan the Pious (Quest Giver)
Chief Engineer Boltwrench (Quest Giver)

② Crusaders' Pinnacle
Marshal Ivalius (Quest Giver)

③ The Valley of Lost Hope
Ground Commander Koup (Quest Giver)

④ Ymirheim
Frazzle Geargrinder (Quest Giver)

⑤ The Broken Front
Dying Soldier (Quest Giver)

⑥ Icecrown Citadel
Captain Kendall (Quest Giver)

⑦ Aldur'thar
Kibli Killohertz (Quest Giver)

① The Shadow Vault
Baron Sliver (Quest Giver)
Duchess Mynx <Ebon Blade Quartermaster>
Duke Lankral (Quest Giver)
The Leaper (Quest Giver)
Biloblow <Poisons>
Vile (Quest Giver)
Vaelen the Flayed (Quest Giver)
Keritose Bloodblade (Quest Giver)

② Blackwatch
Darkrider Arly (Quest Giver)
Crusader Olakin Sainrith (Quest Giver)

③ Ufrang's Hall
Vaelen the Flayed (Quest Giver)

④ Njorndar Village
The Bone Witch (Quest Giver)

⑤ The Underhalls
Bethod Feigr (Quest Giver)

⑥ Valhalas
Geirrvif (Quest Giver)

⑦ Death's Rise
Lord-Commander Arete (Quest Giver)
Aurochs Grimbane (Quest Giver)
Setaal Darkmender (Quest Giver)
Uzo Deathcaller (Quest Giver)

⑧ The Argent Vanguard
Highlord Tirion Fordring (Quest Giver)
Veteran Crusader Aliocha Segard <Argent Crusade Quartermaster>
Crusade Commander Entari (Quest Giver)
Father Gustav (Quest Giver)
Crusader Lord Dalfors (Quest Giver)
Penumbrius (Quest Giver)
Siegemaster Fezzik (Quest Giver)

⑨ Valley of Echoes
The Ebon Watcher (Quest Giver)
Crusade Architect Silas (Quest Giver)
Crusade Engineer Spitzpatrick (Quest Giver)
Father Gustav (Quest Giver)

⑩ Crusaders' Pinnacle
Highlord Tirion Fordring (Quest Giver)

⑪ Saronite Mines
Darkspeaker R'khem (Quest Giver)

⑫ Naz'anak: The Forgotten Depths
Pulsing Crystal (Quest Giver)
Matthias Lehner (Quest Giver)

⑬ The Valley of Lost Hope
Matthias Lehner (Quest Giver)

⑭ Sindragosa's Fall
Matthias Lehner (Quest Giver)

⑮ The Court of Bones
Matthias Lehner (Quest Giver)

⑯ Silent Vigil
Crusader Bridenbrad (Quest Giver)
Bridenbrad's Possessions (Quest Giver)

⑰ Rise of Suffering
Vereth the Cunning (Quest Giver)

① Orgrim's Hammer
Koltira Deathweaver (Quest Giver)
Brother Keltan (Quest Giver)
Sky-Reaver Korm Blackscar (Quest Giver)
Warbringer Davos Rioht (Quest Giver)
Chief Engineer Copperclaw (Quest Giver)

② Crusaders' Pinnacle
Warlord Hork Strongbrow (Quest Giver)

③ The Bombardment
Ground Commander Xutjja (Quest Giver)

④ Ymirheim
Blast Thunderbomb (Quest Giver)

⑤ The Broken Front
Dying Berserker (Quest Giver)

⑥ Icecrown Citadel
Sergeant Kregga (Quest Giver)

⑦ Aldur'thar
Fringe Engineer Tezzla (Quest Giver)

Borean Tundra

Crystalsong Forest

Dalaran

Dragonblight

Grizzly Hills

Howling Fjord

Icecrown

Sholazar Basin

The Storm Peaks

Zul'Drak

THE SAVAGE THICKET

THE GLIMMERING PILLAR

THE MAKERS' PERCH

THE SUNTOUCHED PILLAR

WILDGROWTH MANGAL

RAINSPEAKER CANOPY

NESINGWARY BASE CAMP

RIVER'S HEART

FRENZY HIL

THE MOSSLIGHT PILLAR

THE SKYREACH PILLAR

SHOLAZAR BASIN

A RAINSPEAKER CANOPY

B THE LIFEBLOOD PILLAR

C NESINGWARY BASE CAMP

ICECROWN

THE AVALANCHE

THE LOST LANDS

THE MAKERS' OVERLOOK

THE LIFEBLOOD PILLAR

WINTERGRASP

K THE MAKERS' OVERLOOK

J THE SKYREACH PILLAR

I THE AVALANCHE

H WAYGATE

G RIVER'S HEART

D THE MAKERS' PERCH

E THE SAVAGE THICKET

F THE BONEFIELDS

SHOLAZAR BASIN

The jungle-like environment of Sholazar Basin is an anomaly on the cold continent of Northrend. This rich ecosystem, complete with many varieties of flora and fauna is protected by the titan-erected pillars that protect the basin from the harsh weather of Northrend and from invading Scourge. That safety is now in question though as one of the pillars has fallen in the east and the Scourge are streaming down the Avalanche into Sholazar Basin from bordering Icecrown, threatening to push further into the area.

The Scourge are not the only dangers here. The jungles teem with aggressive wildlife and to the north lies the Savage Thicket, home to the terrifying Primordial Drakes. Hemet Nesingwary has established a camp in the west as there is plenty of good hunting to be had. The gorlocs, an arctic cousin to the more familiar murlocs, live in the basin as well, their separate tribes forming an alliance known as the Oracles and they seek to protect their interests in the area. The wolvars, known as the Frenzyheart Tribe, have made Sholazar Basin their home after having been driven out of their former homeland by the Scourge. Their aggressive nature often causes clashes with the gorlocs in the area.

Sholazar Basin offers plenty of paying work for adventurers level 75-78. Visit Nesing-wary's Camp or Lakeside Landing to get started. The Oracles can use your assistance as well in Rainspeaker Canopy and at their other settlements, as can the Frenzyheart Tribe. Keep in mind that the tensions are such between the Frenzyheart Tribe and the Oracles that once you begin offering your services to one side, the other wants nothing to do with you.

Legend

Herbs	Minerals	Reputation Information
Tiger Lily	Saronite	Frenzyheart Tribe (Both)
Adder's Tongue	Rich Saronite	The Oracles (Both)
	Titanium	

Sholazar Basin Legend

(1) Nesingwary Base Camp
Korg the Cleaver (Quest Giver)
Professor Calvert (Quest Giver)
Debaar (Quest Giver)
Buck Cantwell (Quest Giver)
Weslex Quickwrench (Quest Giver)
Chad (Quest Giver)
Drostan (Quest Giver)
Hemet Nesingwary (Quest Giver)
Grimbooze Thunderbrew (Quest Giver)

(2) Frenzyheart Hill
Rejek (Quest Giver)
High-Shaman Rakjak (Quest Giver)
Elder Harkek (Quest Giver)
Vekgar (Quest Giver)
Goregek the Gorilla Hunter (Quest Giver)
Tanak <Frenzyheart Quartermaster>

(3) Dorian's Outpost
Zootfizzle (Quest Giver)
Colvin Norrington (Quest Giver)
Dorian Drakestalker (Quest Giver)

(4) Makers' Overlook
Timeworn Coffer (Quest Giver)

(5) The Sundered Strand
Moodle (Quest Giver)
Zepik the Gorloc Hunter (Quest Giver)
Jaloot (Quest Giver)

(6) Lakeside Landing
Pilot Vic (Quest Giver)
Tamara Wobblesprocket (Quest Giver)

(7) Rainspeaker Rapids
Avatar of Freya (Quest Giver)

(8) Oracle Soo-rahm (Quest Giver)

(9) Rainspeaker Canopy
High-Oracle Soo-say (Quest Giver)
Lafoo (Quest Giver)
Oracle Soo-dow (Quest Giver)
Oracle Soo-nee (Quest Giver)
Geen <Oracles Quartermaster>

(10) The Lifeblood Pillar
Cultist Corpse (Quest Giver)

(11) Swindlegrin's Dig
Engineer Helice (Quest Giver)

(12) Mistwhisper Refuge
Mistcaller Soo-gan (Quest Giver)

(13) Injured Rainspeaker Oracle (Quest Giver)

(14) Tracker Gekgek (Quest Giver)

(15) Wildgrowth Mangal
Monte Muzzleshot (Quest Giver)

Borean Tundra

Crystalsong Forest

Dalaran

Dragonblight

Grizzly Hills

Howling Fjord

Icecrown

Sholazar Basin

The Storm Peaks

Zul'Drak

ULDUAR

SNOWDRIFT
PLAINS (H)

GROM'ARSH
CRASH SITE
(E)

TERRACE
OF THE
MAKERS (G)

VALKYRION

TEMPLE
OF STORMS

BRUNNHILDAR VILLAGE
(F)

ICECROWN

(D)
FROSTHOLD

K3
(A)

(B)

THE STORM PEAKS

(A) K3

(B) GARM

(C) CAMP TUNKA'LO

THE NORTH SEA

THUNDERFALL

CAMP TUNKA'LO

DUN NIFFELEM

ZUL'DRAK

J DUN NIFFELEM

I THUNDERFALL

H SNOWDRIFT PLAINS

G TERRACE OF THE MAKERS

D FROSTHOLD

E GROM'ARSH CRASH SITE

F BRUNNHILDAR VILLAGE

The Storm Peaks

The frozen, unforgiving landscape of the Storm Peaks is marked by the towering mountains that give this area its name. Both the Alliance and the Horde have established modest footholds in the area as have the goblins—always on the lookout for profit.

Though the land is harsh, this mountainous region is somewhat densely populated. In the northeast lies Camp Tunka'lo, home to a hardy tribe of Taunka who have allied themselves with the Horde. Directly south of them lies Dun Niffelem, home to the Sons of Hodir. These giants don't trust strangers easily but are steadfast allies once you earn their respect. Brunnhildar Village, home to a fierce race of female warriors, can be found in the southern part of the zone. Bouldercrag's Refuge, in the northwest, houses stout Earthern warriors who are working to thwart the Iron Rune Dwarves who have pushed into their land. In the southwest, the race of frost dwarves known as the Frostborn have allied themselves with the Alliance and can be found at Frosthold.

In the north, the stunning Terrace of the Makers rises up out of the mountainsides, a testament to the skill of the ancient race who built it. Ulduar in the far north is another example of their architecture and holds the ominous Halls of Lightning and Halls of Stone.

Players level 76-80 do not lack for things to do here. A good place to start is at the Goblin camp, K3, near the southern edge of the zone. The K3 Goblins as well as members of your faction have work for you, but not all areas are friendly to you when you first enter the zone. You must prove yourself to some of the factions here before they ask you for your aid.

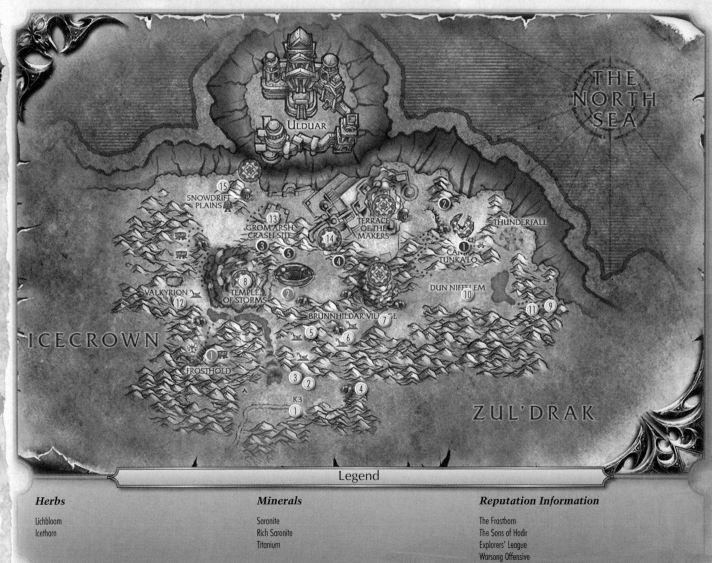

Legend

Herbs

Lichbloom
Icethorn

Minerals

Saronite
Rich Saronite
Titanium

Reputation Information

The Frostborn
The Sons of Hodir
Explorers' League
Warsong Offensive

166

The Storm Peaks Legend

1 Frosthold
Lagnus (Quest Giver)
Fjorlin Frostbrow (Quest Giver)
Rork Sharpchin (Quest Giver)
Yorg Stormheart (Quest Giver)
Archaeologist Andorin (Quest Giver)
Glorthal Stiffbeard (Quest Giver)

2 Foot Steppes
Creteus (Quest Giver)

1 K3
Ricket (Quest Giver)
Jeer Sparksocket (Quest Giver)
Gretchen Fizzlespark (Quest Giver)

2 Snowblind Hills
Tore Rumblewrench (Quest Giver)

3 Crystalweb Cavern
Injured Goblin Miner (Quest Giver)

4 Garm's Rise
Gino (Quest Giver)

5 The Forlorn Mine
Lok'lira the Crone (Quest Giver)
Mildred the Cruel (Quest Giver)

6 Brunnhildar Village
Lok'lira the Crone (After being released) (Quest Giver)
Thyra Kvinnshal (Quest Giver)
Iva the Vengeful (Quest Giver)
Astrid Bjornrittar (Quest Giver)
Gretta the Arbiter (Quest Giver)

7 Valley of Ancient Winters
Brijana (Quest Giver)

8 Temple of Storms
Thorim (Quest Giver)

9 Fjorn's Anvil
Fjorn's Anvil (Quest Giver)

10 Dun Niffelem
King Jokkum (Quest Giver)
Lillehoff <The Sons of Hodir Quartermaster>
Njormeld (Quest Giver)
Fjorn's Anvil (Quest Giver)
Hodir's Helm (Quest Giver)
Hodir's Horn (Quest Giver)
Hodir's Spear (Quest Giver)
Frostworg Denmother (Quest Giver)
Arngrim the Insatiable (Quest Giver)
Calder (Quest Giver)

11 Fjorn's Anvil
Njormeld (Quest Giver)

12 Valkyrion
Harpoon Crate (Quest Giver)

13 The Inventor's Library
Inventor's Library Console (Quest Giver)

14 Temple of Invention
Brann Bronzebeard (Quest Giver)

15 Bouldercrag's Refuge
Bouldercrag the Rockshaper (Quest Giver)
Bruor Ironbane (Quest Giver)

1 Camp Tunka'lo
Xarantaur (Quest Giver)

2 Frostfloe Deep
Chieftain Swiftspear (Quest Giver)

3 Grom'arsh Crash-Site
Bloodguard Lorga (Quest Giver)
Olut Alegut (Quest Giver)
Boktar Bloodfury (Quest Giver)
Moteha Windborn (Quest Giver)

4 Gimorak's Den
Tracker Val'zij (Quest Giver)

5 The Foot Steppes
Khaliisi (Quest Giver)

THE STORM PEAKS

ALTAR OF RHUNOK

ALTAR OF SSERATUS

VOLTARUS

THRYM'S END

THE ARGENT STAND

ZIN

EBON WATCH

LIGHT'S BREACH

ZERAMAS

ZUL'DRAK

Drak'Tharon Keep

Ⓐ DRAK'MABWA

Ⓑ THE ARGENT STAND

Ⓒ THRYM

K GUNDRAK

J VOLTARUS

I THE ALTAR OF RHUNOK

H KOLRAMAS

G ALTAR OF HAR'KOA

GRIZZLY HILLS

GUNDRAK

ZOL'MAZ STRONGHOLD

ALTAR OF MAM'TOTH

ALTAR OF QUETZ'LUN

ALTAR OF HAR'KOA

RAMAS

D LIGHT'S BREACH

E ALTAR OF SSERATUS

F THE AMPITHEATRE OF ANGUISH

169

ZUL'DRAK

The northeastern region of Northrend known as Zul'Drak is home to the Drakkari Ice Trolls. From their capital of Gundrak they have fiercely ruled the region for generations and can be found throughout the area, making trouble for unwary adventurers. The Scourge have set up several necropoli from which they are launching attacks against the Drakkari on several fronts. The Drakkari have turned on their own gods in a desperate attempt to beat back the Lich King's forces and have become even more bloodthirsty and less rational than usual.

In large part due to the Scourge activity, the Argent Crusade has moved into the region in force, claiming several outposts for themselves and battling both the battle hardened Drakkari and the Scourge. The Knights of the Ebon Blade have also set up camp at Ebon Watch and follow a similar agenda to the Argent Crusade in this area.

Not all battles are over territory; some take place for glory alone! At the center of Zul'drak stands the Amphitheatre of Anguish. Even now, surrounded by hostile Drakkari and threatened by the Scourge, the contests continue. Speak with Gurgthock the Fight Promoter in the Arena to pit your battle skills against a string of champions.

Players level 74-77 can find many challenges here. Though neither the Alliance or Horde have outposts in the zone, the Argent Crusade and The Knights of the Ebon Watch welcome the aid of adventurers in battling the invading Scourge.

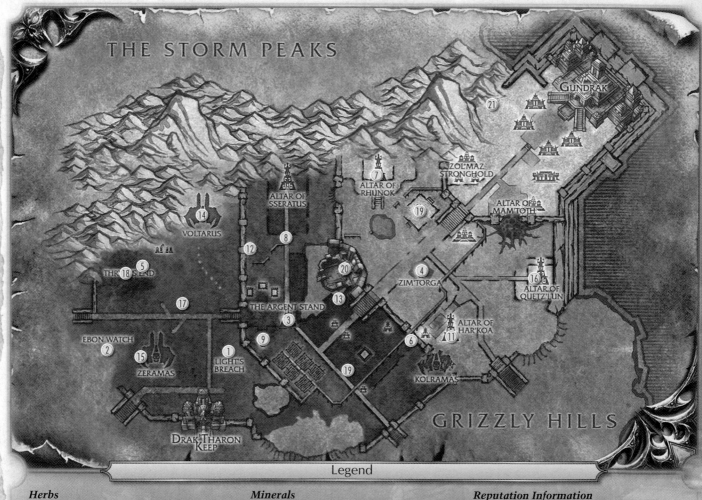

Legend

Herbs	Minerals	Reputation Information
Talandra's Rose	Cobalt	Argent Crusade (Both)
Goldclover	Rich Cobalt	Knights of the Ebon Blade (Both)
Tiger Lily	Saronite	

Zul'Drak Legend

1. **Light's Breach**
   Crusader Lord Lantinga (Quest Giver)
   Elder Shaman Moky (Quest Giver)
   Chief Rageclaw (Quest Giver)

2. **Ebon Watch**
   Stefan Vadu (Quest Giver)
   Bloodrose Datura (Quest Giver)
   Deathdrip <Poison Supplies>

3. **The Argent Stand**
   Commander Kunz (Quest Giver)
   Commander Falstaav (Quest Giver)
   Apprentice Pestlepot (Quest Giver)
   Hexxer Ubungo (Quest Giver)
   Sub-Lieutenant Jax (Quest Giver)
   Magister Teronus III (Quest Giver)
   Avenger Metz (Quest Giver)

4. **Zim'Torga**
   Zim'Torga (Quest Giver)
   Witch Doctor Khufu (Quest Giver)
   Element-Tamer Dagoda (Quest Giver)
   Chronicler To'kini (Quest Giver)
   Scalper Ahunae (Quest Giver)
   Chin'ika <Poison Supplier>

5. **Thrym's End**
   Gymer (Quest Giver)

6. **Drak'Sotra**
   Specialist Cogwheel (Quest Giver)
   Dr. Rogers (Quest Giver)
   Captain Rupert (Quest Giver)
   Sergeant Moonshard (Quest Giver)

7. **Altar of Rhunok**
   Spirit of Rhunok (Quest Giver)

8. **Altar of Sseratus**
   Sergeant Stackhammer (Quest Giver)
   Corporal Maga (Quest Giver)

9. **Zim'Abwa**
   Zim'Abwa (Quest Giver)

10. **Zim'Rhuk**
    Zim'Rhuk (Quest Giver)

11. **Altar of Har'koa**
    Har'koa (Quest Giver)

12. **Heb'Valok**
    Captain Arnath (Quest Giver)
    Alchemist Finklestein (Quest Giver)

13. **Drak'Agal**
    Captain Grondel (Quest Giver)

14. **Voltarus**
    Overlord Drakuru (Quest Giver)

15. **Reliquary of Agony**
    Gristlegut (Quest Giver)

16. **Altar of Quetz'lun**
    Quetz'lun's Spirit (Quest Giver)

17. **Crusader Forward Camp**
    Engineer Reed (Quest Giver)
    Crusader MacKellar (Quest Giver)

18. **Thyrm's End**
    Gerk (Quest Giver)

19. **Drak'Sotra**
    Captain Brandon (Quest Giver)

20. **Amphitheater of Anguish**
    Gurgthock (Quest Giver)

21. **Dubra'Jin**
    Chronicler Bah'Kini (Quest Giver)

Borean Tundra

Crystalsong Forest

Dalaran

Dragonblight

Grizzly Hills

Howling Fjord

Icecrown

Sholazar Basin

The Storm Peaks

Zul'Drak

WORLD DUNGEONS

Utgarde Keep

DUNGEON INFORMATION

Location:	Howling Fjord
Faction:	Both
Suggested Levels:	68-72 (group of five)
Primary Enemies:	Humanoids
Damage Types:	Fire, Shadow, Nature, Frost
Time to Complete:	45 Minutes

In service to the Lich King, elite Vrykul known as Dragonflayers have flocked to Utgarde Keep, preparing for an all out assault on Howling Fjord. If allowed to complete their preparations, the Dragonflayer army will storm outwards, leaving nothing but blood and flames in its wake, destroying the region and endangering all of Northrend. You must strike now, while they are still building their army within the keep. Decimate their forces and take down their leaders to eliminate this threat to both Alliance and Horde alike.

deal of damage in a short amount of time. For these encounters, having a backup healer makes things a bit easier as well.

No matter how good your tank and healer are, without some firepower to take the enemies down, they are just delaying the inevitable. There are several groups of foes that contain four enemies, so some form of crowd control is vital. Classes that can provide crowd control, whether it is the form of a trap, Sap, Polymorph or anything else, and can dish out the damage are most desirable. Because the majority of the foes here are humanoid, a rogue's Sap is very reliable. If you are short on crowd control, but have an extra healer, have a priest use Mind Control on tougher pulls to even out the odds a bit.

GETTING TO UTGARDE KEEP

Utgarde Keep is situated near the center of Howling Fjord. Alliance characters can reach it by taking the road south out of Fort Wildervar or north from Valgarde. Horde characters can reach the Keep by traveling west from Vengeance Landing, going up the lift then following the road, or by traveling north from New Agamand. Both factions should watch out for the Vrykul encampments as they near the keep.

REPUTATION GAINS

Action	Faction	Reputation Gain
Quest: A Score to Settle	Horde Expedition	500

THE ENEMY GARRISON

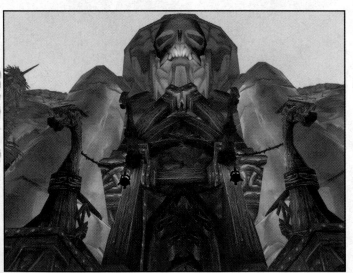

BOSSES

Prince Keleseth	72 Elite
Dalronn the Controller	72 Elite
Skarvald the Constructor	72 Elite
Ingvar the Plunderer	72 Elite

WHO TO BRING

For many players, Utgarde Keep is the first dungeon they face in Northrend. A well balanced group offers the most advantages here, but you can certainly be flexible with your group makeup. As with most dungeons, you need a tank, a dedicated healer, and some damage dealers. Also, make sure you have a good handle on crowd control. Any of the tanking classes should be able to handle the minions here fairly easily as long as they get healed, and the boss fights, while challenging, can be handled by any good tank as well. In this dungeon, none of the tanking classes has a distinct advantage over the others.

Next to a tank, quality healing is the most important element of a group venturing into the keep. While this is generally a good rule for any encounter, it is especially true here where some of the creatures you face have strong attacks that cause a great

Troops

Dragonflayer Bonecrusher	70-71 Elite
Notes: Head Crack (decreases Stamina by 36), Knockdown Spin (knockdown enemies in melee range)	
Dragonflayer Forge Master	70 Elite
Notes: Burning Brand (increases fire damage taken), Cauterize (removes debuffs from allies)	
Dragonflayer Heartsplitter	70-71 Elite
Notes: Throw, Piercing Jab (decreases armor by 15% per stack), Wing Clip	
Dragonflayer Ironhelm	70 Elite
Notes: Heroic Strike, Ringing Slap (spell interrupt)	
Dragonflayer Metalworker	70 Elite
Notes: Sunder Armor, Heated Weapon (Fire damage)	
Dragonflayer Overseer	70 Elite
Notes: Charge, Battle Shout, Demoralizing Shout	
Dragonflayer Runecaster	70-71 Elite
Notes: Njord's Rune of Protection (damage shield), Bolthorn's Rune of Flame (Fire damage)	
Dragonflayer Spiritualist	70 Elite
Notes: Healing Wave, Lightning Bolt, Flame Shock	
Dragonflayer Strategist	70 Elite
Notes: Hurl Dagger (targets random party member), Blind, Ticking Bomb (AoE Fire damage)	
Dragonflayer Weaponsmith	70 Elite
Notes: Concussion Blow, Cleave	
Enslaved Proto-Drake	70 Elite
Notes: Rend, Knock Away (knockback), Flame Breath (Fire damage cone attack)	
Frenzied Geist	70
Notes: Fixate (attacks a target, regardless of other attacks and taunts)	
Proto-Drake Handler	70 Elite
Notes: Debilitating Strike (reduces melee damage done by 75%), Throw	
Proto-Drake Rider	70 Elite
Notes: Throw, Piercing Jab (decreases armor by 15% per stack), Wing Clip	
Savage Worg	70
Notes: Pounce (leaps to target), Enrage (increases attack speed 100%)	
Tunneling Ghoul	70
Notes: Decrepify (Strength -100, movement -30%)	
Vrykul Skeleton	70
Notes: Decrepify (Strength -100, movement -30%)	

QUESTS

A Score to Settle

Faction	Horde Only
Quest Level	68 to obtain
Quest Giver	High Executor Anselm
Goal	Slay Prince Keleseth
Experience Gained	30,150
Rewards	Wraps of the San'layn, Runecaster's Bracers, Vendetta Bindings, Vambraces of the Vengeance Bringer

High Executor Anselm is not going to suffer the insults of Keleseth while the prince builds up his forces in Utgarde Keep. You must make your way through the Dragonflayer forces to Reaver's Hall in the keep to face Prince Keleseth.

You must complete the quest, Report to Anselm, before obtaining A Score to Settle.

Ingvar Must Die!

Faction	Horde Only
Quest Level	68 to obtain
Quest Giver	Dark Ranger Marrah
Goal	Kill Ingvar the Plunderer then take his head to High Executor Anselm in Vengeance Landing.
Experience Gained	25,150
Rewards	Executioner's Band, Ring of Decimation, Signet of Swift Judgment

You can find Dark Ranger Marrah inside Utgarde Keep on the stairs you see just after entering. She is the last surviving member of her recon party and she needs your help. Once you approach the stairs, she reveals herself to you. The Vrykul are savage fighters and she hopes that slaying their leader brings chaos to their ranks. For this task she needs you to make your way through the whole keep until you face Ingvar the Plunderer. Once he is defeated, make sure all party members who have the quest pick up his head before returning to High Executor Anselm.

Into Utgarde!

Faction	Alliance Only
Quest Level	68 to obtain
Quest Giver	Defender Mordun
Goal	Execute Ingvar the Plunderer then take his head to Vice Admiral Keller in Valgarde.
Experience Gained	20,100
Rewards	Executioner's Band, Ring of Decimation, Signet of Swift Judgment

Defender Mordun has seen his share of battles, and he knows that the Vrykul are fearless in a fight. Travel to Utgarde Keep and slay Ingvar the Plunderer, who the Vrykul hold in high esteem, in hopes that this blow turns the tide of battle. Once you have ended the Plunderer's reign, make sure that all party members who have this quest pick up his severed head.

You must first complete the quest, Fresh Legs, from Scout Valory in Valgarde to obtain this quest.

Disarmament

Faction	Alliance Only
Quest Level	68 to obtain
Quest Giver	Defender Mordun
Goal	Enter Utgarde Keep and steal five Vrykul Weapons.
Experience Gained	40,200
Rewards	Amulet of the Tranquil Mind, Razor-Blade Pendant, Necklace of Fragmented Light, Woven Steel Necklace

Defender Mordun has felt the bite of Vrykul weapons and know they are uncannily sharp and nasty. Enter Utgarde Keep and collect five of them so that perhaps he can learn their secrets.

DISARMAMENT

Faction	Horde Only
Quest Level	68 to obtain
Quest Giver	Dark Ranger Marrah
Goal	Enter Utgarde Keep and steal five Vrykul Weapons.
Experience Gained	40,200
Rewards	Necklace of Calm Skies, Hundred Tooth Necklace, Amulet of Constrained Power, Tiled-Stone Pendant

Dark Ranger Marrah has seen how easily the Vrykul weapons cut through her companions. Enter Utgarde Keep and collect five of them and deliver them to High Executor Anselm so that perhaps he can learn their secrets.

Before ascending the stairs, make sure your party is ready for battle. Take care of any summoning, buffing, or other preparations now. At the top of the stairs, past Dark Ranger Marrah, lies the Furnace of Hate. Before you can make your way into its fiery center you must take out the two Dragonflayer Ironhelms standing guard at the top of the stairs. Ironhelms are fond of using Ringing Slap to interrupt any casting, so make sure they stay far away from your healers. Though your group should be able to handle these two with little difficulty, use this first battle to practice your tactics. Set up an attack order and assign raid icons to each foe. This way everyone knows which Dragonflayer to attack first, and which needs to be crowd controlled. Which symbols you use is unimportant, as long as you stay consistent throughout the dungeon run. Make sure everyone understands his or her responsibilities, especially if your party offers more than one method of crowd control. There is no sense in the mage polymorphing a target the rogue is getting ready to sap for instance. Discussing everyone's role beforehand helps you avoid unnecessary deaths as you are just making your way into the Keep.

Once the two guards have been handled, you are ready to take on the Metalworkers and Weaponsmiths that you can see in the hallway here. The two alcoves, one to the left and one to the right contain two Metalworkers at all times and one of the two Weaponsmiths wandering the hallway join them intermittently. Set your group near the top of the stairs, making sure no one goes down the stairs and gets out of Line of Sight, and get ready to pull the two Metalworkers out of the left alcove. Wait until the Weaponsmith has walked away, being careful that the other Weaponsmith is not walking too close, and pull the Metalworkers back to your position. If a rogue is providing your main means of crowd control, you have to Sap one of them before pulling of course, but otherwise, use your crowd control on the second foe once it has pulled back near your party. This keeps it out of the way of the wandering Weaponsmith. Metalworkers can Sunder your armor as well as use Heated Weapon, which causes fire damage, so make sure your healers are on their toes. Repeat this tactic with the Metalworkers in the right alcove as well. Once these have been taken care of, you can pull the two Weaponsmiths separately as they patrol. These guys like to give you a solid knock with Concussion Blow, so be ready to deal with the short stun. When the hallway is clear, move to the far end to enter the Furnace of Hate.

The Furnace holds three forges with a group of two Dragonflayer Metalworkers or Weaponsmiths and one Dragonflayer Forge Master at each. If you have more than one person on crowd control, be sure to take two of these three out of action and concentrate on them one at a time. The Forge Master casts Burning Brand, which increases the fire damage you take, so you don't want him in play at the same time as the Metalworkers with their Heated Weapon if at all possible. You must take out two groups of these to proceed past the Furnace of Hate. Taking down the third and last group isn't necessary, but it is good experience.

THE FIRE IS NOT YOUR FRIEND

The Furnace is separated by large swathes of red hot flames. Stay clear of the fire to avoid taking a good sized chunk of unnecessary damage. There is plenty of room to maneuver in here without getting singed. As you clear each group, a portion of the fire dies out, allowing you to continue.

DRAGONFLAYER PENS

Once you have passed the Furnace of Hate, you reach the Dragonflayer Pens. Like the name suggests, this is where the Dragonflayers keep their Enslaved Proto-Drakes. Be cautious as you enter this room. Directly to the left of the entrance is a lone Enslaved Proto-Drake. While you can skip this fight if you are very careful, the safest thing is to just take this monster out first. These large drakes have a few nasty attacks, including Flame Breath and Knock Away, which can knock the tank back. Have your tank turn the monster toward the wall and away from the rest of the party to minimize the damage of Flame Breath, as well as prevent him from being knocked into another group. Healers should be ready to deal with this damage, as well as the damage over time that the monster's Rend inflicts.

After taking on the lone Proto-Drake, you are ready to clear out the rest of the room. There are three pulls consisting of one Enslaved Proto-Drake and one Proto-Drake Handler each. They are spaced far enough apart so that you can safely pull them to you and create effective crowd control. Control the Handler while focusing your fire on the Enslaved Proto-Drake. Make sure you remember to turn it so that its Fire Breath doesn't hit the whole party. Once the Drake is down, take out the Handler. The Proto-Drake Handlers deal out decent damage, and they can perform Debilitating Strike, which reduces the melee damage done by 75%. Be mindful that if your tank is depending mostly on damage to hold aggro, this debuff can seriously degrade the tank's threat and the rest of the party should manage their damage output accordingly. Once these three groups have been taken care of you are ready to move on to the last group in the room which consists of two Handlers and one Proto-Drake. While having two Handlers can make this a bit more difficult, the same strategy applies. Crowd control at least one of the Handlers, two if you are able to, and take out the Proto-Drake. If you need to take on more than one at a time, make sure everyone is focusing on the same target. A prolonged fight here can be quite dangerous.

Waste Not Want Not

Enslaved Proto-Drakes are skinnable, so be sure to grab the extra Borean Leather off of them if you have a skinner in your party.

Directly past the Dragonflayer Pens are a group of three Dragonflayers which can include any combination of an Ironhelm, Runecaster, and a Strategist. Crowd control the Strategist, and the Ironhelm if possible, and concentrate on the Runecaster. Interrupt his spellcasting as much as possible, and if you have a mage in your party, use Spellsteal when the Runecaster casts Njord's Rune of Protection to remove this advantage from your foe and take it for yourself. Once the Runecaster lies dead at your feet, take on the Strategist. The Strategist can Blind and Hurls Daggers at targets that don't have aggro. Make sure the healers are ready to take care of this sometimes unexpected damage, as well as from the Strategist's Ticking Bomb. Without his friends, the Ironhelm poses little challenge. Watch out for his Ringing Slap and wear him down. Once you have dealt with these three, you are ready to face the first boss.

REAVERS' HALL

When you move your party inside the hall you see a grand table with four Dragonflayers, two on the left and two on the right. These can be any combination of Runecasters, Strategists, and Ironhelms. Prince Keleseth, the first boss, is pacing the floor at the back of the hall. Unless you get too close, he won't aggro you until you have taken out the last of the four Dragonflayers. Crowd control as many of the four as you are able, and concentrate on taking them down as quickly as possible. While all forms of crowd control are helpful here, having a mage to polymorph the final Dragonflayer is extremely helpful. If you can keep this last foe out of commission, you can heal up, regenerate mana, and get ready to face Prince Keleseth. Once you are ready, take on the fourth and last Dragonflayer. As soon as he goes down, Keleseth joins the fight.

PRINCE KELESETH

The Prince can be challenging, but is quite manageable as long as your group stays on their toes and communicates well. Any items, potions, or spells that mitigate shadow damage are very helpful here. His main form of offense is a Shadow Bolt which deals quite a bit of damage. Make sure your tank has gained a good amount of threat before showering the prince with DPS. A few minutes after you engage him, Keleseth summons a group of Vrykul Skeletons. They approach through a doorway to the right of where you entered the hall. Give the tank a chance to get their attention. They don't do a great deal of damage, but enough so that you don't want them beating their bony fists against less heavily armored members of your party. These foes can cast Decrepify which lowers your Strength by 100 and your Movement speed by 30%—a significant debuff! Once the tank has gathered them up, use whatever area of effect damage you have available to eliminate them. They aren't particularly hardy creatures and it doesn't take much to do the job. Of course, being undead, they don't stay down for long and you have to take them out more than once during the fight.

Though this fight is pretty straightforward, Keleseth does have another trick up his voluminous sleeves—Frost Tomb. Every so often, he casts Frost Tomb on a random party member. This freezes a player in place, and they can't act until the Frost Tomb has been shattered. The tombs don't have a lot of health, so a few good shots from a DPS class take care of it. When someone is Frost Tombed, everyone, with the exception of the tank, should focus on breaking it as quickly as possible. This is especially true if the tank or the healer finds themselves frozen. Most deaths that occur during this encounter take place because the healer is trapped in a Frost Tomb and Keleseth wreaks havoc on the tank and the rest of the party before the healer is freed. Stay sharp and take care of the Frost Tombs immediately and the fight goes pretty smoothly.

Once you have defeated Prince Keleseth, you can move out of the hall and into the next hallway. Here you encounter a Dragonflayer Overseer surrounded by a group of Tunneling Ghouls. Have your tank focus on the Overseer, who is elite, while also using area of effect abilities to keep the attention of the non-elite Tunneling Ghouls. Have your DPS classes take down the Ghouls before tackling the much tougher Overseer. Like the Vrykul Skeletons you just faced, the Tunneling Ghouls can cast Decrepify, making it a bit easier for them to get their moldering claws on you. The Overseer is fond of using Battle Shout and Demoralizing Shout, as well as Charging, so make sure your tank keeps up the threat on this bruiser. You face two groups like this, as well as a few Tunneling Ghouls on their own as you make your way down the passage. Here you also find some of the Keep's more disturbing inhabitants, Frenzied Geists. These unnatural creatures are small, but they need to be taken out quickly. They possess the ability to Fixate on a target, focusing their attacks on this individual, ignoring regular rules of threat. Focus your fire on one at a time to eliminate these patrols before they do serious damage.

NJORN STAIR

Another Overseer patrols down the stairs. As you make your way up the stairs, you face several groups of Dragonflayers on each landing. They are spaced far enough apart that you can take on only one group at a time, as long as you are careful. Each group can contain combinations of Dragonflayer Strategists, Ironhelms, Runecasters and their Savage Worgs. Handle these foes just like you did earlier in the keep. Keep an eye out for the Strategists' dirty tricks like Blind and Ticking Bomb, while interrupting the Runecasters' spells and mitigating the Ironhelms' damage as much as possible. Keep your group together and move cautiously up the stairs. With groups of Dragonflayers around almost every corner, "exploring" without the group can be easily fatal. Watch out for the Dragonflayer and Savage Worg patrolling down the stairs so you don't get more on one pull than you intend.

NIDVAR STAIR

Once you reach the Nidvar Stair, you must make your way past two separate groups of two Tunneling Ghouls and three Frenzied Geists. Focus your fire and take down each target in turn. Because these creatures are undead, having a Priest shackle one of them is a great way to keep it out of the fight until you are ready for it. Once you have eliminated these two groups, you are ready to face the second boss encounter.

DALRONN THE CONTROLLER AND SKARVALD THE CONSTRUCTOR

This time you face not one, but two, bosses working to stop your progress through the keep. Dalronn the Controller is a powerful caster. He uses Shadow Bolts offensively and also casts Debilitate which decreases the magical and physical damage you do, making the fight that much harder. Skarvald the Constructor uses his massive bulk to hit hard with Stone Strike. He also Charges players who do not have aggro, which can be quite troublesome for casters. Both of these enemies attack at once and you must deal with them both before the fight is over. Have your tank occupy Skarvald, while your DPS focuses on taking out Dalronn. Any spells or potions that mitigate Shadow damage are extremely helpful here.

Once the Controller is down, you may think that the fight is soon over, but Dalronn doesn't let a little thing like death put him out of commission! He continues to cast on you for as long as Skarvald is also alive and you can't hurt him while he is dead. The same is true of Skarvald should you decide to kill him first. Once Dalronn dies, switch your DPS to Skarvald and burn him down as quickly as possible. It is imperative that your healer is on his or her toes as your party can take a great deal of damage during this time. Once both bosses have been killed, their spirits dissipate and the battle is yours!

Head up the stairs where you find a Dragonflayer Bonecrusher, a Spiritualist, and a Savage Worg. Take out the non-elite Worg first to quickly eliminate one source of damage. If your group is using crowd control, keep the Spiritualist out of the combat to avoid her Healing Wave while you destroy the Bonecrusher. Watch out for his Head Crack which reduces your Stamina. At the top of the stairs you face a group of four Dragonflayers. Follow the same strategy to make your way through this obstacle to reach the top of the keep.

TYR'S TERRACE

As you step out onto the Terrace, you are faced with a group of four Dragonflayers consisting of a Bonecrusher, Heartsplitter and two Savage Worgs. Eliminate the non-elite Savage Worgs quickly to easily lower the damage output of your foes, then take out the Heartsplitter. With his heavier armor, it is best to keep the Bonecrusher under crowd control until you are ready for him. As you round the corner after this group of mobs, you encounter a Proto-Drake Rider and his Enslaved Proto-Drake. Although you can see more of these flying around the keep, this one is the only Rider that comes down to face you and he stays on his Drake during the battle. Watch out for his Piercing Jab which reduces your armor, as well as the Flame Breath spewed out in a frontal cone by the Proto-Drake. Keep any non-melee classes at range to avoid it.

Directly past the Proto-Drake Rider you step down a few stairs to reach another group of Dragonflayers and their Savage Worgs. This group is similar to the one you faced when entering Tyr's Terrace and should be handled in the same way. Once you have eliminated this final obstacle, you are ready to face the final boss.

INGVAR THE PLUNDERER

This final and most difficult encounter requires your party to be on its toes at all times. Make your way down the walkway towards him, but stop before entering the circular area to prepare for the battle. Before engaging him, make sure everyone has consumables at the ready, and that all buffs are in place. Any items, potions, or spells that can mitigate Shadow damage are very useful here as well.

Once you are ready, have your tank move into position and keep non-melee classes at range. Ingvar deals a great deal of melee damage so you must be prepared to keep the tank up from the start. Keep Ingvar close to the center of the circle, making sure everyone stays in line of sight of the healers. The pillars surrounding the area can sometimes make this difficult so each party member needs to make sure they are positioned correctly to receive heals.

In addition to his strong melee attack, Ingvar also has Smash. This move hits everyone in a cone in front of him with a huge amount of Physical damage, and causes almost certain death. When Ingvar starts to do this move he stands still. Everyone, including the tank, needs to get behind him to avoid this potentially battle ending blow. The Plunderer also does Staggering Roar, a bellowing shout that deals more Physical damage and interrupts any casting. Make sure nobody is casting when he starts to shout, as this will prevent them from casting for 6 seconds.

Once you wear him down, the battle is not yet over. For his dark service, Ingvar is resurrected by Annhylde the Caller and now faces you as an undead monstrosity! His melee attacks still do Physical damage, but all of his abilities now do Shadow damage, so any potions or abilities that mitigate Shadow damage are really helpful here. His Smash has been replaced by Dark Smash. This move is just as dangerous, and should be avoided by getting behind him when he starts to cast it. The Plunderer's Staggering Roar has been replaced with Dreadful

Roar, which works the same way, but now deals Shadow damage and silences for even longer. Just like before, make sure no one is casting when he starts to shout. Also, every cast of Dreadful Roar places a stacking debuff on the party that increases Shadow Damage taken by 5%.

He also casts Woe Strike. When placed on a target, this curse does damage to the target and causes anyone directly healing someone who has it to take damage. This debuff can be removed with abilities that remove curses, but if that is not possible then healers must be very observant during this fight. Keep HoT's up as much as possible and only direct heal when absolutely necessary while the curse is up.

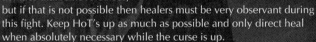

Finally, Ingvar has an ability called Shadow Axe. The Plunderer flings his weapon at a random party member, where it will spin around violently at that location and damage all nearby party members. All players, including the tank, must move away from the spinning axe as quickly as possible to prevent them from taking a heavy amount of Shadow damage. Be mindful of all of your surroundings, and burn him down quickly! For once Dreadful Roar stacks high enough, no amount of healing will keep players alive through The Plunderer's Shadow damage abilities. Once Ingvar falls a second time, you have vanquished Utgarde Keep!

The Nexus

DUNGEON INFORMATION

Location:	Borean Tundra
Faction:	Both
Suggested Levels:	70-73 (group of five)
Primary Enemies:	Humanoid, Elemental, Dragonkin
Damage Types:	Frost, Arcane, Fire, Nature
Time to Complete:	1 Hour

Deep within the reaches of the frozen wastes of Coldarra, the Nexus stands, an icy stronghold of Malygos' power over this land. Inside his minions twist and shape the Arcane Energies he seeks to control, warping the land's creatures and tearing rifts in the very fabric of the universe. Few are willing to risk these halls where Malygos's will reigns supreme. For those brave few, honor and glory await.

WHO TO BRING

The Nexus offers the opportunity to face many different types of foes and a well balanced group is best here, with opportunities for any class to be useful. A strong tank is desirable, especially one skilled in holding agro from multiple mobs. You also need a dedicated healer, as some of the foes you face here can really deal out the damage. Beyond those two key elements, you can be pretty flexible in recruiting your group. It helps a great deal to have some form of crowd control, and one of the boss fights is much easier if you have a mage to Polymorph, although it can be handled without that if necessary.

One of the main advantages your group can have is a high DPS output. Several of the fights in The Nexus get harder the longer they go on, and being able to shut down the enemy quickly gives you a distinct advantage.

GETTING TO THE NEXUS

The Nexus is located in the Borean Tundra, in the heart of the northwestern section known as Coldarra. To reach The Nexus, Horde characters should travel north from Warsong Hold and Alliance characters can journey northwest from Valiance Keep, both following the road to reach Amber Ledge. Once there, speak to Surristrasz to get the flight path to the Transitus Shield. From there, travel west out of the Transitus Shield, following the path into the ravine where it curves north and leads down a ramp into The Nexus.

THE ENEMY GARRISON

BOSSES

Grand Magus Telestra	*72 Elite*
Anomalus	*72 Elite*
Ormorok the Tree Shaper	*72 Elite*
Keristrasza	*73 Elite*

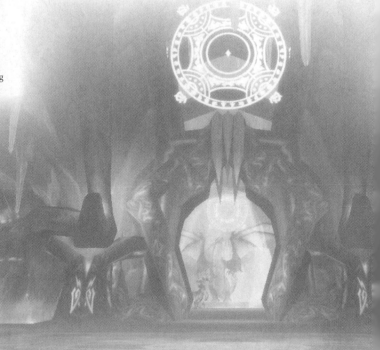

TROOPS

Alliance/Horde Berserker	71 Elite
Notes: Bloodlust (increases attack speed by 30%), War Stomp (knockback), Frenzy (increases attack apeed by 15% per stack)	
Alliance/Horde Cleric	71 Elite
Notes: Flash Heal, Power Word: Shield, Shadow Word: Death	
Alliance/Horde Commander	71 Elite
Notes: Battle Shout, Whirlwind (high damage), Charge	
Alliance/Horde Ranger	71 Elite
Notes: Rapid Shot (can hit anyone in the party), Incendiary Shot	
Azure Enforcer	71 Elite
Notes: Cleave, Mortal Strike	
Azure Magus	72 Elite
Notes: Frost Bolt, Arcane Shock (Arcane damage)	
Azure Scale-Binder	71 Elite
Notes: Heal, Arcane Blast,	
Azure Warder	72 Elite
Notes: Mana Shield, Silence, strong melee swing	
Chaotic Rift	71 Elite
Notes: Chaotic Energy Burst (Arcane damage AoE), Summons Crazed Mana-Wraiths	
Crazed Mana-Wraith	71
Notes: Arcane Missiles	
Crazed Mana-Surge	71 Elite
Notes: Mana Burn, Arcane Nova, When it dies, has the effect Loose Mana (restores mana to all in range)	
Crystalline Frayer	71
Notes: Crystal Bloom (damage increase), Ensnare (movement speed reduction), When it dies, has the effect Aura of Regeneration (restores health and mana to all in range), Seed Pod (revives itself after dying)	
Crystalline Keeper	71 Elite
Notes: Crystal Bark (reflects damage and stuns), Crystal Strike (Arcane damage)	
Crystalline Protector	71 Elite
Notes: Thunderclap, Crystal Chains (root), Shard Spray (Arcane damage)	
Crystalline Tender	71 Elite
Notes: Tranquility, Toughen Hide (increases Armor and Magic Resistance)	
Mage Hunter Ascendant	71 Elite
Notes: Freezing Trap, Cone of Cold, Frostbolt, Arcane Trap (Arcane damage AoE), Polymorph, Arcane Explosion, Immolation Trap, Fireball, Rain of Fire, Aura of Arcane Haste (hits all allies, spell casting speed increases 15%, damage by 150)	
Mage Hunter Initiate	71 Elite
Notes: Renew, Magic Burn (damage over time Arcane damage), Drain Mana	
Mage Slayer	71 Elite
Notes: Draw Magic (Reduces damage and healing done by 225 per stack), Spell Lock (Silence)	
Steward	71 Elite
Notes: Arcane Torrent, Spellbreaker (reduces magic damage done by 75%)	

QUESTS

POSTPONING THE INEVITABLE

Faction	Both
Quest Level	69 to obtain
Quest Giver	Archmage Berinand
Goal	Use the Interdimensional Refabricator near the rift in the Nexus.
Experience Gained	25,150
Rewards	Time-Twisted Wraps, Time-Stop Gloves, Bindings of Sabotage, Gauntlets of the Disturbed Giant

Archmage Berinand has discovered that Azeroth's ley lines are being redirected to the Nexus. He would love to study this phenomenon, but it has the unfortunate side effect of weakening the fabric of the universe! Journey deep within the Nexus and use the Interdimensional Refabricator that Berinand gives you to slow down the effect. After defeating Anomalus, stand on the edge of his platform and activate the Refabricator. You must complete the quest, Reading the Meters, to obtain this quest.

PRISONER OF WAR

Faction	Both
Quest Level	69 to obtain
Quest Giver	Raelorasz
Goal	Enter the Nexus and release Keristrasza.
Experience Gained	40,200
Rewards	Cloak of Azure Lights, Mantle of Keristrasza, Shroud of Fluid Strikes

Malygos has taken Keristrasza as his consort! Though she would never submit willingly, he will eventually bend her to his will if you don't spare her from this fate. You must defeat all of the other bosses in the Nexus before you are able to free Keristrasza and save her from this indignity. You must complete the quest, Springing the Trap, to obtain Prisoner of War.

QUICKENING

Faction	Both
Quest Level	69 to obtain
Quest Giver	Archmage Berinand
Goal	Enter the Nexus and collect 5 Arcane Splinters from Crystalline Protectors.
Experience Gained	20,100
Rewards	Sandals of Mystical Evolution, Treads of Torn Future, Spiked Treads of Mutation, Invigorating Sabatons, Boots of the Unbowed Protector

The incredible arcane energies swirling around the Nexus are transforming the Ancients into something new. Archmage Berinand believes that there is another stage to their metamorphosis and needs you to enter the Nexus and find some proof of this final stage. You can find Crystalline Protectors deep within the Nexus in the area known as The Singing Grove. You must have completed Secrets of the Ancients to obtain this quest.

HAVE THEY NO SHAME

Faction	Both
Quest Level	68 to obtain
Quest Giver	Librarian Serrah
Goal	Enter the Nexus and recover Berinand's Research.
Experience Gained	25,150
Rewards:	Shoulders of the Northern Lights, Cured Mammoth Hide Mantle, Tundra Tracker's Shoulderguards, Tundra Pauldrons

A group of Alliance or Horde (depending on your alignment) adventurers have stolen a book named Berinand's Research from Librarian Serrah. Venture into the Nexus and retrieve it from the Hall of Stasis.

AXIS OF ALIGNMENT

Upon entering the Nexus, you find yourself in the Axis of Alignment. From here there are three paths that lead you further into the dungeon—one to the left, right, and straight ahead. Two Azure Magus and one Azure Warder patrol these paths and walk into the Axis of Alignment as well. Keep your group near the entrance while you make your battle preparations to avoid being surprised by one or both of these foes.

When you are ready, wait for the patrolling enemy to walk in from the right and pull it close to the entrance. If it is an Azure Warder, be ready to deal with his powerful blows, for he is a strong melee fighter. If it is an Azure Magus, be wary of their nasty Frostbolt, as well as their Arcane Shock. Any spells, items, or abilities which can mitigate these types of damage are helpful when facing them. Keep a close eye on their casting bar and interrupt their spells as much as possible to avoid taking unnecessary damage. Once the enemy on the right is down, wait for the enemy on the left to come up the ramp. Fight them near the entrance as well.

MAKE YOUR OWN WAY

The Nexus is laid out in such a way that you can tackle the three bosses in any order you want, always leaving Keristrasza for last. If you like to explore, feel free to start with another path out of the Axis of Alignment to tackle the content in a different order.

Follow the leftmost ramp and be ready for a patrol consisting of a Mage Hunter Ascendant and two Mage Slayers to meet you on this ramp. Mage Hunter Ascendants are powerful foes. There are three types of Mage Hunter Ascendants, not two. There are three types of Mage Hunter Ascendant: Fire, Frost, and Arcane. Fire has abilities like Fireball, Immolation Trap, and Rain of Fire. Frost has abilities like Freezing Trap, Cone of Cold, and Frostbolt. Arcane has an Arcane Trap, Polymorph, and Arcane Explosion. It's impossible to tell which Mage Hunter Ascendant is which before fighting them, so be ready for anything before engaging. All types of Ascendants also cast Aura of Arcane Haste. This hits all of their allies and gives them a 15% increase to Spell Casting Speed, as well as an increase to their damage output, making the Ascendant even more dangerous when part of a group. Whenever you face one, be ready to interrupt the Ascendant's spells when possible, and make sure your healers are paying close attention. The Mage Hunter Ascendants can put out a great deal of damage fairly quickly. If circumstances permit, crowd control the Ascendant while tackling the accompanying Mage Slayers.

These demon dogs are much more dangerous than they look. They have a decent attack but their real threat lies in their abilities Draw Magic and Spell Lock. Draw Magic reduces damage and healing by 225 per stack, making it difficult to take down your enemies and keep your allies on their feet. Spell Lock is a targeted Silence and the Mage Slayers keep this on you as much as possible, making you rely heavily on physical damage to take them out. Once you have eliminated this patrol, you are ready to continue down the ramp.

HALL OF STASIS

The ramp leads to a larger corridor containing several groups of enemies, each entombed in their own icy prison. Even though each foe is in its own block of ice, some of them are still grouped, so be cautious. These frozen foes contain Alliance/ Horde Rangers, Alliance/Horde Berserkers, Alliance/Horde Clerics, and an Alliance/ Horde Commander. You face the opposite faction of your own.

The first pull to the right of the doorway comes singly, most of the rest come in groups of two or three. It is important to make good use of any crowd control you have here. In any group, always take out the Clerics first. They can cast Flash Heal, prolonging the fight, Power Word: Shield, to mitigate the damage you are dishing out to them, and Shadow Word: Death, an instant cast high damage blast. Once they are out of the fight, concentrate on any Rangers you face. These enemies can cast Incendiary Shot and favor Rapid Shot, which can hit anyone in your party.

When facing one of these groups, crowd control the Berserkers whenever possible because they are swift killing machines. They can cast both Bloodlust and Frenzy, both of which increase their attack speed, leaving you very little breathing room in a fight. They also have War Stomp, a knockback ability, which can by very annoying to casters in particular, so keep your distance from these foes unless you are dealing melee damage.

Toward the far end of the corridor you encounter the Commander. He uses Battle Shout to embolden his allies and likes to Charge party members, interrupting their casting. Perhaps his most dangerous move is Whirlwind. This high damage move hits anyone around him and can be devastating to anyone at low health.

Make sure you are pulling these last few frozen groups toward you, keeping clear of the end of the corridor where the ramp leads up. Another group consisting of a Mage Hunter Ascendant and two Mage Slayers patrols down this ramp, and you don't want to tangle with them until you have cleared all of the frozen Alliance foes. Once you have cleared the way, and are ready for the next fight, wait at the end of the corridor for this patrol to come to you and take them out like you did the first group you faced. When you are finished you area ready to head up the ramp into the Librarium.

THE LIBRARIUM

As you enter the Librarium, you see a group of three containing a Steward, Mage Hunter Initiate, and Mage Hunter Ascendant directly in front of you. By now you are familiar with the tricks of the Mage Hunter Ascendant, but the Steward and Mage Hunter Initiate are formidable opponents as well. If possible, use your crowd control on the Mage Hunter Ascendant and focus your attacks on the Initiate first. These foes can cast Renew, Magic Burn, and Drain Mana. Magic Burn is a single target spell similar to Immolation, but with Arcane damage. They don't have a lot of hit points though and can be taken out fairly quickly. Next, focus on the Steward. His use of Arcane Torrent, which functions as an area of effect silence, is very annoying, especially to any casters in your group. Make sure you keep everyone's health topped off while fighting him so that you aren't in dire need of a heal while silenced.

There is another group further down the hall, but you can ignore them as long as you are careful and prepare to pull the group of four from the room to the right. This group is a random assortment of Mage Hunter Ascendants, Mage Hunter Initiates, and Stewards. Crowd control as many of these foes as you can, being careful not to go too far into the room. You don't want Telestra to notice you just yet. Using line of sight, pull this group around the doorway back out to you in the hall, far away from other groups. They pose the same challenges you faced before, with the additional enemy making things a little more difficult. Once you have cleared them out of the way, you are ready to face the Grand Magus Telestra.

GRAND MAGUS TELESTRA

Telestra is a powerful mage who isn't going to be beaten without putting up a spectacular fight. Have your tank run in to engage her first, and move the rest of your party into her chamber. Do as much damage as you can to her during this first phase. She likes to Ice Nova you and casts Fire Bombs, but her most dangerous tactic during this phase of the fight is to fling the entire party around the room. Make sure you have instant damage spells and heals at your fingertips as these are the only thing you can cast during this.

At approximately 50% health she splits into three aspects: Frost, Fire, and Arcane. Polymorph or trap the Arcane aspect to avoid Time Stop and Critter. Time Stop holds you in place, and you can't perform any actions, while Critter does just what you would expect and you find yourself bounding around as a little harmless critter. Make sure any group member with Dispel is ready to return anyone who finds themselves in this predicament back to their original form so they can quickly get back to the fight.

As long as the Arcane aspect is under control, focus on taking down the Frost aspect first. Her Ice Barbs and Blizzard can be quite damaging so you want her out of the picture. Once her icy side is down, take on the Fire aspect. She can use Fire Blast and Scorch to damage you but if you concentrate on her she falls quickly. This leaves you with the Arcane aspect. With your entire group focusing on this aspect, Telestra is soon forced back into her original form.

Once she resumes this form, the fight continues much like it did before she split. She can again fling you about the room, so be ready with instant cast spells. She won't have you flying around the entire time, so be ready to burn her down when your feet once again hit the floor. Defeat the Grand Magus and you have gone a long way toward lessening the power of the Nexus itself.

When you are finished with Telestra, head straight out of her chamber into the hallway across from it. Stay to the left and watch for a wandering patrol of two Mage Slayers and a Mage Hunter Ascendant. Once it walks back down the hallway leading forward, take on the group to the left of the Steward, Mage Hunter Initiate, and Mage Hunter Ascendant. When they are clear, wait for the patrol to come back up the hallway and clear them out. If you need a break between these groups to heal up, retreat to the safety of Telestra's chamber. Once you have defeated both groups, follow the hallway forward into The Rift.

THE RIFT

Continue into The Rift until you see a ramp leading up. At the top of this ramp is a group of four made up of Azure Scale-Binders and Azure Enforcers. These dragonkin are powerful denizens of the Nexus and must be handled with care. The Azure Scale-Binders should always be either crowd controlled, or taken out first, to prevent them from healing themselves and their allies. Their Arcane Blast can also be a dangerous source of damage if you are already injured. The Enforcers are the muscle of the Azure dragonkin. In addition to their strong melee attack, their Cleave and Mortal Strike make them formidable foes in close combat. It is best to handle these one at a time, but if this isn't an option, make sure your tank has a good amount of threat on them because a few of their hits on a lightly armored class can do devastating damage.

The next group of three you see also includes Azure Enforcers and Azure Scale-Binders. Although they are busy dealing with the Chaotic Rift, you pose a much greater threat and they won't hesitate to attack you if you come in range. Before going all the way up the ramp, have one of your ranged damage dealers target the Chaotic Rift and blow it up. It doesn't take much to destroy these, but left alone they spawn numerous non-elite Crazed Mana-Wraiths, which cause unneeded damage in battle. Once the Rift is taken care of, deal with this group of Azure dragonkin much like you handled the group before.

Once this ramp is clear, head down the ramp on the side where you see a Chaotic Rift. Destroy the Rift as before, eliminating the Crazed Mana-Wraiths as well. They are low in health and can be taken out with targeted attacks or with area of effect abilities fairly easily.

Head to the left around the bottom of the ramp to see a Crazed Mana-Surge surrounded by five Crazed Mana-Wraiths. Have your tank focus on the Mana-Surge while the rest of your group quickly takes out the Wraiths before turning their attention back to the Crazed Mana-Surge. These Surges can cast a Mana Burn and an Arcane Nova, hitting anyone nearby. When they die they grant the effect Loose Mana which regenerates mana to anyone in range. Stay within the effect to refill your mana reserves, then take down the group of two Crazed Mana-Surges and three Crazed Mana-Wraiths on the right. Once this group has been cleared, head up the ramp to the right.

Take out the Chaotic Rift from range, being careful not to get too close to agro the three Crazed Mana-Surges and Crazed Mana-Wraiths here. Once the Rift is destroyed, you are ready to take on the Surges. Make sure you are focusing on one target at a time in order to take them down as quickly as possible. If you have reliable area of effect damage in your party, it is a good idea to use it on the Crazed Mana-Wraiths so that their Arcane Missiles don't chew you up while you are fighting the Crazed Mana-Surges. Once you have cleared this landing, make sure you are ready to face Anomalus.

ANOMALUS

Anomalus is an elemental who manipulates the arcane energies in this place to attack any who dare to enter his domain. Though he does mainly melee damage, he also casts Spark which hurls an Arcane bolt at an enemy. Any items or spells that help mitigate Arcane damage are very useful in this fight. Send your tank in to draw Anomalus' attention while everyone moves up onto his platform. At first, this battle is pretty standard: damage Anomalus as much as possible while making sure everyone's health is kept up.

Soon after the battle starts, Anomalus creates a chaotic Rift, shouting, "Reality...unwoven." As soon as the Rift appears, Anomalus begins to Charge Rifts, channeling his arcane energy into it and increasing its attack range and the rate at which it expels Crazed Mana-Wraiths. He also casts Rift Shield which makes him invulnerable while the Chaotic Rift is in place. However, he is concentrating on the rifts and won't attack while you take them down. As soon as a Rift appears, focus all of your energy into destroying it. Make sure the tank is ready to pick Anomalus back up as he once again becomes vulnerable once the Rift goes down.

You need to repeat these tactics several times throughout the fight. As the battle wages on, Anomalus creates Chaotic Rifts more frequently, and does not stop attacking or become invulnerable as they pop up. Use area of effect damage to take out any Chaotic Wraiths that make it through the Rifts before you destroy them. Once you defeat Anomalus any remaining Rifts or Wraiths disappear.

POSTPONING THE INEVITABLE

If you have the quest, Postponing the Inevitable, remember to use the Interdimensional Refabricator here before moving on.

Once you have recovered from your battle with Anomalus, go back down the ramp you came up and drop down to your left where there are no enemies. Once you drop down you see a Crazed Mana-Surge surrounded by Crazed Mana-Wraiths. Take them down as you did the similar groups before to move on.

In front of the large doorway leading to the Singing Grove there is a Chaotic Rift flanked by two Azure Enforcers with an Azure Scale-Binder standing behind them. Take out the Rift from afar and deal with the dragonkin. All three come as one group even though the Scale-Binder sometimes looks as if she were too far away.

THE SINGING GROVE

Follow the left path into the Singing Grove, clearing any of the small Crystalline Frayers you come across. These minute flowers can Ensnare you, but they are non-elite and pose no serious threat. Once you destroy them, they hibernate in a Seed Pod and give off an Aura of Regeneration. This Aura regenerates your health and mana while you are in range, but be careful as the Frayers regenerate their own health as well. Once they emerge from the Seed Pods they will attack you again. Keep moving forward at all times to avoid continually fighting the same groups of Crystalline Frayers.

As you follow the left path you also encounter patrols of Crystalline Keepers and Crystalline Tenders. The Tenders have Tranquility and can cast Toughen Bark, which increases their armor and magic resists. The Keepers cast a dispellable buff on themselves called Crystal Bark which deals Arcane damage to all attackers and has a chance to stun them. Keepers also have Crystal Strike, which deals Arcane damage. Always take down the Tenders first to prevent them from healing.

Once the way is clear, head to the left and take on the Crystalline Protector. This large mutated ancient uses Thunderclap to cause Nature damage and reduce the Attack Speed and Movement of its foes. It can also use Crystal Chains to lock you in place for six seconds. Unless you are the tank, try to move behind the Crystalline Protector to avoid its Shard Spray. This deals Arcane damage in a cone in front of the Protector, damaging anyone in its path.

Continue left, hugging the right wall, making your way through the patrol of Crystalline Keepers and Tenders as you did before. Once they are eliminated, destroy the Crystalline Protector here as well. There are several Crystalline Frayers that stand in your way as well. Remember to keep moving so that they don't respawn on top of you. Follow the path around to the right and clear your way through another Crystalline Protector and yet more Frayers, as well as another patrol of Crystalline Tenders and Crystalline Keepers to reach the next boss.

ORMOROK THE TREE-SHAPER

Ormorok is an easily managed boss as long as everyone pays close attention to the battle. Once you are ready to face him, head up the small ramp into his area. If you aren't a melee fighter, try to stay at range from him to avoid his Trample. Ormorok raises his mighty foot and brings his considerable bulk down on a player, causing a great deal of damage.

The Tree Shaper can also cast Spell Reflection, causing magical spells to be reflected back at the caster and it has four charges. This makes it very important, especially for high damage casters, to keep an eye on Ormorok and be ready when his Spell Reflection is up. Because it has charges, you don't want to just wait for it to go down. Cast low damage spells at him to use up the charges, once again making him vulnerable to your more devastating attacks.

Perhaps Ormorok's most dangerous ability is his Crystal Spikes. In intervals throughout the fight, Ormorok casts these spikes, which erupt from the ground and shoot out in all directions from the Tree Shaper. When he first casts these, they appear as small spikes on the ground. If they appear near you, immediately move to avoid being tossed into the air and damaged by the spikes. It is very important that all party members keep a look out for Crystal Spikes. Being caught by them just once can turn the tide of battle for the worse. When he reaches low health, Ormorok goes into a Frenzy, increasing his physical damage output by 100%. Healers need to be ready to heal this extra damage and tanks need to be ready to use any damage mitigating abilities if it looks like the healer is having trouble keeping up. Once Ormorok the Tree-Shaper falls, you are ready to make your way to the final challenge of the Nexus.

After defeating Ormorok, the Crystalline Frayers are all destroyed. Head back the way you came, hugging the left wall. The path leads through two patrols of Crystalline Keepers and Crystalline Tenders and past two Crystalline Protectors. You need to eliminate each group to make it past them and back out into the Axis of Alignment where you can see Keristrasza in her frozen prison.

As you enter Keristrasza's chamber, there is a lone Azure Magus or Azure Warder patrolling the area. You can take it out without worrying about disturbing the boss. Watch out for its strong melee swing and area of effect Silence.

KERISTRASZA

Malygos has imprisoned Keristrasza, meaning to make her his new consort. By making your way through the Nexus you have proven that you can save her from this indignity. Unfortunately for Keristrasza, the only release from Malygos' control is death. To free the great dragon, click on the three containment spheres, each named for one of the three bosses you have defeated. Make sure everyone is ready before clicking on the final containment sphere.

Once free, Keristrasza is still under Malygos's control and ready for a fight. She poses a double threat with both her maw and her tail. Everyone except the tank should try to stay on her sides. Her Tail Sweep deals a good chunk of damage and knocks you back, which can be deadly if it interrupts a much needed heal.

She also casts Intense Cold. This debuff hits everyone in the party but can be broken by movement or jumping. It deals periodic damage and also slows the attack and casting speeds of anyone afflicted. Once the debuff hits you, you must move or jump. Tanks should not move around to break Intense Cold, but only jump. If a tank moves, Keristrasza will move, and players will have trouble staying at her sides. It is very important that every member of the group keep an eye out for Intense Cold. Once you get it, move immediately, even if you are in the middle of casting. To make this more difficult, Keristrasza can also cast Crystal Chains. These freeze you in place, preventing you from being able to move, which lets Intense Cold stack up on you.

Just as the Tail Sweep makes her backside a dangerous place, Keristrasza's Crystalfire Breath inflicts Frostfire damage to everyone in a cone in front of her. Not only does this cause a great deal of damage, it slows your movement speed and deals damage over time. Once you beat her down to low health, Keristrasza becomes Enraged, which increases her physical damage and attack speed. Make sure the healer keeps a very close eye on the tank, as this really increases Keristrasza's damage output. Burn her down as quickly as you can.

Although you weren't able to completely free her from Malygos's control, with her death you have saved Keristrasza from a far worse fate.

AZJOL-NERUB

DUNGEON INFORMATION

Location:	Dragonblight
Faction:	Both
Suggested Levels:	72-74 (group of five)
Primary Enemies:	Undead
Damage Types:	Shadow, Nature
Time to Complete:	1 hour

Azjol-Nerub was once the proud underground kingdom of the Nerubians. Now, its towering architecture and expansive chambers are home to the Scourge! Anub'arak, the traitor king, has given his allegiance to the Lich King and he uses Azjol-Nerub as a breeding ground for his army of Anub'ar Scourge. Many who enter the caverns never again see the light of day, but more still come. Some know that the once rich kingdom still holds treasures for those brave enough to risk its dangers. Others come not for riches but because they know what is at stake should the armies of Azjol-Nerub be ready when Arthas calls.

WHO TO BRING

Like most dungeons, you can't go wrong with a good strong tank. Several of the fights include multiple foes so you need someone who can generate threat on multiple targets effectively. Having some Nature resistance isn't required, but it does help mitigate the damage.

While a healer of any type works well for dealing with the damage output of these foes, Priests have a distinct advantage for these encounters. The mobs in Azjol-Nerub are Undead and the extra crowd control is very, very useful, especially during the tougher encounters. So much so, that you may want to consider spending a DPS slot for a Shadow Priest. That way you get crowd control, devastating DPS, and in a pinch, back up healing.

Beyond that, all types of DPS classes work well here. Hunters are especially great for their Aspect of the Wild, increasing Nature Resistance, since many of the enemies here deal that type of damage.

GETTING TO AZJOL-NERUB

Azjol-Nerub is located in the western part of Dragonblight, bordering Wintergrasp. Horde characters can most easily reach it by traveling west from Agmar's Hammer, while Alliance characters can take the road north, from Star's Rest. The entrance to the caverns is guarded by several Anub'ar, hostile to both factions, so be cautious in your approach.

THE ENEMY GARRISON

BOSSES

Krik'thir the Gatewatcher	74 Elite
Hadronox	74 Elite
Anub'arak	74 Elite

TROOPS

Animated Bones	72-73
Notes: Created by Anub'ar Necromancers	
Anub'ar Assassin	73
Notes: Backstab	
Anub'ar Brood Keeper	72
Notes: Non-aggressive	
Anub'ar Champion	73
Notes: Rend, Pummel	
Anub'ar Crusher	74 Elite
Notes: Frenzy, Smash (deals a great amount of damage and knocks the target up into the air)	
Anub'ar Crypt Fiend	73
Notes: Infected Wound (increases the Physical damage taken for 20 seconds), Crushing Webs (immobilizes and Nature damage over time)	
Anub'ar Darter	73
Notes: Dart (Damage over time)	
Anub'ar Guardian	73 Elite
Notes: Sunder Armor, Strike (increases melee damage)	
Anub'ar Necromancer	73
Notes: Shadowbolt, Animate Bones (Animates a pile of bones every three seconds for nine seconds)	
Anub'ar Prime Guard	74 Elite
Notes: Drain Power (damage reduced by 1%, and increases your damage by 2% per stack), Mark of Darkness (500 damage per second, 1800 damage to nearby friends when healed)	
Anub'ar Shadowcaster	72 Elite
Notes: Shadowbolt, Shadow Nova (area of effect)	
Anub'ar Skirmisher	72 Elite
Notes: Backstab	
Anub'ar Venomancer	73 Elite
Notes: Poison Bolt (Nature damage over time)	
Anub'ar Warrior	72 Elite
Notes: Cleave, Strike (inflicts increased melee damage)	
Anub'ar Webspinner	72 Elite
Notes: Web Shot (Nature damage, reduces movement speed by 10% per stack, up to 7 times), Web Wrap (encases the target in webbing for 10 seconds unless removed)	
Skittering Infector	72
Notes: Acid Splash (area of effect Nature damage over time)	
Skittering Swarmer	72
Notes: Dangerous in large numbers	
Watcher Gashra	74 Elite
Notes: Infected Bite (Nature damage over time, increases physical damage taken by 20% for 9 seconds), Web Wrap (encases the target in webbing for 10 seconds unless removed), Enrage (increases caster's attack speed by 300% but lowers damage dealt by 50%)	
Watcher Narjil	74 Elite
Notes: Blinding Webs (area of effect Blind for 4 seconds), Infected Bite (Nature damage over time, increases Physical damage taken by 20% for 9 seconds), Web Wrap (encases the target in webbing for 10 seconds unless removed),	
Watcher Silthik	74 Elite
Notes: Poison Spray (Nature damage over time), Infected Bite (Nature damage over time, increases Physical damage taken by 20% for 9 seconds), Web Wrap (encases the target in webbing for 10 seconds unless removed)	

QUESTS

DEATH TO THE TRAITOR KING

Faction	Both
Quest Level	72 to obtain
Quest Giver	Kilix the Unraveler
Goal	Defeat Anub'arak in Azjol-Nerub. Return to Kilix with Anub'arak's Broken Husk
Experience Gained	41,500
Rewards	Kilix's Silk Slippers, Don Soto's Boots, Husk Shard Sabatons, or Greaves of the Traitor.

Anub'arak, the traitor king, makes his home in the once proud underland of Azjol-Nerub. He has pledged himself and his undead army to serve the Lich King. Kill this traitor and bring his Broken Husk to Kilix. You can find Anub'arak deep within Azjol'Nerub.

DON'T FORGET THE EGGS!

Faction	Both
Quest Level	72 to obtain
Quest Giver	Kilix the Unraveler
Goal	Enter Azjol-Nerub and destroy six Nerubian Scourge Eggs.
Experience Gained	25,950
Rewards	Expelling Gauntlets, Purging Handguards, Wraps of Quelled Bane, or Gloves of Banished Infliction.

Throughout Azjol-Nerub, the Scourge Nerubians carefully nurture eggs to increase their numbers. Destroy these as you come across them to keep them from building their army!

THE GILDED GATE

Don't stray too far from the entrance until your group is ready to fight. Make sure everyone is fully buffed and ready before anyone goes exploring down the downwards sloping path. Two Scourge infected Anub'ar, one Webspinner and one Warrior, patrol this path from the base of the slope all the way up to the entrance. This is a good fight to get you used to these creatures before venturing in further. The Warrior comes right up into melee range and can use Strike, to increase melee damage, and Cleave, so make sure any who doesn't have to be near him, isn't. The Webpinner tends to hang back, using Web Shot to dish out Nature damage and reduce its target's movement speed, and Web Wrap which encases its target in a web, immobilizing it for ten seconds unless it is removed.

From here, you can see the first boss, but you have to take care of its minions first! There are three groups of three Anub'ar guarding Krik'thir, each with a named foe and two other Anub'ar. The group on the left contains Watcher Silthik, an Anub'ar Shadowcaster, and an Anub'ar Skirmisher. Crowd control Silthik and focus your fire on the Shadowcaster. He dishes out Shadow damage in both targeted and area of effect varieties, but goes down pretty quickly. Next, destroy the Skirmisher before moving on to Silthik. If your group has no form of crowd control that works on Silthik, take him out first. The Watcher has a couple of nasty Nature Damage over Time abilities as well as Web Wrap, so he is the most dangerous of the group. When fighting these three, be sure to pull them back to the base of the ramp; don't fight them in the room with the others. If you get too close and pull aggro from another group you quickly get swamped with too many bugs at once.

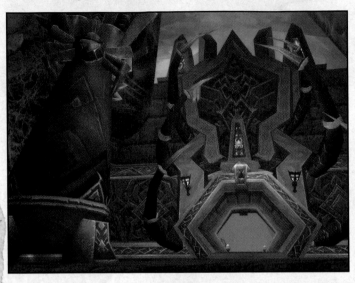

Web Wrap

If a party member becomes encased in webbing, tear it off of them quickly instead of waiting the full ten seconds for it to wear off. It may seem short, but that time can make all the difference during a battle.

Shackle the warrior if possible and concentrate on the less hardy Webspinner. If crowd control isn't available, have the tank handle both mobs while concentrating your fire. Even though this is a relatively easy pull, make sure you establish a kill order to get the group practiced in using one in here. Once the Webspinner is down you can take out the warrior.

At the base of the ramp you face a three-pull consisting of a Warrior, a Webspinner, and a Skirmisher. Crowd control the Warrior and concentrate on the Webspinner once again. The Skirmisher can Backstab, so make sure to look out for this attack. Once the Webspinner is dead, move on to the Skirmisher and finish off the Warrior. If there were any issues with following the kill order you set up, take care of them now, before moving on to the harder pulls. Use any items or spells that mitigate Nature or Shadow damage before beginning the next fight.

As soon as the third bug dies, the second group comes at you. It contains Watcher Gashra, An Anub'ar Warrior and another Skirmisher. As before, crowd control the Watcher. If this is not possible make it your first target. When Gashra is crowd controlled take on the Skirmisher first, to quickly eliminate one source of damage and move on to the Warrior. These guys are pretty tough but with a whole party focusing on them they go down pretty quickly. Like Silthik, Watcher Gashra can use Infected Bite and Web Wrap to make things interesting. Remember to remove Web Wrap as soon as a party member becomes afflicted. Gashra also uses Enrage. This increases her attacking speed by 300%, but reduces the damage dealt by 50%. When Gashra is Enraged, make sure your healer is ready to deal with the extra damage if needed. As before, once the second group is defeated, the third one comes.

This last group contains Watcher Narjil, an Anub'ar Warrior and an Anub'ar Shadowcaster. Control this last watcher and deal with the Shadowcaster, then Warrior, as you did before. Like its fellow Watchers, Narjil uses Infected Bite and Web Wrap but can also use Blinding Webs. Narjil shoots a sticky webbing into a target's eye, causing Blind for four seconds. Although the duration may seem short, it can be bad news if it happens at a critical time, especially if it delays a heal or a taunt. Once these go down, you have a moment as the boss readies its attack.

SCRAMBLE SOME EGGS

Here you see the first of the Nerubian Eggs you must destroy for the Don't Forget the Eggs quest. Everyone in the group who has the quest gets credit for them as long as they are nearby, so make sure you destroy them all after the battle.

KRIK'THIR THE GATEWATCHER

You don't really have any downtime before facing the boss, so any abilities which help regenerate health and mana are useful here. Krik'thir comes at you with some pretty nasty abilities. If you don't have to be within melee range, stay back. Krik'thir casts Curse of Fatigue which is an area of effect curse dealing Shadow damage and slowing movement speed, as well as attack and casting speed. Be sure to remove this whenever possible. The boss also uses Mind Flay quite liberally, dealing Shadow damage and reducing movement speed.

As if worrying about the Gatewatcher weren't enough to keep you busy, he also summons a troop of Skittering Infectors and Skittering Swarmers. These are non-elite foes, but there are a lot of them. As soon as they converge on your group, use area of effect damage to take them out as quickly as possible. The Infectors have an area of effect Nature damage ability, Acid Splash, while the Swarmers just try to overwhelm you with their numbers. Have the tank hold the attention of the boss, and as many of these little critters as she can handle while the rest of the group takes them down.

When Krik'thir reaches 10% health he goes into a Frenzy! This increases his attack speed by 50% and the damage he deals by 100%, so the change is quite significant. The Tank should use any damage mitigating abilities available and the healer must be ready to deal with this increase in damage. Once you have taken care of the Gatewatcher, you can move through the gate.

HADRONOX'S LAIR

Once you have passed through the gate, go forward across the ramp and down the web to the right to enter the Lair. Although it may not look it, the webbing is quite solid. Stop near the base of the ramp. Here you see a large Anub'ar Crusher, an Anub'ar Crypt Fiend, and a Anub'ar Champion in the center of this chamber. There are several creepy crawlies behind them walking down the stairs, so be careful when pulling these. Mark a definite kill order as it is very important here that everyone is on the same page.

Take out the Crypt Fiend first. It is easy to kill and can use Infected Wound, which increases the Physical damage taken, and Crushing Webs, which immobilize. Both of these abilities help out the other Anub'ar trying to kill you. Next, go for the Champion. It is also non-elite and can be taken down

quickly. When that is done, move onto the Crusher. This bug Smashes its target, inflicting a hefty slice of damage and knocks them up in the air. It also uses Frenzy, which increases its attack speed and damage output. This Anub'ar deals out a great deal of damage fairly quickly. Healers must be on their toes if everyone is to survive this fight.

Once you pull the original group of three, two similar groups spawn there. These groups can contain Anub'ar Necromancers also, which summon skeletons to fight. They don't last long and pose little threat unless your party is ailing. Kill these two groups as you did the first, then move back and wait for Hadronox to move up to the center. Notice that hordes of non-elite Anub'ar are swarming toward the boss. Stay tucked back in the corner by the base of the ramp. A few of the non-elites may come over and attack, but as long as you don't venture down the webbing further, they are easily taken care of. Do not move down to engage Hadronox until she is in the center and has killed the majority of the critters attacking her.

HADRONOX

Even for seasoned adventurers, the sight of this giant spider can be daunting. Not only is she an arachnophobe's worst nightmare, you just watched her annihilate hordes of Anub'ar attackers with very little effort. Fear not, with a little caution and a lot of bravery, you can win your way past her.

Use any abilities or items that help mitigate Nature damage before beginning the fight. Send your tank in and have everyone who doesn't have to be in melee range stay out, and try not to stand too close together. Hadronox has a rather nasty Acid Cloud which deals Nature damage to anyone caught inside of it. She can also Pierce Armor, so make sure the healer keeps an eye on the tank for when this happens so that the sudden increase in damage doesn't catch the healer by surprise.

Being a giant spider has its advantages and even when you stay at range Hadronox can still get you with her Web Grab. This deals a hefty bit of damage, and pulls you toward her. This puts you right in range for her Leech Poison ability. This allows her to steal up to 500 health PER SECOND from each person in range and if she kills someone while using this ability she gains 10% health. Healers need to make sure everyone's health stays topped off during this fight to combat this danger. The longer this fight goes on, the more dangerous it is. Pile on the DPS to take her down as quickly as possible.

PASSAGE OF LOST FIENDS

Head through the doorway where you saw Hadronox emerge to reach the Passage of Lost Fiends. Swallow your fear and drop down the hole in the floor. Don't worry, it is safer than it looks. Probably.

THE BROOD PIT

At the end of the Passage is the Brood Pit. Here you see several non-aggressive Brood Keepers. There is no need to, but you can kill these for extra experience. Make sure you rest here and recuperate from the Hadronox fight before moving on. There are also more Nerubian Eggs if you still need to destroy some for the Don't Forget the Eggs quest.

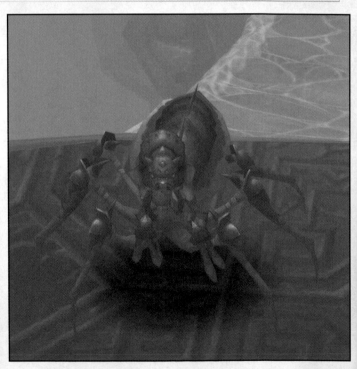

The path leads around through the gate where the traitor king, Anub'arak resides. Head through the gate and down the ramp to face his two Anub'ar Prime Guards. Crowd control one and pull the other to you. These Guards can Drain Power, decreasing your damage output by 1% per stack, but their real danger lies in their Mark of Darkness. This ability causes 500 damage per second, but also causes 1800 damage to everyone nearby if the target is healed. It is a good idea to keep non-melee classes well back because of this. After finishing off one, take out the other guard and prepare to face the ruler of Azjol-Nerub.

ANUB'ARAK

Anub'arak is a powerful foe, and it is important for everyone in your group to be on their toes during this fight. Before moving down to engage him, make sure everyone is fully buffed and at full health and mana. This is not a quick fight and everyone should be prepared to endure it.

Send in your tank and have him spin Anub'arak around so that the rest of the group is never in front of him. He has a Pound ability which deals massive, massive amounts of damage to everyone in front of him. The healer needs to be on the lookout for this ability and ready to heal the tank quickly.

At approximately 66%, 33%, and 15% health, Anub'arak burrows into the ground, becoming invulnerable for a short time, and a few things happen. He uses Impale, which fires spikes up through the floor, ignoring armor and damaging anyone nearby. While he is submerged, several Anub'ar Guardians, Darters, and Assassin's join the fight. The Darters and Assassins are quickly handled, as they are non-elites. Have the tank grab the elite Guardians and hold aggro on them as the group focuses fire on them. When Anub'arak reemerges the tank should pick him up, along with any of the remaining Anub'ar if possible.

Pick off any of these which are harrying the more vulnerable members of your party. As the fight progresses, more and more of these spawn at a faster rate.

You must also deal with Locust Swarm. Anub'arak summons swarms of locusts to come to his aid, dealing Nature damage to everyone. He also summons Carrion Beetles, but if you have successfully handled everything else, they are of little concern.

This fight is somewhat of an endurance fight. You must split your efforts between getting Anub'arak down and dealing with all of his minions. If you just deal with the minions, the fight never ends and if you focus on Anub'arak you are overwhelmed by his servants before you can fell him. Pay close attention and make good use of abilities that root, freeze, or otherwise control the lesser mobs. The entire group needs to pay attention not only to what they are doing, but also to whether other group members need help. Getting through this fight is only possible when everyone works together and performs their jobs well. With patience and perseverance you win the day.

Congratulations, you have cleared out Azjol-Nerub! By defeating Anub'arak you have dealt a severe blow to the Nerubian Scourge! Though their kind has not been annihilated, the work you have done here has set back their plans and put a dent in their growing armies.

DRAK'THARON KEEP

DUNGEON INFORMATION

Location:	Grizzly Hills
Faction:	Both
Suggested Levels:	74-76 (group of five)
Primary Enemies:	Humanoid, Undead, Beast
Damage Types:	Nature, Shadow
Time to Complete:	1-1.5 Hours

Drak'Tharon Keep is the fort Arthas resided in during his search for Frostmourne. Until recently, it belonged to the Drakkari Trolls, but for the most part, the Scourge have taken it over. A few groups of Drakkari still fight the Scourge inside, but theirs is a losing battle. The Scourge use the keep to hold the mountain pass between Grizzly Hills and Zul'Drak, and they can easily defend it against a force ten times the size of their own. While both sides are distracted a small party may be able to make their way inside, dealing a blow to both enemies.

WHO TO BRING

Drak'Tharon Keep is a challenging dungeon, requiring players to communicate well and work together to survive. A well balanced group offers the most advantages here, but you can certainly be flexible with your group makeup. As with most dungeons, you need a tank, a dedicated healer, and some damage dealers. Also, crowd control is always helpful, and absolutely vital in certain areas. Any of the tanking classes should be able to handle the minions here fairly easily as long as the healer is on his or her toes, and the boss fights, while challenging, can be handled by any good tank as well.

Next to a tank, having a great healer is most important to a group daring to brave Drak'Tharon. While this is generally a good rule for any fight, the high damage dealers inside make this especially necessary. For these encounters, having a back up healer makes things a bit easier also.

There are several groups that contain multiple enemies, so some form of crowd control is vital. Classes that can provide crowd control, whether it is the form of a trap, Sap, Polymorph or anything else, and can dish out the damage are most desirable. Because the majority of the foes here are undead, a Priest's Shackle is highly useful, and there are many fights that a Mage's Polymorph can help with.

GETTING TO DRAK'THARON KEEP

Drak'Tharon Keep is located in the northwestern part of Grizzly Hills, on the border of Zul'Drak. To reach it, Horde characters should travel north from Conquest Hold in Grizzly Hills while Alliance characters can most easily reach it by traveling northwest from Amberpine Lodge. Both factions can travel south from Light's Breach in Zul'Drak to reach the keep as well.

THE ENEMY GARRISON

BOSSES

Trollgore	76 Elite
Novos the Summoner	76 Elite
King Dred	76 Elite
The Prophet Tharon'ja	76 Elite

TROOPS

Crystal Handler	75 Elite
Notes: Flash of Darkness (Shadow damage)	
Darkweb Hatchling	74
Notes: Small spiders, dangerous in large numbers	
Darkweb Recluse	75 Elite
Notes: Poison Spit (Nature damage), Encasing Webs(increases time between attacks and casting speed by 100%)	
Drakkari Bat	75
Notes: Dangerous in a colony	
Drakkari Commander	75-76 Elite
Notes: Whirlwind,Battle Shout, Frenzy	
Drakkari Guardian	75-76 Elite
Notes: Hamstring, Shield Bash, Heal	
Drakkari Gutripper	74-75 Elite
Notes: Gut Rip (reduces stamina by 15% for 6 seconds)	
Drakkari Raptor Mount	75
Notes: Sharp teeth	
Drakkari Scytheclaw	74 Elite
Notes: Rend	
Drakkari Shaman	75 Elite
Notes: Lightning Bolt, Chain Heal	
Fetid Troll Corpse	74
Notes: Physical attack	
Flesheating Ghoul	74-75 Elite
Notes: Pierce Armor, Frenzy	
Ghoul Tormentor	72-73 Elite
Notes: Cleave, Flesh Rot	
Hulking Corpse	74 Elite
Notes: Strong Physical Attack	
Risen Drakkari Bat Rider	76 Elite
Notes: Curse of Blood (Increases damage taken by up to 500 for 8 seconds), Impale	
Risen Drakkari Death Knight	76 Elite
Notes: Icy Touch, Fear (single target), Deafening Roar	
Risen Drakkari Handler	75 Elite
Notes: Hooked Net (root), Backhand (stun), Shoot	
Risen Drakkari Soulmage	74 Elite
Notes: Shadow Blast, Blood Siphon (steals health), Void Zone (Shadow damage)	
Risen Drakkari Warrior	74-75 Elite
Notes: Crush Armor, Ghost Strike (Physical damage)	
Risen Shadowcaster	75 Elite
Notes: Shadow Bolt	
Scourge Brute	76 Elite
Notes: Knockdown, Mortal Strike, Dark Weapon (Shadow damage)	
Scourge Reanimator	74-75 Elite
Notes: Cripple (reduces strength and movement speed by 50% and increases time between attacks), Frostbolt, Unholy Frenzy (Increases an ally's attack speed by 35% for 15 seconds, but also deals Shadow damage to that ally)	
Wretched Belcher	74-75 Elite
Notes: Disease Cloud, Bile Vomit (Disease - Nature damage over time), Cleave	

QUESTS

CLEANSING DRAK'THARON

Faction	Both
Quest Level	73 to obtain
Quest Giver	Image of Drakuru
Goal	Use Drakuru's Elixir at his brazier inside of Drak'Tharon. This requires 5 Enduring Mojo.
Experience Gained	31,450
Rewards	Shroud of Temptation, Enticing Sabatons, Shackles of Dark Whispers, Shoulders of the Seducer

Drakuru needs your help to drive the Scourge from Drak'Tharon. To summon him you need to collect five Enduring Mojo from the Drakkari survivors within the keep. To do this, free the Darkweb Victims in the Draknid Lair and defeat them to collect the Mojo. Use it to summon Drakuru once you reach the top of the keep. You must complete Voices From the Dust to obtain this quest.

SEARCH AND RESCUE

Faction	Both
Quest Level	72 to obtain
Quest Giver	Mack Fearsen
Goal	Enter Drak'Tharon Keep and find out what has become of Kurzel.
Experience Gained	20,750
Rewards	Kurzel's Angst, Kurzel's Rage, Kurzel's Warband

Mack is sure Kurzel has stubbornly went off on her own to investigate the keep. Enter Drak'Tharon and make your way to the Draknid Lair. Once you have eliminated the spiders, free the Darkweb victims until you find Kurzel. You must complete Seared Scourge to obtain this quest.

HEAD GAMES

Faction	Both
Quest Level	72 to obtain
Quest Giver	Kurzel
Goal	Use Kurzel's Blouse Scrap in the remains of Novos the Summoner, then take the Ichor Stained Cloth back to Mack in Granite Springs.
Experience Gained	41,500
Rewards	Shameful Cuffs, Scorned Bands, Accused Wristguards, or Disavowed Bracers.

Once you've freed Kurzel from the Darkwebs in the Draknid Lair, she asks for your help in teaching Mack a lesson. Kurzel isn't pleased that Mack and the boys let her wander off to Drak'Tharon on her own and wants you to take a scrap of her blouse and rub it in the ichors staining the floor after you destroy Novos the Summoner. Return this scrap to Mack to make him feel guilty. You must complete Search and Rescue to obtain this quest.

The last group in this hallway at first appears to only consist of two Risen Drakkari Warriors, but as you approach them they do the smart thing and get backup, another Warrior and a Soulmage. As a group of four undead, it gets a little difficult if you don't have any way to crowd control them, so be sure to have a kill order established and allow the tank to get sufficient threat before the rest of the group joins in.

THE WARLORD'S TERRACE

The next room is all about timing your pulls. There are three groups of three Ghouls spread around the room, and two Wretched Belchers that path in circles around half of the room. The ghoul groups contain a random assortment of Flesheating Ghouls and Ghoul Tormenters. Each of Wretched Belchers patrols in a circle around half of the room. Your best bet is to wait until both Wretched Belchers are clear of the first group of ghouls and pull them to you, out of the room. The Ghouls aren't too challenging one on one, but as a group they can be really be troublesome. Try to Shackle or Trap one away from the group so that there is less damage to heal through. If this isn't an option, make sure that the tank has sufficient threat before you start blasting away. These Scourge can really tear into soft juicy caster flesh!

Next, wait for the Wretched Belcher that patrols closest to the door to be away from the other groups and pull it. This large mass of nightmare has a highly damaging Cleave, so make sure everyone that doesn't need to be close to it stays back. It also has a tendency to spew Bile Vomit on anyone nearby, which causes Nature damage over time, and is pretty gross besides. You want to take on only one of these at a time. If you should accidentally pull two, try to shackle one and pull the other back down the steps into the hallway you just cleared. The Wretched Belcher that patrols around the other half of the room walks around the remaining two groups of ghouls, so pull the closest group of ghouls while he is near the far group. Then you pull the remaining Wretched Belcher when he is near the door, followed by the last group of ghouls to safely clear the room.

TROLLGORE

Trollgore can be found at the top of the stairs fighting off groups of three smaller trolls that you can see fly in from somewhere in Zul'Drak. This continues throughout the fight, as three trolls fly in and start attacking Trollgore randomly. Trollgore has an area of effect attack that instantly kills the trolls attacking him, and hurts any players in range. This attack is followed by more area of effect damage in Corpse Explosions, which he uses on the now-dead trolls nearby.

Your healer must be on his or her toes since Trollgore dishes out so much party-wide damage. It might not seem like a significant amount at first, but Trollgore has Consume, a stacking buff that increases all of his damage done by 2% every time he cannibalizes a corpse with it. He can use this on either the Trolls that rush in to attack him, or on player corpses nearby. Not only does he hit the tank harder as the fight drags on, his AoE attacks hit everyone else harder as well. His damage buff is time based rather than health percentage based, so the faster you can kill him the easier it is to collect your loot.

DRAKNID LAIR

The next room is home to some creepy crawlies. As you approach you notice a few tiny, non-elite Darkweb Hatchlings running back and forth in the room, and two groups of elite Darkweb Recluses standing around. There is a group of two Recluses immediately to the left upon entering the room, and another group of three to the right. The small Hatchlings are not much of a threat, so don't be too worried about accidentally pulling them with the big spiders. If you do happen to pull a mixed group, kill the non-elites first.

The Darkweb Recluses have a nasty Poison Spit which deals Nature damage and, being spiders, they like to try to catch you with Encasing Web which increases your casting time and time between attacks by 100%. If these tricks fail to do you in the Recluses attempt to run back to their nest once they reach anywhere between fifty to twenty percent health. If they manage to get there before you kill them, they return with four more of the Hatchlings. Be sure to mark the elites for a specific attack order because you don't want to have to deal with two or more of them running away and bringing back friends. Be ready to use any abilities or spells you can to slow them down or stop them in their tracks. Even though the Hatchlings don't hit too hard on their own, having eight of them running around can cause some trouble!

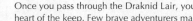

FREE THE VICTIMS!

The Draknid Lair contains more than the spiders you faced, it also contains still wriggling Darkweb Victims! Most of these web casings contain a Drakkari Guardian, but one of them is the prison of Kurzel, the female orc you need to find for the quest Search and Rescue. Once you free Kurzel and talk to her, she starts the quest Head Games that requires you to use Kurzel's Blouse Scrap on the corpse of Novos the Summoner in the next room.

Slaying the unfortunate Drakkari Guardians lets you gather the Enduring Mojo you need for the Cleansing Drak'Tharon quest as well. You can also get this from other Drakkari who have not yet been touched by the Scourge.

TEMPLE OF THE FORGOTTEN

Once you pass through the Draknid Lair, you are well on your way into the inner heart of the keep. Few brave adventurers make it this far. Sharpen your weapons and ready your spells as you venture into the Temple of the Forgotten.

NOVOS THE SUMMONER

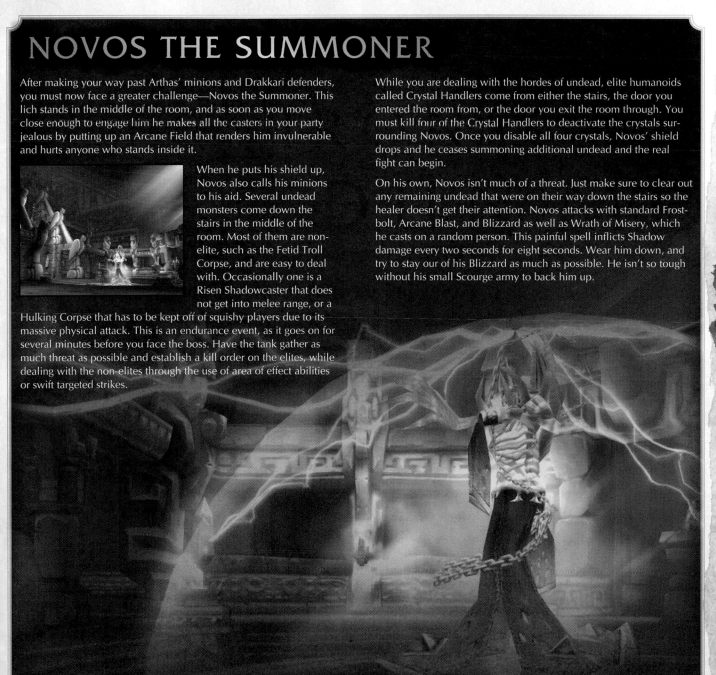

After making your way past Arthas' minions and Drakkari defenders, you must now face a greater challenge—Novos the Summoner. This lich stands in the middle of the room, and as soon as you move close enough to engage him he makes all the casters in your party jealous by putting up an Arcane Field that renders him invulnerable and hurts anyone who stands inside it.

When he puts his shield up, Novos also calls his minions to his aid. Several undead monsters come down the stairs in the middle of the room. Most of them are non-elite, such as the Fetid Troll Corpse, and are easy to deal with. Occasionally one is a Risen Shadowcaster that does not get into melee range, or a Hulking Corpse that has to be kept off of squishy players due to its massive physical attack. This is an endurance event, as it goes on for several minutes before you face the boss. Have the tank gather as much threat as possible and establish a kill order on the elites, while dealing with the non-elites through the use of area of effect abilities or swift targeted strikes.

While you are dealing with the hordes of undead, elite humanoids called Crystal Handlers come from either the stairs, the door you entered the room from, or the door you exit the room through. You must kill four of the Crystal Handlers to deactivate the crystals surrounding Novos. Once you disable all four crystals, Novos' shield drops and he ceases summoning additional undead and the real fight can begin.

On his own, Novos isn't much of a threat. Just make sure to clear out any remaining undead that were on their way down the stairs so the healer doesn't get their attention. Novos attacks with standard Frostbolt, Arcane Blast, and Blizzard as well as Wrath of Misery, which he casts on a random person. This painful spell inflicts Shadow damage every two seconds for eight seconds. Wear him down, and try to stay out of his Blizzard as much as possible. He isn't so tough without his small Scourge army to back him up.

AVIARY

Now that you have defeated Novos, you are ready to proceed deeper into the keep. In the Aviary you find a large group of non-elite Drakkari Bats and one elite Risen Drakkari Bat Rider in the middle of them. The rider can be quite annoying with strong melee attacks and Curse of Blood which increases the amount of damage you take for eight seconds. Have your tank grab the attention of the Bat Rider and give them enough time to gain threat on the Bats as well. Once the tank has established a good amount of threat, have your DPS take out the Bats with area of effect abilities. Make sure the healer is keeping a close eye on health during this.

If your tank does not have the ability to tank multitudes of monsters at once, it is best to single target each of the mobs so casters don't pull hate and get killed by all the bats. They can be quite dangerous as a group.

RAPTOR PENS

The Aviary leads to the outdoor portion of the keep, where you are greeted by a Risen Drakkari Handler and his raptor pets—two Drakkari Gutrippers on either side of him, and when engaged he dismounts to let his Drakkari Raptor Mount join the battle. The handler attacks like a Hunter; he uses Hooked Net to keep the tank in place and runs a few steps away to begin shooting. You can use whatever crowd control you have available on him so the tank doesn't have to worry about tanking the three raptors and running around after the Handler. If this isn't an option, have your ranged DPS take him down first so you don't have to deal with his constant running and shooting.

The mount is non-elite, so take it out quickly before moving on to the Gutrippers. These monstrosities have strong melee attacks and can Gut Rip you, reducing your stamina by 15% for six seconds.

Watch Your Step

As you get further outdoors you approach the raptor pen which contains the next boss, a giant Devilsaur named King Dred, king of all the raptors in Drak'Tharon Keep. Be careful not to go near the pen because it does not block line of sight and the Drakkari Scytheclaws come after you if you get too close.

The next group is made up of two Risen Drakkari Handlers and mounts. Crowd control at least one of the Handlers if possible and eliminate the non-elite mounts quickly. Once this is done, carefully pull the other raptors out of the pen with the boss. If you aren't careful you can accidentally pull him as well, so only pull the raptors as he walks away. These Drakkari Scytheclaws are similar to the other raptors you have already put down. Watch out for their nasty Rend ability and be ready to heal through it. Once you have cleared these guys out, you are ready to face King Dred.

KING DRED

The next boss can be skipped by carefully moving around his pen if you desire, but why would you want to pass up a great fight?! This giant Devilsaur hits moderately hard and also causes multiple bleeds on his target. When you see the emote, "King Dred lashes out wildly," be ready for his special moves. He uses Mangling Slash, which does damage and increase the damage taken from bleeds by 125%, in conjunction with Grievous Bite. This bleed move can be devastating because it deals a great amount of damage every two seconds until the target is fully healed. Healers have to really be on the look out for this bleed effect. The massive Devilsaur also uses Piercing Slash to deal damage and reduce its target's armor by 75%, severely upping the Devilsaur's damage output. Also, be on the look out for King Dred to "Raise his claw menacingly." This gives you a split second warning that he is going to attack three times in rapid succession. If your healer is unprepared for this your tank can go down unexpectedly and end the battle right then and there.

King Dred also has Bellowing Roar, a fear that affects all enemies within 35 yards for four seconds, so be prepared. Be aware of raptors in the rear of the pen, and pull the boss as far away as you can, near the pen opening, so no one gets feared into them. Having a Shaman to lay down a Tremor Totem is a plus on this boss, but not completely necessary.

With King Dred dealt with you head up the stairs that are parallel to the raptor pen. Here you find two Drakkari Guardians fighting a Scourge Brute and a Risen Drakkari Warrior. If you want to let them do the work for you, wait until they are at about half health before pulling them, as that is about the point their health goes back up. There is one Drakkari Shaman in the group, and it uses Chain Heal on its allies so either crowd control it or kill it first. The next group consists of two Drakkari Guardians and two Drakkari Shamans, so make sure to keep them from healing each other. The Shamans can cast Lightning Bolt, but this heal is their main danger, since it prolongs the fight.

Next you face a lone troll Death Knight. His main abilities are Icy Touch and Fear. Make sure to pull him away from the groups behind him so no one gets Feared into them. He hits harder than the troll warriors, but not by much. Since he is a single target, concentrate all of your fire on him and take him out. Next is a lone Drakkari Commander. He buffs himself with Battle Shout and has a nasty Whirlwind attack which everyone but the tank needs to avoid. Be sure to rest up if necessary before tackling the next few pulls.

To the left is a group of two Drakkari Shaman and two Drakkari Guardians standing watch, with two more Guardians fighting Risen Drakkari Warriors nearby. This is a tricky pull because sometimes the Guardians and Risen Drakkari Warriors join the fight several seconds after you engage the group of Shamans and Guardians, making it a group of eight enemies to deal with. Establish a kill order and use whatever crowd control is available to you, making sure to stop the Shamans from healing as much as possible. This is by far the most challenging fight you face outside of a boss battle.

Up the stairs you have to face two Risen Drakkari Death Knights together. Double fears can cause a lot of trouble. Pull these guys back to the stairs so if you get feared you are unlikely to run into another group. Make sure everyone stays on the same target and doesn't pass the tank in threat in case he or she gets the fear. There is a single patrolling Risen Drakkari Death Knight, so be careful not to pull him with the first two. Take out the patrol and the following pair of Risen Drakkari Death Knights at the base of the next staircase and you are home free to the final boss of Drak'Tharon Keep.

THE PROPHET THARON'JA

This skeletal dragon is looking for some flesh to cover his bones, and yours looks good to him! Once your are ready, walk up this last set of stairs and have your tank engage the Prophet while the rest of the group takes up positions around him. Once the tank has established sufficient threat, throw everything you've got at Tharon'ja.

Several times throughout the fight he turns everyone in the party into skeletons, giving you a new set of skills. They include Touch of Life, which steals health from the target, with a five second cooldown, Bone Armor, which absorbs damage for ten seconds, with a ten second cooldown, Taunt; and Slaying Strike, which does a good amount of damage. The tank should still have Tharon'ja's attention despite the transition, so everyone else can focus on using Slaying Strike, including your healer. Tharon'ja also drops Poison Clouds. As soon as you see one drop near you, immediately move out of the way. Don't wait to finish the move or spell you are casting. Everyone should keep up Bone Armor in order to absorb the first bit of damage from the Poison Cloud. If you take damage as the tank or from the Poison Clouds, use Touch of Life. It is on a short cool down, so you cannot spam it and should save it for when you do take some damage. After a few minutes, Tharon'ja casts Return Flesh on you which returns the party to their normal selves.

The transformation stuns you for a few seconds, which is another reason you need to get out of the Poison Clouds as quickly as you can. With some bad luck it is possible that a Poison Cloud appears on top of you just before a transformation and kills you before you can get out. If this happens to your tank or your only healer, then it is difficult to salvage the battle.

Tharon'ja also shoots an Eye Beam at a random person that does a decent amount of damage, but is easily survivable. He also gives you the Curse of Life, which deals Shadow damage until you are at 50% of your health, as well as damaging you with Lightning Breath and Shadow Volley.

By paying close attention to the battle you can survive everything the boss throws at you and his loot is yours!

Congratulations, you have now cleared Drak'Tharon Keep!

CLEANSING DRAK'THARON

If you have collected the Enduring Mojo for the Cleansing Drak' Tharon quest, you can use it here to summon Drakuru.

In addition to the large scale PvP offered by the battlegrounds, World of Warcraft also offers smaller, more organized PvP in the form of Arena Matches. In Arena play, preformed teams pit their skills against other similarly rated teams for honor, glory, and much more tangible rewards. You must be level 80 to participate in ranked Arena Matches, but players of lower level can still have fun in practice matches called Skirmishes. To get started all you need is at least one willing partner.

Making a Team

Forming an Arena Team is quick and easy, but there are a couple of things to consider before you form your team. First, you need to decide which size of team you wish to make. If you and one of your friends are always playing at the same time, then a 2v2 team would be best for you. If you've got a larger group of committed friends, then go for a 5v5 team. You can start, or join, more than one size of team, but you can only be on one team of each size. For instance, you can have your own 2v2, 3v3, and 5v5 teams if you want, but you can't be on two different 2v2 teams.

The second thing you need to do is decide on a name. You want to pick a name that is descriptive, inspiring, or even just amusing, but be sure to exercise the same good judgment with your team name as you would a character name. Your team name is going to stay with you for quite some time, so select a name that you really like, and remember than an offensive one may land you in trouble. Once you have made these decisions, you are ready to make your team. Visit one of the Arena Promoters to create your team Charter. You can find Arena Organizers in the following locations:

Arena Organizer	Location	Zone
"King Dond"	The Ring of Trials	Nagrand
Steamwheedle Sam	Circle of Blood	Blade's Edge Mountains
Bip Nigstrom	Gadgetzan	Tanaris
"Baroness" Llana, Kanika Goldwell	Sewers	Dalaran
Greela "The Grunt" Crankchain	The Ring of Valor	Orgrimmar

Team charters aren't overly expensive, but they do take some startup gold. The cost is well worth it for the chance at glory, and some nice pieces of equipment, that participating in the arena can earn you.

Team	Cost
2v2	80g
3v3	120g
5v5	200g

Once you have purchased your Team Charter, you must select your team colors and logo. Once chosen, these are displayed on your PvP tab and in the World of Warcraft Armory listing for Arena Teams, as well as on your flag during battles, so it is important that you choose something you are happy showing off to other players.

To Battle!

Once you are ready, speak to an Arena Battlemaster, located near arenas and in major cities, to join a queue. Select which type of match you want to queue up for and then select whether you are looking for a Skirmish or a Ranked Match. Skirmishes are great, especially for new teams. They give you the opportunity to fight in the arena without impacting your Team Standing. Of course, they also don't earn you any Arena Points, but they are good practice for honing your arena skills. If your team is new to PvP, or even just new to playing together, spending some time skirmishing can really pay off.

PATIENCE IS A VIRTUE...

If you belong to more than one arena team, it is possible to queue up for more than one type of match at the same time. While this may cut down on the time you have to wait to find a match, remember that if you decline any match once it comes up, it counts as a loss. So, if two matches "pop" at once, you automatically lose the one you don't join, which negatively affects your Team Ranking. If you choose to take your chances like this, be sure to always leave the remaining queue as soon as you accept a match.

PREPARATION

Regardless of the arena, every match starts with the opposing teams in designated areas. All existing buffs disappear, along with any conjured items. This ensures that a team doesn't have any unfair advantages, like Soulstones, or extra buffs, from players not on their team. Pets are dismissed when you enter the arena, but you can summon them back before the battle begins. Any spells or abilities that have less than a fifteen minute cooldown timer are reset, so that they are ready to be used in the upcoming contest. Spells and abilities with longer cooldowns cannot be used in the arena at all.

The only consumables allowed are conjured items and bandages, so make sure you are well prepared before the battle begins. Everyone's health and mana is set to full and each team has about one minute to use any spells or abilities they desire at no mana, rage, energy, soul shard, or runic cost. This should be more than enough time for everyone to prepare for the upcoming battle!

What to Wear

During the preparation time you can change your armor as much as you like, but once the battle begins you are not allowed to equip or unequip any items besides your weapons, so make sure you start the battle fully dressed!

THE FIGHT

Once the preparation countdown expires the battle begins! Though your tactics change depending on factors such as location, class, skill, and opponents, your goal never does. You must be the last challenger standing. Whether you are playing in a 2v2 match or a 5v5, the team with at least one member alive when all the opponents are dead is the undisputed victor.

There is no time limit on arena matches so some are over fairly quickly, while others can lock two teams in intense battle for quite some time. Because matches are made based on your team's ranking, you usually find yourself facing teams of equal ability. This means that most battles are challenging and exciting and take all your attention and skill to win.

I See You!

Each arena is equipped with power ups lasting fifteen seconds which allow you to see stealthed or invisible opponents. This gives you some defense against players who may try to avoid a fight by hiding. Using one of these power ups increases the damage you take by 5%.

The Arenas

Each arena presents its own unique challenges and when you sign up for a match, you can never be sure which arena you may find yourself in. This ensures that a team can't just do battle in their favorite arena and must instead make their strategy flexible enough for any of the locations!

RUINS OF LORDAERON

Lordaeron was once a shining Alliance capital, its streets bustling with trade and travelers. Hammered into haunted ruins by the Scourge, its bleak walls and forgotten paths provide an excellent place for teams to pit their wills against one another.

Though mostly flat, this medium size arena has a few distinguishing features that teams can use to their advantage. Each team begins in the Pit. If you need to eat, drink, or bandage, ducking around the doorway of the Pit can often give you enough cover to take care of these tasks. On one side of the arena stands a small lonely graveyard. Most of the tombstones are too small to have any impact on the battle, but a few of them are large enough to cause Line of Sight (LoS) issues for you or the opposing team. Use them to provide some cover when facing enemies near the graveyard.

The most prominent, and perhaps most important feature, is the Coffin at the center of the arena. This raised coffin is surrounded by three pillars, all of which can affect LoS. Many battles in the Ruins center around controlling this feature. Holding the Coffin gives you a tactical advantage due to its raised position and pillars, but it also makes you a target. If you choose to try to control this position, make sure you are always ready and able to repel multiple attacks.

THE RING OF TRIALS

Don't let the rolling green hills of Nagrand lull you into a sense of safety. Though seemingly simple, The Ring of Trials is often home to some of the bloodiest contests in the Arena circuit.

This arena is very straightforward in appearance. It is round and flat, with teams starting on opposite sides of the circle. The center of the arena is a large open space that gives you plenty of room to maneuver, but no protection. Fighting in this space is often an all out war. Four sizeable pillars mark the edges of this open center area and winning teams learn to use them strategically. Support classes can position themselves behind a pillar to avoid ranged damage, coming out into the open only when necessary. Another common tactic has a team hiding behind the pillars, forcing the opposition to come to them, making it much easier to ambush them.

  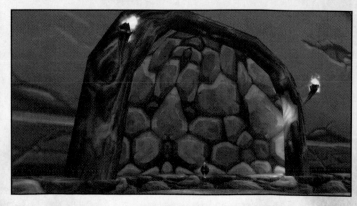

THE CIRCLE OF BLOOD

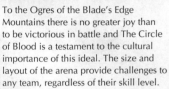

To the Ogres of the Blade's Edge Mountains there is no greater joy than to be victorious in battle and The Circle of Blood is a testament to the cultural importance of this ideal. The size and layout of the arena provide challenges to any team, regardless of their skill level.

This large arena is designed to give opposing teams a great deal of room in which to wage battle and interesting terrain in which to do it. The arena is roughly square in shape, with opposing teams starting on opposite sides. The size of the arena means that you have to move far from the starting pit before being in range to engage the enemy.

The battle area is bisected by a long bridge running the length of the arena which is accessed by ramps on each end. Many battles begin with a race to control this bridge. While it is always a good idea for your team to have a plan before the battle, the size and layout of this arena make it even more important for you to have a strategy in place. Decide before hand if you want to approach the bridge from the ramp closest to you, which gets you to the bridge quickly, or from the far ramp, which gives you a good look at what your opponent is up to.

While the bridge is usually considered the most important feature of the arena, strategically speaking, it is not the only one that gives you an advantage. On either side of the center of the bridge you can find a pillar. These pillars are favorite spots for ranged classes to hold. They offer a good view of the battlefield and offer some protection from attack. Even if you aren't on top, you can still use the pillars to break Line of Sight and give you a little breathing room if you are being attacked from range.

DALARAN SEWERS

The mages of Dalaran don't tolerate violence along the city's well-kept streets but just below them, in the city's underbelly, less reputable businesses flourish and you can always find a fight!

Each team starts in a large pipe above the arena floor. Once the battle starts a stream of water rushes out of the pipe, forcing you out into the center of the arena, so you had better be prepared! The arena consists of a large center platform which is surrounded by a grate. If you are knocked off of the platform, the only way you can get back is via the set of steps in the corner.

There are two large stacks of boxes on opposite corners of the platform which can cause Line of Sight issues. Be sure to keep these in mind when moving around the arena. Just to make things even more interesting, periodically the large pipes in the ceiling rain down a stream of water, blocking Line of Sight in the center of the arena! Your team must learn to work around this so that ranged attacks, or even heals, aren't interrupted when the water starts to flow.

THE RING OF VALOR

Located in Orgrimmar's Valley of Honor, the Ring of Valor has long stood empty, waiting for worthy challengers to pit their skills against one another as a roaring crowd cheers them on.

As the battle begins, two elevators rise up out of the floor of the arena, each bringing an opposing team to the fight. At only ten yards apart, you can easily see who you face before the spiked gates on the elevators drop and the fight starts. Once the battle commences, the elevators become just part of the arena floor, and do not move for the duration of the battle.

At four points along the oval of the arena a pillar periodically raises and lowers. You can ride the pillar up and away from melee attacks, but remember that by doing this you may be hindering your own ability to attack. Also, a line of spikes juts up out of the floor between the elevators and the pillars at certain intervals. Before either of these two things happen, the gears on the walls begin to turn, so you have some warning before the pillars move or the spikes come into play.

TEAM RATING

Every team has a Team Rating. This rating reflects how experienced and skilled a team is and can change with each match. New arena teams start with a Rating of 1500. If you win a match your team's Rating goes up—lose a match and it goes down. How much your Rating changes depends on the Rating of the opposing team. For instance, losing to a team with a higher Team Rating doesn't lower your own rating quite as far as losing to an inferiorly rated team does. Similarly, winning against a lesser rated team nets you a smaller gain than triumphing over a team with a Rating higher than your own. Your Team Rating is used to match you against teams with similar ratings for arena bouts, so the better your team performs, the more challenging foes you are able to face.

ARENA POINTS

Though bragging rights are great, participating in the arena earns you more concrete rewards in the form of Arena Points. These points are calculated at the end of each week using your Team Rating. To be eligible to receive any Arena Points at all, your team must have participated in a minimum of ten matches, and individual players must have participated in at least 30% of the matches played to collect Arena Points. No matter how many Arena Teams you belong to, you can only collect Arena Points from one team each week. The amount of Points you receive is calculated from the team performance that gets you the most points. You can save up to 5,000 Arena Points if you choose to, and best of all, once earned you don't lose them unless you spend them.

Sometimes it is hard waiting until the end of the week to see how many Arena Points you have been awarded. This is where the Arena Calculator comes in. Accessed from the main World of Warcraft website, this calculator does all the heavy math for you and lets you know where you stand based on your Team Rating, as well as lets you plan on how active you should be in the arena to earn yourself the desired rewards.

AFTER THE BATTLE

After each contest, a Post Match Summary appears. It gives you information such as the time the match lasted, the players involved on each team, and the healing, damage, and killing blows performed by each player. It also lists the rating adjustment for each player. This gives you a clear idea of how your team, and your opponent, performed.

ARENA REWARDS

Arena Points are so important because they are the currency you need to purchase some of the best equipment available. Each arena season presents new rewards on which to spend your hard earned Arena Points! Many of the items are geared toward PvP play with stats like Resilience, but the epic gear is also loaded with stats to help in PvE situations as well. Arena Rewards are a great way for players who don't participate in raids to get awesome gear. In addition to equipment, excelling in the arena can also earn a team prestigious arena titles so that anyone who sees a player knows how good they are. Each season presents new and more powerful rewards for arena participation, so it is always a good idea to keep your team in practice!

Name	Extended Cost	Stats
Savage Gladiator's Waraxe	Honor: 3200, Arena: 175	Axe: Physical 237-440, 2.6, 130.2 Equip: Increases attack power by 66., +49 Stamina, Equip: Improves critical strike rating by 22., Equip: Improves your resilience rating by 22.
Savage Gladiator's Touch of Defeat	Honor: 3200, Arena: 175	Wand: Fire 318-591, 1.9, 239.2 Equip: Increases spell power by 28., +27 Stamina, +12 Intellect, Equip: Improves critical strike rating by 16., Equip: Improves your resilience rating by 16.
Savage Gladiator's Baton of Light	Honor: 3200, Arena: 175	Wand: Fire 318-591, 1.9, 239.2 Equip: Increases spell power by 28., +27 Stamina, +12 Intellect, +16 Spirit, Equip: Improves your resilience rating by 16.
Savage Gladiator's War Edge	Honor: 3200, Arena: 175	Thrown: Physical 178-267, 1.9, 117.1 Equip: Increases attack power by 48., +36 Stamina, Equip: Improves critical strike rating by 16., Equip: Improves your resilience rating by 16.
Savage Gladiator's Idol of Steadfastness	Honor: 3200, Arena: 175	Idol: Your Moonfire spell grants spell power.
Savage Gladiator's Idol of Tenacity	Honor: 3200, Arena: 175	Idol: Increases the spell power of the final healing value of your Lifebloom.
Savage Gladiator's Totem of Indomitability	Honor: 3200, Arena: 175	Totem: Your Lava Lash ability also grants attack power.
Savage Gladiator's Totem of Survival	Honor: 3200, Arena: 175	Totem: Your Shock spells grant spell power.
Savage Gladiator's Totem of the Third Wind	Honor: 3200, Arena: 175	Totem: Increases spell power of Lesser Healing Wave.
Savage Gladiator's Libram of Justice	Honor: 3200, Arena: 175	Libram: Increases spell power of Flash of Light.
Savage Gladiator's Piercing Touch	Honor: 3200, Arena: 175	Wand: Fire 318-591, 1.9, 239.2 Equip: Increases spell power by 28., +27 Stamina, +12 Intellect, Equip: Improves your resilience rating by 16., Increases your spell penetration.
Savage Gladiator's Idol of Resolve	Honor: 3200, Arena: 175	Idol: Your Mangle ability also grants you attack power.
Savage Gladiator's Libram of Fortitude	Honor: 3200, Arena: 175	Libram: Your Crusader Strike ability also grants you attack power.
Savage Gladiator's Sigil of Strife	Honor: 3200, Arena: 175	Sigil: Your Plague Strike ability also grants you attack power.
Hateful Gladiator's Waraxe	Honor: 3200, Arena: 350	Axe: Physical 261-485, 2.6, 143.5 Equip: Increases attack power by 76., +58 Stamina, Equip: Improves critical strike rating by 26., Equip: Improves your resilience rating by 25.
Hateful Gladiator's Baton of Light	Honor: 3200, Arena: 350	Wand: Fire 350-651, 1.9, 263.4 Equip: Increases spell power by 33., +31 Stamina, +13 Intellect, +19 Spirit, Equip: Improves your resilience rating by 18.
Hateful Gladiator's Touch of Defeat	Honor: 3200, Arena: 350	Wand: Fire 350-651, 1.9, 263.4 Equip: Increases spell power by 33., +31 Stamina, +13 Intellect, Equip: Improves critical strike rating by 19., Equip: Improves your resilience rating by 18.
Hateful Gladiator's War Edge	Honor: 3200, Arena: 350	Thrown: Physical 196-295, 1.9, 129.2 Equip: Increases attack power by 56., +42 Stamina, Equip: Improves critical strike rating by 18., Equip: Improves your resilience rating by 18.
Hateful Gladiator's Idol of Tenacity	Honor: 3200, Arena: 350	Idol: Increases the spell power of the final healing value of your Lifebloom.
LK Arena 4 Druid Healer Relic	Honor: 3200, Arena: 350	Idol: Increases the spell power of the final healing value of your Lifebloom.
Hateful Gladiator's Totem of Survival	Honor: 3200, Arena: 350	Totem: Your Shock spells grant spell power.
Hateful Gladiator's Libram of Justice	Honor: 3200, Arena: 350	Libram: Increases spell power of Flash of Light.

Name	Extended Cost	Stats
Hateful Gladiator's Sigil of Strife	Honor: 3200, Arena: 350	Sigil: Your Plague Strike ability also grants you attack power.
Hateful Gladiator's Piercing Touch	Honor: 3200, Arena: 350	Wand: Fire 350-651, 1.9, 263.4 Equip: Increases spell power by 33., +31 Stamina, +13 Intellect, Equip: Improves your resilience rating by 18., Increases your spell penetration.
Hateful Gladiator's Idol of Steadfastness	Honor: 3200, Arena: 350	Idol: Your Moonfire spell grants spell power.
Hateful Gladiator's Idol of Resolve	Honor: 3200, Arena: 350	Idol: Your Mangle ability also grants you attack power.
Hateful Gladiator's Totem of the Third Wind	Honor: 3200, Arena: 350	Totem: Increases spell power of Lesser Healing Wave.
Hateful Gladiator's Totem of Indomitability	Honor: 3200, Arena: 350	Totem: Your Lava Lash ability also grants you attack power.
Hateful Gladiator's Libram of Fortitude	Honor: 3200, Arena: 350	Libram: Your Crusader Strike ability also grants you attack power .
Savage Gladiator's Plate Gauntlets	Honor: 3600, Arena: 200	Plate: 1354, Socket Bonus: +4 Critical Strike Rating, Socket: Blue, +50 Strength, +85 Stamina, Equip: Improves critical strike rating by 23., Equip: Improves your resilience rating by 30., Hamstring Rage cost reduced.
Savage Gladiator's Scaled Gauntlets	Honor: 3600, Arena: 200	Plate: 1354, Socket Bonus: +4 Critical Strike Rating, Socket: Blue, +50 Strength, +85 Stamina, Equip: Improves critical strike rating by 23., Equip: Improves your resilience rating by 30., Increases the damage dealt by your Crusader Strike ability.
Savage Gladiator's Dreadplate Gauntlets	Honor: 3600, Arena: 200	Plate: 1354, Socket Bonus: +4 Critical Strike Rating, Socket: Blue, +50 Strength, +85 Stamina, Equip: Improves critical strike rating by 23., Equip: Improves your resilience rating by 30., Reduces the cooldown of your Strangulate.
Savage Gladiator's Ornamented Gloves	Honor: 3600, Arena: 200	Plate: 1354, Socket Bonus: +2 mana per 5 sec., Socket: Blue, +66 Stamina, +28 Intellect, Equip: Increases spell power by 59., Equip: Improves critical strike rating by 22., Equip: Improves your resilience rating by 30., Increases the critical effect chance of your Flash of Light %.
Savage Gladiator's Ringmail Gauntlets	Honor: 3600, Arena: 200	Mail: 758, Socket Bonus: +2 mana per 5 sec., Socket: Blue, +66 Stamina, +28 Intellect, Equip: Increases spell power by 59., Equip: Restores 9 mana per 5 sec., Equip: Improves your resilience rating by 30., Improves the range of all Shock spells yards.
Savage Gladiator's Mail Gauntlets	Honor: 3600, Arena: 200	Mail: 758, Socket Bonus: +2 mana per 5 sec., Socket: Blue, +66 Stamina, +28 Intellect, Equip: Increases spell power by 59., Equip: Improves critical strike rating by 22., Equip: Improves your resilience rating by 30., Improves the range of all Shock spells yards.
Savage Gladiator's Linked Gauntlets	Honor: 3600, Arena: 200	Mail: 758, Socket Bonus: +4 Critical Strike Rating, Socket: Blue, Equip: Increases attack power by 60., +39 Agility, +66 Stamina, +21 Intellect, Equip: Improves critical strike rating by 30., Equip: Improves your resilience rating by 30., Improves the range of all Shock spells yards.
Savage Gladiator's Chain Gauntlets	Honor: 3600, Arena: 200	Mail: 758, Socket Bonus: +4 Critical Strike Rating, Socket: Blue, Equip: Increases attack power by 60., +39 Agility, +66 Stamina, +21 Intellect, Equip: Improves critical strike rating by 30., Equip: Improves your resilience rating by 30., Reduces the cooldown of your Tranquilizing Shot.
Savage Gladiator's Kodohide Gloves	Honor: 3600, Arena: 200	Leather: 341, Socket Bonus: +4 Spirit, Socket: Blue, Equip: Increases spell power by 59., +66 Stamina, +28 Intellect, +22 Spirit, Equip: Improves your resilience rating by 30., Reduces the cast time of your Cyclone spell.

Name	Extended Cost	Stats
Savage Gladiator's Wyrmhide Gloves	Honor: 3600, Arena: 200	Leather: 341, Socket Bonus: +4 Spirit, Socket: Blue, Equip: Increases spell power by 59., +66 Stamina, +28 Intellect, Equip: Improves critical strike rating by 22., Equip: Improves your resilience rating by 30., Reduces the cast time of your Cyclone spell.
Savage Gladiator's Chopper	Honor: 3600, Arena: 200	Axe: Physical 237-440, 2.6, 130.2 Equip: Increases attack power by 66., +49 Stamina, Equip: Improves critical strike rating by 22., Equip: Improves your resilience rating by 22.
Savage Gladiator's Hacker	Honor: 3600, Arena: 200	Axe: Physical 136-254, 1.5, 130 Equip: Increases attack power by 66., +49 Stamina, Equip: Improves critical strike rating by 22., Equip: Improves your resilience rating by 22.
Savage Gladiator's Mutilator	Honor: 3600, Arena: 200	Dagger: Physical 164-305, 1.8, 130.3 Equip: Increases attack power by 66., +49 Stamina, Equip: Improves critical strike rating by 22., Equip: Improves your resilience rating by 22.
Savage Gladiator's Shiv	Honor: 3600, Arena: 200	Dagger: Physical 127-237, 1.4, 130 Equip: Increases attack power by 66., +49 Stamina, Equip: Improves critical strike rating by 22., Equip: Improves your resilience rating by 22.
Savage Gladiator's Left Ripper	Honor: 3600, Arena: 200	Fist Weapon: Physical 136-254, 1.5, 130 Equip: Increases attack power by 66., +49 Stamina, Equip: Improves critical strike rating by 22., Equip: Improves your resilience rating by 22.
Savage Gladiator's Bonecracker	Honor: 3600, Arena: 200	Mace: Physical 136-254, 1.5, 130 Equip: Increases attack power by 66., +49 Stamina, Equip: Improves critical strike rating by 22., Equip: Improves your resilience rating by 22.
Savage Gladiator's Quickblade	Honor: 3600, Arena: 200	Sword: Physical 136-254, 1.5, 130 Equip: Increases attack power by 66., +49 Stamina, Equip: Improves critical strike rating by 22., Equip: Improves your resilience rating by 22.
Savage Gladiator's Endgame	Honor: 3600, Arena: 200	Equip: Increases spell power by 50., +49 Stamina, +21 Intellect, Equip: Improves critical strike rating by 29., Equip: Improves your resilience rating by 28.
Savage Gladiator's Reprieve	Honor: 3600, Arena: 200	Equip: Increases spell power by 50., +49 Stamina, +21 Intellect, +29 Spirit, Equip: Improves your resilience rating by 28.
Savage Gladiator's Left Render	Honor: 3600, Arena: 200	Fist Weapon: Physical 237-440, 2.6, 130.2 Equip: Increases attack power by 66., +49 Stamina, Equip: Improves critical strike rating by 22., Equip: Improves your resilience rating by 22.
Savage Gladiator's Felweave Handguards	Honor: 3600, Arena: 200	Cloth: 181, Socket Bonus: +5 Spell Power, Socket: Blue, Equip: Increases spell power by 59., +66 Stamina, +28 Intellect, Equip: Improves critical strike rating by 22., Equip: Improves your resilience rating by 30., Gives you a chance to avoid interruption caused by damage while casting Fear.
Savage Gladiator's Silk Handguards	Honor: 3600, Arena: 200	Cloth: 181, Socket Bonus: +5 Spell Power, Socket: Blue, Equip: Increases spell power by 59., +66 Stamina, +28 Intellect, Equip: Improves critical strike rating by 22., Equip: Improves your resilience rating by 30., Gives you chance to avoid interruption caused by damage while casting Polymorph.
Savage Gladiator's Satin Gloves	Honor: 3600, Arena: 200	Cloth: 181, Socket Bonus: +5 Spell Power, Socket: Blue, Equip: Increases spell power by 59., +66 Stamina, +28 Intellect, Equip: Improves critical strike rating by 22., Equip: Improves your resilience rating by 30., Reduces the cooldown of your Psychic Scream ability.
Savage Gladiator's Mooncloth Gloves	Honor: 3600, Arena: 200	Cloth: 181, Socket Bonus: +4 Spirit, Socket: Blue, Equip: Increases spell power by 59., +66 Stamina, +28 Intellect, +22 Spirit, Equip: Improves your resilience rating by 30., Reduces the cooldown of your Psychic Scream ability.

Name	Extended Cost	Stats
Savage Gladiator's Dragonhide Gloves	Honor: 3600, Arena: 200	Leather: 341, Socket Bonus: +4 Critical Strike Rating, Socket: Blue, Equip: Increases attack power by 58., +50 Agility, +66 Stamina, Equip: Improves critical strike rating by 22., Equip: Improves your resilience rating by 30., Reduces the energy cost of your Maim.
Savage Gladiator's Leather Gloves	Honor: 3600, Arena: 200	Leather: 341, Socket Bonus: +4 Critical Strike Rating, Socket: Blue, Equip: Increases attack power by 58., +50 Agility, +66 Stamina, Equip: Improves critical strike rating by 22., Equip: Improves your resilience rating by 30., Reduces the cost of your Kick.
Savage Gladiator's Grimoire	Honor: 3600, Arena: 200	Equip: Increases spell power by 50., +49 Stamina, +21 Intellect, Equip: Improves your resilience rating by 28., Increases your spell penetration.
Hateful Gladiator's Plate Gauntlets	Honor: 3600, Arena: 400	Plate: 1401, Socket Bonus: +4 Critical Strike Rating, Socket: Blue, +58 Strength, +99 Stamina, Equip: Improves critical strike rating by 27., Equip: Improves your resilience rating by 35., Harmstring Rage cost reduced.
Hateful Gladiator's Scaled Gauntlets	Honor: 3600, Arena: 400	Plate: 1401, Socket Bonus: +4 Critical Strike Rating, Socket: Blue, +58 Strength, +99 Stamina, Equip: Improves critical strike rating by 27., Equip: Improves your resilience rating by 35., Increases the damage dealt by your Crusader Strike ability.
Hateful Gladiator's Dreadplate Gauntlets	Honor: 3600, Arena: 400	Plate: 1401, Socket Bonus: +4 Critical Strike Rating, Socket: Blue, +58 Strength, +99 Stamina, Equip: Improves critical strike rating by 27., Equip: Improves your resilience rating by 35., Reduces the cooldown of your Strangulate.
Hateful Gladiator's Ringmail Gauntlets	Honor: 3600, Arena: 400	Mail: 784, Socket Bonus: +2 mana per 5 sec., Socket: Blue, +76 Stamina, +33 Intellect, Equip: Increases spell power by 68., Equip: Restores 11 mana per 5 sec., Equip: Improves your resilience rating by 35., Improves the range of all Shock spells yards.
Hateful Gladiator's Mail Gauntlets	Honor: 3600, Arena: 400	Mail: 784, Socket Bonus: +2 mana per 5 sec., Socket: Blue, +76 Stamina, +33 Intellect, Equip: Increases spell power by 68., Equip: Improves critical strike rating by 27., Equip: Improves your resilience rating by 35., Improves the range of all Shock spells yards.
Hateful Gladiator's Ornamented Gloves	Honor: 3600, Arena: 400	Plate: 1401, Socket Bonus: +2 mana per 5 sec., Socket: Blue, +76 Stamina, +33 Intellect, Equip: Increases spell power by 68., Equip: Improves critical strike rating by 27., Equip: Improves your resilience rating by 35., Increases the critical effect chance of your Flash of Light.
Hateful Gladiator's Linked Gauntlets	Honor: 3600, Arena: 400	Mail: 784, Socket Bonus: +4 Critical Strike Rating, Socket: Blue, Equip: Increases attack power by 72., +44 Agility, +76 Stamina, +25 Intellect, Equip: Improves critical strike rating by 35., Equip: Improves your resilience rating by 35., Improves the range of all Shock spells yards.
Hateful Gladiator's Chain Gauntlets	Honor: 3600, Arena: 400	Mail: 784, Socket Bonus: +4 Critical Strike Rating, Socket: Blue, Equip: Increases attack power by 72., +44 Agility, +76 Stamina, +25 Intellect, Equip: Improves critical strike rating by 35., Equip: Improves your resilience rating by 35., Reduces the cooldown of your Tranquilizing Shot.
Hateful Gladiator's Kodohide Gloves	Honor: 3600, Arena: 400	Leather: 353, Socket Bonus: +4 Spirit, Socket: Blue, Equip: Increases spell power by 68., +76 Stamina, +33 Intellect, +27 Spirit, Equip: Improves your resilience rating by 35., Reduces the cast time of your Cyclone spell
Hateful Gladiator's Wyrmhide Gloves	Honor: 3600, Arena: 400	Leather: 353, Socket Bonus: +4 Spirit, Socket: Blue, Equip: Increases spell power by 68., +76 Stamina, +33 Intellect, Equip: Improves critical strike rating by 27., Equip: Improves your resilience rating by 35., Reduces the cast time of your Cyclone spell.

Name	Extended Cost	Stats
Hateful Gladiator's Leather Gloves	Honor: 3600, Arena: 400	Leather: 353, Socket Bonus: +4 Critical Strike Rating, Socket: Blue, Equip: Increases attack power by 66., +58 Agility, +76 Stamina, Equip: Improves critical strike rating by 27., Equip: Improves your resilience rating by 35., Reduces the cost of your Kick.
Hateful Gladiator's Silk Handguards	Honor: 3600, Arena: 400	Cloth: 188, Socket Bonus: +5 Spell Power, Socket: Blue, Equip: Increases spell power by 68., +76 Stamina, +33 Intellect, Equip: Improves critical strike rating by 27., Equip: Improves your resilience rating by 35., Gives you chance to avoid interruption caused by damage while casting Polymorph.
Hateful Gladiator's Felweave Handguards	Honor: 3600, Arena: 400	Cloth: 188, Socket Bonus: +5 Spell Power, Socket: Blue, Equip: Increases spell power by 68., +76 Stamina, +33 Intellect, Equip: Improves critical strike rating by 27., Equip: Improves your resilience rating by 35., Gives you chance to avoid interruption caused by damage while casting Fear.
Hateful Gladiator's Hacker	Honor: 3600, Arena: 400	Axe: Physical 150-280, 1.5, 143.3 Equip: Increases attack power by 76., +58 Stamina, Equip: Improves critical strike rating by 26., Equip: Improves your resilience rating by 25.
Hateful Gladiator's Chopper	Honor: 3600, Arena: 400	Axe: Physical 261-485, 2.6, 143.5 Equip: Increases attack power by 76., +58 Stamina, Equip: Improves critical strike rating by 26., Equip: Improves your resilience rating by 25.
Hateful Gladiator's Shiv	Honor: 3600, Arena: 400	Dagger: Physical 140-261, 1.4, 143.2 Equip: Increases attack power by 76., +58 Stamina, Equip: Improves critical strike rating by 26., Equip: Improves your resilience rating by 25.
Hateful Gladiator's Left Render	Honor: 3600, Arena: 400	Fist Weapon: Physical 261-485, 2.6, 143.5 Equip: Increases attack power by 76., +58 Stamina, Equip: Improves critical strike rating by 26., Equip: Improves your resilience rating by 25.
Hateful Gladiator's Bonecracker	Honor: 3600, Arena: 400	Mace: Physical 150-280, 1.5, 143.3 Equip: Increases attack power by 76., +58 Stamina, Equip: Improves critical strike rating by 26., Equip: Improves your resilience rating by 25.
Hateful Gladiator's Quickblade	Honor: 3600, Arena: 400	Sword: Physical 150-280, 1.5, 143.3 Equip: Increases attack power by 76., +58 Stamina, Equip: Improves critical strike rating by 26., Equip: Improves your resilience rating by 25.
Hateful Gladiator's Endgame	Honor: 3600, Arena: 400	Equip: Increases spell power by 59., +57 Stamina, +24 Intellect, Equip: Improves critical strike rating by 34., Equip: Improves your resilience rating by 33.
Hateful Gladiator's Left Ripper	Honor: 3600, Arena: 400	Fist Weapon: Physical 150-280, 1.5, 143.3 Equip: Increases attack power by 76., +58 Stamina, Equip: Improves critical strike rating by 26., Equip: Improves your resilience rating by 25.
Hateful Gladiator's Mutilator	Honor: 3600, Arena: 400	Dagger: Physical 180-336, 1.8, 143.3 Equip: Increases attack power by 76., +58 Stamina, Equip: Improves critical strike rating by 26., Equip: Improves your resilience rating by 25.
Hateful Gladiator's Satin Gloves	Honor: 3600, Arena: 400	Cloth: 188, Socket Bonus: +5 Spell Power, Socket: Blue, Equip: Increases spell power by 68., +76 Stamina, +33 Intellect, Equip: Improves critical strike rating by 27., Equip: Improves your resilience rating by 35., Reduces the cooldown of your Psychic Scream.
Hateful Gladiator's Mooncloth Gloves	Honor: 3600, Arena: 400	Cloth: 188, Socket Bonus: +4 Spirit, Socket: Blue, Equip: Increases spell power by 68., +76 Stamina, +33 Intellect, +27 Spirit, Equip: Improves your resilience rating by 35., Reduces the cooldown of your Psychic Scream ability.
Hateful Gladiator's Dragonhide Gloves	Honor: 3600, Arena: 400	Leather: 353, Socket Bonus: +4 Critical Strike Rating, Socket: Blue, Equip: Increases attack power by 66., +58 Agility, +76 Stamina, Equip: Improves critical strike rating by 27., Equip: Improves your resilience rating by 35., Reduces the energy cost of your Maim.

Name	Extended Cost	Stats
Hateful Gladiator's Reprieve	Honor: 3600, Arena: 400	Equip: Increases spell power by 59., +57 Stamina, +24 Intellect, +34 Spirit, Equip: Improves your resilience rating by 33.
Hateful Gladiator's Grimoire	Honor: 3600, Arena: 400	Equip: Increases spell power by 59., +57 Stamina, +24 Intellect, Equip: Improves your resilience rating by 33., Increases your spell penetration.
Savage Gladiator's Ringmail Spaulders	Honor: 4800, Arena: 275	Mail: 909, Socket Bonus: +2 mana per 5 sec., Socket: Yellow, +66 Stamina, +28 Intellect, Equip: Increases spell power by 59., Equip: Restores 12 mana per 5 sec., Equip: Improves your resilience rating by 38.
Savage Gladiator's Mail Spaulders	Honor: 4800, Arena: 275	Mail: 909, Socket Bonus: +2 mana per 5 sec., Socket: Yellow, +66 Stamina, +28 Intellect, Equip: Increases spell power by 59., Equip: Improves critical strike rating by 31., Equip: Improves your resilience rating by 38.
Savage Gladiator's Ornamented Spaulders	Honor: 4800, Arena: 275	Plate: 1625, Socket Bonus: +2 mana per 5 sec., Socket: Yellow, +66 Stamina, +28 Intellect, Equip: Increases spell power by 59., Equip: Improves critical strike rating by 31., Equip: Improves your resilience rating by 38.
Savage Gladiator's Scaled Shoulders	Honor: 4800, Arena: 275	Plate: 1625, Socket Bonus: +4 Critical Strike Rating, Socket: Yellow, +50 Strength, +85 Stamina, Equip: Improves critical strike rating by 31., Equip: Improves your resilience rating by 38.
Savage Gladiator's Dreadplate Shoulders	Honor: 4800, Arena: 275	Plate: 1625, Socket Bonus: +4 Critical Strike Rating, Socket: Yellow, +50 Strength, +85 Stamina, Equip: Improves critical strike rating by 31., Equip: Improves your resilience rating by 38.
Savage Gladiator's Plate Shoulders	Honor: 4800, Arena: 275	Plate: 1625, Socket Bonus: +4 Critical Strike Rating, Socket: Yellow, +50 Strength, +85 Stamina, Equip: Improves critical strike rating by 31., Equip: Improves your resilience rating by 38.
Savage Gladiator's Linked Spaulders	Honor: 4800, Arena: 275	Mail: 909, Socket Bonus: +4 Critical Strike Rating, Socket: Yellow, Equip: Increases attack power by 60., +39 Agility, +66 Stamina, +21 Intellect, Equip: Improves critical strike rating by 39., Equip: Improves your resilience rating by 38.
Savage Gladiator's Chain Spaulders	Honor: 4800, Arena: 275	Mail: 909, Socket Bonus: +4 Critical Strike Rating, Socket: Yellow, Equip: Increases attack power by 60., +39 Agility, +66 Stamina, +21 Intellect, Equip: Improves critical strike rating by 39., Equip: Improves your resilience rating by 38.
Savage Gladiator's Kodohide Spaulders	Honor: 4800, Arena: 275	Leather: 409, Socket Bonus: +4 Spirit, Socket: Yellow, Equip: Increases spell power by 59., +66 Stamina, +28 Intellect, +31 Spirit, Equip: Improves your resilience rating by 38.
Savage Gladiator's Wyrmhide Spaulders	Honor: 4800, Arena: 275	Leather: 409, Socket Bonus: +4 Spirit, Socket: Yellow, Equip: Increases spell power by 59., +66 Stamina, +28 Intellect, Equip: Improves critical strike rating by 31., Equip: Improves your resilience rating by 38.
Savage Gladiator's Leather Spaulders	Honor: 4800, Arena: 275	Leather: 409, Socket Bonus: +4 Critical Strike Rating, Socket: Yellow, Equip: Increases attack power by 58., +50 Agility, +66 Stamina, Equip: Improves critical strike rating by 30., Equip: Improves your resilience rating by 38.
Savage Gladiator's Dragonhide Spaulders	Honor: 4800, Arena: 275	Leather: 409, Socket Bonus: +4 Critical Strike Rating, Socket: Yellow, Equip: Increases attack power by 58., +50 Agility, +66 Stamina, Equip: Improves critical strike rating by 30., Equip: Improves your resilience rating by 38.
Savage Gladiator's Satin Mantle	Honor: 4800, Arena: 275	Cloth: 218, Socket Bonus: +6 Stamina, Socket: Yellow, Equip: Increases spell power by 59., +66 Stamina, +28 Intellect, Equip: Improves critical strike rating by 31., Equip: Improves your resilience rating by 58.

Name	Extended Cost	Stats
Savage Gladiator's Felweave Amice	Honor: 4800, Arena: 275	Cloth: 218, Socket Bonus: +6 Stamina, Socket: Yellow, Equip: Increases spell power by 59., +66 Stamina, +28 Intellect, Equip: Improves critical strike rating by 31., Equip: Improves your resilience rating by 58.
Savage Gladiator's Silk Amice	Honor: 4800, Arena: 275	Cloth: 218, Socket Bonus: +6 Stamina, Socket: Yellow, Equip: Increases spell power by 59., +66 Stamina, +28 Intellect, Equip: Improves critical strike rating by 31., Equip: Improves your resilience rating by 58.
Savage Gladiator's Mooncloth Mantle	Honor: 4800, Arena: 275	Cloth: 218, Socket Bonus: +4 Spirit, Socket: Yellow, Equip: Increases spell power by 59., +66 Stamina, +28 Intellect, +31 Spirit, Equip: Improves your resilience rating by 58.
Hateful Gladiator's Ringmail Spaulders	Honor: 4800, Arena: 550	Mail: 941, Socket Bonus: +2 mana per 5 sec., Socket: Yellow, +76 Stamina, +33 Intellect, Equip: Increases spell power by 68., Equip: Restores 14 mana per 5 sec., Equip: Improves your resilience rating by 44.
Hateful Gladiator's Mail Spaulders	Honor: 4800, Arena: 550	Mail: 941, Socket Bonus: +2 mana per 5 sec., Socket: Yellow, +76 Stamina, +33 Intellect, Equip: Increases spell power by 68., Equip: Improves critical strike rating by 36., Equip: Improves your resilience rating by 44.
Hateful Gladiator's Ornamented Spaulders	Honor: 4800, Arena: 550	Plate: 1681, Socket Bonus: +2 mana per 5 sec., Socket: Yellow, +76 Stamina, +33 Intellect, Equip: Increases spell power by 68., Equip: Improves critical strike rating by 36., Equip: Improves your resilience rating by 44.
Hateful Gladiator's Scaled Shoulders	Honor: 4800, Arena: 550	Plate: 1681, Socket Bonus: +4 Critical Strike Rating, Socket: Yellow, +58 Strength, +99 Stamina, Equip: Improves critical strike rating by 36., Equip: Improves your resilience rating by 44.
Hateful Gladiator's Dreadplate Shoulders	Honor: 4800, Arena: 550	Plate: 1681, Socket Bonus: +4 Critical Strike Rating, Socket: Yellow, +58 Strength, +99 Stamina, Equip: Improves critical strike rating by 36., Equip: Improves your resilience rating by 44.
Hateful Gladiator's Plate Shoulders	Honor: 4800, Arena: 550	Plate: 1681, Socket Bonus: +4 Critical Strike Rating, Socket: Yellow, +58 Strength, +99 Stamina, Equip: Improves critical strike rating by 36., Equip: Improves your resilience rating by 44.
Hateful Gladiator's Linked Spaulders	Honor: 4800, Arena: 550	Mail: 941, Socket Bonus: +4 Critical Strike Rating, Socket: Yellow, Equip: Increases attack power by 72., +44 Agility, +76 Stamina, +25 Intellect, Equip: Improves critical strike rating by 44., Equip: Improves your resilience rating by 44.
Hateful Gladiator's Chain Spaulders	Honor: 4800, Arena: 550	Mail: 941, Socket Bonus: +4 Critical Strike Rating, Socket: Yellow, Equip: Increases attack power by 72., +44 Agility, +76 Stamina, +25 Intellect, Equip: Improves critical strike rating by 44., Equip: Improves your resilience rating by 44.
Hateful Gladiator's Kodohide Spaulders	Honor: 4800, Arena: 550	Leather: 423, Socket Bonus: +4 Spirit, Socket: Yellow, Equip: Increases spell power by 68., +76 Stamina, +33 Intellect, +36 Spirit, Equip: Improves your resilience rating by 44.
Hateful Gladiator's Wyrmhide Spaulders	Honor: 4800, Arena: 550	Leather: 423, Socket Bonus: +4 Spirit, Socket: Yellow, Equip: Increases spell power by 68., +76 Stamina, +33 Intellect, Equip: Improves critical strike rating by 36., Equip: Improves your resilience rating by 44.
Hateful Gladiator's Dragonhide Spaulders	Honor: 4800, Arena: 550	Leather: 423, Socket Bonus: +4 Critical Strike Rating, Socket: Yellow, Equip: Increases attack power by 66., +58 Agility, +76 Stamina, Equip: Improves critical strike rating by 36., Equip: Improves your resilience rating by 44.
Hateful Gladiator's Silk Amice	Honor: 4800, Arena: 550	Cloth: 225, Socket Bonus: +6 Stamina, Socket: Yellow, Equip: Increases spell power by 68., +76 Stamina, +33 Intellect, Equip: Improves critical strike rating by 36., Equip: Improves your resilience rating by 44.

Name	Extended Cost	Stats
Hateful Gladiator's Felweave Amice	Honor: 4800, Arena: 550	Cloth: 225, Socket Bonus: +6 Stamina, Socket: Yellow, Equip: Increases spell power by 68., +76 Stamina, +33 Intellect, Equip: Improves critical strike rating by 36., Equip: Improves your resilience rating by 44.
Hateful Gladiator's Satin Mantle	Honor: 4800, Arena: 550	Cloth: 225, Socket Bonus: +6 Stamina, Socket: Yellow, Equip: Increases spell power by 68., +76 Stamina, +33 Intellect, Equip: Improves critical strike rating by 36., Equip: Improves your resilience rating by 44.
Hateful Gladiator's Mooncloth Mantle	Honor: 4800, Arena: 550	Cloth: 225, Socket Bonus: +4 Spirit, Socket: Yellow, Equip: Increases spell power by 68., +76 Stamina, +33 Intellect, +36 Spirit, Equip: Improves your resilience rating by 44.
Hateful Gladiator's Leather Spaulders	Honor: 4800, Arena: 550	Leather: 423, Socket Bonus: +4 Critical Strike Rating, Socket: Yellow, Equip: Increases attack power by 66., +58 Agility, +76 Stamina, Equip: Improves critical strike rating by 36., Equip: Improves your resilience rating by 44.
Savage Gladiator's Plate Chestpiece	Honor: 6000, Arena: 350	Plate: 2166, Socket Bonus: +6 Resilience Rating, Socket: Red, Yellow, +62 Strength, +115 Stamina, Equip: Improves critical strike rating by 36., Equip: Improves your resilience rating by 52.
Savage Gladiator's Dreadplate Chestpiece	Honor: 6000, Arena: 350	Plate: 2166, Socket Bonus: +6 Resilience Rating, Socket: Red, Yellow, +62 Strength, +115 Stamina, Equip: Improves critical strike rating by 36., Equip: Improves your resilience rating by 52.
Savage Gladiator's Scaled Chestpiece	Honor: 6000, Arena: 350	Plate: 2166, Socket Bonus: +6 Resilience Rating, Socket: Red, Yellow, +62 Strength, +115 Stamina, Equip: Improves critical strike rating by 36., Equip: Improves your resilience rating by 52.
Savage Gladiator's Plate Helm	Honor: 6000, Arena: 350	Plate: 1760, Socket Bonus: +8 Critical Strike Rating, Socket: Meta, Red, +62 Strength, +115 Stamina, Equip: Improves critical strike rating by 36., Equip: Improves your resilience rating by 36.
Savage Gladiator's Dreadplate Helm	Honor: 6000, Arena: 350	Plate: 1760, Socket Bonus: +8 Critical Strike Rating, Socket: Meta, Red, +62 Strength, +115 Stamina, Equip: Improves critical strike rating by 36., Equip: Improves your resilience rating by 36.
Savage Gladiator's Scaled Helm	Honor: 6000, Arena: 350	Plate: 1760, Socket Bonus: +8 Critical Strike Rating, Socket: Meta, Red, +62 Strength, +115 Stamina, Equip: Improves critical strike rating by 36., Equip: Improves your resilience rating by 36.
Savage Gladiator's Ornamented Chestguard	Honor: 6000, Arena: 350	Plate: 2166, Socket Bonus: +6 Resilience Rating, Socket: Red, Yellow, +88 Stamina, +39 Intellect, Equip: Increases spell power by 73., Equip: Improves critical strike rating by 36., Equip: Improves your resilience rating by 51.
Savage Gladiator's Ringmail Armor	Honor: 6000, Arena: 350	Mail: 1212, Socket Bonus: +6 Resilience Rating, Socket: Red, Yellow, +88 Stamina, +39 Intellect, Equip: Increases spell power by 73., Equip: Restores 14 mana per 5 sec., Equip: Improves your resilience rating by 51.
Savage Gladiator's Mail Armor	Honor: 6000, Arena: 350	Mail: 1212, Socket Bonus: +6 Resilience Rating, Socket: Red, Yellow, +88 Stamina, +39 Intellect, Equip: Increases spell power by 73., Equip: Improves critical strike rating by 36., Equip: Improves your resilience rating by 51.
Savage Gladiator's Ringmail Helm	Honor: 6000, Arena: 350	Mail: 985, Socket Bonus: 3 mana per 5 sec, Socket: Meta, Red, +88 Stamina, +39 Intellect, Equip: Increases spell power by 73., Equip: Restores 14 mana per 5 sec., Equip: Improves your resilience rating by 36.
Savage Gladiator's Mail Helm	Honor: 6000, Arena: 350	Mail: 985, Socket Bonus: 3 mana per 5 sec, Socket: Meta, Red, +88 Stamina, +39 Intellect, Equip: Increases spell power by 73., Equip: Improves critical strike rating by 36., Equip: Improves your resilience rating by 36.

Name	Extended Cost	Stats
Savage Gladiator's Ringmail Leggings	Honor: 6000, Arena: 350	Mail: 1061, Socket Bonus: +7 Spell Power, Socket: Red, Blue, +88 Stamina, +39 Intellect, Equip: Increases spell power by 73., Equip: Restores 14 mana per 5 sec., Equip: Improves your resilience rating by 52.
Savage Gladiator's Mail Leggings	Honor: 6000, Arena: 350	Mail: 1061, Socket Bonus: +7 Spell Power, Socket: Red, Blue, +88 Stamina, +39 Intellect, Equip: Increases spell power by 73., Equip: Improves critical strike rating by 36., Equip: Improves your resilience rating by 52.
Savage Gladiator's Ornamented Legplates	Honor: 6000, Arena: 350	Plate: 1895, Socket Bonus: +7 Spell Power, Socket: Red, Blue, +88 Stamina, +39 Intellect, Equip: Increases spell power by 73., Equip: Improves critical strike rating by 36., Equip: Improves your resilience rating by 52.
Deadly Gladiator's Ornamented Headcover	Honor: 6000, Arena: 350	Plate: 1867, Socket Bonus: 3 mana per 5 sec, Socket: Meta, Red, +115 Stamina, +50 Intellect, Equip: Increases spell power by 99., Equip: Improves critical strike rating by 51., Equip: Improves your resilience rating by 50.
Savage Gladiator's Ornamented Headcover	Honor: 6000, Arena: 350	Plate: 1760, Socket Bonus: 3 mana per 5 sec, Socket: Meta, Red, +88 Stamina, +39 Intellect, Equip: Increases spell power by 73., Equip: Improves critical strike rating by 36., Equip: Improves your resilience rating by 36.
Savage Gladiator's Scaled Legguards	Honor: 6000, Arena: 350	Plate: 1895, Socket Bonus: +6 Strength, Socket: Red, Blue, +62 Strength, +115 Stamina, Equip: Improves critical strike rating by 36., Equip: Improves your resilience rating by 52.
Savage Gladiator's Dreadplate Legguards	Honor: 6000, Arena: 350	Plate: 1895, Socket Bonus: +6 Strength, Socket: Red, Blue, +62 Strength, +115 Stamina, Equip: Improves critical strike rating by 36., Equip: Improves your resilience rating by 52.
Savage Gladiator's Plate Legguards	Honor: 6000, Arena: 350	Plate: 1895, Socket Bonus: +6 Strength, Socket: Red, Blue, +62 Strength, +115 Stamina, Equip: Improves critical strike rating by 36., Equip: Improves your resilience rating by 52.
Savage Gladiator's Linked Armor	Honor: 6000, Arena: 350	Mail: 1212, Socket Bonus: +6 Resilience Rating, Socket: Red, Yellow, Equip: Increases attack power by 72., +52 Agility, +90 Stamina, +23 Intellect, Equip: Improves critical strike rating by 52., Equip: Improves your resilience rating by 51.
Savage Gladiator's Chain Armor	Honor: 6000, Arena: 350	Mail: 1212, Socket Bonus: +6 Resilience Rating, Socket: Red, Yellow, Equip: Increases attack power by 72., +52 Agility, +90 Stamina, +23 Intellect, Equip: Improves critical strike rating by 52., Equip: Improves your resilience rating by 51.
Savage Gladiator's Linked Helm	Honor: 6000, Arena: 350	Mail: 985, Socket Bonus: +8 Critical Strike Rating, Socket: Meta, Red, Equip: Increases attack power by 72., +52 Agility, +90 Stamina, +23 Intellect, Equip: Improves critical strike rating by 36., Equip: Improves your resilience rating by 51.
Savage Gladiator's Chain Helm	Honor: 6000, Arena: 350	Mail: 985, Socket Bonus: +8 Critical Strike Rating, Socket: Meta, Red, Equip: Increases attack power by 72., +52 Agility, +90 Stamina, +23 Intellect, Equip: Improves critical strike rating by 36., Equip: Improves your resilience rating by 51.
Savage Gladiator's Linked Leggings	Honor: 6000, Arena: 350	Mail: 1061, Socket Bonus: +6 Agility, Socket: Red, Blue, Equip: Increases attack power by 72., +52 Agility, +90 Stamina, +23 Intellect, Equip: Improves critical strike rating by 52., Equip: Improves your resilience rating by 52.
Savage Gladiator's Chain Leggings	Honor: 6000, Arena: 350	Mail: 1061, Socket Bonus: +6 Agility, Socket: Red, Blue, Equip: Increases attack power by 72., +52 Agility, +90 Stamina, +23 Intellect, Equip: Improves critical strike rating by 52., Equip: Improves your resilience rating by 52.
Savage Gladiator's Kodohide Helm	Honor: 6000, Arena: 350	Leather: 443, Socket Bonus: +8 Spirit, Socket: Meta, Red, Equip: Increases spell power by 73., +88 Stamina, +39 Intellect, +36 Spirit, Equip: Improves your resilience rating by 36.
Savage Gladiator's Kodohide Legguards	Honor: 6000, Arena: 350	Leather: 477, Socket Bonus: +7 Spell Power, Socket: Red, Blue, Equip: Increases spell power by 73., +88 Stamina, +39 Intellect, +36 Spirit, Equip: Improves your resilience rating by 52.
Savage Gladiator's Kodohide Robes	Honor: 6000, Arena: 350	Leather: 545, Socket Bonus: +6 Resilience Rating, Socket: Red, Yellow, Equip: Increases spell power by 73., +88 Stamina, +39 Intellect, +36 Spirit, Equip: Improves your resilience rating by 51.
Savage Gladiator's Wyrmhide Legguards	Honor: 6000, Arena: 350	Leather: 477, Socket Bonus: +7 Spell Power, Socket: Red, Blue, Equip: Increases spell power by 73., +88 Stamina, +39 Intellect, Equip: Improves critical strike rating by 36., Equip: Improves your resilience rating by 52.
Savage Gladiator's Wyrmhide Robes	Honor: 6000, Arena: 350	Leather: 545, Socket Bonus: +6 Resilience Rating, Socket: Red, Yellow, Equip: Increases spell power by 73., +88 Stamina, +39 Intellect, Equip: Improves critical strike rating by 36., Equip: Improves your resilience rating by 51.
Savage Gladiator's Wyrmhide Helm	Honor: 6000, Arena: 350	Leather: 443, Socket Bonus: +8 Spirit, Socket: Meta, Red, Equip: Increases spell power by 73., +88 Stamina, +39 Intellect, Equip: Improves critical strike rating by 36., Equip: Improves your resilience rating by 36.
Savage Gladiator's Leather Helm	Honor: 6000, Arena: 350	Leather: 443, Socket Bonus: +8 Critical Strike Rating, Socket: Meta, Red, Equip: Increases attack power by 46., +62 Agility, +90 Stamina, Equip: Improves critical strike rating by 36., Equip: Improves your resilience rating by 51.
Savage Gladiator's Leather Legguards	Honor: 6000, Arena: 350	Leather: 477, Socket Bonus: +6 Agility, Socket: Red, Blue, Equip: Increases attack power by 78., +62 Agility, +90 Stamina, Equip: Improves critical strike rating by 36., Equip: Improves your resilience rating by 51.
Savage Gladiator's Leather Tunic	Honor: 6000, Arena: 350	Leather: 545, Socket Bonus: +6 Resilience Rating, Socket: Red, Yellow, Equip: Increases attack power by 78., +62 Agility, +90 Stamina, Equip: Improves critical strike rating by 36., Equip: Improves your resilience rating by 51.
Savage Gladiator's Dragonhide Robes	Honor: 6000, Arena: 350	Leather: 545, Socket Bonus: +6 Resilience Rating, Socket: Red, Yellow, Equip: Increases attack power by 78., +62 Agility, +90 Stamina, Equip: Improves critical strike rating by 36., Equip: Improves your resilience rating by 51.
Savage Gladiator's Dragonhide Legguards	Honor: 6000, Arena: 350	Leather: 477, Socket Bonus: +6 Agility, Socket: Red, Blue, Equip: Increases attack power by 78., +62 Agility, +90 Stamina, Equip: Improves critical strike rating by 36., Equip: Improves your resilience rating by 51.
Savage Gladiator's Dragonhide Helm	Honor: 6000, Arena: 350	Leather: 443, Socket Bonus: +8 Critical Strike Rating, Socket: Meta, Red, Equip: Increases attack power by 46., +62 Agility, +90 Stamina, Equip: Improves critical strike rating by 36., Equip: Improves your resilience rating by 51.
Savage Gladiator's Mooncloth Robe	Honor: 6000, Arena: 350	Cloth: 290, Socket Bonus: +6 Resilience Rating, Socket: Red, Yellow, Equip: Increases spell power by 73., +88 Stamina, +39 Intellect, +36 Spirit, Equip: Improves your resilience rating by 51.
Savage Gladiator's Satin Hood	Honor: 6000, Arena: 350	Cloth: 236, Socket Bonus: +8 Resilience Rating, Socket: Meta, Red, Equip: Increases spell power by 73., +88 Stamina, +39 Intellect, Equip: Improves critical strike rating by 36., Equip: Improves your resilience rating by 36.
Deadly Gladiator's Silk Cowl	Honor: 6000, Arena: 350	Cloth: 250, Socket Bonus: +8 Resilience Rating, Socket: Meta, Red, Equip: Increases spell power by 99., +115 Stamina, +50 Intellect, Equip: Improves critical strike rating by 51., Equip: Improves your resilience rating by 50.
Savage Gladiator's Silk Raiment	Honor: 6000, Arena: 350	Cloth: 290, Socket Bonus: +9 Stamina, Socket: Red, Yellow, Equip: Increases spell power by 73., +88 Stamina, +39 Intellect, Equip: Improves critical strike rating by 36., Equip: Improves your resilience rating by 51.

PVP

Arenas

**Arena
Rewards**

World PVP

207

Name	Extended Cost	Stats
Savage Gladiator's Silk Trousers	Honor: 6000, Arena: 350	Cloth: 254, Socket Bonus: +7 Spell Power, Socket: Red, Blue, Equip: Increases spell power by 73., +88 Stamina, +39 Intellect, Equip: Improves critical strike rating by 36., Equip: Improves your resilience rating by 52.
Savage Gladiator's Felweave Trousers	Honor: 6000, Arena: 350	Cloth: 254, Socket Bonus: +7 Spell Power, Socket: Red, Blue, Equip: Increases spell power by 73., +88 Stamina, +39 Intellect, Equip: Improves critical strike rating by 36., Equip: Improves your resilience rating by 52.
Savage Gladiator's Felweave Raiment	Honor: 6000, Arena: 350	Cloth: 290, Socket Bonus: +9 Stamina, Socket: Red, Yellow, Equip: Increases spell power by 73., +88 Stamina, +39 Intellect, Equip: Improves critical strike rating by 36., Equip: Improves your resilience rating by 51.
Savage Gladiator's Felweave Cowl	Honor: 6000, Arena: 350	Cloth: 236, Socket Bonus: +8 Resilience Rating, Socket: Meta, Red, Equip: Increases spell power by 73., +88 Stamina, +39 Intellect, Equip: Improves critical strike rating by 36., Equip: Improves your resilience rating by 36.
Savage Gladiator's Silk Cowl	Honor: 6000, Arena: 350	Cloth: 236, Socket Bonus: +8 Resilience Rating, Socket: Meta, Red, Equip: Increases spell power by 73., +88 Stamina, +39 Intellect, Equip: Improves critical strike rating by 36., Equip: Improves your resilience rating by 36.
Savage Gladiator's Satin Leggings	Honor: 6000, Arena: 350	Cloth: 254, Socket Bonus: +7 Spell Power, Socket: Red, Blue, Equip: Increases spell power by 73., +88 Stamina, +39 Intellect, Equip: Improves critical strike rating by 36., Equip: Improves your resilience rating by 52.
Savage Gladiator's Satin Robe	Honor: 6000, Arena: 350	Cloth: 290, Socket Bonus: +9 Stamina, Socket: Red, Yellow, Equip: Increases spell power by 73., +88 Stamina, +39 Intellect, Equip: Improves critical strike rating by 36., Equip: Improves your resilience rating by 51.
Savage Gladiator's Mooncloth Leggings	Honor: 6000, Arena: 350	Cloth: 254, Socket Bonus: +7 Spell Power, Socket: Red, Blue, Equip: Increases spell power by 73., +88 Stamina, +39 Intellect, +36 Spirit, Equip: Improves your resilience rating by 52.
Savage Gladiator's Mooncloth Hood	Honor: 6000, Arena: 350	Cloth: 236, Socket Bonus: +8 Spirit, Socket: Meta, Red, Equip: Increases spell power by 73., +88 Stamina, +39 Intellect, +36 Spirit, Equip: Improves your resilience rating by 36.
Savage Gladiator's Shield Wall	Honor: 6000, Arena: 350	Shield: 7278 , +82 Stamina, Equip: Improves your resilience rating by 54.
Savage Gladiator's Barrier	Honor: 6000, Arena: 350	Shield: 7278 , Equip: Increases spell power by 50., +49 Stamina, +21 Intellect, Equip: Improves critical strike rating by 29., Equip: Improves your resilience rating by 28.
Savage Gladiator's Redoubt	Honor: 6000, Arena: 350	Shield: 7278 , Equip: Increases spell power by 50., +49 Stamina, +21 Intellect, Equip: Restores 12 mana per 5 sec., Equip: Improves your resilience rating by 28.
Hateful Gladiator's Dreadplate Chestpiece	Honor: 6000, Arena: 700	Plate: 2241, Socket Bonus: +6 Resilience Rating, Socket: Red, Yellow, +74 Strength, +133 Stamina, Equip: Improves critical strike rating by 44., Equip: Improves your resilience rating by 59.
Hateful Gladiator's Scaled Chestpiece	Honor: 6000, Arena: 700	Plate: 2241, Socket Bonus: +6 Resilience Rating, Socket: Red, Yellow, +74 Strength, +133 Stamina, Equip: Improves critical strike rating by 44., Equip: Improves your resilience rating by 59.
Hateful Gladiator's Plate Chestpiece	Honor: 6000, Arena: 700	Plate: 2241, Socket Bonus: +6 Resilience Rating, Socket: Red, Yellow, +74 Strength, +133 Stamina, Equip: Improves critical strike rating by 44., Equip: Improves your resilience rating by 59.
Hateful Gladiator's Plate Helm	Honor: 6000, Arena: 700	Plate: 1821, Socket Bonus: +8 Critical Strike Rating, Socket: Meta, Red, +74 Strength, +133 Stamina, Equip: Improves critical strike rating by 44., Equip: Improves your resilience rating by 59.

Name	Extended Cost	Stats
Hateful Gladiator's Dreadplate Helm	Honor: 6000, Arena: 700	Plate: 1821, Socket Bonus: +8 Critical Strike Rating, Socket: Meta, Red, +74 Strength, +133 Stamina, Equip: Improves critical strike rating by 44., Equip: Improves your resilience rating by 59.
Hateful Gladiator's Scaled Helm	Honor: 6000, Arena: 700	Plate: 1821, Socket Bonus: +8 Critical Strike Rating, Socket: Meta, Red, +74 Strength, +133 Stamina, Equip: Improves critical strike rating by 44., Equip: Improves your resilience rating by 59.
Hateful Gladiator's Ringmail Armor	Honor: 6000, Arena: 700	Mail: 1254, Socket Bonus: +6 Resilience Rating, Socket: Red, Yellow, +102 Stamina, +45 Intellect, Equip: Increases spell power by 87., Equip: Restores 18 mana per 5 sec., Equip: Improves your resilience rating by 59.
Hateful Gladiator's Mail Armor	Honor: 6000, Arena: 700	Mail: 1254, Socket Bonus: +6 Resilience Rating, Socket: Red, Yellow, +102 Stamina, +45 Intellect, Equip: Increases spell power by 87., Equip: Improves critical strike rating by 44., Equip: Improves your resilience rating by 59.
Hateful Gladiator's Ringmail Helm	Honor: 6000, Arena: 700	Mail: 1019, Socket Bonus: 3 mana per 5 sec, Socket: Meta, Red, +102 Stamina, +45 Intellect, Equip: Increases spell power by 87., Equip: Restores 18 mana per 5 sec., Equip: Improves your resilience rating by 43.
Hateful Gladiator's Mail Helm	Honor: 6000, Arena: 700	Mail: 1019, Socket Bonus: 3 mana per 5 sec, Socket: Meta, Red, +102 Stamina, +45 Intellect, Equip: Increases spell power by 87., Equip: Improves critical strike rating by 44., Equip: Improves your resilience rating by 43.
Hateful Gladiator's Ringmail Leggings	Honor: 6000, Arena: 700	Mail: 1097, Socket Bonus: +7 Spell Power, Socket: Red, Blue, +102 Stamina, +45 Intellect, Equip: Increases spell power by 87., Equip: Restores 18 mana per 5 sec., Equip: Improves your resilience rating by 59.
Hateful Gladiator's Mail Leggings	Honor: 6000, Arena: 700	Mail: 1097, Socket Bonus: +7 Spell Power, Socket: Red, Blue, +102 Stamina, +45 Intellect, Equip: Increases spell power by 87., Equip: Improves critical strike rating by 44., Equip: Improves your resilience rating by 59.
Hateful Gladiator's Ornamented Legplates	Honor: 6000, Arena: 700	Plate: 1961, Socket Bonus: +7 Spell Power, Socket: Red, Blue, +102 Stamina, +45 Intellect, Equip: Increases spell power by 87., Equip: Improves critical strike rating by 44., Equip: Improves your resilience rating by 59.
Hateful Gladiator's Ornamented Headcover	Honor: 6000, Arena: 700	Plate: 1821, Socket Bonus: 3 mana per 5 sec, Socket: Meta, Red, +102 Stamina, +45 Intellect, Equip: Increases spell power by 87., Equip: Improves critical strike rating by 44., Equip: Improves your resilience rating by 43.
Hateful Gladiator's Ornamented Chestguard	Honor: 6000, Arena: 700	Plate: 2241, Socket Bonus: +6 Resilience Rating, Socket: Red, Yellow, +102 Stamina, +45 Intellect, Equip: Increases spell power by 87., Equip: Improves critical strike rating by 44., Equip: Improves your resilience rating by 59.
Hateful Gladiator's Scaled Legguards	Honor: 6000, Arena: 700	Plate: 1961, Socket Bonus: +6 Strength, Socket: Red, Blue, +74 Strength, +133 Stamina, Equip: Improves critical strike rating by 44., Equip: Improves your resilience rating by 59.
Hateful Gladiator's Dreadplate Legguards	Honor: 6000, Arena: 700	Plate: 1961, Socket Bonus: +6 Strength, Socket: Red, Blue, +74 Strength, +133 Stamina, Equip: Improves critical strike rating by 44., Equip: Improves your resilience rating by 59.
Hateful Gladiator's Plate Leguards	Honor: 6000, Arena: 700	Plate: 1961, Socket Bonus: +6 Strength, Socket: Red, Blue, +74 Strength, +133 Stamina, Equip: Improves critical strike rating by 44., Equip: Improves your resilience rating by 59.
Hateful Gladiator's Linked Armor	Honor: 6000, Arena: 700	Mail: 1254, Socket Bonus: +6 Resilience Rating, Socket: Red, Yellow, Equip: Increases attack power by 88., +60 Agility, +103 Stamina, +29 Intellect, Equip: Improves critical strike rating by 60., Equip: Improves your resilience rating by 59.

Name	Extended Cost	Stats
Hateful Gladiator's Chain Armor	Honor: 6000, Arena: 700	Mail: 1254, Socket Bonus: +6 Resilience Rating, Socket: Red, Yellow, Equip: Increases attack power by 88., +60 Agility, +102 Stamina, +29 Intellect, Equip: Improves critical strike rating by 60., Equip: Improves your resilience rating by 59.
Hateful Gladiator's Linked Helm	Honor: 6000, Arena: 700	Mail: 1019, Socket Bonus: +8 Critical Strike Rating, Socket: Meta, Red, Equip: Increases attack power by 88., +60 Agility, +103 Stamina, +29 Intellect, Equip: Improves critical strike rating by 44., Equip: Improves your resilience rating by 59.
Hateful Gladiator's Chain Helm	Honor: 6000, Arena: 700	Mail: 1019, Socket Bonus: +8 Critical Strike Rating, Socket: Meta, Red, Equip: Increases attack power by 88., +60 Agility, +103 Stamina, +29 Intellect, Equip: Improves critical strike rating by 44., Equip: Improves your resilience rating by 59.
Hateful Gladiator's Linked Leggings	Honor: 6000, Arena: 700	Mail: 1097, Socket Bonus: +6 Agility, Socket: Red, Blue, Equip: Increases attack power by 88., +60 Agility, +103 Stamina, +29 Intellect, Equip: Improves critical strike rating by 60., Equip: Improves your resilience rating by 59.
Hateful Gladiator's Chain Leggings	Honor: 6000, Arena: 700	Mail: 1097, Socket Bonus: +6 Agility, Socket: Red, Blue, Equip: Increases attack power by 88., +60 Agility, +103 Stamina, +29 Intellect, Equip: Improves critical strike rating by 60., Equip: Improves your resilience rating by 59.
Hateful Gladiator's Kodohide Legguards	Honor: 6000, Arena: 700	Leather: 494, Socket Bonus: +7 Spell Power, Socket: Red, Blue, Equip: Increases spell power by 87., +102 Stamina, +45 Intellect, +44 Spirit, Equip: Improves your resilience rating by 59.
Hateful Gladiator's Wyrmhide Legguards	Honor: 6000, Arena: 700	Leather: 494, Socket Bonus: +7 Spell Power, Socket: Red, Blue, Equip: Increases spell power by 87., +102 Stamina, +45 Intellect, Equip: Improves critical strike rating by 44., Equip: Improves your resilience rating by 59.
Hateful Gladiator's Kodohide Robes	Honor: 6000, Arena: 700	Leather: 564, Socket Bonus: +6 Resilience Rating, Socket: Red, Yellow, Equip: Increases spell power by 87., +102 Stamina, +45 Intellect, +44 Spirit, Equip: Improves your resilience rating by 59.
Hateful Gladiator's Wyrmhide Robes	Honor: 6000, Arena: 700	Leather: 564, Socket Bonus: +6 Resilience Rating, Socket: Red, Yellow, Equip: Increases spell power by 87., +102 Stamina, +45 Intellect, Equip: Improves critical strike rating by 44., Equip: Improves your resilience rating by 59.
Hateful Gladiator's Kodohide Helm	Honor: 6000, Arena: 700	Leather: 458, Socket Bonus: +8 Spirit, Socket: Meta, Red, Equip: Increases spell power by 87., +102 Stamina, +45 Intellect, +44 Spirit, Equip: Improves your resilience rating by 43.
Hateful Gladiator's Wyrmhide Helm	Honor: 6000, Arena: 700	Leather: 458, Socket Bonus: +8 Spirit, Socket: Meta, Red, Equip: Increases spell power by 87., +102 Stamina, +45 Intellect, Equip: Improves critical strike rating by 44., Equip: Improves your resilience rating by 43.
Hateful Gladiator's Leather Tunic	Honor: 6000, Arena: 700	Leather: 564, Socket Bonus: +6 Resilience Rating, Socket: Red, Yellow, Equip: Increases attack power by 90., +73 Agility, +103 Stamina, Equip: Improves critical strike rating by 44., Equip: Improves your resilience rating by 59.
Hateful Gladiator's Leather Legguards	Honor: 6000, Arena: 700	Leather: 494, Socket Bonus: +6 Agility, Socket: Red, Blue, Equip: Increases attack power by 90., +73 Agility, +103 Stamina, Equip: Improves critical strike rating by 44., Equip: Improves your resilience rating by 59.
Hateful Gladiator's Dragonhide Robes	Honor: 6000, Arena: 700	Leather: 564, Socket Bonus: +6 Resilience Rating, Socket: Red, Yellow, Equip: Increases attack power by 90., +73 Agility, +103 Stamina, Equip: Improves critical strike rating by 44., Equip: Improves your resilience rating by 59.
Hateful Gladiator's Dragonhide Legguards	Honor: 6000, Arena: 700	Leather: 494, Socket Bonus: +6 Agility, Socket: Red, Blue, Equip: Increases attack power by 90., +73 Agility, +103 Stamina, Equip: Improves critical strike rating by 44., Equip: Improves your resilience rating by 59.
Hateful Gladiator's Leather Helm	Honor: 6000, Arena: 700	Leather: 458, Socket Bonus: +8 Critical Strike Rating, Socket: Meta, Red, Equip: Increases attack power by 58., +73 Agility, +103 Stamina, Equip: Improves critical strike rating by 44., Equip: Improves your resilience rating by 59.
Hateful Gladiator's Dragonhide Helm	Honor: 6000, Arena: 700	Leather: 458, Socket Bonus: +8 Critical Strike Rating, Socket: Meta, Red, Equip: Increases attack power by 58., +73 Agility, +103 Stamina, Equip: Improves critical strike rating by 44., Equip: Improves your resilience rating by 59.
Hateful Gladiator's Satin Hood	Honor: 6000, Arena: 700	Cloth: 244, Socket Bonus: +8 Resilience Rating, Socket: Meta, Red, Equip: Increases spell power by 87., +102 Stamina, +45 Intellect, Equip: Improves critical strike rating by 44., Equip: Improves your resilience rating by 43.
Hateful Gladiator's Silk Cowl	Honor: 6000, Arena: 700	Cloth: 244, Socket Bonus: +8 Resilience Rating, Socket: Meta, Red, Equip: Increases spell power by 87., +102 Stamina, +45 Intellect, Equip: Improves critical strike rating by 44., Equip: Improves your resilience rating by 43.
Hateful Gladiator's Redoubt	Honor: 6000, Arena: 700	Shield: 7530 , Equip: Increases spell power by 59., +57 Stamina, +24 Intellect, Equip: Restores 14 mana per 5 sec., Equip: Improves your resilience rating by 33.
Hateful Gladiator's Felweave Trousers	Honor: 6000, Arena: 700	Cloth: 263, Socket Bonus: +7 Spell Power, Socket: Red, Blue, Equip: Increases spell power by 87., +102 Stamina, +45 Intellect, Equip: Improves critical strike rating by 44., Equip: Improves your resilience rating by 59.
Hateful Gladiator's Felweave Raiment	Honor: 6000, Arena: 700	Cloth: 300, Socket Bonus: +9 Stamina, Socket: Red, Yellow, Equip: Increases spell power by 87., +102 Stamina, +45 Intellect, Equip: Improves critical strike rating by 44., Equip: Improves your resilience rating by 59.
Hateful Gladiator's Felweave Cowl	Honor: 6000, Arena: 700	Cloth: 244, Socket Bonus: +8 Resilience Rating, Socket: Meta, Red, Equip: Increases spell power by 87., +102 Stamina, +45 Intellect, Equip: Improves critical strike rating by 44., Equip: Improves your resilience rating by 43.
Hateful Gladiator's Silk Trousers	Honor: 6000, Arena: 700	Cloth: 263, Socket Bonus: +7 Spell Power, Socket: Red, Blue, Equip: Increases spell power by 87., +102 Stamina, +45 Intellect, Equip: Improves critical strike rating by 44., Equip: Improves your resilience rating by 59.
Hateful Gladiator's Silk Raiment	Honor: 6000, Arena: 700	Cloth: 300, Socket Bonus: +9 Stamina, Socket: Red, Yellow, Equip: Increases spell power by 87., +102 Stamina, +45 Intellect, Equip: Improves critical strike rating by 44., Equip: Improves your resilience rating by 59.
Hateful Gladiator's Satin Leggings	Honor: 6000, Arena: 700	Cloth: 263, Socket Bonus: +7 Spell Power, Socket: Red, Blue, Equip: Increases spell power by 87., +102 Stamina, +45 Intellect, Equip: Improves critical strike rating by 44., Equip: Improves your resilience rating by 59.
Hateful Gladiator's Satin Robe	Honor: 6000, Arena: 700	Cloth: 300, Socket Bonus: +9 Stamina, Socket: Red, Yellow, Equip: Increases spell power by 87., +102 Stamina, +45 Intellect, Equip: Improves critical strike rating by 44., Equip: Improves your resilience rating by 59.
Hateful Gladiator's Mooncloth Leggings	Honor: 6000, Arena: 700	Cloth: 263, Socket Bonus: +7 Spell Power, Socket: Red, Blue, Equip: Increases spell power by 87., +102 Stamina, +45 Intellect, +44 Spirit, Equip: Improves your resilience rating by 59.

Name	Extended Cost	Stats
Hateful Gladiator's Mooncloth Robe	Honor: 6000, Arena: 700	Cloth: 300, Socket Bonus: +6 Resilience Rating, Socket: Red, Yellow, Equip: Increases spell power by 87., +102 Stamina, +45 Intellect, +44 Spirit, Equip: Improves your resilience rating by 59.
Hateful Gladiator's Mooncloth Hood	Honor: 6000, Arena: 700	Cloth: 244, Socket Bonus: +8 Spirit, Socket: Meta, Red, Equip: Increases spell power by 87., +102 Stamina, +45 Intellect, +44 Spirit, Equip: Improves your resilience rating by 43.
Hateful Gladiator's Shield Wall	Honor: 6000, Arena: 700	Shield: 7530, +96 Stamina, Equip: Improves your resilience rating by 63.
Hateful Gladiator's Barrier	Honor: 6000, Arena: 700	Shield: 7530, Equip: Increases spell power by 59., +57 Stamina, +24 Intellect, Equip: Improves critical strike rating by 34., Equip: Improves your resilience rating by 33.
Savage Gladiator's Cleaver	Honor: 8400, Arena: 475	Axe: Physical 237-440, 2.6, 130.2 Equip: Increases attack power by 66., +49 Stamina, Equip: Improves critical strike rating by 22., Equip: Improves your resilience rating by 22.
Savage Gladiator's Shanker	Honor: 8400, Arena: 475	Dagger: Physical 187-281, 1.8, 130 Equip: Increases attack power by 66., +49 Stamina, Equip: Improves critical strike rating by 22., Equip: Improves your resilience rating by 22.
Savage Gladiator's Pummeler	Honor: 8400, Arena: 475	Mace: Physical 237-440, 2.6, 130.2 Equip: Increases attack power by 66., +49 Stamina, Equip: Improves critical strike rating by 22., Equip: Improves your resilience rating by 22.
Savage Gladiator's Slicer	Honor: 8400, Arena: 475	Sword: Physical 270-406, 2.6, 130 Equip: Increases attack power by 66., +49 Stamina, Equip: Improves critical strike rating by 22., Equip: Improves your resilience rating by 22.
Savage Gladiator's Right Ripper	Honor: 8400, Arena: 475	Fist Weapon: Physical 237-440, 2.6, 130.2 Equip: Increases attack power by 66., +49 Stamina, Equip: Improves critical strike rating by 22., Equip: Improves your resilience rating by 22.
Hateful Gladiator's Cleaver	Honor: 8400, Arena: 950	Axe: Physical 261-485, 2.6, 143.5 Equip: Increases attack power by 76., +58 Stamina, Equip: Improves critical strike rating by 26., Equip: Improves your resilience rating by 25.
Hateful Gladiator's Shanker	Honor: 8400, Arena: 950	Dagger: Physical 206-310, 1.8, 143.3 Equip: Increases attack power by 76., +58 Stamina, Equip: Improves critical strike rating by 26., Equip: Improves your resilience rating by 25.
Hateful Gladiator's Right Ripper	Honor: 8400, Arena: 950	Fist Weapon: Physical 261-485, 2.6, 143.5 Equip: Increases attack power by 76., +58 Stamina, Equip: Improves critical strike rating by 26., Equip: Improves your resilience rating by 25.
Hateful Gladiator's Pummeler	Honor: 8400, Arena: 950	Mace: Physical 261-485, 2.6, 143.5 Equip: Increases attack power by 76., +58 Stamina, Equip: Improves critical strike rating by 26., Equip: Improves your resilience rating by 25.
Hateful Gladiator's Slicer	Honor: 8400, Arena: 950	Sword: Physical 298-448, 2.6, 143.5 Equip: Increases attack power by 76., +58 Stamina, Equip: Improves critical strike rating by 26., Equip: Improves your resilience rating by 25.
Hateful Gladiator's Spellblade	Honor: 10000, Arena: 1150	Dagger: Physical 62-202, 1.6, 82.5 +49 Stamina, +32 Intellect, Equip: Increases spell power by 408., Equip: Improves critical strike rating by 32., Equip: Improves your resilience rating by 32.
Hateful Gladiator's Gavel	Honor: 10000, Arena: 1150	Mace: Physical 62-202, 1.6, 82.5 +49 Stamina, +32 Intellect, Equip: Increases spell power by 408., Equip: Restores 13 mana per 5 sec., Equip: Improves your resilience rating by 32.
Savage Gladiator's Spellblade	Honor: 10000, Arena: 575	Dagger: Physical 57-183, 1.6, 75 +42 Stamina, +28 Intellect, Equip: Increases spell power by 355., Equip: Improves critical strike rating by 28., Equip: Improves your resilience rating by 28.

Name	Extended Cost	Stats
Savage Gladiator's Gavel	Honor: 10000, Arena: 575	Mace: Physical 57-183, 1.6, 75 +42 Stamina, +28 Intellect, Equip: Increases spell power by 355., Equip: Restores 11 mana per 5 sec., Equip: Improves your resilience rating by 28.
Hateful Gladiator's Decapitator	Honor: 12000, Arena: 1400	Axe: Physical 537-806, 3.6, 186.5 Equip: Increases attack power by 178., +135 Stamina, Equip: Improves critical strike rating by 60., Equip: Improves your resilience rating by 59.
Hateful Gladiator's Bonegrinder	Honor: 12000, Arena: 1400	Mace: Physical 537-806, 3.6, 186.5 Equip: Increases attack power by 178., +135 Stamina, Equip: Improves critical strike rating by 60., Equip: Improves your resilience rating by 59.
Hateful Gladiator's Pike	Honor: 12000, Arena: 1400	Polearm: Physical 537-806, 3.6, 186.5 Equip: Increases attack power by 178., +135 Stamina, Equip: Improves critical strike rating by 60., Equip: Improves your resilience rating by 59.
Hateful Gladiator's Greatsword	Honor: 12000, Arena: 1400	Sword: Physical 537-806, 3.6, 186.5 Equip: Increases attack power by 178., +135 Stamina, Equip: Improves critical strike rating by 60., Equip: Improves your resilience rating by 59.
Hateful Gladiator's Staff	Honor: 12000, Arena: 1400	Staff: Physical 176-327, 2, 125.8 +57 Agility, +130 Stamina, Equip: Increases attack power by 1845 in Cat, Bear, Dire Bear, and Moonkin forms only., Equip: Improves critical strike rating by 75., Equip: Improves your resilience rating by 75.
Hateful Gladiator's Rifle	Honor: 12000, Arena: 1400	Gun: Physical 311-467, 3, 129.7 Equip: Increases attack power by 56., +42 Stamina, Equip: Improves critical strike rating by 18., Equip: Improves your resilience rating by 18.
Hateful Gladiator's Longbow	Honor: 12000, Arena: 1400	Bow: Physical 311-467, 3, 129.7 Equip: Increases attack power by 56., +42 Stamina, Equip: Improves critical strike rating by 18., Equip: Improves your resilience rating by 18.
Hateful Gladiator's Heavy Crossbow	Honor: 12000, Arena: 1400	Crossbow: Physical 311-467, 3, 129.7 Equip: Increases attack power by 56., +42 Stamina, Equip: Improves critical strike rating by 18., Equip: Improves your resilience rating by 18.
Hateful Gladiator's Energy Staff	Honor: 12000, Arena: 1400	Staff: Physical 176-327, 2, 125.8 +130 Stamina, +57 Intellect, Equip: Increases spell power by 408., +75 Spirit, Equip: Improves your resilience rating by 75.
Hateful Gladiator's Battle Staff	Honor: 12000, Arena: 1400	Staff: Physical 176-327, 2, 125.8 +130 Stamina, +57 Intellect, Equip: Increases spell power by 408., Equip: Improves critical strike rating by 75., Equip: Improves your resilience rating by 75.
Hateful Gladiator's War Staff	Honor: 12000, Arena: 1400	Staff: Physical 176-327, 2, 125.8 +130 Stamina, +57 Intellect, Equip: Increases spell power by 408., Equip: Improves haste rating by 75., Equip: Improves your resilience rating by 75.
Hateful Gladiator's Focus Staff	Honor: 12000, Arena: 1400	Staff: Physical 176-327, 2, 125.8 +130 Stamina, +57 Intellect, Equip: Increases spell power by 408., Equip: Improves hit rating by 75., Equip: Improves your resilience rating by 75.
Savage Gladiator's Decapitator	Honor: 12000, Arena: 700	Axe: Physical 487-731, 3.6, 169.2 Equip: Increases attack power by 156., +117 Stamina, Equip: Improves critical strike rating by 52., Equip: Improves your resilience rating by 51.
Savage Gladiator's Bonegrinder	Honor: 12000, Arena: 700	Mace: Physical 487-731, 3.6, 169.2 Equip: Increases attack power by 156., +117 Stamina, Equip: Improves critical strike rating by 52., Equip: Improves your resilience rating by 51.
Savage Gladiator's Pike	Honor: 12000, Arena: 700	Polearm: Physical 487-731, 3.6, 169.2 Equip: Increases attack power by 156., +117 Stamina, Equip: Improves critical strike rating by 52., Equip: Improves your resilience rating by 51.

Name	Extended Cost	Stats
Savage Gladiator's Greatsword	Honor: 12000, Arena: 700	Sword: Physical 487-731, 3.6, 169.2 Equip: Increases attack power by 156., +117 Stamina, Equip: Improves critical strike rating by 52., Equip: Improves your resilience rating by 51.
Savage Gladiator's Longbow	Honor: 12000, Arena: 700	Bow: Physical 282-424, 3, 117.7 Equip: Increases attack power by 48., +36 Stamina, Equip: Improves critical strike rating by 16., Equip: Improves your resilience rating by 16.
Savage Gladiator's Heavy Crossbow	Honor: 12000, Arena: 700	Crossbow: Physical 282-424, 3, 117.7 Equip: Increases attack power by 48., +36 Stamina, Equip: Improves critical strike rating by 16., Equip: Improves your resilience rating by 16.
Savage Gladiator's Rifle	Honor: 12000, Arena: 700	Gun: Physical 282-424, 3, 117.7 Equip: Increases attack power by 48., +36 Stamina, Equip: Improves critical strike rating by 16., Equip: Improves your resilience rating by 16.
Savage Gladiator's Staff	Honor: 12000, Arena: 700	Staff: Physical 160-296, 2, 114 +50 Agility, +112 Stamina, Equip: Increases attack power by 1602 in Cat, Bear, Dire Bear, and Moonkin forms only., Equip: Improves critical strike rating by 66., Equip: Improves your resilience rating by 65.
Savage Gladiator's Energy Staff	Honor: 12000, Arena: 700	Staff: Physical 160-296, 2, 114 +112 Stamina, +50 Intellect, Equip: Increases spell power by 355., +66 Spirit, Equip: Improves your resilience rating by 65.
LK Arena 1 Feral Druid Staff	Honor: 12000, Arena: 700	Staff: Physical 160-296, 2, 114
Savage Gladiator's Battle Staff	Honor: 12000, Arena: 700	Staff: Physical 160-296, 2, 114 +112 Stamina, +50 Intellect, Equip: Increases spell power by 355., Equip: Improves critical strike rating by 66., Equip: Improves your resilience rating by 65.
Savage Gladiator's War Staff	Honor: 12000, Arena: 700	Staff: Physical 160-296, 2, 114 +112 Stamina, +50 Intellect, Equip: Increases spell power by 355., Equip: Improves haste rating by 66., Equip: Improves your resilience rating by 65.
Savage Gladiator's Focus Staff	Honor: 12000, Arena: 700	Staff: Physical 160-296, 2, 114 +112 Stamina, +50 Intellect, Equip: Increases spell power by 355., Equip: Improves hit rating by 66., Equip: Improves your resilience rating by 65.
Vengeful Gladiator's Bonecracker	Arena: 1125	Mace: Physical 102-191, 1.5, 97.7 +27 Stamina, Equip: Improves critical strike rating by 19., Equip: Improves your resilience rating by 12., Equip: Improves hit rating by 10., Increases attack power.
Vengeful Gladiator's Chain Gauntlets	Arena: 1125	Mail: 596 , +48 Stamina, +30 Agility, Equip: Improves critical strike rating by 17., Equip: Improves your resilience rating by 21., +13 Intellect, Increases attack power., Increases the damage done by your Multi-Shot %.
Vengeful Gladiator's Dragonhide Gloves	Arena: 1125	Leather: 324 , +40 Stamina, +34 Strength, +19 Intellect, +19 Agility, Equip: Improves your resilience rating by 22., Increases spell power., Reduces the cast time of your Cyclone spell.
Vengeful Gladiator's Dreadweave Gloves	Arena: 1125	Cloth: 283 , +45 Stamina, +25 Intellect, Equip: Improves your resilience rating by 21., Gives you chance to avoid interruption caused by damage while casting Fear., Increases spell power.
Deadly Gladiator's Waraxe	Arena: 1200	Axe: Physical 285-530, 2.6, 156.7 Equip: Increases attack power by 86., +64 Stamina, Equip: Improves critical strike rating by 29., Equip: Improves your resilience rating by 28.
Deadly Gladiator's Baton of Light	Arena: 1200	Wand: Fire 382-711, 1.9, 287.6 Equip: Increases spell power by 37., +36 Stamina, +15 Intellect, +21 Spirit, Equip: Improves your resilience rating by 20.
Deadly Gladiator's Touch of Defeat	Arena: 1200	Wand: Fire 382-711, 1.9, 287.6 Equip: Increases spell power by 37., +31 Stamina, +20 Intellect, Equip: Improves critical strike rating by 21., Equip: Improves your resilience rating by 20.

Name	Extended Cost	Stats
Deadly Gladiator's War Edge	Arena: 1200	Thrown: Physical 214-322, 1.9, 141.1 Equip: Increases attack power by 62., +48 Stamina, Equip: Improves critical strike rating by 21., Equip: Improves your resilience rating by 20.
Deadly Gladiator's Idol of Steadfastness	Arena: 1200	Idol: Your Moonfire spell grants spell power.
Deadly Gladiator's Idol of Resolve	Arena: 1200	Idol: Your Mangle ability also grants attack power.
Deadly Gladiator's Totem of the Third Wind	Arena: 1200	Totem: Increases spell power of Lesser Healing Wave.
LK Arena 4 Death Knight Relic	Arena: 1200	Sigil: Your Plague Strike ability also grants you attack power.
Deadly Gladiator's Piercing Touch	Arena: 1200	Wand: Fire 382-711, 1.9, 287.6 Equip: Increases spell power by 37., +31 Stamina, +20 Intellect, Equip: Improves your resilience rating by 20., Increases your spell penetration.
Deadly Gladiator's Idol of Tenacity	Arena: 1200	Idol: Increases the spell power of the final healing value of your Lifebloom.
Deadly Gladiator's Totem of Survival	Arena: 1200	Totem: Your Shock grant spell power.
Deadly Gladiator's Totem of Indomitability	Arena: 1200	Totem: Your Lava Lash ability also grants attack power.
Deadly Gladiator's Libram of Justice	Arena: 1200	Libram: Increases spell power of Flash of Light.
Deadly Gladiator's Sigil of Strife	Arena: 1200	Sigil: Your Plague Strike ability also grants attack power.
Deadly Gladiator's Libram of Fortitude	Arena: 1200	Libram: Your Crusader Strike ability also grants attack power.
Deadly Gladiator's Plate Gauntlets	Arena: 1350	Plate: 1436, Socket Bonus: +4 Critical Strike Rating, Socket: Blue, +67 Strength, +111 Stamina, Equip: Improves critical strike rating by 32., Equip: Improves your resilience rating by 39., Hamstring Rage cost reduced by $/10;s1.
Deadly Gladiator's Scaled Gauntlets	Arena: 1350	Plate: 1436, Socket Bonus: +4 Critical Strike Rating, Socket: Blue, +67 Strength, +111 Stamina, Equip: Improves critical strike rating by 32., Equip: Improves your resilience rating by 39., Increases the damage dealt by your Crusader Strike ability %.
Deadly Gladiator's Dreadplate Gauntlets	Arena: 1350	Plate: 1436, Socket Bonus: +4 Critical Strike Rating, Socket: Blue, +67 Strength, +111 Stamina, Equip: Improves critical strike rating by 32., Equip: Improves your resilience rating by 39., Reduces the cooldown of your Strangulate onds.
Deadly Gladiator's Ringmail Gauntlets	Arena: 1350	Mail: 804, Socket Bonus: +2 mana per 5 sec., Socket: Blue, +85 Stamina, +37 Intellect, Equip: Increases spell power by 78., Equip: Restores 13 mana per 5 sec., Equip: Improves your resilience rating by 39., Improves the range of all Shock spells yards.
Deadly Gladiator's Mail Gauntlets	Arena: 1350	Mail: 804, Socket Bonus: +2 mana per 5 sec., Socket: Blue, +85 Stamina, +37 Intellect, Equip: Increases spell power by 78., Equip: Improves critical strike rating by 32., Equip: Improves your resilience rating by 39., Improves the range of all Shock spells yards.
Deadly Gladiator's Ornamented Gloves	Arena: 1350	Plate: 1436, Socket Bonus: +2 mana per 5 sec., Socket: Blue, +85 Stamina, +37 Intellect, Equip: Increases spell power by 78., Equip: Improves critical strike rating by 32., Equip: Improves your resilience rating by 39., Increases the critical effect chance of your Flash of Light.
Deadly Gladiator's Linked Gauntlets	Arena: 1350	Mail: 804, Socket Bonus: +4 Critical Strike Rating, Socket: Blue, Equip: Increases attack power by 84., +50 Agility, +85 Stamina, +30 Intellect, Equip: Improves critical strike rating by 39., Equip: Improves your resilience rating by 39., Improves the range of all Shock spells yards.

Name	Extended Cost	Stats
Deadly Gladiator's Chain Gauntlets	Arena: 1350	Mail: 804, Socket Bonus: +4 Critical Strike Rating, Socket: Blue, Equip: Increases attack power by 84., +50 Agility, +85 Stamina, +30 Intellect, Equip: Improves critical strike rating by 39., Equip: Improves your resilience rating by 39., Reduces the cooldown of your Tranquilizing Shot.
Deadly Gladiator's Kodohide Gloves	Arena: 1350	Leather: 362, Socket Bonus: +4 Spirit, Socket: Blue, Equip: Increases spell power by 78., +85 Stamina, +37 Intellect, +32 Spirit, Equip: Improves your resilience rating by 39., Reduces the cast time of your Cyclone spell .
Deadly Gladiator's Wyrmhide Gloves	Arena: 1350	Leather: 362, Socket Bonus: +4 Spirit, Socket: Blue, Equip: Increases spell power by 78., +85 Stamina, +37 Intellect, +32 Spirit, Equip: Improves critical strike rating by 32., Equip: Improves your resilience rating by 39., Reduces the cast time of your Cyclone spell .
Deadly Gladiator's Mooncloth Gloves	Arena: 1350	Cloth: 192, Socket Bonus: +4 Spirit, Socket: Blue, Equip: Increases spell power by 78., +85 Stamina, +37 Intellect, +32 Spirit, Equip: Improves your resilience rating by 39., Reduces the cooldown of your Psychic Scream ability.
Deadly Gladiator's Silk Handguards	Arena: 1350	Cloth: 192, Socket Bonus: +5 Spell Power, Socket: Blue, Equip: Increases spell power by 78., +85 Stamina, +37 Intellect, Equip: Improves critical strike rating by 32., Equip: Improves your resilience rating by 39., Gives you chance to avoid interruption caused by damage while casting Polymorph.
Deadly Gladiator's Felweave Handguards	Arena: 1350	Cloth: 192, Socket Bonus: +5 Spell Power, Socket: Blue, Equip: Increases spell power by 78., +85 Stamina, +37 Intellect, Equip: Improves critical strike rating by 32., Equip: Improves your resilience rating by 39., Gives you chance to avoid interruption caused by damage while casting Fear.
Deadly Gladiator's Hacker	Arena: 1350	Axe: Physical 164-306, 1.5, 156.7 Equip: Increases attack power by 86., +64 Stamina, Equip: Improves critical strike rating by 29., Equip: Improves your resilience rating by 28.
Deadly Gladiator's Chopper	Arena: 1350	Axe: Physical 285-530, 2.6, 156.7 Equip: Increases attack power by 86., +64 Stamina, Equip: Improves critical strike rating by 29., Equip: Improves your resilience rating by 28.
Deadly Gladiator's Left Render	Arena: 1350	Fist Weapon: Physical 285-530, 2.6, 156.7 Equip: Increases attack power by 86., +64 Stamina, Equip: Improves critical strike rating by 29., Equip: Improves your resilience rating by 28.
Deadly Gladiator's Left Ripper	Arena: 1350	Fist Weapon: Physical 164-306, 1.5, 156.7 Equip: Increases attack power by 86., +64 Stamina, Equip: Improves critical strike rating by 29., Equip: Improves your resilience rating by 28.
Deadly Gladiator's Bonecracker	Arena: 1350	Mace: Physical 164-306, 1.5, 156.7 Equip: Increases attack power by 86., +64 Stamina, Equip: Improves critical strike rating by 29., Equip: Improves your resilience rating by 28.
Deadly Gladiator's Quickblade	Arena: 1350	Sword: Physical 164-306, 1.5, 156.7 Equip: Increases attack power by 86., +64 Stamina, Equip: Improves critical strike rating by 29., Equip: Improves your resilience rating by 28.
Deadly Gladiator's Endgame	Arena: 1350	Equip: Increases spell power by 66., +66 Stamina, +29 Intellect, Equip: Improves critical strike rating by 38., Equip: Improves your resilience rating by 37.
Deadly Gladiator's Reprieve	Arena: 1350	Equip: Increases spell power by 66., +66 Stamina, +29 Intellect, +38 Spirit, Equip: Improves your resilience rating by 37.
Deadly Gladiator's Grimoire	Arena: 1350	Equip: Increases spell power by 66., +66 Stamina, +29 Intellect, Equip: Improves your resilience rating by 37., Increases your spell penetration.
Deadly Gladiator's Mutilator	Arena: 1350	Dagger: Physical 197-367, 1.8, 156.7 Equip: Increases attack power by 86., +64 Stamina, Equip: Improves critical strike rating by 29., Equip: Improves your resilience rating by 28.

Name	Extended Cost	Stats
Deadly Gladiator's Shiv	Arena: 1350	Dagger: Physical 153-285, 1.4, 156.4 Equip: Increases attack power by 86., +64 Stamina, Equip: Improves critical strike rating by 29., Equip: Improves your resilience rating by 28.
Deadly Gladiator's Satin Gloves	Arena: 1350	Cloth: 192, Socket Bonus: +5 Spell Power, Socket: Blue, Equip: Increases spell power by 78., +85 Stamina, +37 Intellect, Equip: Improves critical strike rating by 32., Equip: Improves your resilience rating by 39., Reduces the cooldown of your Psychic Scream.
Deadly Gladiator's Dragonhide Gloves	Arena: 1350	Leather: 362, Socket Bonus: +4 Critical Strike Rating, Socket: Blue, Equip: Increases attack power by 74., +67 Agility, +85 Stamina, Equip: Improves critical strike rating by 31., Equip: Improves your resilience rating by 39., Reduces the energy cost of your Maim.
Deadly Gladiator's Leather Gloves	Arena: 1350	Leather: 362, Socket Bonus: +4 Critical Strike Rating, Socket: Blue, Equip: Increases attack power by 74., +67 Agility, +85 Stamina, Equip: Improves critical strike rating by 31., Equip: Improves your resilience rating by 39., Reduces the cost of your Kick.
Vengeful Gladiator's Chain Spaulders	Arena: 1500	Mail: 715, Socket Bonus: +3 Resilience Rating, Socket: Red, Yellow, +45 Stamina, +32 Agility, Equip: Improves critical strike rating by 14., Equip: Improves your resilience rating by 21., +10 Intellect, Increases attack power.
Vengeful Gladiator's Dragonhide Spaulders	Arena: 1500	Leather: 377, Socket Bonus: +3 Resilience Rating, Socket: Red, Yellow, +39 Stamina, +30 Strength, +14 Intellect, +21 Agility, Equip: Improves your resilience rating by 21., Increases spell power.
Vengeful Gladiator's Dreadweave Mantle	Arena: 1500	Cloth: 311, Socket Bonus: +3 Resilience Rating, Socket: Blue, Yellow, +45 Stamina, +10 Intellect, Equip: Improves your resilience rating by 21., Equip: Improves hit rating by 13., Increases spell power.
Deadly Gladiator's Ringmail Spaulders	Arena: 1800	Mail: 964, Socket Bonus: +2 mana per 5 sec., Socket: Yellow, +85 Stamina, +37 Intellect, Equip: Increases spell power by 78., Equip: Restores 17 mana per 5 sec., Equip: Improves your resilience rating by 50.
Deadly Gladiator's Mail Spaulders	Arena: 1800	Mail: 964, Socket Bonus: +2 mana per 5 sec., Socket: Yellow, +85 Stamina, +37 Intellect, Equip: Increases spell power by 78., Equip: Improves critical strike rating by 42., Equip: Improves your resilience rating by 50.
Deadly Gladiator's Ornamented Spaulders	Arena: 1800	Plate: 1723, Socket Bonus: +2 mana per 5 sec., Socket: Yellow, +85 Stamina, +37 Intellect, Equip: Increases spell power by 78., Equip: Improves critical strike rating by 42., Equip: Improves your resilience rating by 50.
Deadly Gladiator's Scaled Shoulders	Arena: 1800	Plate: 1723, Socket Bonus: +4 Critical Strike Rating, Socket: Yellow, +67 Strength, +111 Stamina, Equip: Improves critical strike rating by 42., Equip: Improves your resilience rating by 50.
Deadly Gladiator's Dreadplate Shoulders	Arena: 1800	Plate: 1723, Socket Bonus: +4 Critical Strike Rating, Socket: Yellow, +67 Strength, +111 Stamina, Equip: Improves critical strike rating by 42., Equip: Improves your resilience rating by 50.
Deadly Gladiator's Plate Shoulders	Arena: 1800	Plate: 1723, Socket Bonus: +4 Critical Strike Rating, Socket: Yellow, +67 Strength, +111 Stamina, Equip: Improves critical strike rating by 42., Equip: Improves your resilience rating by 50.
Deadly Gladiator's Linked Spaulders	Arena: 1800	Mail: 964, Socket Bonus: +4 Critical Strike Rating, Socket: Yellow, Equip: Increases attack power by 84., +50 Agility, +85 Stamina, +29 Intellect, Equip: Improves critical strike rating by 50., Equip: Improves your resilience rating by 50.

Name	Extended Cost	Stats
Deadly Gladiator's Chain Spaulders	Arena: 1800	Mail: 964, Socket Bonus: +4 Critical Strike Rating, Socket: Yellow, Equip: Increases attack power by 84., +50 Agility, +85 Stamina, +29 Intellect, Equip: Improves critical strike rating by 50., Equip: Improves your resilience rating by 50.
Deadly Gladiator's Kodohide Spaulders	Arena: 1800	Leather: 434, Socket Bonus: +4 Spirit, Socket: Yellow, Equip: Increases spell power by 78., +85 Stamina, +37 Intellect, +42 Spirit, Equip: Improves your resilience rating by 50.
Deadly Gladiator's Wyrmhide Spaulders	Arena: 1800	Leather: 434, Socket Bonus: +4 Spirit, Socket: Yellow, Equip: Increases spell power by 78., +85 Stamina, +37 Intellect, Equip: Improves critical strike rating by 42., Equip: Improves your resilience rating by 50.
Deadly Gladiator's Leather Spaulders	Arena: 1800	Leather: 434, Socket Bonus: +4 Critical Strike Rating, Socket: Yellow, Equip: Increases attack power by 76., +67 Agility, +85 Stamina, Equip: Improves critical strike rating by 42., Equip: Improves your resilience rating by 49.
Deadly Gladiator's Dragonhide Spaulders	Arena: 1800	Leather: 434, Socket Bonus: +4 Critical Strike Rating, Socket: Yellow, Equip: Increases attack power by 76., +67 Agility, +85 Stamina, Equip: Improves critical strike rating by 42., Equip: Improves your resilience rating by 49.
Deadly Gladiator's Satin Mantle	Arena: 1800	Cloth: 231, Socket Bonus: +6 Stamina, Socket: Yellow, Equip: Increases spell power by 78., +85 Stamina, +37 Intellect, Equip: Improves critical strike rating by 42., Equip: Improves your resilience rating by 50.
Deadly Gladiator's Silk Amice	Arena: 1800	Cloth: 231, Socket Bonus: +6 Stamina, Socket: Yellow, Equip: Increases spell power by 78., +85 Stamina, +37 Intellect, Equip: Improves critical strike rating by 42., Equip: Improves your resilience rating by 50.
Deadly Gladiator's Felweave Amice	Arena: 1800	Cloth: 231, Socket Bonus: +6 Stamina, Socket: Yellow, Equip: Increases spell power by 78., +85 Stamina, +37 Intellect, Equip: Improves critical strike rating by 42., Equip: Improves your resilience rating by 50.
Deadly Gladiator's Mooncloth Mantle	Arena: 1800	Cloth: 231, Socket Bonus: +4 Spirit, Socket: Yellow, Equip: Increases spell power by 78., +85 Stamina, +37 Intellect, +42 Spirit, Equip: Improves your resilience rating by 50.
Vengeful Gladiator's Chain Armor	Arena: 1875	Mail: 954, Socket Bonus: +4 Critical Strike Rating, Socket: Red, Red, Yellow, +57 Stamina, +31 Agility, Equip: Improves critical strike rating by 21., Equip: Improves your resilience rating by 21., +17 Intellect, Increases attack power.
Vengeful Gladiator's Chain Helm	Arena: 1875	Mail: 775, Socket Bonus: +4 Resilience Rating, Socket: Meta, Red, +55 Stamina, +37 Agility, Equip: Improves critical strike rating by 22., Equip: Improves your resilience rating by 22., +19 Intellect, Increases attack power.
Vengeful Gladiator's Chain Leggings	Arena: 1875	Mail: 835 , +58 Stamina, +38 Agility, Equip: Improves critical strike rating by 21., Equip: Improves your resilience rating by 33., +15 Intellect, Increases attack power.
Vengeful Gladiator's Dragonhide Helm	Arena: 1875	Leather: 404, Socket Bonus: +4 Resilience Rating, Socket: Meta, Yellow, +52 Stamina, +36 Strength, +20 Intellect, +27 Agility, Equip: Improves your resilience rating by 25., Increases spell power.
Vengeful Gladiator's Dragonhide Legguards	Arena: 1875	Leather: 417 , +49 Stamina, +43 Strength, +26 Intellect, +29 Agility, Equip: Improves your resilience rating by 29., Increases spell power.
Vengeful Gladiator's Dragonhide Tunic	Arena: 1875	Leather: 498, Socket Bonus: +4 Critical Strike Rating, Socket: Red, Red, Yellow, +48 Stamina, +37 Strength, +19 Intellect, +22 Agility, Equip: Improves your resilience rating by 26., Increases spell power.

Name	Extended Cost	Stats
Vengeful Gladiator's Dreadweave Hood	Arena: 1875	Cloth: 395, Socket Bonus: +4 Resilience Rating, Socket: Meta, Red, +66 Stamina, +20 Intellect, Equip: Improves your resilience rating by 33., Increases spell power.
Vengeful Gladiator's Dreadweave Leggings	Arena: 1875	Cloth: 410 , +69 Stamina, +27 Intellect, Equip: Improves your resilience rating by 33., Increases spell power.
Vengeful Gladiator's Barrier	Arena: 1875	Shield: 5727 , +27 Stamina, Equip: Improves your resilience rating by 27., +19 Intellect, Increases spell power.
Deadly Gladiator's Dreadplate Chestpiece	Arena: 2250	Plate: 2298, Socket Bonus: +6 Resilience Rating, Socket: Red, Yellow, +85 Strength, +150 Stamina, Equip: Improves critical strike rating by 51., Equip: Improves your resilience rating by 66.
Deadly Gladiator's Scaled Chestpiece	Arena: 2250	Plate: 2298, Socket Bonus: +6 Resilience Rating, Socket: Red, Yellow, +85 Strength, +150 Stamina, Equip: Improves critical strike rating by 51., Equip: Improves your resilience rating by 66.
Deadly Gladiator's Plate Chestpiece	Arena: 2250	Plate: 2298, Socket Bonus: +6 Resilience Rating, Socket: Red, Yellow, +85 Strength, +150 Stamina, Equip: Improves critical strike rating by 51., Equip: Improves your resilience rating by 66.
Deadly Gladiator's Scaled Helm	Arena: 2250	Plate: 1867, Socket Bonus: +8 Critical Strike Rating, Socket: Meta, Red, +85 Strength, +150 Stamina, Equip: Improves critical strike rating by 51., Equip: Improves your resilience rating by 66.
Deadly Gladiator's Ornamented Chestguard	Arena: 2250	Plate: 2298, Socket Bonus: +6 Resilience Rating, Socket: Red, Yellow, +115 Stamina, +50 Intellect, Equip: Improves spell power by 98., Equip: Improves critical strike rating by 51., Equip: Improves your resilience rating by 66.
Deadly Gladiator's Ringmail Armor	Arena: 2250	Mail: 1286, Socket Bonus: +6 Resilience Rating, Socket: Red, Yellow, +115 Stamina, +50 Intellect, Equip: Improves spell power by 98., Equip: Restores 20 mana per 5 sec., Equip: Improves your resilience rating by 66.
Deadly Gladiator's Mail Armor	Arena: 2250	Mail: 1286, Socket Bonus: +6 Resilience Rating, Socket: Red, Yellow, +115 Stamina, +50 Intellect, Equip: Improves spell power by 98., Equip: Improves critical strike rating by 51., Equip: Improves your resilience rating by 66.
Deadly Gladiator's Ringmail Helm	Arena: 2250	Mail: 1045, Socket Bonus: 3 mana per 5 sec, Socket: Meta, Red, +115 Stamina, +50 Intellect, Equip: Improves spell power by 99., Equip: Restores 20 mana per 5 sec., Equip: Improves your resilience rating by 50.
Deadly Gladiator's Mail Helm	Arena: 2250	Mail: 1045, Socket Bonus: 3 mana per 5 sec, Socket: Meta, Red, +115 Stamina, +50 Intellect, Equip: Improves spell power by 99., Equip: Improves critical strike rating by 51., Equip: Improves your resilience rating by 50.
Deadly Gladiator's Ringmail Leggings	Arena: 2250	Mail: 1125, Socket Bonus: +7 Spell Power, Socket: Red, Blue, +115 Stamina, +50 Intellect, Equip: Increases spell power by 99., Equip: Restores 20 mana per 5 sec., Equip: Improves your resilience rating by 66.
Deadly Gladiator's Mail Leggings	Arena: 2250	Mail: 1125, Socket Bonus: +7 Spell Power, Socket: Red, Blue, +115 Stamina, +50 Intellect, Equip: Increases spell power by 99., Equip: Improves critical strike rating by 51., Equip: Improves your resilience rating by 66.
Deadly Gladiator's Ornamented Legplates	Arena: 2250	Plate: 2011, Socket Bonus: +7 Spell Power, Socket: Red, Blue, +115 Stamina, +50 Intellect, Equip: Increases spell power by 99., Equip: Improves critical strike rating by 51., Equip: Improves your resilience rating by 66.
Deadly Gladiator's Scaled Legguards	Arena: 2250	Plate: 2011, Socket Bonus: +6 Strength, Socket: Red, Blue, +85 Strength, +150 Stamina, Equip: Improves critical strike rating by 51., Equip: Improves your resilience rating by 66.

Name	Extended Cost	Stats
Deadly Gladiator's Dreadplate Legguards	Arena: 2250	Plate: 2011, Socket Bonus: +6 Strength, Socket: Red, Blue, +85 Strength, +150 Stamina, Equip: Improves critical strike rating by 51., Equip: Improves your resilience rating by 66.
Deadly Gladiator's Plate Legguards	Arena: 2250	Plate: 2011, Socket Bonus: +6 Strength, Socket: Red, Blue, +85 Strength, +150 Stamina, Equip: Improves critical strike rating by 51., Equip: Improves your resilience rating by 66.
Deadly Gladiator's Dreadplate Helm	Arena: 2250	Plate: 1867, Socket Bonus: +8 Critical Strike Rating, Socket: Meta, Red, +85 Strength, +150 Stamina, Equip: Improves critical strike rating by 51., Equip: Improves your resilience rating by 66.
Deadly Gladiator's Plate Helm	Arena: 2250	Plate: 1867, Socket Bonus: +8 Critical Strike Rating, Socket: Meta, Red, +85 Strength, +150 Stamina, Equip: Improves critical strike rating by 51., Equip: Improves your resilience rating by 66.
Deadly Gladiator's Linked Armor	Arena: 2250	Mail: 1286, Socket Bonus: +6 Resilience Rating, Socket: Red, Yellow, Equip: Increases attack power by 102., +68 Agility, +115 Stamina, +35 Intellect, Equip: Improves critical strike rating by 67., Equip: Improves your resilience rating by 66.
Deadly Gladiator's Chain Armor	Arena: 2250	Mail: 1286, Socket Bonus: +6 Resilience Rating, Socket: Red, Yellow, Equip: Increases attack power by 102., +68 Agility, +115 Stamina, +35 Intellect, Equip: Improves critical strike rating by 67., Equip: Improves your resilience rating by 66.
Deadly Gladiator's Linked Helm	Arena: 2250	Mail: 1045, Socket Bonus: +8 Critical Strike Rating, Socket: Meta, Red, Equip: Increases attack power by 102., +68 Agility, +115 Stamina, +34 Intellect, Equip: Improves critical strike rating by 51., Equip: Improves your resilience rating by 66.
Deadly Gladiator's Chain Helm	Arena: 2250	Mail: 1045, Socket Bonus: +8 Critical Strike Rating, Socket: Meta, Red, Equip: Increases attack power by 102., +68 Agility, +115 Stamina, +34 Intellect, Equip: Improves critical strike rating by 51., Equip: Improves your resilience rating by 66.
Deadly Gladiator's Linked Leggings	Arena: 2250	Mail: 1125, Socket Bonus: +6 Agility, Socket: Red, Blue, Equip: Increases attack power by 102., +68 Agility, +115 Stamina, +34 Intellect, Equip: Improves critical strike rating by 67., Equip: Improves your resilience rating by 66.
Deadly Gladiator's Chain Leggings	Arena: 2250	Mail: 1125, Socket Bonus: +6 Agility, Socket: Red, Blue, Equip: Increases attack power by 102., +68 Agility, +115 Stamina, +34 Intellect, Equip: Improves critical strike rating by 67., Equip: Improves your resilience rating by 66.
Deadly Gladiator's Kodohide Legguards	Arena: 2250	Leather: 506, Socket Bonus: +7 Spell Power, Socket: Red, Blue, Equip: Increases spell power by 99., +115 Stamina, +50 Intellect, +51 Spirit, Equip: Improves your resilience rating by 66.
Deadly Gladiator's Wyrmhide Legguards	Arena: 2250	Leather: 506, Socket Bonus: +7 Spell Power, Socket: Red, Blue, Equip: Increases spell power by 99., +115 Stamina, +50 Intellect, Equip: Improves critical strike rating by 51., Equip: Improves your resilience rating by 66.
Deadly Gladiator's Kodohide Robes	Arena: 2250	Leather: 578, Socket Bonus: +6 Resilience Rating, Socket: Red, Yellow, Equip: Increases spell power by 98., +115 Stamina, +50 Intellect, +51 Spirit, Equip: Improves your resilience rating by 66.
Deadly Gladiator's Wyrmhide Robes	Arena: 2250	Leather: 578, Socket Bonus: +6 Resilience Rating, Socket: Red, Yellow, Equip: Increases spell power by 98., +115 Stamina, +50 Intellect, Equip: Improves critical strike rating by 51., Equip: Improves your resilience rating by 66.
Deadly Gladiator's Kodohide Helm	Arena: 2250	Leather: 470, Socket Bonus: +8 Spirit, Socket: Meta, Red, Equip: Increases spell power by 99., +115 Stamina, +50 Intellect, +51 Spirit, Equip: Improves your resilience rating by 50.

Name	Extended Cost	Stats
Deadly Gladiator's Wyrmhide Helm	Arena: 2250	Leather: 470, Socket Bonus: +8 Spirit, Socket: Meta, Red, Equip: Increases spell power by 99., +115 Stamina, +50 Intellect, Equip: Improves critical strike rating by 51., Equip: Improves your resilience rating by 50.
Deadly Gladiator's Leather Tunic	Arena: 2250	Leather: 578, Socket Bonus: +6 Resilience Rating, Socket: Red, Yellow, Equip: Increases attack power by 102., +84 Agility, +115 Stamina, Equip: Improves critical strike rating by 51., Equip: Improves your resilience rating by 66.
Deadly Gladiator's Leather Legguards	Arena: 2250	Leather: 506, Socket Bonus: +6 Agility, Socket: Red, Blue, Equip: Increases attack power by 102., +84 Agility, +115 Stamina, Equip: Improves critical strike rating by 51., Equip: Improves your resilience rating by 66.
Deadly Gladiator's Dragonhide Robes	Arena: 2250	Leather: 578, Socket Bonus: +6 Resilience Rating, Socket: Red, Yellow, Equip: Increases attack power by 102., +84 Agility, +115 Stamina, Equip: Improves critical strike rating by 51., Equip: Improves your resilience rating by 66.
Deadly Gladiator's Dragonhide Legguards	Arena: 2250	Leather: 506, Socket Bonus: +6 Agility, Socket: Red, Blue, Equip: Increases attack power by 102., +84 Agility, +115 Stamina, Equip: Improves critical strike rating by 51., Equip: Improves your resilience rating by 66.
Deadly Gladiator's Leather Helm	Arena: 2250	Leather: 470, Socket Bonus: +8 Critical Strike Rating, Socket: Meta, Red, Equip: Increases attack power by 70., +84 Agility, +115 Stamina, Equip: Improves critical strike rating by 51., Equip: Improves your resilience rating by 66.
Deadly Gladiator's Dragonhide Helm	Arena: 2250	Leather: 470, Socket Bonus: +8 Critical Strike Rating, Socket: Meta, Red, Equip: Increases attack power by 70., +84 Agility, +115 Stamina, Equip: Improves critical strike rating by 51., Equip: Improves your resilience rating by 66.
Deadly Gladiator's Mooncloth Hood	Arena: 2250	Cloth: 250, Socket Bonus: +8 Spirit, Socket: Meta, Red, Equip: Increases spell power by 99., +115 Stamina, +50 Intellect, +51 Spirit, Equip: Improves your resilience rating by 50.
Deadly Gladiator's Mooncloth Robe	Arena: 2250	Cloth: 308, Socket Bonus: +6 Resilience Rating, Socket: Red, Yellow, Equip: Increases spell power by 98., +115 Stamina, +50 Intellect, +51 Spirit, Equip: Improves your resilience rating by 66.
Deadly Gladiator's Mooncloth Leggings	Arena: 2250	Cloth: 269, Socket Bonus: +7 Spell Power, Socket: Red, Blue, Equip: Increases spell power by 99., +115 Stamina, +50 Intellect, +51 Spirit, Equip: Improves your resilience rating by 66.
Deadly Gladiator's Satin Hood	Arena: 2250	Cloth: 250, Socket Bonus: +8 Resilience Rating, Socket: Meta, Red, Equip: Increases spell power by 99., +115 Stamina, +50 Intellect, Equip: Improves critical strike rating by 51., Equip: Improves your resilience rating by 50.
Deadly Gladiator's Shield Wall	Arena: 2250	Shield: 7722 , +108 Stamina, Equip: Improves your resilience rating by 71.
Deadly Gladiator's Felweave Trousers	Arena: 2250	Cloth: 269, Socket Bonus: +7 Spell Power, Socket: Red, Blue, Equip: Increases spell power by 99., +115 Stamina, +50 Intellect, Equip: Improves critical strike rating by 51., Equip: Improves your resilience rating by 66.
Deadly Gladiator's Felweave Raiment	Arena: 2250	Cloth: 308, Socket Bonus: +9 Stamina, Socket: Red, Yellow, Equip: Increases spell power by 98., +115 Stamina, +50 Intellect, Equip: Improves critical strike rating by 51., Equip: Improves your resilience rating by 66.
Deadly Gladiator's Felweave Cowl	Arena: 2250	Cloth: 250, Socket Bonus: +8 Resilience Rating, Socket: Meta, Red, Equip: Increases spell power by 99., +115 Stamina, +50 Intellect, Equip: Improves critical strike rating by 51., Equip: Improves your resilience rating by 50.

Name	Extended Cost	Stats
Deadly Gladiator's Silk Trousers	Arena: 2250	Cloth: 269, Socket Bonus: +7 Spell Power, Socket: Red, Blue, Equip: Increases spell power by 99., +115 Stamina, +50 Intellect, Equip: Improves critical strike rating by 51., Equip: Improves your resilience rating by 66.
Deadly Gladiator's Silk Raiment	Arena: 2250	Cloth: 308, Socket Bonus: +9 Stamina, Socket: Red, Yellow, Equip: Increases spell power by 98., +115 Stamina, +50 Intellect, Equip: Improves critical strike rating by 51., Equip: Improves your resilience rating by 66.
Deadly Gladiator's Satin Leggings	Arena: 2250	Cloth: 269, Socket Bonus: +7 Spell Power, Socket: Red, Blue, Equip: Increases spell power by 99., +115 Stamina, +50 Intellect, Equip: Improves critical strike rating by 51., Equip: Improves your resilience rating by 66.
Deadly Gladiator's Satin Robe	Arena: 2250	Cloth: 308, Socket Bonus: +9 Stamina, Socket: Red, Yellow, Equip: Increases spell power by 98., +115 Stamina, +50 Intellect, Equip: Improves critical strike rating by 51., Equip: Improves your resilience rating by 66.
Deadly Gladiator's Barrier	Arena: 2250	Shield: 7722 , Equip: Increases spell power by 66., +66 Stamina, +29 Intellect, Equip: Improves critical strike rating by 38., Equip: Improves your resilience rating by 37.
Deadly Gladiator's Redoubt	Arena: 2250	Shield: 7722 , Equip: Increases spell power by 66., +66 Stamina, +29 Intellect, Equip: Restores 15 mana per 5 sec., Equip: Improves your resilience rating by 37.
Vengeful Gladiator's Cleaver	Arena: 2625	Axe: Physical 177-330, 2.6, 97.5 +27 Stamina, Equip: Improves critical strike rating by 19., Equip: Improves your resilience rating by 12., Equip: Improves hit rating by 10., Increases attack power.
Deadly Gladiator's Cleaver	Arena: 3150	Axe: Physical 285-530, 2.6, 156.7 Equip: Increases attack power by 86., +64 Stamina, Equip: Improves critical strike rating by 29., Equip: Improves your resilience rating by 28.
Deadly Gladiator's Shanker	Arena: 3150	Dagger: Physical 225-338, 1.8, 156.4 Equip: Increases attack power by 86., +64 Stamina, Equip: Improves critical strike rating by 29., Equip: Improves your resilience rating by 28.
Deadly Gladiator's Right Ripper	Arena: 3150	Fist Weapon: Physical 285-530, 2.6, 156.7 Equip: Increases attack power by 86., +64 Stamina, Equip: Improves critical strike rating by 29., Equip: Improves your resilience rating by 28.
Deadly Gladiator's Pummeler	Arena: 3150	Mace: Physical 285-530, 2.6, 156.7 Equip: Increases attack power by 86., +64 Stamina, Equip: Improves critical strike rating by 29., Equip: Improves your resilience rating by 28.
Deadly Gladiator's Slicer	Arena: 3150	Sword: Physical 325-489, 2.6, 156.5 Equip: Increases attack power by 86., +64 Stamina, Equip: Improves critical strike rating by 29., Equip: Improves your resilience rating by 28.
Deadly Gladiator's Spellblade	Arena: 3150	Dagger: Physical 69-220, 1.6, 90.3 +55 Stamina, +36 Intellect, Equip: Increases spell power by 461., Equip: Improves critical strike rating by 36., Equip: Improves your resilience rating by 36.
Deadly Gladiator's Gavel	Arena: 3150	Mace: Physical 69-220, 1.6, 90.3 +55 Stamina, +36 Intellect, Equip: Increases spell power by 461., Equip: Restores 14 mana per 5 sec., Equip: Improves your resilience rating by 36.
Vengeful Gladiator's Bonegrinder	Arena: 3750	Mace: Physical 365-549, 3.6, 126.9 +55 Stamina, +42 Strength, Equip: Improves critical strike rating by 42., Equip: Improves your resilience rating by 33., Equip: Improves hit rating by 18.
Vengeful Gladiator's Decapitator	Arena: 3750	Axe: Physical 365-549, 3.6, 126.9 +55 Stamina, Equip: Improves critical strike rating by 42., Equip: Improves your resilience rating by 33., Equip: Improves hit rating by 18., Increases attack power.

Name	Extended Cost	Stats
Deadly Gladiator's Decapitator	Arena: 4500	Axe: Physical 586-880, 3.6, 203.6 Equip: Increases attack power by 200., +151 Stamina, Equip: Improves critical strike rating by 67., Equip: Improves your resilience rating by 66.
Deadly Gladiator's Bonegrinder	Arena: 4500	Mace: Physical 586-880, 3.6, 203.6 Equip: Increases attack power by 200., +151 Stamina, Equip: Improves critical strike rating by 67., Equip: Improves your resilience rating by 66.
Deadly Gladiator's Pike	Arena: 4500	Polearm: Physical 586-880, 3.6, 203.6 Equip: Increases attack power by 200., +151 Stamina, Equip: Improves critical strike rating by 67., Equip: Improves your resilience rating by 66.
Deadly Gladiator's Greatsword	Arena: 4500	Sword: Physical 586-880, 3.6, 203.6 Equip: Increases attack power by 200., +151 Stamina, Equip: Improves critical strike rating by 67., Equip: Improves your resilience rating by 66.
Deadly Gladiator's Staff	Arena: 4500	Staff: Physical 192-357, 2, 137.3 +85 Agility, +147 Stamina, Equip: Increases attack power by 2084 in Cat, Bear, Dire Bear, and Moonkin forms only., Equip: Improves critical strike rating by 64., Equip: Improves your resilience rating by 84.
Deadly Gladiator's Rifle	Arena: 4500	Gun: Physical 339-510, 3, 141.5 Equip: Increases attack power by 62., +48 Stamina, Equip: Improves critical strike rating by 21., Equip: Improves your resilience rating by 20.
Deadly Gladiator's Longbow	Arena: 4500	Bow: Physical 339-510, 3, 141.5 Equip: Increases attack power by 62., +48 Stamina, Equip: Improves critical strike rating by 21., Equip: Improves your resilience rating by 20.
Deadly Gladiator's Heavy Crossbow	Arena: 4500	Crossbow: Physical 339-510, 3, 141.5 Equip: Increases attack power by 62., +48 Stamina, Equip: Improves critical strike rating by 21., Equip: Improves your resilience rating by 20.
Deadly Gladiator's Energy Staff	Arena: 4500	Staff: Physical 192-357, 2, 137.3 +147 Stamina, +64 Intellect, Equip: Increases spell power by 461., +85 Spirit, Equip: Improves your resilience rating by 84.
Deadly Gladiator's Battle Staff	Arena: 4500	Staff: Physical 192-357, 2, 137.3 +147 Stamina, +64 Intellect, Equip: Increases spell power by 461., Equip: Improves critical strike rating by 85., Equip: Improves your resilience rating by 84.
Deadly Gladiator's War Staff	Arena: 4500	Staff: Physical 192-357, 2, 137.3 +147 Stamina, +64 Intellect, Equip: Increases spell power by 461., Equip: Improves haste rating by 85., Equip: Improves your resilience rating by 84.
Deadly Gladiator's Focus Staff	Arena: 4500	Staff: Physical 192-357, 2, 137.3 +147 Stamina, +64 Intellect, Equip: Increases spell power by 461., Equip: Improves hit rating by 85., Equip: Improves your resilience rating by 84.
Design: Mystic Sun Crystal	Honor: 1250	Yellow: +12 Resilience Rating
Design: Stormy Chalcedony	Honor: 1250	Blue: +15 Spell Penetration
Design: Durable Huge Citrine	Honor: 1250	Orange: +7 Spell Power and +6 Resilience Rating
Design: Empowered Huge Citrine	Honor: 1250	Orange: +12 Attack Power and +6 Resilience Rating
Design: Lucent Huge Citrine	Honor: 1250	Orange: +6 Agility and +6 Resilience Rating
Design: Resplendent Huge Citrine	Honor: 1250	Orange: +6 Strength and +6 Resilience Rating
Design: Shattered Dark Jade	Honor: 1250	Green: +6 Haste Rating and +8 Spell Penetration
Design: Tense Dark Jade	Honor: 1250	Green: +6 Hit Rating and +8 Spell Penetration
Design: Turbid Dark Jade	Honor: 1250	Green: +6 Resilience Rating and +6 Spirit

Name	Extended Cost	Stats
Design: Steady Dark Jade	Honor: 1250	Green: +6 Resilience Rating and +9 Stamina
Design: Opaque Dark Jade	Honor: 1250	Green: +6 Resilience Rating and +2 Mana every 5 seconds
Design: Mysterious Shadow Crystal	Honor: 1250	
Hateful Gladiator's Bracers of Triumph	Honor: 15800	Plate: 980 , +50 Strength, +73 Stamina, Equip: Improves critical strike rating by 34., Equip: Improves your resilience rating by 33.
Hateful Gladiator's Wristguards of Salvation	Honor: 15800	Mail: 549 , +57 Stamina, +24 Intellect, Equip: Increases spell power by 59., Equip: Restores 14 mana per 5 sec., Equip: Improves your resilience rating by 33.
Hateful Gladiator's Bracers of Salvation	Honor: 15800	Plate: 980 , +57 Stamina, +24 Intellect, Equip: Increases spell power by 59., Equip: Restores 14 mana per 5 sec., Equip: Improves your resilience rating by 33.
Hateful Gladiator's Wristguards of Dominance	Honor: 15800	Mail: 549 , +57 Stamina, +24 Intellect, Equip: Increases spell power by 59., Equip: Improves critical strike rating by 34., Equip: Improves your resilience rating by 33.
Hateful Gladiator's Wristguards of Triumph	Honor: 15800	Mail: 549 , Equip: Increases attack power by 50., +34 Agility, +57 Stamina, +32 Intellect, Equip: Improves critical strike rating by 33., Equip: Improves your resilience rating by 32.
Hateful Gladiator's Armwraps of Salvation	Honor: 15800	Leather: 247 , Equip: Increases spell power by 59., +57 Stamina, +24 Intellect, +34 Spirit, Equip: Improves your resilience rating by 33.
Hateful Gladiator's Armwraps of Triumph	Honor: 15800	Leather: 247 , Equip: Increases attack power by 50., +50 Agility, +57 Stamina, Equip: Improves critical strike rating by 33., Equip: Improves your resilience rating by 32.
Hateful Gladiator's Cuffs of Dominance	Honor: 15800	Cloth: 131 , Equip: Increases spell power by 59., +57 Stamina, +24 Intellect, Equip: Improves critical strike rating by 34., Equip: Improves your resilience rating by 33.
Hateful Gladiator's Cuffs of Salvation	Honor: 15800	Cloth: 131 , Equip: Increases spell power by 59., +57 Stamina, +24 Intellect, +34 Spirit, Equip: Improves your resilience rating by 33.
Hateful Gladiator's Armwraps of Dominance	Honor: 15800	Leather: 247 , Equip: Increases spell power by 59., +57 Stamina, +24 Intellect, Equip: Improves critical strike rating by 33., Equip: Improves your resilience rating by 33.
Hateful Gladiator's Pendant of Dominance	Honor: 19000	Equip: Increases spell power by 59., +57 Stamina, +24 Intellect, Equip: Improves critical strike rating by 34., Equip: Improves your resilience rating by 33.
Hateful Gladiator's Pendant of Subjugation	Honor: 19000	Equip: Increases spell power by 59., +57 Stamina, +24 Intellect, Equip: Improves haste rating by 34., Equip: Improves your resilience rating by 33.
Hateful Gladiator's Pendant of Ascendancy	Honor: 19000	Equip: Increases spell power by 59., +57 Stamina, +24 Intellect, Equip: Improves hit rating by 34., Equip: Improves your resilience rating by 33.
Hateful Gladiator's Pendant of Deliverance	Honor: 19000	Equip: Increases spell power by 59., +57 Stamina, +24 Intellect, +34 Spirit, Equip: Improves your resilience rating by 33.
Hateful Gladiator's Pendant of Salvation	Honor: 19000	Equip: Increases spell power by 59., +57 Stamina, +24 Intellect, Equip: Restores 14 mana per 5 sec., Equip: Improves your resilience rating by 33.
Hateful Gladiator's Cloak of Dominance	Honor: 19000	Cloth: 150 , Equip: Increases spell power by 59., +57 Stamina, +24 Intellect, Equip: Improves critical strike rating by 34., Equip: Improves your resilience rating by 33.
Hateful Gladiator's Cloak of Subjugation	Honor: 19000	Cloth: 150 , Equip: Increases spell power by 59., +57 Stamina, +24 Intellect, Equip: Improves haste rating by 34., Equip: Improves your resilience rating by 33.
Hateful Gladiator's Cloak of Deliverance	Honor: 19000	Cloth: 150 , Equip: Increases spell power by 59., +57 Stamina, +24 Intellect, +34 Spirit, Equip: Improves your resilience rating by 33.
Hateful Gladiator's Cloak of Triumph	Honor: 19000	Cloth: 150 , Equip: Increases attack power by 100., +73 Stamina, Equip: Improves critical strike rating by 34., Equip: Improves your resilience rating by 33.
Hateful Gladiator's Cloak of Victory	Honor: 19000	Cloth: 150 , Equip: Increases attack power by 100., +73 Stamina, Equip: Improves hit rating by 34., Equip: Improves your resilience rating by 33.
Hateful Gladiator's Band of Triumph	Honor: 19000	Equip: Increases attack power by 100., +73 Stamina, Equip: Improves critical strike rating by 34., Equip: Improves your resilience rating by 33.
Hateful Gladiator's Band of Dominance	Honor: 19000	Equip: Increases spell power by 59., +57 Stamina, +24 Intellect, Equip: Improves critical strike rating by 34., Equip: Improves your resilience rating by 33.
Hateful Gladiator's Cloak of Salvation	Honor: 19000	Cloth: 150 , Equip: Increases spell power by 59., +57 Stamina, +24 Intellect, Equip: Restores 14 mana per 5 sec., Equip: Improves your resilience rating by 33.
Hateful Gladiator's Cloak of Ascendancy	Honor: 19000	Cloth: 150 , Equip: Increases spell power by 59., +57 Stamina, +24 Intellect, Equip: Improves hit rating by 34., Equip: Improves your resilience rating by 33.
Hateful Gladiator's Pendant of Victory	Honor: 19000	Equip: Increases attack power by 100., +73 Stamina, Equip: Improves hit rating by 34., Equip: Improves your resilience rating by 33.
Hateful Gladiator's Pendant of Triumph	Honor: 19000	Equip: Increases attack power by 100., +73 Stamina, Equip: Improves critical strike rating by 34., Equip: Improves your resilience rating by 33.
Deadly Gladiator's Bracers of Triumph	Honor: 19700	Plate: 1005 , +56 Strength, +84 Stamina, Equip: Improves critical strike rating by 38., Equip: Improves your resilience rating by 37.
Deadly Gladiator's Bracers of Salvation	Honor: 19700	Plate: 1005 , +66 Stamina, +29 Intellect, Equip: Increases spell power by 66., Equip: Restores 15 mana per 5 sec., Equip: Improves your resilience rating by 37.
Deadly Gladiator's Wristguards of Salvation	Honor: 19700	Mail: 563 , +66 Stamina, +29 Intellect, Equip: Increases spell power by 66., Equip: Restores 15 mana per 5 sec., Equip: Improves your resilience rating by 37.
Deadly Gladiator's Wristguards of Dominance	Honor: 19700	Mail: 563 , +66 Stamina, +29 Intellect, Equip: Increases spell power by 66., Equip: Improves critical strike rating by 38., Equip: Improves your resilience rating by 37.
Deadly Gladiator's Wristguards of Triumph	Honor: 19700	Mail: 563 , Equip: Increases attack power by 74., +38 Agility, +66 Stamina, +29 Intellect, Equip: Improves critical strike rating by 38., Equip: Improves your resilience rating by 37.
Deadly Gladiator's Armwraps of Triumph	Honor: 19700	Leather: 253 , Equip: Increases attack power by 58., +56 Agility, +66 Stamina, Equip: Improves critical strike rating by 38., Equip: Improves your resilience rating by 37.
Deadly Gladiator's Cuffs of Dominance	Honor: 19700	Cloth: 135 , Equip: Increases spell power by 66., +66 Stamina, +29 Intellect, Equip: Improves critical strike rating by 38., Equip: Improves your resilience rating by 37.
Deadly Gladiator's Cuffs of Salvation	Honor: 19700	Cloth: 135 , Equip: Increases spell power by 66., +66 Stamina, +29 Intellect, +38 Spirit, Equip: Improves your resilience rating by 37.
Deadly Gladiator's Armwraps of Dominance	Honor: 19700	Leather: 253 , Equip: Increases spell power by 66., +66 Stamina, +29 Intellect, Equip: Improves critical strike rating by 38., Equip: Improves your resilience rating by 37.
Deadly Gladiator's Armwraps of Salvation	Honor: 19700	Leather: 253 , Equip: Increases spell power by 66., +66 Stamina, +29 Intellect, +38 Spirit, Equip: Improves your resilience rating by 37.

Name	Extended Cost	Stats
Deadly Gladiator's Pendant of Triumph	Honor: 23700	Equip: Increases attack power by 112., +84 Stamina, Equip: Improves critical strike rating by 38., Equip: Improves your resilience rating by 37.
Deadly Gladiator's Pendant of Ascendancy	Honor: 23700	Equip: Increases spell power by 66., +66 Stamina, +29 Intellect, Equip: Improves hit rating by 38., Equip: Improves your resilience rating by 37.
Deadly Gladiator's Pendant of Subjugation	Honor: 23700	Equip: Increases spell power by 66., +66 Stamina, +29 Intellect, Equip: Improves haste rating by 38., Equip: Improves your resilience rating by 37.
Deadly Gladiator's Pendant of Deliverance	Honor: 23700	Equip: Increases spell power by 66., +66 Stamina, +29 Intellect, +38 Spirit, Equip: Improves your resilience rating by 37.
Deadly Gladiator's Pendant of Salvation	Honor: 23700	Equip: Increases spell power by 66., +66 Stamina, +29 Intellect, Equip: Restores 15 mana per 5 sec., Equip: Improves your resilience rating by 37.
Deadly Gladiator's Cloak of Dominance	Honor: 23700	Cloth: 154 , Equip: Increases spell power by 66., +66 Stamina, +29 Intellect, Equip: Improves critical strike rating by 38., Equip: Improves your resilience rating by 37.
Deadly Gladiator's Cloak of Subjugation	Honor: 23700	Cloth: 154 , Equip: Increases spell power by 66., +66 Stamina, +29 Intellect, Equip: Improves haste rating by 38., Equip: Improves your resilience rating by 37.
Deadly Gladiator's Cloak of Ascendancy	Honor: 23700	Cloth: 154 , Equip: Increases spell power by 66., +66 Stamina, +29 Intellect, Equip: Improves hit rating by 38., Equip: Improves your resilience rating by 37.
Deadly Gladiator's Cloak of Salvation	Honor: 23700	Cloth: 154 , Equip: Increases spell power by 66., +66 Stamina, +29 Intellect, Equip: Restores 15 mana per 5 sec., Equip: Improves your resilience rating by 37.
Deadly Gladiator's Cloak of Deliverance	Honor: 23700	Cloth: 154 , Equip: Increases spell power by 66., +66 Stamina, +29 Intellect, +38 Spirit, Equip: Improves your resilience rating by 37.
Deadly Gladiator's Cloak of Triumph	Honor: 23700	Cloth: 154 , Equip: Increases attack power by 112., +84 Stamina, Equip: Improves critical strike rating by 38., Equip: Improves your resilience rating by 37.
Deadly Gladiator's Cloak of Victory	Honor: 23700	Cloth: 154 , Equip: Increases attack power by 112., +84 Stamina, Equip: Improves hit rating by 38., Equip: Improves your resilience rating by 37.
Deadly Gladiator's Band of Victory	Honor: 23700	Equip: Increases attack power by 112., +84 Stamina, Equip: Improves hit rating by 38., Equip: Improves your resilience rating by 37.
Deadly Gladiator's Band of Ascendancy	Honor: 23700	Equip: Increases spell power by 66., +66 Stamina, +29 Intellect, Equip: Improves hit rating by 38., Equip: Improves your resilience rating by 37.
Deadly Gladiator's Pendant of Dominance	Honor: 23700	Equip: Increases spell power by 66., +66 Stamina, +29 Intellect, Equip: Improves critical strike rating by 38., Equip: Improves your resilience rating by 37.
Deadly Gladiator's Pendant of Victory	Honor: 23700	Equip: Increases attack power by 112., +84 Stamina, Equip: Improves hit rating by 38., Equip: Improves your resilience rating by 37.
Hateful Gladiator's Greaves of Salvation	Honor: 24800	Plate: 1541, Socket Bonus: +4 Resilience Rating, Socket: Yellow, +76 Stamina, +33 Intellect, Equip: Increases spell power by 68., Equip: Restores 14 mana per 5 sec., Equip: Improves your resilience rating by 44.
Hateful Gladiator's Girdle of Salvation	Honor: 24800	Plate: 1261, Socket Bonus: +5 Spell Power, Socket: Blue, +76 Stamina, +33 Intellect, Equip: Increases spell power by 68., Equip: Restores 14 mana per 5 sec., Equip: Improves your resilience rating by 44.
Hateful Gladiator's Greaves of Triumph	Honor: 24800	Plate: 1541, Socket Bonus: +4 Resilience Rating, Socket: Yellow, +58 Strength, +99 Stamina, Equip: Improves critical strike rating by 36., Equip: Improves your resilience rating by 44.

Name	Extended Cost	Stats
Hateful Gladiator's Girdle of Triumph	Honor: 24800	Plate: 1261, Socket Bonus: +4 Strength, Socket: Blue, +58 Strength, +99 Stamina, Equip: Improves critical strike rating by 36., Equip: Improves your resilience rating by 44.
Hateful Gladiator's Sabatons of Salvation	Honor: 24800	Mail: 862, Socket Bonus: +4 Resilience Rating, Socket: Yellow, +76 Stamina, +33 Intellect, Equip: Increases spell power by 68., Equip: Restores 14 mana per 5 sec., Equip: Improves your resilience rating by 44.
Hateful Gladiator's Waistguard of Salvation	Honor: 24800	Mail: 705, Socket Bonus: +5 Spell Power, Socket: Blue, +76 Stamina, +33 Intellect, Equip: Increases spell power by 68., Equip: Restores 14 mana per 5 sec., Equip: Improves your resilience rating by 44.
Hateful Gladiator's Waistguard of Dominance	Honor: 24800	Mail: 705, Socket Bonus: +5 Spell Power, Socket: Blue, +76 Stamina, +33 Intellect, Equip: Increases spell power by 68., Equip: Improves critical strike rating by 36., Equip: Improves your resilience rating by 44.
Hateful Gladiator's Sabatons of Dominance	Honor: 24800	Mail: 862, Socket Bonus: +4 Resilience Rating, Socket: Yellow, +76 Stamina, +33 Intellect, Equip: Increases spell power by 68., Equip: Improves critical strike rating by 36., Equip: Improves your resilience rating by 44.
Hateful Gladiator's Sabatons of Triumph	Honor: 24800	Mail: 862, Socket Bonus: +4 Resilience Rating, Socket: Yellow, Equip: Increases attack power by 50., +44 Agility, +76 Stamina, +36 Intellect, Equip: Improves critical strike rating by 44., Equip: Improves your resilience rating by 44.
Hateful Gladiator's Waistguard of Triumph	Honor: 24800	Mail: 705, Socket Bonus: +4 Agility, Socket: Blue, Equip: Increases attack power by 50., +44 Agility, +76 Stamina, +36 Intellect, Equip: Improves critical strike rating by 44., Equip: Improves your resilience rating by 44.
Hateful Gladiator's Belt of Salvation	Honor: 24800	Leather: 317, Socket Bonus: +5 Spell Power, Socket: Blue, Equip: Increases spell power by 68., +76 Stamina, +33 Intellect, +36 Spirit, Equip: Improves your resilience rating by 44.
Hateful Gladiator's Boots of Salvation	Honor: 24800	Leather: 388, Socket Bonus: +4 Resilience Rating, Socket: Yellow, Equip: Increases spell power by 68., +76 Stamina, +33 Intellect, +36 Spirit, Equip: Improves your resilience rating by 44.
Hateful Gladiator's Belt of Triumph	Honor: 24800	Leather: 317, Socket Bonus: +4 Agility, Socket: Blue, Equip: Increases attack power by 66., +58 Agility, +76 Stamina, Equip: Improves critical strike rating by 36., Equip: Improves your resilience rating by 44.
Hateful Gladiator's Boots of Triumph	Honor: 24800	Leather: 388, Socket Bonus: +4 Resilience Rating, Socket: Yellow, Equip: Increases attack power by 66., +58 Agility, +76 Stamina, Equip: Improves critical strike rating by 36., Equip: Improves your resilience rating by 44.
Hateful Gladiator's Slippers of Salvation	Honor: 24800	Cloth: 206, Socket Bonus: +4 Resilience Rating, Socket: Yellow, Equip: Increases spell power by 68., +76 Stamina, +33 Intellect, +36 Spirit, Equip: Improves your resilience rating by 44.
Hateful Gladiator's Slippers of Dominance	Honor: 24800	Cloth: 206, Socket Bonus: +4 Resilience Rating, Socket: Yellow, Equip: Increases spell power by 68., +76 Stamina, +33 Intellect, Equip: Improves critical strike rating by 36., Equip: Improves your resilience rating by 44.
Medallion of the Alliance	Honor: 24800	Equip: Improves your resilience rating by 84., Removes all movement impairing effects and all effects which cause loss of control of your character.
Medallion of the Horde	Honor: 24800	Equip: Improves your resilience rating by 84., Removes all movement impairing effects and all effects which cause loss of control of your character.

Name	Extended Cost	Stats
Hateful Gladiator's Cord of Dominance	Honor: 24800	Cloth: 169, Socket Bonus: +5 Spell Power, Socket: Blue, Equip: Increases spell power by 68., +76 Stamina, +33 Intellect, Equip: Improves critical strike rating by 36., Equip: Improves your resilience rating by 44.
Hateful Gladiator's Cord of Salvation	Honor: 24800	Cloth: 169, Socket Bonus: +5 Spell Power, Socket: Blue, Equip: Increases spell power by 68., +76 Stamina, +33 Intellect, +36 Spirit, Equip: Improves your resilience rating by 44.
Hateful Gladiator's Boots of Dominance	Honor: 24800	Leather: 388, Socket Bonus: +4 Resilience Rating, Socket: Yellow, Equip: Increases spell power by 68., +76 Stamina, +33 Intellect, Equip: Improves critical strike rating by 36., Equip: Improves your resilience rating by 44.
Hateful Gladiator's Belt of Dominance	Honor: 24800	Leather: 317, Socket Bonus: +5 Spell Power, Socket: Blue, Equip: Increases spell power by 68., +76 Stamina, +33 Intellect, Equip: Improves critical strike rating by 36., Equip: Improves your resilience rating by 44.
Formula: Enchant Chest - Exceptional Resilience	Honor: 2500	Item Enhancement: Permanently enchant chest armor to increase resilience rating by 20. Requires a level 60 or higher item.
Deadly Gladiator's Waistguard of Salvation	Honor: 31000	Mail: 723, Socket Bonus: +5 Spell Power, Socket: Blue, +85 Stamina, +37 Intellect, Equip: Increases spell power by 78., Equip: Restores 17 mana per 5 sec., Equip: Improves your resilience rating by 50.
Deadly Gladiator's Greaves of Salvation	Honor: 31000	Plate: 1580, Socket Bonus: +4 Resilience Rating, Socket: Yellow, +85 Stamina, +37 Intellect, Equip: Increases spell power by 78., Equip: Restores 17 mana per 5 sec., Equip: Improves your resilience rating by 50.
Deadly Gladiator's Girdle of Salvation	Honor: 31000	Plate: 1293, Socket Bonus: +5 Spell Power, Socket: Blue, +85 Stamina, +37 Intellect, Equip: Increases spell power by 78., Equip: Restores 17 mana per 5 sec., Equip: Improves your resilience rating by 50.
Deadly Gladiator's Greaves of Triumph	Honor: 31000	Plate: 1580, Socket Bonus: +4 Resilience Rating, Socket: Yellow, +67 Strength, +111 Stamina, Equip: Improves critical strike rating by 42., Equip: Improves your resilience rating by 50.
Deadly Gladiator's Girdle of Triumph	Honor: 31000	Plate: 1293, Socket Bonus: +4 Strength, Socket: Blue, +67 Strength, +111 Stamina, Equip: Improves critical strike rating by 42., Equip: Improves your resilience rating by 50.
Deadly Gladiator's Sabatons of Salvation	Honor: 31000	Mail: 884, Socket Bonus: +4 Resilience Rating, Socket: Yellow, +85 Stamina, +37 Intellect, Equip: Increases spell power by 78., Equip: Restores 17 mana per 5 sec., Equip: Improves your resilience rating by 50.
Deadly Gladiator's Waistguard of Dominance	Honor: 31000	Mail: 723, Socket Bonus: +5 Spell Power, Socket: Blue, +85 Stamina, +37 Intellect, Equip: Increases spell power by 78., Equip: Improves critical strike rating by 42., Equip: Improves your resilience rating by 50.
Deadly Gladiator's Sabatons of Dominance	Honor: 31000	Mail: 884, Socket Bonus: +4 Resilience Rating, Socket: Yellow, +85 Stamina, +37 Intellect, Equip: Increases spell power by 78., Equip: Improves critical strike rating by 42., Equip: Improves your resilience rating by 50.
Deadly Gladiator's Sabatons of Triumph	Honor: 31000	Mail: 884, Socket Bonus: +4 Resilience Rating, Socket: Yellow, Equip: Increases attack power by 84., +41 Agility, +85 Stamina, +37 Intellect, Equip: Improves critical strike rating by 50., Equip: Improves your resilience rating by 50.
Deadly Gladiator's Waistguard of Triumph	Honor: 31000	Mail: 723, Socket Bonus: +4 Agility, Socket: Blue, Equip: Increases attack power by 84., +41 Agility, +85 Stamina, +37 Intellect, Equip: Improves critical strike rating by 50., Equip: Improves your resilience rating by 50.
Deadly Gladiator's Belt of Triumph	Honor: 31000	Leather: 325, Socket Bonus: +4 Agility, Socket: Blue, Equip: Increases attack power by 74., +67 Agility, +85 Stamina, Equip: Improves critical strike rating by 42., Equip: Improves your resilience rating by 49.
Deadly Gladiator's Boots of Triumph	Honor: 31000	Leather: 398, Socket Bonus: +4 Resilience Rating, Socket: Yellow, Equip: Increases attack power by 74., +67 Agility, +85 Stamina, Equip: Improves critical strike rating by 42., Equip: Improves your resilience rating by 49.
Deadly Gladiator's Cord of Salvation	Honor: 31000	Cloth: 173, Socket Bonus: +5 Spell Power, Socket: Blue, Equip: Increases spell power by 78., +85 Stamina, +37 Intellect, +42 Spirit, Equip: Improves your resilience rating by 50.
Deadly Gladiator's Treads of Salvation	Honor: 31000	Cloth: 212, Socket Bonus: +4 Resilience Rating, Socket: Yellow, Equip: Increases spell power by 78., +85 Stamina, +37 Intellect, +42 Spirit, Equip: Improves your resilience rating by 50.
Deadly Gladiator's Treads of Dominance	Honor: 31000	Cloth: 212, Socket Bonus: +4 Resilience Rating, Socket: Yellow, Equip: Increases spell power by 78., +85 Stamina, +37 Intellect, Equip: Improves critical strike rating by 42., Equip: Improves your resilience rating by 50.
Battlemaster's Hostility	Honor: 31000	Equip: Improves critical strike rating by 95., Increases maximum health for $d. Shares cooldown with other Battlemaster's trinkets.
Battlemaster's Accuracy	Honor: 31000	Equip: Improves hit rating by 95., Increases maximum health for $d. Shares cooldown with other Battlemaster's trinkets.
Battlemaster's Avidity	Honor: 31000	Equip: Improves haste rating by 95., Increases maximum health for $d. Shares cooldown with other Battlemaster's trinkets.
Battlemaster's Conviction	Honor: 31000	Equip: Increases attack power by 190., Increases maximum health for $d. Shares cooldown with other Battlemaster's trinkets.
Battlemaster's Bravery	Honor: 31000	Equip: Increases spell power by 111., Increases maximum health for $d. Shares cooldown with other Battlemaster's trinkets.
Deadly Gladiator's Cord of Dominance	Honor: 31000	Cloth: 173, Socket Bonus: +5 Spell Power, Socket: Blue, Equip: Increases spell power by 78., +85 Stamina, +37 Intellect, Equip: Improves critical strike rating by 42., Equip: Improves your resilience rating by 50.
Deadly Gladiator's Boots of Dominance	Honor: 31000	Leather: 398, Socket Bonus: +4 Resilience Rating, Socket: Yellow, Equip: Increases spell power by 78., +85 Stamina, +37 Intellect, Equip: Improves critical strike rating by 42., Equip: Improves your resilience rating by 50.
Deadly Gladiator's Belt of Dominance	Honor: 31000	Leather: 325, Socket Bonus: +5 Spell Power, Socket: Blue, Equip: Increases spell power by 78., +85 Stamina, +37 Intellect, Equip: Improves critical strike rating by 42., Equip: Improves your resilience rating by 50.
Deadly Gladiator's Boots of Salvation	Honor: 31000	Leather: 398, Socket Bonus: +4 Resilience Rating, Socket: Yellow, Equip: Increases spell power by 78., +85 Stamina, +37 Intellect, +42 Spirit, Equip: Improves your resilience rating by 50.
Deadly Gladiator's Belt of Salvation	Honor: 31000	Leather: 325, Socket Bonus: +5 Spell Power, Socket: Blue, Equip: Increases spell power by 78., +85 Stamina, +37 Intellect, +42 Spirit, Equip: Improves your resilience rating by 50.

WINTERGRASP

Wintergrasp lies in southwestern Northrend, nestled between Borean Tundra, Dragonblight, Sholazar Basin, and Icecrown. Though the region was formerly covered by a large frozen lake, it has since been drained leaving only a remnant of its former self in the many smaller bodies of water that dot the landscape. Though the land is harsh and snow-covered, it is not without life. Travelers must watch out for hostile creatures such as Chilled Earth Elementals and Wandering Shadows if they stray too far from the path. There are also nodes of ore and herbs to be found in the frozen ground for those craftsmen brave enough to face the dangers in the area.

Wintergrasp Legend

① **Wintergrasp Fortress**
- A. Fortress Gate
- B. Fortress Tower (SW)
- C. Fortress Tower (SE)
- D. Fortress Tower (NW)
- E. Fortress Tower (NE)
- F. Fortress Vehicle Workshop (W)
- G. Fortress Vehicle Workshop (E)

② **Horde Camp**

③ **Alliance Camp**
④ **West Workshop Graveyard**
⑤ **West Vehicle Workshop**
⑥ **Shadowsight Tower**
⑦ **Westpark Vehicle Workshop**
⑧ **Southwest Graveyard**
⑨ **Winter's Edge Tower**
⑩ **Southeast Graveyard**
⑪ **Eastspark Vehicle Workshop**

⑫ **Flamewatch Tower**
⑬ **East Vehicle Workshop**
⑭ **East Workshop Graveyard**
⑮ **Fortress Graveyard**
⑯ **Eastern Bridge**
⑰ **Central Bridge**
⑱ **Western Bridge**

Wintergrasp is a highly contested area where Horde and Alliance forces are in an almost constant battle for control of the region. Though there are many strategically important areas in this zone for foes to battle over, the main prize is Wintergrasp Fortress.

To level the playing field and avoid players swooping down on their flying mounts to attack, Wintergrasp is a no-fly zone. If you attempt to fly into it you are dismounted, and the snow covered ground isn't nearly as soft as it looks. The only way to reach Wintergrasp initially is to take a portal from Dalaran. One hour before each match starts there is an open portal in Sunreaver's Sanctuary for the Horde and in The Silver Enclave for the Alliance. Once the match begins, these portals are no longer available, though they become available again between matches to the winning side. Once you pick up the flight path in Wintergrasp you can fly there from any connecting flight master at any time, even during a match.

At the start of each match, one faction defends the fortress and the other attacks. If the attackers successfully take the fortress they must defend it during the next match. The attacking faction starts in their own camp. The Horde camp is in the northwest and the Alliance camp is in the northeast. Each camp has its own Flight Master along with a merchant selling rewards in exchange for Stone Keeper's Shards and quest givers. The defending faction houses these NPCs in the fortress, leaving their camp empty of everyone but the Flight Master.

At the start of each match the first thing you want to do is to find some opponents to kill. Wintergrasp doesn't force you into groups like Battle Grounds, but forming a raid group is a good idea. That way you can see where your allies are and better coordinate your fighting. As you gain Honor Kills you gain Wintergrasp Ranks. One you have gained a rank or two, head to the nearest Vehicle Workshop under your faction's control, or grab a few allies and take the nearest one from the enemy!

Once you have control of the shop, speak to the Engineer there to commandeer a Siege Vehicle. Your rank determines what types of vehicle you can command: the higher your rank, the better the vehicle.

Siege Vehicles

HK's	Rank	
2	Corporal	Forsaken Catapult
10	First Lieutenant	The Demolisher, Siege Engine

You cannot take Wintergrasp Fortress without first bringing down its defenses and for that you need Siege Vehicles.

Vehicles

Forsaken Catapult

Requires: Corporal

This is the first siege vehicle you can use in Wintergrasp. It can be used to attack both structures and players, though it has a limited range and doesn't pack the punch of the sturdier siege engines. The Forsaken Catapult can launch Plague Barrels at foes, doing decent damage. You can also cause the vehicle to breath fire at your foes which works great as a defensive weapon. It can be easily destroyed by a few determined players, but as the easiest siege vehicle to build, you can field quite an army of them if you choose.

The Demolisher

Requires: First Lieutenant

The Demolisher holds up to four people—one driver and three passengers. The passengers can attack, and be attacked, when the vehicle is standing still. This vehicle has a long range allowing it to Hurl Boulders, very useful in tearing down walls and towers. Drive it up within range and fire away. The Demolisher is equipped with a Ram which can be used defensively to knock enemies back and can also be used for breaking down walls. If the Ram doesn't do the trick, your passengers can take care of any foes who try to get close enough to dismantle your Demolisher.

Siege Engine

Requires: First Lieutenant

The Siege Engine holds up to four players—a driver, a gunner, and two passengers. The passengers can attack and be attacked when the vehicle is at a stop and the gunner can operate a Fire Cannon mounted on the vehicle to take down foes and building alike. Like the Demolisher, the Siege Engine comes equipped with a Ram to knock back your enemies. This vehicle has a long range and really dishes out the damage.

Your ranks only last for the duration of the match, so each time you need to build up Honor Kills to rise in rank and command your siege vehicles. This insures that everyone who starts is on a level playing field and that regular fighters don't necessarily have an advantage over those that only occasionally visit Wintergrasp.

FEELING OUTNUMBERED?

It can be disheartening to show up for a fight only to realize you were expecting a skirmish while your opponent came ready for full out war! Wintergrasp offers some help for your side if you find yourself constantly outnumbered by granting you Tenacity. Tenacity gives the underdog faction a buff which scales up their abilities depending on just how outnumbered they are, making the battle for Wintergrasp more of a fair fight. Superior numbers still have an advantage, but with Tenacity it is no longer automatically an insurmountable advantage. Smaller forces that work together and use their brains to augment their brawn can still have a good shot at winning.

While the majority of the fighting takes place in the area near the fortress and the Vehicle Workshops, there are also defensive towers in the southern part of the zone.

Each tower comes equipped with faction guards and several Wintergrasp Tower Cannons. These have a long range and can be used to guard the roads running through the area. Like Siege Vehicles, the cannons only function during a match; trying to use them between matches results in their destruction.

Wintergrasp Fortress is well defended. It is surrounded by destructible walls with towers on four of the exterior corners. Along with its main gate, all of these structures are vulnerable to attack from Siege Vehicles. When a portion of the structure is targeted, its health appears in the lower left of your screen so you can see how close it is to falling. Each of the towers is equipped with Cannons which the defenders can use to rain down fire on the attacking forces. These cannons have a fairly decent range so you want to keep a close eye on them and avoid their fire whenever possible.

The Fortress is also equipped with two Siege Vehicle Workshops of its own. The defenders can build and field Siege Vehicles to defend the fortress or to take some of the structures controlled by the attackers. If the defending force controls the exterior Siege Vehicle Workshops, there is little the attackers can do to try to take them back. Both defending players and Siege Vehicles can use the teleporters located in the Keep to reach the exterior. This insures that the enemy can't sneak into the fortress through an open gate.

As with most ventures, you stand a better chance working as a team than you do alone. Stick with a group of your allies and work together to take workshops and towers when attacking. When on defense, use your numbers to take out attacking Siege Vehicles and their passengers before they can do too much damage to the Fortress. Take advantage of the environment to block line of sight when possible and try to spread out the opposing forces. Many of the skills you have honed in PvP battlegrounds serve you well here.

At the end of the timed match whichever faction has control of the Wintergrasp Fortress gets to keep it for the next four hours in order to have a chance to reap the benefits. The winners receive a buff, Essence of Wintergrasp, and can now see Greater Elemental Spirits and can collect Stone Keeper's Shards. The fortress holds special merchants, like the Wintergrasp Quartermaster, who trade items for these shards. The winners are also granted the buff, Rulers of Wintergrasp, which increases the damage they do. Within the fortress are portals to the various battlegrounds as well as on leading to the Violet Citadel in Dalaran.

The greatest benefit (besides bragging rights) of holding Wintergrasp Fortress is access to The Vault of Archavon. This one boss raid dungeon is available in both 10 and 25 man versions and can only be used by members of the faction that controls Wintergrasp between matches. Archavon the Stone Watcher is no pushover, and you must be level 80 to enter his vault, but the rewards are well worth it.

STRAND OF THE ANCIENTS

The Strand of the Ancients is a new 15-man battleground set on an island off the southern coast of Dragonblight. Here among the remnants of Titan architecture is the resting place of a legendary Titan artifact, desperately sought by both the Alliance and the Horde who seek to unlock its mysteries.

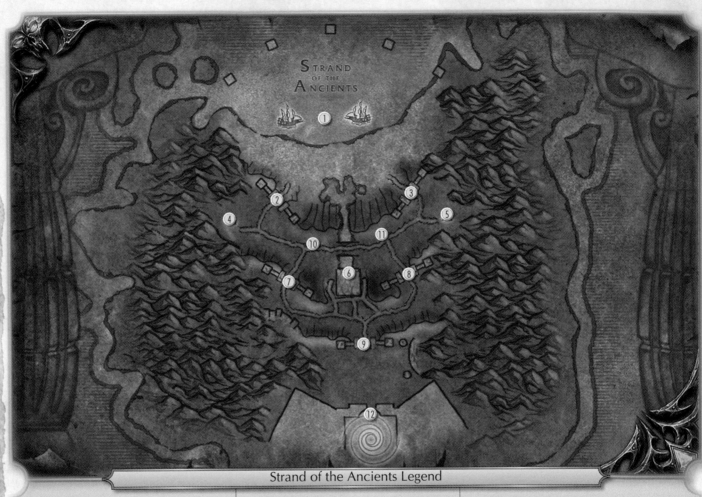

Strand of the Ancients Legend

1. The Frostbreaker and The Graceful Maiden
2. Gate of the Green Emerald
3. Gate of the Blue Sapphire
4. Gorgril Rigspark (Used Demolisher Salesman)
5. Rigger Sparklight (Used Demolisher Salesman)
6. Southern Graveyard
7. Gate of the Purple Amethyst
8. Gate of the Red Sun
9. Gate of the Yellow Moon
10. West Graveyard
11. East Graveyard
12. Chamber of Ancient Relics

To queue up for this battleground speak to the Strand of the Ancients Battlemasters in the major capital cities or click on the portal in Dalaran. The Horde's portal is found in Sunreaver's Sanctuary and the Alliance's portal is located in The Silver Enclave. There are two separate brackets, one for levels 70-79 and the other for level 80 characters which levels the playing field somewhat.

You shouldn't have long to wait to join the battle as each Strand of the Ancients match lasts a maximum of twenty minutes. It is broken up into two parts of ten minutes each. One faction plays the side of the Attackers for the first half while the other defends. Once the time limit is up the teams switch positions and the battle begins anew. Defenders beware though, if the Attackers manage to take the Artifact in less than the allotted time, you are only allowed that same amount of time when it becomes your turn to take the offense!

The goal is to reach, or defend—depending on your position, the powerful Titan Artifact located inside the Chamber of Ancient Relics at the southern end of the Strand. Attackers begin the battle onboard a pair of boats approaching the strand while Defenders begin in the southern part of the zone, near the Chamber of Ancient Relics. While the ships approach, take the opportunity to discuss strategy and apply any buffs to the group and if you are defending, move down into position. As with most undertakings, the key to success is to communicate with your allies and pay close attention to the battle around you.

...Is a Good Offense!

The Battleground Demolisher is everything a good Siege Vehicle should be. It has a long range ability, Hurl Boulder, which is great for attacking Gates, as well as groups of Defenders. For more up close and personal encounters the Demolisher comes equipped with a Ram. This ability damages foes as it knocks them back and can also be used effectively against the Gates. The Demolisher can hold up to three passengers who can be targeted separately from the vehicle and are vulnerable to attack but can also cast or use abilities from the vehicle, even while it is in motion.

Once the ships land, the Attackers disembark and try to push their way up the beach toward either the Gate of the Green Emerald or the Gate of the Blue Sapphire. Defenders may choose to engage the attacking force as they land on the beach to try to keep them from reaching this first set of gates. If this happens, try to engage the Defenders with part of your number while the rest move around to try to get to the gate. Often, the Defenders instead set up near one of the first gates where they can take advantage of its defensive weaponry.

Sometimes the Best Defense...

Each of the five gates is equipped with two stationary Anti-Personnel Cannons which can be manned by any of the defending team. Use the Cannon Blast to hurl a fiery boulder down at attacking opponents, inflicting a fire-based DoT and causing massive damage to not only individual players but their siege vehicles as well. The cannon can be slow at times, making it difficult to hit moving targets, but a well timed shot can make all the difference to a successful defense.

The battleground is three-tiered. The attackers must successfully make their way past the first two destructible gates to reach the next tier on their way to the Chamber holding the Artifact. Attackers should concentrate their firepower on either the Gate of the Green Emerald or the Gate of the Blue Sapphire, not both, as you only need to smash your way through one of them to move up. Defenders need to have at least some support at both gates before the Attackers make their move. Once the Attacking side has committed their forces, the Defenders can move to where they are needed most. Land Mounts are useable within the battleground, so moving quickly to where you are needed is not a problem.

The gates can only be destroyed by using Battleground Demolishers or Barrel Bombs. There is a stack of Bombs and two Demolishers next to the docks of each Attacker ship. If there are no Demolishers available, Attackers should pick up a Barrel Bomb from the starting area. These bombs can be used from your inventory and placed next to a wall, causing huge damage when exploding. More Demolishers and Bombs can be obtained from the Goblin Workshops past the first walls, once the Attacking forces move deeper into the Strand.

Once the attacking forces have breached the first gate, they then move up to the next tier and attempt to repeat the process. Once again there are two gates leading up to the next tier, the Gate of the Purple Amethyst and the Gate of the Red Sun, but you should concentrate your attacks on just one. Always remember as an attacker that you only have ten minutes to reach your goal so you want to focus your efforts to maximize the damage you do.

The battle for the Strand is a difficult one and casualties can be high. Luckily there are three Graveyards carefully located so that little time is wasted running back into the fray if you are killed.

The final obstacle to reaching the top tier is the Gate of the Yellow Moon. Time is often running short by the time the attackers reach this point and both sides should give everything they've got to win here. If this gate is breached there remains only one thin line of defense between the Attackers and the sought after Artifact—the doorway to the Chamber of Relics.

If the Attackers have made it this far the Defenders must throw everything they can at them to halt their advance and try to wait out the timer. Attackers should make sure they've always got Demolishers at the ready to keep up the assault on the gate. Having made it this far, it would be a shame to lose now!

If the Attackers breach the door on the Chamber of Ancient Relics they must click on the Artifact to win this portion of the battle. Once the attackers have claimed the Artifact, or the ten minute time limit has been reached, the teams switch positions and begin the battle again. The victors of the first half receive no extra benefit during the second half of the match, so you always start on an even playing field whether you start on offense or defense. While it is possible for the match to end in a draw, the Strand is much harder to defend than it is to lay siege. More often than not, a single game will be about which team can siege faster, versus which team can siege at all. Regardless, there is always honor and glory to be won on the battlefield!

OLD FRIENDS AND NEW ALLIES

The battle for Northrend is fierce and there are many groups more than willing to reward you for your help once you've proven your worth. With new recipes, mounts, fun vanity pets, and great equipment upgrades, among other things, getting in good with these factions is more than worth your time. Each of these factions offers quests to get you started and gaining reputation with them is not as difficult as it was with some of the groups in the old world. Check out the rewards listed below to get a good idea of what you need to do to get the items you desire.

The Alliance Vanguard (Alliance Only)

The Alliance Vanguard encompasses all of the Alliance forces at work in Northrend, including those of the Explorer's League, the Silver Covenant, the Valiance Expedition, and new allies, the Frostborn. The Vanguard is headquartered at Valgarde in Howling Fjord and in Valiance Keep in the Borean Tundra. They are the first faction that Alliance players encounter when they journey to Northrend and you continue to gain faction with them as you aid their different divisions.

Prove your worthiness to them and you can speak with Logistics Officer Silverstone in Valiance Keep or Logistics Officer Brighton in Valgarde to purchase helpful items like equipment upgrades available only to those who have gained the approval of the Vanguard.

Reputation Level	Name	Purchase Price	Stats
Revered	Shield of the Lion-hearted	39 ⦾ 19 ⦾ 33 ⦾	Shield: 6337, +45 Stamina, Equip: Increases your expertise rating by 31. Equip: Increases defense rating by 32.
Revered	Hammer of the Alliance Vanguard	61 ⦾ 69 ⦾ 1 ⦾	Mace: Physical 118-221, 1.6, 105.9 +36 Stamina, +26 Strength, Equip: Increases your dodge rating by 22.
Revered	Sawed-off Hand Cannon	46 ⦾ 61 ⦾ 1 ⦾	Gun: Physical 208-386, 3.1, 95.8 Equip: Improves hit rating by 18., +17 Agility, +27 Stamina
Revered	Orb of the Eastern Kingdoms	12 ⦾ 80 ⦾ 92 ⦾	Equip: Improves haste rating by 31., +44 Stamina, Equip: Increases spell power by 34.
Revered	Lordaeron's Resolve	37 ⦾ 73 ⦾ 58 ⦾	Shield: 6337, +39 Stamina, +35 Intellect, Equip: Increases spell power by 37.
Revered	Gnomish Magician's Quill	44 ⦾ 39 ⦾ 30 ⦾	Wand: Frost 286-532, 2.1, 194.8 +17 Spirit, +18 Intellect, Equip: Increases spell power by 20.
Revered	Vanguard Soldier's Dagger	59 ⦾ 41 ⦾ 90 ⦾	Dagger: Physical 111-207, 1.5, 106 +36 Stamina, +27 Agility, Equip: Increases attack power by 40.
Exalted	Schematic: Mekgineer's Chopper	400 ⦾	
Exalted	Arcanum of the Savage Gladiator	150 ⦾	Quest: Permanently adds 30 stamina and 25 resilience rating to a head slot item. Does not stack with other enchantments for the selected equipment slot.

EXPLORER'S LEAGUE (Alliance Only)

The Explorer's League has long dedicated itself to learning as much as possible about the origin of the dwarves, and through this pursuit has amassed perhaps the most extensive collection of knowledge in all Azeroth! Their quest for knowledge has led them into Northrend, seeking scraps of knowledge left behind by the Titans. Though exploration and learning are at the heart of their existence, they recognize the threat posed by the Lich King and have put their impressive resources to work against his forces. The Explorer's League has a good sized camp in the Howling Fjord but their members can be found stationed in Alliance bases throughout Northrend.

THE FROSTBORN (Alliance Only)

The Frostborn are a previously unknown race of frost dwarves found in the mountains of the Storm Peaks. Their king, Yorg Stormheart, has opened up their home, Frosthold in the southwestern part of the zone, to Alliance forces. Though they have differences with their dwarven brethren, they also have much in common. These stoic warriors have agreed to join their forces with those of the Alliance in fighting the army of the Lich King.

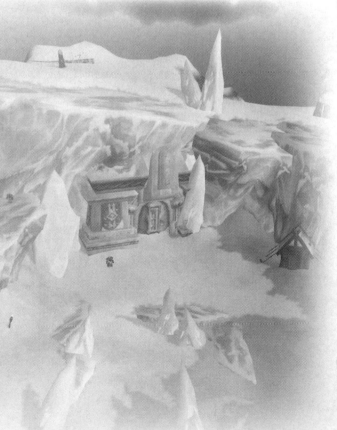

225

The Silver Covenant (Alliance Only)

The Silver Covenant is a militant part of the Kirin Tor. Led by the high elf, Vereesa Windrunner, they disagree with the Kirin Tor's possible acceptance of Blood Elves into their ranks and have separated themselves from the main body of Dalaran's ruling faction. They can be found in The Silver Enclave within Dalaran which is open only to members of the Alliance, as well as at Windrunner's Overlook in the Crystalsong Forest.

Valiance Expedition (Alliance Only)

The Valiance Expedition is the most numerous of the Alliance forces in Northrend. Though it falls under the command of King Varian Wrynn, field commanders direct the day to day activities of the force as they work to thwart the Lich King's plans. Members of the Expedition are found in many places where Alliance forces gather, including Valiance Keep, Valgarde, Westgarde Keep, and in the advance position at Fordragon Hold in the Dragonblight.

THE HORDE EXPEDITION (Horde Only)

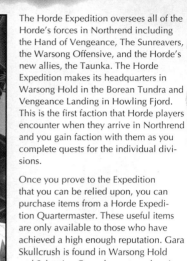

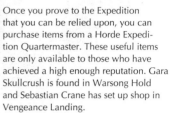

The Horde Expedition oversees all of the Horde's forces in Northrend including the Hand of Vengeance, The Sunreavers, the Warsong Offensive, and the Horde's new allies, the Taunka. The Horde Expedition makes its headquarters in Warsong Hold in the Borean Tundra and Vengeance Landing in Howling Fjord. This is the first faction that Horde players encounter when they arrive in Northrend and you gain faction with them as you complete quests for the individual divisions.

Once you prove to the Expedition that you can be relied upon, you can purchase items from a Horde Expedition Quartermaster. These useful items are only available to those who have achieved a high enough reputation. Gara Skullcrush is found in Warsong Hold and Sebastian Crane has set up shop in Vengeance Landing.

Reputation Level	Name	Purchase Price	Stats
Revered	Bulwark of the Warchief	39 🔘 4 🔘 72 🔘	Shield: 6337, +45 Stamina, Equip: Increases your expertise rating by 31., Equip: Increases defense rating by 32.
Revered	Warsong Punisher	61 🔘 46 🔘 79 🔘	Mace: Physical 118-221, 1.6, 105.9 +36 Stamina, +26 Strength, Equip: Increases your dodge rating by 22.
Revered	Sin'dorei Recurve Bow	46 🔘 43 🔘 88 🔘	Bow: Physical 297-297, 3.1, 95.8 Equip: Improves hit rating by 18., +17 Agility, +27 Stamina
Revered	Charged Wand of the Cleft	47 🔘 11 🔘 92 🔘	Wand: Fire 286-532, 2.1, 194.8 +17 Spirit, +18 Intellect, Equip: Increases spell power by 20.
Revered	Warsong Shanker	63 🔘 5 🔘 40 🔘	Dagger: Physical 111-207, 1.5, 106 +36 Stamina, +27 Agility, Equip: Increases attack power by 40.
Revered	Darkspear Orb	12 🔘 80 🔘 92 🔘	Equip: Improves haste rating by 31., +44 Stamina, Equip: Increases spell power by 34.
Exalted	Arcanum of the Savage Gladiator	150 🔘	Quest: Permanently adds 30 stamina and 25 resilience rating to a head slot item. Does not stack with other enchantments for the selected equipment slot.

THE HAND OF VENGEANCE (Horde Only)

The Hand of Vengeance is the Forsaken division of the Horde forces here in Northrend. None understand better than the Forsaken the danger the Lich King and his Scourge minions pose and they are doing everything in their power to halt the advance of his forces. Members of the Hand can be found in Vengeance Landing and Forsaken outposts in Borean Tundra, as well as at Venomspite in Dragonblight.

THE TAUNKA (Horde Only)

These strong, stoic people are distant cousins to the Tauren and share that race's bond with nature, though the harsh climate of Northrend has shaped the Taunka's relationship with the world differently than that of their ancestral relatives. They recognize the danger that the Lich King poses to not only their own lands, but to all of Northrend and beyond. They have allied themselves with the Horde in hopes of bringing an end to the Lich King. The Taunka can be found in Camp Winterhoof, in Howling Fjord, and Taunka'le Village in Borean Tundra, as well as in other smaller camps like Camp Tunka'lo in the Storm Peaks.

THE SUNREAVERS (Horde Only)

Named after Archmage Aethas Sunreaver, this faction urges the Kirin Tor to admit Blood Elves to its ranks. In this cause they have allied themselves with the Horde and control the area of Dalaran known as Sunreaver's Sanctuary, open only to members of the Horde. They can also be found beneath the city in Crystalsong Forest at Sunreaver's Command.

WARSONG OFFENSIVE (Horde Only)

Led by Garrosh Hellscream, the Warsong Offensive is made up primarily of orcs and trolls. These soldiers are bravely leading the Horde's push into Northrend for they know if they fail to stop the Lich King here in Northrend, they will one day have to face his forces on the plains of Durotar. Members of the Offensive can be found in Warsong Hold in Borean Tundra, Agmar's Hammer in Dragonblight, Conquest Hold in Grizzly Hills and in other smaller camps throughout Northrend.

Reputation Level	Name	Purchase Price
Exalted	Schematic: Mechano-hog	400

ARGENT CRUSADE (Both Factions)

The Argent Crusade was formed when Tirion Fordring claimed the Ashbringer, assumed a leadership role over the Argent Dawn, and drove back the Lich King's forces at Light's Hope Chapel. Though they forced him into a retreat, they realized the danger the Lich King poses and the two factions united as the Argent Crusade to push the fight into Northrend.

The Crusade has a large presence on the continent, primarily in Zul'Drak, at the Argent Stand and Light's Breach, in Dragonblight at Light's Trust, and in Ice Crown at the Argent Vanguard. Once you prove that you are willing to do what it takes to fight back the Scourge you can purchase gear that is only available to those trusted by the Argent Crusade from Veteran Crusader Aliocha Segard stationed in the Argent Vanguard in southeastern Icecrown.

WEARING THE COLORS

Once you gain enough reputation, some of the factions allow you to purchase their tabard. By wearing it you proudly display your allegiance to their cause, referred to as championing, and you are granted bonuses to reputation gains with that faction when fighting in some dungeons. This is a great way to increase your reputation with a faction!

Reputation Level	Name	Purchase Price	Stats
Friendly	Tabard of the Argent Crusade	1 🟤	You champion the cause of the Argent Crusade.All reputation gains while in level 80 dungeons will be applied to your standing with them.
Honored	Arcanum of the Fleeing Shadow	150 🟤	Quest: Permanently adds 25 shadow resist and 30 stamina to a head slot item. Does not stack with other enchantments for the selected equipment slot.
Honored	Cloak of Holy Extermination	21 🟡 9 🟤 13 🟤	Cloth: 140, +57 Stamina, +39 Agility, Equip: Increases your armor penetration rating by 25., Equip: Increases attack power by 52.
Honored	Standard Issue Legguards	46 🟡 18 🟤 42 🟤	Plate: 1831Socket Bonus: +4 Intellect, Socket: Blue, +51 Stamina, +69 Intellect, Equip: Increases spell power by 80., Equip: Improves haste rating by 40.
Honored	Special Issue Legplates	46 🟡 36 🟤 29 🟤	Plate: 1831Socket Bonus: +4 Strength, Socket: Red, +102 Stamina, Equip: Increases defense rating by 69., +30 Strength, Equip: Improves hit rating by 46.
Revered	Design: Guardian's Twilight Opal	4 🟤	Purple: +8 Expertise Rating and +12 Stamina
Revered	Arcanum of the Stalwart Protector	150 🟤	Quest: Permanently adds 37 stamina and 20 defense rating to a head slot item. Does not stack with other enchantments for the selected equipment slot.
Revered	Purifying Torch	52 🟡 35 🟤 6 🟤	Wand: Fire 247-459, 1.6, 220.6 +21 Stamina, Equip: Increases spell power by 26., Equip: Restores 8 mana per 5 sec.
Revered	Argent Skeleton Crusher	89 🟡 56 🟤 27 🟤	Mace: Physical 487-731, 3.6, 169.2 +100 Stamina, +84 Strength, Equip: Increases your armor penetration rating by 77.
Revered	Zombie Sweeper Shotgun	53 🟡 94 🟤 17 🟤	Gun: Physical 238-444, 2.9, 117.6 Equip: Improves critical strike rating by 18., Equip: Improves hit rating by 14., Increases attack power by $s1.
Revered	Fang-Deflecting Faceguard	37 🟡 96 🟤 85 🟤	Plate: 1760, +89 Strength, +87 Stamina, Equip: Increases your armor penetration rating by 78.
Revered	Battle Mender's Helm	32 🟡 72 🟤 90 🟤	Mail: 985, Equip: Increases spell power by 91., +58 Stamina, +60 Intellect, Equip: Improves critical strike rating by 77.
Exalted	Pattern: Brilliant Spellthread	5 🟤	Item Enhancement: Permanently embroiders spellthread into pants, increasing spell power by 50 and Spirit by 20.
Exalted	Polished Regimental Hauberk	61 🟡 23 🟤 79 🟤	Mail: 1254Socket Bonus: +4 Hit Rating, Socket: Yellow, +89 Agility, +69 Stamina, +68 Intellect, Equip: Improves hit rating by 49., Equip: Increases attack power by 104.
Exalted	Helm of Purified Thoughts	53 🟡 67 🟤 12 🟤	Plate: 1821Socket Bonus: +8 Intellect, Socket: Meta, Blue, +99 Stamina, +69 Intellect, Equip: Increases spell power by 84., Equip: Improves critical strike rating by 45.
Exalted	Boots of the Neverending Path	35 🟡 83 🟤 98 🟤	Leather: 388, +49 Stamina, +51 Agility, Equip: Improves hit rating by 66., Equip: Increases attack power by 122.
Exalted	Signet of Hopeful Light	8500 🟤	+42 Stamina, +50 Intellect, Equip: Improves haste rating by 36., Equip: Increases spell power by 58.

Frenzyheart Tribe (Both Factions)

The Frenzyheart are a fierce tribe of wolvar driven from their homeland by the Scourge. They have claimed land in the Sholazar Basin as their new home. Their warlike ways have caused conflict with the Oracles, gorlocs native to Sholazar Basin. Though they don't trust easily, the Frenzyheart tribe is not above rewarding adventurers for aiding their cause.

These wolvar have set up their camp on Frenzyheart Hill in southeastern Sholazar, not far from Rivers Heart. They offer a rewarding questline as well as several daily quests you can complete to aid them in their conflict with the Oracles. Tanak, the Frenzyheart Quartermaster, is found on Frenzyheart Hill and offers a variety of useful equipment and consumables. Once you start helping the Frenzyheart Tribe, the Oracles see this as a sign of aggression and want nothing to do with you.

Changing Sides

The Oracles and the Frenzyheart have a deep hatred of one another and they don't take kindly to their enemy's allies. However, if you wish to change from the Oracles to Frenzyheart you can slay the large cat, Pitch, who is located near the Skyreach Pillar, to trigger a quest from the nearby Frenzyheart Tracker Gekgek. From there you can work your way into the Frenzyheart's good graces.

To switch from the Frenzyheart to the Oracles help the Injured Rainspeaker Oracle, south of Rainspeaker Canopy. This triggers a quest where you escort him back to his village and are then able to do the Oracles quest line.

Reputation Level	Name	Purchase Price	Stats
Friendly	Design: Reckless Huge Citrine	2	Jewel: +7 Spell Power and +6 Haste Rating
Friendly	Roasted Mystery Beast	1 60	Food & Drink: Restores health over time. Must remain seated while eating.
Friendly	Nepeta Leaf	32	Consumable: Increases damage and movement speed. Lasts 30 mins. Can only be used in Sholazar Basin.
Revered	Design: Jagged Forest Emerald	4	Jewel: +8 Critical Strike Rating and +12 Stamina
Revered	Muddied Crimson Gloves	13 70 48	Cloth: 175, +51 Spirit, +37 Stamina, +40 Intellect, Equip: Increases spell power by 60.
Revered	Azure Strappy Pants	32 13 80	Leather: 436, Equip: Increases attack power by 138., Equip: Improves hit rating by 53., +54 Stamina, +67 Agility
Revered	Stolen Vrykul Harpoon	13 85 16	Thrown: Physical 158-295, 2.1, 107.9 Equip: Increases attack power by 44., +17 Agility, +46 Stamina, Equip: Improves haste rating by 10.
Revered	Giant-Sized Gauntlets	25 12 13	Plate: 1308, +40 Strength, Equip: Increases your dodge rating by 51., +77 Stamina, Equip: Improves hit rating by 25.
Revered	Sparkly Shiny Gloves	25 20 87	Plate: 1308, +51 Intellect, Equip: Improves critical strike rating by 37., Equip: Increases spell power by 60., +41 Stamina
Revered	Scavenged Feathery Leggings	43 12 27	Mail: 1025, Equip: Improves haste rating by 40., +68 Intellect, Equip: Increases spell power by 81., +60 Stamina
Revered	Discarded Titanium Legplates	50 48 86	Plate: 1831, +51 Stamina, +69 Intellect, Equip: Increases spell power by 80., Equip: Improves critical strike rating by 53.
Revered	Disgusting Jar	3	Consumable
Exalted	Frenzyheart Insignia of Fury	68	Equip: Improves haste rating by 71., Upon killing a creature that grants you experience, you grow furious, dealing significantly more damage for the next 10 seconds.

The Oracles (Both Factions)

The Oracles are a loose collection of gorloc tribes native to Sholazar Basin. Gorlocs are an evolutionary offshoot of murlocs and they share many similarities to their ancestral relatives, but demonstrate distinct physical differences. The Oracles have long considered themselves the keepers of the leftover Titan technology, even though they don't understand it, and consider the Frenzyheart incursion into their territory to be a grave threat.

You can find the main Oracle encampment at Rainspeaker Canopy. The Oracles here are grateful to any help you can give in their conflict with the wolvar. Like the Frenzyhearts, they have little patience with enemies and don't want anything to do with you once you begin working with the Frenzyheart. Earn their trust though and Geen the Oracles Quartermaster opens up his shop to you.

Changing Sides

The Oracles and the Frenzyheart have a deep hatred of one another and they don't take kindly to their enemy's allies. However, if you wish to change from the Oracles to Frenzyheart you can slay the large cat, Pitch, who is located near the Skyreach Pillar, to trigger a quest from the nearby Frenzyheart Tracker Gekgek. From there you can work your way into the Frenzyheart's good graces.

To switch from the Frenzyheart to the Oracles help the Injured Rainspeaker Oracle, south of Rainspeaker Canopy. This triggers a quest where you escort him back to his village and are then able to do the Oracles quest line.

Reputation Level	Name	Purchase Price	Stats
Friendly	Design: Vivid Dark Jade	2	Jewel: +6 Hit Rating and +9 Stamina
Friendly	Oracle Secret Solution	32	Consumable: Chance to proc poison and increases movement speed. Lasts 30 mins. Can only be used in Sholazar Basin.
Honored	Slow-Roasted Eel	1 60	Food & Drink: Restores health over time. Must remain seated while eating.
Revered	Mysterious Egg	3	Consumable:
Revered	Design: Sundered Forest Emerald	4	Jewel: +8 Critical Strike Rating and +3 Mana every 5 seconds
Revered	Fishy Cinch	14 47 77	Cloth: 158, +37 Intellect, +42 Stamina, +51 Spirit, Equip: Increases spell power by 60.
Revered	Glitterscale Wrap	16 49 60	Leather: 296, Equip: Increases attack power by 102., +60 Stamina, +51 Agility, Equip: Increases your armor penetration rating by 25.
Revered	Shinygem Rod	49 87 12	Wand: Nature 278-516, 1.8, 220.6 +31 Stamina, Equip: Increases spell power by 26., Equip: Improves critical strike rating by 16.
Revered	Toothslice Helm	30 3 76	Mail: 952, +34 Agility, +80 Stamina, Equip: Increases attack power by 138., Equip: Improves critical strike rating by 34., +52 Intellect
Revered	Sharkjaw Cap	30 14 94	Mail: 952, +51 Stamina, +69 Intellect, Equip: Increases spell power by 81., Equip: Improves critical strike rating by 53.
Revered	Gold Star Spaulders	35 24 12	Plate: 1570 , +50 Strength, Equip: Improves critical strike rating by 58., +57 Stamina
Exalted	Oracle Talisman of Ablution	68	Equip: Improves critical strike rating by 71., Restores Mana, Rage, Energy, or Runic Power when you kill a target that grants honor or experience.

KIRIN TOR (Both Factions)

The Kirin Tor is a very closed sect of magic users united to study and protect magical knowledge and artifacts. They rule the floating city of Dalaran, having recently moved the entire city from the shores of Lake Lordaeron to the skies above Northrend. Though they are ruled by Rhonin, who can be found in the Violet Citadel, the Kirin Tor has recently seen a schism in its ranks with The Sunreavers and The Silver Covenant pursuing their own agendas within the Kirin Tor.

Members of the Kirin Tor are found primarily in Dalaran, but are also doing work throughout Northrend in locations such as Amber Ledge in the Borean Tundra, as well as being stationed within both Horde and Alliance outposts. Though their membership is strictly controlled, the Kirin Tor have opened their city to all who would oppose the Lich King and Malygos, and value aid from these allies. Mages start with a reputation of Friendly, giving them an advantage over other classes. Archmage Alvareaux, the Kirin Tor Quartermaster, can be found in the Violet Citadel in Dalaran, offering many useful items for those considered worthy.

Reputation Level	Name	Purchase Price	Stats
Friendly	Tabard of the Kirin Tor	1	You champion the cause of the Kirin Tor. All reputation gains while in level 80 dungeons will be applied to your standing with them.
Honored	Arcanum of the Flame's Soul	150	Quest: Permanently adds 25 fire resist and 30 stamina to a head slot item. Does not stack with other enchantments for the selected equipment slot.
Honored	Lightblade Rivener	65 96 36	Dagger: Physical 134-202, 1.4, 120 +29 Agility, Equip: Improves haste rating by 30., Increases attack power.
Honored	Shroud of Dedicated Research	19 86 36	Cloth: 140, +28 Stamina, +29 Intellect, Equip: Improves haste rating by 38., Equip: Increases spell power by 46.
Honored	Spaulders of Grounded Lightning	31 21 30	Mail: 878, +51 Stamina, Equip: Improves critical strike rating by 34., +34 Agility, Equip: Increases attack power by 68., +34 Intellect, Equip: Improves your resilience rating by 34.
Honored	Helm of the Majestic Stag	25 80	Leather: 428, +51 Stamina, +69 Intellect, Equip: Restores 21 mana per 5 sec., Equip: Increases spell power by 78.
Revered	Flameheart Spell Scalpel	74 12 9	Dagger: Physical 65-206, 1.8, 75.3 +28 Stamina, +33 Intellect, Equip: Improves critical strike rating by 25., Equip: Improves hit rating by 34., Equip: Increases spell power by 355.
Revered	Stave of Shrouded Mysteries	92 98 20	Staff: 260, Physical 232-430, 2.9, 114.1 +77 Strength, Equip: Increases your dodge rating by 56., +117 Stamina, Increases attack power in Cat, Bear, Dire Bear, and Moonkin forms only.
Revered	Girdle of the Warrior Magi	26 37 52	Plate: 1218, Socket: Yellow + Blue, +42 Intellect, +49 Stamina, Equip: Improves critical strike rating by 42., Equip: Increases spell power by 68.
Revered	Mind-Expanding Leggings	37 86 93	Leather: 477, Socket Bonus: +4 Hit Rating, Socket: Red, +78 Agility, +67 Stamina, Equip: Increases your expertise rating by 62., Equip: Increases attack power by 110.
Revered	Arcanum of Burning Mysteries	150	Quest: Permanently adds 30 spell power and 20 critical strike rating to a head slot item. Does not stack with other enchantments for the selected equipment slot.
Exalted	Design: Runed Scarlet Ruby	4	Jewel: +19 Spell Power
Exalted	Pattern: Sapphire Spellthread	5	Item Enhancement: Permanently embroiders spellthread into pants, increasing spell power by 50 and Stamina by 30.
Exalted	Robes of Crackling Flame	40 53 90	Cloth: 300, +66 Stamina, +73 Intellect, Equip: Improves haste rating by 42., Increases spell power., Restores 26 mana per 5 sec.
Exalted	Ghostflicker Waistband	25 42 75	Leather: 317, Socket Bonus: +4 Intellect, Socket: Blue, +42 Intellect, +49 Stamina, Equip: Improves critical strike rating by 41., Equip: Increases spell power by 68.
Exalted	Boots of Twinkling Stars	46 13 26	Mail: 862, +42 Agility, +49 Stamina, +41 Intellect, Equip: Improves haste rating by 58., Equip: Increases attack power by 66.
Exalted	Fireproven Gauntlets	36 5 39	Plate: 1401, +57 Strength, +87 Stamina, Equip: Increases defense rating by 42., Equip: Increases your dodge rating by 33.

KNIGHTS OF THE EBON BLADE (Both Factions)

Having once followed the Lich King, the Knights of the Ebon Blade have broken away from his control under the command of Highlord Darion Mograine. Though they remain tainted by the touch of the Scourge, they have allied themselves with both the Alliance and the Horde to work at bringing down the Lich King.

Their main base is Acherus: The Ebon Hold, the reclaimed necropolis floating above the Eastern Plaguelands, but they can be found in Northrend as well, most notably in Ebon Watch in Zul'Drak, Death's Rise in Icecrown, and at the Shadowvault, also in Icecrown. The Shadowvault is only accessible once you complete several quests, but once it is open to you Duchess Mynx, the Ebon Blade Quartermaster, sells many useful items to those who aid in the Knights' cause.

Reputation Level	Name	Purchase Price	Stats
Friendly	Design: Deadly Huge Citrine	2	Jewel: +6 Agility and +6 Critical Strike Rating
Friendly	Tabard of the Ebon Blade	1	You champion the cause of the Knights of the Ebon Blade. All reputation gains while in level 80 dungeons will be applied to your standing with them.
Honored	Arcanum of Toxic Warding	150	Quest: Permanently adds 25 nature resist and 30 stamina to a head slot item. Does not stack with other enchantments for the selected equipment slot.
Honored	Unholy Persuader	66 48 81	Fist Weapon: Physical 210-390, 2.5, 120 Equip: Increases your armor penetration rating by 29., +30 Agility, +46 Stamina
Honored	Dark Soldier Cape	20 2 9	Cloth: 140, +28 Stamina, +38 Intellect, Equip: Improves hit rating by 29., Equip: Increases spell power by 46.
Honored	Toxin-Tempered Sabatons	35 10 37	Plate: 1439, +51 Strength, +76 Stamina, Equip: Increases defense rating by 34., Increases the block value of your shield.
Honored	Pattern: Nerubian Reinforced Quiver	5	
Revered	Design: Wicked Monarch Topaz	4	Jewel: +16 Attack Power and +8 Critical Strike Rating
Revered	Pattern: Abyssal Bag	5	Soul Bag:
Revered	Arcanum of Torment	150	Quest: Permanently adds 50 attack power and 20 critical strike rating to a head slot item. Does not stack with other enchantments for the selected equipment slot.
Revered	Runeblade of Demonstrable Power		Sword: Physical 474-711, 3.5, 169.3 Equip: Increases attack power by 168., +63 Agility, Equip: Improves critical strike rating by 67., Equip: Improves haste rating by 33.
Revered	Reaper of Dark Souls		Sword: Physical 281-422, 2.7, 130.2 Equip: Increases attack power by 66., +24 Stamina, Equip: Improves critical strike rating by 26., Equip: Improves hit rating by 33.
Revered	Sterile Flesh-Handling Gloves	15 36 83	Cloth: 181, +49 Stamina, +58 Intellect, +41 Spirit, Equip: Increases spell power by 68.
Revered	Spaulders of the Black Arrow	34 85 20	Mail: 909, +42 Stamina, +44 Intellect, Equip: Improves critical strike rating by 33., +58 Agility, Equip: Increases attack power by 88.
Revered	Wound-Binder's Wristguards	17 50 44	Leather: 239, +42 Intellect, +38 Stamina, +36 Spirit, Equip: Increases spell power by 51.
Exalted	Design: Glowing Twilight Opal	4	Jewel: +9 Spell Power and +12 Stamina
Exalted	Belt of Dark Mending	18 70 27	Cloth: 169, +64 Stamina, +50 Intellect, Equip: Improves haste rating by 55., Equip: Increases spell power by 77.
Exalted	Darkheart Chestguard	48 86 48	Leather: 564, Equip: Increases attack power by 180., +88 Agility, +67 Stamina, Equip: Increases your armor penetration rating by 68.
Exalted	Kilt of Dark Mercy	59 7 31	Mail: 1097, Socket Bonus: +2 mana per 5 sec., Socket: Blue, +69 Stamina, +67 Intellect, Equip: Restores 29 mana per 5 sec., Equip: Increases spell power by 104.
Exalted	Death-Inured Sabatons	51 77 55	Plate: 1541, Socket Bonus: +6 Hit Rating, Socket: Blue, Red, +50 Strength, +73 Stamina, Equip: Improves critical strike rating by 66.

The Kalu'ak (Both Factions)

This tribe of tuskarr native to Northrend earn their living primarily through fishing and whaling. Though they are peaceful by nature, they often find it necessary to defend their homes from incursions of Kvaldir and other enemies, and fight fiercely when necessary.

They are one of the first factions that players encounter that are open to both the Horde and Alliance. Their main settlements are Kamagua, in the Howling Fjord, Kaskala, which is under attack from Kvaldir in the Borean Tundra, and Moa'ki Harbor in Dragonblight. They are grateful for any help you can provide and once you have proven yourself a friend to the Kalu'ak you can visit one of their Quartermasters, Tanaika in Kamagua in Howling Fjord or Sairuk at Moa'ki Harbor in Dragonblight to obtain the items listed below.

Reputation Level	Name	Purchase Price	Stats
Friendly	Design: Seer's Dark Jade	2	Jewel: +6 Intellect and +6 Spirit
Friendly	Freshly-Speared Emperor Salmon	1 60	Food & Drink: Restores health over time. Must remain seated while eating.
Honored	Whale-Skin Breastplate	29 60 45	Leather: 474, +38 Agility, +57 Stamina, Equip: Improves haste rating by 55., Equip: Increases attack power by 114.
Honored	Whale-Skin Vest	29 71 87	Leather: 474, +40 Intellect, +51 Stamina, Equip: Improves haste rating by 56., Equip: Increases spell power by 64.
Honored	Ivory-Reinforced Chestguard	43 6 64	Plate: 1886, +84 Stamina, Equip: Increases defense rating by 56., +43 Strength, Equip: Increases your expertise rating by 28.
Honored	Whalebone Carapace	43 22 62	Plate: 1886, +61 Stamina, Equip: Improves critical strike rating by 46., +75 Strength
Honored	Cuttlefish Scale Breastplate	37 18 81	Mail: 1055, +32 Intellect, +56 Agility, +84 Stamina, Equip: Increases attack power by 82.
Honored	Cuttlefish Tooth Ringmail	37 32 51	Mail: 1055, +41 Intellect, +48 Stamina, Equip: Restores 22 mana per 5 sec., Equip: Increases spell power by 65.
Honored	Pigment-Stained Robes	24 97 22	Cloth: 253, +43 Intellect, +42 Stamina, +56 Spirit, Equip: Increases spell power by 66.
Honored	Turtle-Minders Robe	25 6 36	Cloth: 253, +56 Intellect, +55 Stamina, Equip: Improves hit rating by 38., Equip: Increases spell power by 66.
Honored	Design: Defender's Shadow Crystal	2	
Honored	Pattern: Dragonscale Ammo Pouch	5	
Revered	Traditional Flensing Knife	72 36 12	Dagger: Physical 142-265, 1.7, 119.7 +29 Agility, Equip: Increases your armor penetration rating by 21., +28 Stamina, Equip: Increases attack power by 58.
Revered	Totemic Purification Rod	65 70 82	Mace: Physical 85-274, 2.6, 69 Equip: Improves haste rating by 32., +39 Intellect, Equip: Increases spell power by 314., +37 Stamina
Revered	Whale-Stick Harpoon	82 45 45	Polearm: Physical 449-675, 3.6, 156.1 +69 Agility, Equip: Improves hit rating by 40., Equip: Increases attack power by 100., +103 Stamina
Revered	Pattern: Trapper's Traveling Pack	5	
Exalted	Mastercraft Kalu'ak Fishing Pole	128 4 48	Fishing Pole: Physical 447-672, 3, 186.5 , Increases Fishing., Allows underwater breathing.
Exalted	Nurtured Penguin Egg	12	Right Click to summon and dismiss Penguin.

THE SONS OF HODIR (Both Factions)

The Sons of Hodir are an aggressive race of frost giants found in the Storm Peaks. They make their home at Dun Niffelem, the ice carved settlement in the far eastern part of the region. These giants are aggressive to most travelers but you can earn their trust through a series of quests, beginning with *They Took Our Men!* in the goblin camp, K3. This begins a long and extremely entertaining quest line involving Brunnhildar Village and Thorim which leads you to Dun Niffelem.

The giants have several tasks for you, including some which can be done daily, in order to raise you reputation with them. Speak with the Sons of Hodir Quartermaster, Lillehoff, to purchase some very good high level equipment, recipes, enchantments, and even Ice Mammoth mounts!

Reputation Level	Name	Purchase Price	Stats
Honored	Lesser Inscription of the Storm	75 🪙	Quest: Permanently adds 18 spell power and 10 critical strike rating to a shoulder slot item. Does not stack with other enchantments for the selected equipment slot.
Honored	Lesser Inscription of the Crag	75 🪙	Quest: Permanently adds 18 spell power and 4 mana per 5 seconds to a shoulder slot item. Does not stack with other enchantments for the selected equipment slot.
Honored	Lesser Inscription of the Axe	75 🪙	Quest: Permanently adds 30 attack power and 10 critical strike rating. Does not stack with other enchantments for the selected equipment slot.
Honored	Lesser Inscription of the Pinnacle	75 🪙	Quest: Permanently adds 15 dodge rating and 10 defense rating. Does not stack with other enchantments for the selected equipment slot.
Honored	Arcanum of the Frosty Soul	150 🪙	Quest: Permanently adds 25 frost resist and 30 stamina to a head slot item. Does not stack with other enchantments for the selected equipment slot.
Honored	Giant Ring Belt	20 🪙 56 🪙 13 🪙	Mail: 659, +40 Agility, +51 Stamina, +34 Intellect, Equip: Improves critical strike rating by 25., Increases attack power.
Honored	Spaulders of Frozen Knives	25 🪙 79 🪙 74 🪙	Leather: 395, +34 Agility, +51 Stamina, Equip: Improves haste rating by 52., Increases attack power.
Honored	Pattern: Mammoth Mining Bag	5 🪙	Bag
Revered	Reins of the Ice Mammoth	1000 🪙	Mount: Summons and dismisses a rideable Ice Mammoth.
Revered	Ice-Rimed Chopper	91 🪙 96 🪙 17 🪙	Axe: Physical 487-731, 3.6, 169.2 +80 Strength, +117 Stamina, Equip: Improves haste rating by 74.
Revered	Stalactite Chopper	73 🪙 84 🪙 14 🪙	Axe: Physical 237-440, 2.6, 130.2 Equip: Improves critical strike rating by 34., +49 Stamina, Equip: Increases your armor penetration rating by 26., Equip: Increases attack power by 32.
Revered	Broken Stalactite	74 🪙 10 🪙 61 🪙	Dagger: Physical 187-281, 1.8, 130 +26 Agility, Equip: Improves critical strike rating by 33., Equip: Improves hit rating by 28., Equip: Increases attack power by 48.
Revered	Giant-Friend Kilt	37 🪙 18 🪙 91 🪙	Leather: 477, +58 Stamina, +60 Intellect, Equip: Improves critical strike rating by 78., Equip: Increases spell power by 90.
Revered	Spaulders of the Giant Lords	39 🪙 11 🪙 67 🪙	Plate: 1625, +66 Strength, +64 Stamina, Equip: Improves critical strike rating by 58.
Exalted	Design: Smooth Autumn's Glow	4 🪙	Jewel: +16 Critical Strike Rating
Exalted	Pattern: Glacial Bag	5 🪙	Bag
Exalted	Reins of the Grand Ice Mammoth	10000 🪙	Mount: Calls forth the Grand Ice Mammoth! This is a very fast mammoth! Allows two passengers to board. Must be parties with the driver.
Exalted	Greater Inscription of the Axe	100 🪙	Quest: Permanently adds 40 attack power and 15 critical strike rating to shoulder armor. Does not stack with other enchantments for the selected equipment slot.
Exalted	Greater Inscription of the Crag	100 🪙	Quest: Permanently adds 24 spell power and 6 mana per 5 seconds to a shoulder slot item. Does not stack with other enchantments for the selected equipment slot.
Exalted	Greater Inscription of the Pinnacle	100 🪙	Quest: Permanently adds 20 dodge rating and 15 defense rating to shoulder armor. Does not stack with other enchantments for the selected equipment slot.
Exalted	Greater Inscription of the Storm	100 🪙	Quest: Permanently adds 24 spell power and 15 critical strike rating to a shoulder slot item. Does not stack with other enchantments for the selected equipment slot.

THE WYRMREST ACCORD (Both Factions)

As the Blue Dragonflight seeks to control all the magic in the world, the other dragonflights, Red, Green, Bronze, and Black, have united under the Wyrmrest Accord to stand against the Blue Dragonflight and to do what they can against the threat of the Lich King.

Though the dragonflights have representatives, usually in human form, throughout Northrend, their base of operations lies in Wyrmrest Temple in central Dragonblight. It is here that you can find their leader, Alexstrasza the Life-Binder, of the Red Dragonflight, along with representatives of each of the other united dragonflights. Once you have proven yourself an ally, Cielstrasza, the Wyrmrest Accord Quartermaster, makes her wares available to you. You can find her at the top of Wyrmrest Temple. The Accord has several powerful items available, including a Red Drake flying mount!

Reputation Level	Name	Purchase Price	Stats
Friendly	Tabard of the Wyrmrest Accord	1 🪙	You champion the cause of the Wyrmrest Accord. All reputation gains while in level 80 dungeons will be applied to your standing with them.
Honored	Arcanum of the Eclipsed Moon	150 🪙	Quest: Permanently adds 25 arcane resist and 30 stamina to a head slot item. Does not stack with other enchantments for the selected equipment slot.
Honored	Fang of Truth	68 🪙 3 🪙 40 🪙	Sword: Physical 126-234, 1.5, 120 +32 Agility, +29 Stamina, Equip: Increases attack power by 48., Equip: Improves hit rating by 33.
Honored	Cloak of Peaceful Resolutions	20 🪙 48 🪙 68 🪙	Cloth: 140, +64 Stamina, Equip: Increases defense rating by 43., Equip: Improves hit rating by 25., +31 Strength
Honored	Sash of the Wizened Wyrm	14 🪙 6 🪙 36 🪙	Cloth: 158, +37 Stamina, +51 Intellect, Equip: Improves hit rating by 40., Equip: Increases spell power by 60.
Honored	Bracers of Accorded Courtesy	24 🪙 83 🪙 95 🪙	Plate: 916, Socket Bonus: +4 Haste Rating, Socket: Yellow, +29 Intellect, +28 Stamina, Equip: Improves haste rating by 22., Equip: Increases spell power by 46.
Revered	Pattern: Mysterious Bag	5 🪙	Enchanting Bag
Revered	Arcanum of Blissful Mending	150 🪙	Quest: Permanently adds 30 spell power and 8 mana per 5 seconds to a head slot item. Does not stack with other enchantments for the selected equipment slot.
Revered	Breastplate of the Solemn Council	52 🪙 82 🪙 14 🪙	Plate: 2166, Equip: Increases defense rating by 76., +117 Stamina, +49 Strength, Equip: Increases your expertise rating by 56.
Revered	Gavel of the Brewing Storm	75 🪙 73 🪙 12 🪙	Mace: Physical 82-263, 2.3, 75 +49 Stamina, +26 Intellect, Equip: Improves critical strike rating by 24., Equip: Improves haste rating by 25., Equip: Increases spell power by 355.
Revered	Ancestral Sinew Wristguards	14 🪙 11 🪙 82 🪙	Cloth: 127, Socket Bonus: +4 Intellect, Socket: Blue, +31 Stamina, +33 Intellect, +27 Spirit, Equip: Increases spell power by 50.
Revered	Sabatons of Draconic Vigor	37 🪙 12 🪙 85 🪙	Plate: 1489, +44 Strength, +85 Stamina, Equip: Increases defense rating by 58., Equip: Improves hit rating by 29.
Exalted	Design: Glimmering Monarch Topaz	4 🪙	Jewel: +8 Parry Rating and +8 Defense Rating
Exalted	Sandals of Crimson Fury	28 🪙 45 🪙 12 🪙	Cloth: 206, Socket Bonus: +4 Intellect, Socket: Blue, +49 Stamina, +50 Intellect, Equip: Improves haste rating by 51., Equip: Increases spell power by 77.
Exalted	Dragonfriend Bracers	23 🪙 80 🪙	Leather: 247, +49 Agility, +38 Stamina, Equip: Improves critical strike rating by 38., Equip: Increases attack power by 100.
Exalted	Grips of Fierce Pronouncements	28 🪙 66 🪙 59 🪙	Mail: 784, +57 Stamina, +48 Intellect, Equip: Restores 26 mana per 5 sec., Equip: Increases spell power by 77.
Exalted	Legplates of Bloody Reprisal	67 🪙 14 🪙 11 🪙	Plate: 1961, +96 Strength, +117 Stamina, Equip: Increases your armor penetration rating by 90.
Exalted	Reins of the Red Drake	2000 🪙	Mount: Summons and dismisses a rideable Red Drake. This is a very fast mount. This mount can only be summoned in Outland or Northrend.

WHEN GOLD JUST ISN'T ENOUGH

While gold is the currency of choice throughout Azeroth some vendors prefer a different currency and you can barter with other items you find in your travels. The rewards below are open to both the Horde and Alliance.

VENTURE COINS

At Venture Bay, in the southwestern corner of Grizzly Hills, you can obtain Venture Coins for completing quests in the area. You can then trade these coins in at either Grizzly D. Adams, if you are a member of the Alliance, or at Purkom if you are a member of the Horde.

STONE KEEPER'S SHARDS

Stone Keeper's Shards are awarded by doing quests in the zone wide PvP area, Wintergrasp. There are several one-time quests as well as daily quests that reward these shards. When your faction has control of Wintergrasp Fortress you can trade these to the vendors there.

WINTERFIN CLAMS

Gold is of little use to the Winterfin Murlocs, but they love to get their hands on delicious Winterfin Clams! These can be collected from the Winterfin Betrayer camp across the water from the Winterfin Murlocs. Once you perform a task for King Mrgl-Mrgl, the rest of the Winterfin Murlocs trust you and you can then trade the Winterfin Clams you collect to Ahlurglgr the Clam Vendor.

CRAFTED ITEMS AND REWARDS

If you are more the "stay in town and craft" type, you too can barter items for better recipes in some professions. For example, you can receive Dalaran Jewelcrafter's Tokens or Dalaran Cooking Rewards for performing profession oriented quests in Dalaran. You can then trade these tokens into the appropriate vendors, located next to the profession trainers.

CRAFTING

Crafting has always been an integral part of life in Azeroth and this hasn't changed in Wrath of the Lich King. Every profession has been given a lot of love and there are hundreds of new recipes, new materials, and even new perks, such as special abilities, associated with some professions.

As before, each character can learn up to two primary professions, and anyone can learn any or all of the secondary professions, Cooking, First Aid, and Fishing, if they want. Though all the profession received valuable additions and upgrades with this expansion, Wrath of the Lich King also introduces an entirely new profession, Inscription, along with new daily crafting quests.

The following pages include valuable information about each profession, including new materials and recipes, giving you everything you need to continue helping your friends and guildmates with the items you craft, or to just make a nice profit in the Auction House.

Alchemy

Blacksmithing

Cooking

Enchanting

Engineering

First Aid

Fishing

Herbalism

Jewelcrafting

Leatherworking

Mining

Skinning

Tailoring

 INSCRIPTION

Inscription Trainers

Faction	Name	Location
Alliance	Feydin Darkin	Darnassus
Alliance	Thoth	Exodar
Alliance	Elise Brightletter	Ironforge
Alliance	Catarina Stanford	Stormwind
Alliance	Michael Swan (Master Inscription Trainer)	Honor Hold
Alliance	Mindri Dinkles (Grand Master Inscription Trainer)	Valgarde
Alliance	Tink Brightbolt (Grand Master Inscription Trainer)	Valiance Keep
Neutral	Professor Pallin (Grand Master Inscription Trainer)	Dalaran
Horde	Jo'mah	Orgrimmar
Horde	Zantasia	Silvermoon City
Horde	Poshken Hardbinder	Thunder Bluff
Horde	Margaux Parchley	Undercity
Horde	Neferatti (Master Inscription Trainer)	Thrallmar
Horde	Adelene Sunlance (Grand Master Inscription Trainer)	Warsong Hold
Horde	Booker Kells (Grand Master Inscription Trainer)	Vengeance Landing

This brand new profession allows Scribes to create various types of magical writings while mastering their craft. With Inscription, Scribes can manufacture Scrolls, Runes of Power, Glyphs, and other handy items. To practice her art a Scribe must gather the appropriate tools and materials. An Inscription Supplies Vendor can sell you the Virtuoso Inking Set you need to get started, as well as different types of parchment, and even a special ten-slot bag, the Scribe's Satchel, to hold all your Inscription supplies.

To make the inks you need to practice Inscription, you need to first manufacture pigments. To do this you use a process called Milling. Much like Prospecting for a Jewelcrafter, you gain the Milling skill as soon as you take up Inscription. With it, you crush five herbs of the same kind to make the pigments you need. Because of this, Herbalism is a great second profession to pick up if you choose to become a Scribe, though you can always depend on the Auction House or perhaps set up a mutually beneficial arrangement with a friendly Herbalist. Milling different herbs produces different pigments. The common pigments are always produced, with uncommon pigments resulting during a smaller percentage of milling attempts. Milling is not trained as a skill by itself, but increasing your Inscription skill allows you to mill higher level herbs. Once you have milled your herbs into pigments you can then use them to create the various inks you need for your Scribe's creations.

MILLING

Common Pigments	
Pigment	**Herbs**
Alabaster Pigment	Peacebloom, Silverleaf, Earthroot
Dusky Pigment	Mageroyal, Swiftthistle, Briarthorn, Stranglekelp, Bruiseweed
Golden Pigment	Wild Steelbloom, Grave Moss, Kingsblood, Liferoot
Emerald Pigment	Fadeleaf, Goldthorn, Khadgar's Whisker, Wintersbite
Violet Pigment	Firebloom, Purple Lotus, Arthas' Tears, Sungrass, Blindweed, Ghost Mushroom, Gromsblood
Silvery Pigment	Golden Sansam, Dreamfoil, Mountain Silversage, Plaguebloom, Icecap
Nether Pigment	Felweed, Dreaming Glory, Terocone, Ragveil, Ancient Lichen, Netherbloom, Nightmare Vine, Mana Thistle
Azure Pigment	Goldclover, Talandra's Rose, Tiger Lilly, Adder's Tongue, Lichbloom, Icethorn, Deadnettle

Uncommon Pigments	
Pigment	**Herbs**
Verdant Pigment	Mageroyal, Swiftthistle, Briarthorn, Stranglekelp, Bruiseweed
Burnt Pigment	Wild Steelbloom, Grave Moss, Kingsblood, Liferoot
Indigo Pigment	Fadeleaf, Goldthorn, Khadgar's Whisker, Wintersbite
Ruby Pigment	Firebloom, Purple Lotus, Arthas' Tears, Sungrass, Blindweed, Ghost Mushroom, Gromsblood
Sapphire Pigment	Golden Sansam, Dreamfoil, Mountain Silversage, Plaguebloom, Icecap
Ebon Pigment	Felweed, Dreaming Glory, Terocone, Ragveil, Ancient Lichen, Netherbloom, Nightmare Vine, Mana Thistle
Icy Pigment	Goldclover, Talandra's Rose, Tiger Lilly, Adder's Tongue, Lichbloom, Icethorn, Deadnettle

Scribes have several different types of items they can make with their inks and parchment, including two of the most common, Scrolls and Glyphs. Scrolls are similar to those you once picked up off the still twitching bodies of your enemies. They can be used once to increase such things as Stamina or Intellect for a short time. These are great to have on hand for when you are getting ready to face a tough fight—sometimes that little extra oomph is all you need.

Glyphs are more permanent additions to your character. Each character has a tab for Glyphs in their Spellbook & Abilities with spaces for three Major and three Minor Glyphs, though not all of them are available at first. As their name implies, Major Glyphs affect your abilities in a substantial way, making them last longer or do more damage for example. Minor Glyphs also affect your abilities, but in less important ways. For example, one Minor Glyph can make a Mage's Polymorph spell turn the target into a penguin instead of a sheep, another may increase the range of a certain spell.

To use a Glyph, you must be near a Lexicon of Power, usually located near Inscription Trainers. Once placed in a slot, the Glyph is used and cannot be removed, though it can be overwritten, much like gems in sockets. You can always put another Glyph in, but you destroy the existing Glyph by doing so. Major Glyphs are learned from your trainer while Minor Glyphs are learned only through Minor Inscription Research. Each time you use this ability you create a handful of random scrolls which you already know how to make, but you have a chance to learn to create a Minor Glyph. This ability is on a long cooldown so be sure to use it every time it is available to increase your repertoire of Minor Glyphs.

Another very useful creation is Vellum. This allows Enchanters to place their enchants on Vellum which can then be traded to other characters, sent through the mail, or even sold in the Auction House. You may suddenly find yourself very popular among Enchanters! If you choose to procure your herbs through the Auction House or other means besides picking them yourself, Enchanting is a great second profession to pick up with Inscription. Scribes can also make special tarot items which begin quests specific to their profession, along with offhand items that give significant boosts to some stats.

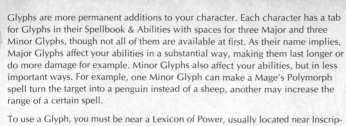

Inscription

Spellname	SkillRank	Source	Reagents
Scroll of Agility	15	Trained	2 Ivory Ink, 1 Light Parchment
Scroll of Strength	15	Trained	2 Ivory Ink, 1 Light Parchment
Scroll of Recall	35	Trained	1 Light Parchment, 1 Moonglow Ink
Bleached Vellum	35	Trained	1 Moonglow Ink, 1 Light Parchment
Moonglow Ink	35	Trained	2 Alabaster Pigment
Scroll of Intellect II	75	Trained	1 Midnight Ink, 1 Light Parchment
Scroll of Spirit II	75	Trained	1 Midnight Ink, 1 Light Parchment
Scroll of Stamina II	75	Trained	1 Midnight Ink, 1 Light Parchment
Treated Vellum	75	Trained	3 Midnight Ink, 1 Light Parchment
Midnight Ink	75	Trained	1 Dusky Pigment
Minor Inscription Research	75	Trained	1 Moonglow Ink, 2 Light Parchment
Glyph of Rejuvenation	80	Trained	1 Midnight Ink, 1 Light Parchment
Glyph of Frost Nova	80	Trained	1 Moonglow Ink, 1 Light Parchment
Glyph of Hunter's Mark	80	Trained	1 Midnight Ink, 1 Light Parchment
Glyph of Spiritual Attunement	80	Trained	1 Midnight Ink, 1 Light Parchment
Glyph of Backstab	80	Trained	1 Midnight Ink, 1 Light Parchment
Glyph of Power Word: Shield	80	Trained	1 Midnight Ink, 1 Light Parchment
Scroll of Strength II	80	Trained	1 Midnight Ink, 1 Light Parchment
Glyph of Wrath	85	Trained	1 Midnight Ink, 1 Light Parchment
Glyph of Rapid Charge	85	Trained	1 Midnight Ink, 1 Light Parchment
Glyph of Flame Shock	85	Trained	1 Midnight Ink, 1 Light Parchment
Glyph of Corruption	85	Trained	1 Midnight Ink, 1 Light Parchment
Hunter's Ink	85	Trained	1 Verdant Pigment
Scroll of Agility II	85	Trained	1 Midnight Ink, 1 Light Parchment
Glyph of Maul	90	Trained	1 Midnight Ink, 1 Light Parchment
Glyph of Ice Armor	90	Trained	1 Midnight Ink, 1 Light Parchment
Glyph of Serpent Sting	90	Trained	1 Midnight Ink, 1 Light Parchment
Glyph of Hammer of Justice	90	Trained	1 Midnight Ink, 1 Light Parchment
Glyph of Evasion	95	Trained	2 Midnight Ink, 1 Light Parchment
Glyph of Heroic Strike	95	Trained	2 Midnight Ink, 1 Light Parchment
Glyph of Psychic Scream	95	Trained	2 Midnight Ink, 1 Light Parchment
Glyph of Lightning Shield	95	Trained	2 Midnight Ink, 1 Light Parchment
Glyph of Healthstone	95	Trained	2 Midnight Ink, 1 Light Parchment
Glyph of Entangling Roots	100	Trained	1 Lion's Ink, 1 Light Parchment
Glyph of Arcane Explosion	100	Trained	1 Lion's Ink, 1 Light Parchment
Glyph of Arcane Shot	100	Trained	1 Lion's Ink, 1 Light Parchment
Lion's Ink	100	Trained	1 Golden Pigment
Glyph of Holy Light	105	Trained	1 Lion's Ink, 1 Common Parchment

Inscription

Spellname	SkillRank	Source	Reagents
Glyph of Eviscerate	105	Trained	1 Lion's Ink, 1 Common Parchment
Glyph of Fade	105	Trained	1 Lion's Ink, 1 Common Parchment
Mysterious Tarot	110	Trained	1 Light Parchment, 1 Hunter's Ink
Glyph of Rending	110	Trained	1 Lion's Ink, 1 Common Parchment
Glyph of Fire Nova Totem	110	Trained	1 Lion's Ink, 1 Common Parchment
Glyph of Health Funnel	110	Trained	1 Lion's Ink, 1 Common Parchment
Mystic Tome	110	Trained	10 Light Parchment, 5 Hunter's Ink
Glyph of Healing Touch	115	Trained	1 Lion's Ink, 1 Common Parchment
Glyph of Arcane Missiles	115	Trained	1 Lion's Ink, 1 Common Parchment
Glyph of Aspect of the Monkey	115	Trained	1 Lion's Ink, 1 Common Parchment
Glyph of Judgement	120	Trained	2 Lion's Ink, 1 Common Parchment
Glyph of Expose Armor	120	Trained	2 Lion's Ink, 1 Common Parchment
Glyph of Flash Heal	120	Trained	2 Lion's Ink, 1 Common Parchment
Glyph of Hamstring	125	Trained	2 Lion's Ink, 1 Common Parchment
Glyph of Flametongue Weapon	125	Trained	2 Lion's Ink, 1 Common Parchment
Glyph of Fear	125	Trained	2 Lion's Ink, 1 Common Parchment
Dawnstar Ink	125	Trained	1 Verdant Pigment, 1 Golden Pigment
Tome of the Dawn	125	Trained	5 Dawnstar Ink, 10 Common Parchment
Book of Survival	125	Trained	5 Dawnstar Ink, 10 Common Parchment
Strange Tarot	125	Trained	2 Dawnstar Ink, 1 Common Parchment
Glyph of Moonfire	130	Trained	2 Lion's Ink, 1 Common Parchment
Glyph of Blink	130	Trained	2 Lion's Ink, 1 Common Parchment
Glyph of Immolation Trap	130	Trained	2 Lion's Ink, 1 Common Parchment
Glyph of Lay on Hands	135	Trained	2 Lion's Ink, 1 Common Parchment
Glyph of Garrote	135	Trained	2 Lion's Ink, 1 Common Parchment
Glyph of Inner Fire	135	Trained	2 Lion's Ink, 1 Common Parchment
Glyph of Sunder Armor	140	Trained	2 Lion's Ink, 1 Common Parchment
Glyph of Lightning Bolt	140	Trained	2 Lion's Ink, 1 Common Parchment
Glyph of Imp	140	Trained	2 Lion's Ink, 1 Common Parchment
Glyph of Insect Swarm	150	Trained	1 Jadefire Ink, 1 Common Parchment
Glyph of Multi-Shot	150	Trained	1 Jadefire Ink, 1 Common Parchment
Jadefire Ink	150	Trained	1 Emerald Pigment
Scroll of Stamina III	155	Trained	5 Jadefire Ink, 5 Common Parchment
Glyph of Evocation	155	Trained	1 Jadefire Ink, 1 Common Parchment
Glyph of Righteous Defense	155	Trained	1 Jadefire Ink, 1 Common Parchment
Scroll of Spirit III	160	Trained	5 Jadefire Ink, 5 Common Parchment
Glyph of Gouge	160	Trained	1 Jadefire Ink, 1 Common Parchment
Glyph of Renew	160	Trained	1 Jadefire Ink, 1 Common Parchment

Spellname	SkillRank	Source	Reagents
Scroll of Intellect III	165	Trained	5 Jadefire Ink, 5 Common Parchment
Glyph of Strength of Earth Totem	165	Trained	1 Jadefire Ink, 1 Common Parchment
Glyph of Shadow Bolt	165	Trained	1 Jadefire Ink, 1 Common Parchment
Glyph of Rebirth	170	Trained	2 Jadefire Ink, 1 Common Parchment
Glyph of Overpower	170	Trained	1 Jadefire Ink, 1 Common Parchment
Scroll of Strength III	170	Trained	5 Jadefire Ink, 5 Common Parchment
Glyph of Icy Veins	175	Trained	2 Jadefire Ink, 1 Common Parchment
Glyph of Aimed Shot	175	Trained	2 Jadefire Ink, 1 Common Parchment
Royal Ink	175	Trained	1 Indigo Pigment, 1 Emerald Pigment
Scroll of Agility III	175	Trained	5 Jadefire Ink, 5 Common Parchment
Tome of Kings	175	Trained	5 Royal Ink, 10 Common Parchment
Royal Guide of Escape Routes	175	Trained	5 Royal Ink, 10 Common Parchment
Arcane Tarot	175	Trained	2 Royal Ink, 1 Common Parchment
Glyph of Cleansing	180	Trained	2 Jadefire Ink, 1 Common Parchment
Glyph of Shadow Word: Pain	180	Trained	2 Jadefire Ink, 1 Common Parchment
Glyph of Sap	185	Trained	2 Jadefire Ink, 1 Common Parchment
Glyph of Frost Shock	185	Trained	2 Jadefire Ink, 1 Common Parchment
Glyph of Revenge	190	Trained	2 Jadefire Ink, 1 Common Parchment
Glyph of Voidwalker	190	Trained	2 Jadefire Ink, 1 Common Parchment
Glyph of Rip	200	Trained	1 Celestial Ink, 1 Common Parchment
Glyph of Deterrence	200	Trained	1 Celestial Ink, 1 Common Parchment
Celestial Ink	200	Trained	1 Violet Pigment
Certificate of Ownership	200	Trained	2 Celestial Ink, 1 Common Parchment
Inscribed Vellum	200	Trained	1 Celestial Ink, 1 Common Parchment
Scroll of Recall II	200	Trained	1 Common Parchment, 1 Celestial Ink
Scroll of Stamina IV	205	Trained	5 Celestial Ink, 5 Heavy Parchment
Glyph of Improved Scorch	205	Trained	1 Celestial Ink, 1 Heavy Parchment
Glyph of Consecration	205	Trained	1 Celestial Ink, 1 Heavy Parchment
Scroll of Spirit IV	210	Trained	5 Celestial Ink, 5 Heavy Parchment
Glyph of Sinister Strike	210	Trained	1 Celestial Ink, 1 Heavy Parchment
Glyph of Smite	210	Trained	1 Celestial Ink, 1 Heavy Parchment
Scroll of Intellect IV	215	Trained	5 Celestial Ink, 5 Heavy Parchment
Glyph of Healing Stream Totem	215	Trained	1 Celestial Ink, 1 Heavy Parchment
Glyph of Searing Pain	215	Trained	1 Celestial Ink, 1 Heavy Parchment
Glyph of Starfire	220	Trained	1 Celestial Ink, 1 Heavy Parchment
Glyph of Barbaric Insults	220	Trained	1 Celestial Ink, 1 Heavy Parchment
Scroll of Strength IV	220	Trained	5 Celestial Ink, 5 Heavy Parchment
Glyph of Ice Block	225	Trained	2 Celestial Ink, 1 Heavy Parchment
Glyph of Disengage	225	Trained	2 Celestial Ink, 1 Heavy Parchment
Fiery Ink	225	Trained	1 Ruby Pigment, 1 Violet Pigment
Scroll of Agility IV	225	Trained	5 Celestial Ink, 5 Heavy Parchment
Fire Eater's Guide	225	Trained	5 Fiery Ink, 10 Heavy Parchment
Book of Stars	225	Trained	5 Fiery Ink, 1 Celestial Ink, 10 Heavy Parchment
Shadowy Tarot	225	Trained	2 Fiery Ink, 1 Heavy Parchment
Glyph of Crusader Strike	230	Trained	2 Celestial Ink, 1 Heavy Parchment
Glyph of Dispel Magic	230	Trained	1 Celestial Ink, 1 Heavy Parchment
Glyph of Slice and Dice	235	Trained	2 Celestial Ink, 1 Heavy Parchment
Glyph of Lesser Healing Wave	235	Trained	2 Celestial Ink, 1 Heavy Parchment
Fine Vellum	235	Trained	1 Fiery Ink, 1 Heavy Parchment
Glyph of Cleaving	240	Trained	1 Celestial Ink, 1 Heavy Parchment
Glyph of Soulstone	240	Trained	2 Celestial Ink, 1 Heavy Parchment
Scroll of Stamina V	250	Trained	5 Shimmering Ink, 5 Heavy Parchment
Shimmering Ink	250	Trained	1 Silvery Pigment
Scroll of Spirit V	255	Trained	5 Shimmering Ink, 5 Heavy Parchment
Scroll of Intellect V	260	Trained	5 Shimmering Ink, 5 Heavy Parchment
Glyph of Shred	260	Trained	1 Shimmering Ink, 1 Heavy Parchment
Glyph of Freezing Trap	260	Trained	1 Shimmering Ink, 1 Heavy Parchment
Glyph of Exorcism	265	Trained	1 Shimmering Ink, 1 Heavy Parchment
Glyph of Bone Shield	265	Trained	1 Shimmering Ink, 1 Heavy Parchment

Spellname	SkillRank	Source	Reagents
Scroll of Strength V	265	Trained	5 Shimmering Ink, 5 Heavy Parchment
Glyph of Fear Ward	270	Trained	1 Shimmering Ink, 1 Heavy Parchment
Glyph of Frost Strike	270	Trained	1 Shimmering Ink, 1 Heavy Parchment
Scroll of Agility V	270	Trained	5 Shimmering Ink, 5 Heavy Parchment
Glyph of Water Mastery	275	Trained	1 Shimmering Ink, 1 Heavy Parchment
Glyph of Shadowburn	275	Trained	1 Shimmering Ink, 1 Heavy Parchment
Ink of the Sky	275	Trained	1 Sapphire Pigment, 1 Silvery Pigment
Stormbound Tome	275	Trained	8 Ink of the Sky, 1 Heavy Parchment
Manual of Clouds	275	Trained	8 Ink of the Sky, 10 Heavy Parchment
Darkmoon Card	275	Trained	5 Ink of the Sky, 1 Heavy Parchment
Glyph of Mana Gem	280	Trained	1 Shimmering Ink, 1 Heavy Parchment
Glyph of Icy Touch	280	Trained	1 Shimmering Ink, 1 Heavy Parchment
Glyph of Sprint	285	Trained	1 Shimmering Ink, 1 Heavy Parchment
Glyph of Execution	285	Trained	1 Shimmering Ink, 1 Heavy Parchment
Glyph of Death Grip	285	Trained	1 Shimmering Ink, 1 Heavy Parchment
Scroll of Intellect VI	300	Trained	5 Ethereal Ink, 5 Heavy Parchment
Scroll of Spirit VI	300	Trained	5 Ethereal Ink, 5 Heavy Parchment
Scroll of Stamina VI	300	Trained	5 Ethereal Ink, 5 Heavy Parchment
Glyph of Flash of Light	300	Trained	1 Ethereal Ink, 1 Heavy Parchment
Glyph of Plague Strike	300	Trained	1 Ethereal Ink, 1 Heavy Parchment
Glyph of Earthliving Weapon	300	Trained	1 Ethereal Ink, 1 Heavy Parchment
Ethereal Ink	300	Trained	1 Nether Pigment
Scroll of Agility VI	300	Trained	5 Ethereal Ink, 5 Heavy Parchment
Scroll of Strength VI	300	Trained	5 Ethereal Ink, 5 Heavy Parchment
Glyph of Feint	305	Trained	1 Ethereal Ink, 1 Heavy Parchment
Glyph of Unbreakable Armor	305	Trained	1 Ethereal Ink, 1 Resilient Parchment
Glyph of Rake	310	Trained	1 Ethereal Ink, 1 Resilient Parchment
Glyph of Rune Tap	310	Trained	1 Ethereal Ink, 1 Resilient Parchment
Glyph of Rapid Fire	315	Trained	1 Ethereal Ink, 1 Resilient Parchment
Glyph of Holy Nova	315	Trained	1 Ethereal Ink, 1 Resilient Parchment
Glyph of Sweeping Strikes	320	Trained	1 Ethereal Ink, 1 Resilient Parchment
Glyph of Blood Strike	320	Trained	1 Ethereal Ink, 1 Resilient Parchment
Glyph of Mage Armor	325	Trained	2 Ethereal Ink, 1 Resilient Parchment
Glyph of Succubus	325	Trained	2 Ethereal Ink, 1 Resilient Parchment
Darkflame Ink	325	Trained	1 Ebon Pigment, 1 Nether Pigment
Hellfire Tome	325	Trained	6 Darkflame Ink, 10 Resilient Parchment
Book of Clever Tricks	325	Trained	6 Darkflame Ink, 10 Resilient Parchment
Greater Darkmoon Card	325	Trained	3 Darkflame Ink, 1 Resilient Parchment, 3 Primal Life
Glyph of Scourge Strike	330	Trained	2 Ethereal Ink, 1 Resilient Parchment
Glyph of Windfury Weapon	330	Trained	2 Ethereal Ink, 1 Resilient Parchment
Glyph of Arcane Power	335	Trained	2 Ethereal Ink, 1 Resilient Parchment
Glyph of Seal of Command	335	Trained	2 Ethereal Ink, 1 Resilient Parchment
Glyph of Ambush	340	Trained	2 Ethereal Ink, 1 Resilient Parchment
Glyph of Death Strike	340	Trained	2 Ethereal Ink, 1 Resilient Parchment
Glyph of Whirlwind	345	Trained	1 Ethereal Ink, 1 Resilient Parchment
Glyph of Vampiric Blood	345	Trained	2 Ethereal Ink, 1 Resilient Parchment
Scroll of Stamina VII	350	Trained	5 Ink of the Sea, 5 Resilient Parchment
Glyph of Frenzied Regeneration	350	Trained	2 Ethereal Ink, 1 Resilient Parchment
Glyph of Hurricane	350	Trained	1 Ink of the Sea, 1 Resilient Parchment
Glyph of Water Elemental	350	Trained	1 Ink of the Sea, 1 Resilient Parchment
Glyph of Aspect of the Beast	350	Trained	1 Ink of the Sea, 1 Resilient Parchment
Glyph of Frost Trap	350	Trained	2 Ethereal Ink, 1 Resilient Parchment
Glyph of Crippling Poison	350	Trained	1 Ink of the Sea, 1 Resilient Parchment
Glyph of Mind Flay	350	Trained	2 Ethereal Ink, 1 Resilient Parchment
Glyph of Mind Soothe	350	Trained	1 Ink of the Sea, 1 Resilient Parchment
Glyph of the Ghoul	350	Trained	2 Ethereal Ink, 1 Resilient Parchment
Glyph of Chain Lightning	350	Trained	1 Ink of the Sea, 1 Resilient Parchment
Glyph of Banish	350	Trained	2 Ethereal Ink, 1 Resilient Parchment
Glyph of Felhunter	350	Trained	1 Ink of the Sea, 1 Resilient Parchment
Ink of the Sea	350	Trained	2 Azure Pigment

CRAFTING

Inscription

Alchemy

Blacksmithing

Cooking

Enchanting

Engineering

First Aid

Fishing

Herbalism

Jewelcrafting

Leatherworking

Mining

Skinning

Tailoring

Inscription			
Spellname	SkillRank	Source	Reagents
Imbued Vellum	350	Trained	1 Ink of the Sea, 1 Resilient Parchment
Scroll of Recall III	350	Trained	1 Ink of the Sea, 1 Resilient Parchment
Scroll of Spirit VII	355	Trained	5 Ink of the Sea, 5 Resilient Parchment
Scroll of Intellect VII	360	Trained	5 Ink of the Sea, 5 Resilient Parchment
Scroll of Strength VII	365	Trained	5 Ink of the Sea, 5 Resilient Parchment
Scroll of Agility VII	370	Trained	5 Ink of the Sea, 5 Resilient Parchment
Glyph of Innervate	375	Trained	1 Ink of the Sea, 1 Resilient Parchment
Glyph of Mangle	375	Trained	1 Ink of the Sea, 1 Resilient Parchment
Glyph of Swiftmend	375	Trained	1 Ink of the Sea, 1 Resilient Parchment
Glyph of Ice Lance	375	Trained	1 Ink of the Sea, 1 Resilient Parchment
Glyph of Invisibility	375	Trained	1 Ink of the Sea, 1 Resilient Parchment
Glyph of Molten Armor	375	Trained	1 Ink of the Sea, 1 Resilient Parchment
Glyph of Bestial Wrath	375	Trained	1 Ink of the Sea, 1 Resilient Parchment
Glyph of Improved Aspect of the Hawk	375	Trained	1 Ink of the Sea, 1 Resilient Parchment
Glyph of Trueshot Aura	375	Trained	1 Ink of the Sea, 1 Resilient Parchment
Glyph of Volley	375	Trained	1 Ink of the Sea, 1 Resilient Parchment
Glyph of Seal of Light	375	Trained	1 Ink of the Sea, 1 Resilient Parchment
Glyph of Seal of Wisdom	375	Trained	1 Ink of the Sea, 1 Resilient Parchment
Glyph of Turn Evil	375	Trained	1 Ink of the Sea, 1 Resilient Parchment
Glyph of Blade Flurry	375	Trained	1 Ink of the Sea, 1 Resilient Parchment
Glyph of Ghostly Strike	375	Trained	1 Ink of the Sea, 1 Resilient Parchment
Glyph of Rupture	375	Trained	1 Ink of the Sea, 1 Resilient Parchment
Glyph of Mind Control	375	Trained	1 Ink of the Sea, 1 Resilient Parchment
Glyph of Prayer of Healing	375	Trained	1 Ink of the Sea, 1 Resilient Parchment
Glyph of Shackle Undead	375	Trained	1 Ink of the Sea, 1 Resilient Parchment
Glyph of Strangulate	375	Trained	1 Ink of the Sea, 1 Resilient Parchment
Glyph of Chain Heal	375	Trained	1 Ink of the Sea, 1 Resilient Parchment
Glyph of Mana Tide Totem	375	Trained	1 Ink of the Sea, 1 Resilient Parchment
Glyph of Stormstrike	375	Trained	1 Ink of the Sea, 1 Resilient Parchment
Glyph of Conflagrate	375	Trained	1 Ink of the Sea, 1 Resilient Parchment
Glyph of Howl of Terror	375	Trained	1 Ink of the Sea, 1 Resilient Parchment
Glyph of Siphon Life	375	Trained	1 Ink of the Sea, 1 Resilient Parchment
Snowfall Ink	375	Trained	2 Icy Pigment, 2 Azure Pigment
Northrend Inscription Research	385	Trained	3 Ink of the Sea, 1 Snowfall Ink, 5 Resilient Parchment
Glyph of Growl	400	Trained	1 Ink of the Sea, 1 Resilient Parchment
Glyph of Lifebloom	400	Trained	1 Ink of the Sea, 1 Resilient Parchment
Glyph of Regrowth	400	Trained	1 Ink of the Sea, 1 Resilient Parchment
Glyph of Starfall	400	Trained	1 Ink of the Sea, 1 Resilient Parchment
Glyph of Fireball	400	Trained	1 Ink of the Sea, 1 Resilient Parchment
Glyph of Frostbolt	400	Trained	1 Ink of the Sea, 1 Resilient Parchment
Glyph of Polymorph	400	Trained	1 Ink of the Sea, 1 Resilient Parchment
Glyph of Remove Curse	400	Trained	1 Ink of the Sea, 1 Resilient Parchment
Glyph of Aspect of the Viper	400	Trained	1 Ink of the Sea, 1 Resilient Parchment
Glyph of Snake Trap	400	Trained	1 Ink of the Sea, 1 Resilient Parchment
Glyph of Steady Shot	400	Trained	1 Ink of the Sea, 1 Resilient Parchment
Glyph of Avenger's Shield	400	Trained	1 Ink of the Sea, 1 Resilient Parchment
Glyph of Avenging Wrath	400	Trained	1 Ink of the Sea, 1 Resilient Parchment
Glyph of Hammer of Wrath	400	Trained	1 Ink of the Sea, 1 Resilient Parchment
Glyph of Adrenaline Rush	400	Trained	1 Ink of the Sea, 1 Resilient Parchment
Glyph of Deadly Throw	400	Trained	1 Ink of the Sea, 1 Resilient Parchment
Glyph of Hemorrhage	400	Trained	1 Ink of the Sea, 1 Resilient Parchment
Glyph of Preparation	400	Trained	1 Ink of the Sea, 1 Resilient Parchment
Glyph of Shiv	400	Trained	1 Ink of the Sea, 1 Resilient Parchment
Glyph of Circle of Healing	400	Trained	1 Ink of the Sea, 1 Resilient Parchment
Glyph of Lightwell	400	Trained	1 Ink of the Sea, 1 Resilient Parchment
Glyph of Mass Dispel	400	Trained	1 Moonglow Ink, 1 Resilient Parchment
Glyph of Shadow Word: Death	400	Trained	1 Ink of the Sea, 1 Resilient Parchment
Glyph of Spirit of Redemption	400	Trained	1 Ink of the Sea, 1 Resilient Parchment
Glyph of Earth Elemental Totem	400	Trained	1 Ink of the Sea, 1 Resilient Parchment

Inscription			
Spellname	SkillRank	Source	Reagents
Glyph of Earth Shock	400	Trained	1 Ink of the Sea, 1 Resilient Parchment
Glyph of Fire Elemental Totem	400	Trained	1 Ink of the Sea, 1 Resilient Parchment
Glyph of Healing Wave	400	Trained	1 Ink of the Sea, 1 Resilient Parchment
Glyph of Totem of Wrath	400	Trained	1 Ink of the Sea, 1 Resilient Parchment
Glyph of Curse of Agony	400	Trained	1 Ink of the Sea, 1 Resilient Parchment
Glyph of Death Coil	400	Trained	1 Ink of the Sea, 1 Resilient Parchment
Glyph of Felguard	400	Trained	1 Ink of the Sea, 1 Resilient Parchment
Glyph of Immolate	400	Trained	1 Ink of the Sea, 1 Resilient Parchment
Glyph of Unstable Affliction	400	Trained	1 Ink of the Sea, 1 Resilient Parchment
Glyph of Fire Blast	400	Trained	1 Ink of the Sea, 1 Resilient Parchment
Iron-bound Tome	400	Trained	5 Snowfall Ink, 10 Resilient Parchment, 1 Frozen Orb
Faces of Doom	400	Trained	5 Snowfall Ink, 10 Resilient Parchment, 1 Frozen Orb
Enchanted Vellum	400	Trained	3 Ink of the Sea, 1 Resilient Parchment
Darkmoon Card of the North	400	Trained	1 Resilient Parchment, 6 Snowfall Ink, 2 Eternal Life
Master's Inscription of the Axe	400	Trained	1 Snowfall Ink
Master's Inscription of the Crag	400	Trained	1 Snowfall Ink
Master's Inscription of the Pinnacle	400	Trained	1 Snowfall Ink
Master's Inscription of the Storm	400	Trained	1 Snowfall Ink
Scroll of Intellect VIII	425	Trained	5 Ink of the Sea, 5 Resilient Parchment
Scroll of Spirit VIII	425	Trained	5 Ink of the Sea, 5 Resilient Parchment
Scroll of Stamina VIII	425	Trained	5 Ink of the Sea, 5 Resilient Parchment
Scroll of Agility VIII	430	Trained	5 Ink of the Sea, 5 Resilient Parchment
Scroll of Strength VIII	430	Trained	5 Ink of the Sea, 5 Resilient Parchment
Scroll of Stamina			1 Ivory Ink, 1 Light Parchment
Scroll of Intellect			1 Ivory Ink, 1 Light Parchment
Scroll of Spirit			1 Ivory Ink, 1 Light Parchment
Ivory Ink			1 Alabaster Pigment
Glyph of Wyvern Sting			1 Ink of the Sea, 1 Resilient Parchment
Glyph of Blocking			1 Ink of the Sea, 1 Resilient Parchment
Glyph of Bloodthirst			1 Ink of the Sea, 1 Resilient Parchment
Glyph of Devastate			1 Ink of the Sea, 1 Resilient Parchment
Glyph of Intervene			1 Ink of the Sea, 1 Resilient Parchment
Glyph of Mortal Strike			1 Ink of the Sea, 1 Resilient Parchment
Glyph of Resonating Power			1 Ink of the Sea, 1 Resilient Parchment
Glyph of Last Stand			1 Ink of the Sea, 1 Resilient Parchment
Glyph of Taunt			1 Ink of the Sea, 1 Resilient Parchment
Glyph of Victory Rush			1 Ink of the Sea, 1 Resilient Parchment
Glyph of Anti-Magic Shell			1 Ink of the Sea, 1 Resilient Parchment
Glyph of Blood Boil			1 Ink of the Sea, 1 Resilient Parchment
Glyph of Blood Tap			1 Ethereal Ink, 1 Resilient Parchment
Glyph of Chains of Ice			1 Ink of the Sea, 1 Resilient Parchment
Glyph of Dark Command			1 Ink of the Sea, 1 Resilient Parchment
Glyph of Death and Decay			1 Ink of the Sea, 1 Resilient Parchment
Glyph of Death's Embrace			1 Ethereal Ink, 1 Heavy Parchment
Glyph of Horn of Winter			1 Ethereal Ink, 1 Resilient Parchment
Glyph of Icebound Fortitude			1 Ink of the Sea, 1 Resilient Parchment
Glyph of Obliterate			1 Ink of the Sea, 1 Resilient Parchment
Glyph of Rune Strike			1 Ink of the Sea, 1 Resilient Parchment
Glyph of Raise Dead			1 Ethereal Ink, 1 Heavy Parchment
Glyph of Corpse Explosion			1 Ethereal Ink, 1 Heavy Parchment
Glyph of Pestilence			1 Ethereal Ink, 1 Heavy Parchment
Glyph of Aquatic Form			1 Lion's Ink, 1 Light Parchment
Glyph of Challenging Roar			1 Jadefire Ink, 1 Common Parchment
Glyph of Rebirth			1 Lion's Ink, 1 Light Parchment
Glyph of Thorns			1 Midnight Ink, 1 Light Parchment
Glyph of the Wild			1 Midnight Ink, 1 Light Parchment
Glyph of the Pack			1 Celestial Ink, 1 Common Parchment

Inscription

Spellname	SkillRank	Source	Reagents
Glyph of Scare Beast			1 Midnight Ink, 1 Light Parchment
Glyph of Revive Pet			1 Midnight Ink, 1 Light Parchment
Glyph of Possessed Strength			1 Midnight Ink, 1 Light Parchment
Glyph of Mend Pet			1 Midnight Ink, 1 Light Parchment
Glyph of Feign Death			1 Jadefire Ink, 1 Common Parchment
Glyph of Arcane Intellect			1 Midnight Ink, 1 Light Parchment
Glyph of Fire Ward			1 Lion's Ink, 1 Light Parchment
Glyph of Frost Armor			1 Midnight Ink, 1 Light Parchment
Glyph of Frost Ward			1 Lion's Ink, 1 Common Parchment
Glyph of Slow Fall			1 Midnight Ink, 1 Light Parchment
Glyph of the Penguin			1 Midnight Ink, 1 Light Parchment
Glyph of Blessing of Kings			1 Lion's Ink, 1 Light Parchment
Glyph of Blessing of Wisdom			1 Midnight Ink, 1 Light Parchment
Glyph of Lay on Hands			1 Midnight Ink, 1 Light Parchment
Glyph of Blessing of Might			1 Midnight Ink, 1 Light Parchment
Glyph of Sense Undead			1 Lion's Ink, 1 Light Parchment
Glyph of the Warhorse			1 Jadefire Ink, 1 Common Parchment
Glyph of Fading			1 Midnight Ink, 1 Light Parchment
Glyph of Fortitude			1 Midnight Ink, 1 Light Parchment
Glyph of Levitate			1 Jadefire Ink, 1 Common Parchment
Glyph of Shackle Undead			1 Lion's Ink, 1 Light Parchment
Glyph of Shadow Protection			1 Jadefire Ink, 1 Common Parchment
Glyph of Shadowfiend			1 Ink of the Sea, 1 Resilient Parchment
Glyph of Blurred Speed			1 Midnight Ink, 1 Light Parchment
Glyph of Distract			1 Lion's Ink, 1 Common Parchment
Glyph of Pick Lock			1 Lion's Ink, 1 Light Parchment
Glyph of Pick Pocket			1 Midnight Ink, 1 Light Parchment
Glyph of Safe Fall			1 Celestial Ink, 1 Common Parchment
Glyph of Vanish			1 Lion's Ink, 1 Common Parchment
Glyph of Astral Recall			1 Jadefire Ink, 1 Common Parchment
Glyph of Renewed Life			1 Jadefire Ink, 1 Common Parchment
Glyph of Water Breathing			1 Lion's Ink, 1 Common Parchment
Glyph of Water Shield			1 Lion's Ink, 1 Light Parchment
Glyph of Water Walking			1 Jadefire Ink, 1 Common Parchment
Glyph of Unending Breath			1 Lion's Ink, 1 Light Parchment
Glyph of Drain Soul			1 Midnight Ink, 1 Light Parchment
Glyph of Curse of Exhaustion			1 Jadefire Ink, 1 Common Parchment
Glyph of Enslave Demon			1 Jadefire Ink, 1 Common Parchment
Glyph of Kilrogg			1 Lion's Ink, 1 Common Parchment
Glyph of Souls			1 Ink of the Sea, 1 Resilient Parchment
Glyph of Battle			1 Midnight Ink, 1 Light Parchment
Glyph of Bloodrage			1 Midnight Ink, 1 Light Parchment
Glyph of Charge			1 Midnight Ink, 1 Light Parchment
Glyph of Mocking Blow			1 Lion's Ink, 1 Light Parchment
Glyph of Thunder Clap			1 Midnight Ink, 1 Light Parchment
Glyph of Victory Rush			1 Ethereal Ink, 1 Resilient Parchment
Glyph of Dash			1 Jadefire Ink, 1 Common Parchment
Glyph of Ghost Wolf			1 Lion's Ink, 1 Light Parchment
Glyph of Seal of Blood			1 Ink of the Sea, 1 Resilient Parchment
Glyph of Seal of Righteousness			1 Ink of the Sea, 1 Resilient Parchment
Glyph of Seal of Vengeance			1 Ink of the Sea, 1 Resilient Parchment

Alchemy

Alchemy Trainers

Faction	Grand Master Trainer	Location
Alliance	Lanolis Dewdrop	Valgarde
Alliance	Falorn Nightwhisper	Valiance Keep
Neutral	Linzy Blackbolt	Dalaran
Horde	Wilhelmina Rindel	Vengeance Landing
Horde	Arthur Henslowe	Warsong Hold

Alchemists have always been highly sought after for their valuable potions, elixirs, flasks and transmutation abilities. Northrend provides new herbs with which to work, making Alchemists more in demand than ever. Mix up valuable concoctions using these new ingredients to give your group an added edge in battle.

 MIXOLOGY

All those hours spent hunched over your equipment, learning to combine both mundane and exotic ingredients into useful and sometime lifesaving concoctions has given you an affinity for your own creations. Mixology is a passive skill, which Alchemist get automatically, that gives you an added benefit to elixirs and flasks that you create and then use, making them more effective or longer lasting. It only works on your own creations, so be sure to keep yourself supplied from your own lab at all times.

Alchemy

Spellname	SkillRank	Source	Reagents
Mixology	50	Trained	
Resurgent Healing Potion	350	Trained	2 Goldclover, 1 Imbued Vial
Wrath Elixir	355	Trained	1 Goldclover, 2 Deadnettle, 1 Imbued Vial
Icy Mana Potion	360	Trained	2 Talandra's Rose, 1 Imbued Vial
Spellpower Elixir	365	Trained	1 Goldclover, 1 Tiger Lily, 1 Imbued Vial
Pygmy Oil	375	Trained	1 Pygmy Suckerfish
Guru's Elixir	375	Trained	3 Pygmy Oil, 1 Imbued Vial
Crazy Alchemist's Potion	375	Trained	2 Goldclover, 1 Imbued Vial
Lesser Flask of Toughness	375	Trained	4 Deadnettle, 1 Goldclover, 1 Imbued Vial
Mighty Arcane Protection Potion	375	Found	2 Crystallized Earth, 1 Imbued Vial
Mighty Frost Protection Potion	375	Found	2 Crystallized Fire, 1 Imbued Vial
Mighty Shadow Protection Potion	375	Found	2 Crystallized Life, 1 Imbued Vial

Inscription

Alchemy

Blacksmithing

Cooking

Enchanting

Engineering

First Aid

Fishing

Herbalism

Jewelcrafting

Leatherworking

Mining

Skinning

Tailoring

Alchemy

Spellname	SkillRank	Source	Reagents
Mighty Fire Protection Potion	375	Found	2 Crystallized Water, 1 Imbued Vial
Mighty Nature Protection Potion	375	Found	2 Crystallized Shadow, 1 Imbued Vial
Potion of Nightmares	380	Trained	1 Goldclover, 2 Talandra's Rose, 1 Imbued Vial
Elixir of Spirit	385	Trained	3 Talandra's Rose, 1 Imbued Vial
Elixir of Mighty Strength	385	Trained	2 Tiger Lily, 1 Imbued Vial
Elixir of Mighty Fortitude	390	Trained	4 Goldclover, 1 Imbued Vial
Elixir of Mighty Agility	395	Trained	2 Goldclover, 2 Adder's Tongue, 1 Imbued Vial
Indestructible Potion	395	Trained	2 Icethorn, 1 Lichbloom, 1 Imbued Vial
Transmute: Titanium	395	Trained	2 Cobalt Bar, 8 Saronite Bar, 2 Crystallized Life
Elixir of Mighty Thoughts	395	Trained	2 Deadnettle, 1 Talandra's Rose, 1 Imbued Vial
Mercurial Alchemist Stone	400	Trained	20 Goldclover, 2 Eternal Life, 1 Frost Lotus
Indestructible Alchemist Stone	400	Trained	20 Deadnettle, 12 Pygmy Oil, 1 Frost Lotus
Mighty Alchemist Stone	400	Trained	15 Adder's Tongue, 15 Tiger Lily, 1 Frost Lotus
Northrend Alchemy Research	400	Trained	12 Goldclover, 12 Adder's Tongue, 4 Talandra's Rose, 4 Tiger Lily, 4 Enchanted Vial
Runic Healing Potion	405	Trained	1 Goldclover, 2 Icethorn, 1 Imbued Vial
Runic Mana Potion	410	Trained	2 Lichbloom, 1 Goldclover, 1 Imbued Vial
Endless Rejuvenation Potion	410	Trained	10 Runic Healing Potion, 10 Runic Mana Potion, 1 Enchanted Vial
Transmute: Earthsiege Diamond	425	Trained	1 Dark Jade, 1 Huge Citrine, 1 Eternal Fire
Transmute: Skyflare Diamond	430	Trained	1 Bloodstone, 1 Chalcedony, 1 Eternal Air
Flask of the Frost Wyrm	435	Trained	5 Icethorn, 5 Lichbloom, 1 Frost Lotus, 1 Enchanted Vial
Flask of Stoneblood	435	Trained	7 Lichbloom, 3 Crystallized Life, 1 Frost Lotus, 1 Enchanted Vial
Flask of Endless Rage	435	Trained	7 Lichbloom, 3 Fire Leaf, 1 Frost Lotus, 1 Enchanted Vial
Flask of Pure Mojo	435	Trained	7 Icethorn, 3 Pygmy Oil, 1 Frost Lotus, 1 Enchanted Vial
Transmute: Eternal Life to Shadow			1 Eternal Life
Transmute: Eternal Life to Fire			1 Eternal Life
Transmute: Eternal Fire to Water			1 Eternal Fire
Transmute: Eternal Fire to Life			1 Eternal Fire
Transmute: Eternal Air to Water			1 Eternal Air
Transmute: Eternal Air to Earth			1 Eternal Air
Transmute: Eternal Shadow to Earth			1 Eternal Shadow
Transmute: Eternal Shadow to Life			1 Eternal Shadow
Transmute: Eternal Earth to Air			1 Eternal Earth
Transmute: Eternal Earth to Shadow			1 Eternal Earth
Transmute: Eternal Water to Air			1 Eternal Water
Transmute: Eternal Water to Fire			1 Eternal Water
Powerful Rejuvenation Potion			2 Talandra's Rose, 2 Lichbloom, 1 Imbued Vial
Transmute: Eternal Might			1 Eternal Air, 1 Eternal Earth, 1 Eternal Fire, 1 Eternal Water
Elixir of Protection			2 Icethorn, 1 Crystallized Earth, 1 Imbued Vial
Potion of Speed			2 Adder's Tongue, 1 Pygmy Oil, 1 Imbued Vial
Potion of Wild Magic			2 Lichbloom, 1 Pygmy Oil, 1 Imbued Vial
Elixir of Mighty Mageblood			1 Goldclover, 2 Lichbloom, 1 Imbued Vial
Endless Mana Potion			10 Runic Mana Potion, 1 Enchanted Vial
Elixir of Accuracy			2 Tiger Lily, 1 Talandra's Rose, 1 Imbued Vial
Elixir of Deadly Strikes			1 Goldclover, 2 Adder's Tongue, 1 Imbued Vial
Elixir of Mighty Defense			2 Icethorn, 1 Crystallized Life, 1 Imbued Vial
Elixir of Expertise			1 Goldclover, 2 Adder's Tongue, 1 Imbued Vial
Elixir of Armor Piercing			2 Tiger Lily, 1 Imbued Vial
Elixir of Lightning Speed			1 Deadnettle, 1 Crystallized Life, 1 Imbued Vial

BLACKSMITHING

Blacksmithing Trainers

Faction	Grand Master Trainer	Location
Alliance	Argo Strongstout	Valiance Keep
Alliance	Rosina Rivet	Valgarde
Alliance	Brandig	Frosthold
Neutral	Alard Schmied	Dalaran
Horde	Crog Steelspine	Warsong Hold
Horde	Borus Ironbender	Agmar's Hammer
Horde	Josric Fame	Venomspite
Horde	Kristen Smythe	Vengeance Landing

Blacksmiths have the ability to create some spectacular gear on par with that found in many dank crypts, dark caves, and other out of the way places. Now, these skilled craftsmen can create an item with one extra socket, allowing you to socket an additional gem. Furthermore, they have an additional perk that grants them two more. The new metals found in Northrend have given skilled Blacksmiths the right materials they need to take their craft to the next level, giving a potential buyer many options in obtaining powerful gear. Granted, meeting up with a skilled Blacksmith in a brightly lit city may lack the mystique of trudging through forgotten fortresses and cavernous keeps, but you usually don't have to pry equipment out of the cold dead hands of your Blacksmith before equipping it!

Blacksmithing

Spellname	SkillRank	Source	Reagents
Cobalt Belt	350	Trained	4 Cobalt Bar
Cobalt Boots	350	Trained	4 Cobalt Bar
Cobalt Skeleton Key	350	Trained	4 Cobalt Bar
Cobalt Shoulders	360	Trained	4 Cobalt Bar
Cobalt Triangle Shield	360	Trained	4 Cobalt Bar
Cobalt Bracers	360	Trained	4 Cobalt Bar
Cobalt Legplates	370	Trained	5 Cobalt Bar
Cobalt Helm	370	Trained	5 Cobalt Bar
Cobalt Gauntlets	370	Trained	5 Cobalt Bar
Cobalt Chestpiece	375	Trained	6 Cobalt Bar
Spiked Cobalt Helm	375	Trained	6 Cobalt Bar
Reinforced Cobalt Shoulders	375	Found	4 Cobalt Bar
Reinforced Cobalt Helm	375	Found	4 Cobalt Bar
Reinforced Cobalt Legplates	375	Found	4 Cobalt Bar
Reinforced Cobalt Chestpiece	375	Found	4 Cobalt Bar
Cobalt Rod	375	Trained	4 Cobalt Bar
Spiked Cobalt Boots	380	Trained	7 Cobalt Bar
Sturdy Cobalt Quickblade	380	Trained	8 Cobalt Bar

Blacksmithing

Spellname	SkillRank	Source	Reagents
Cobalt Tenderizer	380	Trained	8 Cobalt Bar
Spiked Cobalt Shoulders	385	Trained	7 Cobalt Bar
Spiked Cobalt Chestpiece	385	Trained	7 Cobalt Bar
Sure-fire Shuriken	385	Trained	7 Cobalt Bar
Forged Cobalt Claymore	385	Trained	10 Cobalt Bar
Saronite Defender	390	Trained	6 Cobalt Bar, 4 Saronite Bar
Spiked Cobalt Gauntlets	390	Trained	8 Cobalt Bar
Saronite Protector	390	Trained	6 Cobalt Bar, 4 Saronite Bar
Honed Cobalt Cleaver	390	Trained	12 Cobalt Bar, 4 Saronite Bar, 2 Crystallized Fire
Notched Cobalt War Axe	390	Trained	10 Cobalt Bar
Tempered Saronite Belt	395	Trained	6 Cobalt Bar, 5 Saronite Bar
Tempered Saronite Legplates	395	Trained	5 Cobalt Bar, 5 Saronite Bar, 1 Crystallized Earth
Spiked Cobalt Belt	395	Trained	8 Cobalt Bar
Spiked Cobalt Legplates	395	Trained	8 Cobalt Bar
Brilliant Saronite Legplates	395	Trained	5 Cobalt Bar, 5 Saronite Bar, 1 Crystallized Water
Savage Cobalt Slicer	395	Trained	8 Cobalt Bar, 6 Saronite Bar, 2 Crystallized Fire
Brilliant Saronite Belt	395	Trained	6 Cobalt Bar, 5 Saronite Bar
Tempered Saronite Boots	400	Trained	3 Cobalt Bar, 8 Saronite Bar
Tempered Saronite Breastplate	400	Trained	6 Cobalt Bar, 5 Saronite Bar, 1 Crystallized Earth
Spiked Cobalt Bracers	400	Trained	8 Cobalt Bar
Horned Cobalt Helm	400	Trained	8 Cobalt Bar
Brilliant Saronite Gauntlets	400	Trained	3 Cobalt Bar, 8 Saronite Bar
Saronite Ambusher	400	Trained	12 Cobalt Bar, 4 Saronite Bar, 1 Crystallized Shadow
Socket Bracer	400	Trained	4 Saronite Bar, 1 Eternal Earth
Socket Gloves	400	Trained	4 Saronite Bar, 1 Eternal Shadow
Brilliant Saronite Bracers	400	Trained	3 Cobalt Bar, 8 Saronite Bar
Tempered Saronite Helm	405	Trained	12 Saronite Bar, 1 Crystallized Earth
Tempered Saronite Shoulders	405	Trained	12 Saronite Bar
Brilliant Saronite Boots	405	Trained	12 Saronite Bar
Saronite Shiv	405	Trained	12 Saronite Bar, 2 Crystallized Shadow
Deadly Saronite Dirk	405	Trained	7 Saronite Bar, 2 Crystallized Air
Brilliant Saronite Pauldrons	405	Trained	12 Saronite Bar
Saronite Bulwark	410	Trained	14 Saronite Bar
Tempered Saronite Bracers	410	Trained	13 Saronite Bar
Furious Saronite Beatstick	410	Trained	15 Saronite Bar, 2 Crystallized Earth
Cudgel of Saronite Justice	410	Trained	15 Saronite Bar, 2 Crystallized Water
Saronite Spellblade	410	Trained	15 Saronite Bar, 2 Crystallized Fire
Tempered Saronite Gauntlets	415	Trained	14 Saronite Bar
Brilliant Saronite Breastplate	415	Trained	14 Saronite Bar, 1 Crystallized Water
Corroded Saronite Edge	415	Trained	16 Saronite Bar, 1 Crystallized Fire
Corroded Saronite Woundbringer	415	Trained	14 Saronite Bar, 1 Crystallized Fire
Saronite Mindcrusher	415	Trained	20 Saronite Bar, 2 Crystallized Fire
Chestplate of Conquest	415	Trained	14 Saronite Bar, 2 Crystallized Earth
Legplates of Conquest	415	Trained	3 Saronite Bar, 2 Crystallized Earth
Eternal Belt Buckle	415	Trained	4 Saronite Bar, 1 Eternal Earth, 1 Eternal Water, 1 Eternal Shadow
Brilliant Saronite Helm	415	Trained	14 Saronite Bar, 1 Crystallized Water
Vengeance Bindings	420	Trained	12 Saronite Bar, 1 Eternal Fire
Righteous Gauntlets	420	Trained	12 Saronite Bar, 1 Eternal Water
Daunting Handguards	420	Trained	12 Saronite Bar, 1 Eternal Earth
Savage Saronite Bracers	420	Trained	12 Saronite Bar, 1 Eternal Air
Savage Saronite Pauldrons	420	Trained	12 Saronite Bar, 1 Eternal Water
Savage Saronite Waistguard	420	Trained	12 Saronite Bar, 1 Eternal Water
Savage Saronite Walkers	420	Trained	12 Saronite Bar, 1 Eternal Shadow
Savage Saronite Gauntlets	420	Trained	12 Saronite Bar, 1 Eternal Fire
Titanium Rod	420	Trained	2 Saronite Bar, 1 Titanium Bar
Titanium Weapon Chain	420	Trained	2 Saronite Bar, 1 Titanium Bar

Blacksmithing

Spellname	SkillRank	Source	Reagents
Titanium Shield Spike	420	Trained	2 Saronite Bar, 1 Titanium Bar
Ornate Saronite Bracers	420	Trained	12 Saronite Bar, 1 Eternal Air
Ornate Saronite Pauldrons	420	Trained	12 Saronite Bar, 1 Eternal Water
Ornate Saronite Waistguard	420	Trained	12 Saronite Bar, 1 Eternal Water
Ornate Saronite Walkers	420	Trained	12 Saronite Bar, 1 Eternal Shadow
Ornate Saronite Gauntlets	420	Trained	12 Saronite Bar, 1 Eternal Fire
Icebane Girdle	420	Trained	12 Saronite Bar, 2 Eternal Fire, 2 Eternal Water
Icebane Treads	420	Trained	12 Saronite Bar, 2 Eternal Fire, 2 Eternal Water
Helm of Command	425	Trained	14 Saronite Bar, 1 Eternal Fire
Daunting Legplates	425	Trained	14 Saronite Bar, 1 Eternal Earth
Righteous Greaves	425	Trained	14 Saronite Bar, 1 Eternal Water
Savage Saronite Legplates	425	Trained	14 Saronite Bar, 1 Eternal Air
Savage Saronite Hauberk	425	Trained	14 Saronite Bar, 1 Eternal Earth
Savage Saronite Skullshield	425	Trained	14 Saronite Bar, 1 Eternal Shadow
Ornate Saronite Legplates	425	Trained	14 Saronite Bar, 1 Eternal Air
Ornate Saronite Hauberk	425	Trained	14 Saronite Bar, 1 Eternal Earth
Ornate Saronite Skullshield	425	Trained	14 Saronite Bar, 1 Eternal Shadow
Icebane Chestguard	425	Trained	16 Saronite Bar, 3 Eternal Fire, 3 Eternal Water
Titanium Skeleton Key	430	Trained	4 Saronite Bar, 1 Titanium Bar
Titansteel Destroyer	440	Trained	8 Saronite Bar, 8 Titansteel Bar, 2 Frozen Orb
Titansteel Bonecrusher	440	Trained	6 Saronite Bar, 6 Titansteel Bar, 2 Frozen Orb
Titansteel Guardian	440	Trained	6 Saronite Bar, 6 Titansteel Bar, 2 Frozen Orb
Spiked Titansteel Helm	440	Trained	4 Saronite Bar, 4 Titansteel Bar, 1 Frozen Orb
Tempered Titansteel Helm	440	Trained	4 Saronite Bar, 4 Titansteel Bar, 1 Frozen Orb
Brilliant Titansteel Helm	440	Trained	4 Saronite Bar, 4 Titansteel Bar, 1 Frozen Orb
Spiked Titansteel Treads	440	Trained	4 Saronite Bar, 3 Titansteel Bar, 1 Frozen Orb
Tempered Titansteel Treads	440	Trained	4 Saronite Bar, 3 Titansteel Bar, 1 Frozen Orb
Brilliant Titansteel Treads	440	Trained	4 Saronite Bar, 3 Titansteel Bar, 1 Frozen Orb
Titansteel Shanker	440	Trained	6 Saronite Bar, 6 Titansteel Bar, 2 Frozen Orb
Titansteel Shield Wall	440	Trained	4 Saronite Bar, 3 Titansteel Bar, 1 Frozen Orb

COOKING

Cooking Trainers		
Faction	Grand Master Trainer	Location
Alliance	Rollick MacKreel	Valiance Keep
Alliance	Brom Brewbaster	Valgarde
Alliance	Katherine Lee	Dalaran
Horde	Orn Tenderhoof	Warsong Hold
Horde	Awilo Lon'gomba	Dalaran
Horde	Thomas Kolichio	Vengeance Landing

Inscription

Alchemy

Black-
smithing

Cooking

Enchanting

Engineering

First Aid

Fishing

Herbalism

Jewelcrafting

Leatherworking

Mining

Skinning

Tailoring

Nothing beats a freshly cooked meal to bolster your spirits, and other attributes, before going into battle. Cooking trainers have wasted no time in producing succulent recipes from the newly discovered wildlife in Northrend. Because Cooking is a secondary profession it can be learned by anyone, regardless of what other professions they may pursue.

Recipe	Skill Lvl	Source	Reagent(s)
Baked Manta Ray	350	Trained	1 Imperial Manta Ray
Blackened Dragonfin	400	Found	2 Dragonfin Angelfish, 1 Northern Spices
Blackened Worg Steaks	400	Found	1 Worg Haunch, 1 Northern Spices
Critter Bites	400	Found	2 Chilled Meat, 1 Northern Spices
Cuttlesteak	400	Found	1 Moonglow Cuttlefish, 1 Northern Spices
Dalaran Clam Chowder	350	Trained	2 Succulent Clam Meat
Dragonfin Filet	400	Found	1 Dragonfin Angelfish, 1 Northern Spices
Feast	375	Trained	1 Chunk o' Mammoth, 1 Shoveltusk Flank, 1 Wyrm Meat, 4 Chilled Meat
Firecracker Salmon	400	Found	1 Glacial Salmon, 1 Northern Spices
Fish Feast	400	Found	2 Musselback Sculpin, 2 Glacial Salmon, 2 Nettlefish, 4 Northern Spices
Gigantic Feast	425	Found	2 Deep Sea Monsterbelly, 2 Chunk o' Mammoth, 2 Rockfin Grouper, 1 Northern Spices
Grilled Bonescale	350	Trained	1 Bonescale Snapper
Grilled Sculpin	350	Trained	1 Musselback Sculpin
Haunted Herring	350	Found	1 Fangtooth Herring, 1 Essence of Undeath
Hearty Rhino	400	Found	1 Rhino Meat, 1 Northern Spices
Imperial Manta Steak	400	Found	1 Imperial Manta Ray, 1 Northern Spices
Kungaloosh	375	Found	2 Tundra Berries, 1 Savory Snowplum
Last Week's Mammoth	350	Found	1 Chunk o' Mammoth
Mammoth Meal	350	Trained	1 Chunk o' Mammoth
Mega Mammoth Meal	400	Found	2 Chunk o' Mammoth, 1 Northern Spices
Mighty Rhino Dogs	400	Found	2 Rhino Meat, 1 Northern Spices
Northern Stew	350	Found	1 Chilled Meat
Pickled Fangtooth	350	Trained	1 Fangtooth Herring
Poached Nettlefish	350	Trained	1 Nettlefish
Poached Northern Sculpin	400	Found	1 Musselback Sculpin, 1 Northern Spices
Rhino Dogs	350	Trained	1 Rhino Meat
Rhinolicious Wyrmsteak	400	Found	1 Wyrmmeat, 1 Rhino Meat, 1 Northern Spices
Roasted Worg	350	Trained	1 Worg Haunch
Sauteed Goby	350	Trained	1 Barrelhead Goby
Shoveltusk Soup	350	Found	1 Shoveltusk Meat
Shoveltusk Steak	350	Trained	1 Shoveltusk Flank
Small Feast	425	Found	2 Nettlefish, 2 Rhino Meat, 2 Glacial Salmon, 1 Northern Spices
Smoked Rockfin	350	Trained	1 Rockfin Grouper
Smoked Salmon	350	Trained	1 Glacial Salmon
Snapper Extreme	400	Found	3 Bonescale Snappers, 1 Northern Spices
Spiced Mammoth Treats	400	Found	1 Chunk o' Mammoth, 1 Northern Spices
Spiced Wyrm Burger	400	Found	2 Wyrm Meat, 1 Northern Spices
Spicy Blue Nettlefish	400	Found	1 Nettlefish, 1 Northern Spices
Spicy Fried Herring	400	Found	1 Fangtooth Herring, 1 Northern Spices
Succulent Orca Stew	350	Found	1 Succulent Orca Blubber
Tasty Cupcake	350	Found	2 Simple Flour, 1 Northern Egg
Tender Shoveltusk Steak	400	Found	2 Shoveltusk Flank, 1 Northern Spices
Tracker Snacks	400	Found	1 Shoveltusk Flank, 1 Northern Spices
Very Burnt Worg	400	Found	2 Worg Haunch, 1 Northern Spices
Wyrm Delight	350	Trained	1 Wyrm Meat

ENCHANTING

Enchanting Trainers

Faction	Grand Master Trainer	Location
Alliance	Alexis Marlowe	Valiance Keep
Alliance	Elizabeth Jackson	Valgarde
Neutral	Enchanter Nalthanis	Dalaran
Horde	Eorain Dawnstrike	Warsong Hold
Horde	Emil Autumn	Vengeance Landing

Enchanters know that their skill is always in demand and this fact hasn't changed with the push into Northrend. Like other skilled craftsmen, they have taken the opportunity to incorporate the newfound materials the continent offers into their own creations, making some of the strongest enchantments yet seen. With the addition of Inscription, Enchanters can now place their enchants onto Vellum, made by Scribes, giving them the freedom to trade their wares to other players or on the Auction House with the same freedom enjoyed by other craftsmen!

Enchanting

Spellname	SkillRank	Source	Reagents
Enchant Weapon - Scourgebane	350	Found	20 Infinite Dust, Greater Cosmic Essence, 6 Dream Shard
Enchant Cloak - Mighty Armor	350	Found	20 Infinite Dust, 10 Greater Cosmic Essence
Enchant Cloak - Greater Speed	350	Found	24 Infinite Dust, 12 Greater Cosmic Essence
Enchant Shield - Defense	355	Found	10 Infinite Dust, 10 Greater Cosmic Essence
Enchant Boots - Greater Spirit	355	Found	12 Infinite Dust, 5 Greater Cosmic Essence
Enchant Boots - Assault	355	Found	4 Infinite Dust, 4 Lesser Cosmic Essence
Enchant Weapon - Greater Potency	355	Found	2 Infinite Dust, 4 Lesser Cosmic Essence
Enchant Bracers - Striking	360	Trained	6 Infinite Dust
Enchant Gloves - Expertise	365	Found	20 Infinite Dust, 2 Greater Cosmic Essence
Enchant Boots - Greater Vitality	365	Found	14 Infinite Dust, 4 Greater Cosmic Essence
Enchant Weapon - Accuracy	365	Found	40 Infinite Dust, 8 Greater Cosmic Essence, 6 Abyss Crystal
Enchant Gloves - Gatherer	375	Found	1 Greater Cosmic Essence
Enchant Chest - Greater Mana Restoration	375	Found	20 Infinite Dust, 8 Greater Cosmic Essence
Enchant Boots - Greater Fortitude	375	Found	3 Lesser Cosmic Essence, 3 Infinite Dust
Enchant Bracers - Exceptional Intellect	375	Found	10 Infinite Dust
Enchant Cloak - Speed	375	Found	6 Infinite Dust
Runed Cobalt Rod	375	Trained	1 Cobalt Rod, 8 Infinite Dust, 4 Lesser Cosmic Essence, 1 Runed Eternium Rod
Enchant Shield - Greater Intellect	375	Found	12 Infinite Dust

Enchanting

Spellname	SkillRank	Source	Reagents
Enchant Cloak - Major Agility	375	Found	18 Infinite Dust, 6 Greater Cosmic Essence, 2 Dream Shard
Enchant Gloves - Precision	385	Found	15 Infinite Dust, 5 Greater Cosmic Essence
Enchant Chest - Major Health	395	Found	3 Greater Cosmic Essence
Enchant Cloak - Spell Piercing	395	Found	15 Infinite Dust
Enchant Weapon - Berserking	395	Found	20 Infinite Dust, 15 Greater Cosmic Essence, 10 Abyss Crystal
Enchant Cloak - Superior Frost Resistance	400	Found	6 Infinite Dust, 3 Greater Cosmic Essence, 1 Eternal Fire
Enchant Cloak - Superior Nature Resistance	400	Found	15 Infinite Dust, 1 Greater Cosmic Essence, 1 Eternal Shadow
Enchant Weapon - Exceptional Intellect	400	Found	5 Infinite Dust, 12 Greater Cosmic Essence, 2 Dream Shard
Enchant Cloak - Superior Agility	400	Found	9 Infinite Dust
Enchant Weapon - Exceptional Spirit	400	Found	30 Infinite Dust, 2 Dream Shard
Enchant Cloak - Superior Fire Resistance	400	Found	4 Greater Cosmic Essence, 1 Eternal Water
Enchant Cloak - Superior Shadow Resistance	400	Found	12 Infinite Dust, 2 Lesser Cosmic Essence, 1 Eternal Life
Enchant Bracers - Major Spirit	400	Found	16 Infinite Dust, 12 Greater Cosmic Essence
Enchant Cloak - Superior Arcane Resistance	400	Found	20 Infinite Dust, 1 Eternal Earth
Enchant Bracers - Greater Stats	400	Found	16 Infinite Dust, 3 Greater Cosmic Essence
Enchant Ring - Greater Spellpower	400	Trained	8 Infinite Dust, 1 Greater Cosmic Essence
Enchant Ring - Assault	400	Trained	8 Infinite Dust, 1 Greater Cosmic Essence
Enchant Chest - Greater Defense	400	Found	10 Infinite Dust, 1 Eternal Earth
Enchant Ring - Stamina	400	Trained	8 Infinite Dust, 1 Greater Cosmic Essence
Enchant Bracers - Greater Assault	410	Found	25 Infinite Dust, 15 Greater Cosmic Essence, Abyss Crystal
Enchant Weapon - Lifeward	410	Found	4 Abyss Crystal
Enchant Chest - Exceptional Resilience	410	Found	50 Infinite Dust
Enchant Boots - Superior Agility	410	Found	16 Infinite Dust, 6 Greater Cosmic Essence
Enchant Gloves - Greater Blasting	410	Found	30 Infinite Dust, 1 Dream Shard
Enchant Weapon - Giant Slayer	410	Found	Infinite Dust, 8 Greater Cosmic Essence, 6 Dream Shard
Enchant Weapon - Greater Savagery	410	Found	6 Infinite Dust, 2 Greater Cosmic Essence
Enchant Weapon - Black Magic	410	Found	25 Infinite Dust, 15 Greater Cosmic Essence, 10 Abyss Crystal
Enchant Weapon - Massacre	410	Found	40 Infinite Dust, 6 Greater Cosmic Essence, Dream Shard, 6 Abyss Crystal
Enchant Weapon - Superior Potency	410	Found	30 Infinite Dust, 10 Greater Cosmic Essence, 4 Abyss Crystal
Enchant Weapon - Mighty Spellpower	410	Found	40 Infinite Dust, 20 Greater Cosmic Essence, 6 Abyss Crystal
Enchant Gloves - Greater Assault	420	Found	6 Infinite Dust, 1 Greater Cosmic Essence
Enchant Weapon - Icebreaker	420	Found	4 Dream Shard, 4 Eternal Fire
Enchant Bracers - Expertise	420	Found	24 Infinite Dust, 4 Greater Cosmic Essence
Enchant Weapon - Exceptional Agility	420	Found	12 Infinite Dust, 6 Greater Cosmic Essence, 2 Dream Shard, 1 Eternal Air
Enchant Gloves - Major Agility	425	Found	8 Greater Cosmic Essence, 1 Abyss Crystal
Enchant Cloak - Titanweave	425	Found	20 Infinite Dust, 10 Greater Cosmic Essence, 2 Titanium Bar
Enchant Gloves - Exceptional Spellpower	425	Found	4 Infinite Dust, 1 Lesser Cosmic Essence
Enchant Chest - Super Stats	425	Found	4 Infinite Dust, 2 Lesser Cosmic Essence
Enchant Gloves - Armsman	425	Found	2 Dream Shard, 2 Eternal Air, 2 Eternal Earth
Enchant Weapon - Exceptional Spellpower	425	Found	10 Infinite Dust, 2 Greater Cosmic Essence
Enchant Cloak - Shadow Armor	425	Found	20 Infinite Dust, 12 Greater Cosmic Essence, 1 Abyss Crystal

Enchanting

Spellname	SkillRank	Source	Reagents
Enchant Bracers - Greater Spellpower	425	Found	8 Infinite Dust, 4 Lesser Cosmic Essence
Enchant Cloak - Wisdom	425	Found	30 Infinite Dust, 10 Greater Cosmic Essence, 6 Abyss Crystal
Enchant Chest - Exceptional Health	425	Found	20 Infinite Dust, 10 Greater Cosmic Essence
Enchant Boots - Tuskarr's Vitality	425	Found	40 Infinite Dust, 10 Greater Cosmic Essence, 1 Abyss Crystal
Runed Titanium Rod	425	Trained	1 Titanium Rod, 2 Dream Shard, 1 Runed Eternium Rod
Enchant Boots - Icewalker	425	Found	8 Infinite Dust, 1 Crystallized Water
Enchant Gloves - Crusher	425	Found	22 Infinite Dust, 9 Greater Cosmic Essence, 1 Dream Shard
Enchant Chest - Powerful Stats	425	Found	15 Infinite Dust, Greater Cosmic Essence, 4 Abyss Crystal
Enchant Boots - Greater Assault	425	Found	35 Infinite Dust, 5 Greater Cosmic Essence, 4 Abyss Crystal
Enchant Bracers - Superior Spellpower	425	Found	24 Infinite Dust, 16 Greater Cosmic Essence, 2 Abyss Crystal

ENGINEERING

Engineering Trainers

Faction	Grand Master Trainer	Location
Alliance	Sock Brightbolt	Valiance Keep
Alliance	Tisha Longbridge	Valgarde
Neutral	Justin Oshenko	Dalaran
Horde	Chief Engineer Leveny	Warsong Hold
Horde	Jamesina Watterly	Vengeance Landing

Engineers are known for their ingenuity and progressive thinking, and they wasted no time in developing items from the newly discovered ore and other materials in Northrend. They've created some truly unique items, and many of them don't explode very often at all! Skilled Engineers have also discovered a new outlet for their creativity—Tinkering. Tinkering allows an engineer to place a Tinker on a specific piece of their own armor. These function much like an enchant, and only work on the Engineer's own gear. Any piece of gear can only hold either an enchant or a Tinker, not both, so Tinkering gives Engineers a wider range of options than non-engineers have available.

Inscription

Alchemy

Blacksmithing

Cooking

Enchanting

Engineering

First Aid

Fishing

Herbalism

Jewelcrafting

Leatherworking

Mining

Skinning

Tailoring

WORMHOLE: GADGETZAN

 Engineers are always mucking around with the universe, and this time they have uncovered something really useful—a wormhole to Gadgetzan! This ability opens a portal to Gadgetzan in Tanaris for the Engineer and her party. At least that's the way it's supposed to work…

Engineering

Spellname	SkillRank	Source	Reagents
Volatile Blasting Trigger	350	Trained	3 Cobalt Bar, 1 Crystallized Water
Handful of Cobalt Bolts	350	Trained	2 Cobalt Bar
Cobalt Frag Bomb	350	Trained	2 Handful of Cobalt Bolts, 1 Volatile Blasting Trigger
Personal Electromagnetic Pulse Generator	375	Found	4 Overcharged Capacitor
Belt-Clipped Spynoculars	375	Found	4 Cobalt Bar, 2 Sun Crystal
Hand-Mounted Pyro Rocket	375	Found	6 Saronite Bar, 4 Crystallized Fire
Flexweave Underlay	375	Found	12 Frostweave Cloth, 1 Overcharged Capacitor
Nitro Boosts	375	Found	6 Volatile Blasting Trigger, 6 Handful of Cobalt Bolts
Hammer Pick	375	Trained	5 Cobalt Bar
Bladed Pickaxe	375	Trained	5 Cobalt Bar
Explosive Decoy	375	Trained	1 Frostweave Cloth, 3 Volatile Blasting Trigger
Overcharged Capacitor	375	Trained	4 Cobalt Bar, 1 Crystallized Earth
Froststeel Tube	390	Trained	8 Cobalt Bar, 1 Crystallized Water
Diamond-cut Refractor Scope	390	Trained	1 Froststeel Tube, 2 Handful of Cobalt Bolts
Mark "S" Boomstick	400	Trained	10 Saronite Bar, 2 Froststeel Tube, 1 Hair Trigger, 1 Walnut Stock
Hyperspeed Accelerators	400	Trained	6 Saronite Bar, 4 Crystallized Air
Mechano-hog	400	Found	12 Titansteel Bar, 40 Handful of Cobalt Bolts, 2 Arctic Fur, 1 Salvaged Iron Golem Parts, 8 Goblin-machined Piston, 1 Elementium-plated Exhaust Pipe
Mekgineer's Chopper	400	Found	12 Titansteel Bar, 40 Handful of Cobalt Bolts, 2 Arctic Fur, 1 Salvaged Iron Golem Parts, 8 Goblin-machined Piston, 1 Elementium-plated Exhaust Pipe
Saronite Bomb	405	Trained	5 Saronite Bar, 1 Volatile Blasting Trigger
Ultrasafe Bullet Machine	410	Trained	6 Saronite Bar, 4 Volatile Blasting Trigger
Healing Injector Kit	410	Trained	12 Saronite Bar, 2 Handful of Cobalt Bolts
Saronite Arrow Maker	415	Trained	15 Saronite Bar
Mana Injector Kit	415	Trained	12 Saronite Bar, 2 Crystallized Water
Mechanized Snow Goggles	420	Trained	8 Saronite Bar, 2 Borean Leather, 1 Eternal Shadow
Sonic Booster	420	Trained	2 Froststeel Tube, 4 Overcharged Capacitor, 2 Handful of Cobalt Bolts
Noise Machine	420	Trained	2 Froststeel Tube, 2 Overcharged Capacitor, 8 Handful of Cobalt Bolts
Mechanized Snow Goggles	420	Trained	8 Saronite Bar, 2 Borean Leather, 1 Eternal Shadow
Mechanized Snow Goggles	420	Trained	8 Saronite Bar, 2 Borean Leather, 1 Eternal Shadow
Mechanized Snow Goggles	420	Trained	8 Saronite Bar, 2 Borean Leather, 1 Eternal Shadow
Gnomish Lightning Generator	425	Trained	2 Titanium Bar, 8 Saronite Bar, 2 Eternal Water, 2 Eternal Air
Sun Scope	425	Trained	1 Froststeel Tube, 1 Sun Crystal, 1 Autumn's Glow
MOLL-E	425	Trained	8 Saronite Bar, 8 Eternal Air
Gnomish X-Ray Specs	425	Trained	6 Titanium Bar, 2 Dream Shard, 2 Handful of Cobalt Bolts
Global Thermal Sapper Charge	425	Trained	1 Saronite Bar, 1 Volatile Blasting Trigger
Heartseeker Scope	430	Trained	10 Saronite Bar, 2 Twilight Opal
Gnomish Army Knife	435	Trained	10 Saronite Bar, 1 Skinning Knife, 1 Mining Pick, 1 Blacksmith Hammer

Engineering

Spellname	SkillRank	Source	Reagents
Armored Titanium Goggles	440	Trained	8 Titanium Bar, 4 Heavy Borean Leather, 2 Sky Sapphire, 4 Eternal Earth, 1 Frozen Orb
Weakness Spectralizers	440	Trained	8 Titanium Bar, 4 Heavy Borean Leather, 2 Scarlet Ruby, 4 Eternal Air, 1 Frozen Orb
Charged Titanium Specs	440	Trained	8 Titanium Bar, 4 Heavy Borean Leather, 2 Monarch Topaz, 4 Eternal Fire, 1 Frozen Orb
Visage Liquification Goggles	440	Trained	8 Titanium Bar, 4 Heavy Borean Leather, 2 Scarlet Ruby, 4 Eternal Shadow, 1 Frozen Orb
Greensight Gogs	440	Trained	8 Titanium Bar, 4 Heavy Borean Leather, 2 Forest Emerald, 4 Eternal Life, 1 Frozen Orb
Electroflux Sight Enhancers	440	Trained	8 Titanium Bar, 4 Heavy Borean Leather, 2 Autumn's Glow, 4 Eternal Air, 1 Frozen Orb
Truesight Ice Blinders	440	Trained	8 Titanium Bar, 4 Heavy Borean Leather, 2 Twilight Opal, 4 Eternal Water, 1 Frozen Orb
Armor Plated Combat Shotgun	450	Trained	10 Titanium Bar, 20 Saronite Bar, 15 Eternal Air, 15 Eternal Water, 1 Frozen Orb, 1 Walnut Stock
Nesingway 4000	450	Trained	10 Titanium Bar, 1 Frozen Orb, 12 Eternal Fire, 12 Eternal Shadow, 3 Sun Scope, 1 Walnut Stock
Scrapbot Construction Kit			10 Saronite Bar

FIRST AID

First Aid Trainers

Faction	Grand Master Trainer	Location
Alliance	Brynna Wilson	Valiance Keep
Alliance	Anchorite Yazmina	Valgarde
Neutral	Olisarra the Kind	Dalaran
Horde	Nurse Applewood	Warsong Hold
Horde	Sally Tompkins	Vengeance Landing

As always, First Aid is an invaluable skill for any adventurer to have since it doesn't require mana to use and can be done in the heat of battle. As a secondary profession, anyone can learn First Aid and Northrend is full of humanoids, making gathering cloth fairly easy as you make your way across the continent.

Created Item	Skill Lvl	Source	Reagent(s)
Frostweave Bandage	350	Trained	1 Frostweave Cloth
Heavy Frostweave Bandage	400	Trained	2 Frostweave Cloth

FISHING

Fishing Trainers

Faction	Grand Master Trainer	Location
Alliance	Old Man Robert	Valiance Keep
Alliance	Byron Welwick	Valgarde
Neutral	Marcia Chase	Dalaran
Horde	Angelina Soren	Vengeance Landing
Horde	Fishy Ser'ji	Warsong Hold

A true fisherman sees every body of water as an opportunity to increase his or her bragging rights and the lakes, streams, and even oceans of Northrend are no exception. With the Find Fish ability you can now sniff out good fishing spots just as Herbalists and Miners can easily seek out plants and ore nodes. When you are using this ability schools of fish appear on your mini-map, making them easier to find so you spend more time with your pole in the water than looking for a good spot.

HERBALISM

Herbalism Trainers

Faction	Grand Master Trainer	Location
Alliance	Fayin Whisperleaf	Valgarde
Alliance	Kira Moondancer	Valiance Keep
Neutral	Dorothy Egan	Dalaran
Horde	Tansy Wildmane	Warsong Hold
Horde	Marjory Kains	Vengeance Landing

Herbalism is the foundation of both Alchemy and Inscription. As such, an Herbalist's vast botanical knowledge is always in high demand. Many new species of plants have been found thriving in Northrend, even in the harsher climates.

LIFEBLOOD

As an Herbalist you have a strong connection with the flora around you. Lifeblood uses your skill in Herbalism to absorb energy and nutrients from the earth, healing you. This ability can be used every few minutes and is a substantial help to any adventurer, especially non-healing classes.

Herb	Skill Level	Herb	Skill Level
Goldclover	350	Frozen Herb	415
Firethorn	360	Lichbloom	425
Talandra's Rose	385	Adder's Tongue	430
Tiger Lily	400	Icethorn	435

JEWELCRAFTING

Jewelcrafting Trainers

Faction	Grand Master Trainer	Location
Alliance	Ounhulo	Valgarde
Alliance	Alestos	Valiance Keep
Neutral	Timothy Jones	Dalaran
Horde	Carter Tiffens	Vengeance Landing
Horde	Geba'li	Warsong Hold

Jewelcrafters are never at a loss for profitable work and the expansion has given them a whole host of new recipes with which to hone their profession. There are great new necklaces, rings, and trinkets, as well as tons of new, very powerful gems available. Break out your Jeweler's Kit and get to grinding those gems to outfit your own gear, help out your friends, or just make a tidy profit!

GEM PERFECTION

This new ability gives you the chance to cut uncommon quality Northrend gems into perfect gems, giving them an added boost to whichever stat they effect. For example, a Precise Bloodstone gives you +12 Expertise, while a Perfect Precise Bloodstone grants +14 Expertise!

Inscription

Alchemy

Blacksmithing

Cooking

Enchanting

Engineering

First Aid

Fishing

Herbalism

Jewel-crafting

Leatherworking

Mining

Skinning

Tailoring

Jewelcrafting

Spellname	SkillRank	Source	Reagents
Bold Bloodstone	350	Trained	1 Bloodstone
Delicate Bloodstone	350	Trained	1 Bloodstone
Runed Bloodstone	350	Trained	1 Bloodstone
Bright Bloodstone	350	Trained	1 Bloodstone
Flashing Bloodstone	350	Trained	1 Bloodstone
Fractured Bloodstone	350	Trained	1 Bloodstone
Brilliant Sun Crystal	350	Trained	1 Sun Crystal
Smooth Sun Crystal	350	Trained	1 Sun Crystal
Rigid Sun Crystal	350	Trained	1 Sun Crystal
Thick Sun Crystal	350	Trained	1 Sun Crystal
Quick Sun Crystal	350	Trained	1 Sun Crystal
Mystic Sun Crystal	350	Found	1 Sun Crystal
Sovereign Shadow Crystal	350	Trained	1 Shadow Crystal
Shifting Shadow Crystal	350	Trained	1 Shadow Crystal
Tenuous Shadow Crystal	350	Trained	1 Shadow Crystal
Glowing Shadow Crystal	350	Trained	1 Shadow Crystal
Purified Shadow Crystal	350	Trained	1 Shadow Crystal
Royal Shadow Crystal	350	Trained	1 Shadow Crystal
Mysterious Shadow Crystal	350	Found	1 Shadow Crystal
Balanced Shadow Crystal	350	Trained	1 Shadow Crystal
Infused Shadow Crystal	350	Trained	1 Shadow Crystal
Defender's Shadow Crystal	350	Found	1 Shadow Crystal
Puissant Shadow Crystal	350	Trained	1 Shadow Crystal
Guardian's Shadow Crystal	350	Trained	1 Shadow Crystal
Inscribed Huge Citrine	350	Trained	1 Huge Citrine
Etched Huge Citrine	350	Trained	1 Huge Citrine
Champion's Huge Citrine	350	Trained	1 Huge Citrine
Resplendent Huge Citrine	350	Found	1 Huge Citrine
Fierce Huge Citrine	350	Trained	1 Huge Citrine
Deadly Huge Citrine	350	Found	1 Huge Citrine
Glinting Huge Citrine	350	Trained	1 Huge Citrine
Lucent Huge Citrine	350	Found	1 Huge Citrine
Deft Huge Citrine	350	Trained	1 Huge Citrine
Luminous Huge Citrine	350	Trained	1 Huge Citrine
Potent Huge Citrine	350	Trained	1 Huge Citrine
Veiled Huge Citrine	350	Trained	1 Huge Citrine
Durable Huge Citrine	350	Found	1 Huge Citrine
Reckless Huge Citrine	350	Found	1 Huge Citrine
Wicked Huge Citrine	350	Trained	1 Huge Citrine
Pristine Huge Citrine	350	Trained	1 Huge Citrine
Empowered Huge Citrine	350	Found	1 Huge Citrine
Stark Huge Citrine	350	Trained	1 Huge Citrine
Stalwart Huge Citrine	350	Trained	1 Huge Citrine
Accurate Huge Citrine	350	Trained	1 Huge Citrine
Resolute Huge Citrine	350	Trained	1 Huge Citrine
Timeless Dark Jade	350	Trained	1 Dark Jade
Jagged Dark Jade	350	Trained	1 Dark Jade
Vivid Dark Jade	350	Found	1 Dark Jade
Enduring Dark Jade	350	Trained	1 Dark Jade
Steady Dark Jade	350	Found	1 Dark Jade
Forceful Dark Jade	350	Trained	1 Dark Jade
Seer's Dark Jade	350	Found	1 Dark Jade
Misty Dark Jade	350	Trained	1 Dark Jade
Shining Dark Jade	350	Trained	1 Dark Jade
Turbid Dark Jade	350	Found	1 Dark Jade
Intricate Dark Jade	350	Trained	1 Dark Jade
Dazzling Dark Jade	350	Trained	1 Dark Jade
Sundered Dark Jade	350	Trained	1 Dark Jade
Lambent Dark Jade	350	Trained	1 Dark Jade

Jewelcrafting

Spellname	SkillRank	Source	Reagents
Opaque Dark Jade	350	Found	1 Dark Jade
Energized Dark Jade	350	Trained	1 Dark Jade
Radiant Dark Jade	350	Trained	1 Dark Jade
Tense Dark Jade	350	Found	1 Dark Jade
Shattered Dark Jade	350	Found	1 Dark Jade
Solid Chalcedony	350	Trained	1 Chalcedony
Sparkling Chalcedony	350	Trained	1 Chalcedony
Lustrous Chalcedony	350	Trained	1 Chalcedony
Stormy Chalcedony	350	Found	1 Chalcedony
Precise Bloodstone	350	Trained	1 Bloodstone
Bloodstone Band	350	Trained	2 Crystallized Earth, 1 Bloodstone
Sun Rock Ring	350	Trained	2 Crystallized Earth, 1 Sun Crystal
Dark Jade Focusing Lens	350	Trained	1 Dark Jade
Crystal Citrine Necklace	350	Trained	2 Crystallized Earth, 1 Huge Citrine
Crystal Chalcedony Amulet	350	Trained	2 Crystallized Earth, 1 Chalcedony
Subtle Bloodstone	360	Trained	1 Bloodstone
Regal Shadow Crystal	360	Trained	1 Shadow Crystal
Glimmering Huge Citrine	360	Trained	1 Huge Citrine
Shadow Crystal Focusing Lens	360	Trained	1 Shadow Crystal
Enchanted Pearl	360	Trained	1 Northsea Pearl, 1 Infinite Dust
Shadow Jade Focusing Lens	370	Trained	1 Shadow Crystal, 1 Dark Jade
Earthshadow Ring	370	Trained	1 Eternal Earth, 2 Shadow Crystal
Jade Ring of Slaying	370	Trained	1 Eternal Earth, 2 Dark Jade
Jade Dagger Pendant	380	Trained	1 Eternal Earth, 2 Huge Citrine, 2 Dark Jade
Blood Sun Necklace	380	Trained	1 Eternal Earth, 1 Bloodstone, 2 Sun Crystal, 1 Chalcedony
Bright Scarlet Ruby	390	Trained	1 Scarlet Ruby
Sparkling Sky Sapphire	390	Trained	1 Sky Sapphire
Brilliant Autumn's Glow	390	Trained	1 Autumn's Glow
Balanced Twilight Opal	390	Trained	1 Twilight Opal
Pristine Monarch Topaz	390	Trained	1 Monarch Topaz
Dazzling Forest Emerald	390	Trained	1 Forest Emerald
Bold Dragon's Eye	390	Found	1 Dragon's Eye
Delicate Dragon's Eye	390	Found	1 Dragon's Eye
Runed Dragon's Eye	390	Found	1 Dragon's Eye
Bright Dragon's Eye	390	Found	1 Dragon's Eye
Subtle Dragon's Eye	390	Found	1 Dragon's Eye
Flashing Dragon's Eye	390	Found	1 Dragon's Eye
Brilliant Dragon's Eye	390	Found	1 Dragon's Eye
Fractured Dragon's Eye	390	Found	1 Dragon's Eye
Lustrous Dragon's Eye	390	Found	1 Dragon's Eye
Mystic Dragon's Eye	390	Found	1 Dragon's Eye
Precise Dragon's Eye	390	Found	1 Dragon's Eye
Quick Dragon's Eye	390	Found	1 Dragon's Eye
Rigid Dragon's Eye	390	Found	1 Dragon's Eye
Smooth Dragon's Eye	390	Found	1 Dragon's Eye
Solid Dragon's Eye	390	Found	1 Dragon's Eye
Sparkling Dragon's Eye	390	Found	1 Dragon's Eye
Stormy Dragon's Eye	390	Found	1 Dragon's Eye
Thick Dragon's Eye	390	Found	1 Dragon's Eye
Enchanted Tear	390	Trained	1 Siren's Tear, 4 Infinite Dust
Stoneguard Band	390	Trained	2 Eternal Earth
Shadowmight Ring	390	Trained	1 Eternal Earth, 1 Eternal Shadow
Bold Scarlet Ruby	400	Found	1 Scarlet Ruby
Delicate Scarlet Ruby	400	Found	1 Scarlet Ruby
Runed Scarlet Ruby	400	Found	1 Scarlet Ruby
Subtle Scarlet Ruby	400	Found	1 Scarlet Ruby
Flashing Scarlet Ruby	400	Found	1 Scarlet Ruby
Fractured Scarlet Ruby	400	Found	1 Scarlet Ruby

Jewelcrafting			
Spellname	SkillRank	Source	Reagents
Precise Scarlet Ruby	400	Found	1 Scarlet Ruby
Solid Sky Sapphire	400	Found	1 Sky Sapphire
Lustrous Sky Sapphire	400	Found	1 Sky Sapphire
Stormy Sky Sapphire	400	Found	1 Sky Sapphire
Smooth Autumn's Glow	400	Found	1 Autumn's Glow
Rigid Autumn's Glow	400	Found	1 Autumn's Glow
Thick Autumn's Glow	400	Found	1 Autumn's Glow
Mystic Autumn's Glow	400	Found	1 Autumn's Glow
Quick Autumn's Glow	400	Found	1 Autumn's Glow
Sovereign Twilight Opal	400	Found	1 Twilight Opal
Shifting Twilight Opal	400	Found	1 Twilight Opal
Tenuous Twilight Opal	400	Found	1 Twilight Opal
Glowing Twilight Opal	400	Found	1 Twilight Opal
Purified Twilight Opal	400	Found	1 Twilight Opal
Royal Twilight Opal	400	Found	1 Twilight Opal
Mysterious Twilight Opal	400	Found	1 Twilight Opal
Infused Twilight Opal	400	Found	1 Twilight Opal
Regal Twilight Opal	400	Found	1 Twilight Opal
Defender's Twilight Opal	400	Found	1 Twilight Opal
Puissant Twilight Opal	400	Found	1 Twilight Opal
Guardian's Twilight Opal	400	Found	1 Twilight Opal
Inscribed Monarch Topaz	400	Found	1 Monarch Topaz
Etched Monarch Topaz	400	Found	1 Monarch Topaz
Champion's Monarch Topaz	400	Found	1 Monarch Topaz
Resplendent Monarch Topaz	400	Found	1 Monarch Topaz
Deadly Monarch Topaz	400	Found	1 Monarch Topaz
Glinting Monarch Topaz	400	Found	1 Monarch Topaz
Lucent Monarch Topaz	400	Found	1 Monarch Topaz
Deft Monarch Topaz	400	Found	1 Monarch Topaz
Luminous Monarch Topaz	400	Found	1 Monarch Topaz
Potent Monarch Topaz	400	Found	1 Monarch Topaz
Veiled Monarch Topaz	400	Found	1 Monarch Topaz
Durable Monarch Topaz	400	Found	1 Monarch Topaz
Reckless Monarch Topaz	400	Found	1 Monarch Topaz
Wicked Monarch Topaz	400	Found	1 Monarch Topaz
Empowered Monarch Topaz	400	Found	1 Monarch Topaz
Stark Monarch Topaz	400	Found	1 Monarch Topaz
Stalwart Monarch Topaz	400	Found	1 Monarch Topaz
Glimmering Monarch Topaz	400	Found	1 Monarch Topaz
Accurate Monarch Topaz	400	Found	1 Monarch Topaz
Timeless Forest Emerald	400	Found	1 Forest Emerald
Jagged Forest Emerald	400	Found	1 Forest Emerald
Vivid Forest Emerald	400	Found	1 Forest Emerald
Enduring Forest Emerald	400	Found	1 Forest Emerald
Steady Forest Emerald	400	Found	1 Forest Emerald
Forceful Forest Emerald	400	Found	1 Forest Emerald
Seer's Forest Emerald	400	Found	1 Forest Emerald
Misty Forest Emerald	400	Found	1 Forest Emerald
Shining Forest Emerald	400	Found	1 Forest Emerald
Turbid Forest Emerald	400	Found	1 Forest Emerald
Intricate Forest Emerald	400	Found	1 Forest Emerald
Sundered Forest Emerald	400	Found	1 Forest Emerald
Lambent Forest Emerald	400	Found	1 Forest Emerald
Opaque Forest Emerald	400	Found	1 Forest Emerald
Energized Forest Emerald	400	Found	1 Forest Emerald
Radiant Forest Emerald	400	Found	1 Forest Emerald
Tense Forest Emerald	400	Found	1 Forest Emerald

Jewelcrafting			
Spellname	SkillRank	Source	Reagents
Shattered Forest Emerald	400	Found	1 Forest Emerald
Fierce Monarch Topaz	400	Found	1 Monarch Topaz
Resolute Monarch Topaz	400	Found	1 Monarch Topaz
Effulgent Skyflare Diamond	400	Found	1 Skyflare Diamond
Tireless Skyflare Diamond	400	Found	1 Skyflare Diamond
Forlorn Skyflare Diamond	400	Found	1 Skyflare Diamond
Impassive Skyflare Diamond	400	Found	1 Skyflare Diamond
Chaotic Skyflare Diamond	400	Found	1 Skyflare Diamond
Destructive Skyflare Diamond	400	Found	1 Skyflare Diamond
Ember Skyflare Diamond	400	Found	1 Skyflare Diamond
Enigmatic Skyflare Diamond	400	Found	1 Skyflare Diamond
Swift Skyflare Diamond	400	Found	1 Skyflare Diamond
Thundering Skyflare Diamond	400	Found	1 Skyflare Diamond
Insightful Earthsiege Diamond	400	Found	1 Earthsiege Diamond
Bracing Earthsiege Diamond	400	Found	1 Earthsiege Diamond
Eternal Earthsiege Diamond	400	Found	1 Earthsiege Diamond
Powerful Earthsiege Diamond	400	Found	1 Earthsiege Diamond
Relentless Earthsiege Diamond	400	Found	1 Earthsiege Diamond
Austere Earthsiege Diamond	400	Found	1 Earthsiege Diamond
Persistent Earthsiege Diamond	400	Found	1 Earthsiege Diamond
Trenchant Earthsiege Diamond	400	Found	1 Earthsiege Diamond
Invigorating Earthsiege Diamond	400	Found	1 Earthsiege Diamond
Beaming Earthsiege Diamond	400	Found	1 Earthsiege Diamond
Revitalizing Skyflare Diamond	400	Found	1 Skyflare Diamond
Ruby Hare	400	Trained	2 Titanium Bar, 2 Scarlet Ruby, 1 Autumn's Glow
Twilight Serpent	400	Trained	2 Titanium Bar, 2 Twilight Opal, 1 Monarch Topaz
Sapphire Owl	400	Trained	2 Titanium Bar, 2 Sky Sapphire, 1 Forest Emerald
Emerald Boar	400	Trained	2 Titanium Bar, 2 Forest Emerald, 1 Scarlet Ruby
Titanium Impact Band	400	Found	2 Titanium Bar, 4 Dragon's Eye, 4 Eternal Fire, 4 Eternal Shadow, 1 Frozen Orb
Titanium Earthguard Ring	400	Found	2 Titanium Bar, 4 Dragon's Eye, 4 Eternal Earth, 4 Eternal Life, 1 Frozen Orb
Titanium Spellshock Ring	400	Found	2 Titanium Bar, 4 Dragon's Eye, 4 Eternal Water, 4 Eternal Air, 1 Frozen Orb
Titanium Impact Choker	400	Found	2 Titanium Bar, 4 Dragon's Eye, 6 Eternal Air, 6 Eternal Fire, 1 Frozen Orb
Titanium Earthguard Chain	400	Found	2 Titanium Bar, 4 Dragon's Eye, 6 Eternal Life, 6 Eternal Earth, 1 Frozen Orb
Titanium Spellshock Necklace	400	Found	2 Titanium Bar, 4 Dragon's Eye, 6 Eternal Shadow, 6 Eternal Water, 1 Frozen Orb
Ring of Earthen Might	400	Found	2 Titanium Bar, 2 Eternal Earth
Ring of Scarlet Shadows	400	Found	2 Titanium Bar, 3 Eternal Shadow, 1 Scarlet Ruby
Windfire Band	400	Found	2 Titanium Bar, 1 Eternal Air, 2 Eternal Fire
Ring of Northern Tears	400	Found	2 Titanium Bar, 1 Eternal Water, 4 Northsea Pearl
Savage Titanium Ring	400	Found	4 Titanium Bar, 4 Eternal Fire
Savage Titanium Band	400	Found	4 Titanium Bar, 4 Eternal Fire
Titanium Frostguard Ring	400	Found	2 Titanium Bar, 3 Eternal Water, 3 Eternal Fire, 1 Frozen Orb
Monarch Crab	400	Trained	2 Titanium Bar, 2 Monarch Topaz, 1 Forest Emerald
Dream Signet	420	Trained	1 Titanium Bar, 1 Forest Emerald, 1 Dream Shard
Gem Perfection			

Inscription

Alchemy

Blacksmithing

Cooking

Enchanting

Engineering

First Aid

Fishing

Herbalism

Jewel-crafting

Leatherworking

Mining

Skinning

Tailoring

LEATHERWORKING

Leatherworking			
Spellname	SkillRank	Source	Reagents
Mammoth Mining Bag	375	Found	8 Heavy Borean Leather
Black Chitinguard Boots	375	Found	25 Nerubian Chitin, 6 Crystallized Water
Dark Arctic Leggings	375	Found	6 Heavy Borean Leather, 4 Crystallized Shadow
Dark Arctic Chestpiece	375	Found	5 Heavy Borean Leather, 5 Crystallized Shadow
Bracers of Shackled Souls	375	Found	1 Heart of Darkness, 1 Void Crystal, 2 Primal Life, 2 Primal Shadow, 2 Fel Scales
Dragonscale Ammo Pouch	375	Found	20 Icy Dragonscale, 2 Heavy Borean Leather
Nerubian Reinforced Quiver	375	Found	20 Nerubian Chitin, 2 Heavy Borean Leather
Iceborne Shoulderpads	380	Trained	10 Borean Leather
Iceborne Belt	380	Trained	10 Borean Leather
Arctic Shoulderpads	380	Trained	10 Borean Leather
Arctic Belt	380	Trained	10 Borean Leather
Frostscale Gloves	380	Trained	10 Borean Leather
Frostscale Boots	380	Trained	10 Borean Leather
Nerubian Shoulders	380	Trained	10 Borean Leather
Nerubian Boots	380	Trained	10 Borean Leather
Cloak of Harsh Winds	380	Trained	16 Borean Leather, 4 Crystallized Air
Arctic Wristguards	385	Trained	12 Borean Leather
Arctic Helm	385	Trained	14 Borean Leather
Frostscale Bracers	385	Trained	12 Borean Leather
Frostscale Helm	385	Trained	14 Borean Leather
Iceborne Wristguards	385	Trained	12 Borean Leather
Iceborne Helm	385	Trained	14 Borean Leather
Nerubian Bracers	385	Trained	12 Borean Leather
Nerubian Helm	385	Trained	14 Borean Leather
Heavy Borean Leather	390	Trained	6 Borean Leather
Heavy Borean Armor Kit	395	Trained	4 Heavy Borean Leather
Cloak of Tormented Skies	395	Trained	6 Heavy Borean Leather, 5 Crystallized Air, 5 Crystallized Water
Dark Frostscale Leggings	395	Trained	4 Heavy Borean Leather, 5 Crystallized Water
Dark Frostscale Breastplate	395	Trained	6 Heavy Borean Leather, 4 Crystallized Water
Dark Iceborne Leggings	395	Trained	4 Heavy Borean Leather, 5 Crystallized Shadow
Dark Iceborne Chestguard	395	Trained	6 Heavy Borean Leather, 4 Crystallized Shadow
Dark Nerubian Leggings	395	Trained	4 Heavy Borean Leather, 5 Crystallized Water
Dark Nerubian Chestpiece	395	Trained	6 Heavy Borean Leather, 4 Crystallized Water
Nerubian Leg Armor	400	Trained	4 Heavy Borean Leather, 1 Nerubian Chitin
Fur Lining - Stamina	400	Trained	1 Arctic Fur
Fur Lining - Spell Power	400	Trained	1 Arctic Fur
Fur Lining - Fire Resist	400	Found	1 Arctic Fur
Fur Lining - Frost Resist	400	Found	1 Arctic Fur
Fur Lining - Shadow Resist	400	Found	1 Arctic Fur
Fur Lining - Nature Resist	400	Found	1 Arctic Fur
Fur Lining - Arcane Resist	400	Found	1 Arctic Fur
Nerubian Leg Reinforcements	400	Trained	2 Nerubian Chitin
Dragonstompers	400	Trained	35 Icy Dragonscale
Bugsquashers	400	Trained	35 Nerubian Chitin
Scaled Icewalkers	400	Trained	30 Icy Dragonscale, 2 Crystallized Shadow
Eviscerator's Facemask	400	Found	12 Heavy Borean Leather, 1 Eternal Air
Eviscerator's Shoulderpads	400	Found	10 Heavy Borean Leather, 1 Eternal Air
Eviscerator's Chestguard	400	Found	12 Heavy Borean Leather, 1 Eternal Air
Eviscerator's Bindings	400	Found	8 Heavy Borean Leather, 1 Eternal Air
Eviscerator's Gauntlets	400	Found	10 Heavy Borean Leather, 1 Eternal Air
Eviscerator's Waistguard	400	Found	10 Heavy Borean Leather, 1 Eternal Air
Eviscerator's Legguards	400	Found	12 Heavy Borean Leather, 1 Eternal Air
Eviscerator's Treads	400	Found	10 Heavy Borean Leather, 1 Eternal Air
Overcast Headguard	400	Found	12 Heavy Borean Leather, 1 Eternal Water
Overcast Spaulders	400	Found	10 Heavy Borean Leather, 1 Eternal Water

Leatherworking Trainers		
Faction	Grand Master Trainer	Location
Alliance	Rosemary Bovard	Valiance Keep
Alliance	Bernadette Dexter	Valgarde
Neutral	Diane Cannings	Dalaran
Horde	Awan Iceborn	Taunka'le Village
Horde	Gunter Hansen	Vengeance Landing

The leather found on the fierce, hardy creatures of Northrend has given Leatherworkers the materials they need to take their craft further, and they have wasted no time in coming up with new patterns incorporating it into their profession. You can find great new armors and bags, along with new, stronger armor kits. The cold weather has also taught them how to make Fur Linings. These bracer upgrades can only be used on the Leatherworker's own bracers and work similarly to an enchant. They can be used in place of a regular enchant, but you cannot have both on one item.

Leatherworking			
Spellname	SkillRank	Source	Reagents
Borean Armor Kit	350	Trained	4 Borean Leather
Iceborne Leggings	370	Trained	12 Borean Leather
Iceborne Gloves	370	Trained	8 Borean Leather
Arctic Chestpiece	370	Trained	12 Borean Leather
Arctic Boots	370	Trained	8 Borean Leather
Frostscale Leggings	370	Trained	12 Borean Leather
Frostscale Belt	370	Trained	8 Borean Leather
Nerubian Legguards	370	Trained	8 Borean Leather
Nerubian Gloves	370	Trained	12 Borean Leather
Iceborne Chestguard	375	Trained	12 Borean Leather
Iceborne Boots	375	Trained	10 Borean Leather
Arctic Leggings	375	Trained	12 Borean Leather
Arctic Gloves	375	Trained	10 Borean Leather
Frostscale Chestguard	375	Trained	12 Borean Leather
Frostscale Shoulders	375	Trained	10 Borean Leather
Nerubian Chestguard	375	Trained	12 Borean Leather
Nerubian Belt	375	Trained	10 Borean Leather
Trapper's Traveling Pack	375	Found	8 Heavy Borean Leather

Leatherworking

Spellname	SkillRank	Source	Reagents
Overcast Chestguard	400	Found	12 Heavy Borean Leather, 1 Eternal Water
Overcast Bracers	400	Found	8 Heavy Borean Leather, 1 Eternal Water
Overcast Handwraps	400	Found	10 Heavy Borean Leather, 1 Eternal Water
Overcast Belt	400	Found	10 Heavy Borean Leather, 1 Eternal Water
Overcast Leggings	400	Found	12 Heavy Borean Leather, 1 Eternal Water
Overcast Boots	400	Found	10 Heavy Borean Leather, 1 Eternal Water
Swiftarrow Helm	400	Found	12 Heavy Borean Leather, 1 Eternal Air
Swiftarrow Shoulderguards	400	Found	10 Heavy Borean Leather, 1 Eternal Air
Swiftarrow Hauberk	400	Found	12 Heavy Borean Leather, 1 Eternal Air
Swiftarrow Bracers	400	Found	8 Heavy Borean Leather, 1 Eternal Air
Swiftarrow Gauntlets	400	Found	10 Heavy Borean Leather, 1 Eternal Air
Swiftarrow Belt	400	Found	10 Heavy Borean Leather, 1 Eternal Air
Swiftarrow Leggings	400	Found	12 Heavy Borean Leather, 1 Eternal Air
Swiftarrow Boots	400	Found	10 Heavy Borean Leather, 1 Eternal Air
Stormhide Crown	400	Found	12 Heavy Borean Leather, 1 Eternal Water
Stormhide Shoulders	400	Found	10 Heavy Borean Leather, 1 Eternal Water
Stormhide Hauberk	400	Found	12 Heavy Borean Leather, 1 Eternal Water
Stormhide Wristguards	400	Found	8 Heavy Borean Leather, 1 Eternal Water
Stormhide Grips	400	Found	10 Heavy Borean Leather, 1 Eternal Water
Stormhide Belt	400	Found	10 Heavy Borean Leather, 1 Eternal Water
Stormhide Legguards	400	Found	12 Heavy Borean Leather, 1 Eternal Water
Stormhide Stompers	400	Found	10 Heavy Borean Leather, 1 Eternal Water
Giantmaim Legguards	400	Found	12 Heavy Borean Leather, 6 Eternal Water, 6 Eternal Air, 1 Frozen Orb
Giantmaim Bracers	400	Found	10 Heavy Borean Leather, 5 Eternal Water, 5 Eternal Air, 1 Frozen Orb
Revenant's Breastplate	400	Found	12 Heavy Borean Leather, 12 Eternal Water, 1 Frozen Orb
Revenant's Treads	400	Found	10 Heavy Borean Leather, 10 Eternal Water, 1 Frozen Orb
Trollwoven Spaulders	400	Found	10 Heavy Borean Leather, 6 Eternal Fire, 6 Eternal Shadow, 1 Frozen Orb
Trollwoven Girdle	400	Found	10 Heavy Borean Leather, 5 Eternal Fire, 5 Eternal Shadow, 1 Frozen Orb
Earthgiving Legguards	400	Found	12 Heavy Borean Leather, 6 Eternal Life, 6 Eternal Water, 1 Frozen Orb
Earthgiving Boots	400	Found	10 Heavy Borean Leather, 5 Eternal Life, 5 Eternal Water, 1 Frozen Orb
Polar Vest	400	Found	10 Heavy Borean Leather, 3 Eternal Fire, 3 Eternal Water, 8 Nerubian Chitin, 1 Frozen Orb
Polar Cord	400	Found	8 Heavy Borean Leather, 2 Eternal Fire, 2 Eternal Water, 4 Nerubian Chitin, 1 Frozen Orb
Polar Boots	400	Found	8 Heavy Borean Leather, 2 Eternal Fire, 2 Eternal Water, 4 Nerubian Chitin, 1 Frozen Orb
Icy Scale Chestguard	400	Found	10 Heavy Borean Leather, 3 Eternal Fire, 3 Eternal Water, 8 Icy Dragonscale, 1 Frozen Orb
Icy Scale Belt	400	Found	8 Heavy Borean Leather, 2 Eternal Fire, 2 Eternal Water, 4 Icy Dragonscale, 1 Frozen Orb
Icy Scale Boots	400	Found	8 Heavy Borean Leather, 2 Eternal Fire, 2 Eternal Water, 4 Icy Dragonscale, 1 Frozen Orb
Jormungar Leg Armor	405	Trained	5 Heavy Borean Leather, 1 Jormungar Scale
Jormungar Leg Reinforcements	405	Trained	2 Jormungar Scale
Pack of Endless Pockets	415	Trained	8 Heavy Borean Leather
Virulent Spaulders	420	Trained	12 Heavy Borean Leather, 2 Eternal Fire
Eaglebane Bracers	420	Trained	40 Icy Dragonscale
Nightshock Girdle	420	Trained	10 Heavy Borean Leather, 2 Eternal Shadow
Seafoam Gauntlets	420	Trained	10 Heavy Borean Leather, 2 Eternal Water
Jormscale Footpads	420	Trained	6 Heavy Borean Leather, 20 Jormungar Scale
Purehorn Spaulders	420	Trained	30 Nerubian Chitin
Frosthide Leg Armor	425	Trained	2 Arctic Fur, 2 Nerubian Chitin
Icescale Leg Armor	425	Trained	2 Arctic Fur, 2 Icy Dragonscale
Fur Lining - Attack Power	425	Found	1 Arctic Fur
Razorstrike Breastplate	425	Trained	15 Heavy Borean Leather, 1 Eternal Air
Nightshock Hood	425	Trained	14 Heavy Borean Leather, 2 Eternal Shadow

Leatherworking

Spellname	SkillRank	Source	Reagents
Leggings of Visceral Strikes	425	Trained	12 Heavy Borean Leather, 2 Eternal Air
Wildscale Breastplate	425	Trained	25 Heavy Borean Leather
Ice Striker's Cloak	440	Trained	2 Arctic Fur, 6 Eternal Fire, 4 Eternal Shadow, 1 Frozen Orb
Durable Nerubhide Cape	440	Trained	2 Arctic Fur, 40 Nerubian Chitin, 1 Frozen Orb
Bracers of Deflection			8 Heavy Borean Leather, 6 Eternal Air

 MINING

Mining Trainers

Faction	Grand Master Trainer	Location
Alliance	Fendrig Redbeard	Valiance Keep
Alliance	Grumbol Stoutpick	Valgarde
Neutral	Jedidiah Handers	Dalaran
Horde	Brunna Ironaxe	Warsong Hold
Horde	Jonathan Lewis	Vengeance Landing

The continent of Northrend has yielded up new ores for Miners to dig their picks into. In expanding their craft, Miners can combine these ores with other materials found here to create truly special metal bars suitable for use in several other professions. Because of the new Engineering and Blacksmithing recipes especially, Miners find their product in high demand and clearing out every node you see is well worth your time.

Ore	Skill Level
Cobalt	350
Rich Cobalt Node	375
Saronite	400
Rich Saronite Node	425
Titanium	450

TOUGHNESS

 All that hard work you've done Mining has made you extra tough. You maximum health is increased. The higher your Mining skill, the more benefit you see from Toughness.

Mining

Spellname	SkillRank	Source	Reagents
Smelt Cobalt	350	Trained	1 Cobalt Ore
Smelt Saronite	400	Trained	2 Saronite Ore
Smelt Titansteel	450	Trained	3 Titanium Bar, 1 Eternal Fire, 1 Eternal Earth, 1 Eternal Shadow
Smelt Titanium	450	Trained	2 Titanium Ore

Inscription

Alchemy

Blacksmithing

Cooking

Enchanting

Engineering

First Aid

Fishing

Herbalism

Jewelcrafting

Leather-working

Mining

Skinning

Tailoring

Skinning

Skinning Trainers

Faction	Grand Master Trainer	Location
Alliance	Trapper Jack	Valiance Keep
Alliance	Frederic Burrhus	Valgarde
Neutral	Derik Marks	Dalaran
Horde	Tiponi Stormwhisper	Taunka'le Village
Horde	Roberta Jacks	Vengeance Landing

The tough hides of the creatures of Northrend can prove challenging to even an experienced skinner at first, but with a little practice you can soon be filling your packs with Borean Leather to use for crafting or to sell for a nice pile of gold. Be sure to skin everything you come across. Not only is Borean Leather very useful, but some of Northrend's inhabitants yield valuable scales or chitin as well.

MASTER OF ANATOMY

 Skinning can be a dirty job, but it has its rewards beyond the price the leather fetches you. All the time you spent carefully skinning carcasses has given you a broader anatomical knowledge, increasing your critical strike rating. The higher you Skinning skill, the higher your rating.

Tailoring

Tailoring Trainers

Faction	Grand Master Trainer	Location
Alliance	Darin Goodstitch	Valiance Keep
Alliance	Benjamin Clegg	Valgarde
Neutral	Charles Worth	Dalaran
Horde	Raenah	Warsong Hold
Horde	Alexandra McQueen	Vengeance Landing

In pushing into Northrend, Tailors have learned to make good use of the Frostweave cloth and other materials found there. They can now learn many new recipes, including new Spellthreads to apply to pants and Embroidery to beef up their own cloaks. Tailors find their wares in great demand among the cloth wearing set. They can also now manufacture an assortment of Flying Carpets! Yes, you read that correctly—Flying Carpets! Engineers no longer have sole bragging rights on manufactured mounts.

NORTHERN CLOTH SCAVENGING

 A tailor can never have too much cloth! With this in mind, a good tailor is always on the lookout for salvageable cloth, often seeing bits other less trained eyes may miss. This ability gives you the chance to pick up extra cloth off of any Northrend humanoids above and beyond that found in regular loot.

Tailoring

Spellname	SkillRank	Source	Reagents
Bolt of Frostweave	350	Trained	5 Frostweave Cloth
Frostwoven Shoulders	350	Trained	3 Bolt of Frostweave, 1 Eternium Thread
Frostwoven Wristwraps	350	Trained	3 Bolt of Frostweave, 1 Eternium Thread
Northern Cloth Scavenging	350	Found	
Frostweave Net	360	Trained	6 Frostweave Cloth
Frostwoven Robe	360	Trained	4 Bolt of Frostweave, 1 Eternium Thread
Frostwoven Gloves	360	Trained	3 Bolt of Frostweave, 1 Eternium Thread
Red Lumberjack Shirt	360	Found	4 Bolt of Frostweave, 1 Red Dye
Blue Lumberjack Shirt	360	Found	4 Bolt of Frostweave, 1 Blue Dye
Yellow Lumberjack Shirt	360	Found	4 Bolt of Frostweave, 1 Yellow Dye
Green Lumberjack Shirt	360	Found	4 Bolt of Frostweave, 1 Green Dye
Red Workman's Shirt	360	Found	4 Bolt of Frostweave, 1 Red Dye
Blue Workman's Shirt	360	Found	4 Bolt of Frostweave, 1 Blue Dye
Rustic Workman's Shirt	360	Found	4 Bolt of Frostweave, 1 Yellow Dye
Green Workman's Shirt	360	Found	4 Bolt of Frostweave, 1 Green Dye
Frostwoven Belt	370	Trained	3 Bolt of Frostweave, 1 Eternium Thread
Frostwoven Boots	375	Trained	4 Bolt of Frostweave, 1 Eternium Thread
Frostwoven Cowl	380	Trained	5 Bolt of Frostweave, 1 Eternium Thread
Frostwoven Leggings	380	Trained	5 Bolt of Frostweave, 1 Eternium Thread
Mystic Frostwoven Shoulders	385	Trained	7 Bolt of Frostweave, 4 Eternium Thread, 1 Northsea Pearl
Mystic Frostwoven Wristwraps	385	Trained	5 Bolt of Frostweave, 4 Eternium Thread, 2 Northsea Pearl
Mystic Frostwoven Robe	390	Trained	8 Bolt of Frostweave, 4 Eternium Thread, 1 Northsea Pearl
Moonshroud	390	Found	1 Bolt of Imbued Frostweave, 2 Eternal Life
Ebonweave	390	Found	1 Bolt of Imbued Frostweave, 2 Eternal Shadow
Spellweave	390	Found	1 Bolt of Imbued Frostweave, 2 Eternal Fire
Abyssal Bag	390	Found	4 Ebonweave, 2 Spellweave, 1 Eternium Thread
Glacial Bag	390	Found	4 Moonshroud, 4 Ebonweave, 1 Eternium Thread

Tailoring

Spellname	SkillRank	Source	Reagents
Mysterious Bag	390	Found	4 Spellweave, 2 Moonshroud, 1 Eternium Thread
Frostweave Bag	390	Found	6 Bolt of Imbued Frostweave, 2 Eternium Thread
Brilliant Spellthread	390	Found	8 Eternal Life, 1 Iceweb Spider Silk, 3 Eternium Thread, 1 Frozen Orb
Sapphire Spellthread	390	Found	8 Eternal Fire, 1 Iceweb Spider Silk, 3 Eternium Thread, 1 Frozen Orb
Cloak of the Moon	390	Trained	7 Bolt of Frostweave, 1 Northsea Pearl
Wispcloak	390	Found	5 Bolt of Imbued Frostweave, 6 Eternal Life, 4 Eternal Water, 1 Siren's Tear, 1 Frozen Orb
Deathchill Cloak	390	Found	5 Bolt of Imbued Frostweave, 6 Eternal Fire, 4 Eternal Shadow, 1 Siren's Tear, 1 Frozen Orb
Hat of Wintry Doom	390	Found	1 Ebonweave, 6 Bolt of Imbued Frostweave, 4 Iceweb Spider Silk, 1 Eternium Thread
Silky Iceshard Boots	390	Found	1 Spellweave, 5 Bolt of Imbued Frostweave, 2 Heavy Borean Leather, 4 Iceweb Spider Silk, 1 Eternium Thread
Deep Frozen Cord	390	Found	1 Spellweave, 4 Bolt of Imbued Frostweave, 4 Iceweb Spider Silk, 1 Eternium Thread
Frostmoon Pants	390	Found	1 Moonshroud, 6 Bolt of Imbued Frostweave, 4 Iceweb Spider Silk, 1 Eternium Thread
Light Blessed Mittens	390	Found	1 Moonshroud, 4 Bolt of Imbued Frostweave, 4 Iceweb Spider Silk, 1 Eternium Thread
Aurora Slippers	390	Found	1 Moonshroud, 4 Bolt of Imbued Frostweave, 2 Heavy Borean Leather, 4 Iceweb Spider Silk, 1 Eternium Thread
Duskweave Leggings	395	Trained	8 Bolt of Frostweave, 1 Eternium Thread
Duskweave Belt	395	Trained	7 Bolt of Frostweave, 1 Eternium Thread
Duskweave Cowl	395	Trained	8 Bolt of Frostweave, 1 Eternium Thread
Cloak of Frozen Spirits	395	Trained	8 Bolt of Frostweave, 1 Northsea Pearl
Bolt of Imbued Frostweave	400	Trained	3 Bolt of Frostweave, 2 Infinite Dust
Duskweave Wristwraps	400	Trained	8 Bolt of Frostweave, 1 Eternium Thread
Shining Spellthread	400	Trained	2 Crystallized Life, 1 Iceweb Spider Silk, 3 Eternium Thread
Azure Spellthread	400	Trained	2 Crystallized Fire, 1 Iceweb Spider Silk, 3 Eternium Thread
Moonshroud Robe	400	Found	8 Moonshroud, 6 Bolt of Imbued Frostweave, 1 Eternium Thread, 1 Frozen Orb
Moonshroud Gloves	400	Found	4 Moonshroud, 4 Bolt of Imbued Frostweave, 1 Eternium Thread, 1 Frozen Orb
Ebonweave Robe	400	Found	8 Ebonweave, 6 Bolt of Imbued Frostweave, 1 Eternium Thread, 1 Frozen Orb
Ebonweave Gloves	400	Found	4 Ebonweave, 4 Bolt of Imbued Frostweave, 1 Eternium Thread, 1 Frozen Orb
Spellweave Robe	400	Found	8 Spellweave, 6 Bolt of Imbued Frostweave, 1 Eternium Thread, 1 Frozen Orb

Tailoring

Spellname	SkillRank	Source	Reagents
Spellweave Gloves	400	Found	4 Spellweave, 4 Bolt of Imbued Frostweave, 1 Eternium Thread, 1 Frozen Orb
Duskweave Robe	405	Trained	10 Bolt of Frostweave, 1 Eternium Thread
Duskweave Gloves	405	Trained	9 Bolt of Frostweave, 1 Eternium Thread
Master's Spellthread	405	Trained	1 Azure Spellthread, 5 Crystallized Life
Sanctified Spellthread	405	Trained	1 Shining Spellthread, 5 Crystallized Fire
Duskweave Shoulders	410	Trained	10 Bolt of Frostweave, 1 Eternium Thread
Duskweave Boots	410	Trained	10 Bolt of Frostweave, 1 Eternium Thread
Flying Carpet	410	Trained	4 Bolt of Imbued Frostweave, 4 Sun Crystal, 4 Green Dye, 2 Yellow Dye, 2 Iceweb Spider Silk
Black Duskweave Leggings	415	Trained	5 Bolt of Imbued Frostweave, 2 Iceweb Spider Silk, 2 Eternium Thread
Black Duskweave Wristwraps	415	Trained	4 Bolt of Imbued Frostweave, 2 Iceweb Spider Silk, 2 Eternium Thread
Frostsavage Belt	415	Trained	3 Bolt of Imbued Frostweave, 3 Crystallized Fire, 3 Crystallized Earth, 2 Eternium Thread
Frostsavage Bracers	415	Trained	3 Bolt of Imbued Frostweave, 3 Crystallized Fire, 3 Crystallized Earth, 2 Eternium Thread
Lightweave Embroidery	420	Trained	1 Moonshroud, 1 Eternium Thread
Darkglow Embroidery	420	Trained	1 Ebonweave, 1 Eternium Thread
Swordguard Embroidery	420	Trained	1 Spellweave, 1 Eternium Thread
Black Duskweave Robe	420	Trained	5 Bolt of Imbued Frostweave, 2 Iceweb Spider Silk, 2 Eternium Thread
Frostsavage Shoulders	420	Trained	3 Bolt of Imbued Frostweave, 4 Crystallized Fire, 4 Crystallized Earth, 2 Eternium Thread
Frostsavage Boots	420	Trained	3 Bolt of Imbued Frostweave, 4 Crystallized Fire, 4 Crystallized Earth, 2 Eternium Thread
Frostsavage Gloves	420	Trained	3 Bolt of Imbued Frostweave, 4 Crystallized Fire, 4 Crystallized Earth, 2 Eternium Thread
Frostsavage Robe	420	Trained	4 Bolt of Imbued Frostweave, 5 Crystallized Fire, 5 Crystallized Earth, 2 Eternium Thread
Frostsavage Leggings	420	Trained	4 Bolt of Imbued Frostweave, 5 Crystallized Fire, 5 Crystallized Earth, 2 Eternium Thread
Frostsavage Cowl	420	Trained	4 Bolt of Imbued Frostweave, 5 Crystallized Fire, 5 Crystallized Earth, 2 Eternium Thread
Glacial Waistband	420	Trained	4 Bolt of Imbued Frostweave, 2 Eternal Fire, 2 Eternal Water, 2 Eternium Thread, 1 Frozen Orb
Glacial Slippers	420	Trained	4 Bolt of Imbued Frostweave, 2 Eternal Fire, 2 Eternal Water, 2 Eternium Thread, 1 Frozen Orb
Magnificent Flying Carpet	425	Trained	12 Bolt of Imbued Frostweave, 4 Monarch Topaz, 4 Red Dye, 2 Yellow Dye, 4 Iceweb Spider Silk
Glacial Robe	425	Trained	6 Bolt of Imbued Frostweave, 3 Eternal Fire, 3 Eternal Water, 3 Eternium Thread, 1 Frozen Orb
Duskweave Boots			1 Frostwoven Boots, 2 Crystallized Shadow

Inscription

Alchemy

Blacksmithing

Cooking

Enchanting

Engineering

First Aid

Fishing

Herbalism

Jewelcrafting

Leatherworking

Mining

Skinning

Tailoring

ACHERUS: THE EBON HOLD

Title	Location	Faction	Race & Class	Group #	Starter	Finisher	Prerequisite	Reputation	XP	Money
Welcome!	Acherus: The Ebon Hold	All	All Death Knight		Ebon Hold Gift Voucher	Siouxsie the Banshee				
CHOICE OF: 1 Diablo Stone, 1 Panda Collar, 1 Zergling Leash										

AHK'KAHET: THE OLD KINGDOM

Title	Location	Faction	Race & Class	Group #	Starter	Finisher	Prerequisite	Reputation	XP	Money
The Faceless Ones	Ahn'kahet: The Old Kingdom	All	All		Kilix the Unraveler	Kilix the Unraveler			42300	
CHOICE OF: 1 Mantle of Thwarted Evil, 1 Shoulderpads of Abhorrence, 1 Shoulderplates of the Abolished, 1 Epaulets of the Faceless Ones										
All Things in Good Time	Ahn'kahet: The Old Kingdom	All	All		Kilix the Unraveler	Kilix the Unraveler			33100	22 20
Funky Fungi	Ahn'kahet: The Old Kingdom	All	All		Ooze-covered Fungus	Kilix the Unraveler			42300	
Proof of Demise: Herald Volazj	Ahn'kahet: The Old Kingdom	All	All		Archmage Lan'dalock	Archmage Lan'dalock		75 with Kirin Tor	44100	22 20
REWARD: 2 Emblem of Heroism										

AZJOL-NERUB

Title	Location	Faction	Race & Class	Group #	Starter	Finisher	Prerequisite	Reputation	XP	Money
Death to the Traitor King	Azjol-Nerub	All	All		Kilix the Unraveler	Kilix the Unraveler			41500	
CHOICE OF: 1 Kilix's Silk Slippers, 1 Don Soto's Boots, 1 Husk Shard Sabatons, 1 Greaves of the Traitor										
Don't Forget the Eggs!	Azjol-Nerub	All	All		Kilix the Unraveler	Kilix the Unraveler			25950	11 20
CHOICE OF: 1 Expelling Gauntlets, 1 Purging Handguards, 1 Wraps of Quelled Bane, 1 Gloves of Banished Infliction										
Proof of Demise: Anub'arak	Azjol-Nerub	All	All		Archmage Lan'dalock	Archmage Lan'dalock		75 with Kirin Tor	44100	22 20
REWARD: 2 Emblem of Heroism										

BOREAN TUNDRA

Title	Location	Faction	Race & Class	Group #	Starter	Finisher	Prerequisite	Reputation	XP	Money
Winterfin Commerce	Borean Tundra	All	All		King Mrgl-Mrgl's Spare Suit, King Mrgl-Mrgl	Ahlurglgr	Learning to Communicate		20100	4 70
Oh Noes, the Tadpoles!	Borean Tundra	All	All		King Mrgl-Mrgl's Spare Suit, King Mrgl-Mrgl	King Mrgl-Mrgl	Winterfin Commerce	250 with Cenarion Expedition	20100	4 70
CHOICE OF: 1 Lobstrock Slicer, 1 Tidal Boon, 1 Sinking Pauldrons, 1 Shimmering Band										
Them!	Borean Tundra	All	All		Brglmurgl	Brglmurgl	Winterfin Commerce		20100	4 70
I'm Being Blackmailed By My Cleaner	Borean Tundra	All	All		King Mrgl-Mrgl's Spare Suit, King Mrgl-Mrgl	Mrmrglmr	Oh Noes, the Tadpoles!		2000	
Grmmurggll Mrllggrl Glrggl!!!	Borean Tundra	All	All		Mrmrglmr	Mrmrglmr	I'm Being Blackmailed By My Cleaner		20100	4 70
Succulent Orca Stew	Borean Tundra	All	All		Cleaver Bmurglbrm	Cleaver Bmurglbrm	I'm Being Blackmailed By My Cleaner		20100	4 70
REWARD: 20 Succulent Orca Stew										
The Spare Suit	Borean Tundra	All	All		Mrmrglmr	King Mrgl-Mrgl	Grmmurggll Mrllggrl Glrggl!!!	10 with Cenarion Expedition	2000	
Surrender... Not!	Borean Tundra	All	All		King Mrgl-Mrgl's Spare Suit, King Mrgl-Mrgl	King Mrgl-Mrgl	The Spare Suit	350 with Cenarion Expedition	25400	10
CHOICE OF: 1 Lost Sea Oculus, 1 Soggy Hide Pauldrons, 1 Rusty Mesh Leggings, 1 Bogstrok Plate Gloves										
Keymaster Urmgrgl	Borean Tundra	All	All		Glrglrglr	Glrglrglr	Learning to Communicate		20100	4 70
Escape from the Winterfin Caverns	Borean Tundra	All	All		Lurgglbr	King Mrgl-Mrgl	Learning to Communicate	250 with Cenarion Expedition	20100	4 70
CHOICE OF: 1 Shell Smasher, 1 Amphibious Speargun, 1 Scepter of the Winterfin, 1 Fish-Eye Poker, 1 Mrgl Blade, 1 Glimmering Orca Tooth										
Learning to Communicate	Borean Tundra	All	All		King Mrgl-Mrgl's Spare Suit, King Mrgl-Mrgl	King Mrgl-Mrgl		250 with Cenarion Expedition	20100	4 70
Too Close For Comfort	Borean Tundra	Horde	All		Endorah	Librarian Donathan	The Defense of Warsong Hold, The Defense of Warsong Hold, The Defense of Warsong Hold		10050	2 40
Nick of Time	Borean Tundra	All	All		Midge	Librarian Donathan	Plug the Sinkholes		10050	2 40
Monitoring the Rift: Cleftcliff Anomaly	Borean Tundra	All	All		Librarian Garren	Librarian Garren			15100	3 70
Monitoring the Rift: Sundered Chasm	Borean Tundra	All	All		Librarian Garren	Librarian Garren	Monitoring the Rift: Cleftcliff Anomaly		15100	3 70
Hellscream's Vigil	Borean Tundra	Horde	All		Warsong Recruitment Officer	Garrosh Hellscream		10 with Warsong Offensive	2000	

BOREAN TUNDRA

Title	Location	Faction	Race & Class	Group #	Starter	Finisher	Prerequisite	Reputation	XP	Money
Hellscream's Vigil	Borean Tundra	Horde	All		Warsong Recruitment Officer	Garrosh Hellscream	Hero of the Mag'har	10 with Warsong Offensive	2000	
Prison Break	Borean Tundra	All	All		Librarian Donathan	Librarian Donathan			20100	4🜚70🜚
Abduction	Borean Tundra	All	All		Librarian Donathan	Librarian Donathan	Prison Break		20100	4🜚70🜚
Report to Steeljaw's Caravan	Borean Tundra	Horde	All		Overlord Bor'gorok	Grunt Ragefist		10 with The Taunka	2000	
We Strike!	Borean Tundra	Horde	All		Longrunner Proudhoof	Overlord Bor'gorok		350 with Warsong Offensive, 350 with The Taunka	25400	10🜚
CHOICE OF: 1 Dusk Watcher's Belt, 1 Shadewrap Gloves, 1 Tundrastrider Boots, 1 Warsong's Fervor										
The Honored Dead	Borean Tundra	Horde	All		Grunt Ragefist	Grunt Ragefist		250 with Warsong Offensive	20100	4🜚70🜚
Put Them to Rest	Borean Tundra	Horde	All		Grunt Ragefist	Grunt Ragefist		250 with Warsong Offensive	20100	4🜚70🜚
The Defense of Warsong Hold	Borean Tundra	Horde	All		High Overlord Saurfang	Overlord Razgor		10 with Warsong Offensive	2000	
The Defense of Warsong Hold	Borean Tundra	Horde	All		High Overlord Saurfang	Overlord Razgor		10 with Warsong Offensive	2000	
The Defense of Warsong Hold	Borean Tundra	Horde	All		High Overlord Saurfang	Overlord Razgor		10 with Warsong Offensive	2000	
Taking Back Mightstone Quarry	Borean Tundra	Horde	All		Overlord Razgor	Overlord Razgor	The Defense of Warsong Hold, The Defense of Warsong Hold, The Defense of Warsong Hold	250 with Warsong Offensive	20100	
Thassarian, My Brother	Borean Tundra	All	All		Leryssa	William Allerton	Plug the Sinkholes		10050	
The Late William Allerton	Borean Tundra	All	All		William Allerton	Leryssa	Thassarian, My Brother	150 with Valiance Expedition	15100	
CHOICE OF: 1 Seafarer Boots, 1 Seaspeaker Legguards, 1 Talisman of the Tundra, 1 Seabone Heaume										
Lost and Found	Borean Tundra	All	All		Leryssa	James Deacon	The Late William Allerton	75 with Valiance Expedition	10050	
Cutting Off the Source	Borean Tundra	Horde	All		Overlord Razgor	Overlord Razgor	Taking Back Mightstone Quarry	250 with Warsong Offensive	20100	
CHOICE OF: 1 Combatant Greatsword, 1 Warsong Longbow, 1 Writhing Longstaff, 1 Medic's Morning Star, 1 Soldier's Spiked Mace, 1 Vicious Spellblade										
In Wine, Truth	Borean Tundra	All	All		James Deacon	Old Man Colburn	Lost and Found	150 with Valiance Expedition	15100	
REWARD: 5 Caraway Burnwine										
A Deserter	Borean Tundra	Alliance	All		Old Man Colburn	Private Brau	In Wine, Truth	25 with Valiance Expedition	5050	
The Honored Ancestors	Borean Tundra	All	All		Elder Atkanok	Elder Atkanok		250 with The Kalu'ak	20300	5🜚
Patience is a Virtue that We Don't Need	Borean Tundra	Horde	All		Quartermaster Holgoth	Quartermaster Holgoth	The Defense of Warsong Hold, The Defense of Warsong Hold, The Defense of Warsong Hold	250 with Warsong Offensive	20100	
The Lost Spirits	Borean Tundra	All	All		Elder Atkanok	Elder Atkanok	The Honored Ancestors	250 with The Kalu'ak	20300	5🜚
Bury Those Cockroaches!	Borean Tundra	Horde	All		Quartermaster Holgoth	Quartermaster Holgoth	Patience is a Virtue that We Don't Need	250 with Warsong Offensive	20100	
CHOICE OF: 1 Marshwalker Legguards, 1 Tundrastrider Coif, 1 Mightstone Breastplate, 1 Warsong's Wrath										
Picking Up the Pieces	Borean Tundra	All	All		Elder Atkanok	Elder Atkanok	The Lost Spirits	250 with The Kalu'ak	20300	5🜚
Leading the Ancestors Home	Borean Tundra	All	All		Elder Atkanok	Elder Atkanok	Picking Up the Pieces	350 with The Kalu'ak	25400	10🜚
CHOICE OF: 1 Seafarer Mantle, 1 Iceflow Collar, 1 Whalehunter Leggings, 1 Freed Shackles										
Taken by the Scourge	Borean Tundra	Horde	All		Foreman Mortuus	Foreman Mortuus	The Defense of Warsong Hold, The Defense of Warsong Hold, The Defense of Warsong Hold	250 with Warsong Offensive	20100	
CHOICE OF: 1 Weathered Worker Cloak, 1 Marshwalker Boots, 1 Westrift Handcovers, 1 Mightstone Legplates										
Reclaiming the Quarry	Borean Tundra	All	All		Etaruk	Etaruk		250 with The Kalu'ak	20300	5🜚
Karuk's Oath	Borean Tundra	All	All		Karuk	Karuk		350 with The Kalu'ak	25150	
CHOICE OF: 1 Blubber Carver, 1 Compact Arrow Launcher, 1 Medicine Stick, 1 Shark Stabber, 1 Claw of the Tuskarr, 1 Spirit Channeller's Rod										
Untold Truths	Borean Tundra	Horde	All		Shadowstalker Barthus	Shadowstalker Luther	Taking Back Mightstone Quarry	25 with Warsong Offensive	5050	
Nerub'ar Secrets	Borean Tundra	Horde	All		Shadowstalker Luther	Shadowstalker Barthus	Untold Truths	25 with Warsong Offensive	5050	
Message to Hellscream	Borean Tundra	Horde	All		Shadowstalker Barthus	Garrosh Hellscream	Nerub'ar Secrets	25 with Warsong Offensive	5050	
Hampering Their Escape	Borean Tundra	All	All		Etaruk	Etaruk	Reclaiming the Quarry	350 with The Kalu'ak	20300	5🜚
Reinforcements Incoming...	Borean Tundra	Horde	All		Garrosh Hellscream	Shadowstalker Ickoris	Message to Hellscream	25 with Warsong Offensive	5050	
Gamel the Cruel	Borean Tundra	All	All		Karuk	Karuk	Karuk's Oath	250 with The Kalu'ak	20100	4🜚70🜚
CHOICE OF: 1 Wharfmaster's Hat, 1 Seaspeaker Mantle, 1 Rigid Tuskring, 1 Giant Turtle Collar										

Title	Location	Faction	Race & Class	Group #	Starter	Finisher	Prerequisite	Reputation	XP	Money
A Father's Words	Borean Tundra	All	All		Karuk	Veehja	Gamel the Cruel	150 with The Kalu'ak	15100	
The Tablet of Leviroth	Borean Tundra	All	All		Karuk	Karuk		75 with The Kalu'ak		
Secrets of Riplash	Borean Tundra	All	All		Veehja	Veehja		150 with The Kalu'ak	15100	
A Visit to the Curator	Borean Tundra	All	All		Etaruk	Etaruk	Hampering Their Escape	250 with The Kalu'ak	20300	5
CHOICE OF: 1 Sealskin Bindings, 1 Seaspeaker Gloves, 1 Icechill Buckler, 1 Lost Crusader Waistguard										
The Sky Will Know	Borean Tundra	Horde	All		Spirit Talker Snarlfang	Imperean			2000	
The Trident of Naz'jan	Borean Tundra	All	All		Veehja	Veehja	A Father's Words		20100	
The Emissary	Borean Tundra	All	All		Veehja	Karuk	The Trident of Naz'jan	500 with The Kalu'ak	30150	
CHOICE OF: 1 Iceflow Wristwraps, 1 Whalehunter Gloves, 1 Sharkproof Coif, 1 Seabone Legplates										
Boiling Point	Borean Tundra	All	All		Imperean	Imperean	The Sky Will Know		20300	5
Shrouds of the Scourge	Borean Tundra	Horde	All		Chieftain Wintergale	Chieftain Wintergale	Patching Up, Deploy the Shake-n-Quake!	250 with The Taunka	20300	5
Return to the Spirit Talker	Borean Tundra	Horde	All		Imperean	Spirit Talker Snarlfang	Motes of the Enraged	10 with Warsong Offensive	2000	
The Bad Earth	Borean Tundra	Horde	All		Chieftain Wintergale	Chieftain Wintergale	Shrouds of the Scourge	250 with The Taunka	20300	5
Vision of Air	Borean Tundra	Horde	All		Spirit Talker Snarlfang	Spirit Talker Snarlfang	Return to the Spirit Talker	10 with Warsong Offensive	2000	
CHOICE OF: 1 Mender's Cover, 1 Regenerative Hide Harness, 1 Chilled Mail Boots, 1 Icy Ripper Ring										
What the Cold Wind Brings...	Borean Tundra	Horde	All		Ith'rix's Hardened Carapace	High Overlord Saurfang		250 with Warsong Offensive	20100	
CHOICE OF: 1 Sweltering Leggings, 1 Marshwalker Waistguard, 1 Plainhunter's Epaulettes, 1 Battle Leader's Breastplate										
Blending In	Borean Tundra	Horde	All		Chieftain Wintergale	Chieftain Wintergale	The Bad Earth	250 with The Taunka	20300	5
Wind Master To'bor	Borean Tundra	Horde	All		Overlord Razgor	Wind Master To'bor	Cutting Off the Source	10 with Warsong Offensive	2000	
Farseer Grimwalker's Spirit	Borean Tundra	Horde	All		Spirit Talker Snarlfang	Farseer Grimwalker's Spirit	Vision of Air	250 with Warsong Offensive	20100	4 70
Magic Carpet Ride	Borean Tundra	Horde	All		Wind Master To'bor	Gorge the Corpsegrinder	Wind Master To'bor	10 with Warsong Offensive	2000	
Kaganishu	Borean Tundra	Horde	All		Farseer Grimwalker's Spirit	Farseer Grimwalker's Spirit	Farseer Grimwalker's Spirit	250 with Warsong Offensive	20300	5
Return My Remains	Borean Tundra	Horde	All		Farseer Grimwalker's Spirit	Spirit Talker Snarlfang	Kaganishu	350 with Warsong Offensive	25150	9 40
CHOICE OF: 1 Lost Marksman's Rifle, 1 Dry Earth Circle, 1 Idol of the Plainstalker, 1 Libram of Furious Blows, 1 Totem of the Tundra, 1 Branch of Everlasting Flame										
Revenge Upon Magmoth	Borean Tundra	Horde	All		Ortrosh	Ortrosh	Vision of Air	250 with Horde Expedition	20100	4 70
CHOICE OF: 1 Layered Frost Robes, 1 Reinforced Caribou-Hide Helm, 1 Spiked Magmoth Mantle, 1 Amberplate Legguards										
Words of Power	Borean Tundra	Horde	All		Chieftain Wintergale	Chieftain Wintergale	Blending In	250 with The Taunka	20300	5
A Courageous Strike	Borean Tundra	Horde	All		Durm Icehide	Durm Icehide	Blending In	250 with The Taunka	20300	5
Tank Ain't Gonna Fix Itself	Borean Tundra	Horde	All		Gorge the Corpsegrinder	Mobu	Magic Carpet Ride	10 with Warsong Offensive	2000	
Mobu's Pneumatic Tank Transjigamarig	Borean Tundra	Horde	All		Mobu	Mobu	Tank Ain't Gonna Fix Itself	250 with Warsong Offensive	20100	
Super Strong Metal Plates!	Borean Tundra	Horde	All		Mobu	Mobu	Tank Ain't Gonna Fix Itself	250 with Warsong Offensive	20100	
Dirty, Stinkin' Snobolds!	Borean Tundra	All	All		Crafty Wobblesprocket	Crafty Wobblesprocket	The Mechagnomes	250 with Valiance Expedition	20100	4 70
The Borean Inquisition	Borean Tundra	All	All		Librarian Donathan	Librarian Normantis	Abduction		5050	
Neutralizing the Cauldrons	Borean Tundra	Horde	All		Sage Aeire	Sage Aeire	Blending In	250 with The Taunka	20300	5
CHOICE OF: 1 Layered Frost Hood, 1 Rhinohide Wristwraps, 1 Spiked Magmoth Gloves, 1 Chilled Pauldrons										
The Art of Persuasion	Borean Tundra	All	All		Archmage Evanor, Librarian Normantis	Librarian Normantis	The Borean Inquisition		15100	3 70
Motes of the Enraged	Borean Tundra	All	All		Imperean	Imperean	Boiling Point		20100	4 70
Just a Few More Things...	Borean Tundra	All	All		Crafty Wobblesprocket	Crafty Wobblesprocket	Dirty, Stinkin' Snobolds!	250 with Valiance Expedition	20100	4 70
Tanks a lot...	Borean Tundra	Horde	All		Mobu	Gorge the Corpsegrinder	Mobu's Pneumatic Tank Transjigamarig, Super Strong Metal Plates!	25 with Warsong Offensive	5050	
The Plains of Nasam	Borean Tundra	Horde	All		Gorge the Corpsegrinder	Garrosh Hellscream	Tanks a lot...	500 with Warsong Offensive	30150	
CHOICE OF: 1 Gorge's Loungewear, 1 Warsong Scout Spaulders, 1 Tank Commander's Treads, 1 Gorge's Breastplate of Bloodrage										
Hah... You're Not So Big Now!	Borean Tundra	All	All		Crafty Wobblesprocket	Crafty Wobblesprocket	Just a Few More Things...	250 with Valiance Expedition	20100	4 70
CHOICE OF: 1 Wizzlenob Shoulder Covers, 1 Reinforced Elastic Band, 1 Ring-Ridden Wrist Protectors, 1 Thin Dexterity Enhancing Tube										
The Spire of Blood	Borean Tundra	Horde	All		Vial of Fresh Blood	Snow Tracker Grumm	Blending In	150 with The Taunka	15250	3 90
Into the Mist	Borean Tundra	All	All		Waltor of Pal'ea	Waltor of Pal'ea		250 with The Kalu'ak	20100	

BOREAN TUNDRA

Title	Location	Faction	Race & Class	Group #	Starter	Finisher	Prerequisite	Reputation	XP	Money
Burn in Effigy	Borean Tundra	All	All		Waltor of Pal'ea	Waltor of Pal'ea	Into the Mist	250 with The Kalu'ak	20100	
CHOICE OF: 1 Seafarer Boots, 1 Seaspeaker Legguards, 1 Talisman of the Tundra, 1 Seabone Heaume										
Plan B	Borean Tundra	All	All		Crafty Wobblesprocket	Crafty Wobblesprocket	Hah... You're Not So Big Now!	250 with Valiance Expedition	20100	4🥈70🥉
Shatter the Orbs!	Borean Tundra	Horde	All		Snow Tracker Grumm	Snow Tracker Junek	The Spire of Blood	250 with The Taunka	20300	5🥈
Horn of the Ancient Mariner	Borean Tundra	All	All		Waltor of Pal'ea	Waltor of Pal'ea		250 with The Kalu'ak	20100	
Orabus the Helmsman	Borean Tundra	All	All		Waltor of Pal'ea	Waltor of Pal'ea	Horn of the Ancient Mariner	250 with The Kalu'ak	20100	14🥈10🥉
CHOICE OF: 1 Transborean Bracers, 1 Floodplain Vest, 1 Pugnacious Collar, 1 Mendicant's Treads										
Seek Out Karuk!	Borean Tundra	All	All		Waltor of Pal'ea	Karuk	Burn in Effigy, Orabus the Helmsman	250 with The Kalu'ak	20100	
Sharing Intelligence	Borean Tundra	All	All		Archmage Evanor, Librarian Normantis	Librarian Donathan	The Art of Persuasion	2000		48🥉
Escaping the Mist	Borean Tundra	Horde	All		Mootoo the Younger	Elder Mootoo		350 with Warsong Offensive	25150	
CHOICE OF: 1 Transborean Wraps, 1 Floodplain Shoulderpads, 1 Westrift Wristguards, 1 Condor-Bone Star										
It Was The Orcs, Honest!	Borean Tundra	All	All		Crafty Wobblesprocket	Crafty Wobblesprocket	Plan B	350 with Valiance Expedition	25400	10🥈
CHOICE OF: 1 Frostbiter, 1 Hungering Greatstaff, 1 Shivering Healer's Cloak, 1 Jagged Icefist, 1 Frostspeaker Collar										
A Race Against Time	Borean Tundra	All	All		Librarian Donathan	Librarian Donathan	Sharing Intelligence		20100	4🥈70🥉
Enlistment Day	Borean Tundra	All	All		Recruitment Officer Blythe	General Arlos		10 with Valiance Expedition	2000	
Get Me Outa Here!	Borean Tundra	All	All		Bonker Togglevolt	Fizzcrank Fullthrottle		350 with Valiance Expedition	25400	10🥈
CHOICE OF: 1 Lost Marksman's Rifle, 1 Dry Earth Circle, 1 Idol of the Plainstalker, 1 Libram of Furious Blows, 1 Totem of the Tundra, 1 Branch of Everlasting Flame										
Sage Highmesa is Missing	Borean Tundra	Horde	All		Greatmother Taiga	Sage Highmesa		10 with The Taunka	2000	
A Proper Death	Borean Tundra	Horde	All		Sage Highmesa	Sage Highmesa	Sage Highmesa is Missing	250 with The Taunka	20100	4🥈70🥉
Merciful Freedom	Borean Tundra	Horde	All		Shadowstalker Canarius	Shadowstalker Canarius	Reinforcements Incoming...	250 with Warsong Offensive	20100	
Stop the Plague	Borean Tundra	Horde	All		Sage Highmesa	Sage Highmesa	A Proper Death	250 with The Taunka	20100	4🥈70🥉
CHOICE OF: 1 Sweltering Handwraps, 1 Rhinohide Mask, 1 Plainhunter's Waistband, 1 Chilled Shoulderplates										
Find Bristlehorn	Borean Tundra	Horde	All		Sage Highmesa	Longrunner Bristlehorn	Stop the Plague	250 with The Taunka	20100	
Reforging the Key	Borean Tundra	All	All		Librarian Donathan	Surristrasz	A Race Against Time			
Taking Wing	Borean Tundra	All	All		Surristrasz	Warmage Anzim	Reforging the Key		2000	48🥉
Rescuing Evanor	Borean Tundra	All	All		Warmage Anzim	Archmage Evanor	Taking Wing		20100	4🥈70🥉
CHOICE OF: 1 Sweltering Belt, 1 Charred Treads, 1 Glimmering Ringmail Gloves, 1 Seething Waistguard										
Dragonspeak	Borean Tundra	All	All		Archmage Evanor	Surristrasz	Rescuing Evanor		10050	2🥈40🥉
Fallen Necropolis	Borean Tundra	Horde	All		Sage Highmesa	Sage Highmesa	Stop the Plague	250 with The Taunka	20100	4🥈70🥉
CHOICE OF: 1 Layered Frost Sandals, 1 Vial of Renewal, 1 Reinforced Caribou-Hide Chestguard, 1 Amberplate Waistguard										
Scouting the Sinkholes	Borean Tundra	Horde	All		Greatfather Mahan	Greatfather Mahan		250 with The Taunka	20100	4🥈70🥉
The Heart of the Elements	Borean Tundra	Horde	All		Greatfather Mahan	Wind Tamer Barah	Scouting the Sinkholes	250 with The Taunka	20100	4🥈70🥉
The Warsong Farms	Borean Tundra	Horde	All		Shadowstalker Ickoris	Shadowstalker Ickoris	Reinforcements Incoming...	250 with Warsong Offensive	20100	
The Doctor and the Lich-Lord	Borean Tundra	Horde	All		Longrunner Bristlehorn	Sage Highmesa	Find Bristlehorn	250 with The Taunka	20300	5🥈
Damned Filthy Swine	Borean Tundra	Horde	All		Farmer Torp	Farmer Torp		250 with Warsong Offensive	20100	
Return with the Bad News	Borean Tundra	Horde	All		Sage Highmesa	Greatmother Taiga	The Doctor and the Lich-Lord	350 with The Taunka	25150	9🥈40🥉
CHOICE OF: 1 Shivering Healer's Ring, 1 Reinforced Caribou-Hide Boots, 1 Spiked Magmoth Chestpiece, 1 Amberplate Headguard, 1 Greatmother's Talisman of Cleansing										
Bring 'Em Back Alive	Borean Tundra	Horde	All		Farmer Torp	Farmer Torp	Damned Filthy Swine	250 with Warsong Offensive	20100	
CHOICE OF: 1 Transborean Cover, 1 Marshwalker Chestpiece, 1 Westrift Leggings, 1 Mightstone Pauldrons										
Check in With Bixie	Borean Tundra	All	All		Mordle Cogspinner	Bixie Wrenchshanker	What's the Matter with the Transmatter?	10 with Valiance Expedition	2000	
Oh Great... Plagued Magnataur!	Borean Tundra	All	All		Bixie Wrenchshanker	Bixie Wrenchshanker	Check in With Bixie	250 with Valiance Expedition	20100	4🥈70🥉
There's Something Going On In Those Caves	Borean Tundra	All	All		Bixie Wrenchshanker	Bixie Wrenchshanker	Oh Great... Plagued Magnataur!	250 with Valiance Expedition	20100	4🥈70🥉
CHOICE OF: 1 Sweltering Handwraps, 1 Rhinohide Mask, 1 Plainhunter's Waistband, 1 Chilled Shoulderplates										
The Horn of Elemental Fury	Borean Tundra	Horde	All		Wind Tamer Barah	Wind Tamer Barah	The Heart of the Elements	250 with The Taunka	20100	4🥈70🥉
Rats, Tinky Went into the Necropolis!	Borean Tundra	All	All		Bixie Wrenchshanker	Tinky Wickwhistle	There's Something Going On In Those Caves	250 with Valiance Expedition	20100	
Might As Well Wipe Out the Scourge	Borean Tundra	All	All		Bixie Wrenchshanker	Bixie Wrenchshanker	There's Something Going On In Those Caves	250 with Valiance Expedition	20100	4🥈70🥉
CHOICE OF: 1 Layered Frost Sandals, 1 Vial of Renewal, 1 Reinforced Caribou-Hide Chestguard, 1 Amberplate Waistguard										

Title	Location	Faction	Race & Class	Group #	Starter	Finisher	Prerequisite	Reputation	XP	Money
I'm Stuck in this Damned Cage... But Not For Long!	Borean Tundra	All	All		Tinky Wickwhistle	Tinky Wickwhistle	Rats, Tinky Went into the Necropolis!	250 with Valiance Expedition	20300	
Let Bixie Know	Borean Tundra	All	All		Tinky Wickwhistle	Bixie Wrenchshanker	I'm Stuck in this Damned Cage... But Not For Long!	10 with Valiance Expedition	2000	
Back to the Airstrip	Borean Tundra	All	All		Bixie Wrenchshanker	Fizzcrank Fullthrottle	Let Bixie Know	350 with Valiance Expedition	25150	9⬤40⬤
CHOICE OF: 1 Shivering Healer's Ring, 1 Reinforced Caribou-Hide Boots, 1 Spiked Magmoth Chestpiece, 1 Amberplate Headguard, 1 Hypergizmatic Energy Booster										
King Mrgl-Mrgl	Borean Tundra	All	All		Supply Master Taz'ishi	King Mrgl-Mrgl			2000	
Get to Getry	Borean Tundra	Horde	All		Shadowstalker Ickoris	Shadowstalker Getry	The Warsong Farms	10 with Warsong Offensive	2000	
King Mrgl-Mrgl	Borean Tundra	All	All		Mordle Cogspinner	King Mrgl-Mrgl	The Mechagnomes		2000	
Foolish Endeavors	Borean Tundra	Horde	All		Shadowstalker Getry	Garrosh Hellscream	Get to Getry	500 with Warsong Offensive	30150	
CHOICE OF: 1 Reinforced Mendicant's Cowl, 1 Graven Shoveltusk Pendant, 1 Benign Crusader's Plate, 1 Ermine Ruff Cloak										
The Collapse	Borean Tundra	Horde	All		Wind Tamer Barah	Wind Tamer Barah	The Horn of Elemental Fury	350 with The Taunka	25150	9⬤40⬤
CHOICE OF: 1 Sweltering Cuffs, 1 Rhinohide Gloves, 1 Plainhunter's Chestpiece, 1 Chilled Greaves										
Distress Call	Borean Tundra	All	All		Airman Skyhopper	Fizzcrank Fullthrottle	Plug the Sinkholes	10 with Valiance Expedition	2000	
The Mechagnomes	Borean Tundra	All	All		Fizzcrank Fullthrottle	Jinky Wingnut		10 with Valiance Expedition	2000	
Nork Bloodfrenzy's Charge	Borean Tundra	Horde	All		Garrosh Hellscream	Warden Nork Bloodfrenzy	Foolish Endeavors	10 with Warsong Offensive	2000	
What's the Matter with the Transmatter?	Borean Tundra	All	All		Mordle Cogspinner	Mordle Cogspinner	The Mechagnomes	250 with Valiance Expedition	20100	4⬤70⬤
Coward Delivery... Under 30 Minutes or it's Free	Borean Tundra	Horde	All		Warden Nork Bloodfrenzy	Scout Tungok	Nork Bloodfrenzy's Charge	150 with Warsong Offensive	15100	
Re-Cursive	Borean Tundra	All	All		Jinky Wingnut	Jinky Wingnut	The Mechagnomes	250 with Valiance Expedition	20100	4⬤70⬤
CHOICE OF: 1 Layered Frost Hood, 1 Rhinohide Wristwraps, 1 Spiked Magmoth Gloves, 1 Chilled Pauldrons										
Scouting the Sinkholes	Borean Tundra	All	All		Abner Fizzletorque	Abner Fizzletorque	Emergency Protocol: Section 8.2, Paragraph D	250 with Valiance Expedition	20100	9⬤40⬤
Vermin Extermination	Borean Tundra	Horde	All		Scout Tungok	Scout Tungok	Coward Delivery... Under 30 Minutes or it's Free	250 with Warsong Offensive	20100	
CHOICE OF: 1 Transborean Mantle, 1 Floodplain Cover, 1 Scout's Signet Ring, 1 Chestguard of Salved Wounds										
Fueling the Project	Borean Tundra	All	All		Abner Fizzletorque	Abner Fizzletorque	Scouting the Sinkholes	250 with Valiance Expedition	20100	4⬤70⬤
The Wondrous Bloodspore	Borean Tundra	Horde	All		Bloodmage Laurith	Bloodmage Laurith		250 with Warsong Offensive	20100	
Pollen from the Source	Borean Tundra	Horde	All		Bloodmage Laurith	Bloodmage Laurith	The Wondrous Bloodspore	250 with Warsong Offensive	20100	
A Bot in Mammoth's Clothing	Borean Tundra	All	All		Abner Fizzletorque	Abner Fizzletorque	Fueling the Project	250 with Valiance Expedition	20100	4⬤70⬤
A Suitable Test Subject	Borean Tundra	Horde	All		Bloodmage Laurith	Bloodmage Laurith	Pollen from the Source	10 with Warsong Offensive	2000	
The Invasion of Gammoth	Borean Tundra	Horde	All		Bloodmage Laurith	Primal Mighthorn	A Suitable Test Subject	10 with Warsong Offensive	2000	
Gammothra the Tormentor	Borean Tundra	Horde	All		Primal Mighthorn	Primal Mighthorn	The Invasion of Gammoth	250 with Warsong Offensive	20100	
Trophies of Gammoth	Borean Tundra	Horde	All		Primal Mighthorn	Garrosh Hellscream	Gammothra the Tormentor	150 with Warsong Offensive	15100	
CHOICE OF: 1 Transborean Leggings, 1 Marshwalker Pauldrons, 1 Tundrastrider Ringmail, 1 Mightstone Helm										
Deploy the Shake-n-Quake!	Borean Tundra	All	All		Abner Fizzletorque	Abner Fizzletorque	A Bot in Mammoth's Clothing	350 with Valiance Expedition	25150	9⬤40⬤
CHOICE OF: 1 Sweltering Cuffs, 1 Rhinohide Gloves, 1 Plainhunter's Chestpiece, 1 Chilled Greaves										
Massive Moth Omelet?	Borean Tundra	Horde	All		Massive Glowing Egg	Bloodmage Laurith		250 with Warsong Offensive	20100	
Finding Pilot Tailspin	Borean Tundra	All	All		Fizzcrank Fullthrottle	Iggy "Tailspin" Cogtoggle	Re-Cursive	10 with Valiance Expedition	2000	
A Little Bit of Spice	Borean Tundra	Alliance	All		Iggy "Tailspin" Cogtoggle	Iggy "Tailspin" Cogtoggle	Finding Pilot Tailspin	250 with Valiance Expedition	20100	4⬤70⬤
A Time for Heroes	Borean Tundra	Alliance	All		General Arlos	Sergeant Hammerhill	Enlistment Day	10 with Valiance Expedition	2000	
Lupus Pupus	Borean Tundra	Alliance	All		Iggy "Tailspin" Cogtoggle	Iggy "Tailspin" Cogtoggle	A Little Bit of Spice	250 with Valiance Expedition	20100	4⬤70⬤
The Ultrasonic Screwdriver	Borean Tundra	All	All		The Ultrasonic Screwdriver	Crafty Wobblesprocket		10 with Valiance Expedition	2000	
Master and Servant	Borean Tundra	All	All		Crafty Wobblesprocket	Crafty Wobblesprocket	The Ultrasonic Screwdriver	350 with Valiance Expedition	25150	9⬤40⬤
CHOICE OF: 1 Layered Frost Robes, 1 Reinforced Caribou-Hide Helm, 1 Spiked Magmoth Mantle, 1 Amberplate Legguards										
Traversing the Rift	Borean Tundra	All	All		Surristrasz	Archmage Berinand	Dragonspeak		15100	3⬤70⬤
Lefty Loosey, Righty Tighty	Borean Tundra	All	All		Jinky Wingnut	Jinky Wingnut	Re-Cursive	350 with Valiance Expedition	25150	9⬤40⬤
A Soldier in Need	Borean Tundra	All	All		Medic Hawthorn	Medic Hawthorn		150 with Valiance Expedition	15100	
REWARD: 2 Super Rejuvenation Potion										

BOREAN TUNDRA

Title	Location	Faction	Race & Class	Group #	Starter	Finisher	Prerequisite	Reputation	XP	Money
Cultists Among Us	Borean Tundra	All	All		Symbol of Death, Cultist Shrine	Captain "Lefty" Lugsail		75 with Valiance Expedition	10050	
Notify Arlos	Borean Tundra	All	All		Admiral Cantlebree	General Arlos	Cultists Among Us	10 with Valiance Expedition	2000	
Enemies of the Light	Borean Tundra	All	All		Harbinger Vurenn	Harbinger Vurenn	Notify Arlos	250 with Valiance Expedition	20100	
CHOICE OF: 1 Marshwalker Legguards, 1 Tundrastrider Coif, 1 Mightstone Breastplate, 1 Harbinger's Wrath										
Further Investigation	Borean Tundra	All	All		Harbinger Vurenn	Vindicator Yaala	Enemies of the Light	25 with Valiance Expedition	5050	
The Hunt is On	Borean Tundra	All	All		Vindicator Yaala	Vindicator Yaala	Further Investigation	250 with Valiance Expedition	20100	
CHOICE OF: 1 Transborean Leggings, 1 Marshwalker Pauldrons, 1 Tundrastrider Ringmail, 1 Mightstone Helm										
Emergency Protocol: Section 8.2, Paragraph C	Borean Tundra	Alliance	All		Iggy "Tailspin" Cogtoggle	Iggy "Tailspin" Cogtoggle	Lupus Pupus	250 with Valiance Expedition	20100	4🟡70⚪
Emergency Protocol: Section 8.2, Paragraph D	Borean Tundra	Alliance	All		Iggy "Tailspin" Cogtoggle	Iggy "Tailspin" Cogtoggle	Emergency Protocol: Section 8.2, Paragraph C	250 with Valiance Expedition	20100	4🟡70⚪
The Siege	Borean Tundra	Alliance	All		Sergeant Hammerhill	Sergeant Hammerhill	A Time for Heroes	250 with Valiance Expedition	20100	4🟡70⚪
CHOICE OF: 1 Combatant Greatsword, 1 Valiance Longbow, 1 Writhing Longstaff, 1 Medic's Morning Star, 1 Soldier's Spiked Mace, 1 Vicious Spellblade										
The Gearmaster	Borean Tundra	All	All		Jinky Wingnut	Fizzcrank Fullthrottle	Lefty Loosey, Righty Tighty	350 with Valiance Expedition	25400	10⚪
CHOICE OF: 1 Mender's Cover, 1 Regenerative Hide Harness, 1 Chilled Mail Boots, 1 Icy Ripper Ring										
A Mission Statement	Borean Tundra	All	All		Arch Druid Lathorius	Arch Druid Lathorius		10 with Cenarion Expedition	2050	
Unfit for Death	Borean Tundra	All	All		Zaza	Zaza	A Mission Statement	250 with Cenarion Expedition	20300	
Ears of Our Enemies	Borean Tundra	All	All		Arch Druid Lathorius	Arch Druid Lathorius	A Mission Statement	250 with Cenarion Expedition	20300	5⚪
Can't Get Ear-nough...	Borean Tundra	All	All		Arch Druid Lathorius	Arch Druid Lathorius	Ears of Our Enemies	150 with Cenarion Expedition	20300	
The Culler Cometh	Borean Tundra	All	All	2	Zaza	Zaza	Unfit for Death	250 with Cenarion Expedition	20300	5⚪
CHOICE OF: 1 Nymph Stockings, 1 Binder's Links, 1 Assailant Shroud, 1 Plainwatcher Legplates										
Happy as a Clam	Borean Tundra	All	All		Hierophant Cenius	Hierophant Cenius	A Mission Statement	250 with Cenarion Expedition	20300	
The Abandoned Reach	Borean Tundra	All	All		Hierophant Cenius	Hierophant Liandra	Happy as a Clam	10 with Cenarion Expedition	2050	
Not On Our Watch	Borean Tundra	All	All		Hierophant Liandra	Hierophant Liandra	The Abandoned Reach	250 with Cenarion Expedition	20300	
The Nefarious Clam Master...	Borean Tundra	All	All		Hierophant Liandra	Hierophant Cenius	Not On Our Watch	250 with Cenarion Expedition	20300	
CHOICE OF: 1 Nimble Blade, 1 Rod of Poacher Punishment, 1 G.E.H.T.A., 1 Borean Ward, 1 Wand of the Keeper, 1 Dowsing Rod										
Give Fizzcrank the News	Borean Tundra	All	All		Iggy "Tailspin" Cogtoggle	Fizzcrank Fullthrottle	Emergency Protocol: Section 8.2, Paragraph D	350 with Valiance Expedition	25150	9🟡40⚪
CHOICE OF: 1 Mantle of Congealed Anger, 1 Reinforced Caribou-Hide Leggings, 1 Spiked Magmoth Helm, 1 Amberplate Grips										
Help Those That Cannot Help Themselves	Borean Tundra	All	All		Arch Druid Lathorius	Arch Druid Lathorius	A Mission Statement	250 with Cenarion Expedition	20300	
Khu'nok Will Know	Borean Tundra	All	All		Arch Druid Lathorius	Khu'nok the Behemoth	Help Those That Cannot Help Themselves	150 with Cenarion Expedition	15250	
Kaw the Mammoth Destroyer	Borean Tundra	All	All		Khu'nok the Behemoth	Arch Druid Lathorius	Khu'nok Will Know	350 with Cenarion Expedition	25400	
CHOICE OF: 1 D.E.H.T.A. Overshirt, 1 Faux Leather Hood, 1 Ethical Epaulettes, 1 Moral Sabatons										
Load 'er Up!	Borean Tundra	Horde	All		Fezzix Geartwist	Fezzix Geartwist			20100	4🟡70⚪
Ned, Lord of Rhinos...	Borean Tundra	All	All	2	Killinger the Den Watcher	Killinger the Den Watcher	A Mission Statement	350 with Cenarion Expedition	25400	
CHOICE OF: 1 Regenerative Cloth, 1 Denwatcher's Leggings, 1 Farseer's Headpiece, 1 Plainkeeper Blockade										
Emergency Supplies	Borean Tundra	All	All		Fizzcrank Recon Pilot	Fezzix Geartwist			20100	4🟡70⚪
Ride to Taunka'le Village	Borean Tundra	Horde	All		Ambassador Talonga	Sage Earth and Sky	The Defense of Warsong Hold, The Defense of Warsong Hold, The Defense of Warsong Hold	10 with The Taunka	2000	
Death From Above	Borean Tundra	Alliance	All		Sergeant Hammerhill	Sergeant Hammerhill	The Siege	250 with Valiance Expedition	20100	4🟡70⚪
What Are They Up To?	Borean Tundra	Horde	All		Sage Earth and Sky	Sage Earth and Sky		250 with The Taunka	20100	4🟡70⚪
The Assassination of Harold Lane	Borean Tundra	All	All	3	Arch Druid Lathorius	Arch Druid Lathorius		500 with Cenarion Expedition	30450	
CHOICE OF: 1 Band of Wholesome Preservation, 1 Ring of Indignant Rage, 1 Activist's Signet of Blasting										
The Power of the Elements	Borean Tundra	Horde	All		Dorain Frosthoof	Dorain Frosthoof	Load 'er Up!	250 with The Taunka	20100	4🟡70⚪
Patching Up	Borean Tundra	Horde	All		Fezzix Geartwist	Fezzix Geartwist	The Power of the Elements		25150	9🟡40⚪
CHOICE OF: 1 Wizzlenob Shoulder Covers, 1 Reinforced Elastic Band, 1 Ring-Ridden Wrist Protectors, 1 Thin Dexterity Enhancing Tube										
Master the Storm	Borean Tundra	Horde	All		Sage Earth and Sky	Sage Earth and Sky	What Are They Up To?	250 with The Taunka	20100	4🟡70⚪

261

Title	Location	Faction	Race & Class	Group #	Starter	Finisher	Prerequisite	Reputation	XP	Money
Weakness to Lightning	Borean Tundra	Horde	All		Sage Earth and Sky	Sage Earth and Sky	Master the Storm	250 with The Taunka	20100	4🟡 70🔴
Plug the Sinkholes	Borean Tundra	Alliance	All		Sergeant Hammerhill	Sergeant Hammerhill	Death From Above	250 with Valiance Expedition	20100	
CHOICE OF: 1 Transborean Cover, 1 Marshwalker Chestpiece, 1 Westrift Leggings, 1 Mightstone Pauldrons										
Breaking Through	Borean Tundra	Horde	All	3	Chieftain Wintergale	Chieftain Wintergale	Words of Power	350 with The Taunka	25150	9🟡 40🔴
CHOICE OF: 1 Chain of Vigilant Thought, 1 Clutch of Undying Will, 1 Choker of Forceful Redemption										
Souls of the Decursed	Borean Tundra	Horde	All		Greatmother Taiga	Greatmother Taiga	Master the Storm	250 with The Taunka	20100	4🟡 70🔴
Military? What Military?	Borean Tundra	Alliance	All		Gerald Green	Plagued Grain		150 with Valiance Expedition	15100	
Pernicious Evidence	Borean Tundra	Alliance	All		Plagued Grain	Gerald Green	Military? What Military?	75 with Valiance Expedition	10050	
It's Time for Action	Borean Tundra	Alliance	All		Gerald Green	Gerald Green	Pernicious Evidence	250 with Valiance Expedition	20100	4🟡 70🔴
CHOICE OF: 1 Transborean Bracers, 1 Floodplain Vest, 1 Pugnacious Collar, 1 Mendicant's Treads										
Fruits of Our Labor	Borean Tundra	Alliance	All		Gerald Green	Gerald Green	It's Time for Action	250 with Valiance Expedition	20100	
Cleaning Up the Pools	Borean Tundra	Horde	All		Iron Eyes	Iron Eyes	Master the Storm	250 with The Taunka	20100	4🟡 70🔴
CHOICE OF: 1 Mantle of Congealed Anger, 1 Reinforced Caribou-Hide Leggings, 1 Spiked Magmoth Helm, 1 Amberplate Grips										
The Sub-Chieftains	Borean Tundra	Horde	All		Sage Earth and Sky	Sage Earth and Sky	Weakness to Lightning	350 with The Taunka	25150	9🟡 40🔴
CHOICE OF: 1 Frostbiter, 1 Frostspeaker Collar, 1 Hungering Greatstaff, 1 Jagged Icefist, 1 Shivering Healer's Cloak										
Reference Material	Borean Tundra	Alliance	All		Jeremiah Hawning	Jeremiah Hawning	Pernicious Evidence	150 with Valiance Expedition	15100	4🟡 70🔴
Defeat the Gearmaster	Borean Tundra	Horde	All		Greatmother Taiga	Greatmother Taiga	Souls of the Decursed	350 with The Taunka	25400	10🟡
CHOICE OF: 1 Taut Driftwood Bow, 1 Stave of the Spiritcaller, 1 Earthborn Greaves, 1 Fireborn Warhammer, 1 Stave of the Windborn										
Take No Chances	Borean Tundra	Alliance	All		Wendy Darren	Wendy Darren	Pernicious Evidence	250 with Valiance Expedition	20100	4🟡 70🔴
CHOICE OF: 1 Transborean Mantle, 1 Floodplain Cover, 1 Scout's Signet Ring, 1 Chestguard of Salved Wounds										
Hellscream's Champion	Borean Tundra	Horde	All		Garrosh Hellscream	Chieftain Wintergale	The Plains of Nasam, Foolish Endeavors, Trophies of Gammoth	500 with Warsong Offensive	30150	
CHOICE OF: 1 Borean Smasher, 1 Axe of Frozen Death, 1 Staff of the Purposeful Mendicant, 1 Fury of the Raging Dragon, 1 Fang of the Desolate Soul, 1 Tower of the Infinite Mind										
Cultists Among Us	Borean Tundra	All	All		Cultist Shrine	Captain "Lefty" Lugsail		75 with Valiance Expedition	10050	
Word on the Street	Borean Tundra	All	All		Mark Hanes	Leryssa	Plug the Sinkholes		2000	
Farshire	Borean Tundra	Alliance	All		Sergeant Hammerhill	Gerald Green	Plug the Sinkholes	10 with Valiance Expedition	2000	
The Fall of Taunka'le Village	Borean Tundra	Horde	All		Chieftain Wintergale	Mother Tauranook	Breaking Through	10 with The Taunka, 10 with Warsong Offensive	2050	
Across Transborea	Borean Tundra	Horde	All		Mother Tauranook	Wartook Iceborn	The Fall of Taunka'le Village	250 with The Taunka, 250 with Warsong Offensive	20300	
Cowards and Fools	Borean Tundra	Alliance	All		Private Brau	Ataika	A Deserter	75 with Valiance Expedition	10050	
Buying Some Time	Borean Tundra	Alliance	All		Thassarian	Thassarian	Finding the Phylactery	250 with Valiance Expedition	20300	
CHOICE OF: 1 Dusk Watcher's Belt, 1 Shadewrap Gloves, 1 Tundrastrider Boots, 1 Death Knight's Anguish										
Words of Power	Borean Tundra	Alliance	All		Thassarian	Thassarian	Buying Some Time	250 with Valiance Expedition	20300	5🟡
Surrounded!	Borean Tundra	All	All		Corporal Venn	Corporal Venn	The Son of Karkut	250 with Valiance Expedition	20300	
CHOICE OF: 1 Sweltering Leggings, 1 Marshwalker Waistguard, 1 Plainhunter's Epaulettes, 1 Battle Leader's Breastplate										
Preparing for the Worst	Borean Tundra	All	All		Utaik	Utaik		250 with The Kalu'ak	20300	5🟡
CHOICE OF: 1 Seafarer Cinch, 1 Whalehunter Cuffs, 1 Sharkproof Boots, 1 Clam Collector Gauntlets										
Not Without a Fight!	Borean Tundra	All	All		Ataika	Ataika		250 with The Kalu'ak	20300	5🟡
CHOICE OF: 1 Iceflow Footwraps, 1 Waverunner Waistband, 1 Landlocked Wristguards, 1 Deep Sea Tuskring										
Muahit's Wisdom	Borean Tundra	All	All		Ataika	Elder Muahit	Not Without a Fight!	250 with The Kalu'ak	20300	
Finding the Phylactery	Borean Tundra	Alliance	All		Thassarian	Thassarian		250 with Valiance Expedition	20100	
Spirits Watch Over Us	Borean Tundra	All	All		Elder Muahit	Elder Muahit	Muahit's Wisdom	150 with The Kalu'ak	15250	3🟡 90🔴
One Last Delivery	Borean Tundra	Alliance	All		Gerald Green	Hilda Stoneforge	Fruits of Our Labor	25 with Valiance Expedition	5050	
Weapons for Farshire	Borean Tundra	Alliance	All		Hilda Stoneforge	Gerald Green	One Last Delivery	25 with Valiance Expedition	5050	
Call to Arms!	Borean Tundra	Alliance	All		Gerald Green	Gerald Green	Weapons for Farshire	250 with Valiance Expedition	20100	
CHOICE OF: 1 Indomitable Choker of Light, 1 Chain of the Tolling Bell, 1 Pendant of Revolutionary Thought										

BOREAN TUNDRA

Title	Location	Faction	Race & Class	Group #	Starter	Finisher	Prerequisite	Reputation	XP	Money
The Tides Turn	Borean Tundra	All	All		Elder Muahit	Elder Muahit	Spirits Watch Over Us	250 with The Kalu'ak	20100	
CHOICE OF: 1 Blubber Grinder, 1 Zook's Walking Stick, 1 Fin Carver, 1 Edge of the Tuskarr, 1 Manual of the Tides										
Navigation Charts (Deprecated)	Borean Tundra	All	All		Karuk	Karuk	Karuk's Oath	250 with The Kalu'ak	20100	4 70
Last Rites	Borean Tundra	Alliance	All	3	Thassarian	Thassarian	Words of Power	500 with Valiance Expedition	30450	15
CHOICE OF: 1 Borean Smasher, 1 Axe of Frozen Death, 1 Staff of the Purposeful Mendicant, 1 Fury of the Raging Dragon, 1 Fang of the Desolate Soul, 1 Tower of the Infinite Mind										
Repurposed Technology	Borean Tundra	Alliance	All		Jeremiah Hawning	Jeremiah Hawning	Reference Material	250 with Valiance Expedition	20100	
CHOICE OF: 1 Weathered Worker Cloak, 1 Marshwalker Boots, 1 Westrift Handcovers, 1 Mightstone Legplates										
The Son of Karkut	Borean Tundra	All	All		Ataika	Corporal Venn	Cowards and Fools	250 with Valiance Expedition	20300	
A Little Help Here? DEPRECATED	Borean Tundra	All	All		Corporal Venn	Corporal Venn		250 with Valiance Expedition	20300	5
Thassarian, the Death Knight	Borean Tundra	All	All		Corporal Venn	Thassarian	Surrounded!	25 with Valiance Expedition	5100	
DEPRECATED	Borean Tundra	All	All		Lieutenant Dumont	Lieutenant Dumont	DEPRECAED	250 with Valiance Expedition	20750	
DEPRECATED	Borean Tundra	All	All		Suspicious Dirt Mound	Cartographer Tobias	Descent into Darkness	250 with Valiance Expedition	20750	
A Diplomatic Mission	Borean Tundra	All	All		Counselor Talbot	Karuk	Notify Arlos		2000	
DEPRECAED	Borean Tundra	All	All		Lieutenant Dumont	Lieutenant Dumont		250 with Valiance Expedition	20750	
Cruelty of the Kvaldir	Borean Tundra	All	All		Karuk	Karuk		150 with The Kalu'ak	15100	
To Bor'gorok Outpost, Quickly!	Borean Tundra	Horde	All		Sauranok the Mystic	Spirit Talkor Snarlfang	The Defense of Warsong Hold, The Defense of Warsong Hold, The Defense of Warsong Hold	10 with Warsong Offensive	2000	
Veehja's Revenge	Borean Tundra	All	All		Veehja	Veehja	A Father's Words		25150	9 40
Monitoring the Rift: Winterfin Cavern	Borean Tundra	All	All		Librarian Garren	Librarian Garren	Monitoring the Rift: Sundered Chasm		25150	9 40
CHOICE OF: 1 Cavernous Gauntlets, 1 Spaulders of Echoing Truth, 1 Wristguards of Rocky Horror, 1 Girdle of Ripped Space										
Herald of War	Borean Tundra	Horde	All		High Overlord Saurfang	Thrall	Darkness Stirs	250 with Warsong Offensive, 250 with Orgrimmar	20750	

COLDARRA

Title	Location	Faction	Race & Class	Group #	Starter	Finisher	Prerequisite	Reputation	XP	Money
Reading the Meters	Coldarra	All	All		Archmage Berinand	Archmage Berinand			20100	4 70
Secrets of the Ancients	Coldarra	All	All		Archmage Berinand	Archmage Berinand			20100	4 70
Nuts for Berries	Coldarra	All	All		Librarian Serrah	Librarian Serrah			20100	4 70
Keep the Secret Safe	Coldarra	All	All		Librarian Serrah	Librarian Serrah	Nuts for Berries		20100	4 70
CHOICE OF: 1 Cauterizing Chain Strand, 1 Seared Scale Cape, 1 Gauntlets of the Crimson Guardian, 1 Serrah's Star										
Basic Training	Coldarra	All	All		Raelorasz	Raelorasz			20100	4 70
Drake Hunt	Coldarra	All	All		Raelorasz	Raelorasz	Hatching a Plan		20100	4 70
CHOICE OF: 1 Sweltering Robes, 1 Charred Drakehide Belt, 1 Flame Infused Bindings, 1 Helm of the Crimson Drakonid										
Cracking the Code	Coldarra	All	All		Raelorasz	Raelorasz	Drake Hunt		20100	4 70
Hatching a Plan	Coldarra	All	All		Raelorasz	Raelorasz	Basic Training		20100	4 70
?????	Coldarra	All	All				Cracking the Code			
Drake Hunt	Coldarra	All	All		Raelorasz	Raelorasz	Drake Hunt		20100	4 70
Puzzling...	Coldarra	All	All		Scintillating Fragment	Raelorasz			20100	4 70
The Cell	Coldarra	All	All		Raelorasz	Raelorasz	Puzzling...		20100	4 70
REWARD: 1 Augmented Arcane Prison										
Keristrasza	Coldarra	All	All		Keristrasza	Keristrasza	The Cell		2000	48
Bait and Switch	Coldarra	All	All		Keristrasza	Keristrasza	Keristrasza		20100	4 70
Saragosa's End	Coldarra	All	All		Keristrasza	Keristrasza	Bait and Switch		20100	4 70
CHOICE OF: 1 Flame Hardened Waistband, 1 Flame Hardened Wristbindings, 1 Cauterizing Chain Leggings, 1 Fury of the Crimson Drake										
Mustering the Reds	Coldarra	All	All		Keristrasza	Raelorasz	Saragosa's End		10050	2 40
Springing the Trap	Coldarra	All	All		Raelorasz	Raelorasz	Mustering the Reds		20100	4 70
CHOICE OF: 1 Crimson Will, 1 Serrated Scale Shank, 1 Fiery Prod, 1 Rod of the Crimson Keeper, 1 Smoldering Talon, 1 Scaled Flame Cloak										
Corastrasza	Coldarra	All	All		Librarian Serrah	Corastrasza			5500	1 90
Aces High!	Coldarra	All	All		Corastrasza	Corastrasza	Corastrasza		27550	14 80
CHOICE OF: 1 Assault Hauberk, 1 Incursion Vestments, 1 Vest of the Assailant, 1 Besieging Breastplate										

DRAGONBLIGHT

Title	Location	Faction	Race & Class	Group #	Starter	Finisher	Prerequisite	Reputation	XP	Money
Let Nothing Go To Waste	Dragonblight	All	All		Elder Ko'nani	Elder Ko'nani		250 with The Kalu'ak	20300	5
Slay Loguhn	Dragonblight	All	All		Elder Ko'nani	Elder Ko'nani	Let Nothing Go To Waste	350 with The Kalu'ak	25650	10 60
CHOICE OF: 1 Sharkdiver's Bracers, 1 Gleaming Tuskring, 1 Sea Rusted Gauntlets, 1 Baleen Braided Collar										

Title	Location	Faction	Race & Class	Group #	Starter	Finisher	Prerequisite	Reputation	XP	Money
Planning for the Future	Dragonblight	All	All		Trapper Mau'i	Trapper Mau'i		250 with The Kalu'ak	20300	5🟤
A Tauren Among Taunka	Dragonblight	Horde	All		Wartook Iceborn	Emissary Brighthoof	Across Transborea	10 with The Taunka, 10 with Warsong Offensive	2050	
Into the Fold	Dragonblight	Horde	All		Emissary Brighthoof	Emissary Brighthoof		250 with The Taunka, 250 with Warsong Offensive	20300	
The Taunka and the Tauren	Dragonblight	Horde	All		Senior Sergeant Juktok	Emissary Brighthoof		10 with The Taunka, 10 with Warsong Offensive	2050	
Pride of the Horde	Dragonblight	Horde	All		Blood Guard Roh'kill	Blood Guard Roh'kill		250 with Warsong Offensive	20300	

CHOICE OF: 1 Spiderwarder Braces, 1 Glade Wanderer Belt, 1 Breastplate of Sizzling Chitin, 1 Scarab of Isanoth, 1 Legplates of the Agmar Preserver

Title	Location	Faction	Race & Class	Group #	Starter	Finisher	Prerequisite	Reputation	XP	Money
Blood Oath of the Horde	Dragonblight	Horde	All		Emissary Brighthoof	Emissary Brighthoof	Into the Fold	150 with The Taunka, 150 with Warsong Offensive	15250	
Your Presence is Required at Stars' Rest	Dragonblight	Alliance	All		Emissary Skyhaven	Image of Archmage Modera		10 with Kirin Tor	2050	
Your Presence is Required at Agmar's Hammer	Dragonblight	Horde	All		Envoy Ripfang	Image of Archmage Aethas Sunreaver		10 with Kirin Tor	2050	
Rifle the Bodies	Dragonblight	All	All		Image of Archmage Aethas Sunreaver	Image of Archmage Aethas Sunreaver		250 with Kirin Tor	20300	5🟤
Rifle the Bodies	Dragonblight	All	All		Image of Archmage Modera	Image of Archmage Modera		250 with Kirin Tor	20300	5🟤
Prevent the Accord	Dragonblight	All	All		Image of Archmage Modera	Image of Archmage Modera	Rifle the Bodies	350 with Kirin Tor	25650	10🟤 60🟤

CHOICE OF: 1 Kirin Tor Initiate's Cowl, 1 Violet Stalker Bracers, 1 Azurehunter Legguards, 1 Dalaran Sentry Headguard

Title	Location	Faction	Race & Class	Group #	Starter	Finisher	Prerequisite	Reputation	XP	Money
Prevent the Accord	Dragonblight	All	All		Image of Archmage Aethas Sunreaver	Image of Archmage Aethas Sunreaver	Rifle the Bodies	350 with Kirin Tor	25650	10🟤 60🟤

CHOICE OF: 1 Kirin Tor Initiate's Cowl, 1 Violet Stalker Bracers, 1 Azurehunter Legguards, 1 Dalaran Sentry Headguard

Title	Location	Faction	Race & Class	Group #	Starter	Finisher	Prerequisite	Reputation	XP	Money
Avenge this Atrocity!	Dragonblight	All	All		Ethenial Moonshadow	Ethenial Moonshadow			20300	5🟤
Agmar's Hammer	Dragonblight	Horde	All		Emissary Brighthoof	Overlord Agmar	Blood Oath of the Horde	150 with Warsong Offensive	15250	
Tua'kea's Crab Traps	Dragonblight	All	All		Tua'kea	Tua'kea	Slay Loguhn	250 with The Kalu'ak	20300	5🟤
Signs of Big Watery Trouble	Dragonblight	All	All		Wrecked Crab Trap	Tua'kea		10 with The Kalu'ak	2050	50🟤
End Arcanimus	Dragonblight	All	All		Ethenial Moonshadow	Ethenial Moonshadow	Avenge this Atrocity!		25650	10🟤 60🟤

CHOICE OF: 1 Fading Handwraps, 1 Ring of the Afterlife, 1 Deathtouched Boots, 1 Crystalplate Pauldrons

Title	Location	Faction	Race & Class	Group #	Starter	Finisher	Prerequisite	Reputation	XP	Money
Test Quest for Craig	Dragonblight	All	All	2	[Demo] Craig Amai	[Demo] Craig Amai		250 with The League of Arathor, 250 with Orgrimmar	10050	
The Bait	Dragonblight	All	All		Tua'kea	Tua'kea	Signs of Big Watery Trouble	250 with The Kalu'ak	20300	5🟤
Meat on the Hook	Dragonblight	All	All		Tua'kea	Tua'kea	The Bait	350 with The Kalu'ak	25650	10🟤 60🟤

CHOICE OF: 1 Fisherman's Earwarmer, 1 Moa'ki Thresherhide Tunic, 1 Sharkdiver's Leggings, 1 Crustacean Stompers

Title	Location	Faction	Race & Class	Group #	Starter	Finisher	Prerequisite	Reputation	XP	Money
Sweet Revenge	Dragonblight	All	All		Stone Hunk O' Gargoyle				20500	5🟤 30🟤
A Letter Home	Dragonblight	All	All		A Letter Home				20500	5🟤 30🟤
Sweeter Revenge	Dragonblight	All	All				Sweet Revenge		20500	5🟤 30🟤
Recording the Fallen	Dragonblight	All	All						20500	5🟤 30🟤
A Scarlet Among Us	Dragonblight	All	All						20500	5🟤 30🟤
Spiritual Insight	Dragonblight	All	All		Toalu'u the Mystic	Toalu'u the Mystic	Slay Loguhn	250 with The Kalu'ak	20300	5🟤
Elder Mana'loa	Dragonblight	All	All		Toalu'u the Mystic	Elder Mana'loa	Spiritual Insight	250 with The Kalu'ak	20300	5🟤
Freedom for the Lingering	Dragonblight	All	All		Elder Mana'loa	Elder Mana'loa	Elder Mana'loa	250 with The Kalu'ak	20300	5🟤
Conversing With the Depths	Dragonblight	All	All		Elder Mana'loa	Toalu'u the Mystic	Freedom for the Lingering	500 with The Kalu'ak	25400	10🟤

CHOICE OF: 1 Chilled Headsmasher, 1 Imported Ironshod Crossbow, 1 Staff of the Spiked Beast, 1 Carved Dragonbone Mace, 1 Gleaming Iceblade, 1 Frostbite Warstaff

Title	Location	Faction	Race & Class	Group #	Starter	Finisher	Prerequisite	Reputation	XP	Money
Message from the West	Dragonblight	Horde	All		Messenger Torvus	Messenger Torvus	Hellscream's Champion	150 with Warsong Offensive	15250	
Victory Nears...	Dragonblight	Horde	All		Overlord Agmar	Senior Sergeant Juktok	Agmar's Hammer	10 with Warsong Offensive	2050	
From the Depths of Azjol-Nerub	Dragonblight	Horde	All		Senior Sergeant Juktok	Senior Sergeant Juktok	Victory Nears...	250 with Warsong Offensive	20300	
Black Blood of Yogg-Saron	Dragonblight	Horde	All		Borus Ironbender	Borus Ironbender	Victory Nears...	250 with Warsong Offensive	20300	
An Enemy in Arthas	Dragonblight	All	All		Kilix the Unraveler	Kilix the Unraveler			20300	
The Lost Empire	Dragonblight	Horde	All		Kilix the Unraveler	Overlord Agmar	An Enemy in Arthas	150 with Horde Expedition	15250	

CHOICE OF: 1 Wastewind Cinch, 1 Snowfall Reaver Gloves, 1 Iceshear Bindings, 1 Stonepath Sabatons

DRAGONBLIGHT

Title	Location	Faction	Race & Class	Group #	Starter	Finisher	Prerequisite	Reputation	XP	Money
Nozzlerust Defense	Dragonblight	All	All		Narf	Narf			20750	5 60
Stocking Up	Dragonblight	All	All		Xink	Xink			20750	5 60
Shaved Ice	Dragonblight	All	All		Zivlix	Zivlix			20750	5 60
Soft Packaging	Dragonblight	All	All		Zivlix	Zivlix	Shaved Ice		20750	5 60
Something That Doesn't Melt	Dragonblight	All	All		Zivlix	Zivlix	Soft Packaging		20750	5 60
CHOICE OF: 1 Refractive Shoulderpads, 1 Hyper-amplified Natural Leather Vest, 1 Tightened Chainmesh Boots, 1 Automated Weapon Coater, 1 Thunder Capacitor											
Scourge Armaments	Dragonblight	Horde	All		Borus Ironbender	Borus Ironbender	Black Blood of Yogg-Saron	250 with Warsong Offensive	20300	
CHOICE OF: 1 Wastewind Leggings, 1 Snowfall Reaver Leggings, 1 Anub'ar-Husk Helm, 1 Stonepath Chestguard											
Hard to Swallow	Dragonblight	All	All		Xink	Xink	Soft Packaging		20750	5 60
Lumber Hack	Dragonblight	All	All		Xink	Xink	Something That Doesn't Melt		20750	5 60
CHOICE OF: 1 Mounted Boneshredder, 1 Coldwind Scratching Pole, 1 Composite Harpyspine Staff, 1 Compact Explosive Delivery Device, 1 Reactive Waraxe, 1 Infused Dragonbone Splinter											
Rustling Some Feathers	Dragonblight	All	All		Narf	Narf	Something That Doesn't Melt		20750	5 60
Harp on This!	Dragonblight	All	All		Narf	Narf	Something That Doesn't Melt		25950	11 20
CHOICE OF: 1 Miraculous Waistwarming Band, 1 Narf's Explosiveproof Strand, 1 Serrated Chain Links, 1 Experimental Utility Belt											
The Might of the Horde	Dragonblight	Horde	All		Senior Sergeant Juktok	Senior Sergeant Juktok	From the Depths of Azjol-Nerub	250 with Warsong Offensive	20300	
CHOICE OF: 1 Frontrunner's Blessed Handwraps, 1 Snowfall Reaver Boots, 1 Westwind Waistband, 1 Stonepath Gauntlets											
A Strange Device	Dragonblight	All	All		Goramosh's Strange Device	Image of Archmage Modera	Rifle the Bodies	75 with Kirin Tor	10150	
Marked for Death: High Cultist Zangus	Dragonblight	Horde	All		Captain Gort	Captain Gort	Victory Nears...	250 with Warsong Offensive	20300	
The Flesh-Bound Tome	Dragonblight	Horde	All		Flesh-bound Tome	Captain Gort	Marked for Death: High Cultist Zangus	250 with Warsong Offensive	20300	
A Strange Device	Dragonblight	All	All		Goramosh's Strange Device	Image of Archmage Aethas Sunreaver	Rifle the Bodies	75 with Kirin Tor	10150	
Projections and Plans	Dragonblight	All	All		Image of Archmage Modera	Image of Archmage Modera	A Strange Device	250 with Kirin Tor	20300	5
Projections and Plans	Dragonblight	All	All		Image of Archmage Aethas Sunreaver	Image of Archmage Aethas Sunreaver	A Strange Device	250 with Kirin Tor	20300	5
Strength of Icemist	Dragonblight	Horde	All		Greatmother Icemist	Banthok Icemist	From the Depths of Azjol-Nerub	150 with Horde Expedition, 150 with The Taunka	15250	
Chains of the Anub'ar	Dragonblight	Horde	All		Banthok Icemist	Banthok Icemist	Strength of Icemist	250 with Horde Expedition, 250 with The Taunka	20300	
CHOICE OF: 1 Wastewind Pauldrons, 1 Snowfall Reaver Pauldrons, 1 Anub'ar-Husk Shoulderguards, 1 Stonepath Pauldrons											
The Focus on the Beach	Dragonblight	All	All		Image of Archmage Modera	Image of Archmage Modera	Projections and Plans	250 with Kirin Tor	20300	5
The Focus on the Beach	Dragonblight	All	All		Image of Archmage Aethas Sunreaver	Image of Archmage Aethas Sunreaver	Projections and Plans	250 with Kirin Tor	20300	5
A Letter for Home	Dragonblight	Alliance	All		Captain Malin's Letter	Commander Saia Azuresteel		250 with Valiance Expedition	20300	5
Return of the High Chief	Dragonblight	Horde	All		Banthok Icemist	Overlord Agmar	Chains of the Anub'ar	500 with Horde Expedition, 500 with The Taunka	30750	
Attack by Air!	Dragonblight	Horde	All		Senior Sergeant Juktok	Valnok Windrager	The Might of the Horde	10 with Warsong Offensive	2050	
Blightbeasts be Damned!	Dragonblight	Horde	All		Valnok Windrager	Valnok Windrager	Attack by Air!	250 with Warsong Offensive	20300	
CHOICE OF: 1 Wastewind Bracers, 1 Glade Wanderer Bracers, 1 Scourge Ghoul Collar, 1 Petrified Bone Chestguard											
Slim Pickings	Dragonblight	All	All		Zort	Zort			20750	5 60
Messy Business	Dragonblight	All	All		Zort	Zort	Slim Pickings		20750	5 60
Apply This Twice a Day	Dragonblight	All	All		Zort	Ko'char the Unbreakable	Messy Business		20750	5 60
REWARD: 1 Zort's Protective Elixir											
Worm Wrangler	Dragonblight	All	All		Zort	Zort	Apply This Twice A Day		20750	5 60
Stomping Grounds	Dragonblight	All	All		Ko'char the Unbreakable	Ko'char the Unbreakable	Slim Pickings		20750	5 60
Really Big Worm	Dragonblight	All	All	3	Ko'char the Unbreakable	Ko'char the Unbreakable	Apply This Twice A Day		31150	16 80
CHOICE OF: 1 Thin Jormungar Legwraps, 1 Rattlebore Slayer Leggings, 1 Ice Heart Chestguard, 1 Crystalplate Legguards											
Atop the Woodlands	Dragonblight	All	All		Image of Archmage Modera	Image of Archmage Modera	The Focus on the Beach	250 with Kirin Tor	20300	5
CHOICE OF: 1 Kirin Tor Initiate's Sandals, 1 Violet Stalker Shoulderpads, 1 Azurehunter Handguards, 1 Dalaran Sentry Wristbraces											
Atop the Woodlands	Dragonblight	All	All		Image of Archmage Aethas Sunreaver	Image of Archmage Aethas Sunreaver	The Focus on the Beach	250 with Kirin Tor	20300	5
CHOICE OF: 1 Kirin Tor Initiate's Sandals, 1 Violet Stalker Shoulderpads, 1 Azurehunter Handguards, 1 Dalaran Sentry Wristbraces											
A Letter for Home	Dragonblight	Horde	All		Lieutenant Ta'zinni's Letter	Overlord Agmar		250 with Warsong Offensive	20300	5
Wanted: Magister Keldonus	Dragonblight	Horde	All	3	Wanted!	Captain Gort		350 with Warsong Offensive	25950	11 20
CHOICE OF: 1 Magister's Bane, 1 Mageslayer Rifle, 1 Endurance of the Spell Warder, 1 Backtwister, 1 Bloodsmeared Brutalizer, 1 Keldonus's Missing Spellshard											

Title	Location	Faction	Race & Class	Group #	Starter	Finisher	Prerequisite	Reputation	XP	Money
Wanted: Gigantaur	Dragonblight	Horde	All	3	Wanted!	Captain Gort		350 with Horde Expedition	25950	11 🟡 20 🟤
CHOICE OF: 1 Chaos Mender Cloak, 1 Lothalar Woodwalker Bracers, 1 Ridgehunter Gauntlets, 1 Plated Magnataur Leggings										
Wanted: Dreadtalon	Dragonblight	Horde	All	3	Wanted!	Captain Gort		350 with Warsong Offensive	25950	11 🟡 20 🟤
CHOICE OF: 1 Feathers of the Dragon Wastes, 1 Lothalar Woodwalker Shoulders, 1 Ridgehunter Chestguard, 1 Dreadtalon's Clutch										
Strengthen the Ancients	Dragonblight	All	All		Sarendryana	Sarendryana	The Focus on the Beach	250 with Valiance Expedition	20300	5 🟤
CHOICE OF: 1 Bracers of Nature's Fury, 1 Lothalar Woodwalker Belt, 1 Star's Rest Treads, 1 Bark Covered Pauldrons										
To Dragon's Fall	Dragonblight	Horde	All	5	Captain Gort	Rokhan	Wanted: Magister Keldonus, Wanted: Gigantaur, Wanted: Dreadtalon	10 with Warsong Offensive	2100	
Strengthen the Ancients	Dragonblight	Horde	All		Earthwarden Grife	Earthwarden Grife	The Focus on the Beach	250 with Horde Expedition	20300	5 🟤
CHOICE OF: 1 Bracers of Nature's Fury, 1 Lothalar Woodwalker Belt, 1 Star's Rest Treads, 1 Bark Covered Pauldrons										
Sarathstra, Scourge of the North	Dragonblight	Horde	All	5	Rokhan	Captain Gort	To Dragon's Fall	500 with Warsong Offensive	31450	17 🟡 70 🟤
CHOICE OF: 1 Wrap of Vigorous Destruction, 1 Belt of Vengeful Purification, 1 Links of Righteous Persecution, 1 Girdle of Forceful Annihilation										
Search Indu'le Village	Dragonblight	All	All		Image of Archmage Modera	Mage-Commander Evenstar	Atop the Woodlands	250 with Kirin Tor	20300	5 🟤
Containing the Rot	Dragonblight	Horde	All		Soar Hawkfury	Soar Hawkfury	Victory Nears...	250 with Warsong Offensive	20300	
The Good Doctor...	Dragonblight	Horde	All		Soar Hawkfury	Doctor Sintar Malefious	Containing the Rot	10 with Warsong Offensive	2050	
In Search of the Ruby Lilac	Dragonblight	Horde	All		Blight Doctor, Blight Doctor, Doctor Sintar Malefious	Doctor Sintar Malefious	The Good Doctor...	250 with Warsong Offensive	20500	
Return to Soar	Dragonblight	Horde	All		Blight Doctor, Blight Doctor, Doctor Sintar Malefious	Soar Hawkfury	In Search of the Ruby Lilac	10 with Warsong Offensive	2050	
Search Indu'le Village	Dragonblight	All	All		Image of Archmage Aethas Sunreaver	Mage-Commander Evenstar	Atop the Woodlands	250 with Kirin Tor	20300	5 🟤
The End of the Line	Dragonblight	All	All		Mage-Commander Evenstar	Image of Archmage Modera	Search Indu'le Village	350 with Kirin Tor	25400	10 🟤
CHOICE OF: 1 Daschal's Discarded Shiv, 1 Mace of the Violet Guardian, 1 Staff of the Ley Mender, 1 Mana Infused Claw, 1 Tome of the Violet Tower										
The End of the Line	Dragonblight	All	All		Mage-Commander Evenstar	Image of Archmage Aethas Sunreaver	Search Indu'le Village	350 with Kirin Tor	25400	10 🟤
CHOICE OF: 1 Daschal's Discarded Shiv, 1 Mace of the Violet Guardian, 1 Staff of the Ley Mender, 1 Mana Infused Claw, 1 Tome of the Violet Tower										
Where the Wild Things Roam	Dragonblight	Horde	All		Soar Hawkfury	Soar Hawkfury	Return to Soar	250 with Warsong Offensive	20500	5 🟡 30 🟤
CHOICE OF: 1 Battleworn Magnataur Crusher, 1 Crossbow of the Hardened Ranger, 1 Moonrest Garden Stave, 1 Keen Woodland Shank, 1 Spiked Coldwind Club, 1 Staff of Ruby Wood										
Stiff Negotiations	Dragonblight	All	All		Narf	Zort	Lumber Hack, Harp on This!		15550	4 🟡 40 🟤
Koltira and the Language of Death	Dragonblight	Horde	All		Captain Gort	Koltira Deathweaver	The Flesh-Bound Tome	10 with Warsong Offensive	2050	
Travel to Moa'ki Harbor	Dragonblight	All	All		Hotawa	Elder Ko'nani	The Tides Turn	10 with The Kalu'ak	2050	
CHOICE OF: 1 Wandering Healer's Kilt, 1 Durable Worghide Cape, 1 Choker of the Northern Wind, 1 Grips of the Windswept Plains										
Travel to Moa'ki Harbor	Dragonblight	All	All		Anuniaq	Elder Ko'nani	Avenge Iskaal	10 with The Kalu'ak	2050	
CHOICE OF: 1 Wandering Healer's Kilt, 1 Durable Worghide Cape, 1 Choker of the Northern Wind, 1 Grips of the Windswept Plains										
Gaining an Audience	Dragonblight	All	All		Image of Archmage Modera	Tariolstrasz	The End of the Line	25 with The Wyrmrest Accord	5100	
Gaining an Audience	Dragonblight	All	All		Image of Archmage Aethas Sunreaver	Tariolstrasz	The End of the Line	25 with The Wyrmrest Accord	5100	
Informing the Queen	Dragonblight	All	All		Tariolstrasz	Alexstrasza the Life-Binder	The Steward of Wyrmrest Temple	10 with The Wyrmrest Accord	2100	
Informing the Queen	Dragonblight	All	All		Tariolstrasz	Alexstrasza the Life-Binder	The Steward of Wyrmrest Temple	10 with The Wyrmrest Accord	2100	
In Service of Blood	Dragonblight	Horde	All		Koltira Deathweaver	Koltira Deathweaver	Koltira and the Language of Death	250 with Warsong Offensive	20500	
In Service of the Unholy	Dragonblight	Horde	All		Koltira Deathweaver	Koltira Deathweaver	Koltira and the Language of Death	350 with Warsong Offensive	25650	
In Service of Frost	Dragonblight	Horde	All		Koltira Deathweaver	Koltira Deathweaver	Koltira and the Language of Death	250 with Warsong Offensive	20500	
The Power to Destroy	Dragonblight	Horde	All		Koltira Deathweaver	Koltira Deathweaver	In Service of Blood, In Service of the Unholy, In Service of Frost	250 with Warsong Offensive	20500	
The Translated Tome	Dragonblight	Horde	All		Koltira Deathweaver	Captain Gort	The Power to Destroy	500 with Warsong Offensive	30750	15 🟡 90 🟤
CHOICE OF: 1 Wastewind Headcover, 1 Snowfall Reaver Breastplate, 1 Anub'ar-Husk Leggings, 1 Stonepath Helm										
All Hail Roanauk!	Dragonblight	Horde	All		Overlord Agmar	Overlord Agmar	Return of the High Chief	250 with Warsong Offensive	20500	
CHOICE OF: 1 Suntouched Flowers, 1 Honorborn Cloak, 1 Petrified Bone Footguards, 1 Oath Signet										

DRAGONBLIGHT

Title	Location	Faction	Race & Class	Group #	Starter	Finisher	Prerequisite	Reputation	XP	Money
Pest Control	Dragonblight	Alliance	All		Duane	Duane		250 with Valiance Expedition	20500	5🟤 30🟠
Canyon Chase	Dragonblight	Alliance	All		Duane	Duane	Pest Control	250 with Valiance Expedition	20500	5🟤 30🟠
CHOICE OF: 1 Wyrmward Cover, 1 Canyon Runner's Vest, 1 Wyrmchaser's Waistguard, 1 Wyrmbane Wristguards										
Pest Control	Dragonblight	Horde	All		Kontokanis	Kontokanis		250 with Warsong Offensive	20500	5🟤 30🟠
Canyon Chase	Dragonblight	Horde	All		Kontokanis	Kontokanis	Pest Control	250 with Warsong Offensive	20500	5🟤 30🟠
CHOICE OF: 1 Wyrmward Cover, 1 Canyon Runner's Vest, 1 Wyrmchaser's Waistguard, 1 Wyrmbane Wristguards										
Disturbing Implications	Dragonblight	All	All		Emblazoned Battle Horn	Aurastrasza		250 with The Wyrmrest Accord	20500	5🟤 30🟠
Disturbing Implications	Dragonblight	All	All		Emblazoned Battle Horn	Aurastrasza		250 with The Wyrmrest Accord	20500	5🟤 30🟠
One of a Kind	Dragonblight	All	All	2	Aurastrasza	Aurastrasza	Disturbing Implications, Disturbing Implications	250 with The Wyrmrest Accord	20500	5🟤 30🟠
Mighty Magnataur	Dragonblight	All	All	2	Aurastrasza	Aurastrasza	One of a Kind	250 with The Wyrmrest Accord	20500	5🟤 30🟠
Reclusive Runemaster	Dragonblight	All	All	3	Aurastrasza	Aurastrasza	Mighty Magnataur	350 with The Wyrmrest Accord	25950	11🟤 20🟠
Wanton Warlord	Dragonblight	All	All	3	Aurastrasza	Aurastrasza	Reclusive Runemaster	350 with The Wyrmrest Accord	31150	16🟤 80🟠
CHOICE OF: 1 Battered Magnataur Dualblade, 1 Longbow of the Ruby Rider, 1 Shortblade of the Ruby Ally, 1 Taigasha, 1 Emme's Lost Spellblade, 1 Life Binder Talisman										
The Lost Courier	Dragonblight	All	All		Private Casey	Courier Lanson		25 with Valiance Expedition	5100	
The Liquid Fire of Elune	Dragonblight	Alliance	All		Warden Jodi Moonsong	Warden Jodi Moonsong		250 with Valiance Expedition	20300	5🟤
Kill the Cultists	Dragonblight	Alliance	All		Warden Jodi Moonsong	Warden Jodi Moonsong	The Liquid Fire of Elune	250 with Valiance Expedition	20300	5🟤
The Favor of Zangus	Dragonblight	Alliance	All		The Favor of Zangus	Warden Jodi Moonsong	The Liquid Fire of Elune	10 with Valiance Expedition	2050	
The High Cultist	Dragonblight	Alliance	All		Warden Jodi Moonsong	Warden Jodi Moonsong	The Favor of Zangus	350 with Valiance Expedition	25400	10🟤
CHOICE OF: 1 Wastewind Leggings, 1 Snowfall Reaver Leggings, 1 Anub'ar-Husk Helm, 1 Stonepath Chestguard										
Of Traitors and Treason	Dragonblight	All	All		Courier Lanson	Palena Silvercloud		10 with Valiance Expedition	2050	
High Commander Halford Wyrmbane	Dragonblight	All	All		Palena Silvercloud	High Commander Halford Wyrmbane	Of Traitors and Treason	10 with Valiance Expedition	2050	
To Venomspite!	Dragonblight	Horde	All		Tobias Sarkhoff	Chief Plaguebringer Middleton	Give it a Name	10 with The Hand of Vengeance	2050	
The Forsaken Blight and You: How Not to Die	Dragonblight	Horde	All		Chief Plaguebringer Middleton	Chief Plaguebringer Middleton		250 with The Hand of Vengeance	20300	
CHOICE OF: 1 Wastewind Handwraps, 1 Spiritfury Bands, 1 Belt of Ghostly Essence, 1 Wraithshimmer Legplates										
Imbeciles Abound!	Dragonblight	Horde	All		Blight Doctor, Blight Doctor, Doctor Sintar Malefious	Chief Plaguebringer Middleton		25 with The Hand of Vengeance	5100	
Emerald Dragon Tears	Dragonblight	Horde	All		Chief Plaguebringer Middleton	Chief Plaguebringer Middleton	The Forsaken Blight and You: How Not to Die	250 with The Hand of Vengeance	20300	
Wanted: The Scarlet Onslaught	Dragonblight	Horde	All		Wanted Poster	High Executor Wroth		250 with The Hand of Vengeance	20300	5🟤
Blighted Last Rites	Dragonblight	Horde	All		Apothecary Vicky Levine	Apothecary Vicky Levine		10 with The Hand of Vengeance	2050	50🟠
Materiel Plunder	Dragonblight	Horde	All		Quartermaster Bartlett	Quartermaster Bartlett		250 with The Hand of Vengeance	20300	5🟤
Let Them Not Rise!	Dragonblight	Horde	All		Apothecary Vicky Levine	Apothecary Vicky Levine	Blighted Last Rites	250 with The Hand of Vengeance	20300	5🟤
CHOICE OF: 1 Chilled Headsmasher, 1 Imported Ironshod Crossbow, 1 Staff of the Spiked Beast, 1 Carved Dragonbone Mace, 1 Gleaming Iceblade, 1 Frostbite Warstaff										
Fresh Remounts	Dragonblight	Horde	All		Hansel Bauer	Hansel Bauer	Materiel Plunder	250 with The Hand of Vengeance	20300	5🟤
Spread the Good Word	Dragonblight	Horde	All		Chief Plaguebringer Middleton	Chief Plaguebringer Middleton	Emerald Dragon Tears	250 with The Hand of Vengeance	20300	
The Forsaken Blight	Dragonblight	Horde	All		Chief Plaguebringer Middleton	Doctor Sintar Malefious	Spread the Good Word	150 with The Hand of Vengeance	15250	
CHOICE OF: 1 Battlement Enforcer's Axe, 1 Siege Captain's Gun, 1 Mace of the Fallen Raven Priest, 1 Idol of the Wastes, 1 Stronghold Battlemace, 1 Bloodtinged Spellblade										
The Kor'kron Vanguard!	Dragonblight	All	All		Overlord Agmar	Saurfang the Younger	All Hail Roanauk!, The Forsaken Blight, Blightbeasts be Damned!	25 with Warsong Offensive	5150	
CHOICE OF: 1 Implacable Zombie Crushers, 1 Reinforced Traveler's Boots, 1 Sandals of Chaos Resolution, 1 Treads of the Valiant Struggle										
Stealing from the Siegesmiths	Dragonblight	Horde	All		Deathguard Molder	Deathguard Molder	Let Them Not Rise!	250 with The Hand of Vengeance	20300	5🟤
Bombard the Ballistae	Dragonblight	Horde	All		Deathguard Molder	Deathguard Molder	Stealing from the Siegesmiths	250 with The Hand of Vengeance	20300	5🟤
CHOICE OF: 1 Ritual Neckguard, 1 Saboteur's Wrap, 1 Siegemaster's Torch Ring										
Need to Know	Dragonblight	Horde	All		Spy Mistress Repine	Spy Mistress Repine	Stealing from the Siegesmiths	250 with The Hand of Vengeance	20300	5🟤

Title	Location	Faction	Race & Class	Group #	Starter	Finisher	Prerequisite	Reputation	XP	Money
Naxxramas and the Fall of Wintergarde	Dragonblight	All	All		High Commander Halford Wyrmbane	Gryphon Commander Urik		10 with Valiance Expedition	2050	
Flight of the Wintergarde Defender	Dragonblight	All	All		Gryphon Commander Urik	Gryphon Commander Urik	Naxxramas and the Fall of Wintergarde	250 with Valiance Expedition	20300	
The Spy in New Hearthglen	Dragonblight	Horde	All		Spy Mistress Repine	Agent Skully	Need to Know	250 with The Hand of Vengeance	20300	5 🥈
A Means to an End	Dragonblight	Horde	All		Apothecary Vicky Levine	Apothecary Vicky Levine	Stealing from the Siegesmiths	250 with The Hand of Vengeance	20300	5 🥈
Fire Upon the Waters	Dragonblight	Horde	All		Apothecary Vicky Levine	Apothecary Vicky Levine	A Means to an End	250 with The Hand of Vengeance	20300	5 🥈
CHOICE OF: 1 Highseas Wristwraps, 1 Glade Wanderer Boots, 1 Westwind Shoulderguards, 1 Sinner's Repentance										
No Mercy for the Captured	Dragonblight	Horde	All		Spy Mistress Repine	High Executor Wroth	Wanted: The Scarlet Onslaught	250 with The Hand of Vengeance	20300	5 🥈
Return to the High Commander	Dragonblight	All	All		Gryphon Commander Urik	High Commander Halford Wyrmbane	Flight of the Wintergarde Defender	10 with Valiance Expedition	2050	
CHOICE OF: 1 Frontrunner's Blessed Handwraps, 1 Snowfall Reaver Boots, 1 Westwind Waistband, 1 Stonepath Gauntlets										
Torture the Torturer	Dragonblight	Horde	All		High Executor Wroth	High Executor Wroth	No Mercy for the Captured	250 with The Hand of Vengeance	20300	5 🥈
CHOICE OF: 1 Wastewind Garments, 1 Snowfall Reaver Hood, 1 Iceshear Pauldrons, 1 Crystalplate Gauntlets										
Rescue from Town Square	Dragonblight	All	All		High Commander Halford Wyrmbane	High Commander Halford Wyrmbane	Return to the High Commander	250 with Valiance Expedition	20300	
Without a Prayer	Dragonblight	Horde	All		Agent Skully	Agent Skully	The Spy in New Hearthglen	250 with The Hand of Vengeance	20300	5 🥈
The Fate of the Dead	Dragonblight	Alliance	All		Commander Lynore Windstryke	Commander Lynore Windstryke	Return to the High Commander	250 with Valiance Expedition	20300	
CHOICE OF: 1 Wastewind Cinch, 1 Snowfall Reaver Gloves, 1 Iceshear Bindings, 1 Stonepath Sabatons										
The Perfect Dissemblance	Dragonblight	Horde	All		Agent Skully	Agent Skully	Without a Prayer	250 with The Hand of Vengeance	20300	5 🥈
No Place to Run	Dragonblight	All	All		Serinar	Serinar	The Obsidian Dragonshrine	250 with The Wyrmrest Accord	20750	5 🥈 60 🥉
No One to Save You	Dragonblight	All	All		Serinar	Serinar	The Obsidian Dragonshrine	250 with The Wyrmrest Accord	20750	5 🥈 60 🥉
The Best of Intentions	Dragonblight	All	All		Serinar	Serinar	No Place to Run	250 with The Wyrmrest Accord	20750	5 🥈 60 🥉
Culling the Damned	Dragonblight	All	All		Serinar	Serinar	The Best of Intentions	250 with The Wyrmrest Accord	20750	5 🥈 60 🥉
Defiling the Defilers	Dragonblight	All	All		Serinar	Serinar	The Best of Intentions	250 with The Wyrmrest Accord	20750	5 🥈 60 🥉
Tales of Destruction	Dragonblight	All	All		Serinar	Nalice	Neltharion's Flame	10 with The Wyrmrest Accord	2100	56 🥉
Neltharion's Flame	Dragonblight	All	All		Serinar	Serinar	Defiling the Defilers	350 with The Wyrmrest Accord	26200	11 🥈 80 🥉
CHOICE OF: 1 High Priest Forith's Robes, 1 Wyrm-slave Collar, 1 Legplates of the Conquered Knight, 1 Lord Prestor's Drape										
Not In Our Mine	Dragonblight	All	All		Highlord Leoric Von Zeldig	Highlord Leoric Von Zeldig	The Demo-gnome	250 with Valiance Expedition	20300	
The Rod of Compulsion	Dragonblight	Horde	All		Torturer's Rod	High Executor Wroth	No Mercy for the Captured	75 with The Hand of Vengeance	10150	2 🥈 50 🥉
The Bleeding Ore	Dragonblight	All	All		Siege Engineer Quarterflash	Siege Engineer Quarterflash	The Demo-gnome	250 with Valiance Expedition	20300	
The Denouncement	Dragonblight	Horde	All		High Executor Wroth	High Executor Wroth	The Rod of Compulsion	350 with The Hand of Vengeance	25650	10 🥈 60 🥉
CHOICE OF: 1 Robe of Calcified Tears, 1 Torturer's Fleshwoven Leggings, 1 Paingiver Wristguards, 1 Sabatons of the Enforcer										
A Fall From Grace	Dragonblight	Horde	All		Agent Skully	Agent Skully	The Perfect Dissemblance	250 with The Hand of Vengeance	20500	5 🥈 30 🥉
The Demo-gnome	Dragonblight	All	All		High Commander Halford Wyrmbane	Siege Engineer Quarterflash	Return to the High Commander	5 with Valiance Expedition		
The Search for Slinkin	Dragonblight	All	All		Siege Engineer Quarterflash	Slinkin the Demo-gnome	The Demo-gnome	250 with Valiance Expedition	20300	
Leave Nothing to Chance	Dragonblight	All	All		Slinkin the Demo-gnome	Siege Engineer Quarterflash	The Search for Slinkin	350 with Valiance Expedition	25400	
CHOICE OF: 1 Suntouched Flowers, 1 Honorborn Cloak, 1 Petrified Bone Footguards, 1 Oath Signet										
Understanding the Scourge War Machine	Dragonblight	All	All		Siege Engineer Quarterflash	High Commander Halford Wyrmbane	Leave Nothing to Chance, The Bleeding Ore	10 with Valiance Expedition	2050	
Imprints on the Past	Dragonblight	All	All		Zelig the Visionary	Zelig the Visionary	Return to the High Commander	250 with Valiance Expedition	20300	
CHOICE OF: 1 Visionary's Robes, 1 Guiding Gloves of the Seer, 1 Foresight's Anticipation, 1 Vigilant Skullcap										
The Truth Will Out	Dragonblight	Horde	All		Agent Skully	High Executor Wroth	A Fall From Grace	250 with The Hand of Vengeance	20300	5 🥈
Do Unto Others	Dragonblight	Horde	All	3	High Executor Wroth	High Executor Wroth	The Truth Will Out	350 with The Hand of Vengeance	25650	10 🥈 60 🥉
CHOICE OF: 1 Bindings of the Forceful Vanquisher, 1 Cuffs of the Decapitator, 1 Wristguards of the Remorseful, 1 Purity-Anointed Warbands										
Orik Trueheart and the Forgotten Shore	Dragonblight	All	All		Zelig the Visionary	Orik Trueheart	Imprints on the Past	25 with Valiance Expedition	5100	
The Murkweed Elixir	Dragonblight	All	All		Orik Trueheart	Orik Trueheart	Orik Trueheart and the Forgotten Shore	250 with Valiance Expedition, 250 with Argent Crusade	20300	

DRAGONBLIGHT

Title	Location	Faction	Race & Class	Group #	Starter	Finisher	Prerequisite	Reputation	XP	Money
The Forgotten Tale	Dragonblight	All	All		Orik Trueheart	Orik Trueheart	The Murkweed Elixir	250 with Valiance Expedition, 250 with Argent Crusade	20300	
Of Traitors and Treason	Dragonblight	All	All		Captain Adams	Greer Orehammer	All Hail the Conqueror of Skorn!	10 with Valiance Expedition	2050	
High Commander Halford Wyrmbane	Dragonblight	All	All		Greer Orehammer	High Commander Halford Wyrmbane	Of Traitors and Treason	10 with Valiance Expedition	2050	
The Truth Shall Set Us Free	Dragonblight	All	All		Orik Trueheart	Orik Trueheart	The Forgotten Tale	500 with Valiance Expedition, 500 with Argent Crusade	30450	
Funding the War Effort	Dragonblight	Horde	All		Quartermaster Bartlett	Quartermaster Bartlett		250 with The Hand of Vengeance	20300	5🥈
CHOICE OF: 1 Warblade of the Forgotten Footman, 1 Valonforth's Remembrance, 1 Hood of the Forgotten Rifleman, 1 Chestpiece of the Forgotten Captain, 1 Circlet of the Forgotten Mercenary										
Beachfront Property	Dragonblight	Horde	All		Surveyor Hansen	Surveyor Hansen		250 with The Hand of Vengeance	20300	5🥈
Parting Thoughts	Dragonblight	All	All		Orik Trueheart	Zelig the Visionary	The Truth Shall Set Us Free	25 with Valiance Expedition	5100	
CHOICE OF: 1 Warblade of the Forgotten Footman, 1 Valonforth's Remembrance, 1 Hood of the Forgotten Rifleman, 1 Chestpiece of the Forgotten Captain, 1 Circlet of the Forgotten Mercenary										
Find Durkon!	Dragonblight	All	All		High Commander Halford Wyrmbane	Cavalier Durkon	Rescue from Town Square	10 with Valiance Expedition	2050	
The Noble's Crypt	Dragonblight	Alliance	All		Cavalier Durkon	Cavalier Durkon	Find Durkon!	250 with Valiance Expedition	20300	
CHOICE OF: 1 Wastewind Garments, 1 Snowfall Reaver Hood, 1 Iceshear Pauldrons, 1 Crystalplate Gauntlets										
Secrets of the Scourge	Dragonblight	Alliance	All		Flesh-bound Tome (MISSING !: Task 23203)	Cavalier Durkon	Find Durkon!	25 with Valiance Expedition	5150	
Mystery of the Tome	Dragonblight	All	All		Cavalier Durkon	High Commander Halford Wyrmbane	Secrets of the Scourge	10 with Valiance Expedition	2050	
Understanding the Language of Death	Dragonblight	All	All		High Commander Halford Wyrmbane	Inquisitor Hallard	Mystery of the Tome	10 with Valiance Expedition	2050	
A Righteous Sermon	Dragonblight	All	All		Mayor Godfrey, Inquisitor Hallard	High Commander Halford Wyrmbane	Understanding the Language of Death	250 with Valiance Expedition	20500	
CHOICE OF: 1 Highseas Wristwraps, 1 Glade Wanderer Boots, 1 Westwind Shoulderguards, 1 Sinner's Repentance										
Into Hostile Territory	Dragonblight	All	All		High Commander Halford Wyrmbane	Duke August Foehammer	A Righteous Sermon, Understanding the Scourge War Machine	25 with Valiance Expedition	5150	
Steamtank Surprise	Dragonblight	All	All		Duke August Foehammer	Ambo Cash	Into Hostile Territory	350 with Valiance Expedition	25650	
CHOICE OF: 1 Ritual Neckguard, 1 Saboteur's Wrap, 1 Siegemaster's Torch Ring										
Defending Wyrmrest Temple	Dragonblight	All	All		Lord Afrasastrasz	Lord Afrasastrasz	Report to Lord Afrasastrasz	250 with The Wyrmrest Accord	20750	5🥈60🥉
Heated Battle	Dragonblight	All	All		Ceristrasz	Ceristrasz	Report to the Ruby Dragonshrine	250 with The Wyrmrest Accord	20750	5🥈60🥉
Return to the Earth	Dragonblight	All	All		Ceristrasz	Ceristrasz	Heated Battle	250 with The Wyrmrest Accord	20750	5🥈60🥉
Through Fields of Flame	Dragonblight	All	All		Ceristrasz	Ceristrasz	Return to the Earth	250 with The Wyrmrest Accord	26200	11🥈80🥉
CHOICE OF: 1 Treads of the Charred Canyon, 1 Scourgeslayer Belt, 1 Wyrmfire Gloves, 1 Conscript's Ruby Waistguard										
The Fate of the Ruby Dragonshrine	Dragonblight	All	All		Ruby Brooch	Krasus		350 with The Wyrmrest Accord	5250	1🥇50🥈
Report to Lord Afrasastrasz	Dragonblight	All	All		Alexstrasza the Life-Binder	Lord Afrasastrasz	Informing the Queen, Informing the Queen	10 with The Wyrmrest Accord	2100	
Wanted: Kreug Oathbreaker	Dragonblight	All	All	5	Wanted!, Wanted!	Highlord Leoric Von Zeldig	Return to the High Commander	350 with Valiance Expedition	25950	11🥈20🥉
CHOICE OF: 1 Wastewind Bracers, 1 Glade Wanderer Bracers, 1 Scourge Ghoul Collar, 1 Petrified Bone Chestguard										
A Disturbance In The West	Dragonblight	All	All		Vas the Unstable	Rodney Wells		10 with Valiance Expedition	2050	
To Stars' Rest!	Dragonblight	Alliance	All		Rodney Wells	Image of Archmage Modera	A Disturbance In The West	10 with Valiance Expedition	2050	
Wanted: High Shaman Bloodpaw	Dragonblight	All	All	3	Wanted!, Wanted!	Highlord Leoric Von Zeldig	Return to the High Commander	350 with Valiance Expedition	25950	11🥈20🥉
CHOICE OF: 1 Battleworn Magnataur Crusher, 1 Crossbow of the Hardened Ranger, 1 Moonrest Garden Stave, 1 Keen Woodland Shank, 1 Spiked Coldwind Club, 1 Staff of Ruby Wood										
Wanted: Onslaught Commander Iustus	Dragonblight	All	All	4	Wanted!, Wanted!	Highlord Leoric Von Zeldig	Return to the High Commander	350 with Valiance Expedition	25950	11🥈20🥉
CHOICE OF: 1 Sabatons of the Enforcer, 1 Paingiver Wristguards, 1 Robe of the Justicebringer, 1 Legpads of the Inquisitor										
The Obsidian Dragonshrine	Dragonblight	All	All		Nalice	Serinar		10 with The Wyrmrest Accord	2100	56🥉
Heated Battle	Dragonblight	All	All		Vargastrasz	Vargastrasz	Report to the Ruby Dragonshrine	250 with The Wyrmrest Accord	20750	5🥈60🥉
Return to the Earth	Dragonblight	All	All		Vargastrasz	Vargastrasz	Heated Battle	250 with The Wyrmrest Accord	20750	5🥈60🥉
Through Fields of Flame	Dragonblight	All	All		Vargastrasz	Vargastrasz	Return to the Earth	250 with The Wyrmrest Accord	26200	11🥈80🥉
CHOICE OF: 1 Treads of the Charred Canyon, 1 Scourgeslayer Belt, 1 Wyrmfire Gloves, 1 Conscript's Ruby Waistguard										
zzOLD The Fate of the Ruby Dragonshrine	Dragonblight	All	All		Alexstrasza the Life-Binder	Alexstrasza the Life-Binder				

Title	Location	Faction	Race & Class	Group #	Starter	Finisher	Prerequisite	Reputation	XP	Money
Cycle of Life	Dragonblight	All	All		Nishera the Garden Keeper	Nishera the Garden Keeper		250 with The Wyrmrest Accord	20750	5🟡 60⚪
Scattered To The Wind	Dragonblight	Alliance	All		Ambo Cash	Ambo Cash	Steamtank Surprise	250 with Valiance Expedition	20500	
The Plume of Alystros	Dragonblight	All	All	3	Nishera the Garden Keeper	Nishera the Garden Keeper	Cycle of Life	350 with The Wyrmrest Accord	25950	11🟡 20⚪
CHOICE OF: 1 Alystros's Plume Cinch, 1 Ancient Dreamer's Leggings, 1 Verdant Linked Boots, 1 Belt of the Emerald Guardian										
The Chain Gun And You	Dragonblight	Alliance	All		Ambo Cash	Ambo Cash	Scattered To The Wind	350 with Valiance Expedition	25650	
Seeds of the Lashers	Dragonblight	All	All		Lord Itharius	Lord Itharius		250 with The Wyrmrest Accord	20750	5🟡 60⚪
That Which Creates Can Also Destroy	Dragonblight	All	All		Lord Itharius	Lord Itharius	Seeds of the Lashers	500 with The Wyrmrest Accord	31150	16🟡 80⚪
CHOICE OF: 1 Mantle of Itharius, 1 Gloves of the Emerald Stalker, 1 Verdant Hunter's Guise, 1 Breastplate of Nature's Ire										
Report to the Ruby Dragonshrine	Dragonblight	Alliance	All		Lauriel Trueblade	Ceristrasz	Speak with your Ambassador	10 with The Wyrmrest Accord	2100	56⚪
Report to the Ruby Dragonshrine	Dragonblight	Horde	All		Golluck Rockfist	Vargastrasz	Speak with your Ambassador	10 with The Wyrmrest Accord	2100	56⚪
Breaking Off A Piece	Dragonblight	Alliance	All		Yord "Calamity" Icebeard	Yord "Calamity" Icebeard	Steamtank Surprise	250 with Valiance Expedition	20500	
CHOICE OF: 1 Wastewind Pauldrons, 1 Snowfall Reaver Pauldrons, 1 Anub'ar-Husk Shoulderguards, 1 Stonepath Pauldrons										
Plunderbeard Must Be Found!	Dragonblight	Alliance	All		Ambo Cash	Plunderbeard	The Chain Gun And You	75 with Valiance Expedition	10250	
My Old Enemy	Dragonblight	All	All	3	Commander Eligor Dawnbringer	Commander Eligor Dawnbringer		350 with Valiance Expedition	25650	10🟡 60⚪
CHOICE OF: 1 Battlement Enforcer's Axe, 1 Siege Captain's Gun, 1 Mace of the Fallen Raven Priest, 1 Stronghold Battlemace, 1 Bloodtinged Spellblade, 1 Idol of the Wastes										
Plunderbeard's Journal	Dragonblight	Alliance	All		Plunderbeard	Ambo Cash	Plunderbeard Must Be Found!	250 with Valiance Expedition	20500	
Chasing Icestorm: The 7th Legion Front	Dragonblight	Alliance	All		Ambo Cash	Legion Commander Tyralion	Plunderbeard's Journal	25 with Valiance Expedition	5150	
Chasing Icestorm: Thel'zan's Phylactery	Dragonblight	All	All		Legion Commander Tyralion	High Commander Halford Wyrmbane	Chasing Icestorm: The 7th Legion Front	350 with Valiance Expedition	25650	
CHOICE OF: 1 Wastewind Headcover, 1 Snowfall Reaver Breastplate, 1 Anub'ar-Husk Leggings, 1 Stonepath Helm										
Return to Sender	Dragonblight	All	All		Xink	Xink			2100	56⚪
Mystery of the Infinite	Dragonblight	All	All		Chromie	Chromie		350 with The Wyrmrest Accord	26200	11🟡 80⚪
CHOICE OF: 1 Dagger of the Returning Past, 1 Time-Bending Smasher, 1 Timeshattered Spire, 1 Twig of Happy Reminders										
Finality	Dragonblight	All	All		High Commander Halford Wyrmbane	Legion Commander Yorik	Chasing Icestorm: Thel'zan's Phylactery	10 with Valiance Expedition	2050	
An End And A Beginning	Dragonblight	All	All		Legion Commander Yorik	High Commander Halford Wyrmbane	Finality	250 with Valiance Expedition	20500	
To Fordragon Hold!	Dragonblight	All	All		High Commander Halford Wyrmbane	Highlord Bolvar Fordragon	An End And A Beginning	500 with Valiance Expedition	30750	
CHOICE OF: 1 Implacable Zombie Crushers, 1 Reinforced Traveler's Boots, 1 Sandals of Chaos Resolution, 1 Treads of the Valiant Struggle										
What Secrets Men Hide	Dragonblight	All	All		Zelig the Visionary	Zelig the Visionary	Parting Thoughts	250 with Valiance Expedition	20500	
The Return of the Crusade?	Dragonblight	Alliance	All		Commander Lynore Windstryke	Commander Lynore Windstryke	Parting Thoughts		20500	5🟡 30⚪
REWARD: 5 Runic Healing Potion										
The Path of Redemption	Dragonblight	All	All		High Commander Halford Wyrmbane	High Commander Halford Wyrmbane	Parting Thoughts	250 with Valiance Expedition	20500	
Frostmourne Cavern	Dragonblight	All	All		Zelig the Visionary	Zelig the Visionary	What Secrets Men Hide	350 with Valiance Expedition	25650	
CHOICE OF: 1 Wrap of Vigorous Destruction, 1 Belt of Vengeful Purification, 1 Links of Righteous Persecution, 1 Girdle of Forceful Annihilation										
The High Executor Needs You	Dragonblight	Horde	All		Senior Sergeant Juktok	High Executor Wroth		10 with The Hand of Vengeance	2100	
Audience With The Dragon Queen	Dragonblight	All	All		Highlord Bolvar Fordragon	Alexstrasza the Life-Binder	To Fordragon Hold!	10 with Valiance Expedition, 10 with The Wyrmrest Accord	2100	
Audience With The Dragon Queen	Dragonblight	All	All		Saurfang the Younger	Alexstrasza the Life-Binder	The Kor'kron Vanguard!	10 with Warsong Offensive, 10 with The Wyrmrest Accord	2100	
Galakrond and the Scourge	Dragonblight	All	All		Alexstrasza the Life-Binder	Torastrasza	Audience With The Dragon Queen, Audience With The Dragon Queen			
On Ruby Wings	Dragonblight	All	All		Torastrasza	Alexstrasza the Life-Binder	Galakrond and the Scourge	350 with The Wyrmrest Accord	25950	
CHOICE OF: 1 Scourgeslayer Cover, 1 Wyrmfire Links, 1 Chestplate of the Ruby Champion, 1 Will of the Red Dragonflight										
Return To Angrathar	Dragonblight	All	All		Alexstrasza the Life-Binder	Highlord Bolvar Fordragon	On Ruby Wings	500 with Valiance Expedition	31150	
Return To Angrathar	Dragonblight	All	All		Alexstrasza the Life-Binder	Saurfang the Younger	On Ruby Wings	500 with Warsong Offensive	31150	
The Call Of The Crusade	Dragonblight	All	All		Tilda Darathan	Crusader Valus		25 with Argent Crusade	5200	

DRAGONBLIGHT

Title	Location	Faction	Race & Class	Group #	Starter	Finisher	Prerequisite	Reputation	XP	Money
The Cleansing Of Jintha'kalar	Dragonblight	All	All		Crusader Valus	Crusader Valus		250 with Argent Crusade	20750	5🟡 60⚪
CHOICE OF: 1 Scourgeslayer's Shank, 1 Claw of the Undead Ravager, 1 Joint-Severing Quickblade, 1 Wand of Purifying Fire, 1 Wand of Blinding Light									
Speak with your Ambassador	Dragonblight	Alliance	All		Tariolstrasz	Lauriel Trueblade	Gaining an Audience	10 with Valiance Expedition	2050	
Speak with your Ambassador	Dragonblight	Horde	All		Tariolstrasz	Golluck Rockfist	Gaining an Audience	10 with Warsong Offensive	2050	
The Steward of Wyrmrest Temple	Dragonblight	All	All		Ceristrasz	Tariolstrasz	Through Fields of Flame	10 with The Wyrmrest Accord	2100	
The Steward of Wyrmrest Temple	Dragonblight	All	All		Vargastrasz	Tariolstrasz	Through Fields of Flame	10 with The Wyrmrest Accord	2100	
Into the Breach!	Dragonblight	All	All		Crusader Valus	Sergeant Riannah	The Cleansing Of Jintha'kalar		2100	60⚪
Darkness Stirs	Dragonblight	Horde	All		Alexstrasza the Life-Binder	High Overlord Saurfang	Return To Angrathar	500 with Warsong Offensive	31150	
Mystery of the Infinite, Redux	Dragonblight	All	All		Chromie	Chromie	Mystery of the Infinite	350 with The Wyrmrest Accord	27550	14🟡 80⚪
CHOICE OF: 1 Futuresight Rune, 1 Rune of Finite Variation, 1 Rune of Infinite Power									
Reborn From The Ashes	Dragonblight	Alliance	All		Alexstrasza the Life-Binder	King Varian Wrynn	Return To Angrathar	500 with Stormwind, 500 with Valiance Expedition	31150	
Fate, Up Against Your Will	Dragonblight	Alliance	All		King Varian Wrynn	Thrall	Reborn From The Ashes	250 with Stormwind, 250 with Valiance Expedition	20750	
A Royal Coup	Dragonblight	Alliance	All		Thrall	King Varian Wrynn	Fate, Up Against Your Will	250 with Stormwind, 250 with Valiance Expedition	20750	
The Killing Time	Dragonblight	Alliance	All		King Varian Wrynn	Broll Bearmantle	A Royal Coup	10 with Stormwind, 10 with Valiance Expedition	2100	
The Key to the Focusing Iris	Dragonblight	All	All		Key to the Focusing Iris	Alexstrasza the Life-Binder		500 with The Wyrmrest Accord	33100	22🟡 20⚪
REWARD: 1 Key to the Focusing Iris									
The Heroic Key to the Focusing Iris	Dragonblight	All	All		Heroic Key to the Focusing Iris	Alexstrasza the Life-Binder		500 with The Wyrmrest Accord	44100	
REWARD: 1 Heroic Key to the Focusing Iris									
The Battle For The Undercity	Dragonblight	Alliance	All		Broll Bearmantle	King Varian Wrynn	The Killing Time	500 with Stormwind, 500 with Valiance Expedition	41500	
REWARD: 1 Medallion of Heroism AND CHOICE OF: 1 Wrynn's Leggings of Foresight, 1 Wrynn's Leggings of Valor, 1 Wrynn's Leggings of Wisdom, 1 Wrynn's Legguards of Brutality, 1 Wrynn's Legguards of Heroism, 1 Wrynn's Legplates of Carnage									

DRAK'THARON KEEP

Title	Location	Faction	Race & Class	Group #	Starter	Finisher	Prerequisite	Reputation	XP	Money
Search and Rescue	Drak'Tharon Keep	All	All		Mack Fearsen	Kurzel	Seared Scourge		20750	5🟡 60⚪
CHOICE OF: 1 Kurzel's Angst, 1 Kurzel's Rage, 1 Kurzel's Warband									
Cleansing Drak'Tharon	Drak'Tharon Keep	All	All		Image of Drakuru	Drakuru	Voices From the Dust		31450	17🟡 70⚪
CHOICE OF: 1 Shroud of Temptation, 1 Enticing Sabatons, 1 Shackles of Dark Whispers, 1 Shoulders of the Seducer									
Head Games	Drak'Tharon Keep	All	All		Kurzel	Mack Fearsen	Search and Rescue		41500	
CHOICE OF: 1 Shameful Cuffs, 1 Scorned Bands, 1 Accused Wristguards, 1 Disavowed Bracers									
Proof of Demise: The Prophet Tharon'ja	Drak'Tharon Keep	All	All		Archmage Lan'dalock	Archmage Lan'dalock		75 with Kirin Tor	44100	22🟡 20⚪
REWARD: 2 Emblem of Heroism									

GRIZZLY HILLS

Title	Location	Faction	Race & Class	Group #	Starter	Finisher	Prerequisite	Reputation	XP	Money
Find Kurun!	Grizzly Hills	All	All		Fallen Earthen Warrior	Kurun			2100	
Raining Down Destruction	Grizzly Hills	All	All		Kurun	Kurun			20950	5🟡 90⚪
Filling the Cages	Grizzly Hills	All	All		Samir	Samir			20750	5🟡 60⚪
CHOICE OF: 1 Grinder of Reverse Emancipation, 1 Warbling Crossbow, 1 Mace of Helotry, 1 Spike of Renounced Autonomy, 1 Yoke Slasher, 1 Sword of the Caged Mind									
Into the Breach	Grizzly Hills	All	All		Kurun	Kurun	Rallying the Troops		20950	5🟡 90⚪
CHOICE OF: 1 Forge-Scarred Sandals, 1 Iron-Shatter Leggings, 1 Flame-Tested Chestguard, 1 Grips of Flawed Temper									
The Damaged Journal	Grizzly Hills	Alliance	All		Battered Journal	Torthen Deepdig			20950	5🟡 90⚪
The Runic Keystone	Grizzly Hills	Alliance	All		Explorers' League Surveyor, Torthen Deepdig	Torthen Deepdig	The Damaged Journal		20950	5🟡 90⚪
Truce?	Grizzly Hills	All	All		Drakuru	Drakuru	Filling the Cages		10250	
Vial of Visions	Grizzly Hills	All	All		Drakuru	Drakuru	Truce?		20750	
Subject to Interpretation	Grizzly Hills	All	All		Drakuru	Image of Drakuru	Vial of Visions		20750	5🟡 60⚪
CHOICE OF: 1 Ethereal Hood, 1 Drakuru's Ghastly Helm, 1 Helm of Spirit Links, 1 Spiritforged Helm									
The Runic Prophecies	Grizzly Hills	Alliance	All		Explorers' League Surveyor, Torthen Deepdig	Torthen Deepdig	The Runic Keystone		20950	5🟡 90⚪
CHOICE OF: 1 Wayfinder's Bracers, 1 Discoverer's Mitts, 1 Trailbreaker's Spaulders, 1 Waywalker's Girdle									

Title	Location	Faction	Race & Class	Group #	Starter	Finisher	Prerequisite	Reputation	XP	Money
REUSE	Grizzly Hills	All	All		Captain Gryan Stoutmantle	Captain Gryan Stoutmantle			2100	
Softening the Blow	Grizzly Hills	All	All		Captain Gryan Stoutmantle	Brugar Stoneshear			20950	
Brothers in Battle	Grizzly Hills	Alliance	All		Brugar Stoneshear	Brugar Stoneshear	Softening the Blow		20950	5🥈90🥉
Uncovering the Tunnels	Grizzly Hills	Alliance	All		Brugar Stoneshear	Brugar Stoneshear	Brothers in Battle		20950	5🥈90🥉
Sacrifices Must be Made	Grizzly Hills	All	All		Image of Drakuru	Image of Drakuru	Subject to Interpretation		20750	5🥈60🥉
The Fate of Orlond	Grizzly Hills	Alliance	All		Brugar Stoneshear	Surveyor Orlond	Uncovering the Tunnels		15700	
Steady as a Rock?	Grizzly Hills	Alliance	All		Surveyor Orlond	Brugar Stoneshear	The Fate of Orlond		26200	4🥈60🥉
CHOICE OF: 1 Dusty Miner's Leggings, 1 Ectoplasm Stained Wristguards, 1 Ghostridden Waistguard, 1 Shocksteel Shoulderguards										
The Damaged Journal	Grizzly Hills	Horde	All		Battered Journal	Sage Paluna		250 with The Taunka	20950	5🥈90🥉
Mr. Floppy's Perilous Adventure	Grizzly Hills	All	All		Emily	Squire Walter			20750	5🥈60🥉
CHOICE OF: 1 Path-Cutter's Cord, 1 Boots of Safe Travel, 1 Legguards of Unerring Navigation, 1 Bracers of the Chaperon										
Seared Scourge	Grizzly Hills	All	All		Mack Fearsen	Mack Fearsen	Scourgekabob		20750	5🥈60🥉
Seared Scourge	Grizzly Hills	All	All		Mack Fearsen	Mack Fearsen	Seared Scourge		20300	5🥈
Heart of the Ancients	Grizzly Hills	All	All		Image of Drakuru	Heart of the Ancients	Sacrifices Must be Made		20750	
REWARD: 1 Heart of the Ancients										
Deciphering the Journal	Grizzly Hills	Horde	All		Sage Paluna	Sage Paluna	The Damaged Journal	250 with The Taunka	20950	5🥈90🥉
The Runic Prophecies	Grizzly Hills	Horde	All		Sage Paluna	Sage Paluna	Deciphering the Journal	250 with The Taunka	20950	5🥈90🥉
CHOICE OF: 1 Wayfinder's Bracers, 1 Discoverer's Mitts, 1 Trailbreaker's Spaulders, 1 Waywalker's Girdle										
Voices From the Dust	Grizzly Hills	All	All		Image of Drakuru	Image of Drakuru	My Heart is in Your Hands		20950	5🥈90🥉
CHOICE OF: 1 Wispy Shoulderpads, 1 Helm of Rising Smoke, 1 Plane-shifted Boots, 1 Spiritforged Legguards, 1 Vengeful Spirit Beads										
Rallying the Troops	Grizzly Hills	All	All		Kurun	Kurun	Raining Down Destruction		20950	5🥈90🥉
Pounding the Iron	Grizzly Hills	Horde	All		Scout Vor'takh	Scout Vor'takh	Deciphering the Journal	250 with Warsong Offensive	20950	5🥈70🥉
An Expedient Ally	Grizzly Hills	All	All		Scout Vor'takh	Kurun			2100	
Gavrock	Grizzly Hills	All	All		Kurun	Gavrock	Into the Breach		2100	
Dun-da-Dun-tah!	Grizzly Hills	All	All		Harrison Jones	Harkor			20950	5🥈90🥉
CHOICE OF: 1 Sandals of Quick Escape, 1 Coiled Leather Gauntlets, 1 Whip-Stitched Wristguards, 1 Load-Bearing Girdle										
Runes of Compulsion	Grizzly Hills	All	All		Gavrock	Gavrock	Gavrock		20950	5🥈90🥉
Latent Power	Grizzly Hills	All	All		Gavrock	Gavrock	Runes of Compulsion		20950	5🥈90🥉
Free at Last	Grizzly Hills	All	All		Gavrock	Gavrock	Latent Power		26200	11🥈80🥉
CHOICE OF: 1 Liberator's Blade, 1 Branch of the Roaming Spirit, 1 Spire of Soaring Rumination, 1 Bondsniper, 1 Talon of Freedom										
Descent into Darkness	Grizzly Hills	All	All		Mikhail's Journal	Lieutenant Dumont		75 with Valiance Expedition	10400	
CHOICE OF: 1 Abandoned Hood, 1 Discarded Miner's Jerkin, 1 Patched Trapper Pauldrons, 1 Rusty Cave Stompers										
Report to Gryan Stoutmantle... Again	Grizzly Hills	All	All		Lieutenant Dumont	Captain Gryan Stoutmantle	Descent into Darkness	25 with Valiance Expedition	5200	
Nice to Meat You	Grizzly Hills	All	All		Harkor	Harkor			15700	5🥈90🥉
Therapy	Grizzly Hills	All	All		Harkor	Harkor			20950	5🥈90🥉
CHOICE OF: 1 Kilt of Peaceful Reclamation, 1 Leggings of Anger Management, 1 Handguards of Extermination, 1 Chestguard of Expressed Fury, 1 Therapeutic Cloak										
It Takes Guts....	Grizzly Hills	All	All		Kraz	Kraz			20950	5🥈90🥉
Drak'aguul's Mallet	Grizzly Hills	All	All		Kraz	Kraz	It Takes Guts....		20950	5🥈90🥉
CHOICE OF: 1 Bell-Ringer's Shoulderpads, 1 Waistguard of Expedient Procurement, 1 Polished Staghorn Helm, 1 Hammer-Holder's Gauntlets										
See You on the Other Side	Grizzly Hills	All	All		Kraz	Gan'jo	Drak'aguul's Mallet		20950	5🥈90🥉
Check Up on Raegar	Grizzly Hills	Alliance	All		Brugar Stoneshear	Raegar Breakbrow	Steady as a Rock?		2100	
The Perfect Plan	Grizzly Hills	Alliance	All		Raegar Breakbrow	Raegar Breakbrow	Check Up on Raegar		20950	5🥈90🥉
Why Fabricate When You Can Appropriate?	Grizzly Hills	Alliance	All		Raegar Breakbrow	Raegar Breakbrow	The Perfect Plan		20950	5🥈90🥉
We Have the Power	Grizzly Hills	Alliance	All		Raegar Breakbrow	Raegar Breakbrow	Why Fabricate When You Can Appropriate?		20950	5🥈90🥉
Sasha's Hunt	Grizzly Hills	All	All		Sasha	Sasha	Fate and Coincidence		20950	5🥈90🥉
CHOICE OF: 1 Bloody Bulwark, 1 Wolfslayer's Crest, 1 Scepter of Passionate Reprisal, 1 Staff of Righteous Vengeance										
Chill Out, Mon	Grizzly Hills	All	All		Gan'jo	Kraz	See You on the Other Side		20950	
... Or Maybe We Don't	Grizzly Hills	Alliance	All		Raegar Breakbrow	Raegar Breakbrow	We Have the Power		20950	5🥈90🥉
Jin'arrak's End	Grizzly Hills	All	All		Kraz	Kraz	Chill Out, Mon		20950	5🥈90🥉
CHOICE OF: 1 Axe of the Warlord's Demise, 1 Beaked Dagger, 1 Serrated Cold-Iron Slicer, 1 Branch of Insightful Dreams, 1 Jagged Troll Render, 1 Glowing Voodoo Orb										
The Iron Thane and His Anvil	Grizzly Hills	Alliance	All		Raegar Breakbrow	Raegar Breakbrow	... Or Maybe We Don't		26200	11🥈80🥉
CHOICE OF: 1 Grounded Gloves, 1 Crackpot Spaulders, 1 Short-Circuiting Boots, 1 Golem-Rider's Greaves										
Blackout	Grizzly Hills	Alliance	All		Raegar Breakbrow	Raegar Breakbrow	... Or Maybe We Don't		20950	5🥈90🥉
Hollowstone Mine	Grizzly Hills	All	All		Captain Gryan Stoutmantle	Petrov	Report to Gryan Stoutmantle... Again		2100	
Souls at Unrest	Grizzly Hills	All	All		Petrov	Petrov	Hollowstone Mine		20950	5🥈90🥉
CHOICE OF: 1 Specially Treated Robes, 1 Bearskin Helm, 1 Hide-Lined Chestguard, 1 Carapace of the Fallen										
A Name from the Past	Grizzly Hills	All	All		Petrov	Captain Gryan Stoutmantle	Souls at Unrest		5250	
Ruuna the Blind	Grizzly Hills	All	All		Private Arun	Ruuna the Blind	A Name from the Past		5250	
Solstice Village	Grizzly Hills	All	All		Sasha	Sasha	Ruuna the Blind			
The Evil Below	Grizzly Hills	All	All		Sasha	Sasha	Sasha's Hunt			
Hour of the Worg	Grizzly Hills	All	All	3	Sasha	Sasha	A Sister's Pledge		31450	17🥈70🥉
CHOICE OF: 1 Furred Worgslayer Spaulders, 1 Fangsever Shoulderguards, 1 Keen Razorfang Spaulders, 1 Worg-Rendering Shoulderguards, 1 Bone-Polished Iceplate Shoulders										

Title	Location	Faction	Race & Class	Group #	Starter	Finisher	Prerequisite	Reputation	XP	Money
An Intriguing Plan	Grizzly Hills	All	All		Tormak the Scarred	Prospector Rokar	The Unexpected 'Guest'	250 with The Taunka	20950	5 90
Blackriver Brawl	Grizzly Hills	Horde	All		Raider Captain Kronn	Raider Captain Kronn		250 with Horde Expedition	20750	5 60
Gray Worg Hides	Grizzly Hills	Horde	All		Hidetrader Jun'ik	Hidetrader Jun'ik		250 with Horde Expedition	20750	5 60
CHOICE OF: 1 Abandoned Hood, 1 Discarded Miner's Jerkin, 1 Patched Trapper Pauldrons, 1 Rusty Cave Stompers										
A Minor Substitution	Grizzly Hills	Horde	All		Hidetrader Jun'ik	Hidetrader Jun'ik	Gray Worg Hides	250 with Horde Expedition	20750	
CHOICE OF: 1 Specially Treated Robes, 1 Bearskin Helm, 1 Hide-Lined Chestguard, 1 Carapace of the Fallen										
Jun'ik's Coverup	Grizzly Hills	Horde	All		Hidetrader Jun'ik	Hidetrader Jun'ik	A Minor Substitution	75 with Horde Expedition	10400	
Delivery to Krenna	Grizzly Hills	Horde	All		Hidetrader Jun'ik	Conqueror Krenna	Jun'ik's Coverup	75 with Horde Expedition	10400	
The Captive Prospectors	Grizzly Hills	Alliance	All		Mountaineer Kilian	Mountaineer Kilian	Steady as a Rock?, Free at Last		20950	5 90
Looking the Part	Grizzly Hills	Alliance	All		Mountaineer Kilian	Mountaineer Kilian	The Captive Prospectors		20950	5 90
Cultivating an Image	Grizzly Hills	Alliance	All		Mountaineer Kilian	Mountaineer Kilian	Looking the Part		20950	5 90
Put on Your Best Face for Loken	Grizzly Hills	Alliance	All		Mountaineer Kilian	Mountaineer Kilian	Cultivating an Image		20950	5 90
CHOICE OF: 1 Spaulders of Foresight, 1 Belt of Keen Hearing, 1 Shoulderpads of Imminent Disaster, 1 Whispering Stompers										
Say Hello to My Little Friend	Grizzly Hills	All	All		Prigmon	Harkor	Shimmercap Stew		20750	5 60
The Unexpected 'Guest'	Grizzly Hills	Horde	All		Tormak the Scarred	Tormak the Scarred		250 with The Taunka	20950	5 90
From the Ground Up	Grizzly Hills	All	All		Prospector Rokar	Prospector Rokar	An Intriguing Plan	250 with The Taunka	20950	5 90
We Have the Power	Grizzly Hills	All	All		Prospector Rokar	Prospector Rokar	Why Fabricate When You Can Appropriate?	250 with The Taunka	20950	5 90
... Or Maybe We Don't	Grizzly Hills	All	All		Prospector Rokar	Prospector Rokar	We Have the Power	250 with The Taunka	20950	5 90
Bringing Down the Iron Thane	Grizzly Hills	All	All		Prospector Rokar	Tormak the Scarred	... Or Maybe We Don't	350 with The Taunka	26200	11 80
CHOICE OF: 1 Grounded Gloves, 1 Crackpot Spaulders, 1 Short-Circuiting Boots, 1 Golem-Rider's Greaves										
The Overseer's Shadow	Grizzly Hills	Horde	All		Scout Vor'takh	Scout Vor'takh	In the Name of Loken		20950	5 90
Cultivating an Image	Grizzly Hills	Horde	All		Scout Vor'takh	Scout Vor'takh	The Overseer's Shadow		20950	5 90
Loken's Orders	Grizzly Hills	Horde	All		Scout Vor'takh	Scout Vor'takh	Cultivating an Image		20950	5 90
In the Name of Loken	Grizzly Hills	Horde	All		Scout Vor'takh	Scout Vor'takh	Free at Last, The Runic Prophecies		15700	4 60
Vordrassil's Fall	Grizzly Hills	Horde	All		Windseer Grayhorn	Windseer Grayhorn	Attack on Silverbrook	250 with Warsong Offensive	20750	
CHOICE OF: 1 Robe of Expurgation, 1 Wax-Coated Chestguard, 1 Acid-Resistant Hauberk, 1 Chestplate of Untimely Rewards										
Good Troll Hunting	Grizzly Hills	All	All		Sergeant Thurkin	Samir	My Enemy's Friend		5200	1 44
Troll Season!	Grizzly Hills	All	All		Lieutenant Dumont	Samir	Replenishing the Storehouse		15400	4 10
Replenishing the Storehouse	Grizzly Hills	All	All		Master Woodsman Anderhol	Master Woodsman Anderhol		250 with Valiance Expedition	20750	5 60
The Darkness Beneath	Grizzly Hills	Horde	All		Windseer Grayhorn	Windseer Grayhorn	Attack on Silverbrook	250 with Warsong Offensive	20750	
Them or Us!	Grizzly Hills	All	All		Master Woodsman Anderhol	Master Woodsman Anderhol		150 with Valiance Expedition	15550	4 40
Take Their Rear!	Grizzly Hills	All	All		Master Woodsman Anderhol	Master Woodsman Anderhol	Replenishing the Storehouse	250 with Valiance Expedition	20750	5 60
Eagle Eyes	Grizzly Hills	All	All		Master Woodsman Anderhol	Master Woodsman Anderhol	Them or Us!	250 with Valiance Expedition	20750	5 60
The Failed World Tree	Grizzly Hills	All	All		Hierophant Thayreen	Hierophant Thayreen	A Swift Response	250 with Valiance Expedition	20750	
CHOICE OF: 1 Robe of Expurgation, 1 Wax-Coated Chestguard, 1 Acid-Resistant Hauberk, 1 Chestplate of Untimely Rewards										
A Dark Influence	Grizzly Hills	All	All		Hierophant Thayreen	Hierophant Thayreen	A Swift Response	250 with Warsong Offensive	20750	
Secrets of the Flamebinders	Grizzly Hills	Alliance	All		Woodsman Drake	Woodsman Drake	A Tentative Pact	250 with Valiance Expedition	20750	5 60
Thinning the Ranks	Grizzly Hills	Alliance	All		Woodsman Drake	Woodsman Drake	A Tentative Pact	250 with Valiance Expedition	20750	5 60
Mmm... Amberseeds!	Grizzly Hills	All	All		Amberseed	Master Woodsman Anderhol		75 with Valiance Expedition	5150	
Just Passing Through	Grizzly Hills	All	All		Master Woodsman Anderhol	Master Woodsman Anderhol	Mmm... Amberseeds!	250 with Valiance Expedition	20500	5 30
Doing Your Duty	Grizzly Hills	All	All		Master Woodsman Anderhol	Master Woodsman Anderhol	Just Passing Through	150 with Valiance Expedition	15400	
CHOICE OF: 1 Rancid Signet, 1 Fetid Loop, 1 Mildly Tarnished Ring										
A Possible Link	Grizzly Hills	Horde	All		Windseer Grayhorn	Windseer Grayhorn	The Failed World Tree, A Dark Influence	350 with Warsong Offensive	25950	
CHOICE OF: 1 Instigator's Gloves, 1 Shackles of Sanity, 1 Helm of the Furbolg Purifier, 1 Blood-Spattered Spaulders										
The Bear God's Offspring	Grizzly Hills	Horde	All		Windseer Grayhorn	Windseer Grayhorn	Vordrassil's Fall, The Darkness Beneath	150 with Warsong Offensive	15700	

Title	Location	Faction	Race & Class	Group #	Starter	Finisher	Prerequisite	Reputation	XP	Money
[Deprecated] Sewing Your Seed	Grizzly Hills	All	All				Doing Your Duty			
Ursoc, the Bear God	Grizzly Hills	Horde	All	3	Windseer Grayhorn	Windseer Grayhorn	Destroy the Sapling, Vordrassil's Seeds	500 with Warsong Offensive	31450	17🟡 70⚪
REWARD: 1 Bulwark of the Tormented God AND CHOICE OF: 1 Kilt of Deific Torment, 1 Pants of Purified Wind, 1 Greaves of Sanctified Dissolution, 1 Legguards of Dissolved Hope, 1 Leggings of Forceful Purification										
Destroy the Sapling	Grizzly Hills	Horde	All		Windseer Grayhorn	Windseer Grayhorn	A Possible Link, The Bear God's Offspring	250 with Warsong Offensive	20950	
Vordrassil's Seeds	Grizzly Hills	Horde	All		Windseer Grayhorn	Windseer Grayhorn	A Possible Link, The Bear God's Offspring	250 with Warsong Offensive	20750	
CHOICE OF: 1 Hoarder's Necklace, 1 Band of the Tender, 1 Drape of the Possessive Soul										
Shredder Repair	Grizzly Hills	Alliance	All		Synipus	Synipus			20750	5🟡 60⚪
REWARD: 1 Key to Refurbished Shredder										
A Possible Link	Grizzly Hills	All	All		Hierophant Thayreen	Hierophant Thayreen	The Failed World Tree, A Dark Influence	350 with Valiance Expedition	25950	
CHOICE OF: 1 Instigator's Gloves, 1 Shackles of Sanity, 1 Helm of the Furbolg Purifier, 1 Blood-Spattered Spaulders										
Children of Ursoc	Grizzly Hills	All	All		Hierophant Thayreen	Hierophant Thayreen	Vordrassil's Fall, The Darkness Beneath	150 with Warsong Offensive	15700	
Vordrassil's Sapling	Grizzly Hills	All	All		Hierophant Thayreen	Hierophant Thayreen	A Possible Link, The Bear God's Offspring	250 with Valiance Expedition	20950	
Ursoc, the Bear God	Grizzly Hills	All	All	3	Hierophant Thayreen	Hierophant Thayreen	Destroy the Sapling, Vordrassil's Seeds	500 with Valiance Expedition	31450	17🟡 70⚪
REWARD: 1 Bulwark of the Tormented God AND CHOICE OF: 1 Kilt of Deific Torment, 1 Pants of Purified Wind, 1 Greaves of Sanctified Dissolution, 1 Legguards of Dissolved Hope, 1 Leggings of Forceful Purification										
Vordrassil's Seeds	Grizzly Hills	All	All		Hierophant Thayreen	Hierophant Thayreen	A Possible Link, The Bear God's Offspring	250 with Valiance Expedition	20950	
CHOICE OF: 1 Hoarder's Necklace, 1 Band of the Tender, 1 Drape of the Possessive Soul										
The Thane of Voldrune	Grizzly Hills	Alliance	All		Woodsman Drake	Woodsman Drake	Secrets of the Flamebinders, Thinning the Ranks	250 with Valiance Expedition	20750	5🟡 60⚪
CHOICE OF: 1 Headbinder's Crown, 1 Tunic of the Rectified Thane, 1 Legguards of Refuted Feudalism, 1 Skull-Reshaper's Helm, 1 Thane-Reaper's Signet										
The Flamebinders' Secrets	Grizzly Hills	Horde	All		Sergeant Nazgrim	Sergeant Nazgrim	The Conqueror's Task	250 with Warsong Offensive	20750	5🟡 60⚪
A Show of Strength	Grizzly Hills	Horde	All		Sergeant Nazgrim	Sergeant Nazgrim	The Conqueror's Task	250 with Warsong Offensive	20750	5🟡 60⚪
The Thane of Voldrune	Grizzly Hills	Horde	All		Sergeant Nazgrim	Sergeant Nazgrim	The Flamebinders' Secrets, A Show of Strength	250 with Warsong Offensive	20750	5🟡 60⚪
CHOICE OF: 1 Headbinder's Crown, 1 Tunic of the Rectified Thane, 1 Legguards of Refuted Feudalism, 1 Skull-Reshaper's Helm, 1 Thane-Reaper's Signet										
Pieces Parts	Grizzly Hills	Alliance	All		Pipthwack	Pipthwack			20750	5🟡 60⚪
Shred the Alliance	Grizzly Hills	Horde	All		Grekk	Grekk		250 with Warsong Offensive	20750	5🟡 60⚪
REWARD: 1 Key to Refurbished Shredder										
A Bear of an Appetite	Grizzly Hills	All	All		Hugh Glass	Hugh Glass			20950	5🟡 90⚪
Making Repairs	Grizzly Hills	Horde	All		Lurz	Lurz		250 with Warsong Offensive	20750	5🟡 60⚪
Keep 'Em on Their Heels	Grizzly Hills	Horde	All		Commander Bargok	Commander Bargok		250 with Warsong Offensive	20750	5🟡 60⚪
Overwhelmed!	Grizzly Hills	Horde	All		Aumana	Aumana		250 with Warsong Offensive	20750	5🟡 60⚪
Kick 'Em While They're Down	Grizzly Hills	Alliance	All		Sergeant Hartsman	Sergeant Hartsman		250 with Valiance Expedition	20750	5🟡 60⚪
Local Support	Grizzly Hills	All	All		Lieutenant Dumont	Lieutenant Dumont		250 with Valiance Expedition	20750	
CHOICE OF: 1 Bramble-Proof Leggings, 1 Patchhide Pants, 1 Legguards of Swift Pursuit, 1 Snaptooth Legplates, 1 Injured Trapper's Cloak										
Close the Deal	Grizzly Hills	All	All		Lieutenant Dumont	Ivan	Local Support	25 with Valiance Expedition	5200	
A Tentative Pact	Grizzly Hills	All	All		Ivan	Lieutenant Dumont	Close the Deal	25 with Valiance Expedition	5200	
An Exercise in Diplomacy	Grizzly Hills	All	All		Lieutenant Dumont	Envoy Ducal	A Tentative Pact	250 with Valiance Expedition	10400	
Life or Death	Grizzly Hills	Alliance	All		Rheanna	Rheanna		250 with Valiance Expedition	20750	5🟡 60⚪
Northern Hospitality	Grizzly Hills	All	All		Sergei	Sergei	An Exercise in Diplomacy		20750	11🟡 20⚪
CHOICE OF: 1 Insignia of Bloody Fire, 1 Mendicant's Charm, 1 Talon of Hatred										
Test of Mettle	Grizzly Hills	All	All		Sergei	Captured Trapper	Northern Hospitality, Wolfsbane Root		15550	
Words of Warning	Grizzly Hills	All	All		Captured Trapper	Caged Prisoner	Test of Mettle	250 with Valiance Expedition	15550	
Wolfsbane Root	Grizzly Hills	Alliance	All		Katja	Katja			20750	4🟡 40⚪
CHOICE OF: 1 Herbalist's Pauldrons, 1 Girdle of Growing Vines, 1 Pruning Pendant, 1 Drape of Horticultural Sanitization										
Escape from Silverbrook	Grizzly Hills	All	All		Caged Prisoner	Lieutenant Dumont	Words of Warning	250 with Valiance Expedition	20750	
CHOICE OF: 1 Raiment of the Caged Beast, 1 Boots of Internal Strife, 1 Wristguard of the Tormented Soul, 1 Sabatons of Crushed Humanity, 1 Worgslayer's Ring										
A Swift Response	Grizzly Hills	All	All		Lieutenant Dumont	Lieutenant Dumont	Escape from Silverbrook	250 with Valiance Expedition	20750	5🟡 60⚪
Down With Captain Zorna!	Grizzly Hills	Alliance	All	3	Baron Freeman	Baron Freeman			20750	5🟡 60⚪
REWARD: 10 Venture Coin										

GRIZZLY HILLS

Title	Location	Faction	Race & Class	Group #	Starter	Finisher	Prerequisite	Reputation	XP	Money
Crush Captain Brightwater!	Grizzly Hills	Horde	All		General Khazgar	General Khazgar			20750	5🟡60🟠
REWARD: 10 Venture Coin										
Keep Them at Bay!	Grizzly Hills	Alliance	All		Lieutenant Stuart	Lieutenant Stuart			20750	5🟡60🟠
REWARD: 10 Venture Coin										
Keep Them at Bay	Grizzly Hills	Horde	All		Centurion Kaggrum	Centurion Kaggrum			20750	5🟡60🟠
REWARD: 10 Venture Coin										
Smoke 'Em Out	Grizzly Hills	Alliance	All		Sergeant Downey	Sergeant Downey			20750	5🟡60🟠
REWARD: 10 Venture Coin										
Smoke 'Em Out	Grizzly Hills	Horde	All		Stone Guard Ragetotem	Stone Guard Ragetotem			20750	5🟡60🟠
REWARD: 10 Venture Coin										
Out of Body Experience	Grizzly Hills	All	All		Ruuna the Blind	Ruuna the Blind	Ruuna's Request		10500	
Ruuna's Request	Grizzly Hills	All	All		Ruuna the Blind	Ruuna the Blind	Ruuna the Blind		20950	
CHOICE OF: 1 Foreseer's Girdle, 1 Pauldrons of the Prophet, 1 Gossamer-Stained Grips, 1 Thought-Purifying Protector										
Fate and Coincidence	Grizzly Hills	All	All		Ruuna the Blind	Sasha	Out of Body Experience		5250	
Anatoly Will Talk	Grizzly Hills	All	All		Sasha	Sasha	Fate and Coincidence		15700	
CHOICE OF: 1 Solstice Signet, 1 Tatjana's Pendant, 1 Seal of the Slumbering Wolf										
A Sister's Pledge	Grizzly Hills	All	All		Sasha	Anya	Anatoly Will Talk		10500	
My Enemy's Friend	Grizzly Hills	Horde	All		Conqueror Krenna, Conqueror Krenna	Conqueror Krenna	The Thane of Voldrune		20950	
CHOICE OF: 1 Bramble-Proof Leggings, 1 Patchhide Pants, 1 Legguards of Swift Pursuit, 1 Snaptooth Legplates, 1 Injured Trapper's Cloak										
Attack on Silverbrook	Grizzly Hills	Horde	All		Conqueror Krenna, Conqueror Krenna	Conqueror Krenna	My Enemy's Friend	250 with Warsong Offensive	20750	
CHOICE OF: 1 Raiment of the Caged Beast, 1 Boots of Internal Strife, 1 Wristguard of the Tormented Soul, 1 Sabatons of Crushed Humanity, 1 Worgslayer's Ring										
Mounting Up	Grizzly Hills	Alliance	All		Squire Percy	Squire Percy			20950	5🟡90🟠
The Horse Hollerer	Grizzly Hills	Horde	All		Soulok Stormfury	Soulok Stormfury		250 with The Taunka	20950	5🟡90🟠
Tactical Clemency	Grizzly Hills	All	All		Gorgonna	Captured Trapper	Gorgonna	25 with Warsong Offensive	5200	
Mikhail's Journal	Grizzly Hills	Horde	All		Mikhail's Journal	Conqueror Krenna		75 with Warsong Offensive	10400	
Gorgonna	Grizzly Hills	Horde	All		Conqueror Krenna, Conqueror Krenna	Gorgonna	Mikhail's Journal	75 with Warsong Offensive	10400	
Ruuna the Blind	Grizzly Hills	All	All		Gorgonna	Ruuna the Blind	Tactical Clemency		5250	
DEPRECATED	Grizzly Hills	Horde	All		Gorgonna	Gorgonna		25 with Warsong Offensive	5250	
The Conquest Pit: Bear Wrestling!	Grizzly Hills	Horde	All	3	Grennix Shivwiggle	Bookie Vel'jen	Tactical Clemency, Delivery to Krenna		25950	11🟡20🟠
The Conquest Pit: Mad Furbolg Fighting	Grizzly Hills	Horde	All	3	Grennix Shivwiggle	Bookie Vel'jen	The Conquest Pit: Bear Wrestling!		25950	16🟡80🟠
The Conquest Pit: Blood and Metal	Grizzly Hills	Horde	All	3	Grennix Shivwiggle	Bookie Vel'jen	The Conquest Pit: Mad Furbolg Fighting		25950	16🟡80🟠
The Conquest Pit: Death Is Likely	Grizzly Hills	Horde	All	3	Grennix Shivwiggle	Bookie Vel'jen	The Conquest Pit: Blood and Metal		31450	17🟡70🟠
The Conquest Pit: Final Showdown	Grizzly Hills	Horde	All	3	Grennix Shivwiggle	Gorgonna	The Conquest Pit: Death Is Likely	500 with Warsong Offensive	31450	17🟡70🟠
CHOICE OF: 1 Grips of Torrential Power, 1 Shining Buckle Gauntlets, 1 Handguards of Deluded Might, 1 Charged Earthlink Grips, 1 Handguards of the Sanguine Gladiator										
Riding the Red Rocket	Grizzly Hills	Horde	All		General Gorlok	General Gorlok			20750	5🟡60🟠
REWARD: 10 Venture Coin										
Seeking Solvent	Grizzly Hills	Horde	All		Gurtor	Gurtor			20750	5🟡60🟠
REWARD: 4 Venture Coin										
Always Seeking Solvent	Grizzly Hills	Horde	All		Gurtor	Gurtor	Seeking Solvent		20750	5🟡60🟠
REWARD: 2 Venture Coin										
Supplemental Income	Grizzly Hills	Horde	All		Provisioner Lorkran	Provisioner Lorkran		250 with Warsong Offensive	20750	
Riding the Red Rocket	Grizzly Hills	Alliance	All		Commander Howser	Commander Howser			20750	5🟡60🟠
REWARD: 10 Venture Coin										
Seeking Solvent	Grizzly Hills	Alliance	All		Barblefink	Barblefink			20750	5🟡60🟠
REWARD: 4 Venture Coin										
Blackriver Skirmish	Grizzly Hills	All	All		Scout Captain Carter	Scout Captain Carter		250 with Valiance Expedition	20750	5🟡60🟠
REWARD: 10 Venture Coin										
Always Seeking Solvent	Grizzly Hills	Alliance	All		Barblefink	Barblefink	Seeking Solvent			
REWARD: 2 Venture Coin										
Onward to Camp Oneqwah	Grizzly Hills	Horde	All		Sergeant Nazgrim	Scout Vor'takh	The Thane of Voldrune	25 with The Taunka	5200	
Eyes Above	Grizzly Hills	Horde	All		Windseer Grayhorn	Windseer Grayhorn	My Enemy's Friend	150 with Warsong Offensive	15550	4🟡40🟠
CHOICE OF: 1 Insignia of Bloody Fire, 1 Mendicant's Charm, 1 Talon of Hatred										
The Conqueror's Task	Grizzly Hills	Horde	All		Conqueror Krenna, Conqueror Krenna	Sergeant Nazgrim			5200	
Shimmercap Stew	Grizzly Hills	All	All		Prigmon	Prigmon	Scourgekabob		20950	5🟡90🟠
Scourgekabob	Grizzly Hills	All	All		Prigmon	Mack Fearsen	Vial of Visions		5200	1🟡44🟠

GRIZZLY HILLS

Title	Location	Faction	Race & Class	Group #	Starter	Finisher	Prerequisite	Reputation	XP	Money
To Conquest Hold, But Be Careful!	Grizzly Hills	Horde	All		High Executor Wroth	Conqueror Krenna		10 with Warsong Offensive	2100	
The Hills Have Us	Grizzly Hills	All	All		Gryphon Commander Urik	Lieutenant Dumont		25 with Valiance Expedition	5150	
Shifting Priorities	Grizzly Hills	Horde	All		Scout Vor'takh	Sergeant Riannah			2100	60
Reallocating Resources	Grizzly Hills	All	All		Captain Gryan Stoutmantle	Sergeant Riannah			2100	60
My Heart is in Your Hands	Grizzly Hills	All	All		Heart of the Ancients	Image of Drakuru	Heart of the Ancients		20750	

GUNDRAK

Title	Location	Faction	Race & Class	Group #	Starter	Finisher	Prerequisite	Reputation	XP	Money
Gal'darah Must Pay	Gundrak	All	All		Tol'mar	Tol'mar	Unfinished Business		27000	6 80
CHOICE OF: 1 Sly Mojo Sash, 1 Strange Voodoo Belt, 1 Ranger's Belt of the Fallen Empire, 1 Clasp of the Fallen Demi-God										
For Posterity	Gundrak	All	All		Chronicler Bah'Kini	Chronicler Bah'Kini			27000	13 60
CHOICE OF: 1 Lion's Head Ring, 1 Ring of Foul Mojo, 1 Solid Platinum Band, 1 Voodoo Signet										
One of a Kind	Gundrak	All	All		Chronicler Bah'Kini	Chronicler Bah'Kini			27000	13 60
CHOICE OF: 1 Fur-lined Moccasins, 1 Rhino Hide Kneeboots, 1 Scaled Boots of Fallen Hope, 1 Slippers of the Mojo Dojo, 1 Trollkickers										
Proof of Demise: Gal'darah	Gundrak	All	All		Archmage Lan'dalock	Archmage Lan'dalock		75 with Kirin Tor	44100	22 20
REWARD: 2 Emblem of Heroism										

HALLS OF LIGHTNING

Title	Location	Faction	Race & Class	Group #	Starter	Finisher	Prerequisite	Reputation	XP	Money
Whatever it Takes!	Halls of Lightning	All	All		King Jokkum	King Jokkum	The Reckoning	500 with The Sons of Hodir	27550	14 80
CHOICE OF: 1 Robes of Lightning, 1 Hardened Tongue Tunic, 1 Lightningbringer's Hauberk, 1 Breastplate of Jagged Stone										
Diametrically Opposed	Halls of Lightning	All	All		King Jokkum	King Jokkum	The Reckoning		27550	14 80
CHOICE OF: 1 Lightning Infused Mantle, 1 Charred Leather Shoulderguards, 1 Stormforged Shoulders, 1 Pauldrons of Extinguished Hatred, 1 Mantle of Volkhan										
Timear Foresees Titanium Vanguards in your Future!	Halls of Lightning	All	All		Archmage Timear	Archmage Timear		75 with Kirin Tor	33100	14 80
CHOICE OF: 1 Kirin Tor Commendation Badge, 1 Argent Crusade Commendation Badge, 1 Ebon Blade Commendation Badge, 1 Wyrmrest Commendation Badge										
Proof of Demise: Loken	Halls of Lightning	All	All		Archmage Lan'dalock	Archmage Lan'dalock		75 with Kirin Tor	44100	22 20
REWARD: 2 Emblem of Heroism										

HALLS OF STONE

Title	Location	Faction	Race & Class	Group #	Starter	Finisher	Prerequisite	Reputation	XP	Money
Halls of Stone	Halls of Stone	All	All		Brann Bronzebeard (1), Brann Bronzebeard	Brann Bronzebeard			43200	
CHOICE OF: 1 Mantle of the Intrepid Explorer, 1 Shoulderpads of the Adventurer, 1 Spaulders of Lost Secrets, 1 Pauldrons of Reconnaissance										
Proof of Demise: Sjonnir The Ironshaper	Halls of Stone	All	All		Archmage Lan'dalock	Archmage Lan'dalock		75 with Kirin Tor	44100	22 20
REWARD: 2 Emblem of Heroism										

HOWLING FJORD

Title	Location	Faction	Race & Class	Group #	Starter	Finisher	Prerequisite	Reputation	XP	Money
Break the Blockade	Howling Fjord	Alliance	All		Bombardier Petrov	Bombardier Petrov		250 with Valiance Expedition	20100	4 70
Scare the Guano Out of Them!	Howling Fjord	Alliance	All		Engineer Feknut	Engineer Feknut		250 with Valiance Expedition	20100	4 70
CHOICE OF: 1 Icestriker Bands, 1 Reinforced Tuskhide Hauberk, 1 Bloodbinder's Girdle, 1 Ice-Crusted Cape										
Shoveltusk Soup Again?	Howling Fjord	Alliance	All		Chef Kettleblack	Chef Kettleblack		250 with Valiance Expedition	20100	4 70
REWARD: 20 Shoveltusk Soup										
The Clutches of Evil	Howling Fjord	All	All		Captain Adams	Captain Adams		250 with Valiance Expedition	20100	4 70
The New Plague	Howling Fjord	Horde	All		Apothecary Lysander	Apothecary Lysander		250 with Horde Expedition	20100	4 70
CHOICE OF: 1 Blauvelt's Special Occasion Gloves, 1 Nimblefinger Scaled Gloves, 1 Antique Reinforced Legguards, 1 Imperious Worghide Cap										
Spiking the Mix	Howling Fjord	Horde	All		Apothecary Lysander	Apothecary Lysander	The New Plague		10050	2 40
Test at Sea	Howling Fjord	Horde	All		Apothecary Lysander	Apothecary Lysander	Spiking the Mix	250 with The Hand of Vengeance	20100	4 70
CHOICE OF: 1 Frost-Trimmed Gauntlets, 1 Azure Chain Hauberk, 1 Ramshorn-Inlaid Shoulders, 1 Runed Clamshell Choker										
My Daughter	Howling Fjord	Alliance	All		Old Man Stonemantle	Overseer Irena Stonemantle	Leader of the Deranged	10 with Explorers' League	2000	
See to the Operations	Howling Fjord	Alliance	All		Overseer Irena Stonemantle	Steel Gate Chief Archaeologist		10 with Explorers' League	2000	
[Temporarily Deprecated Awaiting a New Mob] Finlay Is Gutless	Howling Fjord	Alliance	All		Finlay Fletcher	Finlay Fletcher		250 with Valiance Expedition	20100	4 70
Root Causes	Howling Fjord	All	All		Ember Clutch Ancient	Ember Clutch Ancient			25150	
CHOICE OF: 1 Dark Iron Signet, 1 Flint-Reinforced Spaulders, 1 Cold-Iron Armbands, 1 Arcanum-Bound Bracers										
Mage-Lieutenant Malister	Howling Fjord	All	All		Captain Adams	Mage-Lieutenant Malister	The Clutches of Evil	10 with Valiance Expedition	2000	
Two Wrongs...	Howling Fjord	All	All		Mage-Lieutenant Malister	Mage-Lieutenant Malister	Mage-Lieutenant Malister	250 with Valiance Expedition	20100	4 70
CHOICE OF: 1 Indigo Robe of Replenishment, 1 Interlinked Chain Girdle, 1 Beneficent Skullcap, 1 Iron-Studded Leggings										

Howling Fjord

Title	Location	Faction	Race & Class	Group #	Starter	Finisher	Prerequisite	Reputation	XP	Money
One Last Time	Howling Fjord	Alliance	All		Tarnished Promise Ring	Overseer Irena Stonemantle		250 with Explorers' League	20300	5
One Size Does Not Fit All	Howling Fjord	Alliance	All		Cannoneer Ely	Cannoneer Ely		250 with Valiance Expedition	20100	4 70
Report to Scout Knowles	Howling Fjord	All	All		Captain Adams	Scout Knowles	Two Wrongs...	10 with Valiance Expedition	2000	
Mission: Eternal Flame	Howling Fjord	All	All		Scout Knowles	Scout Knowles	Report to Scout Knowles	250 with Valiance Expedition	20100	4 70
CHOICE OF: 1 Bone-Inlaid Bracers, 1 Embossed Ermine Girdle, 1 Magdun Spaulders, 1 Runeplate Helm										
Danger! Explosives!	Howling Fjord	Alliance	All		Sapper Steelring	Sapper Steelring	Two Wrongs...	250 with Explorers' League	20100	4 70
Reports from the Field	Howling Fjord	Horde	All		High Executor Anselm	High Executor Anselm	War is Hell	150 with The Hand of Vengeance	15100	
Send Them Packing	Howling Fjord	Alliance	All		Explorer Abigail	Explorer Abigail	Two Wrongs...	250 with Explorers' League	20100	4 70
Let Them Eat Crow	Howling Fjord	Horde	All		Pontius	Pontius		250 with The Hand of Vengeance	20100	4 70
Hell Has Frozen Over...	Howling Fjord	Alliance	All		Macalroy	Vice Admiral Keller			1250	
The Windrunner Fleet	Howling Fjord	Horde	All		High Executor Anselm	Captain Harker	Reports from the Field	25 with Horde Expedition	5050	
Ambushed!	Howling Fjord	Horde	All		Captain Harker	Captain Harker	The Windrunner Fleet	150 with Horde Expedition	20100	4 70
CHOICE OF: 1 Bone-Threaded Harness, 1 Benevolent Hood, 1 Nerubian Inner Husk										
Of Keys and Cages	Howling Fjord	Alliance	All		Father Levariol	Father Levariol	All Hail the Conqueror of Skorn!	250 with Valiance Expedition	20100	4 70
Guide Our Sights	Howling Fjord	Horde	All		Captain Harker	Dark Ranger Lyana	Ambushed!	250 with The Hand of Vengeance	20100	
Landing the Killing Blow	Howling Fjord	Horde	All		Dark Ranger Lyana	Dark Ranger Lyana	Guide Our Sights	350 with The Hand of Vengeance	25150	9 40
CHOICE OF: 1 Bramblethorn Greatstaff, 1 Coldstone Cutlass, 1 Cragthumper, 1 Earthspike, 1 Elekk-Horn Crossbow, 1 Pacifying Pummeler										
Report to Anselm	Howling Fjord	Horde	All		Dark Ranger Lyana	High Executor Anselm	Landing the Killing Blow	75 with The Hand of Vengeance	10050	
Dealing With Gjalerbron	Howling Fjord	All	All		Captain Adams	Captain Adams	All Hail the Conqueror of Skorn!	250 with Valiance Expedition	20100	4 70
Necro Overlord Mezhen	Howling Fjord	All	All		Captain Adams	Captain Adams	Dealing With Gjalerbron	350 with Valiance Expedition	25400	10
CHOICE OF: 1 Drape of Munificence, 1 Dusk-Linked Leggings, 1 Gold-Plated Coldsteel Girdle, 1 Worgskin Shoulders										
Gjalerbron Attack Plans	Howling Fjord	All	All		Gjalerbron Attack Plans	Mage-Lieutenant Malister		250 with Valiance Expedition	20300	5
The Frost Wyrm and its Master	Howling Fjord	All	All	2	Mage-Lieutenant Malister	Mage-Lieutenant Malister	Gjalerbron Attack Plans	350 with Valiance Expedition	25400	10
CHOICE OF: 1 Earthwell Footwraps, 1 Magispike Helm, 1 Silversteel Gauntlets, 1 Lost Vrykul Signet										
In Service to the Light	Howling Fjord	Alliance	All		Father Levariol	Father Levariol	Of Keys and Cages	250 with Valiance Expedition	20100	4 70
CHOICE OF: 1 Regal Pantaloons, 1 Loam-Stained Greaves, 1 Tribal Chestguard, 1 Worgtooth Pendant										
Leader of the Deranged	Howling Fjord	Alliance	All		Sapper Steelring	Sapper Steelring	Danger! Explosives!	250 with Explorers' League	20100	4 70
CHOICE OF: 1 Wrathwrought Shoulderpads, 1 Whispersteel Handguards, 1 Feather-Lined Shoulderpads, 1 Spiked Skullguard										
Trail of Fire	Howling Fjord	Horde	All		Apothecary Hanes	Apothecary Lysander		350 with Horde Expedition	25150	9 40
CHOICE OF: 1 Coldspike Longbow, 1 Regal Sceptre, 1 Worn Vrykul Smasher, 1 Whelpling-Skull Zapper, 1 Ice-Rimed Dagger, 1 Stoneblade Slicer										
If Valgarde Falls...	Howling Fjord	Alliance	All		Vice Admiral Keller	Vice Admiral Keller	Hell Has Frozen Over...	250 with Valiance Expedition	12650	4 40
Rescuing the Rescuers	Howling Fjord	Alliance	All		Vice Admiral Keller	Vice Admiral Keller	If Valgarde Falls...	250 with Valiance Expedition	12650	4 40
CHOICE OF: 1 Earthspike, 1 Elekk-Horn Crossbow, 1 Pacifying Pummeler, 1 Bramblethorn Greatstaff, 1 Coldstone Cutlass, 1 Cragthumper										
Towers of Certain Doom	Howling Fjord	All	All		Westguard Sergeant	Westguard Sergeant	Operation: Skornful Wrath	250 with Valiance Expedition	20100	4 70
Gruesome, But Necessary	Howling Fjord	All	All		Westguard Sergeant	Westguard Sergeant	Operation: Skornful Wrath	250 with Valiance Expedition	20100	4 70
Burn Skorn, Burn!	Howling Fjord	All	All		Westguard Sergeant	Westguard Sergeant	Operation: Skornful Wrath	250 with Valiance Expedition	20100	4 70
Operation: Skornful Wrath	Howling Fjord	All	All		Captain Adams	Westguard Sergeant	Mission: Plague This!	10 with Valiance Expedition	2000	
Stop the Ascension!	Howling Fjord	Alliance	All		Vrykul Scroll of Ascension	Father Levariol	Operation: Skornful Wrath	350 with Valiance Expedition	25400	10
CHOICE OF: 1 Supple Doeskin Moccasins, 1 Shock-Bound Spaulders, 1 Onyx Grips, 1 Rejuvenating Cord										
All Hail the Conqueror of Skorn!	Howling Fjord	All	All		Westguard Sergeant	Captain Adams	Gruesome, But Necessary, Burn Skorn, Burn!, Towers of Certain Doom	350 with Valiance Expedition	25400	10
CHOICE OF: 1 Sun-fired Striders, 1 Shaleground Bracers, 1 Puissance-Infused Pendant, 1 Vineweven Tunic										
Fresh Legs	Howling Fjord	Alliance	All		Scout Valory	Defender Mordun			2000	48
Sniff Out the Enemy	Howling Fjord	Horde	All		Pontius	Dragonskin Scroll	Let Them Eat Crow	150 with Horde Expedition	15100	
The Dragonskin Map	Howling Fjord	Horde	All		Dragonskin Scroll	High Executor Anselm	Sniff Out the Enemy	75 with Horde Expedition	10050	

277

Title	Location	Faction	Race & Class	Group #	Starter	Finisher	Prerequisite	Reputation	XP	Money
Prisoners of Wyrmskull	Howling Fjord	Alliance	All		Vice Admiral Keller	Vice Admiral Keller	Rescuing the Rescuers	250 with Valiance Expedition	12650	4🥈 40🥉
Skorn Must Fall!	Howling Fjord	All	All		Chieftain Ashtotem	Winterhoof Brave	Mimicking Nature's Call	10 with The Taunka	2000	
Gruesome, But Necessary	Howling Fjord	All	All		Winterhoof Brave	Winterhoof Brave	Skorn Must Fall!	250 with The Taunka	20100	4🥈 70🥉
Burn Skorn, Burn!	Howling Fjord	All	All		Winterhoof Brave	Winterhoof Brave	Skorn Must Fall!	250 with The Taunka	20100	4🥈 70🥉
Towers of Certain Doom	Howling Fjord	All	All		Winterhoof Brave	Winterhoof Brave	Skorn Must Fall!	250 with The Taunka	20100	4🥈 70🥉
Stop the Ascension!	Howling Fjord	Horde	All		Vrykul Scroll of Ascension	Greatmother Ankha	Skorn Must Fall!	350 with The Taunka	25400	10🥈
CHOICE OF: 1 Supple Doeskin Moccasins, 1 Shock-Bound Spaulders, 1 Onyx Grips, 1 Rejuvenating Cord										
The Conqueror of Skorn!	Howling Fjord	All	All		Winterhoof Brave	Chieftain Ashtotem	Gruesome, But Necessary, Burn Skorn, Burn!, Towers of Certain Doom	350 with The Taunka	25400	10🥈
CHOICE OF: 1 Sun-fired Striders, 1 Shaleground Bracers, 1 Puissance-Infused Pendant, 1 Vineweven Tunic										
Dealing With Gjalerbron	Howling Fjord	Horde	All		Chieftain Ashtotem	Chieftain Ashtotem	The Conqueror of Skorn!	250 with The Taunka	20100	4🥈 70🥉
Necro Overlord Mezhen	Howling Fjord	Horde	All		Chieftain Ashtotem	Chieftain Ashtotem	Dealing With Gjalerbron	350 with The Taunka	25400	10🥈
CHOICE OF: 1 Drape of Munificence, 1 Dusk-Linked Leggings, 1 Gold-Plated Coldsteel Girdle, 1 Worgskin Shoulders										
Of Keys and Cages	Howling Fjord	Horde	All		Greatmother Ankha	Greatmother Ankha	The Conqueror of Skorn!	250 with The Taunka	20100	4🥈 70🥉
Gjalerbron Attack Plans	Howling Fjord	Horde	All		Gjalerbron Attack Plans	Celea Frozenmane		250 with The Taunka	20300	5🥈
The Frost Wyrm and its Master	Howling Fjord	Horde	All	2	Celea Frozenmane	Celea Frozenmane	Gjalerbron Attack Plans	350 with The Taunka	25400	10🥈
CHOICE OF: 1 Earthwell Footwraps, 1 Magispike Helm, 1 Silversteel Gauntlets, 1 Lost Vrykul Signet										
The Walking Dead	Howling Fjord	Horde	All		Greatmother Ankha	Greatmother Ankha	Of Keys and Cages	250 with The Taunka	20100	4🥈 70🥉
CHOICE OF: 1 Regal Pantaloons, 1 Loam-Stained Greaves, 1 Tribal Chestguard, 1 Worgtooth Pendant										
Down to the Wire	Howling Fjord	Alliance	All		Gil Grisert	Gil Grisert		250 with Valiance Expedition	20100	4🥈 70🥉
CHOICE OF: 1 Artfully Tooled Leggings, 1 Songscale Breastplate, 1 Cold-Forged Bronze Legplates, 1 Shimmering Cold-Iron Band										
War is Hell	Howling Fjord	Horde	All		High Executor Anselm	High Executor Anselm		250 with The Hand of Vengeance	20100	
Hasty Preparations	Howling Fjord	Horde	All		Ahota Whitefrost	Ahota Whitefrost		250 with The Taunka	20100	4🥈 70🥉
CHOICE OF: 1 Artfully Tooled Leggings, 1 Songscale Breastplate, 1 Cold-Forged Bronze Legplates, 1 Shimmering Cold-Iron Band										
The Human League	Howling Fjord	Alliance	All		Beltrand McSorf	Pulroy the Archaeologist	Rescuing the Rescuers	25 with Valiance Expedition	3150	
Zedd's Probably Dead	Howling Fjord	Alliance	All		Pulroy the Archaeologist	Zedd	The Human League	25 with Valiance Expedition	3150	
Making the Horn	Howling Fjord	Horde	All		Nokoma Snowseer	Nokoma Snowseer			20100	4🥈 70🥉
And Then There Were Two...	Howling Fjord	Alliance	All		Zedd	Glorenfeld	Zedd's Probably Dead	150 with Valiance Expedition	9500	
The Depths of Depravity	Howling Fjord	Alliance	All		Glorenfeld	Glorenfeld	And Then There Were Two...	250 with Valiance Expedition	20100	
Return to Valgarde	Howling Fjord	Alliance	All		Glorenfeld	Beltrand McSorf	Stunning Defeat at the Ring	250 with Valiance Expedition	5050	1🥈 20🥉
CHOICE OF: 1 Deacon's Wraps, 1 Stretch-Hide Spaulders, 1 Streamlined Stompers, 1 Scavenged Tirasian Plate										
Green Eggs and Whelps	Howling Fjord	Horde	All		Plaguebringer Tillinghast	Plaguebringer Tillinghast		250 with The Hand of Vengeance	20100	4🥈 70🥉
Draconis Gastritis	Howling Fjord	Horde	All		Plaguebringer Tillinghast	Plaguebringer Tillinghast	Green Eggs and Whelps	250 with The Hand of Vengeance	20100	4🥈 70🥉
CHOICE OF: 1 Indigo Robe of Replenishment, 1 Interlinked Chain Girdle, 1 Beneficent Skullcap, 1 Iron-Studded Leggings										
Mimicking Nature's Call	Howling Fjord	Horde	All		Nokoma Snowseer	Nokoma Snowseer	Making the Horn		20100	4🥈 70🥉
CHOICE OF: 1 Braxley's Backyard Moonshine, 1 Gholamcloth Wrap, 1 Appointed Scalemail Leggings, 1 Inscribed Worghide Treads										
A Lesson in Fear	Howling Fjord	Horde	All		Sergeant Gorth	Sergeant Gorth	The Offensive Begins	250 with Horde Expedition	20100	4🥈 70🥉
CHOICE OF: 1 Grounded Pants, 1 Hex-Linked Stronghelm, 1 Nimblefinger Band, 1 Stoneground Cleaver										
Baleheim Bodycount	Howling Fjord	Horde	All		Sergeant Gorth	Sergeant Gorth	A Lesson in Fear	250 with The Hand of Vengeance	25150	9🥈 40🥉
CHOICE OF: 1 Deacon's Wraps, 1 Stretch-Hide Spaulders, 1 Streamlined Stompers, 1 Scavenged Tirasian Plate										
The Yeti Next Door	Howling Fjord	Alliance	All		Foreman Colbey	Foreman Colbey		250 with Valiance Expedition	20100	4🥈 70🥉
CHOICE OF: 1 Braxley's Backyard Moonshine, 1 Gholamcloth Wrap, 1 Appointed Scalemail Leggings, 1 Inscribed Worghide Treads										
Baleheim Must Burn!	Howling Fjord	Horde	All		Sergeant Gorth	Sergeant Gorth	A Lesson in Fear	150 with Horde Expedition	15100	
The Artifacts of Steel Gate	Howling Fjord	Horde	All		Sage Mistwalker	Sage Mistwalker		250 with The Taunka	20100	4🥈 70🥉
CHOICE OF: 1 Crackling Cloak, 1 Unsparing Band, 1 Worg-Fang Talisman										
Find Sage Mistwalker	Howling Fjord	Horde	All		Greatmother Ankha	Sage Mistwalker	The Conqueror of Skorn!	10 with The Taunka	2000	

Title	Location	Faction	Race & Class	Group #	Starter	Finisher	Prerequisite	Reputation	XP	Money
The Shining Light	Howling Fjord	All	All		Ares the Oathbound	Ares the Oathbound	Rescuing the Rescuers	250 with Valiance Expedition	20100	
CHOICE OF: 1 Coldspike Longbow, 1 Ice-Rimed Dagger, 1 Regal Sceptre, 1 Stoneblade Slicer, 1 Whelpling-Skull Zapper, 1 Worn Vrykul Smasher										
Guided by Honor	Howling Fjord	All	All		Ares the Oathbound	Lord Irulon Trueblade	The Shining Light	75 with Valiance Expedition, 75 with Argent Crusade	10050	4🟡70🔴
Dragonflayer Battle Plans	Howling Fjord	Alliance	All		Vice Admiral Keller	Vice Admiral Keller	Prisoners of Wyrmskull	250 with Valiance Expedition	12650	4🟡40🔴
CHOICE OF: 1 Benevolent Hood, 1 Blood-Stained Chain Leggings, 1 Bone-Threaded Harness, 1 Nerubian Inner Husk										
To Westguard Keep!	Howling Fjord	All	All		Vice Admiral Keller	Captain Adams	Dragonflayer Battle Plans	25 with Valiance Expedition	3150	
Preying Upon the Weak	Howling Fjord	Alliance	All		Trapper Jethan	Trapper Jethan			12650	4🟡40🔴
CHOICE OF: 1 Fizznik's Patented Earwarmer, 1 Earth-Infused Leggings, 1 Master Artilleryman Boots, 1 Arcanum Shield										
The Offensive Begins	Howling Fjord	Horde	All		High Executor Anselm	Sergeant Gorth	The Dragonskin Map	10 with Horde Expedition	2000	
Rivenwood Captives	Howling Fjord	Horde	All		Longrunner Skycloud	Longrunner Skycloud		250 with The Taunka	20300	5🔴
CHOICE OF: 1 Icestriker Bands, 1 Reinforced Tuskhide Hauberk, 1 Bloodbinder's Girdle, 1 Ice-Crusted Cape										
Keeping Watch on the Interlopers	Howling Fjord	Horde	All		Junat the Wanderer	Apothecary Malthus	Making the Horn, Suppressing the Elements, Hasty Preparations		2000	
What's in That Brew?	Howling Fjord	Horde	All		Apothecary Malthus	Apothecary Malthus		250 with The Hand of Vengeance	20100	4🟡70🔴
The Ring of Judgement	Howling Fjord	Alliance	All		Glorenfeld	Daegarn	The Depths of Depravity	10 with Valiance Expedition	2000	
Stunning Defeat at the Ring	Howling Fjord	Alliance	All		Daegarn	Glorenfeld	The Ring of Judgement	250 with Valiance Expedition	20100	
Brains! Brains! Brains!	Howling Fjord	Horde	All		Apothecary Grick	Apothecary Grick		250 with The Hand of Vengeance	20100	4🟡70🔴
CHOICE OF: 1 Fizznik's Patented Earwarmer, 1 Earth-Infused Leggings, 1 Master Artilleryman Boots, 1 Arcanum Shield										
The Enigmatic Frost Nymphs	Howling Fjord	Alliance	All		Lieutenant Maeve	Lurielle	Down to the Wire, The Yeti Next Door, I'll Try Anything!		1250	
The Ambush	Howling Fjord	Horde	All		Sergeant Gorth	Lydell	Baleheim Bodycount, Baleheim Must Burn!	350 with The Hand of Vengeance	25150	9🟡40🔴
New Agamand	Howling Fjord	Horde	All		Apothecary Lysander	Chief Plaguebringer Harris	Test at Sea	10 with The Hand of Vengeance	2000	
A Tailor-Made Formula	Howling Fjord	Horde	All		Chief Plaguebringer Harris	Chief Plaguebringer Harris	New Agamand	250 with The Hand of Vengeance	20100	
CHOICE OF: 1 Acid-Etched Knuckles, 1 Featherweight Claymore, 1 Fullered Coldsteel Dagger, 1 Hair-Trigger Blunderbuss										
Apply Heat and Stir	Howling Fjord	Horde	All		Chief Plaguebringer Harris	Chief Plaguebringer Harris	A Tailor-Made Formula	150 with The Hand of Vengeance	15100	
Field Test	Howling Fjord	Horde	All		Chief Plaguebringer Harris	Chief Plaguebringer Harris	Apply Heat and Stir	250 with The Hand of Vengeance	20100	4🟡70🔴
CHOICE OF: 1 Munificent Bulwark, 1 Tome of Alacrity										
Time for Cleanup	Howling Fjord	Horde	All		Chief Plaguebringer Harris	"Hacksaw" Jenny	Field Test		5050	
Parts for the Job	Howling Fjord	Horde	All		"Hacksaw" Jenny	"Hacksaw" Jenny	Time for Cleanup	250 with Horde Expedition	20100	4🟡70🔴
CHOICE OF: 1 Crystalline Star, 1 Shock-Resistant Hood, 1 Banded Chain Gloves, 1 Munificent Legguards										
Warning: Some Assembly Required	Howling Fjord	Horde	All		"Hacksaw" Jenny	"Hacksaw" Jenny	Parts for the Job	250 with Horde Expedition	25150	9🟡40🔴
CHOICE OF: 1 Flexible Leather Footwraps, 1 Fire-Purifying Tunic, 1 Inescapable Girdle, 1 Light-Bound Chestguard										
Suppressing the Elements	Howling Fjord	Horde	All		Wind Tamer Kagan	Wind Tamer Kagan		250 with The Taunka	20100	4🟡70🔴
The Frozen Glade	Howling Fjord	Horde	All		Nokoma Snowseer	Lurielle	Hasty Preparations, Making the Horn, Suppressing the Elements		2000	
Spirits of the Ice	Howling Fjord	All	All		Lurielle	Lurielle			20100	4🟡70🔴
The Fallen Sisters	Howling Fjord	All	All		Lurielle	Lurielle	Spirits of the Ice		20100	4🟡70🔴
Wild Vines	Howling Fjord	All	All		Lurielle	Lurielle	Spirits of the Ice		20100	4🟡70🔴
Spawn of the Twisted Glade	Howling Fjord	All	All		Lurielle	Lurielle	The Fallen Sisters, Wild Vines		20100	4🟡70🔴
The Cleansing	Howling Fjord	Horde	All		Sage Mistwalker	Sage Mistwalker	The Artifacts of Steel Gate	250 with The Taunka	20100	4🟡70🔴
Seeds of the Blacksouled Keepers	Howling Fjord	All	All		Lurielle	Lurielle	The Fallen Sisters, Wild Vines		20100	4🟡70🔴
CHOICE OF: 1 Drape of Distilled Hatred, 1 Blacksoul Protector's Hauberk, 1 Root of the Everlasting										
The Cleansing	Howling Fjord	Alliance	All		Watcher Moonleaf	Watcher Moonleaf		250 with Valiance Expedition	20100	4🟡70🔴
In Worg's Clothing	Howling Fjord	Horde	All		Sage Mistwalker	Ulfang	The Cleansing		20100	
Alpha Worg	Howling Fjord	Horde	All		Ulfang	Sage Mistwalker	Eyes of the Eagle	350 with The Taunka	25150	9🟡40🔴
CHOICE OF: 1 Gholamweave Leggings, 1 Darksteel Ringmail Greaves, 1 Worgblood Berserker's Hauberk, 1 Proto-Drake Tooth Spaulders										
In Worg's Clothing	Howling Fjord	Alliance	All		Watcher Moonleaf	Ulfang	The Cleansing		20100	

Title	Location	Faction	Race & Class	Group #	Starter	Finisher	Prerequisite	Reputation	XP	Money
Alpha Worg	Howling Fjord	Alliance	All		Ulfang	Watcher Moonleaf	Eyes of the Eagle	350 with Valiance Expedition	25150	9⊚40⊚
CHOICE OF: 1 Gholamweave Leggings, 1 Darksteel Ringmail Greaves, 1 Worgblood Berserker's Hauberk, 1 Proto-Drake Tooth Spaulders										
Mission: Package Retrieval	Howling Fjord	All	All		Scout Knowles	Scout Knowles	Mission: Eternal Flame	250 with Valiance Expedition	20100	4⊚70⊚
Mission: Forsaken Intel	Howling Fjord	All	All		Scout Knowles	Peppy Wrongnozzle	Mission: Package Retrieval	10 with Valiance Expedition	2000	
I'll Try Anything!	Howling Fjord	Alliance	All		Christopher Sloan	Christopher Sloan		250 with Valiance Expedition	12650	4⊚40⊚
Absholutely... Thish Will Work!	Howling Fjord	Alliance	All		Peppy Wrongnozzle	Peppy Wrongnozzle	Mission: Forsaken Intel	75 with Valiance Expedition	10050	2⊚40⊚
You Tell Him ...Hic!	Howling Fjord	All	All		Peppy Wrongnozzle	Captain Adams	Absholutely... Thish Will Work!	10 with Valiance Expedition	2000	
Mission: Plague This!	Howling Fjord	All	All		Captain Adams	Captain Adams	You Tell Him ...Hic!	350 with Valiance Expedition	25150	9⊚40⊚
CHOICE OF: 1 Coldstone-Inlaid Waistguard, 1 Flamebinder Handwraps, 1 Purestrike Bracers, 1 Emeraldscale Pauldrons										
Into the World of Spirits	Howling Fjord	Alliance	All		Thoralius the Wise	Thoralius the Wise	Rescuing the Rescuers	250 with Valiance Expedition	20100	
The Echo of Ymiron	Howling Fjord	Alliance	All		Thoralius the Wise	Thoralius the Wise	Into the World of Spirits	250 with Valiance Expedition	20100	
Anguish of Nifflevar	Howling Fjord	Alliance	All		Thoralius the Wise	Thoralius the Wise	The Echo of Ymiron	250 with Valiance Expedition	20100	
CHOICE OF: 1 Blauvelt's Special Occasion Gloves, 1 Nimblefinger Scaled Gloves, 1 Antique Reinforced Legguards, 1 Imperious Worghide Cap										
The Book of Runes	Howling Fjord	Alliance	All		Prospector Belvar	Prospector Belvar	Down to the Wire, The Yeti Next Door, I'll Try Anything!	250 with Explorers' League	20100	4⊚70⊚
The Rune of Command	Howling Fjord	Alliance	All		Prospector Belvar	Prospector Belvar	Mastering the Runes	250 with Explorers' League	20100	4⊚70⊚
Mastering the Runes	Howling Fjord	Alliance	All		Prospector Belvar	Prospector Belvar	The Book of Runes	250 with Explorers' League	20100	4⊚70⊚
The Book of Runes	Howling Fjord	Horde	All		Longrunner Pembe	Longrunner Pembe	Hasty Preparations, Making the Horn, Suppressing the Elements	250 with The Taunka	20100	4⊚70⊚
Mastering the Runes	Howling Fjord	Horde	All		Longrunner Pembe	Longrunner Pembe	The Book of Runes	250 with The Taunka	20100	4⊚70⊚
The Rune of Command	Howling Fjord	Horde	All		Longrunner Pembe	Longrunner Pembe	Mastering the Runes	250 with The Taunka	20100	4⊚70⊚
March of the Giants	Howling Fjord	Alliance	All	2	Researcher Aderan	Researcher Aderan	Down to the Wire, The Yeti Next Door, I'll Try Anything!	250 with Valiance Expedition	20300	5⊚
The Lodestone	Howling Fjord	Alliance	All	3	Researcher Aderan	Researcher Aderan	March of the Giants	250 with Valiance Expedition	20300	5⊚
Demolishing Megalith	Howling Fjord	Alliance	All	3	Researcher Aderan	Researcher Aderan	The Lodestone	350 with Valiance Expedition	25400	10⊚
March of the Giants	Howling Fjord	Horde	All	2	Sage Edan	Sage Edan	Hasty Preparations, Making the Horn, Suppressing the Elements	250 with The Taunka	20300	5⊚
The Lodestone	Howling Fjord	Horde	All	3	Sage Edan	Sage Edan	March of the Giants	250 with The Taunka	20300	5⊚
Demolishing Megalith	Howling Fjord	Horde	All	3	Sage Edan	Sage Edan	The Lodestone	350 with The Taunka	25400	10⊚
I've Got a Flying Machine!	Howling Fjord	Alliance	All		Steel Gate Chief Archaeologist	Steel Gate Chief Archaeologist	See to the Operations	250 with Explorers' League	20100	4⊚70⊚
REWARD: 5 Super Healing Potion AND CHOICE OF: 1 Crackling Cloak, 1 Unsparing Band, 1 Worg-Fang Talisman										
Steel Gate Patrol	Howling Fjord	Alliance	All		Steel Gate Chief Archaeologist	Steel Gate Chief Archaeologist	I've Got a Flying Machine!	250 with Explorers' League	20100	4⊚70⊚
REWARD: 2 Super Healing Potion										
Where is Explorer Jaren?	Howling Fjord	Alliance	All		Overseer Irena Stonemantle	Explorer Jaren		10 with Explorers' League	2000	
And You Thought Murlocs Smelled Bad!	Howling Fjord	Alliance	All		Explorer Jaren	Explorer Jaren		250 with Explorers' League	20100	4⊚70⊚
It's a Scourge Device	Howling Fjord	Alliance	All		Scourge Device	Explorer Jaren		10 with Explorers' League	2000	
Bring Down Those Shields	Howling Fjord	Alliance	All		Explorer Jaren	Explorer Jaren	It's a Scourge Device	350 with Explorers' League	25150	9⊚40⊚
CHOICE OF: 1 Earthbinder's Regenerating Band, 1 Ramshorn Greathelm, 1 Ghoul-Crushing Stompers, 1 Infused Coldstone Rune										
And You Thought Murlocs Smelled Bad!	Howling Fjord	Horde	All		Apothecary Anastasia	Apothecary Anastasia		250 with The Hand of Vengeance	20100	4⊚70⊚
It's a Scourge Device	Howling Fjord	Horde	All		Scourge Device	Apothecary Anastasia		10 with The Hand of Vengeance	2000	
Bring Down Those Shields	Howling Fjord	Horde	All		Apothecary Anastasia	Apothecary Anastasia	It's a Scourge Device	350 with The Hand of Vengeance	25150	9⊚40⊚
CHOICE OF: 1 Earthbinder's Regenerating Band, 1 Ramshorn Greathelm, 1 Ghoul-Crushing Stompers, 1 Infused Coldstone Rune										
Everything Must Be Ready	Howling Fjord	Alliance	All		Quartermaster Brevin	Gil Grisert	Necro Overlord Mezhen, Mission: Plague This!	10 with Valiance Expedition	1250	44⊚
The One That Got Away	Howling Fjord	Alliance	All		Christopher Sloan	Christopher Sloan	I'll Try Anything!	250 with Valiance Expedition	20100	4⊚70⊚

Howling Fjord

Title	Location	Faction	Race & Class	Group #	Starter	Finisher	Prerequisite	Reputation	XP	Money
Camp Winterhoof	Howling Fjord	Horde	All		Cormath the Courier	Chieftain Ashtotem	Parts for the Job	10 with The Taunka	1250	
Brother Betrayers	Howling Fjord	All	All		Ulfang	Ulfang	In Worg's Clothing		20100	
Brother Betrayers	Howling Fjord	All	All		Ulfang	Ulfang	In Worg's Clothing		20100	
Eyes of the Eagle	Howling Fjord	All	All		Ulfang	Ulfang	Brother Betrayers		20100	
Eyes of the Eagle	Howling Fjord	All	All		Ulfang	Ulfang	Brother Betrayers		20100	
We Call Him Steelfeather	Howling Fjord	Alliance	All		Gil Grisert	Gil Grisert	Down to the Wire	150 with Valiance Expedition	9500	3 40
The Path to Payback	Howling Fjord	Alliance	All		Guard Captain Zorek	Guard Captain Zorek	Rescuing the Rescuers	250 with Valiance Expedition	20100	4 70
It Goes to 11...	Howling Fjord	Alliance	All		Lieutenant Icehammer	Lieutenant Icehammer	Harpoon Master Yavus	350 with Valiance Expedition	25150	9 40
CHOICE OF: 1 Frost-Trimmed Gauntlets, 1 Azure Chain Hauberk, 1 Ramshorn-Inlaid Shoulders, 1 Runed Clamshell Choker										
Trident of the Son	Howling Fjord	All	All		Old Icefin	Old Icefin			20100	4 70
The Enemy's Legacy	Howling Fjord	Horde	All		Scribe Seguine	Scribe Seguine		250 with Horde Expedition	20100	
Shield Hill	Howling Fjord	Horde	All		"Hacksaw" Jenny	"Hacksaw" Jenny		250 with Horde Expedition	20100	4 70
CHOICE OF: 1 Coldstone-Inlaid Waistguard, 1 Flamebinder Handwraps, 1 Purestrike Bracers, 1 Emeraldscale Pauldrons										
Locating the Mechanism	Howling Fjord	Alliance	All		Guard Captain Zorek	Guard Captain Zorek	The Path to Payback	250 with Valiance Expedition	20100	
Meet Lieutenant Icehammer...	Howling Fjord	Alliance	All		Guard Captain Zorek	Lieutenant Icehammer	Locating the Mechanism	10 with Valiance Expedition	2000	
Keeper Witherleaf	Howling Fjord	All	All		Lurielle	Lurielle	Spawn of the Twisted Glade, Seeds of the Blacksouled Keepers		25150	9 40
Drop It then Rock It!	Howling Fjord	Alliance	All		Lieutenant Icehammer	Lieutenant Icehammer	Meet Lieutenant Icehammer...	250 with Valiance Expedition	20100	
Harpoon Master Yavus	Howling Fjord	Alliance	All		Lieutenant Icehammer	Lieutenant Icehammer	Drop It then Rock It!	250 with Valiance Expedition	20100	4 70
Sleeping Giants	Howling Fjord	All	All		Mage-Lieutenant Malister	Mage-Lieutenant Malister	Of Keys and Cages	250 with Valiance Expedition	20100	4 70
Sleeping Giants	Howling Fjord	Horde	All		Ahota Whitefrost	Ahota Whitefrost	Of Keys and Cages	250 with The Taunka	20100	4 70
Forgotten Treasure	Howling Fjord	All	All		Spectral Sailor, Black Conrad's Ghost, Handsome Terry	Handsome Terry	Street "Cred"		20100	
Let's Go Surfing Now	Howling Fjord	Alliance	All		Lieutenant Icehammer	Guard Captain Zorek	It Goes to 11...	10 with Valiance Expedition	2000	
Daggercap Divin'	Howling Fjord	Alliance	All		Harold Lagras	Harold Lagras		250 with Valiance Expedition	20100	4 70
The Explorers' League Outpost	Howling Fjord	Alliance	All		Beltrand McSorf	Stanwad	Return to Valgarde	10 with Valiance Expedition	2000	
The Slumbering King	Howling Fjord	All	All		Mezhen's Writings	Captain Adams	Dealing With Gjalerbron	350 with Valiance Expedition	25400	10
The Slumbering King	Howling Fjord	Horde	All		Mezhen's Writings	Chieftain Ashtotem	Dealing With Gjalerbron	350 with The Taunka	25400	10
The Fragrance of Money	Howling Fjord	All	All		Spectral Sailor, Black Conrad's Ghost, Handsome Terry	Handsome Terry	Forgotten Treasure		20100	4 70
Feeding the Survivors	Howling Fjord	All	All		Elder Atuik	Elder Atuik		250 with The Kalu'ak	20100	4 70
Arming Kamagua	Howling Fjord	All	All		Elder Atuik	Elder Atuik	Feeding the Survivors	250 with The Kalu'ak	20100	4 70
Avenge Iskaal	Howling Fjord	All	All		Elder Atuik	Elder Atuik	Arming Kamagua	350 with The Kalu'ak	20100	
Zeh'gehn Sez	Howling Fjord	All	All		Zeh'gehn	Handsome Terry	A Traitor Among Us		10050	
Trust is Earned	Howling Fjord	Alliance	All		Hidalgo the Master Falconer	Hidalgo the Master Falconer		250 with Valiance Expedition	20100	
DEPRECATED	Howling Fjord	All	All							
Handsome Terry	Howling Fjord	All	All		Handsome Terry	Handsome Terry			15100	
Pirates of the North Seas	Howling Fjord	All	All		Grezzix Spindlesnap	Grezzix Spindlesnap			5050	
Gambling Debt	Howling Fjord	All	All		Taruk	Taruk	Forgotten Treasure		15100	
The Ransacked Caravan	Howling Fjord	Alliance	All		Hidalgo the Master Falconer	Hidalgo the Master Falconer	Trust is Earned	250 with Valiance Expedition, 250 with Explorers' League	20100	
Jack Likes His Drink	Howling Fjord	All	All		Taruk	Taruk	Gambling Debt		15100	9 40
Dead Man's Debt	Howling Fjord	All	All		Taruk	Taruk	Jack Likes His Drink		25150	
REWARD: 1 Black Conrad's Treasure										
Falcon Versus Hawk	Howling Fjord	Alliance	All		Hidalgo the Master Falconer	Hidalgo the Master Falconer	The Ransacked Caravan	250 with Valiance Expedition, 250 with Explorers' League	20100	
Swabbin' Soap	Howling Fjord	All	All		Scuttle Frostprow	Scuttle Frostprow			20100	4 70

Title	Location	Faction	Race & Class	Group #	Starter	Finisher	Prerequisite	Reputation	XP	Money
There Exists No Honor Among Birds	Howling Fjord	Alliance	All		Hidalgo the Master Falconer	Hidalgo the Master Falconer	Falcon Versus Hawk	350 with Valiance Expedition, 350 with Explorers' League	25150	9🔘 40🔘
CHOICE OF: 1 Flexible Leather Footwraps, 1 Fire-Purifying Tunic, 1 Inescapable Girdle, 1 Light-Bound Chestguard										
The Jig is Up	Howling Fjord	All	All	3	Annie Bonn	Annie Bonn	Meet Number Two		25150	
CHOICE OF: 1 Sailor's Knotted Charm, 1 First Mate's Pocketwatch, 1 Strike of the Seas										
The Way to His Heart...	Howling Fjord	All	All		Anuniaq	Anuniaq	Swabbin' Soap	250 with The Kalu'ak	20100	4🔘 70🔘
A Traitor Among Us	Howling Fjord	All	All		Spectral Sailor, Black Conrad's Ghost, Handsome Terry	Zeh'gehn	The Fragrance of Money		5050	
Problems on the High Bluff	Howling Fjord	Alliance	All		Stanwad	Walt	The Explorers' League Outpost	10 with Valiance Expedition, 10 with Explorers' League	2000	
Tools to Get the Job Done	Howling Fjord	Alliance	All		Walt	Walt		250 with Valiance Expedition, 250 with Explorers' League	20100	
A Carver and a Croaker	Howling Fjord	All	All		Spectral Sailor, Black Conrad's Ghost, Handsome Terry	Zeh'gehn	Zeh'gehn Sez		5050	
Out of My Element?	Howling Fjord	Alliance	All		Donny	Donny		250 with Valiance Expedition, 250 with Explorers' League	12650	
Outpost Over Yonder...	Howling Fjord	Alliance	All		Donny	Stanwad		25 with Valiance Expedition, 25 with Explorers' League	5050	
"Crowleg" Dan	Howling Fjord	All	All		Zeh'gehn	Handsome Terry	A Carver and a Croaker		25150	
Meet Number Two	Howling Fjord	All	All		Spectral Sailor, Black Conrad's Ghost, Handsome Terry	Annie Bonn	"Crowleg" Dan		5050	
We Can Rebuild It	Howling Fjord	Alliance	All		Walt	Walt	Tools to Get the Job Done	250 with Explorers' League, 250 with Valiance Expedition	20100	
We Have the Technology	Howling Fjord	Alliance	All		Walt	Walt	Tools to Get the Job Done	250 with Explorers' League, 250 with Valiance Expedition	20100	
Iron Rune Constructs and You: Rocket Jumping	Howling Fjord	Alliance	All		Walt	Walt	We Can Rebuild It, We Have the Technology	10 with Explorers' League, 10 with Valiance Expedition	2000	
Iron Rune Constructs and You: Collecting Data	Howling Fjord	Alliance	All		Walt	Walt	Iron Rune Constructs and You: Rocket Jumping	10 with Explorers' League, 10 with Valiance Expedition	2000	
Iron Rune Constructs and You: The Bluff	Howling Fjord	Alliance	All		Walt	Walt	Iron Rune Constructs and You: Collecting Data	10 with Explorers' League, 10 with Valiance Expedition	2000	
Lightning Infused Relics	Howling Fjord	Alliance	All		Walt	Walt	Iron Rune Constructs and You: The Bluff	350 with Explorers' League, 350 with Valiance Expedition	25150	14🔘 10🔘
CHOICE OF: 1 Crystalline Star, 1 Shock-Resistant Hood, 1 Banded Chain Gloves, 1 Munificent Legguards										
The Delicate Sound of Thunder	Howling Fjord	Alliance	All		Walt	Walt	Iron Rune Constructs and You: The Bluff	350 with Explorers' League, 350 with Valiance Expedition	25150	9🔘 40🔘
CHOICE OF: 1 Acid-Etched Knuckles, 1 Featherweight Claymore, 1 Fullered Coldsteel Dagger, 1 Hair-Trigger Blunderbuss										
News From the East	Howling Fjord	All	All		Walt	Captain Adams	Lightning Infused Relics, The Delicate Sound of Thunder	10 with Explorers' League, 10 with Valiance Expedition	2000	
CHOICE OF: 1 Munificent Bulwark, 1 Tome of Alacrity										
The Dead Rise!	Howling Fjord	All	All		Orfus of Kamagua	Orfus of Kamagua		250 with The Kalu'ak	20100	
Elder Atuik and Kamagua	Howling Fjord	All	All		Orfus of Kamagua	Elder Atuik	The Dead Rise!	75 with The Kalu'ak	10050	
Grezzix Spindlesnap	Howling Fjord	All	All		Elder Atuik	Grezzix Spindlesnap	Elder Atuik and Kamagua	10 with The Kalu'ak	2000	
Street "Cred"	Howling Fjord	All	All		Grezzix Spindlesnap	"Silvermoon" Harry	Grezzix Spindlesnap	25 with The Kalu'ak	5050	
"Scoodles"	Howling Fjord	All	All		"Silvermoon" Harry	"Silvermoon" Harry	Street "Cred"	250 with The Kalu'ak	20100	
The Staff of Storm's Fury	Howling Fjord	All	All		"Silvermoon" Harry	Orfus of Kamagua	"Scoodles"	250 with The Kalu'ak	20100	

HOWLING FJORD

Title	Location	Faction	Race & Class	Group #	Starter	Finisher	Prerequisite	Reputation	XP	Money
The Frozen Heart of Isuldof	Howling Fjord	All	All		"Silvermoon" Harry	Orfus of Kamagua	"Scoodles"	250 with The Kalu'ak	20100	
The Lost Shield of the Aesirites	Howling Fjord	All	All		"Silvermoon" Harry	Captain Ellis	"Scoodles"	150 with The Kalu'ak	15100	
Mutiny on the Mercy	Howling Fjord	All	All		Captain Ellis	Captain Ellis	The Lost Shield of the Aesirites	150 with The Kalu'ak	15100	
Sorlof's Booty	Howling Fjord	All	All		Captain Ellis	Captain Ellis	Mutiny on the Mercy	150 with The Kalu'ak	15100	
The Shield of the Aesirites	Howling Fjord	All	All		Captain Ellis	Orfus of Kamagua	Sorlof's Booty	250 with The Kalu'ak	20100	
The Ancient Armor of the Kvaldir	Howling Fjord	All	All		"Silvermoon" Harry	Orfus of Kamagua	"Scoodles"	250 with The Kalu'ak	20100	
A Return to Resting	Howling Fjord	All	All		Orfus of Kamagua	Orfus of Kamagua		250 with The Kalu'ak	20100	
Return to Atuik	Howling Fjord	All	All		Orfus of Kamagua	Elder Atuik	A Return to Resting	500 with The Kalu'ak	30150	14🟡 10⚪
CHOICE OF: 1 Horn of the Herald, 1 Mender of the Oncoming Dawn, 1 Fury of the Encroaching Storm										
Orfus of Kamagua	Howling Fjord	All	All		Lunk-tusk	Orfus of Kamagua		25 with The Kalu'ak	5050	
Give it a Name	Howling Fjord	Horde	All		Chief Plaguebringer Harris	Tobias Sarkhoff		10 with The Hand of Vengeance	2050	
Adding Injury to Insult	Howling Fjord	Horde	All		Lydell	Lydell	The Ambush	350 with Horde Expedition	25150	9🟡 40⚪
CHOICE OF: 1 Bone-Inlaid Bracers, 1 Embossed Ermine Girdle, 1 Magdun Spaulders, 1 Runeplate Helm										
Against Nifflevar	Howling Fjord	Horde	All		Ranger Captain Areiel	Ranger Captain Areiel		250 with The Hand of Vengeance	20100	
Howling Fjord: aa - A - LK FLAG	Howling Fjord	All	All							
Help for Camp Winterhoof	Howling Fjord	Horde	All		Longrunner Nanik	Chieftain Ashtotem		10 with The Taunka	2000	

ICECROWN

Title	Location	Faction	Race & Class	Group #	Starter	Finisher	Prerequisite	Reputation	XP	Money
To the Rise with all Due Haste!	Icecrown	All	All		Baron Sliver	Lord-Commander Arete	Ebon Blade Prisoners	10 with Knights of the Ebon Blade	2200	
The Story Thus Far...	Icecrown	All	All		Lord-Commander Arete	Lord-Commander Arete	Ebon Blade Prisoners	10 with Knights of the Ebon Blade	2200	
Blood in the Water	Icecrown	All	All		Lord-Commander Arete	Lord-Commander Arete	The Story Thus Far...	250 with Knights of the Ebon Blade	22050	7🟡 40⚪
From Their Corpses, Rise!	Icecrown	All	All		Setaal Darkmender	Setaal Darkmender	The Story Thus Far...	250 with Knights of the Ebon Blade	22050	7🟡 40⚪
You'll Need a Gryphon	Icecrown	All	All		Lord-Commander Arete	Uzo Deathcaller	Blood in the Water	250 with Knights of the Ebon Blade	22050	7🟡 40⚪
CHOICE OF: 1 Gryphon Rider's Bracers, 1 Gryphon Hide Moccasins, 1 Gauntlets of Urgency, 1 Helmet of the Dedicated										
No Fly Zone	Icecrown	All	All		Uzo Deathcaller	Uzo Deathcaller	You'll Need a Gryphon	250 with Knights of the Ebon Blade	22050	7🟡 40⚪
Intelligence Gathering	Icecrown	All	All		Aurochs Grimbane	Aurochs Grimbane	The Story Thus Far...	250 with Knights of the Ebon Blade	22050	7🟡 40⚪
In Strict Confidence	Icecrown	All	All		Lord-Commander Arete	Lord-Commander Arete	The Grand (Admiral's) Plan	250 with Knights of the Ebon Blade	22050	7🟡 40⚪
CHOICE OF: 1 Arete's Command, 1 Growler's Intimidation, 1 Curved Assassin's Dagger, 1 Interrogator's Flaming Knuckles, 1 Staff of Interrogation										
Second Chances	Icecrown	All	All	5	Lord-Commander Arete	Lord-Commander Arete	In Strict Confidence	350 with Knights of the Ebon Blade	27550	14🟡 80⚪
The Admiral Revealed	Icecrown	All	All	5	Lord-Commander Arete	Lord-Commander Arete	Second Chances	350 with Knights of the Ebon Blade	27550	14🟡 80⚪
CHOICE OF: 1 Amulet of the Crusade, 1 The Severed Noose of Westwind, 1 Emeline's Locket, 1 Reinforced Titanium Neckguard										
It's All Fun and Games	Icecrown	All	All		Thassarian	Baron Sliver		250 with Knights of the Ebon Blade	22050	7🟡 40⚪
I Have an Idea, But First...	Icecrown	All	All		Baron Sliver	Baron Sliver	It's All Fun and Games, It's All Fun and Games	250 with Knights of the Ebon Blade	22050	7🟡 40⚪
It's All Fun and Games	Icecrown	All	All		Koltira Deathweaver	Baron Sliver		250 with Knights of the Ebon Blade	22050	7🟡 40⚪
Free Your Mind	Icecrown	All	All		Baron Sliver	Baron Sliver	I Have an Idea, But First...	350 with Knights of the Ebon Blade	27550	14🟡 80⚪
CHOICE OF: 1 Lady Nightswood's Engagement Ring, 1 Signet of Baron Sliver, 1 Shadow Vault Shawl, 1 Chain of the Sovereign										
If He Cannot Be Turned	Icecrown	All	All		Baron Sliver	Thassarian	Free Your Mind		27550	14🟡 80⚪
If He Cannot Be Turned	Icecrown	All	All		Baron Sliver	Koltira Deathweaver	Free Your Mind		27550	14🟡 80⚪
The Shadow Vault	Icecrown	All	All		Thassarian	Baron Sliver	If He Cannot Be Turned	10 with Knights of the Ebon Blade	2200	74⚪
CHOICE OF: 1 Softly Glowing Orb, 1 Chuchu's Tiny Box of Horrors, 1 Thorny Rose Brooch										
The Shadow Vault	Icecrown	All	All		Koltira Deathweaver	Baron Sliver	If He Cannot Be Turned	10 with Knights of the Ebon Blade	2200	74⚪
CHOICE OF: 1 Softly Glowing Orb, 1 Chuchu's Tiny Box of Horrors, 1 Thorny Rose Brooch										
The Duke	Icecrown	All	All		Baron Sliver	Duke Lankral	The Shadow Vault, The Shadow Vault	10 with Knights of the Ebon Blade	2200	

283

Title	Location	Faction	Race & Class	Group #	Starter	Finisher	Prerequisite	Reputation	XP	Money
Honor Challenge	Icecrown	All	All		Duke Lankral	Duke Lankral	The Duke	250 with Knights of the Ebon Blade	22050	7🜚 40🜚
Shadow Vault Decree	Icecrown	All	All		Duke Lankral	Duke Lankral	Honor Challenge	250 with Knights of the Ebon Blade	22050	7🜚 40🜚
CHOICE OF: 1 Duke Lankral's Velvet Slippers, 1 Vest of Jotunheim, 1 Thane's Restraints, 1 Blackened Breastplate of the Vault										
Get the Key	Icecrown	All	All		Vaelen the Flayed	Vaelen the Flayed	Honor Challenge	250 with Knights of the Ebon Blade	22050	7🜚 40🜚
Let the Baron Know	Icecrown	All	All		Vaelen the Flayed	Baron Sliver	Get the Key	25 with Knights of the Ebon Blade	5500	1🜚 90🜚
Eliminate the Competition	Icecrown	All	All		The Leaper	The Leaper	The Duke	250 with Knights of the Ebon Blade	22050	7🜚 40🜚
CHOICE OF: 1 Sigrid's Mittens, 1 Efrem's Bracers, 1 Gauntlet's of Onu'zun, 1 Chestplate of the Glacial Crusader, 1 Iron Coffin Lid										
Ebon Blade Prisoners	Icecrown	All	All		Vaelen the Flayed	Vaelen the Flayed	Let the Baron Know	250 with Knights of the Ebon Blade	22050	7🜚 40🜚
CHOICE OF: 1 Shadow Vault Cowl, 1 Gloves of the Flayed, 1 Links of the Battlemender, 1 Ebon Pauldrons										
Crush Dem Vrykuls!	Icecrown	All	All		Vile	Vile	Let the Baron Know	250 with Knights of the Ebon Blade	22050	7🜚 40🜚
CHOICE OF: 1 Vile's Uglystick, 1 Vrykul Crusher, 1 Wrought-Iron Staff, 1 Vile's Poker, 1 Bow of Bone and Sinew										
Leave Our Mark	Icecrown	All	All		Baron Sliver	Baron Sliver	Let the Baron Know	250 with Knights of the Ebon Blade	22050	7🜚 40🜚
The Bone Witch	Icecrown	All	All		The Leaper	The Bone Witch	Eliminate the Competition	10 with Knights of the Ebon Blade	2200	74🜚
Scourge Tactics	Icecrown	All	All		Crusade Commander Entari	Crusade Commander Entari	Honor Above All Else	250 with Argent Crusade	21600	6🜚 80🜚
Honor Above All Else	Icecrown	All	All		Highlord Tirion Fordring	Crusade Commander Entari		10 with Alliance Vanguard	2150	
Defending The Vanguard	Icecrown	All	All		Crusader Lord Dalfors	Crusader Lord Dalfors	Honor Above All Else	250 with Argent Crusade	21600	6🜚 80🜚
CHOICE OF: 1 Touch of Light, 1 Argent Girdle, 1 Crusader's Locket, 1 Enchanted Plate Waistguard										
Curing The Incurable	Icecrown	All	All		Father Gustav	Father Gustav	Honor Above All Else	250 with Argent Crusade	21600	6🜚 80🜚
CHOICE OF: 5 Runic Healing Potion, 5 Runic Mana Potion										
Deep in the Bowels of The Underhalls	Icecrown	All	All		The Bone Witch	The Bone Witch	The Bone Witch	250 with Knights of the Ebon Blade	22050	7🜚 40🜚
The Sum is Greater than the Parts	Icecrown	All	All		Dr. Terrible's "Building a Better Flesh Giant"	The Bone Witch	The Bone Witch	350 with Knights of the Ebon Blade	27550	14🜚 80🜚
CHOICE OF: 1 Bone Witch's Drape, 1 Belt of Njorndar, 1 Glaciel Ranger's Leggings, 1 Rings of Nergeld										
If There Are Survivors...	Icecrown	All	All		Crusade Commander Entari	Penumbrius	Scourge Tactics, Curing The Incurable, Defending The Vanguard		2150	
Into The Wild Green Yonder	Icecrown	All	All		Penumbrius	Highlord Tirion Fordring	If There Are Survivors...	350 with Argent Crusade	27000	13🜚 60🜚
Revenge for the Vargul	Icecrown	All	All		Bethod Feigr	Bethod Feigr	The Bone Witch	350 with Knights of the Ebon Blade	27550	14🜚 80🜚
CHOICE OF: 1 Mantle of the Underhalls, 1 Boots of the Fallen Thane, 1 Circlet of Suffering, 1 Gauntlets of the Holy Gladiator, 1 Illska's Greatcloak										
A Tale of Valor	Icecrown	All	All		Highlord Tirion Fordring	Crusader Bridenbrad		10 with Argent Crusade	2200	74🜚
Shoot 'Em Up	Icecrown	All	All		The Leaper	The Leaper	Ebon Blade Prisoners	250 with Knights of the Ebon Blade	22050	7🜚 40🜚
A Cold Front Approaches	Icecrown	All	All		Highlord Tirion Fordring	Siegemaster Fezzik	Into The Wild Green Yonder	10 with Argent Crusade	2150	
Vile Like Fire!	Icecrown	All	All		Vile	Vile	Crush Dem Vrykuls!	250 with Knights of the Ebon Blade	22050	7🜚 40🜚
A Hero Remains	Icecrown	All	All		Crusader Bridenbrad	Highlord Tirion Fordring	A Tale of Valor	250 with Argent Crusade	22050	7🜚 40🜚
The Keeper's Favor	Icecrown	All	All		Highlord Tirion Fordring	Keeper Remulos	A Hero Remains	150 with Argent Crusade	16550	5🜚 80🜚
Hope Within the Emerald Nightmare	Icecrown	All	All		Keeper Remulos	Keeper Remulos	The Keeper's Favor		22050	7🜚 40🜚
The Boon of Remulos	Icecrown	All	All		Keeper Remulos	Crusader Bridenbrad	Hope Within the Emerald Nightmare	250 with Argent Crusade	22050	7🜚 40🜚
Time Yet Remains	Icecrown	All	All		Crusader Bridenbrad	Highlord Tirion Fordring	The Boon of Remulos	10 with Argent Crusade	2200	74🜚
The Touch of an Aspect	Icecrown	All	All		Highlord Tirion Fordring	Alexstrasza the Life-Binder	Time Yet Remains	150 with Argent Crusade	16550	5🜚 80🜚
Dahlia's Tears	Icecrown	All	All		Alexstrasza the Life-Binder	Alexstrasza the Life-Binder	The Touch of an Aspect		22050	7🜚 40🜚
The Boon of Alexstrasza	Icecrown	All	All		Alexstrasza the Life-Binder	Crusader Bridenbrad	Dahlia's Tears	250 with Argent Crusade	22050	7🜚 40🜚
Hope Yet Remains	Icecrown	All	All		Crusader Bridenbrad	Highlord Tirion Fordring	The Boon of Alexstrasza	10 with Argent Crusade	2200	74🜚
The Will of the Naaru	Icecrown	All	All		Highlord Tirion Fordring	A'dal	Hope Yet Remains	150 with Argent Crusade	16550	5🜚 80🜚
The Boon of A'dal	Icecrown	All	All		A'dal	Crusader Bridenbrad	The Will of the Naaru	250 with Argent Crusade	22050	7🜚 40🜚

Title	Location	Faction	Race & Class	Group #	Starter	Finisher	Prerequisite	Reputation	XP	Money
Light Within the Darkness	Icecrown	All	All		Bridenbrad's Possessions	Highlord Tirion Fordring	The Boon of A'dal	500 with Argent Crusade	33100	22 20
CHOICE OF: 1 Bridenbrad's Sash, 1 Belt of the Never-Forgotten, 1 Chained Belt of Remembrance, 1 Girdle of Eternal Memory, 1 Signet of Bridenbrad										
Vandalizing Jotunheim	Icecrown	All	All		Duke Lankral	Duke Lankral	Let the Baron Know	250 with Knights of the Ebon Blade	22050	7 40
Vaelen Has Returned	Icecrown	All	All		Baron Sliver	Vaelen the Flayed	Let the Baron Know	10 with Knights of the Ebon Blade	2200	
The Last Line Of Defense	Icecrown	All	All		Siegemaster Fezzik	Siegemaster Fezzik	A Cold Front Approaches	500 with Argent Crusade	32400	
CHOICE OF: 1 Cannoneer's Morale, 1 Fezzik's Pocketwatch, 1 Cannoneer's Fuselighter										
The Art of Being a Water Terror	Icecrown	All	All		The Bone Witch	The Bone Witch	The Sum is Greater than the Parts	250 with Knights of the Ebon Blade	22050	7 40
CHOICE OF: 1 Pantaloons of the Water Magi, 1 Spear-Sisters Mantle, 1 Links of the Sleep-Watcher, 1 Jotunheim Shackles										
Reading the Bones	Icecrown	All	All		The Bone Witch	The Bone Witch	The Bone Witch	250 with Knights of the Ebon Blade	22050	7 40
CHOICE OF: 1 Fate Rune of Baneful Intent, 1 Fate Rune of Fleet Feet, 1 Fate Rune of Nigh Invincibility, 1 Fate Rune of Primal Energy, 1 Fate Rune of Unsurpassed Vigor										
Reading the Bones	Icecrown	All	All		The Bone Witch	The Bone Witch	Reading the Bones	10 with Knights of the Ebon Blade		
CHOICE OF: 1 Fate Rune of Baneful Intent, 1 Fate Rune of Fleet Feet, 1 Fate Rune of Nigh Invincibility, 1 Fate Rune of Primal Energy, 1 Fate Rune of Unsurpassed Vigor										
Once More Unto The Breach, Hero	Icecrown	All	All Warrior, Paladin, Hunter, Rogue, Priest, Shaman, Mage, Warlock, Druid		Highlord Tirion Fordring	The Ebon Watcher	The Last Line Of Defense	10 with Argent Crusade, 10 with Knights of the Ebon Blade	2150	
Once More Unto The Breach, Hero	Icecrown	All	All Death Knight		Highlord Tirion Fordring	The Ebon Watcher	The Last Line Of Defense	10 with Argent Crusade, 10 with Knights of the Ebon Blade	2150	
Blackwatch	Icecrown	All	All		Baron Sliver	Darkrider Arly		10 with Knights of the Ebon Blade	2200	74
The Restless Dead	Icecrown	All	All		Father Gustav	Father Gustav	Once More Unto The Breach, Hero, Once More Unto The Breach, Hero	250 with Argent Crusade	21600	
CHOICE OF: 1 Blade of Echoes, 1 The Argent Resolve, 1 Hand of Gustav, 1 Staff of Redeemed Souls										
Where Are They Coming From?	Icecrown	All	All		Darkrider Arly	Darkrider Arly		150 with Knights of the Ebon Blade	16550	5 80
The Purging Of Scourgeholme	Icecrown	All	All		The Ebon Watcher	The Ebon Watcher	Once More Unto The Breach, Hero, Once More Unto The Breach, Hero	250 with Argent Crusade, 250 with Knights of the Ebon Blade	21600	
Destroying the Altars	Icecrown	All	All		Darkrider Arly	Darkrider Arly	Where Are They Coming From?	250 with Knights of the Ebon Blade	22050	7 40
Death's Gaze	Icecrown	All	All		Darkrider Arly	Darkrider Arly	Where Are They Coming From?	250 with Knights of the Ebon Blade	22050	7 40
Through the Eye	Icecrown	All	All		The Bone Witch	The Bone Witch	The Art of Being a Water Terror	250 with Knights of the Ebon Blade	22050	7 40
The Scourgestone	Icecrown	All	All		The Ebon Watcher	The Ebon Watcher	Once More Unto The Breach, Hero, Once More Unto The Breach, Hero	250 with Argent Crusade, 250 with Knights of the Ebon Blade	21600	6 80
The Air Stands Still	Icecrown	All	All		The Ebon Watcher	The Ebon Watcher	The Scourgestone, The Purging Of Scourgeholme	500 with Argent Crusade, 500 with Knights of the Ebon Blade	32700	
CHOICE OF: 1 Leiah's Footpads, 1 Sixen's Skullcap, 1 Cobalt's Shoulderguards, 1 Jayde's Reinforced Handguards										
The Stone That Started A Revolution	Icecrown	All	All		Crusade Architect Silas (Chapter IV), Crusade Architect Silas	Crusade Architect Silas	Once More Unto The Breach, Hero, Once More Unto The Breach, Hero	250 with Argent Crusade	21800	
CHOICE OF: 1 Adepts Wristwraps, 1 Girdle of Reprieve, 1 Architect's Spaulders, 1 Stability Girdle										
Find the Ancient Hero	Icecrown	All	All		The Bone Witch	The Bone Witch	Through the Eye	250 with Knights of the Ebon Blade	22050	7 40
Spill Their Blood	Icecrown	All	All		Darkrider Arly	Darkrider Arly	Destroying the Altars, Death's Gaze	250 with Knights of the Ebon Blade	22050	7 40
It Could Kill Us All	Icecrown	All	All		Crusade Engineer Spitzpatrick	Crusade Engineer Spitzpatrick	Once More Unto The Breach, Hero, Once More Unto The Breach, Hero	250 with Argent Crusade	21800	7 10
Jagged Shards	Icecrown	All	All		Jagged Shard	Crusader Olakin Sainrith	Destroying the Altars, Death's Gaze	250 with Argent Crusade	22050	7 40
Not-So-Honorable Combat	Icecrown	All	All	5	The Bone Witch	The Bone Witch	Find the Ancient Hero	350 with Knights of the Ebon Blade	27550	14 80
CHOICE OF: 1 Wristguard of the Bone Witch, 1 Njorndar Furywraps, 1 Iskalder's Fate, 1 Battlescar Spirebands										
I'm Smelting... Smelting!	Icecrown	All	All		Crusader Olakin Sainrith	Crusader Olakin Sainrith	Jagged Shards	250 with Argent Crusade	22050	7 40
Into The Frozen Heart Of Northrend	Icecrown	All	All		Father Gustav	Highlord Tirion Fordring		250 with Argent Crusade	21800	

Title	Location	Faction	Race & Class	Group #	Starter	Finisher	Prerequisite	Reputation	XP	Money
The Runesmiths of Malykriss	Icecrown	All	All		Crusader Olakin Sainrith	Crusader Olakin Sainrith	Jagged Shards	250 with Argent Crusade	22050	7 40
The Battle For Crusaders' Pinnacle	Icecrown	All	All		Highlord Tirion Fordring	Father Gustav	Into The Frozen Heart Of Northrend	250 with Argent Crusade	21800	7 10
Banshee's Revenge	Icecrown	All	All	5	The Bone Witch	The Bone Witch	Not-So-Honorable Combat	500 with Knights of the Ebon Blade	33100	22 20
CHOICE OF: 1 Vengance Shiv, 1 Quickblade of Cold Return, 1 The Witching Grimoie, 1 Bonecaster's Endgame, 1 Bulwark of Redemption										
New Recruit	Icecrown	All	All		Vereth the Cunning	Vereth the Cunning	Vereth the Cunning	250 with Knights of the Ebon Blade	22050	7 40
Killing Two Scourge With One Skeleton	Icecrown	All	All		Darkrider Arly	Darkrider Arly	A Visit to the Doctor, By Fire Be Purged	250 with Knights of the Ebon Blade	22050	7 40
CHOICE OF: 1 Fleshwerk Shackles, 1 Fleshwerk Wristguards, 1 Flesh-scaled Bracers, 1 Hardened Bone Wrist Protectors										
The Vile Hold	Icecrown	All	All		Vereth the Cunning	Vereth the Cunning	New Recruit	250 with Knights of the Ebon Blade	22050	7 40
CHOICE OF: 1 Lithe Stalker's Cord, 1 Cunning Leather Tunic, 1 Enchanted Bracelets of the Scout, 1 Legplates of Dominion										
Generosity Abounds	Icecrown	All	All		Vereth the Cunning	Vereth the Cunning	The Vile Hold	250 with Knights of the Ebon Blade	22050	7 40
Matchmaker	Icecrown	All	All		Vereth the Cunning	Vereth the Cunning	The Vile Hold	250 with Knights of the Ebon Blade	22050	7 40
A Visit to the Doctor	Icecrown	All	All		Darkrider Arly	Darkrider Arly	I'm Smelting... Smelting!, The Runesmiths of Malykriss	250 with Knights of the Ebon Blade	22050	7 40
Vereth the Cunning	Icecrown	All	All		Keritose Bloodblade	Vereth the Cunning	Seeds of Chaos, Amidst the Confusion	75 with Knights of the Ebon Blade	11050	3 70
The Crusaders' Pinnacle	Icecrown	All	All		Father Gustav	Highlord Tirion Fordring	The Battle For Crusaders' Pinnacle	500 with Argent Crusade	32700	
CHOICE OF: 1 The Argent Skullcap, 1 Tirion's Headwrap, 1 Crusader's Coif, 1 The Argent Crown, 1 The Crusader's Resolution										
Stunning View	Icecrown	All	All		Vereth the Cunning	Vereth the Cunning	The Vile Hold	250 with Knights of the Ebon Blade	22050	7 40
The Rider of the Unholy	Icecrown	All	All	5	Vereth the Cunning	Vereth the Cunning	Generosity Abounds, Matchmaker, Stunning View	350 with Knights of the Ebon Blade	27550	14 80
CHOICE OF: 1 Discarded Slaughterhouse Gloves, 1 Blood-encrusted Boots, 1 Plated Legs of the Unholy, 1 Frail Bone Wand										
The Rider of Frost	Icecrown	All	All	5	Vereth the Cunning	Vereth the Cunning	Generosity Abounds, Matchmaker, Stunning View	350 with Knights of the Ebon Blade	27550	14 80
CHOICE OF: 1 Sapph's Cleaver, 1 Frost Climber's Hatchet, 1 Icy Quick Edge, 1 Axe of the Cunning										
The Rider of Blood	Icecrown	All	All	5	Vereth the Cunning	Vereth the Cunning	Generosity Abounds, Matchmaker, Stunning View	350 with Knights of the Ebon Blade	27550	14 80
CHOICE OF: 1 Blood-forged Circle, 1 Grotesque Butcher's Pants, 1 Blood-stalker's Cover, 1 Breastplate of Splattered Blood										
The Fate of Bloodbane	Icecrown	All	All	5	Vereth the Cunning	Vereth the Cunning	The Rider of the Unholy, The Rider of Frost, The Rider of Blood	500 with Knights of the Ebon Blade	33100	22 20
CHOICE OF: 1 Bloodbane Shroud, 1 Bloodbane Cloak, 1 Bloodbane's Fall, 1 Bloodbane's Resolve										
Parting Gifts	Icecrown	All	All		Keritose Bloodblade	Keritose Bloodblade	A Short Fuse, A Short Fuse	10 with Knights of the Ebon Blade	2200	74
An Undead's Best Friend	Icecrown	All	All		Keritose Bloodblade	Keritose Bloodblade	Parting Gifts	250 with Knights of the Ebon Blade	22050	7 40
Honor is for the Weak	Icecrown	All	All		Keritose Bloodblade	Keritose Bloodblade	Parting Gifts	250 with Knights of the Ebon Blade	22050	7 40
From Whence They Came	Icecrown	All	All		Keritose Bloodblade	Keritose Bloodblade	Parting Gifts	250 with Knights of the Ebon Blade	22050	7 40
Seeds of Chaos	Icecrown	All	All		Keritose Bloodblade	Keritose Bloodblade	An Undead's Best Friend, Honor is for the Weak, From Whence They Came	250 with Knights of the Ebon Blade	22050	7 40
CHOICE OF: 1 Weeping Mantle, 1 Fur-lined Helm, 1 Chain Gloves of the Quarry, 1 Grimy Saronite Pauldrons, 1 Bloodblade										
Amidst the Confusion	Icecrown	All	All							
Amidst the Confusion	Icecrown	All	All		Keritose Bloodblade	Keritose Bloodblade	An Undead's Best Friend, Honor is for the Weak, From Whence They Came	250 with Knights of the Ebon Blade	22050	7 40
Regaining Control	Icecrown	All	All							
Preparing the Delivery	Icecrown	All	All							
Outliving Usefulness	Icecrown	All	All							
By Fire Be Purged	Icecrown	All	All		Crusader Olakin Sainrith	Crusader Olakin Sainrith	I'm Smelting... Smelting!, The Runesmiths of Malykriss	250 with Argent Crusade	22050	7 40
CHOICE OF: 1 Fair Touch of the Crusader, 1 Olakin's Enchanted Torch, 1 Fleshwerk Throwing Glaive										
He's Gone to Pieces	Icecrown	All	All		Darkrider Arly	Darkrider Arly	Killing Two Scourge With One Skeleton	250 with Knights of the Ebon Blade	22050	7 40
Battle at Valhalas	Icecrown	All	All		The Bone Witch	Geirrvif	Banshee's Revenge		2200	
Battle at Valhalas: Fallen Heroes	Icecrown	All	All	5	Geirrvif	Gjonner the Merciless	Battle at Valhalas		33100	22 20
Battle at Valhalas: Khit'rix the Dark Master	Icecrown	All	All	5	Geirrvif	Gjonner the Merciless	Battle at Valhalas: Fallen Heroes		33100	22 20

Title	Location	Faction	Race & Class	Group #	Starter	Finisher	Prerequisite	Reputation	XP	Money
Battle at Valhalas: The Return of Sigrid Iceborn	Icecrown	All	All	5	Geirrvif	Gjonner the Merciless	Battle at Valhalas: Khit'rix the Dark Master		33100	22 20
CHOICE OF: 5 Runic Healing Potion, 5 Runic Mana Potion										
Battle at Valhalas: Carnage!	Icecrown	All	All	5	Geirrvif	Gjonner the Merciless	Battle at Valhalas: The Return of Sigrid Iceborn		33100	22 20
Battle at Valhalas: Thane Deathblow	Icecrown	All	All	5	Geirrvif	Gjonner the Merciless	Battle at Valhalas: Carnage!		33100	22 20
Battle at Valhalas: Final Challenge	Icecrown	All	All	5	Geirrvif	Gjonner the Merciless	Battle at Valhalas: Thane Deathblow		33100	22 20
CHOICE OF: 1 Robes of Refrained Celebration, 1 Battleplate of Unheard Ovation, 1 Chestguard of Unwanted Success, 1 Tunic of the Unduly Victorious										
Putting Olakin Back Together Again	Icecrown	All	All		Darkrider Arly	Darkrider Arly	He's Gone to Pieces	250 with Knights of the Ebon Blade	22050	7 40
I'm Not Dead Yet!	Icecrown	All	All		Father Kamaros	Absalan the Pious	Destroying the Altars, Death's Gaze	250 with Argent Crusade	22050	7 40
Orgrim's Hammer	Icecrown	All	All		Warlord Hork Strongbrow	Sky-Reaver Korm Blackscar	The Crusaders' Pinnacle	25 with Warsong Offensive	5450	
The Skybreaker	Icecrown	All	All		Marshal Ivalius	High Captain Justin Bartlett	The Crusaders' Pinnacle	25 with Valiance Expedition	5450	
Judgment Day Comes!	Icecrown	All	All		Absalan the Pious	Highlord Tirion Fordring		25 with Argent Crusade	5400	
Judgment Day Comes!	Icecrown	All	All		Brother Keltan	Highlord Tirion Fordring		25 with Argent Crusade	5400	
The Broken Front	Icecrown	All	All		Sky-Reaver Korm Blackscar	Sky-Reaver Korm Blackscar	Orgrim's Hammer		22050	7 40
I'm Not Dead Yet!	Icecrown	All	All		Father Kamaros	Brother Keltan	Destroying the Altars, Death's Gaze		22050	7 40
Avenge Me!	Icecrown	All	All		Sky-Reaver Korm Blackscar	Sky-Reaver Korm Blackscar			22050	7 40
The Broken Front	Icecrown	All	All		High Captain Justin Bartlett	High Captain Justin Bartlett	The Skybreaker		22050	7 40
Finish Me!	Icecrown	All	All		High Captain Justin Bartlett	High Captain Justin Bartlett			22050	7 40
No Mercy!	Icecrown	All	All		High Captain Justin Bartlett	High Captain Justin Bartlett	The Broken Front		22050	7 40
Make Them Pay!	Icecrown	All	All		Sky-Reaver Korm Blackscar	Sky-Reaver Korm Blackscar	The Broken Front		22050	7 40
The Flesh Giant Champion	Icecrown	All	All		Darkrider Arly	Darkrider Arly	Putting Olakin Back Together Again	350 with Knights of the Ebon Blade	27550	14 80
CHOICE OF: 1 Mantle of the Flesh Giant, 1 Shoulderpads of Fleshwerks, 1 Giant Champion's Spaulders, 1 Pauldrons of Morbidus										
Army of the Damned	Icecrown	All	All		Matthias Lehner	Matthias Lehner	Do Your Worst		27550	
Poke and Prod	Icecrown	All	All		Sky-Reaver Korm Blackscar, Koltira Deathweaver	Koltira Deathweaver	Takes One to Know One		22050	7 40
CHOICE OF: 1 Ring of the Fallen Shadow Adept, 1 Hulking Abomination Hide Cloak, 1 Amulet of the Malefic Necromancer										
Good For Something?	Icecrown	All	All		Sky-Reaver Korm Blackscar	Chief Engineer Copperclaw	The Broken Front		2200	74
Volatility	Icecrown	Horde	All		Chief Engineer Copperclaw	Chief Engineer Copperclaw	Good For Something?		22050	7 40
CHOICE OF: 1 Smuggler's Bracers, 1 Glacier-walker's Mukluks, 1 Skycaptain's Belt, 1 Plated Bracelet of the Skies										
Opportunity	Icecrown	Horde	All		Koltira Deathweaver	Sergeant Kregga	Orgrim's Hammer, The Shadow Vault	75 with Warsong Offensive	11050	
Takes One to Know One	Icecrown	All	All		Sky-Reaver Korm Blackscar	Koltira Deathweaver	The Broken Front		2200	
Volatility	Icecrown	Horde	All		Chief Engineer Copperclaw	Chief Engineer Copperclaw	Volatility		22050	7 40
Blow it Up!	Icecrown	Horde	All		Sergeant Kregga	Saronite Bomb Stack	Establishing Superiority		2200	74
A Short Fuse	Icecrown	All	All		Saronite Bomb Stack	Pulsing Crystal	Blow it Up!		2200	74
That's Abominable!	Icecrown	Horde	All		Koltira Deathweaver	Koltira Deathweaver	Poke and Prod		22050	7 40
CHOICE OF: 1 Slippers of the Broken Front, 1 Mantle of Reanimation, 1 Geist Stalker Leggings, 1 Scourgebane Pauldrons										
Time to Hide	Icecrown	All	All		Matthias Lehner	Matthias Lehner	A Voice in the Dark		22050	5 80
CHOICE OF: 1 Scourgehammer, 1 Shooter's Glory, 1 Pilot's Knife, 1 Mace of the Final Command, 1 Blunt Brainwasher, 1 Ritualist's Bloodletter										
That's Abominable!	Icecrown	Horde	All		Koltira Deathweaver	Koltira Deathweaver	That's Abominable!		22050	7 40
Against the Giants	Icecrown	Horde	All	5	Koltira Deathweaver	Koltira Deathweaver	Poke and Prod		27550	14 80
Coprous the Defiled	Icecrown	Horde	All	5	Koltira Deathweaver	Koltira Deathweaver	Against the Giants		27550	14 80
Basic Chemistry	Icecrown	Horde	All	5	Koltira Deathweaver	Koltira Deathweaver	Against the Giants		22050	7 40
CHOICE OF: 1 Newt-Eye Ring, 1 Frog-Toe Band, 1 Bat-Wool Signet										
King of the Mountain	Icecrown	Alliance	All		Frazzle Geargrinder	Frazzle Geargrinder	Get to Ymirheim!	250 with Valiance Expedition	22050	7 40
Neutralizing the Plague	Icecrown	Horde	All	5	Koltira Deathweaver	Koltira Deathweaver	Basic Chemistry		33100	22 20
Return to the Surface	Icecrown	All	All		Matthias Lehner	Koltira Deathweaver	Time to Hide		11050	3 70
King of the Mountain	Icecrown	Horde	All		Blast Thunderbomb	Blast Thunderbomb	Get to Ymirheim!	250 with Warsong Offensive	22050	7 40
Assault by Ground	Icecrown	Alliance	All		Ground Commander Koup	Ground Commander Koup	Joining the Assault	250 with Valiance Expedition	22050	7 40
...All the Help We Can Get.	Icecrown	All	All		High Captain Justin Bartlett	Thassarian	The Broken Front		2200	
Poke and Prod	Icecrown	Alliance	All		Thassarian	Thassarian	...All the Help We Can Get.		22050	7 40
CHOICE OF: 1 Ring of the Fallen Shadow Adept, 1 Hulking Abomination Hide Cloak, 1 Amulet of the Malefic Necromancer										
That's Abominable!	Icecrown	Alliance	All		Thassarian	Thassarian	Poke and Prod		22050	7 40
CHOICE OF: 1 Slippers of the Broken Front, 1 Mantle of Reanimation, 1 Geist Stalker Leggings, 1 Scourgebane Pauldrons										

Title	Location	Faction	Race & Class	Group #	Starter	Finisher	Prerequisite	Reputation	XP	Money
That's Abominable!	Icecrown	Alliance	All		Thassarian	Thassarian	That's Abominable!		22050	7🪙40🪙
Your Attention, Please	Icecrown	All	All		High Captain Justin Bartlett	Chief Engineer Boltwrench	The Broken Front		2200	
Borrowed Technology	Icecrown	All	All		Chief Engineer Boltwrench	Chief Engineer Boltwrench	Your Attention, Please		22050	7🪙40🪙
CHOICE OF: 1 Smuggler's Bracers, 1 Glacier-walker's Mukluks, 1 Skycaptain's Belt, 1 Plated Bracelet of the Skies										
The Solution Solution	Icecrown	All	All		Chief Engineer Boltwrench	Chief Engineer Boltwrench	Borrowed Technology		22050	7🪙40🪙
Get to Ymirheim!	Icecrown	Horde	All		Chief Engineer Copperclaw	Blast Thunderbomb	Orgrim's Hammer	10 with Warsong Offensive	2200	
Against the Giants	Icecrown	Alliance	All		Thassarian	Thassarian	Poke and Prod		27550	14🪙80🪙
Basic Chemistry	Icecrown	Alliance	All	5	Thassarian	Thassarian	Against the Giants		22050	7🪙40🪙
CHOICE OF: 1 Newt-Eye Ring, 1 Bat-Wool Signet, 1 Frog-Toe Band										
Get to Ymirheim!	Icecrown	All	All		Chief Engineer Boltwrench	Frazzle Geargrinder	The Skybreaker	10 with Valiance Expedition	2200	
Neutralizing the Plague	Icecrown	Alliance	All	5	Thassarian	Thassarian	Basic Chemistry		33100	22🪙20🪙
Coprous the Defiled	Icecrown	Alliance	All	5	Thassarian	Thassarian	Against the Giants		33100	22🪙20🪙
Slaves to Saronite	Icecrown	All	All		Absalan the Pious	Absalan the Pious	The Skybreaker	250 with Argent Crusade	22050	7🪙40🪙
Assault by Ground	Icecrown	Horde	All		Ground Commander Xutjja	Ground Commander Xutjja	Joining the Assault	250 with Warsong Offensive	22050	7🪙40🪙
Slaves to Saronite	Icecrown	All	All		Brother Keltan	Brother Keltan	Orgrim's Hammer	250 with Argent Crusade	22050	7🪙40🪙
Field Repairs	Icecrown	All	All		Koltira Deathweaver	Wrecked Demolisher	Return to the Surface		22050	7🪙40🪙
Do Your Worst	Icecrown	All	All		Matthias Lehner	Matthias Lehner	Field Repairs		22050	7🪙40🪙
CHOICE OF: 1 Demolisher Driver's Dustcoat, 1 Refurbished Demolisher Gear Belt, 1 Drivetrain Chain Leggings, 1 Accelerator Stompers, 1 Demolisher's Grips										
Raise the Barricades	Icecrown	Horde	All		Koltira Deathweaver	Koltira Deathweaver	Need More Info	250 with Knights of the Ebon Blade	22050	7🪙40🪙
Bloodspattered Banners	Icecrown	Horde	All		Koltira Deathweaver	Koltira Deathweaver	Raise the Barricades	250 with Knights of the Ebon Blade	22050	7🪙40🪙
Mind Tricks	Icecrown	All	All	3	Darkspeaker R'khem	Darkspeaker R'khem	Orgrim's Hammer, The Skybreaker		27550	14🪙80🪙
CHOICE OF: 1 The Darkspeaker's Footpads, 1 The Darkspeaker's Treads, 1 The Darkspeaker's Sabatons, 1 The Darkspeaker's Iron Walkers										
Assault by Air	Icecrown	Alliance	All		Ground Commander Koup	Ground Commander Koup	Joining the Assault	250 with Valiance Expedition	22050	7🪙40🪙
Assault by Air	Icecrown	Horde	All		Ground Commander Xutjja	Ground Commander Xutjja	Joining the Assault	250 with Warsong Offensive	22050	7🪙40🪙
The Ironwall Rampart	Icecrown	Horde	All	5	Koltira Deathweaver	Koltira Deathweaver	Raise the Barricades, No Rest For The Wicked	350 with Knights of the Ebon Blade	27550	14🪙80🪙
Blinding the Eyes in the Sky	Icecrown	All	All		Sky-Reaver Korm Blackscar	Sky-Reaver Korm Blackscar	Raise the Barricades	250 with Warsong Offensive	22050	7🪙40🪙
Get the Message	Icecrown	All	All		High Captain Justin Bartlett	High Captain Justin Bartlett	Raise the Barricades	250 with Valiance Expedition	22050	7🪙40🪙
Sneak Preview	Icecrown	Alliance	All		Thassarian	Thassarian	That's Abominable!		16550	5🪙80🪙
The Guardians of Corp'rethar	Icecrown	Horde	All	5	Koltira Deathweaver	Koltira Deathweaver	Before the Gate of Horror	350 with Knights of the Ebon Blade	27550	14🪙80🪙
—	Icecrown	All	All		High Captain Justin Bartlett		That's Abominable!			
Drag and Drop	Icecrown	Alliance	All		Thassarian	Thassarian	Sneak Preview		22050	7🪙40🪙
Chain of Command	Icecrown	Alliance	All		Thassarian	Thassarian	Sneak Preview		22050	7🪙40🪙
CHOICE OF: 1 Cultist's Cowl, 1 Jhaequon's Tunic, 1 Savryn's Muddy Boots, 1 Cultbreaker's Chestguard										
Cannot Reproduce	Icecrown	All	All		Thassarian	Chief Engineer Boltwrench	Sneak Preview		22050	7🪙40🪙
Retest Now	Icecrown	All	All		Chief Engineer Boltwrench	Chief Engineer Boltwrench	Cannot Reproduce		22050	7🪙40🪙
CHOICE OF: 1 Bow of Regression, 1 Twisted Hooligan Whacker, 1 Writhing Mace, 1 Cultist's Cauldron Stirrer, 1 Deadly Razordarts										
Retest Now	Icecrown	All	All		Chief Engineer Boltwrench	Chief Engineer Boltwrench	Retest Now		22050	7🪙40🪙
Drag and Drop	Icecrown	Alliance	All		Thassarian	Thassarian	Drag and Drop		22050	7🪙40🪙
Shatter the Shards	Icecrown	Horde	All	5	Koltira Deathweaver	Koltira Deathweaver	Before the Gate of Horror	350 with Knights of the Ebon Blade	27550	7🪙40🪙
Before the Gate of Horror	Icecrown	Horde	All	5	Koltira Deathweaver	Koltira Deathweaver	Bloodspattered Banners, The Ironwall Rampart	250 with Knights of the Ebon Blade	22050	7🪙40🪙
Blood of the Chosen	Icecrown	Horde	All		Warbringer Davos Rioht	Warbringer Davos Rioht	Orgrim's Hammer	250 with Warsong Offensive	22050	7🪙40🪙
Keeping the Alliance Blind	Icecrown	All	All		Sky-Reaver Korm Blackscar	Sky-Reaver Korm Blackscar	Blinding the Eyes in the Sky	250 with Warsong Offensive	22050	7🪙40🪙
Raise the Barricades	Icecrown	Alliance	All		Thassarian	Thassarian	Need More Info	250 with Knights of the Ebon Blade	22050	7🪙40🪙
Capture More Dispatches	Icecrown	All	All		High Captain Justin Bartlett	High Captain Justin Bartlett	Get the Message	250 with Valiance Expedition	22050	7🪙40🪙
Bloodspattered Banners	Icecrown	Alliance	All		Thassarian	Thassarian	Raise the Barricades	250 with Knights of the Ebon Blade	22050	7🪙40🪙
Before the Gate of Horror	Icecrown	Alliance	All		Thassarian	Thassarian	Bloodspattered Banners, The Ironwall Rampart	250 with Knights of the Ebon Blade	22050	7🪙40🪙
Blood of the Chosen	Icecrown	Alliance	All		Knight-Captain Drosche	Knight-Captain Drosche	The Skybreaker	250 with Valiance Expedition	22050	7🪙40🪙
The Ironwall Rampart	Icecrown	Alliance	All	5	Thassarian	Thassarian	Raise the Barricades, No Rest For The Wicked	350 with Knights of the Ebon Blade	27550	14🪙80🪙

Title	Location	Faction	Race & Class	Group #	Starter	Finisher	Prerequisite	Reputation	XP	Money
The Guardians of Corp'rethar	Icecrown	Alliance	All	5	Thassarian	Thassarian	Before the Gate of Horror	350 with Knights of the Ebon Blade	27550	14🟡80🟡
Shatter the Shards	Icecrown	Alliance	All	5	Thassarian	Thassarian	Before the Gate of Horror	350 with Knights of the Ebon Blade	27550	7🟡40🟡
Joining the Assault	Icecrown	Horde	All		Warbringer Davos Rioht	Ground Commander Xutija	Orgrim's Hammer	25 with Warsong Offensive	5500	1🟡90🟡
Joining the Assault	Icecrown	Alliance	All		Knight-Captain Drosche	Ground Commander Koup	The Skybreaker	25 with Valiance Expedition	5500	1🟡90🟡
Not a Bug	Icecrown	Alliance	All		Thassarian	Thassarian	Drag and Drop		22050	7🟡40🟡
CHOICE OF: 1 Mantle of the Dark Messenger, 1 Gilly's Strangulation Gauntlets, 1 Chain Gloves of the Demonic Minion, 1 Legplates of the Northern Expedition, 1 Gutbuster of Aldur'thar										
Not a Bug	Icecrown	Alliance	All		Thassarian	Thassarian	Not a Bug		22050	7🟡40🟡
Need More Info	Icecrown	Alliance	All		Thassarian	Thassarian	Drag and Drop		22050	7🟡40🟡
No Rest For The Wicked	Icecrown	Alliance	All	5	Thassarian	Thassarian	Need More Info		33100	22🟡20🟡
CHOICE OF: 1 Encrusted Zombie Finger, 1 Polished Zombie Exterminator, 1 Touch of Unlife										
Futility	Icecrown	All	All		Matthias Lehner	Koltira Deathweaver	Army of the Damned	75 with Warsong Offensive	11050	3🟡70🟡
Cradle of the Frostbrood	Icecrown	Horde	All		Koltira Deathweaver	Koltira Deathweaver	Futility	250 with Warsong Offensive	22050	7🟡40🟡
CHOICE OF: 1 Axe of Bloodstained Ice, 1 Wyrmstalker's Bow, 1 Reanimator's Hacker, 1 Corrupter's Shanker, 1 Necrolord's Sacrificial Dagger										
No Rest For The Wicked	Icecrown	Alliance	All	5	Thassarian	Thassarian	No Rest For The Wicked		33100	22🟡20🟡
Sneak Preview	Icecrown	Horde	All		Koltira Deathweaver	Koltira Deathweaver	That's Abominable!		16550	5🟡80🟡
Drag and Drop	Icecrown	Horde	All		Koltira Deathweaver	Koltira Deathweaver	Sneak Preview		22050	7🟡40🟡
Drag and Drop	Icecrown	Horde	All		Koltira Deathweaver	Koltira Deathweaver	Drag and Drop		22050	7🟡40🟡
Chain of Command	Icecrown	Horde	All		Koltira Deathweaver	Koltira Deathweaver	Sneak Preview		22050	7🟡40🟡
CHOICE OF: 1 Cultist's Cowl, 1 Jhaequon's Tunic, 1 Savryn's Muddy Boots, 1 Cultbreaker's Chestguard										
Cannot Reproduce	Icecrown	Horde	All		Koltira Deathweaver	Chief Engineer Copperclaw	Sneak Preview		22050	7🟡40🟡
Retest Now	Icecrown	Horde	All		Chief Engineer Copperclaw	Chief Engineer Copperclaw	Cannot Reproduce		22050	7🟡40🟡
CHOICE OF: 1 Bow of Regression, 1 Twisted Hooligan Whacker, 1 Writhing Mace, 1 Cultist's Cauldron Stirrer, 1 Deadly Razordarts										
Retest Now	Icecrown	Horde	All		Chief Engineer Copperclaw	Chief Engineer Copperclaw	Retest Now		22050	7🟡40🟡
Not a Bug	Icecrown	Horde	All		Chief Engineer Copperclaw	Koltira Deathweaver	Drag and Drop		22050	7🟡40🟡
CHOICE OF: 1 Mantle of the Dark Messenger, 1 Gilly's Strangulation Gauntlets, 1 Chain Gloves of the Demonic Minion, 1 Legplates of the Northern Expedition, 1 Gutbuster of Aldur'thar										
Where Dragons Fell	Icecrown	All	All		Matthias Lehner	Matthias Lehner	Futility		22050	7🟡40🟡
Time for Answers	Icecrown	All	All		Matthias Lehner	Matthias Lehner	Where Dragons Fell		5500	1🟡90🟡
The Hunter and the Prince	Icecrown	All	All		Matthias Lehner	Matthias Lehner	Time for Answers		27550	14🟡80🟡
CHOICE OF: 1 Gloves of Tormented Recollection, 1 Gloves of Troubled Memory, 1 Leggings of the Turning Point, 1 Bloodstained Helmet										
Knowledge is a Terrible Burden	Icecrown	All	All		Matthias Lehner	Koltira Deathweaver	The Hunter and the Prince	75 with Valiance Expedition	11050	
Argent Aid	Icecrown	Horde	All		Koltira Deathweaver	Highlord Tirion Fordring	Knowledge is a Terrible Burden		16550	
Tirion's Gambit	Icecrown	All	All		Highlord Tirion Fordring	Highlord Tirion Fordring	Argent Aid	500 with Argent Crusade, 500 with Knights of the Ebon Blade, 500 with Valiance Expedition, 500 with Warsong Offensive	33100	22🟡20🟡
CHOICE OF: 1 Blade of the Empty Void, 1 Hammer of Wrenching Change, 1 Knife of the Tarnished Soul, 1 Stave of Youthful Sorrow										
Not a Bug	Icecrown	Horde	All		Koltira Deathweaver	Koltira Deathweaver	Not a Bug		22050	7🟡40🟡
Need More Info	Icecrown	Horde	All		Koltira Deathweaver	Koltira Deathweaver	Drag and Drop		22050	7🟡40🟡
No Rest For The Wicked	Icecrown	Horde	All	5	Koltira Deathweaver	Koltira Deathweaver	Need More Info		33100	22🟡20🟡
CHOICE OF: 1 Polished Zombie Exterminator, 1 Encrusted Zombie Finger, 1 Touch of Unlife										
No Rest For The Wicked	Icecrown	Horde	All	5	Koltira Deathweaver	Koltira Deathweaver	No Rest For The Wicked		33100	22🟡20🟡
Fringe Science Benefits	Icecrown	Horde	All		Fringe Engineer Tezzla	Fringe Engineer Tezzla	Volatility		22050	7🟡40🟡
Amped for Revolt!	Icecrown	Horde	All		Fringe Engineer Tezzla	Fringe Engineer Tezzla	Fringe Science Benefits		22050	7🟡40🟡
Total Ohmage: The Valley of Lost Hope!	Icecrown	Horde	All		Fringe Engineer Tezzla	Fringe Engineer Tezzla	Fringe Science Benefits		22050	7🟡40🟡
Chief Engineer Copperclaw	Icecrown	Horde	All		Chief Engineer Copperclaw	Chief Engineer Copperclaw			2200	74🟡
Green Technology	Icecrown	Horde	All		Chief Engineer Copperclaw	Fringe Engineer Tezzla	Volatility		2200	74🟡
Leading the Charge	Icecrown	Alliance	All		Kibli Killohertz	Kibli Killohertz	Borrowed Technology		22050	7🟡40🟡
Watts My Target	Icecrown	Alliance	All		Kibli Killohertz	Kibli Killohertz	Leading the Charge		22050	7🟡40🟡
Putting the Hertz: The Valley of Lost Hope	Icecrown	Alliance	All		Kibli Killohertz	Kibli Killohertz	Leading the Charge		22050	7🟡40🟡
Killohertz	Icecrown	All	All		Chief Engineer Boltwrench	Kibli Killohertz	Borrowed Technology		2200	74🟡
Exploiting an Opening	Icecrown	All	All		Thassarian	Captain Kendall	The Skybreaker, The Shadow Vault	75 with Valiance Expedition	11050	
Set it Off!	Icecrown	All	All		Captain Kendall	Saronite Bomb Stack	Securing the Perimeter		2200	74🟡
A Short Fuse	Icecrown	All	All		Saronite Bomb Stack	Pulsing Crystal	Set it Off!		2200	74🟡
Time to Hide	Icecrown	All	All		Matthias Lehner	Matthias Lehner	A Voice in the Dark		22050	5🟡80🟡
CHOICE OF: 1 Scourgehammer, 1 Shooter's Glory, 1 Pilot's Knife, 1 Mace of the Final Command, 1 Blunt Brainwasher, 1 Ritualist's Bloodletter										
Return to the Surface	Icecrown	All	All		Matthias Lehner	Thassarian	Time to Hide	75 with Valiance Expedition	11050	3🟡70🟡
Field Repairs	Icecrown	All	All		Thassarian	Wrecked Demolisher	Return to the Surface		22050	7🟡40🟡

Title	Location	Faction	Race & Class	Group #	Starter	Finisher	Prerequisite	Reputation	XP	Money
Do Your Worst	Icecrown	All	All		Matthias Lehner	Matthias Lehner	Field Repairs		22050	7🟡 40🔴
CHOICE OF: 1 Demolisher Driver's Dustcoat, 1 Refurbished Demolisher Gear Belt, 1 Drivetrain Chain Leggings, 1 Accelerator Stompers, 1 Demolisher's Grips										
Army of the Damned	Icecrown	All	All		Matthias Lehner	Matthias Lehner	Do Your Worst		27550	
Futility	Icecrown	All	All		Matthias Lehner	Thassarian	Army of the Damned	75 with Valiance Expedition	11050	3🟡 70🔴
Sindragosa's Fall	Icecrown	Alliance	All		Thassarian	Thassarian	Futility	250 with Valiance Expedition	22050	7🟡 40🔴
CHOICE OF: 1 Axe of Bloodstained Ice, 1 Wyrmstalker's Bow, 1 Reanimator's Hacker, 1 Corrupter's Shanker, 1 Necrolord's Sacrificial Dagger										
Where Dragons Fell	Icecrown	All	All		Matthias Lehner	Matthias Lehner	Futility		22050	7🟡 40🔴
Time for Answers	Icecrown	All	All		Matthias Lehner	Matthias Lehner	Where Dragons Fell		5500	1🟡 90🔴
The Hunter and the Prince	Icecrown	All	All		Matthias Lehner	Matthias Lehner	Time for Answers		27550	14🟡 80🔴
CHOICE OF: 1 Gloves of Tormented Recollection, 1 Gloves of Troubled Memory, 1 Leggings of the Turning Point, 1 Bloodstained Helmet										
Knowledge is a Terrible Burden	Icecrown	All	All		Matthias Lehner	Thassarian	The Hunter and the Prince		11050	
Tirion's Help	Icecrown	Alliance	All		Thassarian	Highlord Tirion Fordring	Knowledge is a Terrible Burden		16550	
Tirion's Gambit	Icecrown	All	All		Highlord Tirion Fordring	Highlord Tirion Fordring	Tirion's Help	500 with Argent Crusade, 500 with Knights of the Ebon Blade, 500 with Valiance Expedition, 500 with Warsong Offensive	33100	22🟡 20🔴
CHOICE OF: 1 Blade of the Empty Void, 1 Knife of the Tarnished Soul, 1 Hammer of Wrenching Change, 1 Stave of Youthful Sorrow										
Static Shock Troops: the Bombardment	Icecrown	Alliance	All		Kibli Killohertz	Kibli Killohertz	Leading the Charge		22050	7🟡 40🔴
Riding the Wavelength: The Bombardment	Icecrown	Horde	All		Fringe Engineer Tezzla	Fringe Engineer Tezzla	Fringe Science Benefits		22050	7🟡 40🔴
Aces High!	Icecrown	All	All		Corastrasza	Corastrasza	Aces High!		22050	7🟡 40🔴
Preparations for War	Icecrown	All	All		Officer Van Rossem	High Captain Justin Bartlett		25 with Valiance Expedition	5500	1🟡 90🔴
Preparations for War	Icecrown	All	All		Sky-Reaver Klum	Sky-Reaver Korm Blackscar		25 with Warsong Offensive	5500	1🟡 90🔴

ICECROWN CITADEL

Title	Location	Faction	Race & Class	Group #	Starter	Finisher	Prerequisite	Reputation	XP	Money
Establishing Superiority	Icecrown Citadel	Horde	All		Sergeant Kregga	Sergeant Kregga	Opportunity		22050	7🟡 40🔴
CHOICE OF: 1 Shock-Proof Head Protector, 1 Hulking Horror Tunic, 1 Gloves of the Mad Bomber, 1 Icewalker's Spikes										
Securing the Perimeter	Icecrown Citadel	All	All		Captain Kendall	Captain Kendall	Exploiting an Opening	250 with Valiance Expedition	22050	7🟡 40🔴
CHOICE OF: 1 Shock-Proof Head Protector, 1 Hulking Horror Tunic, 1 Gloves of the Mad Bomber, 1 Icewalker's Spikes										

SHATTRATH CITY

Title	Location	Faction	Race & Class	Group #	Starter	Finisher	Prerequisite	Reputation	XP	Money
Onwards to Northrend!	Shattrath City	Alliance	All		Herald of the Alliance	Alliance Recruiter				
Onwards to Northrend!	Shattrath City	Horde	All		Herald of the Horde	Horde Recruiter			1250	
Welcome to Sholazar Basin	Sholazar Basin	All	All		Monte Muzzleshot	Hemet Nesingway	Where in the World is Hemet Nesingway?		10600	3🟡 10🔴
PvP Test	Sholazar Basin	All	All		Test PvP Questgiver	Test PvP Questgiver				
Rhino Mastery: The Test	Sholazar Basin	All	All		Hemet Nesingway	Hemet Nesingway	Have a Part, Give a Part, Wipe That Grin Off His Face		21150	6🟡 20🔴
Where in the World is Hemet Nesingway?	Sholazar Basin	All	All		Archmage Pentarus	Monte Muzzleshot			2100	
Need an Engine, Take an Engine	Sholazar Basin	All	All		Weslex Quickwrench	Weslex Quickwrench			15850	4🟡 80🔴
Have a Part, Give a Part	Sholazar Basin	All	All		Weslex Quickwrench	Weslex Quickwrench	Need an Engine, Take an Engine		21150	6🟡 20🔴
Venture Co. Misadventure	Sholazar Basin	All	All		Debaar	Debaar			21150	6🟡 20🔴
Wipe That Grin Off His Face	Sholazar Basin	All	All		Debaar	Debaar	Venture Co. Misadventure		21150	6🟡 20🔴
CHOICE OF: 1 Ogre-Crushing Wristguards, 1 Bracers of the Rejuvenated Forest, 1 Spitelinked Bracers, 1 Roaming Wristguards										
Rhino Mastery: The Chase	Sholazar Basin	All	All		Hemet Nesingway	Oracle Soo-rahm	Rhino Mastery: The Test		2100	
Playing Along	Sholazar Basin	All	All		High-Shaman Rakjak	High-Shaman Rakjak		350 with Frenzyheart Tribe	5350	1🟡 66🔴
The Ape Hunter's Slave	Sholazar Basin	All	All		High-Shaman Rakjak	High-Shaman Rakjak	Playing Along	350 with Frenzyheart Tribe	21400	6🟡 50🔴
Tormenting the Softknuckles	Sholazar Basin	All	All		Goregek the Gorilla Hunter	High-Shaman Rakjak	Playing Along	500 with Frenzyheart Tribe	21400	6🟡 50🔴
The Underground Menace	Sholazar Basin	All	All		Elder Harkek	High-Shaman Rakjak	Flown the Coop!	500 with Frenzyheart Tribe	21400	6🟡 50🔴

SHATTRATH CITY

Title	Location	Faction	Race & Class	Group #	Starter	Finisher	Prerequisite	Reputation	XP	Money
Flown the Coop!	Sholazar Basin	All	All		Elder Harkek	Elder Harkek	The Wasp Hunter's Apprentice, The Sapphire Queen	350 with Frenzyheart Tribe	21400	6🟡 50🔴
CHOICE OF: 1 Stained Coop Warmer, 1 Egg-Warming Boots, 1 Straw-Lined Leggings, 1 Cracked Nest Stabilizer										
The Wasp Hunter's Apprentice	Sholazar Basin	All	All		High-Shaman Rakjak	High-Shaman Rakjak	The Ape Hunter's Slave, Tormenting the Softknuckles	350 with Frenzyheart Tribe	21400	6🟡 50🔴
The Sapphire Queen	Sholazar Basin	All	All		Elder Harkek	High-Shaman Rakjak	The Ape Hunter's Slave, Tormenting the Softknuckles	500 with Frenzyheart Tribe	21400	6🟡 50🔴
CHOICE OF: 1 Chitin-Reinforced Hood, 1 Stinger-Proof Chestguard, 1 Insect-Filtering Faceguard, 1 Bug-Smashing Pauldrons										
Mischief in the Making	Sholazar Basin	All	All		High-Shaman Rakjak	High-Shaman Rakjak	Flown the Coop!	350 with Frenzyheart Tribe	21400	6🟡 50🔴
A Rough Ride	Sholazar Basin	All	All		High-Shaman Rakjak	Zepik the Gorloc Hunter	Mischief in the Making, The Underground Menace	350 with Frenzyheart Tribe	5350	1🟡 66🔴
Lightning Definitely Strikes Twice	Sholazar Basin	All	All		Zepik the Gorloc Hunter	Zepik the Gorloc Hunter	A Rough Ride	500 with Frenzyheart Tribe	21400	6🟡 50🔴
CHOICE OF: 1 Gloves of the Crackling Storm, 1 Static-Dispersing Shoulderpads, 1 Belt of Trapped Lightning, 1 Zepik's Grounded Legplates										
The Mist Isn't Listening	Sholazar Basin	All	All		Zepik the Gorloc Hunter	Zepik the Gorloc Hunter	A Rough Ride	350 with Frenzyheart Tribe	21400	6🟡 50🔴
Hoofing It	Sholazar Basin	All	All		Zepik the Gorloc Hunter	High-Shaman Rakjak	The Mist Isn't Listening, Lightning Definitely Strikes Twice	350 with Frenzyheart Tribe	21400	6🟡 50🔴
Just Following Orders	Sholazar Basin	All	All		High-Shaman Rakjak	Injured Rainspeaker Oracle	Hoofing It		21400	6🟡 50🔴
An Offering for Soo-rahm	Sholazar Basin	All	All		Oracle Soo-rahm	Oracle Soo-rahm	Rhino Mastery: The Chase		21150	6🟡 20🔴
The Bones of Nozronn	Sholazar Basin	All	All		Oracle Soo-rahm	Hemet Nesingwary	An Offering for Soo-rahm		15850	4🟡 80🔴
Reclamation	Sholazar Basin	All	All		Avatar of Freya	Avatar of Freya	Back Through the Waygate		32400	20🟡 40🔴
CHOICE OF: 1 Gaze of the Punishing Construct, 1 Helm of the Avenging Protector, 1 Headguard of Vast Destruction, 1 Helm of Towering Rage, 1 Greathelm of the Titan Protectorate										
The Etymidian	Sholazar Basin	All	All		Avatar of Freya	The Etymidian	Powering the Waygate - The Maker's Overlook		21600	
Dreadsaber Mastery: Becoming a Predator	Sholazar Basin	All	All		Buck Cantwell	Buck Cantwell	Wipe That Grin Off His Face, Have a Part, Give a Part		21150	6🟡 20🔴
Dreadsaber Mastery: Stalking the Prey	Sholazar Basin	All	All		Buck Cantwell	Buck Cantwell	Dreadsaber Mastery: Becoming a Predator		21150	6🟡 20🔴
Crocolisk Mastery: The Trial	Sholazar Basin	All	All		Debaar	Debaar	Dreadsaber Mastery: Becoming a Predator, Rhino Mastery: The Test		21150	6🟡 20🔴
Rhino Mastery: The Kill	Sholazar Basin	All	All		Hemet Nesingwary	Hemet Nesingwary	The Bones of Nozronn		26450	12🟡 40🔴
CHOICE OF: 1 Nimblefoot Moccasins, 1 Toenail Belt, 1 Shaved Rhinohorn Chestguard, 1 Rhino-Tail Girdle										
Dreadsaber Mastery: Ready to Pounce	Sholazar Basin	All	All		Buck Cantwell	Buck Cantwell	Dreadsaber Mastery: Stalking the Prey		21150	6🟡 20🔴
CHOICE OF: 1 Scrap-Hide Spaulders, 1 Dreadsaber Tooth Shoulderpads, 1 Pauldrons of Swift Replenishment, 1 Pauldrons of the Silent Mist, 1 Bronzed Dome Protector										
Powering the Waygate - The Maker's Perch	Sholazar Basin	All	All		Avatar of Freya	Avatar of Freya	Freya's Pact		16050	5🟡 10🔴
Crocolisk Mastery: The Plan	Sholazar Basin	All	All		Debaar	Debaar	Crocolisk Mastery: The Trial		21150	6🟡 20🔴
An Issue of Trust	Sholazar Basin	All	All		Avatar of Freya	Avatar of Freya			26750	13🟡
CHOICE OF: 1 Binding of Purified Corpses, 1 Splattered Zombie Wristguards, 1 Skeleton Smashers, 1 Preservative-Stained Gauntlets										
Crocolisk Mastery: The Ambush	Sholazar Basin	All	All		Debaar	Debaar	Crocolisk Mastery: The Plan		21150	6🟡 20🔴
CHOICE OF: 1 Tooth-Marked Girdle, 1 Crocscale Moccasins, 1 Muck-Stained Carapace, 1 Bent Crocolisk Tooth										
Fortunate Misunderstandings	Sholazar Basin	All	All		High-Oracle Soo-say	High-Oracle Soo-say	Just Following Orders	350 with The Oracles	21400	6🟡 50🔴
CHOICE OF: 1 Leggings of Mending Fronds, 1 Ragged Leaf Grips, 1 Belt of Misconceptions, 1 Ring of Misinterpreted Gestures										
Make the Bad Snake Go Away	Sholazar Basin	All	All		High-Oracle Soo-say	High-Oracle Soo-say	Fortunate Misunderstandings	350 with The Oracles	21400	6🟡 50🔴
Gods like Shiny Things	Sholazar Basin	All	All		Lafoo	High-Oracle Soo-say	Fortunate Misunderstandings	350 with The Oracles	21400	6🟡 50🔴
Making Peace	Sholazar Basin	All	All		High-Oracle Soo-say	High-Oracle Soo-say	Make the Bad Snake Go Away	350 with The Oracles	21400	6🟡 50🔴
CHOICE OF: 1 Drape of the Offered Branch, 1 Cloak of the Buzzing Swarm, 1 Lightning Beetle's Cape, 1 Cloak of the Hardened Tortoise										
Back So Soon?	Sholazar Basin	All	All		High-Oracle Soo-say	Mistcaller Soo-gan	Making Peace, Gods like Shiny Things	250 with The Oracles	10700	3🟡 30🔴
The Lost Mistwhisper Treasure	Sholazar Basin	All	All		Mistcaller Soo-gan	Mistcaller Soo-gan	Back So Soon?	350 with The Oracles	21400	6🟡 50🔴
CHOICE OF: 1 Bracers of Prompt Reclamation, 1 Legguards of the Aggressive Emissary, 1 Clear Earthen Scalemail, 1 Handguards of Transient Friendship										
Forced Hand	Sholazar Basin	All	All		Mistcaller Soo-gan	Mistcaller Soo-gan	Back So Soon?	350 with The Oracles	21400	6🟡 50🔴
Home Time!	Sholazar Basin	All	All		Mistcaller Soo-gan	High-Oracle Soo-say	The Lost Mistwhisper Treasure, Forced Hand	250 with The Oracles	10700	3🟡 30🔴
The Angry Gorloc	Sholazar Basin	All	All		High-Oracle Soo-say	Moodle	Home Time!	250 with The Oracles	10700	3🟡 30🔴

Title	Location	Faction	Race & Class	Group #	Starter	Finisher	Prerequisite	Reputation	XP	Money
Lifeblood of the Mosswalker Shrine	Sholazar Basin	All	All		Moodle	Moodle	The Angry Gorloc	350 with The Oracles	21400	6 50
The Mosswalker Savior	Sholazar Basin	All	All		Moodle	Moodle	The Angry Gorloc	350 with The Oracles	21400	6 50
A Hero's Burden	Sholazar Basin	All	All	3	Moodle	Artruis's Phylactery	Lifeblood of the Mosswalker Shrine, The Mosswalker Savior		32100	19 50
CHOICE OF: 1 Choker of Binding, 1 Blood-Infused Pendant, 1 Artruis's Focus Stone, 1 Spiked Collar of Servitude										
Frenzyheart Champion	Sholazar Basin	All	All		Zepik the Gorloc Hunter	Zepik the Gorloc Hunter	A Hero's Burden		10700	3 30
In Search of Bigger Game	Sholazar Basin	All	All				Rhino Mastery: The Kill, Dreadsaber Mastery: Ready to Pounce, Crocolisk Mastery: The Ambush			
Kick, What Kick?	Sholazar Basin	All	All		Drostan	Drostan	Have a Part, Give a Part, Wipe That Grin Off His Face		2100	
The Great Hunter's Challenge	Sholazar Basin	All	All		Drostan	Drostan	Kick, What Kick?		26450	12 40
CHOICE OF: 1 Fingers of Dextrous Decimation, 1 Bracers of Rapid Death, 1 Faceguard of Flawless Aim, 1 Helm of Brutal Slaughter										
In Search of Bigger Game	Sholazar Basin	All	All		Hemet Nesingwary	Dorian Drakestalker	Rhino Mastery: The Kill, Dreadsaber Mastery: Ready to Pounce, Crocolisk Mastery: The Ambush		2150	
Sharpening Your Talons	Sholazar Basin	All	All		Dorian Drakestalker	Dorian Drakestalker	Rhino Mastery: The Kill, Crocolisk Mastery: The Ambush, Dreadsaber Mastery: Ready to Pounce		21400	6 50
Securing the Bait	Sholazar Basin	All	All		Dorian Drakestalker	Dorian Drakestalker	Dreadsaber Mastery: Ready to Pounce, Rhino Mastery: The Kill, Crocolisk Mastery: The Ambush		21400	6 50
A Mammoth Undertaking	Sholazar Basin	All	All		Zootfizzle	Zootfizzle	Securing the Bait, Sharpening Your Talons		16050	5 10
Cultist Incursion	Sholazar Basin	All	All		Cultist Corpse	Avatar of Freya	The Fallen Pillar		16200	6 80
Returned Sevenfold	Sholazar Basin	All	All		Avatar of Freya	Avatar of Freya	An Issue of Trust		21400	6 50
REWARD: 1 Signet of the Avenging Heart AND CHOICE OF: 1 Cowl of the Purifier, 1 Scourgebane Treads, 1 Keeper's Touch, 1 Lifegiver's Ward										
The Fallen Pillar	Sholazar Basin	All	All		Avatar of Freya	Cultist Corpse	Returned Sevenfold		10700	
Powering the Waygate - The Maker's Overlook	Sholazar Basin	All	All		Avatar of Freya	Avatar of Freya	Powering the Waygate - The Maker's Perch		21400	
Post-partum Aggression	Sholazar Basin	All	All		Dorian Drakestalker	Dorian Drakestalker	A Mammoth Undertaking		26750	13
CHOICE OF: 1 Dragon Slayer's Shortbow, 1 Hemet's Trophy Gun, 1 Dorian's Prybar, 1 Nesingwary Brush Burner, 1 Cloak of the Deadliest Game, 1 Polished Protodrake Cloak										
Exterminate the Intruders	Sholazar Basin	All	All		Avatar of Freya	Avatar of Freya	Cultist Incursion		21400	6 50
CHOICE OF: 1 Lifewarden's Raiment, 1 Helm of the Ancient Horn, 1 Treads of Bound Life, 1 Wristguards of Titanic Vengeance										
The Lifewarden's Wrath	Sholazar Basin	All	All		Avatar of Freya	Avatar of Freya	Exterminate the Intruders, Weapons of Destruction		16050	5 10
Freya's Pact	Sholazar Basin	All	All		Avatar of Freya	Avatar of Freya	The Lifewarden's Wrath		2150	
It Could Be Anywhere!	Sholazar Basin	All	All		Chad	Chad			31750	18 60
CHOICE OF: 1 Cloak of Renewed Hope, 1 Pauldrons of Resolution, 1 Boots of Dominance, 1 Ring of Devoted Promises										
Some Make Lemonade, Some Make Liquor	Sholazar Basin	All	All		Grimbooze Thunderbrew	Grimbooze Thunderbrew	Dreadsaber Mastery: Becoming a Predator, Rhino Mastery: The Test		21150	6 20
Still At It	Sholazar Basin	All	All		Grimbooze Thunderbrew	Grimbooze Thunderbrew	Some Make Lemonade, Some Make Liquor		15850	4 80
The Taste Test	Sholazar Basin	All	All		Grimbooze Thunderbrew	Grimbooze Thunderbrew	Still At It		26450	12 40
REWARD: 20 Kungaloosh										
Lakeside Landing	Sholazar Basin	All	All		Hemet Nesingwary	Tamara Wobblesprocket	Rhino Mastery: The Chase, Dreadsaber Mastery: Stalking the Prey, Crocolisk Mastery: The Plan		2150	66
The Part-time Hunter	Sholazar Basin	All	All		Tamara Wobblesprocket	Tamara Wobblesprocket			21150	6 20
My Pet Roc	Sholazar Basin	All	All		Zootfizzle	Zootfizzle	Sharpening Your Talons, Securing the Bait		21400	6 50
Weapons of Destruction	Sholazar Basin	All	All		Avatar of Freya	Avatar of Freya	Cultist Incursion		21400	6 50
Reconnaissance Flight	Sholazar Basin	All	All		Pilot Vic	Pilot Vic	An Embarrassing Incident		21400	6 50
Reagent Agent	Sholazar Basin	All	All		Colvin Norrington	Colvin Norrington	Sharpening Your Talons, Securing the Bait		21400	6 50
CHOICE OF: 1 Field Researcher's Boots, 1 Hydrafang Breeches, 1 Roc Hunter's Bracer, 1 Norrington's Burnished Breastplate										
Uncharted Territory (DEPRECATED)	Sholazar Basin	All	All		Professor Calvert	Professor Calvert			15850	4 80
Burning to Help	Sholazar Basin	All	All		Colvin Norrington	Colvin Norrington			21400	6 50
Engineering a Disaster	Sholazar Basin	All	All		Engineer Helice	Hemet Nesingwary			21150	6 20
Hand of the Oracles	Sholazar Basin	All	All		Jaloot	Jaloot	A Hero's Burden		10700	3 30
A Timeworn Coffer	Sholazar Basin	All	All		Timeworn Coffer	Timeworn Coffer			21600	6 80
CHOICE OF: 1 Aged Watcher's Legwraps, 1 Binding of the Ancient Keeper, 1 Rockhandler's Gloves, 1 Stonebound Chestguard										

SHATTRATH CITY

Title	Location	Faction	Race & Class	Group #	Starter	Finisher	Prerequisite	Reputation	XP	Money
Return of the Lich Hunter	Sholazar Basin	All	All		Zepik the Gorloc Hunter	Elder Harkek	Wolvar Faction Choice Tracker		10700	3🔘30🔘
Return of the Friendly Dryskin	Sholazar Basin	All	All		High-Oracle Soo-say	High-Oracle Soo-say	Oracle Faction Choice Tracker		10700	3🔘30🔘
Aerial Surveillance	Sholazar Basin	All	All		Professor Calvert	Pilot Vic	Have a Part, Give a Part		5350	
An Embarassing Incident	Sholazar Basin	All	All		Pilot Vic	Pilot Vic	Have a Part, Give a Part		21400	6🔘50🔘
Chicken Party!	Sholazar Basin	All	All		Sholazar Daily Test NPC, Elder Harkek	Elder Harkek	Return of the Lich Hunter	250 with Frenzyheart Tribe	21400	6🔘50🔘
Kartak's Rampage	Sholazar Basin	All	All		Sholazar Daily Test NPC, Vekgar	Shaman Jakjek	Return of the Lich Hunter	350 with Frenzyheart Tribe	27000	13🔘60🔘
Appeasing the Great Rain Stone	Sholazar Basin	All	All		Sholazar Daily Test NPC, High-Oracle Soo-say	High-Oracle Soo-say	Return of the Friendly Dryskin	250 with The Oracles	21400	6🔘50🔘
Will of the Titans	Sholazar Basin	All	All		Sholazar Daily Test NPC, Oracle Soo-dow	Lightningcaller Soo-met	Return of the Friendly Dryskin	350 with The Oracles	27000	13🔘60🔘
Song of Wind and Water	Sholazar Basin	All	All		Sholazar Daily Test NPC	Oracle Soo-nee	Return of the Friendly Dryskin	250 with The Oracles	22050	7🔘40🔘
The Heartblood's Strength	Sholazar Basin	All	All		Sholazar Daily Test NPC, Rejek	Rejek	Return of the Lich Hunter	250 with Frenzyheart Tribe	22050	7🔘40🔘
Rejek: First Blood	Sholazar Basin	All	All		Sholazar Daily Test NPC	Rejek	Return of the Lich Hunter	250 with Frenzyheart Tribe	22050	7🔘40🔘
A Cleansing Song	Sholazar Basin	All	All		Sholazar Daily Test NPC	Oracle Soo-nee	Return of the Friendly Dryskin	250 with The Oracles	22050	7🔘40🔘
Song of Reflection	Sholazar Basin	All	All		Sholazar Daily Test NPC	Oracle Soo-nee	Return of the Friendly Dryskin	250 with The Oracles	22050	7🔘40🔘
Song of Fecundity	Sholazar Basin	All	All		Sholazar Daily Test NPC	Oracle Soo-nee	Return of the Friendly Dryskin	250 with The Oracles	22050	7🔘40🔘
Strength of the Tempest	Sholazar Basin	All	All		Sholazar Daily Test NPC	Rejek	Return of the Lich Hunter	250 with Frenzyheart Tribe	22050	7🔘40🔘
A Hero's Headgear	Sholazar Basin	All	All		Sholazar Daily Test NPC	Rejek	Return of the Lich Hunter	250 with Frenzyheart Tribe	22050	7🔘40🔘
Tools of War	Sholazar Basin	All	All		Sholazar Daily Test NPC	Shaman Jakjek	Return of the Lich Hunter	350 with Frenzyheart Tribe	27000	13🔘60🔘
Secret Strength of the Frenzyheart	Sholazar Basin	All	All		Sholazar Daily Test NPC	Shaman Jakjek	Return of the Lich Hunter	350 with Frenzyheart Tribe	27000	13🔘60🔘
Mastery of the Crystals	Sholazar Basin	All	All		Sholazar Daily Test NPC	Lightningcaller Soo-met	Return of the Friendly Dryskin	350 with The Oracles	27000	13🔘60🔘
Power of the Great Ones	Sholazar Basin	All	All		Sholazar Daily Test NPC	Lightningcaller Soo-met	Return of the Friendly Dryskin	350 with The Oracles	27000	13🔘60🔘
The Secret to Kungaloosh (DEPRECATED)	Sholazar Basin	Alliance	All		Grimbooze Thunderbrew	Grimbooze Thunderbrew				
Kungaloosh (DEPRECATED)	Sholazar Basin	Horde	All		Awilo Lon'gomba, Katherine Lee	Katherine Lee				
Back Through the Waygate	Sholazar Basin	All	All		The Etymidian	Avatar of Freya	The Activation Rune		16200	5🔘30🔘
Force of Nature	Sholazar Basin	All	All		Pilot Vic	Avatar of Freya			2150	
A Steak Fit for a Hunter	Sholazar Basin	All	All		Korg the Cleaver	Korg the Cleaver	Rhino Mastery: The Test		21150	6🔘20🔘
Salvaging Life's Strength	Sholazar Basin	All	All		Avatar of Freya	Avatar of Freya	Returned Sevenfold		21400	6🔘50🔘
Aerial Surveillance	Sholazar Basin	All	All		Pilot Vic	Pilot Vic	Have a Part, Give a Part		5350	

STRAND OF THE ANCIENTS

Title	Location	Faction	Race & Class	Group #	Starter	Finisher	Prerequisite	Reputation	XP	Money
Call to Arms: Strand of the Ancients	Strand of the Ancients	Alliance	All		Alliance Brigadier General, Alliance Brigadier General	Alliance Brigadier General				
Call to Arms: Strand of the Ancients	Strand of the Ancients	Horde	All		Horde Warbringer, Horde Warbringer	Horde Warbringer				

THE CULLING OF STRATHOLME

Title	Location	Faction	Race & Class	Group #	Starter	Finisher	Prerequisite	Reputation	XP	Money
Dispelling Illusions	The Culling of Stratholme	All	All		Chromie	Chromie			27550	14🔘80🔘
A Royal Escort	The Culling of Stratholme	All	All		Chromie	Chromie	Dispelling Illusions		44100	
CHOICE OF: 1 Gloves of the Time Guardian, 1 Handwraps of Preserved History, 1 Grips of Chronological Events, 1 Gauntlets of The Culling										
Timear Foresees Infinite Agents in your Future!	The Culling of Stratholme	All	All		Archmage Timear	Archmage Timear		75 with Kirin Tor	33100	14🔘80🔘
CHOICE OF: 1 Kirin Tor Commendation Badge, 1 Argent Crusade Commendation Badge, 1 Ebon Blade Commendation Badge, 1 Wyrmrest Commendation Badge										
Proof of Demise: Mal'Ganis	The Culling of Stratholme	All	All		Archmage Lan'dalock	Archmage Lan'dalock		75 with Kirin Tor	44100	22🔘20🔘
REWARD: 2 Emblem of Heroism										

THE EYE OF ETERNITY

Title	Location	Faction	Race & Class	Group #	Starter	Finisher	Prerequisite	Reputation	XP	Money
Judgment at the Eye of Eternity	The Eye of Eternity	All	All		Krasus	Krasus	The Key to the Focusing Iris	500 with The Wyrmrest Accord	33100	22🔘20🔘
CHOICE OF: 1 Chain of the Ancient Wyrm, 1 Torque of the Red Dragonflight, 1 Pendant of the Dragonsworn, 1 Drakescale Collar										

THE EYE OF ETERNITY

Title	Location	Faction	Race & Class	Group #	Starter	Finisher	Prerequisite	Reputation	XP	Money
Heroic Judgment at the Eye of Eternity	The Eye of Eternity	All	All		Krasus	Krasus	The Heroic Key to the Focusing Iris	1000 with The Wyrmrest Accord	44100	
CHOICE OF: 1 Wyrmrest Necklace of Power, 1 Life-Binder's Locket, 1 Favor of the Dragon Queen, 1 Nexus War Champion Beads										

THE NEXUS

Title	Location	Faction	Race & Class	Group #	Starter	Finisher	Prerequisite	Reputation	XP	Money
Postponing the Inevitable	The Nexus	All	All		Archmage Berinand	Archmage Berinand	Reading the Meters		25150	4🟡70🔴
CHOICE OF: 1 Time-Twisted Wraps, 1 Time-Stop Gloves, 1 Bindings of Sabotage, 1 Gauntlets of the Disturbed Giant										
Quickening	The Nexus	All	All		Archmage Berinand	Archmage Berinand	Secrets of the Ancients		20100	4🟡70🔴
CHOICE OF: 1 Sandals of Mystical Evolution, 1 Treads of Torn Future, 1 Spiked Treads of Mutation, 1 Invigorating Sabatons, 1 Boots of the Unbowed Protector										
Prisoner of War	The Nexus	All	All		Raelorasz	Raelorasz	Springing the Trap		40200	4🟡70🔴
CHOICE OF: 1 Cloak of Azure Lights, 1 Mantle of Keristrasza, 1 Shroud of Fluid Strikes										
Have They No Shame?	The Nexus	All	All		Librarian Serrah	Librarian Serrah			25150	3🟡70🔴
CHOICE OF: 1 Shoulders of the Northern Lights, 1 Cured Mammoth Hide Mantle, 1 Tundra Tracker's Shoulderguards, 1 Tundra Pauldrons										
Have They No Shame?	The Nexus	All	All		Librarian Serrah	Librarian Serrah			25150	3🟡70🔴
CHOICE OF: 1 Shoulders of the Northern Lights, 1 Cured Mammoth Hide Mantle, 1 Tundra Tracker's Shoulderguards, 1 Tundra Pauldrons										
Proof of Demise: Keristrasza	The Nexus	All	All		Archmage Lan'dalock	Archmage Lan'dalock		75 with Kirin Tor	44100	22🟡20🔴
REWARD: 2 Emblem of Heroism										

THE OCULUS

Title	Location	Faction	Race & Class	Group #	Starter	Finisher	Prerequisite	Reputation	XP	Money
The Struggle Persists	The Oculus	All	All		Raelorasz	Belgaristrasz			27550	14🟡80🔴
CHOICE OF: 1 Ring of Temerity, 1 Flourishing Band, 1 Band of Motivation, 1 Staunch Signet										
A Unified Front	The Oculus	All	All		Belgaristrasz	Image of Belgaristrasz	The Struggle Persists		44100	
Mage-Lord Urom	The Oculus	All	All		Image of Belgaristrasz	Image of Belgaristrasz	A Unified Front		44100	
A Wing and a Prayer	The Oculus	All	All		Image of Belgaristrasz	Raelorasz	Mage-Lord Urom		44100	
CHOICE OF: 1 Cuffs of Gratitude, 1 Soaring Wristwraps, 1 Bindings of Raelorasz, 1 Bracers of Reverence										
Timear Foresees Centrifuge Constructs in your Future!	The Oculus	All	All		Archmage Timear	Archmage Timear		75 with Kirin Tor	33100	14🟡80🔴
CHOICE OF: 1 Kirin Tor Commendation Badge, 1 Argent Crusade Commendation Badge, 1 Ebon Blade Commendation Badge, 1 Wyrmrest Commendation Badge										
Proof of Demise: Ley-Guardian Eregos	The Oculus	All	All		Archmage Lan'dalock	Archmage Lan'dalock		75 with Kirin Tor	44100	22🟡20🔴
REWARD: 2 Emblem of Heroism										

THE STORM PEAKS

Title	Location	Faction	Race & Class	Group #	Starter	Finisher	Prerequisite	Reputation	XP	Money
Clean Up	The Storm Peaks	All	All		Jeer Sparksocket	Jeer Sparksocket			21600	6🟡80🔴
Just Around the Corner	The Storm Peaks	All	All		Jeer Sparksocket	Jeer Sparksocket	Clean Up		21600	6🟡80🔴
A Delicate Touch	The Storm Peaks	All	All		Ricket	Ricket	Slightly Unstable		21600	6🟡80🔴
CHOICE OF: 1 Ironwool Bindings, 1 Gale-wind Guard, 1 Plated Skullguard, 1 The "D" Ring										
Opening the Backdoor	The Storm Peaks	All	All		Ricket	Ricket	A Delicate Touch, Bitter Departure, Ample Inspiration		21600	6🟡80🔴
Know No Fear	The Storm Peaks	All	All		Ricket	Ricket	Opening the Backdoor		21600	6🟡80🔴
A Flawless Plan	The Storm Peaks	All	All		Gino	Gino	Opening the Backdoor		21600	6🟡80🔴
Demolitionist Extraordinaire	The Storm Peaks	All	All		Gino	Ricket	A Flawless Plan		2150	68🔴
CHOICE OF: 1 K3 Surgeon's Gloves, 1 Buckshot-Proof Battlesurgeon's Protector, 1 Mammoth Mukluks, 1 Goblin Damage Absorber, 1 Ricket's Beatstick										
Expressions of Gratitude	The Storm Peaks	All	All							
Slightly Unstable	The Storm Peaks	All	All		Jeer Sparksocket	Ricket	Just Around the Corner		2150	68🔴
Reclaimed Rations	The Storm Peaks	All	All		Ricket	Ricket			21600	6🟡80🔴
Ample Inspiration	The Storm Peaks	All	All		Ricket	Ricket	Reclaimed Rations, Expression of Gratitude		21600	6🟡80🔴
CHOICE OF: 1 Mammoth Sinew Cinch, 1 Mammoth Hide Galoshes, 1 Wooly Cowl, 1 Polished Tusk Shackles, 1 K3 Pachyderm Prevention Device										
Moving In	The Storm Peaks	All	All		Tore Rumblewrench	Tore Rumblewrench	Reclaimed Rations		21600	6🟡80🔴
Ore Repossession	The Storm Peaks	All	All		Tore Rumblewrench	Tore Rumblewrench	Reclaimed Rations		21600	6🟡80🔴
Only Partly Forgotten	The Storm Peaks	All	All		Injured Goblin Miner	Injured Goblin Miner			21600	6🟡80🔴
Bitter Departure	The Storm Peaks	All	All		Injured Goblin Miner	Ricket	Only Partly Forgotten		21600	6🟡80🔴
CHOICE OF: 1 Snowblind Butcher, 1 Garm's Ward, 1 Daschal's Serrated Blade, 1 Twisted Reflection										
Overstock	The Storm Peaks	All	All		Ricket	Ricket	Demolitionist Extraordinaire		21600	6🟡80🔴
Not Rain, Nor Snow, Nor Exploding Plane	The Storm Peaks	All	All				Demolitionist Extraordinaire			
All Grown Up	The Storm Peaks	All	All				Demolitionist Extraordinaire			
Expression of Gratitude	The Storm Peaks	All	All		Ricket	Ricket			21600	6🟡80🔴
Tore's Got the Goods	The Storm Peaks	All	All							
The Crone's Bargain	The Storm Peaks	All	All		Lok'lira the Crone, Lok'lira the Crone	Lok'lira the Crone	Leave No Goblin Behind		21800	
They Took Our Men!	The Storm Peaks	All	All		Gretchen Fizzlespark	Gretchen Fizzlespark			21800	
CHOICE OF: 1 Fur-Lined Shoulder Warmers, 1 Fur-Lined Mittens, 1 Summit Bracers, 1 Chestguard of the Frozen Ascent, 1 Frozen Mood Ring										

THE STORM PEAKS

Title	Location	Faction	Race & Class	Group #	Starter	Finisher	Prerequisite	Reputation	XP	Money
Equipment Recovery	The Storm Peaks	All	All		Gretchen Fizzlespark	Gretchen Fizzlespark			21800	7🟡10🟤
Leave No Goblin Behind	The Storm Peaks	All	All		Gretchen Fizzlespark	Lok'lira the Crone	They Took Our Men!		10800	
Going Bearback	The Storm Peaks	All	All		Brijana	Brijana	You'll Need a Bear		22050	7🟡40🟤
Luxurious Getaway!	The Storm Peaks	All	All		Rin Duoctane	Jeer Sparksocket			2150	68🟤
On Brann's Trail	The Storm Peaks	Alliance	All		Archaeologist Andorin	Archaeologist Andorin			22050	7🟡40🟤
Sniffing Out the Perpetrator	The Storm Peaks	All	All		Archaeologist Andorin	Brann Bronzebeard	On Brann's Trail	250 with Explorers' League	22050	7🟡40🟤
Cold Hearted	The Storm Peaks	All	All		Brijana	Brijana	Going Bearback		22050	7🟡40🟤
Pieces to the Puzzle	The Storm Peaks	All	All		Brann Bronzebeard	Brann Bronzebeard	Sniffing Out the Perpetrator	250 with Explorers' League	22050	7🟡40🟤
Data Mining	The Storm Peaks	All	All		Brann Bronzebeard	Brann Bronzebeard	Pieces to the Puzzle	250 with Explorers' League	22050	7🟡40🟤
When All Else Fails	The Storm Peaks	All	All		Ricket	Rork Sharpchin	Demolitionist Extraordinaire, Know No Fear		2150	68🟤
Offering Thanks	The Storm Peaks	Alliance	All		Lagnus	Glorthal Stiffbeard		10 with The Frostborn	2150	68🟤
Missing Scouts	The Storm Peaks	Alliance	All		Glorthal Stiffbeard	Glorthal Stiffbeard	Offering Thanks	250 with The Frostborn	21600	6🟡80🟤
Loyal Companions	The Storm Peaks	Alliance	All		Fjorlin Frostbrow	Fjorlin Frostbrow	Offering Thanks	250 with The Frostborn	21600	6🟡80🟤
CHOICE OF: 1 Boots of the Howling Winds, 1 Hardened Whipping Belt, 1 Broken Chastity Belt, 1 Jawbreakers										
Stemming the Aggressors	The Storm Peaks	Alliance	All		Glorthal Stiffbeard	Glorthal Stiffbeard	Missing Scouts	250 with The Frostborn	21600	6🟡80🟤
Baby Stealers	The Storm Peaks	Alliance	All		Fjorlin Frostbrow	Fjorlin Frostbrow	Loyal Companions	250 with The Frostborn	21600	6🟡80🟤
Sirana Iceshriek	The Storm Peaks	Alliance	All	3	Glorthal Stiffbeard	Glorthal Stiffbeard	Stemming the Aggressors	350 with The Frostborn	27000	13🟡60🟤
CHOICE OF: 1 Wand of Chilled Renewal, 1 Iceshrieker's Touch, 1 Razor-sharp Ice Shards, 1 Weighted Throwing Axe										
Pushed Too Far	The Storm Peaks	Alliance	All		Fjorlin Frostbrow	Fjorlin Frostbrow	The Brothers Bronzebeard, Baby Stealers, The Reckoning	250 with The Frostborn	21600	6🟡80🟤
Ancient Relics	The Storm Peaks	Alliance	All		Rork Sharpchin	Rork Sharpchin		250 with Explorers' League	21600	6🟡80🟤
CHOICE OF: 1 Airy Pale Ale, 1 Worg Tooth Oatmeal Stout, 1 Rork Red Ribbon, 2 Snowfall Lager, 2 Drakefire Chile Ale										
Aid from the Explorer's League	The Storm Peaks	All	All		Brann Bronzebeard	Lagnus	Norgannon's Shell	10 with The Frostborn	2200	74🟤
Norgannon's Shell	The Storm Peaks	All	All		Inventor's Library Console	Brann Bronzebeard	The Library Console	250 with Explorers' League	22050	7🟡40🟤
CHOICE OF: 1 Hardened Vine of the Mauler, 1 Maker's Edge, 1 Maker's Touch, 1 Blade of the Inception, 1 Maiden's Dagger										
The Frostborn King	The Storm Peaks	Alliance	All		Lagnus	Yorg Stormheart	Aid from the Explorer's League	10 with The Frostborn	2200	74🟤
Fervor of the Frostborn	The Storm Peaks	All	All		Yorg Stormheart, Yorg Stormheart	Yorg Stormheart	The Frostborn King	250 with The Frostborn	22050	7🟡40🟤
CHOICE OF: 1 Frosthowl Cinch, 1 Nomadic Bracers, 1 Chestplate of the Northern Ranger, 1 Coldblooded Legplates										
An Experienced Guide	The Storm Peaks	All	All		Yorg Stormheart, Yorg Stormheart	Drom Frostgrip	Fervor of the Frostborn	250 with The Frostborn	22050	7🟡40🟤
Unwelcome Guests	The Storm Peaks	Alliance	All		Fjorlin Frostbrow	Fjorlin Frostbrow	Fervor of the Frostborn	250 with The Frostborn	22050	7🟡40🟤
The Lonesome Watcher	The Storm Peaks	All	All		Drom Frostgrip	Creteus	An Experienced Guide	250 with The Frostborn	22050	7🟡40🟤
The Hidden Relic	The Storm Peaks	All	All		Creteus, Creteus	The Guardian's Charge	Fate of the Titans		22050	7🟡40🟤
Fury of the Frostborn King	The Storm Peaks	All	All		The Guardian's Charge, The Guardian's Charge	Creteus	The Hidden Relic	350 with The Frostborn	22050	7🟡40🟤
The Master Explorer	The Storm Peaks	All	All		Creteus, Creteus	Brann Bronzebeard	Fury of the Frostborn King	10 with Explorers' League	2200	74🟤
The Brothers Bronzebeard	The Storm Peaks	All	All		Brann Bronzebeard, Brann Bronzebeard, Brann Bronzebeard		The Brothers Bronzebeard			
Ancient Relics	The Storm Peaks	Horde	All		Olut Alegut	Olut Alegut		250 with Warsong Offensive	21600	6🟡80🟤
CHOICE OF: 1 Airy Pale Ale, 1 Worg Tooth Oatmeal Stout, 1 Rork Red Ribbon, 2 Snowfall Lager, 2 Drakefire Chile Ale										
The Exiles of Ulduar	The Storm Peaks	All	All		Brann Bronzebeard	Bouldercrag the Rockshaper	Norgannon's Shell		2200	74🟤
The Drakkensryd	The Storm Peaks	All	All		Gretta the Arbiter	Thorim	Lok'lira's Parting Gift		27550	
CHOICE OF: 1 Leggings of the Frozen Wastes, 1 Frost Hardened Bracers, 1 Pauldrons of the Ascent, 1 Light-Touched Mantle, 1 Sharpened Hyldnir Harpoon										
SCRAP-E	The Storm Peaks	All	All		SCRAP-E Access Card	SCRAP-E			22050	7🟡40🟤
The Prototype Console	The Storm Peaks	All	All		SCRAP-E	Prototype Console	SCRAP-E		16550	5🟡80🟤
If Size Mattered...	The Storm Peaks	All	All							
The Missing Bronzebeard	The Storm Peaks	Horde	All		Boktar Bloodfury	Boktar Bloodfury		250 with Warsong Offensive	22050	7🟡40🟤
Making a Harness	The Storm Peaks	All	All		Haylin, Astrid Bjornrittar	Astrid Bjornrittar	Deemed Worthy		22050	
CHOICE OF: 1 Brunnhildar Runed Ring, 1 Yeti Hide Mantle, 1 Brunnhildar Snowkickers, 1 Astrid's Riding Gloves										

Title	Location	Faction	Race & Class	Group #	Starter	Finisher	Prerequisite	Reputation	XP	Money
Mildred the Cruel	The Storm Peaks	All	All		Lok'lira the Crone, Lok'lira the Crone	Mildred the Cruel	The Crone's Bargain		2200	
Discipline	The Storm Peaks	All	All		Mildred the Cruel	Mildred the Cruel	Mildred the Cruel		10900	3⬤60⬤
CHOICE OF: 1 Mildred's Cowl, 1 Cured Proto-Drake Leggings, 1 Mildred's Grasp, 1 Vyrkul Training Helm										
Examples to be Made	The Storm Peaks	All	All		Mildred the Cruel	Mildred the Cruel	Discipline		10900	3⬤60⬤
A Certain Prisoner	The Storm Peaks	All	All		Mildred the Cruel	Lok'lira the Crone	Examples to be Made		5450	
The Nose Knows	The Storm Peaks	Horde	All		Boktar Bloodfury	Khaliisi	The Missing Bronzebeard	10 with Warsong Offensive	2200	74⬤
Sniffing Out the Perpetrator	The Storm Peaks	All	All		Khaliisi	Brann Bronzebeard	The Nose Knows		22050	7⬤40⬤
Speak Orcish, Man!	The Storm Peaks	All	All		Brann Bronzebeard	Moteha Windborn	Sniffing Out the Perpetrator	10 with Warsong Offensive	2200	74⬤
Mending Fences	The Storm Peaks	All	All		Thorim, Thorim	Thorim	Sibling Rivalry	2200000 with The Sons of Hodir	22050	7⬤40⬤
Speaking with the Wind's Voice	The Storm Peaks	Horde	All		Moteha Windborn	Moteha Windborn	Speak Orcish, Man!	250 with Warsong Offensive	22050	7⬤40⬤
Catching up with Brann	The Storm Peaks	All	All		Brann Bronzebeard, Boktar Bloodfury	Boktar Bloodfury	Speaking with the Wind's Voice		16550	5⬤80⬤
A Change of Scenery	The Storm Peaks	All	All		Lok'lira the Crone, Lok'lira the Crone	Lok'lira the Crone	A Certain Prisoner		2200	
The Refiner's Fire	The Storm Peaks	All	All		Slag Covered Metal	Fjorn's Anvil			22050	7⬤40⬤
	The Storm Peaks	All	All		Haylin	Haylin				
Forging an Alliance	The Storm Peaks	All	All		Thorim, Thorim	Njormeld	A Spark of Hope, Mending Fences	250 with The Sons of Hodir	22050	7⬤40⬤
CHOICE OF: 1 Vestments of Dun Niffelem, 1 Njormeld's Pauldrons, 1 Reforged Chain Leggings, 1 Ring of Jokkum										
Aberrations	The Storm Peaks	All	All		Thyra Kvinnshal	Thyra Kvinnshal			22050	7⬤40⬤
Pieces of the Puzzle	The Storm Peaks	All	All		Boktar Bloodfury	Brann Bronzebeard	Catching up with Brann		22050	7⬤40⬤
Data Mining	The Storm Peaks	All	All		Brann Bronzebeard	Brann Bronzebeard	Pieces of the Puzzle		22050	7⬤40⬤
Norgannon's Shell	The Storm Peaks	All	All		Inventor's Library Console	Brann Bronzebeard	The Library Console		22050	7⬤40⬤
CHOICE OF: 1 Hardened Vine of the Mauler, 1 Maker's Edge, 1 Maker's Touch, 1 Blade of the Inception, 1 Maiden's Dagger										
The Earthen of Ulduar	The Storm Peaks	All	All		Brann Bronzebeard	Bouldercrag the Rockshaper	Norgannon's Shell		2200	74⬤
Rare Earth	The Storm Peaks	All	All		Bouldercrag the Rockshaper	Bouldercrag the Rockshaper			22050	7⬤40⬤
Fighting Back	The Storm Peaks	All	All		Bouldercrag the Rockshaper	Bouldercrag the Rockshaper	Rare Earth		22050	7⬤40⬤
Relief for the Fallen	The Storm Peaks	All	All		Bouldercrag the Rockshaper	Bouldercrag the Rockshaper	Rare Earth		22050	7⬤40⬤
Off With Their Black Wings	The Storm Peaks	All	All		Iva the Vengeful	Iva the Vengeful			22050	7⬤40⬤
CHOICE OF: 1 Flowing Valkyrion Robes, 1 Hyldnir Painbringer, 1 Iva's Boots, 1 Proto-Drake Cover, 1 Scaled Proto-Wristguard										
Valkyrion Must Burn	The Storm Peaks	All	All		Harpoon Crate	Iva the Vengeful	The Crone's Bargain		16550	5⬤80⬤
CHOICE OF: 1 Flamebringer's Crown, 1 Steel-tipped Snowboots, 1 Valkyrion Tracker's Chestguard, 1 Wooly Stompers										
A Spark of Hope	The Storm Peaks	All	All		Fjorn's Anvil	Thorim	The Refiner's Fire	2200000 with The Sons of Hodir	16550	5⬤80⬤
Slaves of the Stormforged	The Storm Peaks	All	All		Bouldercrag the Rockshaper	Bouldercrag the Rockshaper	Relief for the Fallen, Fighting Back		22050	7⬤40⬤
The Dark Ore	The Storm Peaks	All	All		Bouldercrag the Rockshaper	Bouldercrag the Rockshaper	Fighting Back, Relief for the Fallen		22050	7⬤40⬤
The Gifts of Loken	The Storm Peaks	All	All		Bouldercrag the Rockshaper	Bouldercrag the Rockshaper	Slaves of the Stormforged, The Dark Ore		22050	7⬤40⬤
CHOICE OF: 1 Leggings of Renewed Hope, 1 Mantle of Bouldercrag, 1 Rockshaper's Resolve, 1 Bouldercrag's Pendant										
You Can't Miss Him	The Storm Peaks	All	All		King Jokkum	Njormeld		75 with The Sons of Hodir	11050	3⬤70⬤
Battling the Elements	The Storm Peaks	All	All		Burly Frost Giant, Njormeld	Njormeld	You Can't Miss Him	250 with The Sons of Hodir	22050	7⬤40⬤
Yulda's Folly	The Storm Peaks	All	All		Iva the Vengeful	Iva the Vengeful			16550	5⬤80⬤
Is That Your Goblin?	The Storm Peaks	All	All		Lok'lira the Crone's Conversation Credit, Lok'lira the Crone	Lok'lira the Crone	A Change of Scenery		11050	
The Hyldsmeet	The Storm Peaks	All	All		Lok'lira the Crone's Conversation Credit, Lok'lira the Crone	Lok'lira the Crone	Is That Your Goblin?		2200	74⬤
Taking on All Challengers	The Storm Peaks	All	All		Lok'lira the Crone's Conversation Credit, Lok'lira the Crone	Lok'lira the Crone	The Hyldsmeet		22050	7⬤40⬤
CHOICE OF: 1 Hyldnir Runeweaver's Garb, 1 Proto-scale Pants, 1 Crown of Hyldnir, 1 Hyldnir Headcracker										
You'll Need a Bear	The Storm Peaks	All	All		Lok'lira the Crone's Conversation Credit, Lok'lira the Crone	Brijana	Taking on All Challengers		11050	
The Brothers Bronzebeard	The Storm Peaks	All	All		Brann Bronzebeard, Brann Bronzebeard, Brann Bronzebeard	Velog Icebellow	The Master Explorer	500 with Explorers' League, 500 with The Frostborn	33100	22⬤20⬤
CHOICE OF: 1 Ring of the Northern Winds, 1 Jagged Ice Band, 1 Amberglow Signet, 1 Iceforged Battle Ring										
In Memoriam	The Storm Peaks	All	All		King Jokkum	King Jokkum	Forging an Alliance	250 with The Sons of Hodir	22050	7⬤40⬤

THE STORM PEAKS

Title	Location	Faction	Race & Class	Group #	Starter	Finisher	Prerequisite	Reputation	XP	Money
A Monument to the Fallen	The Storm Peaks	All	All		King Jokkum	Njormeld	In Memoriam	75 with The Sons of Hodir	11050	3🟤70🟠
Blowing Hodir's Horn	The Storm Peaks	All	All		Hodir's Horn	Hodir's Horn	A Monument to the Fallen	250 with The Sons of Hodir	22050	7🟤40🟠
Facing the Storm	The Storm Peaks	All	All		Bruor Ironbane	Bruor Ironbane	Slaves of the Stormforged, The Dark Ore		22050	7🟤40🟠
Armor of Darkness	The Storm Peaks	All	All		Dark Armor Plate	Bruor Ironbane	Slaves of the Stormforged, The Dark Ore		22050	7🟤40🟠
The Armor's Secrets	The Storm Peaks	All	All		Bruor Ironbane	Bruor Ironbane	Armor of Darkness		22050	7🟤40🟠
Hot and Cold	The Storm Peaks	All	All		Fjorn's Anvil	Fjorn's Anvil		250 with The Sons of Hodir	22050	7🟤40🟠
The Last of Her Kind	The Storm Peaks	All	All		Haylin, Astrid Bjornrittar	Astrid Bjornrittar	Making a Harness		22050	
Valduran the Stormborn	The Storm Peaks	All	All		Bouldercrag the Rockshaper	Bouldercrag the Rockshaper	The Armor's Secrets		27550	14🟤80🟠
CHOICE OF: 1 Lantern of Enchanted Flame, 1 Bloodied Leather Gloves, 1 Belt of the Stormforged, 1 Rockshaper Stompers										
Forging a Head	The Storm Peaks	All	All		Njormeld	Njormeld		250 with The Sons of Hodir	22050	7🟤40🟠
Fate of the Titans	The Storm Peaks	All	All		Creteus, Creteus	Creteus	The Lonesome Watcher		22050	7🟤40🟠
CHOICE OF: 1 Ring of Order, 1 Spiked Iceclimber's Boots, 1 Cuffs of Invention, 1 Mantle of Long Winter										
Mounting Hodir's Helm	The Storm Peaks	All	All		Njormeld	Njormeld	Forging a Head	150 with The Sons of Hodir	5500	1🟤90🟠
Destroy the Forges!	The Storm Peaks	All	All		Bouldercrag the Rockshaper	Bouldercrag the Rockshaper	Valduran the Stormborn		22050	7🟤40🟠
The Slithering Darkness	The Storm Peaks	All	All		Haylin, Astrid Bjornrittar	Astrid Bjornrittar	Making a Harness		22050	7🟤40🟠
CHOICE OF: 1 Jormungar Galoshes, 1 Hibernal Chestguard, 1 Scaled Jormungar Protector, 1 Bjornrittar's Chilled Legguards, 1 Jormungar Fang										
Hit Them Where it Hurts	The Storm Peaks	All	All		Bruor Ironbane	Bruor Ironbane	Valduran the Stormborn		22050	7🟤40🟠
A Colossal Threat	The Storm Peaks	All	All		Bouldercrag the Rockshaper	Bouldercrag the Rockshaper	Destroy the Forges!, Hit Them Where it Hurts		22050	7🟤40🟠
Spy Hunter	The Storm Peaks	All	All		Frostworg Denmother	Frostworg Denmother		250 with The Sons of Hodir	22050	7🟤40🟠
The Warm-Up	The Storm Peaks	All	All		Haylin, Astrid Bjornrittar	Astrid Bjornrittar	The Last of Her Kind		16550	
Into the Pit	The Storm Peaks	All	All		Haylin, Astrid Bjornrittar	Astrid Bjornrittar	The Warm-Up		22050	7🟤40🟠
The Heart of the Storm	The Storm Peaks	All	All		Bouldercrag the Rockshaper	Bouldercrag the Rockshaper	A Colossal Threat		22050	7🟤40🟠
Emergency Measures	The Storm Peaks	Horde	All		Bloodguard Lorga	Bloodguard Lorga		250 with Warsong Offensive	21800	7🟤10🟠
CHOICE OF: 1 Frosthowl Cinch, 1 Nomadic Bracers, 1 Chestplate of the Northern Ranger, 1 Coldblooded Legplates										
Raising Hodir's Spear	The Storm Peaks	All	All		Lorekeeper Randvir	Lorekeeper Randvir		250 with The Sons of Hodir	22050	7🟤40🟠
Thrusting Hodir's Spear	The Storm Peaks	All	All		Hodir's Spear	Hodir's Spear		350 with The Sons of Hodir	27550	14🟤80🟠
The Earthen Oath	The Storm Peaks	All	All		Thorim	Thorim	The Terrace of the Makers		27550	14🟤80🟠
CHOICE OF: 1 Terrace Gazer's Gloves, 1 Bracer of Tarbash, 1 Shoulders of Earthen Might, 1 Thorim's Grasp										
Polishing the Helm	The Storm Peaks	All	All		Hodir's Helm	Hodir's Helm	Mounting Hodir's Helm	250 with The Sons of Hodir	22050	7🟤40🟠
The Iron Colossus	The Storm Peaks	All	All		Bouldercrag the Rockshaper	Bouldercrag the Rockshaper	The Heart of the Storm		33100	22🟤20🟠
CHOICE OF: 1 Snowdrift Pantaloons, 1 Leggings of Heightened Renewal, 1 Jormungar Hide Legguards, 1 Iron Colossus Legplates										
A New Beginning	The Storm Peaks	All	All		Njormeld	Thorim	Forging an Alliance		22050	7🟤40🟠
Krolmir, Hammer of Storms	The Storm Peaks	All	All		Thorim, Thorim	Thorim	Territorial Trespass	350 with The Sons of Hodir	27550	14🟤80🟠
CHOICE OF: 1 Locket of Snowcrest, 1 Storm-weathered Cuffs, 1 Stormstalker's Clutch, 1 Backhanded Grips										
Jormuttar is Soo Fat...	The Storm Peaks	All	All		King Jokkum	King Jokkum		250 with The Sons of Hodir	22050	7🟤40🟠
The Witness and the Hero	The Storm Peaks	Horde	All		Xarantaur	Xarantaur		250 with Warsong Offensive	22050	7🟤40🟠
Loken's Lackeys	The Storm Peaks	All	All		Thorim	Thorim	The Terrace of the Makers		22050	7🟤40🟠
Memories of Stormhoof	The Storm Peaks	Horde	All		Xarantaur	Xarantaur	The Witness and the Hero	250 with Warsong Offensive	22050	7🟤40🟠
Distortions in Time	The Storm Peaks	All	All		Chieftain Swiftspear	Xarantaur	The Witness and the Hero	250 with Warsong Offensive	22050	7🟤40🟠
Feeding Arngrim	The Storm Peaks	All	All		Arngrim the Insatiable	Arngrim the Insatiable		250 with The Sons of Hodir	22050	7🟤40🟠
The Reckoning	The Storm Peaks	All	All		Thorim	King Jokkum	Loken's Lackeys, The Earthen Oath		33100	22🟤20🟠
CHOICE OF: 1 Gloves of the Servant, 1 Rough Climber's Grips, 1 Gauntlets of the Windreacher, 1 Gauntlets of Vigilance										
Where Time Went Wrong	The Storm Peaks	Horde	All		Xarantaur	Xarantaur	Memories of Stormhoof, Distortions in Time	250 with Warsong Offensive	22050	7🟤40🟠
The Hero's Arms	The Storm Peaks	Horde	All		Xarantaur	Xarantaur	Memories of Stormhoof, Distortions in Time		22050	7🟤40🟠
Veranus	The Storm Peaks	All	All		Thorim, Thorim	Thorim	A New Beginning		22050	7🟤40🟠
Territorial Trespass	The Storm Peaks	All	All		Thorim, Thorim	Thorim	Veranus		11050	3🟤70🟠
CHOICE OF: 1 Thorim's Crusher, 1 Thorim's Riding Crop, 1 Crossbow of the Storms, 1 Broodmother's Protector, 1 Razor-sharp Icicle										
Looking for Survivors	The Storm Peaks	All	All		"Honest" Max	"Honest" Max			21400	6🟤50🟠

THE STORM PEAKS

Title	Location	Faction	Race & Class	Group #	Starter	Finisher	Prerequisite	Reputation	XP	Money
The Missing Tracker	The Storm Peaks	Horde	All		Bloodguard Lorga	Tracker Val'zij		75 with Warsong Offensive	11050	3 70
Cave Medicine	The Storm Peaks	Horde	All		Tracker Val'zij	Tracker Val'zij	The Missing Tracker		22050	7 40
There's Always Time for Revenge	The Storm Peaks	Horde	All		Tracker Val'zij	Tracker Val'zij	Cave Medicine	250 with Warsong Offensive	22050	7 40
CHOICE OF: 1 Boots of the Howling Winds, 1 Hardened Whipping Belt, 1 Broken Chastity Belt, 1 Jawbreakers										
The Terrace of the Makers	The Storm Peaks	All	All		Thorim, Thorim	Thorim	Krolmir, Hammer of Storms		11050	
Changing the Wind's Course	The Storm Peaks	Horde	All		Xarantaur	Xarantaur	Where Time Went Wrong, The Hero's Arms	350 with Warsong Offensive	27550	14 80
CHOICE OF: 1 Iceshrieker's Touch, 1 Razor-sharp Ice Shards, 1 Wand of Chilled Renewal, 1 Weighted Throwing Axe										
When All Else Fails	The Storm Peaks	All	All		Ricket	Olut Alegut	Demolitionist Extraordinaire, Know No Fear		2150	68
Prepare for Glory	The Storm Peaks	All	All		Haylin, Astrid Bjornrittar	Lok'lira the Crone	Into the Pit		2200	72
Lok'lira's Parting Gift	The Storm Peaks	All	All		Lok'lira the Crone's Conversation Credit, Lok'lira the Crone	Gretta the Arbiter	Prepare for Glory		5500	
Deemed Worthy	The Storm Peaks	All	All		Brijana	Astrid Bjornrittar	Cold Hearted		11050	3 70
Sibling Rivalry	The Storm Peaks	All	All		Thorim, Thorim	Thorim	The Drakkensryd		16550	5 80
A Voice in the Dark	The Storm Peaks	All	All		Matthias Lehner, Pulsing Crystal	Matthias Lehner	A Short Fuse		2200	
Going After the Core	The Storm Peaks	All	All		Brann Bronzebeard	Brann Bronzebeard	Norgannon's Shell		22050	7 40
The Core's Keeper	The Storm Peaks	All	All		Brann Bronzebeard	Brann Bronzebeard	Going After the Core		22050	7 40
Forging the Keystone	The Storm Peaks	All	All		Brann Bronzebeard	Boktar Bloodfury	The Core's Keeper	350 with Warsong Offensive	27550	14 80
CHOICE OF: 1 Amberglow Signet, 1 Iceforged Battle Ring, 1 Jagged Ice Band, 1 Ring of the Northern Winds										
A Voice in the Dark	The Storm Peaks	All	All		Matthias Lehner, Pulsing Crystal	Matthias Lehner	A Short Fuse		2200	
The Library Console	The Storm Peaks	All	All		Brann Bronzebeard	Inventor's Library Console	Data Mining		11050	3 70
The Library Console	The Storm Peaks	All	All		Brann Bronzebeard	Inventor's Library Console	Data Mining		11050	3 70
The Brothers Bronzebeard	The Storm Peaks	Alliance	All		Velog Icebellow	Velog Icebellow	The Master Explorer	500 with Explorers' League, 500 with The Frostborn	33100	22 20
CHOICE OF: 1 Ring of the Northern Winds, 1 Jagged Ice Band, 1 Amberglow Signet, 1 Iceforged Battle Ring										
Everfrost	The Storm Peaks	All	All		Everfrost Chip	Calder		350 with The Sons of Hodir	21400	6 50
Remember Everfrost!	The Storm Peaks	All	All		Calder	Calder	Everfrost	350 with The Sons of Hodir		6 50
Maintaining Discipline	The Storm Peaks	All	All		Gretta the Arbiter	Gretta the Arbiter	The Drakkensryd		16350	5 50
REWARD: 1 Hyldnir Spoils										
Defending Your Title	The Storm Peaks	All	All		Gretta the Arbiter	Gretta the Arbiter	The Hyldsmeet		22050	7 40
REWARD: 1 Hyldnir Spoils										
Back to the Pit	The Storm Peaks	All	All		Gretta the Arbiter	Gretta the Arbiter	Into the Pit		22050	7 40
REWARD: 1 Hyldnir Spoils										
The Aberrations Must Die	The Storm Peaks	All	All		Gretta the Arbiter	Gretta the Arbiter	The Hyldsmeet, Aberrations		22050	7 40
REWARD: 1 Hyldnir Spoils										
Xarantaur, the Witness	The Storm Peaks	Horde	All		Boktar Bloodfury	Xarantaur	Forging the Keystone	10 with Warsong Offensive	2200	74

THE VIOLET HOLD

Title	Location	Faction	Race & Class	Group #	Starter	Finisher	Prerequisite	Reputation	XP	Money
Discretion is Key	The Violet Hold	All	All		Rhonin	Warden Alturas			2150	66
Containment	The Violet Hold	All	All		Warden Alturas	Warden Alturas	Discretion is Key	500 with Kirin Tor	42800	
CHOICE OF: 1 Tattooed Deerskin Leggings, 1 Conferred Pantaloons, 1 Labyrinthine Legguards, 1 Dalaran Warden's Legplates										
Proof of Demise: Cyanigosa	The Violet Hold	All	All		Archmage Lan'dalock	Archmage Lan'dalock		75 with Kirin Tor	44100	22 20
REWARD: 2 Emblem of Heroism										

UTGARDE KEEP

Title	Location	Faction	Race & Class	Group #	Starter	Finisher	Prerequisite	Reputation	XP	Money
Into Utgarde!	Utgarde Keep	Alliance	All		Defender Mordun	Vice Admiral Keller			20100	4 70
CHOICE OF: 1 Executioner's Band, 1 Ring of Decimation, 1 Signet of Swift Judgment										
Ingvar Must Die!	Utgarde Keep	Horde	All		High Executor Anselm	High Executor Anselm			25150	9 40
CHOICE OF: 1 Executioner's Band, 1 Ring of Decimation, 1 Signet of Swift Judgment										
A Score to Settle	Utgarde Keep	Horde	All		High Executor Anselm	High Executor Anselm	Report to Anselm	500 with Horde Expedition	30150	
CHOICE OF: 1 Wraps of the San'layn, 1 Vendetta Bindings, 1 Runecaster's Bracers, 1 Vambraces of the Vengeance Bringer										
Disarmament	Utgarde Keep	Alliance	All		Defender Mordun	Defender Mordun			40200	
CHOICE OF: 1 Amulet of the Tranquil Mind, 1 Razor-Blade Pendant, 1 Necklace of Fragmented Light, 1 Woven Steel Necklace										

Utgarde Keep

Title	Location	Faction	Race & Class	Group #	Starter	Finisher	Prerequisite	Reputation	XP	Money
Disarmament	Utgarde Keep	Horde	All		High Executor Anselm	High Executor Anselm			40200	
CHOICE OF: 1 Necklace of Calm Skies, 1 Hundred Tooth Necklace, 1 Amulet of Constrained Power, 1 Tiled-Stone Pendant										
Proof of Demise: Ingvar the Plunderer	Utgarde Keep	All	All		Archmage Lan'dalock	Archmage Lan'dalock		75 with Kirin Tor	44100	22 20
REWARD: 2 Emblem of Heroism										
Junk in My Trunk	Utgarde Pinnacle	All	All		Brigg Smallshanks	Brigg Smallshanks			44100	
CHOICE OF: 1 Bauble-Woven Gown, 1 Exotic Leather Tunic, 1 Silver-Plated Battlechest, 1 Gilded Ringmail Hauberk										
Vengeance Be Mine!	Utgarde Pinnacle	All	All		Brigg Smallshanks	Brigg Smallshanks			44100	
CHOICE OF: 1 Cowl of the Vindictive Captain, 1 Headguard of Retaliation, 1 Helmet of Just Retribution, 1 Faceguard of Punishment, 1 Platehelm of Irate Revenge										
Timear Foresees Ymirjar Berserkers in your Future!	Utgarde Pinnacle	All	All		Archmage Timear	Archmage Timear		75 with Kirin Tor	33100	14 80
CHOICE OF: 1 Kirin Tor Commendation Badge, 1 Argent Crusade Commendation Badge, 1 Ebon Blade Commendation Badge, 1 Wyrmrest Commendation Badge										
Proof of Demise: King Ymiron	Utgarde Pinnacle	All	All		Archmage Lan'dalock	Archmage Lan'dalock		75 with Kirin Tor	44100	22 20
REWARD: 2 Emblem of Heroism										

Wintergrasp

Title	Location	Faction	Race & Class	Group #	Starter	Finisher	Prerequisite	Reputation	XP	Money
Warding the Warriors	Wintergrasp	All	All		Sorceress Kaylana, Kanrethad	Sorceress Kaylana			22050	7 40
REWARD: 3 Stone Keeper's Shard										
Bones and Arrows	Wintergrasp	All	All		Bowyer Randolph, Kanrethad	Bowyer Randolph			22050	7 40
REWARD: 3 Stone Keeper's Shard										
A Rare Herb	Wintergrasp	All	All		Anchorite Tessa, Kanrethad	Anchorite Tessa			22050	7 40
REWARD: 3 Stone Keeper's Shard										
No Mercy for the Merciless	Wintergrasp	All	All		Commander Zanneth, Kanrethad	Commander Zanneth			22050	7 40
REWARD: 3 Stone Keeper's Shard										
Slay them all!	Wintergrasp	All	All		Commander Dardosh, Kanrethad	Commander Dardosh			22050	7 40
REWARD: 3 Stone Keeper's Shard										
No Mercy for the Merciless	Wintergrasp	All	All		Commander Zanneth, Kanrethad	Commander Zanneth			22050	7 40
REWARD: 3 Stone Keeper's Shard										
Slay them all!	Wintergrasp	All	All		Commander Dardosh, Kanrethad	Commander Dardosh			22050	7 40
REWARD: 3 Stone Keeper's Shard										
Victory in Wintergrasp	Wintergrasp	All	All		Tactical Officer Ahbramis	Alliance Brigadier General			22050	7 40
REWARD: 1 Stone Keeper's Shard										
Victory in Wintergrasp	Wintergrasp	All	All		Tactical Officer Kilrath	Tactical Officer Kilrath			22050	7 40
REWARD: 1 Stone Keeper's Shard										
Stop the Siege	Wintergrasp	All	All		Lieutenant Murp, Kanrethad	Lieutenant Murp			22050	7 40
REWARD: 3 Stone Keeper's Shard										
Stop the Siege	Wintergrasp	All	All		Senior Demolitionist Legoso, Kanrethad	Commander Zanneth			22050	7 40
REWARD: 3 Stone Keeper's Shard										
Fueling the Demolishers	Wintergrasp	All	All		Siegesmith Stronghoof, Kanrethad	Commander Dardosh		25 with Alliance	22050	7 40
REWARD: 3 Stone Keeper's Shard										
Warding the Walls	Wintergrasp	All	All		Hoodoo Master Fu'jin, Kanrethad	Hoodoo Master Fu'jin			22050	7 40
REWARD: 3 Stone Keeper's Shard										
Bones and Arrows	Wintergrasp	All	All		Vieron Blazefeather, Kanrethad	Vieron Blazefeather			22050	7 40
REWARD: 3 Stone Keeper's Shard										
Healing with Roses	Wintergrasp	All	All		Primalist Mulfort, Kanrethad	Primalist Mulfort			22050	7 40
REWARD: 3 Stone Keeper's Shard										
A Rare Herb	Wintergrasp	All	All		Anchorite Tessa, Kanrethad	Anchorite Tessa			22050	7 40
REWARD: 3 Stone Keeper's Shard										
Bones and Arrows	Wintergrasp	All	All		Bowyer Randolph, Kanrethad	Bowyer Randolph			22050	7 40
REWARD: 3 Stone Keeper's Shard										
Fueling the Demolishers	Wintergrasp	All	All		Siege Master Stouthandle, Kanrethad	Commander Zanneth		25 with Alliance	22050	7 40
REWARD: 3 Stone Keeper's Shard										
Warding the Warriors	Wintergrasp	All	All		Sorceress Kaylana, Kanrethad	Sorceress Kaylana			22050	7 40
REWARD: 3 Stone Keeper's Shard										

Wintergrasp

Title	Location	Faction	Race & Class	Group #	Starter	Finisher	Prerequisite	Reputation	XP	Money
Bones and Arrows	Wintergrasp	All	All		Vieron Blazefeather, Kanrethad	Vieron Blazefeather			22050	7 🪙 40 🪙
REWARD: 3 Stone Keeper's Shard										
Fueling the Demolishers	Wintergrasp	All	All		Siegesmith Stronghoof, Kanrethad	Commander Dardosh			22050	7 🪙 40 🪙
REWARD: 3 Stone Keeper's Shard										
Healing with Roses	Wintergrasp	All	All		Primalist Mulfort, Kanrethad	Primalist Mulfort			22050	7 🪙 40 🪙
REWARD: 3 Stone Keeper's Shard										
Jinxing the Walls	Wintergrasp	All	All		Hoodoo Master Fu'jin, Kanrethad	Hoodoo Master Fu'jin			22050	7 🪙 40 🪙
REWARD: 3 Stone Keeper's Shard										
Defend the Siege	Wintergrasp	All	All		Senior Demolitionist Legoso, Kanrethad	Senior Demolitionist Legoso			22050	7 🪙 40 🪙
REWARD: 3 Stone Keeper's Shard										
Defend the Siege	Wintergrasp	All	All		Lieutenant Murp, Kanrethad	Lieutenant Murp			22050	7 🪙 40 🪙
REWARD: 3 Stone Keeper's Shard										

Zul'Drak

Title	Location	Faction	Race & Class	Group #	Starter	Finisher	Prerequisite	Reputation	XP	Money
Troll Patrol	Zul'Drak	All	All		Kunz Jr., Commander Kunz	Commander Kunz		250 with Argent Crusade	21150	6 🪙 20 🪙
Troll Patrol: High Standards	Zul'Drak	All	All		Captain Brandon	Captain Brandon		75 with Argent Crusade	5300	1 🪙 58 🪙
Defend the Stand	Zul'Drak	All	All		Commander Falstaav	Commander Falstaav		250 with Argent Crusade	21150	6 🪙 20 🪙
Argent Crusade, We Are Leaving!	Zul'Drak	All	All		Sergeant Stackhammer	Sergeant Stackhammer	New Orders for Sergeant Stackhammer	250 with Argent Crusade	21150	6 🪙 20 🪙
CHOICE OF: 1 Embattled Legwraps, 1 Embattled Jerkin, 1 Valiant Belt of Battle, 1 Thick Bracers of Battle										
New Orders for Sergeant Stackhammer	Zul'Drak	All	All		Commander Kunz	Sergeant Stackhammer	Parachutes for the Argent Crusade	10 with Argent Crusade	2100	62 🪙
Trouble at the Altar of Sseratus	Zul'Drak	All	All		Hexxer Ubungo	Hexxer Ubungo	Parachutes for the Argent Crusade		21150	6 🪙 20 🪙
Strange Mojo	Zul'Drak	All	All		Strange Mojo	Hexxer Ubungo			5300	1 🪙 58 🪙
Mopping Up	Zul'Drak	All	All		Corporal Maga	Corporal Maga	New Orders for Sergeant Stackhammer	250 with Argent Crusade	21150	6 🪙 20 🪙
Troll Patrol: Intestinal Fortitude	Zul'Drak	All	All		Captain Rupert	Captain Rupert		250 with Argent Crusade	5300	1 🪙 58 🪙
Precious Elemental Fluids	Zul'Drak	All	All		Hexxer Ubungo	Hexxer Ubungo	Strange Mojo		21150	6 🪙 20 🪙
CHOICE OF: 1 Bloodbinder's Raiment, 1 Bloodletter's Boots, 1 Gauntlets of the Great Sacrifice, 1 Chestplate of the Altar										
Leave No One Behind	Zul'Drak	All	All		Dr. Rogers	Dr. Rogers		250 with Argent Crusade	21150	6 🪙 20 🪙
CHOICE OF: 1 Rescuer's Cloak, 1 Ravager's Skullcap, 1 Rescuer's Binding, 1 Vindicator's Bracers of Sacrifice										
Mushroom Mixer	Zul'Drak	All	All		Hexxer Ubungo	Hexxer Ubungo	Precious Elemental Fluids		21150	6 🪙 20 🪙
Too Much of a Good Thing	Zul'Drak	All	All		Hexxer Ubungo	Hexxer Ubungo	Mushroom Mixer		26450	12 🪙 40 🪙
CHOICE OF: 1 Soothsayer's Garb, 1 Supple Wristguards, 1 Bloodbinder's Links, 1 Brazen Offender's Shoulderplates										
Troll Patrol: Whatdya Want, a Medal?	Zul'Drak	All	All		Captain Grondel	Captain Grondel		25 with Argent Crusade	5300	1 🪙 58 🪙
Gluttonous Lurkers	Zul'Drak	All	All		Apprentice Pestlepot	Alchemist Finklestein	Precious Elemental Fluids	250 with Argent Crusade	21150	6 🪙 20 🪙
Troll Patrol: The Alchemist's Apprentice	Zul'Drak	All	All		Alchemist Finklestein	Alchemist Finklestein		75 with Argent Crusade	5300	1 🪙 58 🪙
Death to the Necromagi	Zul'Drak	All	All		Sergeant Moonshard	Sergeant Moonshard	Throwing Down	250 with Argent Crusade	21150	6 🪙 20 🪙
Skimmer Spinnerets	Zul'Drak	All	All		Specialist Cogwheel	Specialist Cogwheel	Throwing Down	250 with Argent Crusade	21150	6 🪙 20 🪙
Malas the Corrupter	Zul'Drak	All	All	2	Sergeant Moonshard	Sergeant Moonshard	Death to the Necromagi	350 with Argent Crusade	26450	12 🪙 40 🪙
CHOICE OF: 1 Leggings of Fastidious Decapitation, 1 Legguards of Solemn Revenge, 1 Ceremonial Pike Leggings, 1 Legplates of the Vengeful Mendicant										
A Tangled Skein	Zul'Drak	All	All		Specialist Cogwheel	Specialist Cogwheel	Crashed Sprayer	250 with Argent Crusade	21150	6 🪙 20 🪙
CHOICE OF: 1 Blade of Diligence, 1 Knife of the Dutybound, 1 Cleaver of Diligence, 1 Staff of the Dutybound, 1 Dutybound Mace of Purity, 1 Staff of Diligence										
Lab Work	Zul'Drak	All	All		Alchemist Finklestein	Alchemist Finklestein		250 with Argent Crusade	21150	6 🪙 20 🪙
The Drakkari Do Not Need Water Elementals!	Zul'Drak	All	All		Sub-Lieutenant Jax	Sub-Lieutenant Jax	Strange Mojo	250 with Argent Crusade	21150	6 🪙 20 🪙
Troll Patrol	Zul'Drak	All	All		Kunz Jr.	Commander Kunz		250 with Argent Crusade	21150	6 🪙 20 🪙
Troll Patrol: Something for the Pain	Zul'Drak	All	All		Captain Brandon	Captain Brandon		75 with Argent Crusade	5300	1 🪙 58 🪙
The Blessing of Zim'Abwa	Zul'Drak	All	All		Hexxer Ubungo	Zim'Abwa			21150	
Blessing of Zim'Abwa	Zul'Drak	All	All		Zim'Abwa	Zim'Abwa	The Blessing of Zim'Abwa			

Title	Location	Faction	Race & Class	Group #	Starter	Finisher	Prerequisite	Reputation	XP	Money
Troll Patrol: Done to Death	Zul'Drak	All	All		Captain Rupert	Captain Rupert		75 with Argent Crusade	5300	1🟡 58🟠
Crashed Sprayer	Zul'Drak	All	All		Specialist Cogwheel	Specialist Cogwheel	Skimmer Spinnerets	250 with Argent Crusade	21150	6🟡 20🟠
Pure Evil	Zul'Drak	All	All		Captain Rupert	Eitrigg	Death to the Necromagi	250 with Argent Crusade	21150	6🟡 20🟠

CHOICE OF: 1 Soothsayer's Shoulderpads, 1 Gloves of Swift Death, 1 Boots of the Altar, 1 Ritualistic Band of Light

Title	Location	Faction	Race & Class	Group #	Starter	Finisher	Prerequisite	Reputation	XP	Money
Troll Patrol: Creature Comforts	Zul'Drak	All	All		Captain Grondel	Captain Grondel		75 with Argent Crusade	5300	1🟡 58🟠
Troll Patrol	Zul'Drak	All	All		Kunz Jr.	Commander Kunz		250 with Argent Crusade	21150	6🟡 20🟠
Troll Patrol: Can You Dig It?	Zul'Drak	All	All		Captain Brandon	Captain Brandon		75 with Argent Crusade	5300	1🟡 58🟠
Blahblah[PH]	Zul'Drak	All	All		Ancient Drakkari Tablets					
Troll Patrol: Throwing Down	Zul'Drak	All	All		Captain Rupert	Captain Rupert		75 with Argent Crusade	5300	1🟡 58🟠
Troll Patrol: Couldn't Care Less	Zul'Drak	All	All		Captain Grondel	Captain Grondel		75 with Argent Crusade	5300	1🟡 58🟠
Pa'Troll	Zul'Drak	All	All		Commander Kunz	Commander Kunz	Parachutes for the Argent Crusade	250 with Argent Crusade	21150	6🟡 20🟠

CHOICE OF: 1 Pantaloons of the Dutybound, 1 Belt of Service, 1 Wristguards of Service, 1 Ribbed Helm of Servitude, 1 Vile Tome of Tenets

Title	Location	Faction	Race & Class	Group #	Starter	Finisher	Prerequisite	Reputation	XP	Money
Something for the Pain	Zul'Drak	All	All		Captain Brandon	Captain Brandon		75 with Argent Crusade	5300	1🟡 58🟠
Throwing Down	Zul'Drak	All	All		Captain Rupert	Captain Rupert		75 with Argent Crusade	5300	1🟡 58🟠
Creature Comforts	Zul'Drak	All	All		Captain Grondel	Captain Grondel		75 with Argent Crusade	5300	1🟡 58🟠
The Alchemist's Apprentice	Zul'Drak	All	All		Alchemist Finklestein	Alchemist Finklestein		75 with Argent Crusade	5300	1🟡 58🟠
The Alchemist's Apprentice	Zul'Drak	All	All		Alchemist Finklestein	Alchemist Finklestein		75 with Argent Crusade	5300	1🟡 58🟠
Congratulations!	Zul'Drak	All	All		Commander Kunz	Commander Kunz		350 with Argent Crusade	31750	18🟡 60🟠

REWARD: 1 Patroller's Pack

Title	Location	Faction	Race & Class	Group #	Starter	Finisher	Prerequisite	Reputation	XP	Money
Cocooned!	Zul'Drak	All	All		Captain Rupert	Captain Rupert		250 with Argent Crusade	21150	6🟡 20🟠
Stocking the Shelves	Zul'Drak	All	All		Captain Arnath	Captain Arnath	Siphoning the Spirits	250 with Argent Crusade	21150	6🟡 20🟠

CHOICE OF: 1 Knuckle of Victory, 1 Victorious Spellblade, 1 Thorny Bough of the Light, 1 Crusader's Greatblade, 1 High-Strung Bow

Title	Location	Faction	Race & Class	Group #	Starter	Finisher	Prerequisite	Reputation	XP	Money
Clipping Their Wings	Zul'Drak	All	All		Captain Arnath	Captain Arnath	Siphoning the Spirits	250 with Argent Crusade	21150	6🟡 20🟠

CHOICE OF: 1 Braided Bat Sinew, 1 Bat Fur Mitts, 1 Huntsman's Jerkin, 1 Gauntlets of the Gatherer

Title	Location	Faction	Race & Class	Group #	Starter	Finisher	Prerequisite	Reputation	XP	Money
The Blessing of Zim'Torga	Zul'Drak	All	All		Witch Doctor Khufu	Zim'Torga	Too Much of a Good Thing		21400	
Blessing of Zim'Torga	Zul'Drak	All	All		Zim'Torga	Zim'Torga	The Blessing of Zim'Torga		21400	
The Leaders at Jin'Alai	Zul'Drak	All	All		Scalper Ahunae	Scalper Ahunae	To the Witch Doctor		21400	6🟡 50🟠

REWARD: 5 Candy Bar AND CHOICE OF: 1 Soothsayer's Sandals, 1 Supple Belt of the Bloodletter, 1 Boots of the Great Sacrifice, 1 Ring of Ancestral Protectors

Title	Location	Faction	Race & Class	Group #	Starter	Finisher	Prerequisite	Reputation	XP	Money
To the Witch Doctor	Zul'Drak	All	All		Hexxer Ubungo	Witch Doctor Khufu	Too Much of a Good Thing		2150	
Breaking Through Jin'Alai	Zul'Drak	All	All		Witch Doctor Khufu	Witch Doctor Khufu	To the Witch Doctor		21400	
To Speak With Har'koa	Zul'Drak	All	All		Witch Doctor Khufu	Har'koa	Breaking Through Jin'Alai		10700	
You Can Run, But You Can't Hide	Zul'Drak	All	All		Stefan Vadu	Stefan Vadu	Near Miss	250 with Knights of the Ebon Blade	20950	5🟡 90🟠
Kickin' Nass and Takin' Manes	Zul'Drak	All	All		Stefan Vadu	Stefan Vadu	The Ebon Watch		20950	5🟡 90🟠
An Invitation, of Sorts...	Zul'Drak	All	All		Unliving Choker	Stefan Vadu		150 with Knights of the Ebon Blade	15700	4🟡 60🟠
But First My Offspring	Zul'Drak	All	All		Har'koa	Har'koa	To Speak With Har'koa		21400	

CHOICE OF: 1 Soothsayer's Handwraps, 1 Bloodletter's Pants, 1 Spiritist's Focus, 1 Brazen Offender's Helm

Title	Location	Faction	Race & Class	Group #	Starter	Finisher	Prerequisite	Reputation	XP	Money
Darkness Calling	Zul'Drak	All	All		Writhing Choker	Stefan Vadu		150 with Knights of the Ebon Blade	15700	4🟡 60🟠
Relics of the Snow Leopard Goddess	Zul'Drak	All	All		Chronicler To'kini	Chronicler To'kini	Breaking Through Jin'Alai		21400	
Near Miss	Zul'Drak	All	All		Stefan Vadu	Stefan Vadu	An Invitation, of Sorts...	75 with Knights of the Ebon Blade	10500	3🟡
Close Call	Zul'Drak	All	All		Stefan Vadu	Stefan Vadu	Darkness Calling	75 with Knights of the Ebon Blade	10500	3🟡
The Frozen Earth	Zul'Drak	All	All		Element-Tamer Dagoda	Element-Tamer Dagoda	The Leaders at Jin'Alai		21400	6🟡 50🟠

CHOICE OF: 1 Bloodbinder's Wrist Wraps, 1 Supple Bloodbinder's Helm, 1 Bloodbinder's Gauntlets, 1 Band of the Bloodletter

Title	Location	Faction	Race & Class	Group #	Starter	Finisher	Prerequisite	Reputation	XP	Money
Sealing the Rifts	Zul'Drak	All	All		Scalper Ahunae	Scalper Ahunae	The Leaders at Jin'Alai		21400	6🟡 50🟠
Spirit of Rhunok	Zul'Drak	All	All		Spirit of Rhunok	Spirit of Rhunok	But First My Offspring		10700	
Silver Lining	Zul'Drak	All	All		Stefan Vadu	Stefan Vadu	Close Call	250 with Knights of the Ebon Blade	20950	5🟡 90🟠
My Prophet, My Enemy	Zul'Drak	All	All		Spirit of Rhunok	Spirit of Rhunok	Spirit of Rhunok		21400	
An End to the Suffering	Zul'Drak	All	All		Spirit of Rhunok	Spirit of Rhunok	My Prophet, My Enemy		26750	

CHOICE OF: 1 Bloodbinder's Shoulderpads, 1 Drape of the Bloodletter, 1 Belt of the Bloodbinder, 1 Ancestral Chestplates

Title	Location	Faction	Race & Class	Group #	Starter	Finisher	Prerequisite	Reputation	XP	Money
Dressing Down	Zul'Drak	All	All		Stefan Vadu	Stefan Vadu	You Can Run, But You Can't Hide	150 with Knights of the Ebon Blade	15700	4🟤 60🟠
Suit Up!	Zul'Drak	All	All		Stefan Vadu	Stefan Vadu	Silver Lining	150 with Knights of the Ebon Blade	15700	4🟤 60🟠
Plundering Their Own	Zul'Drak	All	All		Chronicler To'kini	Chronicler To'kini	Relics of the Snow Leopard Goddess		21400	
Feedin' Da Goolz	Zul'Drak	All	All		Gristlegut	Gristlegut			20950	
CHOICE OF: 1 Soiled Trousers, 1 Aged Abomination Tripe, 1 Redigested Mail Scraps, 1 Carved Bone Helm, 1 Petrified Ghoul Finger										
Back to Har'koa	Zul'Drak	All	All		Spirit of Rhunok	Har'koa	An End to the Suffering		10700	
The Blessing of Zim'Rhuk	Zul'Drak	All	All		Witch Doctor Khufu	Zim'Rhuk	But First My Offspring		21400	
Blessing of Zim'Rhuk	Zul'Drak	All	All		Zim'Rhuk	Zim'Rhuk	The Blessing of Zim'Rhuk			
Scalps!	Zul'Drak	All	All		Scalper Ahunae	Scalper Ahunae	Sealing the Rifts		21400	6🟤 50🟠
Infiltrating Voltarus	Zul'Drak	All	All		Stefan Vadu	Stefan Vadu		250 with Knights of the Ebon Blade	20950	5🟤 90🟠
CHOICE OF: 1 Sandals of Spying, 1 Double-Agent's Wristwraps, 1 Gauntlets of the Secret Agent, 1 Drape of Duplicity, 1 Fist of Subtlety										
Bringing Down Heb'Jin	Zul'Drak	All	All		Element-Tamer Dagoda	Element-Tamer Dagoda	Sealing the Rifts		21400	6🟤 50🟠
CHOICE OF: 1 Band of Misty Mojo, 1 Supple Mantle of the Bloodletter, 1 Leggings of the Ritual, 1 Gauntlets of the Altar										
Reunited	Zul'Drak	All	All		Overlord Drakuru	Overlord Drakuru	Suit Up!		20950	5🟤 90🟠
Dark Horizon	Zul'Drak	All	All		Overlord Drakuru	Overlord Drakuru	Dressing Down		20950	5🟤 90🟠
I Sense a Disturbance	Zul'Drak	All	All		Har'koa	Har'koa	Back to Har'koa		21400	
Preparations for the Underworld	Zul'Drak	All	All		Har'koa	Har'koa	I Sense a Disturbance		21400	
Seek the Wind Serpent Goddess	Zul'Drak	All	All		Quetz'lun's Spirit	Quetz'lun's Spirit	Preparations for the Underworld		10700	
Foundation for Revenge	Zul'Drak	All	All		Quetz'lun's Spirit	Quetz'lun's Spirit	Setting the Stage		21400	
So Far, So Bad	Zul'Drak	All	All		Stefan Vadu	Stefan Vadu	Infiltrating Voltarus	250 with Knights of the Ebon Blade	20950	5🟤 90🟠
CHOICE OF: 1 Cords of Duplicity, 1 Subtle Boots of the Infiltrator, 1 Helm of Subtle Whispers, 1 Infiltrator's Shield										
Setting the Stage	Zul'Drak	All	All		Quetz'lun's Spirit	Quetz'lun's Spirit	Seek the Wind Serpent Goddess		21400	
It Rolls Downhill	Zul'Drak	All	All		Overlord Drakuru	Overlord Drakuru			20950	5🟤 90🟠
Hell Hath a Fury	Zul'Drak	All	All		Quetz'lun's Spirit	Quetz'lun's Spirit	Foundation for Revenge		26750	
CHOICE OF: 1 Soothsayer's Wristwraps, 1 Bloodletter's Skullcap, 1 Ritualistic Shoulderguards, 1 Ancestral Girdle										
One Last Thing	Zul'Drak	All	All		Quetz'lun's Spirit	Har'koa	Hell Hath a Fury		10700	
Sabotage	Zul'Drak	All	All		Stefan Vadu	Stefan Vadu	Hazardous Materials	250 with Knights of the Ebon Blade	20950	5🟤 90🟠
CHOICE OF: 1 Badge of the Infiltrator, 1 Skins of Subterfuge, 1 Shoulderguards of Subterfuge, 1 Belt of the Betrayer										
Hazardous Materials	Zul'Drak	All	All		Stefan Vadu	Stefan Vadu	So Far, So Bad	250 with Knights of the Ebon Blade	20950	5🟤 90🟠
Blood of a Dead God	Zul'Drak	All	All		Har'koa	Har'koa	One Last Thing		21400	
You Reap What You Sow	Zul'Drak	All	All		Witch Doctor Khufu	Witch Doctor Khufu	Blood of a Dead God		26750	
CHOICE OF: 1 Ritualistic Shield, 1 Supple Bloodbinder's Leggings, 1 Neckcharm of Mighty Mojo, 1 Ancestral Gauntlets, 1 Bloodletter's Blade										
Zero Tolerance	Zul'Drak	All	All		Overlord Drakuru	Overlord Drakuru			20950	5🟤 90🟠
Fuel for the Fire	Zul'Drak	All	All		Overlord Drakuru	Overlord Drakuru			20950	5🟤 90🟠
Wooly Justice	Zul'Drak	All	All		Scalper Ahunae	Scalper Ahunae	You Reap What You Sow		21400	6🟤 50🟠
CHOICE OF: 1 Soothsayer's Hood, 1 Supple Bloodbinder's Boots, 1 Bloodbinder's Shoulderguards, 1 Bloodletter's Legplates, 1 Frigid Crossbow										
Enchanted Tiki Warriors	Zul'Drak	All	All		Element-Tamer Dagoda	Element-Tamer Dagoda	You Reap What You Sow		21400	
Hexed Caches	Zul'Drak	All	All		Chronicler To'kini	Chronicler To'kini	You Reap What You Sow		21400	
CHOICE OF: 1 Bloodbinder's Hood, 1 Supple Vest of the Bloodbinder, 1 Neckcharm of the Bloodletter, 1 Belt of Divine Ancestry										
Disclosure	Zul'Drak	All	All		Overlord Drakuru	Overlord Drakuru	Fuel for the Fire		10500	3🟤
The Key of Warlord Zol'Maz	Zul'Drak	All	All		Har'koa	Har'koa	You Reap What You Sow		26750	
Betrayal	Zul'Drak	All	All		Stefan Vadu	Stefan Vadu	Sabotage	500 with Knights of the Ebon Blade	31750	18🟤 60🟠
CHOICE OF: 1 Betrayer's Choker, 1 Choker of Betrayal, 1 Choker of the Betrayer										
Rampage	Zul'Drak	All	All		Witch Doctor Khufu	Witch Doctor Khufu	The Key of Warlord Zol'Maz		26750	
CHOICE OF: 1 Bloodbinder's Gloves, 1 Supple Vest of the Bloodletter, 1 Bloodletter's Headgear, 1 Ancestral War Boots										
The Gods Have Spoken	Zul'Drak	All	All	3	Witch Doctor Khufu	Har'koa	Rampage		26750	
Convocation at Zol'Heb	Zul'Drak	All	All	3	Har'koa	Har'koa	The Gods Have Spoken		32400	20🟤 40🟠
CHOICE OF: 1 Robe of the Conquered Prophet, 1 Intricate Zandalari Tunic, 1 Chestguard of Rampaging Fury, 1 Links of the Terrified Deity										
Parachutes for the Argent Crusade	Zul'Drak	All	All		Commander Falstaav	Commander Falstaav		250 with Argent Crusade	21150	
CHOICE OF: 1 Crusader's Ripcord, 1 Rescuer's Ripcord, 1 Rescuer's Chestguard, 1 Boots of the Rescuer, 1 Blade of Valorous Service										
DEPRICATED>>Enemy of Our Enemy	Zul'Drak	All	All		Stefan Vadu	Stefan Vadu			2100	60🟤
First Things First	Zul'Drak	All	All		Commander Kunz	Sergeant Riannah			2100	60🟤
Smoke on the Horizon	Zul'Drak	All	All		Witch Doctor Khufu	Sergeant Riannah			2100	60🟤
Taking a Stand	Zul'Drak	All	All		Bloodrose Datura	Commander Falstaav	Kickin' Nass and Takin' Manes		2100	60🟤
Siphoning the Spirits	Zul'Drak	All	All		Captain Arnath	Captain Arnath			20950	5🟤 90🟠
Wanted: Ragemane's Flipper	Zul'Drak	All	All	3	Wanted!	Chief Rageclaw		350 with Argent Crusade	26200	11🟤 80🟠
CHOICE OF: 1 Staff of the Sorrowful Chieftain, 1 Hammer of Quiet Mourning, 1 Cresent of Brooding Fury, 1 Sword of Heartwrenching Slaughter										

Title	Location	Faction	Race & Class	Group #	Starter	Finisher	Prerequisite	Reputation	XP	Money
This Just In: Fire Still Hot!	Zul'Drak	All	All		Elder Shaman Moky	Elder Shaman Moky		250 with Argent Crusade	20950	5🟡90🟤
REWARD: 1 The Fire Extinguisher										
Trolls Is Gone Crazy!	Zul'Drak	All	All		Chief Rageclaw	Chief Rageclaw			20950	5🟡90🟤
CHOICE OF: 1 Emancipator's Robes, 1 Wristguard of Healing Fingers, 1 Freedom-Path Treads, 1 Leggings of the Canny Chief										
Orders From Drakuru	Zul'Drak	All	All		Orders From Drakuru	Crusader Lord Lantinga	In Search Of Answers	250 with Argent Crusade	20950	11🟡80🟤
The Ebon Watch	Zul'Drak	All	All		Crusader Lord Lantinga	Stefan Vadu	Orders From Drakuru	25 with Knights of the Ebon Blade	5250	
Crusader Forward Camp	Zul'Drak	All	All		Crusader Lord Lantinga	Crusader MacKellar	Orders From Drakuru	25 with Argent Crusade	5250	
Making Something Out Of Nothing	Zul'Drak	All	All		Engineer Reed	Engineer Reed	Crusader Forward Camp	250 with Argent Crusade	21150	
In Search Of Answers	Zul'Drak	All	All		Crusader Lord Lantinga	Orders From Drakuru		150 with Argent Crusade	15700	
That's What Friends Are For...	Zul'Drak	All	All		Crusader MacKellar	Crusader MacKellar	Crusader Forward Camp	250 with Argent Crusade	21150	
CHOICE OF: 1 Greenhealer's Gauntlets, 1 Medic's Hood, 1 Purifier's Pantaloons, 1 Horn of Argent Fury										
Light Won't Grant Me Vengeance	Zul'Drak	All	All		Gerk	Gerk	Crusader Forward Camp	350 with Argent Crusade	26450	12🟡40🟤
A Great Storm Approaches	Zul'Drak	All	All		Gymer	Engineer Reed	Crusader Forward Camp		2100	
Gymer's Salvation	Zul'Drak	All	All		Engineer Reed	Engineer Reed	A Great Storm Approaches	250 with Argent Crusade	21150	
Our Only Hope	Zul'Drak	All	All		Engineer Reed	Gymer	Gymer's Salvation	75 with Argent Crusade	10600	
The Storm King's Vengeance	Zul'Drak	All	All		Gymer	Crusader MacKellar	Our Only Hope	500 with Argent Crusade	31750	18🟡60🟤
CHOICE OF: 1 Grips of the Giant-Rider, 1 Horns of Electrified Terror, 1 Bracers of Vengeful Flight, 1 Life-Light Pauldrons, 1 Clutch of the Storm Giant										
The Amphitheater of Anguish: Yggdras!	Zul'Drak	All	All	5	Gurgthock	Wodin the Troll-Servant			32100	19🟡50🟤
The Amphitheater of Anguish: Magnataur!	Zul'Drak	All	All	5	Gurgthock	Wodin the Troll-Servant	The Amphitheater of Anguish: Yggdras!, The Amphitheater of Anguish: Yggdras!		32100	19🟡50🟤
The Amphitheater of Anguish: From Beyond!	Zul'Drak	All	All	5	Gurgthock	Wodin the Troll-Servant	The Amphitheater of Anguish: Magnataur!		32100	19🟡50🟤
The Amphitheater of Anguish: Tuskarrmageddon!	Zul'Drak	All	All	5	Gurgthock	Wodin the Troll-Servant	The Amphitheater of Anguish: From Beyond!		32100	19🟡50🟤
REWARD: 5 Runic Healing Potion, 5 Runic Mana Potion, 20 Heavy Frostweave Bandage										
The Amphitheater of Anguish: Korrak the Bloodrager!	Zul'Drak	All	All	5	Gurgthock	Wodin the Troll-Servant	The Amphitheater of Anguish: Tuskarrmageddon!		32100	19🟡50🟤
The Champion of Anguish	Zul'Drak	All	All	5	Gurgthock	Wodin the Troll-Servant	The Amphitheater of Anguish: Korrak the Bloodrager!		32400	20🟡40🟤
CHOICE OF: 1 Icier Barbed Spear, 1 Chilly Slobberknocker, 1 Wodin's Second-Best Shanker, 1 De-Raged Waraxe, 1 Screw-Sprung Fixer-Upper, 1 Crimson Cranium Crusher										
The Amphitheater of Anguish: Yggdras!	Zul'Drak	All	All	5	Gurgthock	Wodin the Troll-Servant	The Ring of Blood: The Final Challenge		32100	19🟡50🟤
The Champion's Call!	Zul'Drak	All	All	5	Shifty Vickers	Gurgthock			2150	
Unfinished Business	Zul'Drak	All	All		Tol'mar	Tol'mar	Convocation at Zol'Heb		10800	
Just Checkin'	Zul'Drak	All	All		Chronicler To'kini	Chronicler Bah'Kini			10800	

ACHIEVEMENTS

 Did you ever wish you had a way to keep track of all you have accomplished with your characters, or better yet, a new way to brag about them? If so, Blizzard has granted your wish! The new Achievements section keeps a record of almost everything you do in World of Warcraft, like making it through those epic raids, completing all those quests, exploring out of the way areas, and even smaller accomplishments like obtaining a vanity pet, or giving your /love to all the critters of the world.

Your Achievements are organized into different categories such as Quests, Exploration, Dungeons, and many others. Just select a category from the list on the left of the Achievements window to see the list of Achievements in that area. You can also see your most recent Achievements on the Summary page. Each Achievement lists what you need to accomplish to earn that Achievement, and even lists the date you earned it! You can also track Achievements on the right hand side of your screen, much like quests, by checking the Track box under each one.

BUT, I ALREADY DID THAT!

Since Achievements are a new feature of World of Warcraft, it isn't possible to go back and track everything you've done before now. If you want to fill in all of your Achievements you need to revisit a few of your old stomping grounds to do it.

GENERAL	49

QUESTS	19
Classic	5
The Burning Crusade	15
Wrath of the Lich King	22
Exploration	5
Eastern Kingdoms	25
Kalimdor	20
Outland	9
Northrend	11

PLAYER VS. PLAYER	44
Arena	28
Alterac Valley	20
Arathi Basin	17
Eye of the Storm	12
Warsong Gulch	20
Strand of the Ancients	18
Wintergrasp	23

DUNGEONS & RAIDS	27
Classic	27
The Burning Crusade	41
Lich King Dungeon	12
Lich King Heroic	51
Lich King Raid	29
Lich King Heroic Raid	29

PROFESSIONS	3
Cooking	29
Fishing	31
First Aid	7

REPUTATION	15
Classic	5
The Burning Crusade	16
Wrath of the Lich King	13

WORLD EVENTS	14
Lunar Festival	15
Love is in the Air	16
Children's Week	8
Noble Garden	2
Midsummer	20
Brewfest	10
Hallow's End	21
Winter Veil	14

FEATS OF STRENGTH	112

STATISTICS

In addition to keeping track of all that you have achieved, you can also track the minutiae of your character in several different categories with the Statistics tab. For example, do you wonder where all your gold goes? Take a look at your statistics to find out. You can see not only where your gold came from, but where you spent it! You can also take a look at things like your Attributes and Combat.

While it is certainly fun to be able to track your own Achievements, it is even more interesting to compare yours with others. To look at someone's Achievements target them and right click their character portrait then select Compare Achievements from the menu. Your Achievements window opens up and you can see the other person's Achievements to the right of yours. Now you can see exactly how they stack up against you!

As you earn Achievements you get achievement points. The number of points is listed next to every Achievement and they vary based on the difficulty of the Achievement completed. These points are not used to purchase any special items, they simply provide a value that shows how far a character has progressed.

DUNGEONS & RAIDS

CLASSIC

 Deadmines — 10
Defeat Edwin VanCleef.

 Ragefire Chasm — 10
Defeat Taragaman the Hungerer.

 Wailing Caverns — 10
Defeat Mutanus the Devourer.

 Shadowfang Keep — 10
Defeat Archmage Arugal.

 Blackfathom Deeps — 10
Defeat Aku'mai.

Stormwind Stockade — 10
Defeat Bazil Thredd.

Gnomeregan — 10
Defeat Mekgineer Thermaplugg.

10 **Razorfen Kraul**
Defeat Charlga Razorflank.

10 **Razorfen Downs**
Defeat Amnennar the Coldbringer.

10 **Scarlet Monastery**
Defeat the Scarlet Crusade within the Scarlet Monastery.

10 **Uldaman**
Defeat Archaedas.

10 **Zul'Farrak**
Defeat Chief Ukorz Sandscalp.

10 **Maraudon**
Defeat Princess Theradras.

10 **Sunken Temple**
Defeat Shade of Eranikus.

10 **Blackrock Depths**
Defeat Emperor Dagran Thaurissan.

10 **Lower Blackrock Spire**
Defeat Overlord Wyrmthalak.

10 **King of Dire Maul**
Defeat each wing of Dire Maul.

10 **Scholomance**
Defeat the leaders of Scholomance.

10 **Stratholme**
Defeat the evil masterminds inhabiting Stratholme.

10 **Onyxia's Lair**
Defeat Onyxia.

10 **Blackwing Lair**
Defeat Nefarian.

10 **Molten Core**
Defeat Ragnaros.

10 **Temple of Ahn'Qiraj**
Defeat C'Thun.

10 **Zul'Gurub**
Defeat Hakkar.

10 **Ruins of Ahn'Qiraj**
Defeat Ossirian the Unscarred.

10 **Upper Blackrock Spire**
Defeat General Drakkisath.

10 **Leeeeeeeeeeeeroy!**
Kill 50 rookery whelps within 15 seconds.

LICH KING

10 **Utgarde Keep**
Defeat the bosses in Utgarde Keep.

10 **The Nexus**
Defeat the bosses in The Nexus.

10 **The Culling of Stratholme**
Defeat the bosses in Caverns of Time: Stratholme.

Azjol-Nerub

Defeat the bosses in Azjol-Nerub.

 Ahn'kahet: The Old Kingdom

Defeat the bosses in Ahn'kahet: The Old Kingdom.

 Drak'Tharon Keep

Defeat the bosses in Drak'Tharon Keep.

 The Violet Hold

Defeat Cyanigosa in The Violet Hold.

 Gundrak

Defeat the bosses in Gundrak.

 Halls of Stone

Defeat the boss encounters in Halls of Stone.

 Halls of Lightning

Defeat the bosses in Halls of Lightning.

 The Oculus

Defeat the bosses in The Oculus.

 Utgarde Pinnacle

Defeat the bosses in Utgarde Pinnacle.

LICH KING HEROIC

 Heroic: Utgarde Keep

Defeat the Utgarde Keep bosses on Heroic Difficulty.

 Heroic: The Nexus

Defeat The Nexus bosses on Heroic Difficulty.

 Heroic: Azjol-Nerub

Defeat the Azjol-Nerub bosses on Heroic Difficulty.

 Heroic: Ahn'kahet: The Old Kingdom

Defeat the Ahn'kahet: The Old Kingdom bosses on Heroic Difficulty.

 Heroic: Drak'Tharon Keep

Defeat the Drak'Tharon Keep bosses on Heroic Difficulty.

 Heroic: The Violet Hold

Defeat The Violet Hold bosses on Heroic Difficulty.

 Heroic: Gundrak

Defeat the Gundrak bosses on Heroic Difficulty.

 Heroic: Halls of Stone

Defeat the boss encounters inl the Halls of Stone on Heroic Difficulty.

 Heroic: Halls of Lightning

Defeat the Halls of Lightning bosses on Heroic Difficulty.

 Heroic: The Oculus

Defeat The Oculus bosses on Heroic Difficulty.

 Heroic: Utgarde Pinnacle

Defeat the Utgarde Pinnacle bosses on Heroic Difficulty.

 Heroic: The Culling of Stratholme

Defeat the Caverns of Time: Stratholme bosses on Heroic Difficulty.

 Watch Him Die

Defeat Krik'thir the Gatewatcher in Azjol-Nerub on Heroic Difficulty while Watcher Gashra, Watcher Narjil and Watcher Silthik are still alive.

 Hadronox Denied

Defeat Hadronox in Azjol-Nerub on Heroic Difficulty before he webs the top doors and prevents more creatures from spawning.

Defenseless

Defeat Cyanigosa in The Violet Hold without using Defense Control Crystals and with Prison Seal Integrity at 100% while in Heroic Difficulty.

The Culling of Time

Defeat the Infinite Corruptor in The Culling of Stratholme on Heroic Difficulty.

Lightning Struck

Defeat General Bjarngrim in the Halls of Lightning on Heroic Difficulty while he has a Temporary Electrical Charge.

Gotta Go!

Defeat Anub'arak in Azjol-Nerub on Heroic Difficulty in 2 minutes or less.

The Party's Over

Defeat Prince Taldaram in Ahn'kahet on Heroic Difficulty with less than 5 people.

Volazj's Quick Demise

Defeat Herald Volazj in Ahn'kahet on Heroic Difficulty in 2 minutes or less.

What the Eck?

Defeat Gal'darah in Gundrak on Heroic Difficulty while under the effects of Eck Residue.

Lockdown!

Defeat Xevozz, Lavanthor, Ichoron, Zuramat the Obliterator, Erekem and Moragg in The Violet Hold on Heroic Difficulty.

Good Grief

Defeat the Maiden of Grief in the Halls of Stone on Heroic Difficulty in 1 minute or less.

Timely Death

Defeat Loken in the Halls of Lightning on Heroic Difficulty in 2 minutes or less.

Make It Count

Defeat Ley-Guardian Eregos in The Oculus on Heroic Difficulty within 20 minutes of Drakos the Interrogator's death.

Experienced Drake Rider

On three different visits to The Oculus, get credit for defeating Ley-Guardian Eregos while riding an Amber, Emerald and Ruby drake on Heroic Difficulty.

Zombiefest!

Kill 100 Risen Zombies in 1 minute in The Culling of Stratholme on Heroic Difficulty.

Lodi Dodi We Loves the Skadi
Defeat Skadi the Ruthless in Utgarde Pinnacle on Heroic Difficulty within 3 minutes of starting the gauntlet event.

On The Rocks

Defeat Prince Keleseth in Utgarde Keep on Heroic Difficulty without shattering any Frost Tombs.

Intense Cold

Defeat Keristrasza in The Nexus on Heroic Difficulty without allowing Intense Cold to reach more than two stacks.

Chaos Theory

Defeat Anomalus in The Nexus on Heroic Difficulty without destroying any Chaotic Rifts.

Respect Your Elders

Defeat Elder Nadox in Ahn'kahet on Heroic Difficulty without killing any Ahn'kahar Guardians.

Better Off Dred

Engage King Dred in Drak'Tharon Keep on Heroic Difficulty and slay 6 Drakkari Gutrippers or Drakkari Scytheclaw during his defeat.

Less-rabi

Defeat Moorabi in Gundrak on Heroic Difficulty while preventing him from transforming into a mammoth at any point during the encounter.

Dehydration

Defeat Ichoron in the Violet Hold on Heroic Difficulty without allowing any Ichor Globules to merge.

Shatter Resistant

Defeat Volkhan in the Halls of Lightning on Heroic Difficulty without allowing him to shatter more than 4 Brittle Golems.

The Incredible Hulk

Force Svala Sorrowgrave to kill a Scourge Hulk on Heroic Difficulty in Utgarde Pinnacle.

Ruby Void

Defeat Ley-Guardian Eregos in The Oculus on Heroic Difficulty without anyone in your party using a Ruby Drake.

Emerald Void

Defeat Ley-Guardian Eregos in The Oculus on Heroic Difficulty without anyone in your party using an Emerald Drake.

Amber Void

Defeat Ley-Guardian Eregos in The Oculus on Heroic Difficulty without anyone in your party using an Amber Drake.

Volunteer Work

Defeat Jedoga Shadowseeker in Ahn'kahet on Heroic Difficulty without killing any Twilight Volunteers.

Oh Novos!

Defeat Novos the Summoner in Drak'Tharon Keep on Heroic Difficulty without allowing any undead minions to reach the floor.

Snakes. Why'd It Have To Be Snakes?
Defeat Slad'ran in Gundrak on Heroic Difficulty without getting snake wrapped.

Split Personality
Defeat Grand Magus Telestra in The Nexus on Heroic Difficulty after having killed her images within 5 seconds of each other during both splits.

Consumption Junction
Defeat Trollgore in Drak'Tharon Keep on Heroic Difficulty before Consume reaches ten stacks.

Share The Love
Defeat Gal'darah in Gundrak on Heroic Difficulty and have 5 unique party members get impaled throughout the fight.

A Void Dance
Defeat Zuramat the Obliterator in The Violet Hold without killing any void sentries.

Brann Spankin' New
Defeat the Tribunal of Ages encounter in the Halls of Stone on Heroic Difficulty without allowing Brann Bronzebeard to take any damage.

Abuse the Ooze
Defeat Sjonnir the Ironshaper in the Halls of Stone on Heroic Difficulty and kill 5 Formed Oozes during the encounter.

My Girl Loves to Skadi All the Time
Defeat Skadi the Ruthless in Utgarde Pinnacle on Heroic Difficulty after having killed Grauf from 100% to dead in a single pass.

King's Bane
Defeat King Ymiron in Utgarde Pinnacle on Heroic Difficulty without anyone in the party triggering Bane.

LICH KING HEROIC RAID

Heroic: The Arachnid Quarter
Defeat the bosses of The Arachnid Quarter of Naxxramas on Heroic Difficulty.

Heroic: The Construct Quarter
Defeat the bosses of The Construct Quarter of Naxxramas on Heroic Difficulty.

Heroic: The Plague Quarter
Defeat the bosses of The Plague Quarter of Naxxramas on Heroic Difficulty.

Heroic: The Military Quarter
Defeat the bosses of The Military Quarter of Naxxramas on Heroic Difficulty.

Heroic: Sapphiron's Demise
Defeat Sapphiron on Heroic Difficulty in Naxxramas.

Heroic: Kel'Thuzad's Defeat
Defeat Kel'Thuzad on Heroic Difficulty in Naxxramas.

Heroic: The Fall of Naxxramas
Defeat every boss in Naxxramas on Heroic Difficulty.

Heroic: The Dedicated Few
Defeat the bosses of Naxxramas with less than 21 people on Heroic Difficulty.

Heroic: The Spellweaver's Downfall
Defeat Malygos on Heroic Difficulty.

Heroic: Besting the Black Dragonflight
Defeat Sartharion the Onyx Guardian on Heroic Difficulty.

Heroic: Make Quick Werk Of Him
Kill Patchwerk in Naxxramas in 3 minutes or less on Heroic Difficulty.

Heroic: Arachnophobia
Kill Maexxna in Naxxramas within 20 minutes of Anub'Rekhan's death on Heroic Difficulty.

Heroic: A Poke In The Eye
Defeat Malygos on Heroic Difficulty with fewer than 21.

Heroic: You Don't Have An Eternity
Defeat Malygos in 5 minutes or less on Heroic Difficulty.

Heroic: Less Is More
Defeat Sartharion the Onyx Guardian and the Twilight Drakes on Heroic Difficulty with fewer than 21.

 ### Heroic: Gonna Go When the Volcano Blows
Defeat Sartharion the Onyx Guardian on Heroic Difficulty without getting hit by Lava Strike.

 ### Heroic: Twilight Assist
With at least one Twilight Drake still alive, engage and defeat Sartharion the Onyx Guardian on Heroic Difficulty.

 ### Heroic: Twilight Duo
With at least two Twilight Drakes still alive, engage and defeat Sartharion the Onyx Guardian on Heroic Difficulty.

 ### Heroic: The Twilight Zone
With all three Twilight Drakes still alive, engage and defeat Sartharion the Onyx Guardian on Heroic Difficulty.

 ### Heroic: The Safety Dance
Defeat Heigan the Unclean in Naxxramas on Heroic Difficulty without anyone in the raid dying.

 ### Heroic: Momma Said Knock You Out
Defeat Grand Widow Faerlina in Naxxramas on Heroic Difficulty without dispelling frenzy.

 ### Heroic: The Hundred Club
Defeat Sapphiron on Heroic Difficulty in Naxxramas without any member of the raid having a frost resist value over 100.

 ### Heroic: Denyin' the Scion
Deliver a killing blow to a Scion of Eternity while riding on a hover disk on Heroic Difficulty.

 ### Heroic: And They Would All Go Down Together
Defeat the 4 Horsemen in Naxxramas on Heroic Difficulty, ensuring that they all die within 15 seconds of each other.

 ### Heroic: Shocking!
Defeat Thaddius in Naxxramas on Heroic Difficulty without anyone in the raid crossing the negative and positive charges.

 ### Heroic: Subtraction
Defeat Thaddius in Naxxramas on Heroic Difficulty with less than 21 people.

Heroic: Spore Loser
Defeat Loatheb in Naxxramas on Heroic Difficulty without killing any spores.

 ### Heroic: Just Can't Get Enough
Defeat Kel'Thuzad on Heroic Difficulty in Naxxramas while killing at least 18 abominations in his chamber.

 ### The Immortal
Within one raid lockout period, defeat every boss in Naxxramas on Heroic Difficulty without allowing any raid member to die during any of the boss encounters.

LICH KING RAID

 ### The Arachnid Quarter
Defeat the bosses of The Arachnid Quarter of Naxxramas on Normal Difficulty.

 ### The Construct Quarter
Defeat the bosses of The Construct Quarter of Naxxramas on Normal Difficulty.

 ### The Plague Quarter
Defeat the bosses of The Plague Quarter of Naxxramas on Normal Difficulty.

 ### The Military Quarter
Defeat the bosses of The Military Quarter of Naxxramas on Normal Difficulty.

Sapphiron's Demise
Defeat Sapphiron on Normal Difficulty in Naxxramas.

 ### Kel'Thuzad's Defeat
Defeat Kel'Thuzad on Normal Difficulty in Naxxramas.

The Fall of Naxxramas

Defeat every boss in Naxxramas on Normal Difficulty.

The Dedicated Few

Defeat the bosses of Naxxramas on Normal Difficulty with less than 9 people.

The Spellweaver's Downfall

Defeat Malygos on Normal Difficulty.

Less Is More

Defeat Sartharion the Onyx Guardian and the Twilight Drakes with fewer than 9 on Normal Difficulty.

Make Quick Werk Of Him

Defeat Patchwerk in Naxxramas on Normal Difficulty in 3 minutes or less.

Arachnophobia

Defeat Maexxna in Naxxramas within 20 minutes of Anub'Rekhan's death on Normal Difficulty.

A Poke In The Eye

Defeat Malygos with fewer than 9 on Normal Difficulty.

You Don't Have An Eternity

Defeat Malygos in 5 minutes or less on Normal Difficulty.

Besting the Black Dragonflight

Defeat Sartharion the Onyx Guardian on Normal Difficulty.

The Safety Dance

Defeat Heigan the Unclean in Naxxramas on Normal Difficulty without anyone in the raid dying.

Momma Said Knock You Out

Defeat Grand Widow Faerlina in Naxxramas on Normal Difficulty without dispelling frenzy.

Gonna Go When the Volcano Blows

Defeat Sartharion the Onyx Guardian on Normal Difficulty without getting hit by Lava Strike.

Twilight Assist

With at least one Twilight Drake still alive, engage and defeat Sartharion the Onyx Guardian on Normal Difficulty.

Twilight Duo

With at least two Twilight Drakes still alive, engage and defeat Sartharion the Onyx Guardian on Normal Difficulty.

The Twilight Zone

With all three Twilight Drakes still alive, engage and defeat Sartharion the Onyx Guardian on Normal Difficulty.

The Hundred Club

Defeat Sapphiron on Normal Difficulty in Naxxramas without any member of the raid having a frost resist value over 100.

Denyin' the Scion

Deliver a killing blow to a Scion of Eternity while riding on a hover disk on Normal Difficulty.

And They Would All Go Down Together

Defeat the 4 Horsemen in Naxxramas on Normal Difficulty, ensuring that they all die within 15 seconds of each other.

Shocking!

Defeat Thaddius in Naxxramas on Normal Difficulty without anyone in the raid crossing the negative and positive charges.

Subtraction

Defeat Thaddius in Naxxramas on Normal Difficulty with less than 9 people.

Spore Loser

Defeat Loatheb in Naxxramas on Normal Difficulty without killing any spores.

Just Can't Get Enough

Defeat Kel'Thuzad on Normal Difficulty in Naxxramas while killing at least 18 abominations in his chamber.

The Undying

Within one raid lockout period, defeat every boss in Naxxramas on Normal Difficulty without allowing any raid member to die during any of the boss encounters.

THE BURNING CRUSADE

10 **Hellfire Ramparts**
Defeat Omor the Unscarred.

10 **The Blood Furnace**
Defeat Keli'dan the Breaker.

10 **The Slave Pens**
Defeat Quagmirran.

10 **Underbog**
Defeat The Black Stalker.

10 **Mana-Tombs**
Defeat Nexus-Prince Shaffar.

10 **The Escape From Durnholde**
Defeat Epoch Hunter.

10 **Sethekk Halls**
Defeat Talon King Ikiss.

10 **Shadow Labyrinth**
Defeat Murmur.

10 **Opening of the Dark Portal**
Defeat Aeonus.

10 **The Steamvault**
Defeat Warlord Kalithresh.

10 **The Shattered Halls**
Defeat Warchief Kargath Bladefist.

10 **The Mechanar**
Defeat Pathaleon the Calculator.

10 **The Botanica**
Defeat Warp Splinter.

10 **The Arcatraz**
Defeat Harbinger Skyriss.

10 **Magister's Terrace**
Defeat Kael'thas Sunstrider.

10 **Auchenai Crypts**
Defeat Exarch Maladaar.

10 **Heroic: Hellfire Ramparts**
Defeat the leaders of Hellfire Ramparts on Heroic Difficulty.

10 **Heroic: The Blood Furnace**
Defeat Keli'dan the Breaker on Heroic Difficulty.

10 **Heroic: The Slave Pens**
Defeat Quagmirran on Heroic Difficulty.

10 **Heroic: Underbog**
Defeat The Black Stalker on Heroic Difficulty.

10 **Heroic: Mana-Tombs**
Defeat Nexus-Prince Shaffar on Heroic Difficulty.

10 **Heroic: Auchenai Crypts**
Defeat Exarch Maladaar on Heroic Difficulty.

10 Heroic: The Escape From Durnholde
Defeat Epoch Hunter on Heroic Difficulty.

10 Heroic: Sethekk Halls
Defeat Talon King Ikiss on Heroic Difficulty.

10 Heroic: Shadow Labyrinth
Defeat Murmur on Heroic Difficulty.

10 Heroic: Opening of the Dark Portal
Defeat Aeonus on Heroic Difficulty.

10 Heroic: The Steamvault
Defeat Warlord Kalithresh on Heroic Difficulty.

10 Heroic: The Shattered Halls
Defeat Warchief Kargath Bladefist on Heroic Difficulty.

10 Heroic: The Mechanar
Defeat Pathaleon the Calculator on Heroic Difficulty.

10 Heroic: The Botanica
Defeat Warp Splinter on Heroic Difficulty.

10 Heroic: The Arcatraz
Defeat Harbinger Skyriss on Heroic Difficulty.

10 Heroic: Magister's Terrace
Defeat Kael'thas Sunstrider on Heroic Difficulty.

10 Karazhan
Defeat Prince Malchezaar in Karazhan.

10 Zul'Aman
Defeat Zul'jin in Zul'Aman.

10 Gruul's Lair
Defeat Gruul the Dragonkiller in Gruul's Lair.

10 Magtheridon's Lair
Defeat Magtheridon in Magtheridon's Lair.

10 Serpentshrine Cavern
Defeat Lady Vashj in Serpentshrine Cavern.

10 The Battle for Mount Hyjal
Defeat Archimonde in The Battle for Mount Hyjal.

10 Tempest Keep
Defeat Kael'thas Sunstrider in Tempest Keep.

10 The Black Temple
Defeat Illidan Stormrage in The Black Temple.

10 Sunwell Plateau
Defeat Kil'jaeden in Sunwell Plateau.

10 Classic Dungeonmaster
Complete the classic dungeon achievements listed.

10 Outland Dungeonmaster
Complete the Burning Crusade dungeon achievements listed.

20 Classic Raider
Complete the classic raid achievements listed.

20 Outland Raider
Complete the Burning Crusade raid achievements listed.

20 Outland Dungeon Hero
Complete the heroic Burning Crusade dungeon achievements listed.

10 Northrend Dungeonmaster
Complete the Northrend dungeon achievements listed.

20 Northrend Dungeon Hero
Complete the heroic Northrend dungeon achievements listed.

10 Champion of the Frozen Wastes
Defeat the dungeon and raid bosses listed below.

10 Emblem of Heroism
Loot an Emblem of Heroism.

Emblem of Valor — 10
Loot an Emblem of Valor.

 25 Emblems of Heroism — 10
Loot 25 Emblems of Heroism.

 50 Emblems of Heroism — 10
Loot 50 Emblems of Heroism.

 100 Emblems of Heroism — 10
Loot 100 Emblems of Heroism.

 250 Emblems of Heroism — 10
Loot 250 Emblems of Heroism.

 500 Emblems of Heroism — 10
Loot 500 Emblems of Heroism.

 1000 Emblems of Heroism — 10
Loot 1000 Emblems of Heroism.

 25 Emblems of Valor — 10
Loot 25 Emblems of Valor.

 50 Emblems of Valor — 10
Loot 50 Emblems of Valor.

 100 Emblems of Valor — 10
Loot 100 Emblems of Valor.

 250 Emblems of Valor — 10
Loot 250 Emblems of Valor.

 500 Emblems of Valor — 10
Loot 500 Emblems of Valor.

 1000 Emblems of Valor — 10
Loot 1000 Emblems of Valor.

Timear Foresees — 10
Complete the Northrend daily dungeon quests.

 Proof of Demise — 10
Complete the Northrend daily dungeon quests.

 Glory of the Hero — 25
Complete the Heroic Dungeon achievements listed.

 Glory of the Raider — 25
Complete the Normal Difficulty raid achievements listed.

 Heroic: Glory of the Raider — 25
Complete the Heroic Difficulty raid achievements listed.

EXPLORATION

EASTERN KINGDOMS

 Explore Dun Morogh — 10
Explore Dun Morogh, revealing the covered areas of the world map.

 Explore Alterac Mountains — 10
Explore Alterac Mountains, revealing the covered areas of the world map.

 Explore Arathi Highlands — 10
Explore Arathi Highlands, revealing the covered areas of the world map.

 Explore Badlands — 10
Explore Badlands, revealing the covered areas of the world map.

Explore Blasted Lands

Explore Blasted Lands, revealing the covered areas of the world map.

 Explore Stranglethorn Vale

Explore Stranglethorn Vale, revealing the covered areas of the world map.

 Explore Tirisfal Glades

Explore Tirisfal Glades, revealing the covered areas of the world map.

 Explore Swamp of Sorrows

Explore Swamp of Sorrows, revealing the covered areas of the world map.

 Explore Silverpine Forest

Explore Silverpine Forest, revealing the covered areas of the world map.

 Explore Westfall

Explore Westfall, revealing the covered areas of the world map.

 Explore Western Plaguelands

Explore Western Plaguelands, revealing the covered areas of the world map.

 Explore Wetlands

Explore Wetlands, revealing the covered areas of the world map.

 Explore Eastern Plaguelands

Explore Eastern Plaguelands, revealing the covered areas of the world map.

 Explore Ghostlands

Explore Ghostlands, revealing the covered areas of the world map.

 Explore Hillsbrad Foothills

Explore Hillsbrad Foothills, revealing the covered areas of the world map.

 Explore Eversong Woods

Explore Eversong Woods, revealing the covered areas of the world map.

 Explore The Hinterlands

Explore The Hinterlands, revealing the covered areas of the world map.

 Explore Isle of Quel'Danas

Explore Isle of Quel'Danas, revealing the covered areas of the world map.

 Explore Searing Gorge

Explore Searing Gorge, revealing the covered areas of the world map.

 Explore Burning Steppes

Explore Burning Steppes, revealing the covered areas of the world map.

 Explore Elwynn Forest

Explore Elwynn Forest, revealing the covered areas of the world map.

 Explore Deadwind Pass

Explore Deadwind Pass, revealing the covered areas of the world map.

 Explore Duskwood

Explore Duskwood, revealing the covered areas of the world map.

 Explore Loch Modan

Explore Loch Modan, revealing the covered areas of the world map.

 Explore Redridge Mountains

Explore Redridge Mountains, revealing the covered areas of the world map.

KALIMDOR

 10 *Explore Durotar*

Explore Durotar, revealing the covered areas of the world map.

 10 *Explore Mulgore*

Explore Mulgore, revealing the covered areas of the world map.

 10 *Explore The Barrens*

Explore The Barrens, revealing the covered areas of the world map.

 10 *Explore Teldrassil*

Explore Teldrassil, revealing the covered areas of the world map.

 10 *Explore Darkshore*

Explore Darkshore, revealing the covered areas of the world map.

 10 *Explore Ashenvale*

Explore Ashenvale, revealing the covered areas of the world map.

 10 *Explore Thousand Needles*

Explore Thousand Needles, revealing the covered areas of the world map.

 10 *Explore Stonetalon Mountains*

Explore Stonetalon Mountains, revealing the covered areas of the world map.

 10 *Explore Desolace*

Explore Desolace, revealing the covered areas of the world map.

 10 *Explore Feralas*

Explore Feralas, revealing the covered areas of the world map.

 10 *Explore Dustwallow Marsh*

Explore Dustwallow Marsh, revealing the covered areas of the world map.

 10 *Explore Tanaris Desert*

Explore Tanaris Desert, revealing the covered areas of the world map.

 10 *Explore Azshara*

Explore Azshara, revealing the covered areas of the world map.

 10 *Explore Felwood*

Explore Felwood, revealing the covered areas of the world map.

 10 *Explore Un'Goro Crater*

Explore Un'Goro Crater, revealing the covered areas of the world map.

 10 *Explore Moonglade*

Explore Moonglade, revealing the covered areas of the world map.

 10 *Explore Silithus*

Explore Silithus, revealing the covered areas of the world map.

 10 *Explore Winterspring*

Explore Winterspring, revealing the covered areas of the world map.

 10 *Explore Azuremyst Isle*

Explore Azuremyst Isle, revealing the covered areas of the world map.

 10 *Explore Bloodmyst Isle*

Explore Bloodmyst Isle, revealing the covered areas of the world map.

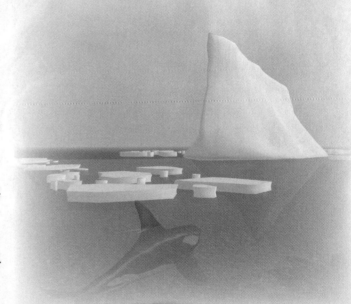

NORTHREND

 10 *Explore Howling Fjord*

Explore Howling Fjord, revealing the covered areas of the world map.

 10 *Explore Borean Tundra*

Explore Borean Tundra, revealing the covered areas of the world map.

Explore Dragonblight

Explore Dragonblight, revealing the covered areas of the world map.

Explore Grizzly Hills

Explore Grizzly Hills, revealing the covered areas of the world map.

Explore Zul'Drak

Explore Zul'Drak, revealing the covered areas of the world map.

Explore Sholazar Basin

Explore Sholazar Basin, revealing the covered areas of the world map.

Explore Storm Peaks

Explore Storm Peaks, revealing the covered areas of the world map.

Explore Icecrown

Explore Icecrown, revealing the covered areas of the world map.

Explore Crystalsong Forest

Explore Crystalsong Forest, revealing the covered areas of the world map.

Northern Exposure

Kill one of the extremely rare and hard to find Northrend creatures.

Frostbitten

Kill all of the extremely rare and hard to find Northrend creatures.

OUTLAND

Explore Netherstorm

Explore Netherstorm, revealing the covered areas of the world map.

Explore Hellfire Peninsula

Explore Hellfire Peninsula, revealing the covered areas of the world map.

Explore Zangarmarsh

Explore Zangarmarsh, revealing the covered areas of the world map.

Explore Shadowmoon Valley

Explore Shadowmoon Valley, revealing the covered areas of the world map.

Explore Blade's Edge Mountains

Explore Blade's Edge Mountains, revealing the covered areas of the world map.

Explore Nagrand

Explore Nagrand, revealing the covered areas of the world map.

Explore Terokkar Forest

Explore Terokkar Forest, revealing the covered areas of the world map.

Medium Rare

Kill one of the extremely rare and hard to find Outland creatures.

Bloody Rare

Kill all of the extremely rare and hard to find Outland creatures.

Explore Eastern Kingdoms

Explore the regions of Eastern Kingdoms.

Explore Kalimdor

Explore the regions of Kalimdor.

Explore Outland

Explore the regions of Outland.

Explore Northrend

Explore the regions of Northrend.

World Explorer

Explore Eastern Kingdoms, Kalimdor, Outland and Northrend.

FEATS OF STRENGTH

 Murky
Proud owner of Murky from the 2005 BlizzCon in Anaheim, California.

 Murloc Costume
Proud owner of the Murloc Costume from the 2007 BlizzCon in Anaheim, California.

 Tyrael's Hilt
Proud owner of Tyrael's Hilt from the 2008 World Wide Invitational in Paris, France.

 Big Blizzard Bear
Proud owner of the Big Blizzard Bear from the 2008 BlizzCon.

 Scarab Lord
Opened the gates of Ahn'Qiraj.

 Merciless Gladiator
Achieved Merciless Gladiator title.

 Vengeful Gladiator
Achieved Vengeful Gladiator title.

 Brutal Gladiator
Achieved Brutal Gladiator title.

 Why? Because It's Red
Obtain a Red Qiraji Resonating Crystal.

 Atiesh, Greatstaff of the Guardian
Completed the quest to obtain Atiesh, Greatstaff of the Guardian.

 Warglaives of Azzinoth
Owner of a set of Warglaives of Azzinoth.

 Thunderfury, Blessed Blade of the Windseeker
Completed the quest to obtain Thunderfury, Blessed Blade of the Windseeker.

 Sulfuras, Hand of Ragnaros
Owner of Sulfuras, Hand of Ragnaros.

Amani War Bear
Owner of Amani War Bear.

 Hand of A'dal
Earned the title, "Hand of A'dal".

 Champion of the Naaru
Earned the title, "Champion of the Naaru".

 Grand Marshal
Earned the title, "Grand Marshal".

 Field Marshal
Earned the title, "Field Marshal".

 Commander
Earned the title, "Commander".

 Lieutenant Commander
Earned the title, "Lieutenant Commander".

 Knight-Champion
Earned the title, "Knight-Champion".

 Knight-Captain
Earned the title, "Knight-Captain".

 Knight
Earned the title, "Knight".

 Sergeant Major
Earned the title, "Sergeant Major".

 Master Sergeant
Earned the title, "Master Sergeant".

 Private
Earned the title, "Private".

 High Warlord
Earned the title, "High Warlord".

 Lieutenant
Earned the title, "Lieutenant General".

Warlord
Earned the title, "Warlord".

General
Earned the title, "General".

Champion
Earned the title, "Champion".

Centurion
Earned the title, "Centurion".

Blood Guard
Earned the title, "Blood Guard".

Senior Sergeant
Earned the title, "Senior Sergeant".

Stone Guard
Earned the title, "Stone Guard".

First Sergeant
Earned the title, "First Sergeant".

Sergeant
Earned the title, "Sergeant".

Scout
Earned the title, "Scout".

Realm First! Obsidian Slayer
Participated in the realm first defeat of Sartharion the Onyx Guardian on Heroic Difficulty.

Realm First! Level 80
First person on the realm to achieve level 80.

Realm First! Level 80 Rogue
First rogue on the realm to achieve level 80.

Realm First! Level 80 Warrior
First warrior on the realm to achieve level 80.

Realm First! Level 80 Mage
First mage on the realm to achieve level 80.

Realm First! Level 80 Death Knight
First death knight on the realm to achieve level 80.

Realm First! Level 80 Hunter
First hunter on the realm to achieve level 80.

Realm First! Level 80 Warlock
First warlock on the realm to achieve level 80.

Realm First! Level 80 Priest
First priest on the realm to achieve level 80.

Realm First! Level 80 Paladin
First paladin on the realm to achieve level 80.

Realm First! Level 80 Druid
First druid on the realm to achieve level 80.

Realm First! Level 80 Shaman
First shaman on the realm to achieve level 80.

Grunt
Earned the title, "Grunt".

Legionnaire
Earned the title, "Legionnaire".

Corporal
Earned the title, "Corporal".

Sergeant
Earned the title, "Sergeant".

Knight-Lieutenant
Earned the title, "Knight-Lieutenant".

Marshal
Earned the title, "Marshal".

319

Collector's Edition: Mini-Diablo
Owner of the World of Warcraft Collector's Edition Mini-Diablo pet.

Collector's Edition: Panda
Owner of the World of Warcraft Collector's Edition Panda pet.

Collector's Edition: Zergling
Owner of the World of Warcraft Collector's Edition Zergling pet.

Collector's Edition: Netherwhelp
Owner of the The Burning Crusade's Collector's Edition Netherwhelp pet.

Collector's Edition: Frost Wyrm Whelp
Owner of the Wrath of the Lich King's Collector's Edition Frost Wyrm Whelp pet.

Thori'dal, the Stars' Fury
Owner of Thori'dal, the Stars' Fury.

Deathcharger's Reins
Obtain the Deathcharger's Reins from Baron Rivendare in Stratholme.

Avast Ye, Admiral!
Obtain the Bloodsail Admiral's Hat... and try to get some fresh air every now and then.

Old School Ride
Owner of one of the original epic mounts that are no longer attainable.

Swift Zulian Tiger
Obtain the Swift Zulian Tiger from High Priest Thekal in Zul'Gurub.

Swift Razzashi Raptor
Obtain the Swift Razzashi Raptor from Bloodlord Mandokir in Zul'Gurub.

Fiery Warhorse's Reins
Obtain the Fiery Warhorse's Reins from Attumen the Huntsman in Karazhan.

Reins of the Raven Lord
Obtain the Reins of the Raven Lord from Anzu in Sethekk Halls.

Swift White Hawkstrider
Obtain the Swift White Hawkstrider from Kael'thas Sunstrider in Magister's Terrace.

Ashes of Al'ar
Obtain the Ashes of Al'ar from Kael'thas Sunstrider in Tempest Keep.

Swift Nether Drake
Obtain the Swift Nether Drake from Arena Season 1 of The Burning Crusade.

Merciless Nether Drake
Obtain the Merciless Nether Drake from Arena Season 2 of The Burning Crusade.

Vengeful Nether Drake
Obtain the Merciless Nether Drake from Arena Season 3 of The Burning Crusade.

The Horseman's Reins
Obtain The Horseman's Reins from The Headless Horseman in the Scarlet Monastery during Hallow's End.

Hero of Shattrath
Gained exalted status with The Scryers and The Aldor.

Yellow Brewfest Stein
Proud owner of the 2007 Vintage Yellow Brewfest Stein.

Blue Brewfest Stein
Proud owner of the 2008 Vintage Blue Brewfest Stein.

Realm First! Magic Seeker
Participated in the realm first defeat of Malygos on Heroic Difficulty.

Realm First! Conqueror of Naxxramas
Participated in the realm first defeat of Kel'Thuzad on Heroic Difficulty in Naxxramas.

Realm First! Level 80 Gnome
First gnome on the realm to achieve level 80.

Realm First! Level 80 Blood Elf
First blood elf on the realm to achieve level 80.

Realm First! Level 80 Draenei
First draenei on the realm to achieve level 80.

Realm First! Level 80 Dwarf
First dwarf on the realm to achieve level 80.

Realm First! Level 80 Human
First human on the realm to achieve level 80.

 ### Realm First! Grand Master Scribe
First person on the realm to achieve 450 skill in inscription.

 ### Realm First! Level 80 Night Elf
First night elf on the realm to achieve level 80.

 ### Realm First! Grand Master Jewelcrafter
First person on the realm to achieve 450 skill in jewelcrafting.

 ### Realm First! Level 80 Orc
First orc on the realm to achieve level 80.

 ### Realm First! Grand Master Leatherworker
First person on the realm to achieve 450 skill in leatherworking.

 ### Realm First! Level 80 Tauren
First tauren on the realm to achieve level 80.

 ### Realm First! Grand Master Miner
First person on the realm to achieve 450 skill in mining.

 ### Realm First! Level 80 Troll
First troll on the realm to achieve level 80.

 ### Realm First! Grand Master Skinner
First person on the realm to achieve 450 skill in skinning.

 ### Realm First! Level 80 Forsaken
First forsaken on the realm to achieve level 80.

 ### Realm First! Grand Master Tailor
First person on the realm to achieve 450 skill in tailoring.

 ### Realm First! Grand Master Blacksmith
First person on the realm to achieve 450 skill in blacksmithing.

 ### Friends In High Places
Obtain a Zhevra mount through the Recruit-a-Friend program.

 ### Realm First! Grand Master Alchemist
First person on the realm to achieve 450 skill in alchemy.

 ### Realm First! Northrend Vanguard
First player on the realm to gain exalted reputation with the Argent Crusade, Wyrmrest Accord, Kirin Tor and Knights of the Ebon Blade.

 ### Realm First! Cooking Grand Master
First person on the realm to achieve 450 skill in cooking.

 ### Competitor's Tabard
Proud owner of a Competitor's Tabard from the 2008 Spirit of Competition event.

 ### Realm First! Grand Master Enchanter
First person on the realm to achieve 450 skill in enchanting.

 ### Spirit of Competition
Proud owner of a Spirit of Competition pet from the 2008 Spirit of Competition event.

 ### Realm First! Grand Master Engineer
First person on the realm to achieve 450 skill in engineering.

 ### Clockwork Rocket Bot
Proud owner of the 2007 Vintage Winter Veil gift, the Clockwork Rocket Bot.

 ### Realm First! First Aid Grand Master
First person on the realm to achieve 450 skill in first aid.

 ### Crashin' Thrashin' Racer
Proud owner of the 2008 Vintage Winter Veil gift, the Crashin' Thrashin' Racer.

 ### Realm First! Grand Master Angler
First person on the realm to achieve 450 skill in fishing.

 ### Tabard of the Protector
Obtained a Tabard of the Protector from the Dark Portal event.

 ### Realm First! Grand Master Herbalist
First person on the realm to achieve 450 skill in herbalism.

 ### Tabard of the Argent Dawn
Obtained a Tabard of the Argent Dawn from the Scourge Invasion event.

GENERAL

Level 10
Reach level 10.

Level 20
Reach level 20.

Level 30
Reach level 30.

Level 40
Reach level 40.

Level 50
Reach level 50.

Level 60
Reach level 60.

Level 70
Reach level 70.

Level 80
Reach level 80.

Plenty of Pets
Collect 15 unique vanity pets.

Did Somebody Order a Knuckle Sandwich?
Raise your unarmed skill to 400.

Shave and a Haircut
Visit a Barber Shop and get your hair cut.

Safe Deposit
Buy 7 additional bank slots.

Epic
Equip an epic item in every slot with a minimum item level of 213.

Superior
Equip a superior item in every slot with a minimum item level of 187.

Greedy
Win a greed roll on a superior or better item above level 185 by rolling 100.

Needy
Win a need roll on a superior or better item above level 185 by rolling 100.

Represent
Obtain a tabard.

Master of Arms
Raise four weapon skills to 400.

Fast and Furious
Learn the journeyman riding skill.

Into The Wild Blue Yonder
Learn the expert riding skill.

Giddy Up!
Learn the apprentice riding skill.

The Right Stuff
Learn the artisan riding skill.

Going Down?
Fall 65 yards without dying.

Can I Keep Him?
Obtain a vanity pet.

Ten Tabards
Collect 10 unique tabards.

Twenty-Five Tabards
Collect 25 unique tabards.

My Sack is "Gigantique"
Equip Haris Pilton's "Gigantique" Bag.

Got My Mind On My Money
Loot 100 gold.

Got My Mind On My Money

Loot 1,000 gold.

 Got My Mind On My Money

Loot 5,000 gold.

 Got My Mind On My Money

Loot 10,000 gold.

 Got My Mind On My Money

Loot 25,000 gold.

 The Keymaster

Obtain the keys listed below.

 To All The Squirrels I've Loved Before

Show the critters of Azeroth how much you /love them.

 Well Read

Read the books listed below.

 Plethora of Pets

Collect 25 unique vanity pets.

 Shop Smart, Shop Pet...Smart

Collect 50 unique vanity pets.

 Friend or Fowl?

Slay 15 turkeys in 3 minutes.

Tastes Like Chicken

Sample 50 different kinds of Azeroth's delectable dishes.

 It's Happy Hour Somewhere

Drink 25 different types of beverages

 Higher Learning

Read the volumes of "The Schools of Arcane Magic" found in Dalaran listed below.

 Armored Brown Bear

Obtain an Armored Brown Bear from Mei Francis in Dalaran.

 Wooly Mammoth

Obtain a Wooly Mammoth from Mei Francis in Dalaran.

 Traveler's Tundra Mammoth

Obtain a Traveler's Tundra Mammoth from Mei Francis in Dalaran.

 Ring of the Kirin Tor

Purchase a Signet of the Kirin Tor or Band of the Kirin Tor in Dalaran.

 Get to the Choppa!

Obtain a Mekgineer's Chopper or a Mechano-hog.

 Stable Keeper

Obtain 10 mounts.

 Filling Up The Barn

Obtain 25 mounts.

 Leading the Cavalry

Obtain 50 mounts.

PLAYER VS. PLAYER

ALTERAC VALLEY

Alterac Valley Victory
Win Alterac Valley.

Alterac Valley Veteran
Complete 100 victories in Alterac Valley.

Stormpike Perfection
Win Alterac Valley without losing a tower or captain. You must also control all of the Horde's towers.

Alterac Grave Robber
Take 50 graveyards in Alterac Valley.

Tower Defense
Defend 50 towers in Alterac Valley.

The Sickly Gazelle
In Alterac Valley, kill an enemy in the Field of Strife before they dismount.

Loyal Defender
In Alterac Valley, kill 50 enemy players in the Hall of the Frostwolf.

Everything Counts
Win Alterac Valley while your team controls both mines.

The Alterac Blitz
Win Alterac Valley in 6 minutes.

Alterac Valley All-Star
In a single Alterac Valley battle, assault a graveyard, defend a graveyard, assault a tower, defend a tower and slay someone in the Field of Strife.

Frostwolf Howler
Obtain a Frostwolf Howler.

Stormpike Battle Charger
Obtain a Stormpike Battle Charger.

Hero of the Frostwolf Clan
Gain exalted reputation with the Frostwolf Clan.

Hero of the Stormpike Guard
Gain exalted reputation with the Stormpike Guard.

Frostwolf Perfection
Win Alterac Valley without losing a tower or captain. You must also control all of the Alliance's towers.

Loyal Defender
In Alterac Valley, kill 50 enemy players in the Hall of the Stormpike.

Everything Counts
Win Alterac Valley while your team controls both mines.

To the Looter Go the Spoils
Loot the Autographed Picture of Foror & Tigule in Alterac Valley.

Master of Alterac Valley
Complete the Alterac Valley achievements listed.

ARATHI BASIN

Disgracin' The Basin

Assault 3 bases in a single Arathi Basin battle.

Arathi Basin Victory

Win Arathi Basin.

Arathi Basin Veteran

Complete 100 victories in Arathi Basin.

Territorial Dominance

Win 10 Arathi Basin matches while controlling all 5 flags.

To The Rescue!

Come to the defense of a base in Arathi Basin 50 times by recapping the flag.

Me and the Cappin' Makin' it Happen

Take 50 flags in Arathi Basin.

Let's Get This Done

Win Arathi Basin in 6 minutes.

Resilient Victory

Overcome a 500 resource disadvantage in a match of Arathi Basin and claim victory.

We Had It All Along *cough*

Win Arathi Basin by 10 points (2000 to 1990).

Arathi Basin Perfection

Win Arathi Basin with a score of 2000 to 0.

Arathi Basin All-Star

Assault and Defend 2 bases in a single Arathi Basin match.

Arathi Basin Assassin

Get five honorable kills at each of the bases in a single Arathi Basin battle.

The Defiler

Gain exalted reputation with The Forsaken Defilers.

Knight of Arathor

Gain exalted reputation with The League of Arathor.

Overly Defensive

Defend 3 bases in a single Arathi Basin battle.

Master of Arathi Basin

Complete the Arathi Basin achievements listed.

ARENA

Step Into The Arena

Win a ranked arena match at level 80.

Mercilessly Dedicated

Win 100 ranked arena matches at level 80.

Just the Two of Us: 1550

Earn a 1550 personal rating in the 2v2 bracket of the arena at level 80.

Just the Two of Us: 1750

Earn a 1750 personal rating in the 2v2 bracket of the arena at level 80.

Just the Two of Us: 2000

Earn a 2000 personal rating in the 2v2 bracket of the arena at level 80.

Three's Company: 1550

10 — Earn a 1550 personal rating in the 3v3 bracket of the arena at level 80.

Three's Company: 1750

10 — Earn a 1750 personal rating in the 3v3 bracket of the arena at level 80.

High Five: 2000

10 — Earn a 2000 personal rating in the 5v5 bracket of the arena at level 80.

Three's Company: 2000

10 — Earn a 2000 personal rating in the 3v3 bracket of the arena at level 80.

High Five: 1550

10 — Earn a 1550 personal rating in the 5v5 bracket of the arena at level 80.

High Five: 1750

10 — Earn a 1750 personal rating in the 5v5 bracket of the arena at level 80.

Hot Streak

10 — Win ten ranked matches in a row at level 80.

Last Man Standing

10 — Be the sole survivor at the end of a ranked 5v5 match at level 80.

World Wide Winner

10 — Win a ranked arena match in Blade's Edge, Nagrand, The Ring of Valor, Dalaran Sewers and the Ruins of Lordaeron at level 80.

Vengefully Dedicated

10 — Win 200 ranked arena matches at level 80.

Brutally Dedicated

10 — Win 300 ranked arena matches at level 80.

Death Touch

10 — Kill someone within 15 seconds of the start of an arena match at level 80.

Steamroller

10 — Win a 5v5 ranked arena match in 45 seconds or less at level 80.

Just the Two of Us: 2200

10 — Earn a 2200 personal rating in the 2v2 bracket of the arena at level 80.

Three's Company: 2200

10 — Earn a 2200 personal rating in the 3v3 bracket of the arena at level 80.

High Five: 2200

10 — Earn a 2200 personal rating in the 5v5 bracket of the arena at level 80.

Hotter Streak

10 — Win ten ranked matches in a row with a rating above 1800 at level 80.

Hot Hot Hot Streak

30 — Win ten ranked matches in a row with a rating above 2000 at level 80.

The Arena Master

50 — Complete the arena achievements listed.

Challenger

10 — Earn the Challenger title in an arena season at level 80.

Gladiator

10 — Earn the Gladiator title in an arena season at level 80.

Duelist

10 — Earn the Duelist title in an arena season at level 80.

Rival

10 — Earn the Rival title in an arena season at level 80.

EYE OF THE STORM

10 *Eye of the Storm Victory*
Win Eye of the Storm.

10 *Eye of the Storm Veteran*
Complete 100 victories in Eye of the Storm.

10 *Storm Glory*
While your team holds 4 of the bases in Eye of the Storm, personally grab the flag and capture it.

10 *Storm Capper*
Personally carry and capture the flag in Eye of the Storm.

10 *Stormtrooper*
Kill 5 flag carriers in a single Eye of the Storm battle.

10 *Flurry*
Win Eye of the Storm in under 6 minutes.

10 *Bound for Glory*
In a single Eye of the Storm match, capture the flag 3 times without dying.

10 *Bloodthirsty Berserker*
Get a killing blow while under the effects of the berserker buff in Eye of the Storm.

10 *Stormy Assassin*
In a single Eye of the Storm battle, get 5 honorable kills at each of the bases.

10 *The Perfect Storm*
Win Eye of the Storm with a score of 2000 to 0.

10 *Eye of the Storm Domination*
Win Eye of the Storm 10 times while holding 4 bases.

25 *Master of Eye of the Storm*
Complete the Eye of the Storm achievements listed.

10 *Take a Chill Pill*
In Eye of the Storm, kill a player who is under the effects of the Berserker power-up.

STRAND OF THE ANCIENTS

10 *Strand of the Ancients Victory*
Win Strand of the Ancients.

10 *Strand of the Ancients Veteran*
Complete 100 victories in Strand of the Ancients.

20 *Storm the Beach*
Win Strand of the Ancients in 6 minutes.

10 *Defense of the Ancients*
Defend the beach without losing any walls.

10 *The Dapper Sapper*
Plant 100 Seaforium charges which successfully damage a wall.

10 *Not Even a Scratch*
Win a Strand of the Ancients battle without losing any siege vehicles.

10 *Artillery Veteran*
Destroy 100 vehicles using a turret.

10 *Drop it!*
Kill 100 players carrying seaforium.

10 *Steady Hands*
Disarm 5 mines in a single battle.

10 *Ancient Protector*
Kill 10 players in the Courtyard of the Ancients in a single battle.

10 *Artillery Expert*
Destroy 5 vehicles using a turret in a single battle.

10 *Drop it now!*
Kill 5 players carrying seaforium in a single battle.

10 *Ancient Courtyard Protector*
Kill 100 players in the Courtyard of the Ancients.

10 *Not Even a Scratch*
Win a Strand of the Ancients battle without losing any siege vehicles.

Explosives Expert 10

Plant 5 Seaforium charges which successfully damage a wall in a single battle.

 Master of Strand of the Ancients 25

Complete the Strand of the Ancients achievements listed.

 Defense of the Ancients 10

Defend the beach without losing any walls.

WARSONG GULCH

 Warsong Gulch Victory 10

Win Warsong Gulch.

 Warsong Gulch Veteran 10

Complete 100 victories in Warsong Gulch.

 Warsong Gulch Perfection 10

Win Warsong Gulch with a score of 3 to 0.

 Capture the Flag 10

Personally carry and capture the flag in Warsong Gulch.

 Persistent Defender 10

Return 50 flags as a defender in Warsong Gulch.

 Warsong Expedience 10

Win Warsong Gulch in under 7 minutes.

 Quick Cap 10

Grab the flag and capture it under 75 seconds.

 Not In My House 10

In a single Warsong Gulch battle, kill 10 flag carriers before they leave the Silverwing Flag Room.

 Ironman 10

In a single Warsong Gulch battle, carry and capture the flag 3 times without dying.

 Supreme Defender 10

Kill 100 flag carriers in Warsong Gulch.

 Save The Day 10

Kill the enemy who is carrying your flag in the opposing team's flag room while the opposing team's flag is at their base, within their control.

 Warsong Outrider 10

Gain exalted reputation with the Warsong Outriders.

 Silverwing Sentinel 10

Gain exalted reputation with the Silverwing Sentinels.

 Frenzied Defender 10

Return 5 flags in a single Warsong Gulch battle.

 Master of Warsong Gulch 25

Complete the Warsong Gulch achievements listed.

 Not In My House 10

In a single Warsong Gulch battle, kill 10 flag carriers before they leave the Warsong Flag Room.

 Supreme Defender 10

Kill 100 flag carriers in Warsong Gulch.

 Not So Fast 10

In Warsong Gulch, kill a player who is under the effects of the speed power-up.

Quick Cap

Grab the flag and capture it under 75 seconds.

 Louder than Bombs

Drop a bomb on a player in Wintergrasp Fortress.

 Leaning Tower

Destroy a tower in Wintergrasp.

 Industrial Warfare

Destroy 20 siege workshops in Wintergrasp.

 Destruction Derby

Destroy each of the vehicles listed below.

 Against the Odds

Win Wintergrasp while having Tenacity.

 All Hail the Timely Bail

Bail out of a plane that has less than 5% health.

 Didn't Stand a Chance

Kill 20 mounted players using a tower cannon.

 Master of Wintergrasp

Complete the Wintergrasp achievements listed.

WINTERGRASP

 Wintergrasp Victory

Win the battle for Wintergrasp.

 Within Our Grasp

Attack Wintergrasp and succeed in 10 minutes or less.

 Wintergrasp Veteran

Win 100 battles for Wintergrasp.

 Black War Mammoth

Obtain a Black War Mammoth.

 Catch Air and Shred

Destroy a plane with a shredder in Wintergrasp.

 Grand Black War Mammoth

Obtain a Grand Black War Mammoth.

 Heroic: Archavon the Stone Watcher

Defeat Archavon the Stone Watcher on Heroic Difficulty.

 50 Stone Keeper's Shards

Obtain 50 Stone Keeper's Shards.

 Archavon the Stone Watcher

Defeat Archavon the Stone Watcher on Normal Difficulty.

 100 Stone Keeper's Shards

Obtain 100 Stone Keeper's Shards.

 Vehicular Gnomeslaughter

Kill 100 players in Wintergrasp using a vehicle or a cannon.

 250 Stone Keeper's Shards

Obtain 250 Stone Keeper's Shards.

500 Stone Keeper's Shards

Obtain 500 Stone Keeper's Shards.

 1000 Stone Keeper's Shards

Obtain 1000 Stone Keeper's Shards.

 Wintergrasp Ranger

Kill 10 players in each of the Wintergrasp areas listed below.

 Damage Control

Do 300,000 damage or healing in a single battle in any battleground.

 The Grim Reaper

Get 30 Honorable Kills in a single battle in any battleground.

 Battlemaster

Complete the battleground achievements listed.

 Wrecking Ball

Get 20 killing blows without dying in a single battle in any battleground.

 An Honorable Kill

Achieve an honorable kill.

 25000 Honorable Kills

Get 25000 honorable kills.

 That Takes Class

Get an honorable, killing blow on one of each class.

 Know Thy Enemy

Get an honorable, killing blow on five different races.

 Make Love, Not Warcraft

Emote /hug on a dead enemy before they release corpse.

 City Defender

Kill 50 enemy players in any of your home cities.

 Gurubashi Arena Master

Loot the Arena Master trinket from the Gurubashi Arena.

 Gurubashi Arena Grand Master

Complete Short John Mithril's quest to obtain the Arena Grand Master trinket.

 10000 Honorable Kills

Get 10000 honorable kills.

 5000 Honorable Kills

Get 5000 honorable kills.

 100 Honorable Kills

Get 100 honorable kills.

 500 Honorable Kills

Get 500 honorable kills.

 1000 Honorable Kills

Get 1000 honorable kills.

 Wrath of the Horde

Kill 5 Alliance players in each of the cities listed below.

 10 *Wrath of the Alliance*

Kill 5 Horde players in each of the cities.

 10 *Death to the Warchief!*

Kill Thrall.

 10 *Bleeding Bloodhoof*

Kill Cairne Bloodhoof.

 10 *Downing the Dark Lady*

Kill Lady Sylvanas Windrunner.

 10 *Killed in Quel'Thalas*

Kill Lor'themar Theron.

 20 *For The Alliance!*

Slay the leaders of the Horde.

 10 *Storming Stormwind*

Kill King Varian Wrynn.

 10 *Death to the King!*

Kill King Magni Bronzebeard.

 10 *Immortal No More*

Kill High Priestess Tyrande Whisperwind.

 10 *Putting Out the Light*

Kill Prophet Velen.

 20 *For The Horde!*

Slay the leaders of the Alliance.

 10 *Freedom of the Horde*

Obtain an Insignia or Medallion of the Horde.

 10 *Freedom of the Alliance*

Obtain an Insignia or Medallion of the Alliance.

 20 *The Conqueror*

Raise your reputation values in Warsong Gulch, Arathi Basin and Alterac Valley to Exalted.

 10 *Call in the Cavalry*

Obtain one of the war mounts through the honor system.

 10 *50000 Honorable Kills*

Get 50000 honorable kills.

 10 *100000 Honorable Kills*

Get 100000 honorable kills.

 20 *The Justicar*

Raise your reputation values in Warsong Gulch, Arathi Basin and Alterac Valley to Exalted.

 10 *Call to Arms!*

Complete each of the Call to Arms daily battleground quests.

 10 *Call to Arms!*

Complete each of the Call to Arms daily battleground quests.

 10 *Know Thy Enemy*

Get an honorable, killing blow on five different races.

City Defender

Kill 50 enemy players in any of your home cities.

 Duel-icious

Win a duel against another player.

 Battlemaster

Complete the battleground achievements listed.

 Grizzled Veteran

Complete the Grizzly Hills PvP daily quests.

 Grizzled Veteran

Complete the Grizzly Hills PvP daily quests.

PROFESSIONS

COOKING

 **Journeyman Cook**

Become a Journeyman Cook.

Expert Cook

Become an Expert Cook.

 Artisan Cook

Become an Artisan Cook.

 Master Cook

Become a Master Cook.

 Grand Master Cook

Become a Grand Master Cook.

 The Cake Is Not A Lie

Bake a Delicious Chocolate Cake.

 Kickin' It Up a Notch

Complete each of The Rokk's 4 cooking daily quests.

 Hail to the Chef

Complete the cooking achievements listed.

 The Northrend Gourmet

Cook 15 of the Northrend recipes.

 The Northrend Gourmet

Cook 30 of the Northrend recipes.

 The Northrend Gourmet

Cook 45 of the Northrend recipes.

 Second That Emotion

Eat each one of the "emotion" foods.

 Critter Gitter

Using Critter Bites, coerce 10 critters to be your pet within 3 minutes or less.

 Our Daily Bread

Complete each of the cooking daily quests offered by Katherine Lee in Dalaran.

 Our Daily Bread

Complete each of the cooking daily quests offered by Awilo Lon'gomba in Dalaran.

 Hail to the Chef

Complete the cooking achievements listed.

Dinner Impossible

Present a Great Feast in each of the battlegrounds.

 Lunch Lady

Learn 25 cooking recipes.

 Short Order Cook

Learn 50 cooking recipes.

 Chef de Partie

Learn 75 cooking recipes.

 Sous Chef

Learn 100 cooking recipes.

 Chef de Cuisine

Learn 160 cooking recipes.

 The Outland Gourmet

Cook each of the Outland cooking recipes.

 Captain Rumsey's Lager

Brew up some of Captain Rumsey's Lager.

 Dalaran Cooking Award

Obtain a Dalaran Cooking Award.

 10 Dalaran Cooking Awards

Obtain 10 Dalaran Cooking Awards.

 25 Dalaran Cooking Awards

Obtain 25 Dalaran Cooking Awards.

 50 Dalaran Cooking Awards

Obtain 50 Dalaran Cooking Awards.

 100 Dalaran Cooking Awards

Obtain 100 Dalaran Cooking Awards.

First Aid

 Journeyman in First Aid

Become a Journeyman in first aid.

 Expert in First Aid

Become an Expert in first aid.

 Artisan in First Aid

Become an Artisan in first aid.

 Master in First Aid

Become a Master in first aid.

 Grand Master in First Aid

Become a Grand Master in first aid.

 Stocking Up

Create 500 Heavy Frostweave Bandages.

 Ultimate Triage

Use a Heavy Frostweave Bandage to heal another player or yourself with less than 5% health.

FISHING

10 Journeyman Fisherman
Become a Journeyman Fisherman.

10 Expert Fisherman
Become an Expert Fisherman.

10 Artisan Fisherman
Become an Artisan Fisherman.

10 Master Fisherman
Become a Master Fisherman.

10 Grand Master Fisherman
Become a Grand Master Fisherman.

10 The Lurker Above
Fish up The Lurker Below in Serpentshrine Cavern.

10 The Fishing Diplomat
Fish something up in Orgrimmar and Stormwind.

10 The Old Gnome and the Sea
Successfully fish from a school.

20 Master Angler of Stranglethorn
Win the Booty Bay fishing contest.

10 Deadliest Catch
Fish up Gahz'ranka in Zul'Gurub using the Mudskunk Lure.

10 Mr. Pinchy's Magical Crawdad Box
Fish your way to Mr. Pinchy's Magical Crawdad Box.

10 One That Didn't Get Away
Catch one of the rare fish in the list below.

10 Old Man Barlowned
Complete each of Old Man Barlo's 5 fishing daily quests listed below.

10 Outland Angler
Catch a fish in each of the specific nodes listed below.

10 Fish Don't Leave Footprints
Learn the ability to find fish.

10 The Scavenger
Successfully fish in each of the junk nodes listed below.

10 Accomplished Angler
Complete the fishing achievements listed.

10 Northrend Angler
Catch a fish in each of the specific nodes listed below.

10 25 Fish
Catch 25 fish.

10 50 Fish
Catch 50 fish.

10 100 Fish
Catch 100 fish.

10 250 Fish
Catch 250 fish.

10 500 Fish
Catch 500 fish.

10 1000 Fish
Catch 1000 fish.

10 Old Crafty
Fish up Old Crafty in Orgrimmar.

10 Old Ironjaw
Fish up Old Ironjaw in Ironforge.

10 There's Gold In That There Fountain
Fish up the gold coins listed below from the Dalaran fountain.

10 I Smell A Giant Rat
Fish up the Giant Sewer Rat from The Underbelly in Dalaran.

QUESTS

CLASSIC

The Green Hills of Stranglethorn

Complete all of Hemet Nesingwary quests in Stranglethorn Vale up to and including The Green Hills of Stranglethorn and Big Game Hunter.

Loremaster of Eastern Kingdoms

Complete 740 quests in Eastern Kingdoms.

Loremaster of Kalimdor

Complete 765 quests in Kalimdor.

A Penny For Your Thoughts

Fish up the copper coins listed below from the Dalaran fountain.

Silver in the City

Fish up the silver coins listed below from the Dalaran fountain.

The Coin Master

Complete the coin fishing achievements listed.

Professional Journeyman

Become a Journeyman in a profession.

Skills to Pay the Bills

Become a Grand Master in fishing, first aid and cooking.

Professional Expert

Become an Expert in a profession.

Professional Artisan

Become an Artisan in a profession.

Professional Master

Become a Master in a profession.

Professional Grand Master

Become a Grand Master in a profession.

Working Day and Night

Become a Grand Master in two professions.

THE BURNING CRUSADE

Loremaster of Outland

Complete the Outland quest achievements listed.

Hills Like White Elekk

Complete all of Hemet Nesingwary quests in Nagrand up to and including The Ultimate Bloodsport.

10 *To Hellfire and Back*

Complete 80 quests in Hellfire Peninsula.

10 *Mysteries of the Marsh*

Complete 54 quests in Zangarmarsh.

10 *Terror of Terokkar*

Complete 63 quests in Terokkar Forest.

10 *Nagrand Slam*

Complete 75 quests in Nagrand.

10 *On the Blade's Edge*

Complete 86 quests in Blade's Edge Mountains.

10 *Into the Nether*

Complete 120 quests in Netherstorm.

10 *Shadow of the Betrayer*

Complete 90 quests in Shadowmoon Valley.

10 *To Hellfire and Back*

Complete 90 quests in Hellfire Peninsula.

10 *Terror of Terokkar*

Complete 68 quests in Terokkar Forest.

10 *Nagrand Slam*

Complete 87 quests in Nagrand.

10 *Bombs Away*

Complete the Fires Over Skettis quest in under 2 minutes 15 seconds while not in a group.

10 *Blade's Edge Bomberman*

Complete the Bomb Them Again! quest in under 2 minutes 15 seconds while not in a group.

WRATH OF THE LICH KING

10 *Loremaster of Northrend*

Complete the Northrend quest achievements listed.

10 *Nothing Boring About Borean*

Complete 130 quests in Borean Tundra.

10 *I've Toured the Fjord*

Complete 130 quests in Howling Fjord.

10 *Might of Dragonblight*

Complete 115 quests in Dragonblight.

10 *The Empire of Zul'Drak*

Complete 100 quests in Zul'Drak.

10 *Fo' Grizzle My Shizzle*

Complete 85 quests in Grizzly Hills.

10 *The Summit of Storm Peaks*

Complete 100 quests in Storm Peaks.

10 *Into the Basin*

Complete 75 quests in Sholazar Basin.

10 *Icecrown: The Final Goal*

Complete 140 quests in Icecrown.

10 *Veteran of the Wrathgate*

Complete the Dragonblight quests leading up to and including the Return to Angrathar.

D.E.H.T.A's Little P.I.T.A.
10
Uphold D.E.H.T.A's beliefs by completing all of the quests up to and including the Assassination of Harold Lane.

 The Snows of
10
Complete all of Hemet Nesingwary quests in Northrend up to and including Post-partum Aggression.

 Honorary Frenzyheart
10
Complete the 8 daily quests for the Frenzyheart.

 Savior of the Oracles
10
Complete the 8 daily quests for the Oracles.

 Rapid Defense
10
Complete the Defending Wyrmrest Temple quest in under 2 minutes while not in a group.

 I've Toured the Fjord
10
Complete 105 quests in Howling Fjord.

 Fo' Grizzle My Shizzle
10
Complete 75 quests in Grizzly Hills.

 Nothing Boring About Borean
10
Complete 150 quests in Borean Tundra.

 Might of Dragonblight
10
Complete 130 quests in Dragonblight.

 Mine Sweeper
10
Get caught in 10 consecutive land mine explosions in the Sparksocket Minefield without landing.

 Guru of Drakuru
10
Complete the main storyline quests involving Drakuru.

 A Simple Re-Quest
10
Complete a daily quest every day for five consecutive days.

 2000 Quests Completed
10
Complete 2000 quests.

 50 Quests Completed
10
Complete 50 quests.

 100 Quests Completed
10
Complete 100 quests.

 250 Quests Completed
10
Complete 250 quests.

 500 Quests Completed
10
Complete 500 quests.

 1000 Quests Completed
10
Complete 1000 quests.

 1500 Quests Completed
10
Complete 1500 quests.

 Hemet Nesingwary: The Collected
10
Complete the Green Hills of Stranglethorn, Hills Like White Elekk and Snows of Northrend achievements.

 5 Daily Quests Complete
10
Complete 5 daily quests.

 50 Daily Quests Complete
10
Complete 50 daily quests.

 200 Daily Quests Complete
10
Complete 200 daily quests.

 500 Daily Quests Complete
10
Complete 500 daily quests.

 1000 Daily Quests Complete
10
Complete 1000 daily quests.

 3000 Quests Completed
50
Complete 3000 quests.

 The Bread Winner
10
Make 10,000 gold from quest rewards.

Of Blood and Anguish
Complete the Ring of Blood quests in Nagrand and the Ampitheater of Anguish quests in Zul'Drak.

The Loremaster
Complete the quest achievements listed.

The Loremaster
Complete the quest achievements listed.

REPUTATION

CLASSIC

They Love Me In That Tunnel
Earn exalted status with Timbermaw Hold.

The Argent Dawn
Earn exalted status with the Argent Dawn.

Hydraxian Waterlords
Earn exalted status with the Hydraxian Waterlords.

Brood of Nozdormu
Earn exalted status with the Brood of Nozdormu.

Hero of the Zandalar Tribe
Earn exalted status with the Zandalar Tribe.

THE BURNING CRUSADE

The Burning Crusader
Raise all of The Burning Crusade dungeon reputations to exalted.

The Burning Crusader
Raise all of The Burning Crusade dungeon reputations to exalted.

Cenarion War Hippogryph
Obtain the Cenarion War Hippogryph from the Cenarion Expedition in Zangarmarsh.

Flying High Over Skettis
Earn exalted status within the Sha'tari Skyguard.

A Quest a Day Keeps the Ogres at Bay
Earn exalted status within Ogri'la.

You're So Offensive
Earn exalted status with the Shattered Sun Offensive.

On Wings of Nether
Earn exalted status with Netherwing.

Oh My, Kurenai
Earn exalted status with the Kurenai.

The Czar of Sporeggar
Earn exalted status with Sporeggar.

Mag'har of Draenor
Earn exalted status with The Mag'har.

Chief Exalted Officer
Earn exalted status with The Consortium.

Shattrath Divided
Earn exalted status with The Scryers or The Aldor.

Sworn to the Deathsworn
Earn exalted status with the Ashtongue Deathsworn.

The Scale of the Sands
Earn exalted status with The Scale of the Sands.

The Violet Eye

Earn exalted status with The Violet Eye.

Skyshattered

Defeat Captain Skyshatter in the Dragonmaw race on Netherwing Ledge.

WRATH OF THE LICH KING

The Argent Crusade

Earn exalted status with the Argent Crusade.

Tuskarrmageddon

Earn exalted status with The Kalu'ak .

Frenzyheart Tribe

Earn exalted status with the Frenzyheart Tribe.

The Oracles

Earn exalted status with the The Oracles.

Mercenary of Sholazar

Earn exalted status with the The Oracles and the Frenzyheart Tribe.

The Wyrmrest Accord

Earn exalted status with The Wyrmrest Accord.

The Kirin Tor

Earn exalted status with The Kirin Tor.

Knights of the Ebon Blade

Earn exalted status with the Knights of the Ebon Blade.

Northrend Vanguard

Gain exalted reputation with the Argent Crusade, Wyrmrest Accord, Kirin Tor and Knights of the Ebon Blade.

The Winds of the North

Gain exalted reputation with Warsong Offensive, The Hand of Vengeance and The Taunka.

The Winds of the North

Gain exalted reputation with Valiance Expedition, Explorers' League and The Silver Covenant.

Ice Mammoth

Obtain a Ice Mammoth.

Grand Ice Mammoth

Obtain a Grand Ice Mammoth.

30 Exalted Reputations

Raise 30 reputations to Exalted.

25 Exalted Reputations

Raise 25 reputations to Exalted.

20 Exalted Reputations

Raise 20 reputations to Exalted.

15 Exalted Reputations

Raise 15 reputations to Exalted.

Somebody Likes Me

Raise a reputation to Exalted.

5 Exalted Reputations

Raise 5 reputations to Exalted.

10 Exalted Reputations

Raise 10 reputations to Exalted.

Ambassador of the Horde — 10

Earn exalted reputation with 5 home cities.

The Diplomat — 25

Raise your reputation level from unfriendly to exalted with Timbermaw Hold, Sporeggar and the Kurenai.

The Diplomat — 25

Raise your reputation level from unfriendly to exalted with Timbermaw Hold, Sporeggar and The Mag'har.

The Argent Champion — 25

Earn exalted status with the Argent Dawn and the Argent Crusade.

Ambassador of the Alliance — 10

Earn exalted reputation with 5 home cities.

Guardian of Cenarius — 25

Earn exalted status with the Cenarion Circle and Cenarion Expedition.

35 Exalted Reputations — 10

Raise 35 reputations to Exalted.

40 Exalted Reputations — 10

Raise 40 reputations to Exalted.

WORLD EVENTS

BREWFEST

Disturbing the Peace — 10

While wearing 3 pieces of Brewfest clothing, get completely smashed and dance in Dalaran.

Dire — 10

Kill Coren Direbrew.

Have Keg, Will Travel — 10

Obtain a brewfest mount.

Brew of the Year — 20

Sample 12 beers featured in the Brew of the Month club.

Strange Brew — 10

Drink the Brewfest beers.

The Brewfest Diet — 10

Eat 8 of the Brewfest foods.

Down With The Dark Iron — 10

Defend the Brewfest camp from the Dark Iron attack and complete the quest, "This One Time, When I Was Drunk…"

Strange Brew — 10

Drink the Brewfest beers.

Drunken Stupor — 10

Fall 65 yards without dying while completely smashed during the Brewfest Holiday.

Does Your Wolpertinger Linger? — 10

Obtain a Wolpertinger pet.

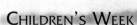

CHILDREN'S WEEK

Veteran Nanny — 50

Acquire Egbert's Egg, Sleepy Willy, and Elekk Training Collar on one character.

School of Hard Knocks — 10

Take your orphan into the battlegrounds and complete the feats.

 Out With It

10 Eat so many Tricky Treats that you get an upset tummy.

 The Savior of

10 Complete one of the quests to save a village from the Headless Horseman.

 Check Your Head

10 Use Weighted Jack-o'-Lanterns to put pumpkin heads on each of the races listed below.

 Sinister Calling

10 Obtain a Sinister Squashling pet and Hallowed Helm.

 Tricks and Treats of Kalimdor

10 Visit the Candy Buckets in Kalimdor.

 Tricks and Treats of Eastern Kingdoms

10 Visit the Candy Buckets in Eastern Kingdoms.

Tricks and Treats of Outland

10 Visit the Candy Buckets in Outland.

 Once An Orphan...

10 Kill 10 enemy players who have an orphan with them.

 Bad Example

10 Eat the sweets listed below while your orphan is watching.

 Daily Chores

10 Complete a daily quest every day for five consecutive days with your orphan out.

 Hail To The King, Baby

10 Defeat King Ymiron in Utgarde Pinnacle with your orphan out.

 Home Alone

10 Use your Hearthstone while your orphan is with you.

 Aw, Isn't It Cute?

10 Obtain one of the Children's Week reward pets.

HALLOW'S END

 Bring Me The Head of... Oh Wait

10 Kill the Headless Horseman.

The Masquerade

10 Get transformed by the Hallowed Wands.

 A Mask for All Occasions

20 Collect the 20 unique Flimsy Masks.

20 ## Tricks and Treats of Azeroth
Complete the Kalimdor, Eastern Kingdoms and Outland Tricks and Treats achievements.

 10 ## Trick or Treat!
Receive a handful of a candy from one of the Candy Buckets located in an inn.

 10 ## The Mask Task
Obtain a Flimsy Mask during Hallow's End.

 10 ## That Sparkling Smile
Show off your sparkling smile by using a Tooth Pick.

 10 ## Rotten Hallow
Ruin Hallow's End for the Horde by completing Sergeant Hartman's quests which involve crashing the wickerman festival and cleaning up the stinkbombs from Southshore.

 10 ## Rotten Hallow
Ruin Hallow's End for the Alliance by completing Darkcaller Yanka's quests which involve going to Southshore, ruining the kegs with rotten eggs and tossing stinkbombs into the town.

 10 ## G.N.E.R.D. Rage
Earn 50 honorable kills while under the influence of the G.N.E.R.D. buff. It's a slap in the face!

LOVE IS IN THE AIR

 10 ## Heartmender
Mend 20 broken hearts with Unbestowed Friendship Bracelets.

 10 ## Shafted!
Shoot 10 players with the Silver Shafted Arrow.

 10 ## Flirt With Disaster
Get completely smashed, put on your best perfume, throw a handful of rose petals on Sraaz and then kiss him. You'll regret it in the morning.

 10 ## Flirt With Disaster
Get completely smashed, put on your best perfume, throw a handful of rose petals on Jeremiah Payson and then kiss him. You'll regret it in the morning.

 10 ## Lonely?
Join someone in Dalaran at their Romantic Picnic during the Love is in the Air celebration.

 10 ## Lovely Luck Is On Your Side
Open a Gift of Adoration and receive a Lovely Black Dress.

 10 ## Nearest and Dearest
Complete the Love is in the Air storyline quest beginning with Dearest Colara or Dearest Elenia.

 10 ## The Rocket's Pink Glare
Shoot off 10 Love Rockets in 20 seconds or less.

 10 ## Nation of Adoration
Obtain a Gift of Adoration from each of the cities listed below.

 10 ## Nation of Adoration
Obtain a Gift of Adoration from each of the cities listed below.

 10 ## Fistful of Love
Use a Handful of Rose Petals on each of the race/class combinations listed below.

 10 ## Perma-Peddle
Obtain a permanent Peddlefeet pet by procuring a Truesilver Shafted Arrow.

 10 ## Be Mine!
Use the Bag of Candies to create each of the hearts listed below.

 10 ## Sweet Tooth
Sample the Love is in the Air candies listed below.

 10 ## My Love is Like a Red, Red Rose
Obtain a Bouquet of Red Roses during the Love is in the Air celebration.

 10 ## I Pitied The Fool
Pity the Love Fool in the locations specified below.

LUNAR FESTIVAL

A Coin of Ancestry

Receive a Coin of Ancestry.

5 Coins of Ancestry

Receive 5 Coins of Ancestry.

10 Coins of Ancestry

Receive 10 Coins of Ancestry.

25 Coins of Ancestry

Receive 25 Coins of Ancestry.

50 Coins of Ancestry

Receive 50 Coins of Ancestry.

Lunar Festival Finery

Purchase a festive pant suit or festive dress with Coins of Ancestry.

Elders of the Dungeons

Honor the Elders which are located inside the dungeons.

Elders of Kalimdor

Honor the Elders which are located in Kalimdor.

Elders of Eastern Kingdoms

Honor the Elders which are located in Eastern Kingdoms

Elders of the Horde

Honor the Elders which are located in the Horde capital cities.

Elders of the Alliance

Honor the Elders which are located in the Alliance capital cities.

Elune's Blessing

Complete the Elune's Blessing quest by defeating Omen.

The Rocket's Red Glare

Shoot off 10 Red Rocket Clusters in 25 seconds or less.

Elders of Northrend

Honor the Elders which are located in Northrend.

Frenzied Firecracker

Shoot off 10 Festival Firecrackers in 30 seconds or less.

MIDSUMMER

Ice the Frost Lord

Slay Ahune in the Slave Pens.

Burning Hot Pole Dance

Dance at the ribbon pole for 60 seconds while wearing completed Midsummer set.

Torch Juggler

Juggle 40 torches in 15 seconds in Dalaran.

Flame Warden of Eastern Kingdoms
Honor the flames of Eastern Kingdoms.

Flame Warden of Kalimdor
Honor the flames of Kalimdor.

Flame Warden of Outland
Honor the flames of Outland.

Flame Keeper of Eastern Kingdoms
Honor the flames of Eastern Kingdoms.

Flame Keeper of Kalimdor
Honor the flames of Kalimdor.

Flame Keeper of Outland
Honor the flames of Outland.

Extinguishing Eastern Kingdoms
Desecrate the Horde's bonfires in Eastern Kingdoms.

Extinguishing Kalimdor
Desecrate the Horde's bonfires in Kalimdor.

Extinguishing Outland
Desecrate the Horde's bonfires in Outland.

Extinguishing Eastern Kingdoms (Alliance)
Desecrate the Alliance's bonfires in Eastern Kingdoms.

Extinguishing Kalimdor (Alliance)
Desecrate the Alliance's bonfires in Kalimdor.

Extinguishing Outland (Alliance)
Desecrate the Alliance's bonfires in Outland.

The Fires of Azeroth
Complete the Flame Warden of Eastern Kingdoms, Kalimdor and Outland achievements.

Desecration of the Horde
Complete the Extinguishing Eastern Kingdoms, Kalimdor and Outland achievements.

The Fires of Azeroth
Complete the Flame Keeper of Eastern Kingdoms, Kalimdor and Outland achievements.

Desecration of the Alliance
Complete the Extinguishing Eastern Kingdoms, Kalimdor and Outland achievements.

King of the Fire Festival
Complete the quest, "A Thief's Reward", by stealing the flames from your enemy's capital cities.

Noble Garden

Sunday's Finest
Discover the White Tuxedo Shirt and Black Tuxedo Pants by opening Brightly Colored Eggs during the Noble Garden celebration.

Dressed for the Occasion
Discover an Elegant Dress by opening Brightly Colored Eggs during the Noble Garden celebration.

Winter Veil

 With a Little Helper from My Friends [10]
Earn 50 honorable kills as a Little Helper from the Winter Wondervolt machine.

 Scrooge [10]
Throw a snowball at Cairne Bloodhoof during the Feast of Winter Veil.

 On Metzen! [10]
Save Metzen the Reindeer.

 'Tis the Season [10]
During the Feast of Winter Veil, wear 3 pieces of winter clothing and eat Graccu's Mince Meat Fruitcake.

 Simply Abominable [10]
Complete the quest to retrieve the stolen Smokywood Pastures' stolen treats and receive a Smokywood Pastures' Thank You.

 Scrooge [10]
Throw a snowball at King Magni Bronzebeard during the Feast of Winter Veil.

 Fa-la-la-la-Ogri'la [10]
Complete the Bomb Them Again! quest while mounted on a flying reindeer during the Feast of Winter Veil.

 Crashin' & Thrashin' [10]
Gain 25 crashes with your Crashin' Thrashin' Racer during the Feast of Winter Veil.

 Bros. Before Ho Ho Ho's [10]
Use Mistletoe on the Horde "Brothers" during the Feast of Winter Veil.

 Bros. Before Ho Ho Ho's [10]
Use Mistletoe on the Alliance "Brothers" during the Feast of Winter Veil.

 Let It Snow [10]
During the Feast of Winter Veil, use a Handful of Snowflakes on each of the race/class combinations listed below.

 The Winter Veil Gourmet [10]
During the Feast of Winter Veil, use your culinary expertise to produce a Gingerbread Cookie, Egg Nog and Hot Apple Cider.

 He Knows If You've Been Naughty [10]
Open one of the presents underneath the Winter Veil tree once they are available.

A Frosty Shake [10]
During the Feast of Winter Veil, use your Winter Veil Disguise kit to become a snowman and then dance with another snowman in Dalaran.

 To Honor One's Elders [30]
Complete the Lunar Festival achievements listed.

 The Flame Warden [20]
Complete the Midsummer achievements listed.

 The Flame Keeper [20]
Complete the Midsummer achievements listed.

 Hallowed Be Thy Name [10]
Complete the Hallow's End achievements listed.

 Hallowed Be Thy Name [10]
Complete the Hallow's End achievements listed.

 Brewmaster [10]
Complete the Brewfest achievements listed.

 Brewmaster [10]
Complete the Brewfest achievements listed.

 Merrymaker [10]
Complete the Winter Veil achievements listed.

 Merrymaker [10]
Complete the Winter Veil achievements listed.

 Fool For Love [10]
Complete the Love is in the Air achievements listed.

 Fool For Love [10]
Complete the Love is in the Air achievements listed.

 For The Children [10]
Complete the Children's Week achievements listed.

 What A Long, Strange Trip It's Been [50]
Complete the world events achievements listed.

Author Acknowledgements

Being involved with a project like this is an amazing experience and we would like to thank Blizzard for creating such an engaging world to explore. Thoroughly getting to know such a well crafted and intriguing place is a monumental task and we couldn't have wished for a better team to do it with. Dexter Hall worked tirelessly right alongside of us and this guide would not have been the same without him. He is not only knowledgeable and hardworking but also one of the best tanks we have ever had the privilege of playing with. Thanks for letting us hit you up at odd hours for info and the occasional strange screenshot! Tommaso Russo, Derek Bates, and Dustin Reynolds came through time and time again collecting information, providing insight, and making themselves available whenever we needed them, never complaining about running through something just one more time. Thanks guys for being such great help, and such great friends. Buck N Uber FTW!

At Brady we would like to thank Brian Shotton and Dan Caparo for working tirelessly to make this book the best it can be, Leigh Davis for giving us the opportunity to work on such an amazing project, and everyone else there who works to put out exceptional product time and time again.

We would also like to thank our parents, Jeff Sims, Linda Taintor, and Lee Allan, for putting up with missed visits, short phone calls, and the general forgetting of birthdays, anniversaries, and other important family events while we work on a project. They are always supportive and excited by each new guide we do, despite the fact that we are pretty certain they have no idea what "a WoW" is.

Brian's Acknowledgements

Once again we have reached the end of a World of Warcraft product. As always, it was an immense amount of work.

I would personally like to thank, Gina Pippin and Ben George at Blizzard for their assistance in getting this title approved and out on time. Their assistance in gathering data, icons, stats, and art must have seemed never-ending. Good news; we did it! Take a break, I won't ask for the Wrath of the Lich King Atlas data for a week.

I would also like to single out Ben for getting Dan and I through the Diablo III line at Blizzcon so quickly—the game is amazing.

Big props for Dan Caparo on his design and all those in production that helped lay it out: Tracy, Colin, and Wil.

Finally, my good friends Jennifer and Kenny Sims, I have known you a long time. This journey started almost three years ago, but here we are. Congratulations on a rockin' book. The quality of text, timeliness of submissions, and patience you exhibited speak to your quality as authors.

ALANINA

Kenny Sims
Author

CYRDDIN

Jennifer Sims
Lead Author

EVILVOOD

Tommaso Russo
Assistant

FEARCEDEATH

Derek Bates
Assistant

KWANAH

Dustin Reynolds
Assistant

LOKNIK

Dexter Hall
Author

MADE EXCLUSIVELY FOR WORLD OF WARCRAFT®

MMO GAMING MOUSE

- Quick access to even more spells and abilities with 15 buttons to bind

- Truly personalized look with 16 million illumination options

- Meets all your gaming needs with the most advanced software available to date

For the ultimate World of Warcraft® experience, go to:

WWW.STEELSERIES.COM/WOW

Check out the World of Warcraft®: Wrath of the Lich King™ Gaming Keyboard and exclusive mouse pads.

AVAILABLE AT:

GameStop
power to the players™
www.gamestop.com

amazon.com
www.amazon.com

newegg.com
www.newegg.com

SteelSeries

TIPS & TRICKS

MMO GAMING MOUSE

CUSTOM MACROS

Here is a break down of the macro dialog:

A) Macro name
B) Macro box showing the sequence of keys that define the action
C) The type of delay used in on the macro.

DELAY OPTIONS :

Text (Auto-delay) - Default setting which automatically applies delays based on the type of macro being created

Record Delay - Set your own delays within the macro

No Delay

D) Ok will create, edit & apply your changes
E) Cancel will discard your changes

HOW TO:

1. Select the button that you wish to assign a macro to. The Button Assignment tab on the right will slide open, showing you the current command bound to that button.

2. In the Button Assignment tab, click New under the Custom Macro section. This will bring up the macro dialog.

3. Create a name that is meaningful and easy to remember. For example, a macro to control your pet could be named Pet Attack or Pet Stay.

4. Select your method of delay, click the macro box and begin typing your macro. If you make a mistake, simply click the clear button to start over.

5. Press Ok and your macro will be saved and automatically assigned to the button you have selected.

6. If you wish to place the macro on a different button, just select button and then the macro, or you can simply drag and drop the macro from the Button Assignment tab to any button you desire.

GETTING STARTED - MANAGING PROFILES

Click on the Character window and enter your character info. Your avatar and description will be retrieved automatically from the WOW Armory and a profile will be created with your character name.

Select a unique illumination color and effect through the Illumination Settings panel (found at the bottom of the interface) for your profile. You can create up to 10 different profiles with any color and effect combo.

ADVANCED TIP:

Bind your profile to any button using the Button Assignment -> Change Profile section. You can also bind Profile Up/Down to cycle through all profiles. Use it to quickly switch between normal and PVP profiles in game - just bind these to the buttons under different colors (i.e. blue for normal and green for PVP) and switch on-the-fly.

ADVANCED TIP:

To share profiles with your friends just click "File Menu" and select either "Export Profile" or "Import Profile".

USING IT IN WORLD OF WARCRAFT:

You may already have combos or macros mapped to your keyboard. Now you can move/add more commands to the mouse.

· For Hunters and Warlocks, it's a handy way to assign pet commands to mouse buttons so you can quickly control their actions during combat.

· For Druids and Warriors, use macros to quickly switching between stances / forms during a fight.

steelseries

BUILD YOUR LEGION!

World of Warcraft® Collectible Miniatures Game

- Premium miniature figures featuring faithful design and highly detailed paints!
- Standard and deluxe starter sets plus three-figure boosters!
- 70 high-quality figures available, including Horde, Alliance, and Monsters!

For more information, visit

WoWMINIS.COM/BG

OFFICIAL STRATEGY GUIDE

Written by Jennifer and Kenny Sims, and Dexter Hall

© 2008 DK/BradyGAMES, a division of Penguin Group (USA) Inc.
BradyGAMES® is a registered trademark of Penguin Group (USA) Inc.
All rights reserved, including the right of reproduction in whole or in part
in any form.

DK/BradyGames, a division of Penguin Group (USA) Inc.
800 East 96th Street, 3rd Floor
Indianapolis, IN 46240

ISBN: 978-0-7440-1021-3

Printing Code: The rightmost double-digit number is the year of the
book's printing; the rightmost single-digit number is the number of the
book's printing. For example, 08-1 shows that the first printing of the book
occurred in 2008.

11 10 09 08   4   3   2   1

Printed in the USA.

BRADYGAMES STAFF

Publisher
David Waybright

Editor-In-Chief
H. Leigh Davis

Licensing Director
Mike Degler

Marketing Director
Debby Neubauer

International Translations
Brian Saliba

CREDITS

Development Editor
Brian Shotton

Screenshot Editor
Michael Owen

Lead Designer
Dan Caparo

Book Designer
Brent Gann

Production Designers
Wil Cruz
Tracy Wehmeyer

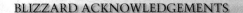

BLIZZARD ACKNOWLEDGEMENTS

Director of Global Licensing
Cory Jones

Licensing Manager
Gina Pippin

Associate Licensing Manager
Ben George

Director, Creative Development
Jeff Donais

Lead Developer Licensed Products
Shawn Carnes

Art Director
Glenn Rane

Blizzard Special Thanks
Andrew Rowe, Kyle Dates, Nathan LaMusaga, Roman Marotte, Paul Della Bitta,
Danielle Vanderlip, Liam Knapp, Jonathan Brown, Andrew Hsu, Daniel Chin, Evan
Crawford, Zachariah Owens, Gloria Soto, Thomas Newcomer